T5-DHR-472

FOUNDATIONS OF ACCOUNTING

Edited by
RICHARD P. BRIEF
New York University

A GARLAND SERIES

Accounting from the Outside

The Collected Papers of Anthony G. Hopwood

Edited with an Introduction by
ANTHONY G. HOPWOOD

GARLAND PUBLISHING, INC.
NEW YORK & LONDON 1988

For a list of Garland's publications in accounting, see the final pages of this volume.

Library of Congress Cataloging-in-Publication Data

Hopwood, Anthony G.
Accounting from the outside.

(Foundations of Accounting)
Bibliography: p.
1. Accounting. 2. Managerial accounting. 3. Accounting—Social aspects.. I. Title. II. Series.
HF5635.H812 1988 657 88-24496
ISBN 0-4280-6124-1 (alk paper)

Design by Renata Gomes

The volumes in this series are printed on acid-free, 250-year-life paper.

Printed in the United States of America

In memory of
my parents

Contents

Selected Editorial Pontifications

Acknowledgements

I would like to acknowledge the help provided by all the publishers in obtaining permission to reprint articles, chapters, and other contributions. Reprint conditions require that specific mention be made of the following:

Papers 5, 12, 24, 25, 28, 29, 35, 36, 37, 38, 39, 40, 41, 42, 43, and 44 are reprinted with permission from *Accounting, Organizations and Society*, Pergamon Press plc.

Papers 6 and 17 are reprinted by permission of Philip Allan Publishers Limited.

Paper 13 is reprinted from Kim B. Clark, Robert H. Hayes, and Christopher Lorenz, eds., *The Uneasy Alliance: Managing the Productivity-Technology Dilemma*, Boston: Harvard Business School Press, 1985. Copyright © 1985 by the President and Fellows of Harvard College. Reprinted by permission.

Papers 14, 26, 31, and 32 are reprinted by permission of Pitman Publishing.

Paper 21 first appeared in *Accountancy* (October, 1981). Reprinted with permission.

Paper 22 is reprinted from *New Forms of Work Organization*, Vol.2 (1979), pp.115–145 by permission of the International Labour Organisation. Copyright 1979, International Labour Organisation, Geneva.

Paper 23 is reprinted by permission of the Macmillan Press Limited.

Observing the Accounting Craft

AN INTRODUCTION

Accounting has always had a certain fascination for me. As a child, I almost left school on two occasions to enter the accountancy profession. Not doing that, I proceeded to study the subject at the London School of Economics and Political Science. Although thereafter I was one of the few who did not seek to enter professional training, I nevertheless decided to continue my probings into accounting at the University of Chicago, in the process first setting aside the possibility of pursuing research in the area of industrial economics and thereafter in the area of finance. And since that time accounting has become a phenomenon for almost continuous observation, curiosity, and inquiry.

The reasons for the fascination are difficult to appreciate, as they are for many things that provide an element of continuity between one's quite distant past and the here and now. The interest arose during a period of rapid accounting development in the United Kingdom. Its involvement with attempts at industrial and financial reconstruction resulted in a certain prominence in media discussions. Accounting was starting to catch the public eye and I might well have been one of those enticed within its web at that time. Its characterization as a seemingly modern and rational form of knowledge and expertise might have influenced the perceptions of a young grammar school boy, not least when a close family member provided a more immediate exemplar of the accountant in action. I remember what might otherwise have been purely social discussions being peppered with tales of new American methods, accounting's involvement in corporate reorganisation, the early stages of the rise of a new breed of financial executives in the United Kingdom, and, not least in significance, the more questionable implications of this for local manufacturing and employment in a relatively poor region of the North of England.

Just such an ambiguity surrounded many of my initial involvements with accounting. Early attempts to join the profession provided some fascinating insights into the social recruitment criteria used by the agents of a seemingly meritocratic occupation. Through family involvements I had the opportunity to witness some of the personal and organizational tensions, anxieties, and contradictions associated with the economic rationalizing concerns of accountants and the other managerial groups with which they were associated. Not only could parts of a local economy be seen as being more readily incorporated into wider patterns of economic forces, but also the management practices with which accounting was associated were seen in ways that provided some insights into how they could shift patterns of influence and discretion within wider organizational settings. Even at that time accounting started to come across as a more multifaceted phenomenon and one that, however technical its procedures might appear, was not isolated from wider patterns of human and social life. Indeed, as I remember it, I was already starting to be aware of the contradictory nature of the accounting task. Despite the aura of professional neutrality and the articulation of its serving a conception of the public interest, accountants were widely known to be the servants of those wishing to follow the letter rather than the spirit of the legislative intent, not least in the area of taxation. Even quite mundane associations with accounting in practice were starting to create an impression of the equivocality of the accountant's craft, if only in terms of the discretionary nature of a final account. There quite obviously was more at stake in accounting than mere financial arithmetic.

My undergraduate years at the London School of Economics only served to increase such impressions. Under the watchful eye of people like Will Baxter, Harold Edey, and Basil Yamey, accounting started to emerge as a more problematic activity. Although the accounting part of a wider study of the social sciences was not extensive at that time, the economic orientation to the subject that was an important part of the intellectual tradition at the LSE (Dev, 1980), provided a means of confronting the technical practice of accounting with a wider framework for its analysis. Costs and profits were portrayed as multifaceted, complex, and conceptual phenomena whose interpretation required a wider, albeit still economic, appreciation of the contexts in which they functioned and had an effect. Whilst certainly not emphasized, some basis for appreciating how political and social concerns might intermingle with and change modes of economic calculation was nevertheless also provided at the LSE at that time, not least in the context of discussions of approaches to forms of social cost-benefit analysis which were then emerging.

In such ways an interest in studying and understanding accounting developed. A more questioning curiosity about accounting started to emerge, providing the basis for an interest in continuing the study *of* accounting rather than seeking a professional indoctrination *in* the subject. In the mid-1960s, however, it was almost impossible to obtain adequate research training in accounting or indeed most other management subjects in the United Kingdom. The major business schools were just about to be established. The research infrastructure was minimal. Being advised of such constraints, I decided to apply to doctoral programmes in the United States. On these grounds the University of Chicago was to become my intellectual base for the next five years.

CHICAGO AND THE EXPLORATION OF ACCOUNTING IN USE

Chicago undoubtedly provided the intellectual basis for the development of my interest in the study of accounting in use. Although the focus of that interest was to change a great deal subsequently, the idea of probing into the actual functioning of the accounting craft originated in and was nurtured by the productive academic environment that Chicago provided. The commitment to the sustained and rigorous study of business phenomena that was such an important part of the intellectual life of the Graduate School of Business at the University of Chicago at that time created an intellectual ethos that was exciting, demanding, and, above all, conducive for experimentation.

It was indeed an exciting time to be studying accounting at Chicago. The rise of an interest in empiricism was still occurring, much fostered by David Green and propagated by him in his doctoral seminars and, not least, in the newly established *Journal of Accounting Research*. New interrelationships were being forged between accounting and economics, quantitative methods, and even the behavioral sciences. Research discussions were couched in philosophical terms. Modern finance theory and its empirical basis were being constructed at the School, amongst other places. Even the student community was itself an exceptionally able and innovative one. Bill Beaver, Philip Brown, Joel Demski, and Mel Greenball, for instance, were all ahead of me on the

Doctoral Programme, and Ray Ball and Ross Watts, amongst others, were to join soon afterwards.

In such an environment research, not surprisingly, had a very high profile and priority. For someone recently arrived from the United Kingdom, it was quite obvious that research was perceived as a professional activity rather than a gentlemanly pursuit. Amongst both the faculty and the doctoral students, I think it fair to say, there was a feeling that knowledge itself was in the process of changing. The old was contrasted with the new and the forces driving the new were explicitly discussed and argued.

My own interest in the behavioral and organizational aspects of accounting emerged by chance in an institution devoted to the extension of quite particular conceptions of economic rationality. Forced to take a course on organization theory to satisfy the course distribution requirements of the doctoral programme, that course, so ably and interestingly taught by Paul Goodman (now of Carnegie-Mellon University), provided me with a new vision of how to study accounting. The interest and challenge was such that I restructured my doctoral studies, setting aside a specialization in finance in order to delve further into the behavioral aspects of accounting systems. Of course there were those who thought such a move ill-advised, but the helpful counsels of George Sorter, the director of the doctoral programme at the time, and particularly Dick Hoffman, a social-psychologist who had himself only recently joined the Chicago faculty from the University of Michigan, greatly eased the intellectual transition that was to result in an attempt to forge some understanding of the interrelationship between accounting and the organizational contexts in which it operated.

The dysfunctional consequences of management accounting systems started to be a topic of particular interest to me. Stimulated by Chris Argyris's pioneering study of *The Impact of Budgets on People* (1952), still possibly wondering about my own early exposure to the more equivocal functioning of accounting, certainly influenced by the social-psychological orientation of a great deal of the behavioral science programme at Chicago, and also intrigued by the then emergent contingency formulations of organization theory, I began to think about exploring the factors that influenced the behavioral and organizational consequences of accounting systems, dysfunctional or otherwise.

A commitment to engage in field research also developed at an early stage for reasons now difficult to reconstruct. Perhaps my very early interest in the actual functioning of accounting played some role. I certainly remember holding the view that accounting was an organizational phenomenon and needed to be studied as such. Seen in such terms, I think that there was a quite genuine interest in the development of an action based, more humanistic basis for appreciating the variety of management responses to accounting, with a view to moving towards a more adequate understanding of how accounting functioned as a significant organizational and social practice. I was also quite definitely worried about the validity of laboratory experimentation, a methodology then just starting to be used in accounting research. A trial experiment using friendly subjects reinforced my doubts about the credibility of the exercise as a basis for understanding the functioning of accounting as an organizational practice. By then I was also familiar with and quite worried about a developing body of research on the social psychology of the psychological experiment, work conveniently ignored by the experimental literature. The laboratory appeared to me to be an ever less obvious site for the exploration of accounting in action. Although I was aware of the difficulties of entering the field, not least for a novice Englishman in Chicago, I was nevertheless convinced that this was what I ought to do even though it created a new precedent for accounting research at Chicago and even though there were those who initially did not look on the proposal with favor.

Research access to a suitable organization was far from easy to negotiate, taking nine anxious months in all. As a research orientated institution, the Chicago Business School had relatively few suitable contacts in industrial and commercial circles at that time. I decided I did not wish to study a traditional insurance company, even though access might have been available. However tempting it initially appeared, I also decided that the impracticalities of field work in Florida were too great. And even greater in Chile! Even the efforts of a future Secretary of State failed to get me into one organization. In the end, however, access was gained to a major steel company and Gary, Indiana, amidst its agonising environmental deprivations, was to become a second home for the next couple of years or so.

"You don't need to be a behavioral scientist to understand this lot. You need to be a bloody anthropologist," advised one of my early shop floor contacts. "You're in the jungle now," he went on to add, describing how almost every department in the steel plant had its own ethnic and cultural identity, mirroring the immigration history of the Mid West. The newest arrivals seemingly always started on the shop floor in the dirty and dangerous early processes, slowly being promoted upwards and, over time, moving into the relatively cleaner and safer later processes of steel making. By the time I was around the descendents of the British, the Germans, and the Scandinavians were way down the line and the first black foreman had been appointed in the blast furnaces.

For somewhat different reasons, an anthropologist of sorts I was to become. Entering the field with quite general interests and hypotheses, and almost no prior studies to rely on, a great deal of time was spent on trying to understand how an amazingly complex and quite sophisticated accounting system functioned, how it became involved with wider organizational processes, and how it had the consequences it had. The initial research efforts were exploratory and observational. I worked on the night shift. I had a hole burnt in my jacket in the blast furnace—an initiation of a sort. I spent an amazing amount of time watching, listening, and talking. Later I was to refer to this in terms of tapping into the linguistic culture of the firm. For over time I became increasingly aware of not only the different ways in which the same accounting system was implicated in organizational processes, but also the subtle distinctions in language that both reflected and shaped the patterns of differential use. These distinctions provided a focus for the final study; the linguistic differences were the basis for further exploration by the use of questionnaires. The latter is something that nearly all subsequent users of the research instrument have ignored, merrily but all too ignorantly proceeding with using it in factory-like style.

The form of the doctoral research was influenced not only by the problem and the exploration of the research site. With such field research being all very new in an accounting context, not least at Chicago, it was made quite clear that a more structured approach to the final research design was required. So questionnaire design, distribution, and analysis entered the research process, as did the complexities of nonparametric statistics. So much so, in fact, that in those distant days when field explorations were new and little understood by the accounting research establishment, and when accounting itself was less assured of its intellectual bases, the highly significant exploratory research was purged from the final text, the latter thereby having the appearance of a more structured, anticipated, confident, and seemingly scientific work.

The resultant study, published in its entirety as *An Accounting System and Managerial Behaviour* (Hopwood, 1973; see also the papers in section one of the present collection), provided some insights into the managerial processes through which accounting data acquired an organizational meaning and significance. Focusing on the differing ways in which different managers used the same accounting system, it cast some light on the ways in which organizational factors could mediate and shape the consequences associated with an accounting system, thereby providing a way of appreciating a diversity of effects rather than a set of inevitable ones, anticipated or otherwise. The study also provided a basis for appreciating how factors such as participation in the budgetary process and other organizational circumstances could influence the change the processes at work, thereby creating a whole range of new problems for investigation in further studies. In more contemporary terms, the study also provided some insights into how organizational cultures and managerial philosophies might shape the significance attached to accounting systems and play some role in influencing their effects.

Perhaps more significantly for me, however, the study undertaken in Chicago had demonstrated that it was possible and meaningful to probe into the actual functioning of accounting. Although I was never myself to extend the precise form of that analysis, a basis for a more widespread interest in observing and questioning accounting in use had been created. Rather than focusing on the technical analysis and elaboration of accounting in isolation from its organizational context, I had started along a path of inquiry concerned with the observation of accounting rather than its propagation, with an exploration of its organizational and social bases rather than the presumption of a technical autonomy, and with an attempt to appreciate the actual consequences of accounting rather than the unproblematic acceptance of its stated rationales.

THE DEVELOPMENT OF AN ORGANIZATIONAL INTEREST

The culture shock on returning to the United Kingdom in 1970 was intellectual as well as social in nature. Having developed my interest in organizational issues in the United States, I had tended to take for granted the social psychological domination of the subject evident at that time and place, and its resulting individualistic orientation (Kassem, 1976). The contrast with a British perspective therefore could not have been more marked, not least with the vibrant organizational research community at the Manchester Business School, which celebrated its links to the substantive disciplines of anthropology, sociology, and even a version of institutional economics. Accordingly I had to set about merging myself in organizational studies afresh, luckily, however, in an environment noted for its excitement, its innovativeness, and its concern with the scholarly, the practical, and the interface between the two.

Working on the text of *Accounting and Human Behaviour* (Hopwood, 1974) provided a most useful way of thinking through what might be at stake with a wider organisational perspective on accounting. It provided a context in which to explore new literatures, to push existing understandings, and to start raising a somewhat different set of questions related to the organizational embeddedness of accounting. Although the text is now a somewhat dated work (albeit one that is still in use), I am still surprised by the apparent novelty of some of the occasional comments and the extent to which it reflected what was then only the beginning of a new way of attempting to perceive the accounting craft. At times even I wonder how I could possibly have thought that way at that time!

A number of influences were starting to reflect themselves in my work. Not only was an expanding interdisciplinary basis evident but also a growing involvement with accounting in practice. Post-experience management teaching was useful in this respect, as were the opportunities that the Manchester Business School provided to work with a mature, ambitious, and intellectually able group of post-graduate students. In a more complex way I was also stimulated by the intellectual agenda created by the Management Control Research Group at the School. Founded by Morris McInnes and Tony Lowe, the group set itself an impossibly ambitious research agenda of both surveying and categorizing the variety of approaches to management control systems functioning in the United Kingdom. At that time there was little prior work to guide such an endeavor. Existing conceptual frameworks and distinctions were woefully inadequate to reflect the diversity of practices in use. And the methodological problems involved in mapping such diversity were very real. Hardly surprisingly the activities of the group generated a fair amount of conflict, an enormous data bank of observations and recordings, and relatively few publications. Be that as it may, the project exposed all of us to the complexities of management accounting in practice and illuminated very forcefully the inadequacies of many existing understandings of the subject. What findings there were pointed to an appreciation of accounting that recognized its involvement with other organizational practices and the ways in which accounting systems were implicated in the construction of organizations as we know them, rather than being mere reflections of the organizational endeavour.

As a result of such experiences a more organizationally grounded appreciation of accounting started to emerge. The technical practice of accounting increasingly came to be related to the organizational and wider contexts in which it functioned. The interrelationships between accounting and organizational structures, aspects of the technological and competitive environments of the enterprise, and the dynamics of the political processes that characterise organizational life started to be explored. Although I was at this time both aware of and influenced by contingent notions of organization developed in the organizational literature, I think that it is fair to say that even then I found such frameworks useful but inadequate, at least as they were then formulated. They provided one way of characterizing the organizational dependency of accounting systems, but they did this in a way that was too deterministic, offered too limited a view of the more complex patterns of interdependency that I increasingly came to see as influencing accounting's functioning in organizations, and ignored the more subtle ways in which flows of accounting information could shift and disturb patterns of influence, power, meaning, and significance within the organizational realm.

Aware of such limitations of more conventional, albeit still emerging, ways of conceiving accounting in an organizational context, a more open personal agenda for probing into the organizational functioning and significance of accounting started to develop. Much interested in the challenge of deriving an approach to teaching in the area, I became increasingly interested in the articulation of quite general but hopefully useful frameworks that might help to improve our understanding of the organizational construction, functioning, and consequences of accounting. Somewhat in contrast but certainly not in conflict, I also developed an interest in both ways of appreciating the quite specific functioning of accounting systems in specific organizations and the research strategies that might result in a more organizationally grounded insight into accounting as it operated. Earlier interests in the "use" of accounting broadened out into interests in the different ways in which accounting systems could be and were caught up in decision and influence processes in organizations. An interest in the micro politics of accounting started to emerge. I became more sensitive to the ways in which accounting changes could influence managerial vocabularies and the articulation of organizational aims, problems, and possibilities. The ways in which accounting got caught up in wider organizational patterns of transformation and change started to become of particular interest. I started at least to talk about the extent to which the elaboration of accounting systems might be a response to organizational crisis. The management of information flows in circumstances characterized by rapid change and disruption became a topic of growing curiosity. The quite complex ways in which accounting could be influenced by organizational restructurings started to enter my research agenda.

Perhaps unfortunately, most of these interests did not result in specific research projects. Rather together they provided a basis for a growing sense of unease with both existing technical appreciations of the accounting craft and the so-called behavioral insights that had emerged by that time. The autonomy attributed to the former and the constrained notions of organizational rationality that were implicit in discussions of them were an increasing source of dissatisfaction, as were the individualistic emphases that were quite explicit in the rise of a behavioral stance in the accounting research community. The inability of the latter to confront a great deal of what I came to see as being at stake in the organizational practice of accounting provided a basis for an intellectual unease with research developments. Increasingly I also put more emphasis on the limitations that such behavioral views had for guiding even pragmatic interests in accounting system design. Perhaps by then the teaching demands evident in a business school environment were making their impact, although not only was I never aware of a conflict between the scholarly and the practical but, in contrast, I became increasingly interested in some of the quite similar demands that both strands of thinking could make on accounting knowledge.

All too clearly, subsequent interests in understanding the dynamics of accounting change were emergent at this time. A focus on grounded inquiry had already been articulated. A multiplicity of rationales for accounting elaboration and development were starting to be appreciated, providing a rich basis for continuing empirical and theoretical inquiries. Although perhaps not quite so well appreciated at that time, an interest in both the scholarly and the practical roles of accounting knowledge was also starting to be made more evident. All told, an agenda for future research, a quite particular theoretical stance, and a perspective on the roles that knowledge might play were all emerging in ways that continued to have a significant influence on the direction of future enthusiasms and inquiries.

INSTITUTIONAL INVOLVEMENTS

It is most likely quite difficult to appreciate some, at least, of these shifting interests outside of the context of a growing involvement with the institutionalization of accounting research. For reasons that I sense owe more to luck than design, I had the opportunity to become an active contributor to three quite significant advancements in the institutional development of accounting research in the United Kingdom at that time. These were the launching of an accounting research initiative by the then Social Science Research Council, the government funding body for research in the human and social sciences; the development of a programme of European accounting research workshops by the newly established European Institute for Advanced Studies in Management, in Brussels, an activity that subsequently gave rise to the creation of the European Accounting Association; and the establishment of a new specialized international research journal concerned with the behavioral, organizational, and social analyses of accounting, *Accounting, Organizations and Society*. All of these activities consumed a vast amount of my time, and some still do so. Although they considerably constrained my own research and writing endeavors, not only did they not stop them but over the years they also had a very considerable influence upon them.

The development of a European network of accounting researchers brought me into contact with very different research traditions, theoretical ways of appreciating accounting, and strategies for engaging in accounting research. It is always difficult to appreciate and disentangle the influences such awarenesses have had on your own work. They invariably leave few specific residues. But I am very conscious of the cumulative impact, not least with respect to the richness of insight and sheer enthusiasm for grounded organizational inquiry that was such an important part of the Scandinavian, and particularly the Swedish, tradition of research in the areas of accounting and information systems in particular and management more generally. My personal contacts and friendships with Scandinavian researchers provided possibilities for direct theoretical influences; they also prompted a reorientation of my organizational interests, away from a model influenced by the North

American academic community and towards one increasingly open to the quite different intellectual traditions of continental Europe. In ways that would be difficult, if not impossible, to chart with precision, I started to develop into a European academic who increasingly could observe both American work and my own earlier inquiries with interest but from a distance.

The full development of a more European tradition of inquiry will, in all probability, be manifested by a younger group of scholars, rather than by those of us who were privileged to have played some role in the creation of a cross-national network of accounting researchers. But I derive a great deal of pleasure from the part I have been able to play in the establishment of that network and I look forward with pleasure to the days when it might result in understandings and insights different from those I personally have been able to utilize.

Different institutional forms can undoubtedly play some role in changing modes of inquiry and the resultant patterns of knowledge and understanding. Indeed it was with just such a view in mind that I sought to establish a new journal that would be exclusively concerned with the organizational, behavioral, and social analyses of accounting. Although it still has an unfinished agenda for intellectual exploration and change, I like to think that *Accounting, Organizations and Society* has already played some role in opening up new areas for inquiry, legitimizing different scholarly traditions, and creating a more international and open research community amongst those interested in probing into the human and social nature of accounting thought and practice.

The initial idea on which *Accounting, Organizations and Society* was based emerged in an educational context. With other colleagues at the Manchester Business School I had designed a role-playing case study based on the affairs of Pergamon Press, an organization that played a not insignificant role in recent British accounting history. Wanting the students to have the opportunity to question actual participants in the affair rather than rely solely on press reports and official documents, key participants were invited to take part in the teaching of the case study. Robert Maxwell, the founder of Pergamon Press, was one of those individuals and, ever the entrepreneur, Mr. Maxwell used the opportunity to inquire into whether I had any ideas for new research journals!

Well, as it happens, I had. At that time I was becoming increasingly conscious of a gap that existed between the potential for an organizational and social understanding of accounting and the editorial policies and concerns of the existing accounting research journals. That idea of a gap gave rise to a proposal for a new journal and after numerous deliberations and consultations *Accounting, Organizations and Society*, the new journal, was launched in 1976.

In retrospect it is interesting to reflect on the enormous gap between the naiveté of the idea and the reality of the journal's establishment. Even getting agreement on the name of the new journal was problematic. Majority opinion was strongly in favor of it being known as the *Journal of Behavioral and Social Accounting*. I, however, was bothered about the constrained view of what would hopefully become a new research area implicit in such a designation. I wanted something more suggestive of the need to openly explore ways in which accounting functioned in organizational and social settings. Whilst the concerns of the 1970s emphasized the specificities of behavioral and social accounting, I envisioned a journal that would encourage the investigation of wider questions relating to the rise of economic calculation in organizations and society. *Accounting, Organizations and Society* emerged as a title that hopefully suggested the possibilities that the new journal might create, rather than being reflective of, the immediate context out of which it emerged.

Now is not the occasion to review the history of *Accounting, Organizations and Society*. I like to think that it has achieved quite a lot, although I am equally conscious of what remains to be achieved. It certainly has consumed an immense amount of my time and energy, and still does so. But my involvement with the journal has been a reciprocal one. Just as I have at least attempted to steer and influence it, so *Accounting, Organizations and Society* has had a very significant influence on me. I have learnt from what it has published; I have gained from the intellectual agendas it has helped to create; and I am wiser as a result of the new networks of enthusiastic researchers that have been associated with the journal. International in scope, the community of those interested in the organizational and social analysis of accounting has established a tradition of open, friendly, and facilitative interchange that has brought together friendship and intellectual curiosity in ways that have been mutually enriching.

THE RISE OF A SOCIAL INTEREST

It was whilst *Accounting, Organizations and Society* was still a very new baby, that I moved to what was then the Oxford Centre for Management Studies (now Templeton College, Oxford) with the explicit brief of establishing a programme of accounting research. Although my stay at Oxford was a relatively short one, it was nevertheless a productive and significant one. An active and successful period of fund raising provided the basis for me to plan a more focused programme of research and to recruit a talented team of researchers that included Stuart Burchell, Colin Clubb, John Hughes, and Janine Nahapiet. Freed from many of the pressures of teaching and academic administration, that newly established research group was quickly able to establish a congenial and very productive mode of operation.

The research agenda of the group was explicit, albeit general. We were all interested in pushing further our understandings of what might be at stake in an organizational and social analysis of accounting. Whilst I and others had pointed to the organizational and social bases and consequences of accounting practices, in many ways such appeals had only served to point to the possibilities of a new way of inquiring into the functioning of accounting. The group was all too aware of this; early discussions focused on "what was at stake" with such a view, which ways of characterizing accounting might enrich the task of directly conceiving accounting within the spheres of the organizational and the social, and what were the theoretical and methodological prerequisites for advancing such a view. The research group was also unanimous that a major focus for such inquiries ought to be the study of accounting change. Rather than seeking to directly explore accounting as it was, we viewed that much more might be gained from exploring accounting in the process of becoming, of changing, of becoming what it was not. In such a context, it was thought, more might be seen of the forces that put accounting into motion and of the organizational and social consequences of disruptions in the accounting craft. Whilst we were well aware that change is a relative matter and that we might, as a consequence, have to focus on accounting elaborations rather than more fundamental shifts, we were nevertheless convinced that even such analyses might provide an empirical richness that would stimulate, provoke, and influence our more theoretical explorations of accounting in the process of becoming what it was not.

The specific empirical interests of the research group were influenced by a mixture of pragmatic and intellectual considerations, as is invariably the case. One project focused on the introduction of budgeting systems into a region of the National Health Service. Another aimed to explore the rise of interest in forms of social accounting in a number of European countries, although given the diversity of such initiatives it also sought to understand the social dynamics that gave rise to social accountings and the different nature of the social significances attached to them. A third project was orientated towards organizational studies of accounting system change. Taken together, the projects resulted in a vast amount of rich empirical material, only some of which has been published as of now. Both the diversity and the depth of the empirical findings served as a vital stimulus to theoretical inquiry, raising, as they did, questions about adequate ways of understanding the forces at work and the ways in which accounting changes emerged out of complex configurations of organizational and social circumstances.

The inquiry resulted in a number of more general contributions to the literature, all of which are collected here. Early concerns to probe into, question, and distance ourselves from many conventional understandings of accounting are reflected in "The Roles of Accounting in Organisations and Society." So aware of the possibilities for different ways of interrogating accounting, some initial statements of our research interests and agenda appeared in "The Development of Accounting in its International Context: Past Concerns and Emergent Issues," a paper that now reads as a very preliminary one indeed, and "'A Message From Mars'—and Other Reminiscences from the Past," a paper that reports on some empirical findings that were to serve as a crucial catalyst for more general theorizing. More mature statements of the research position developed in the group are given in "Accounting in Its Social Context: Towards a History of Value Added in the United Kingdom" and, although written and published appreciably later, in "The Archaeology of Accounting Systems."

Other writings pursue and elaborate upon the approach to the organizational and social analysis of accounting developed in those initial papers. Some of the implications for an organizational understanding of accounting are sketched out in "Management Accounting and Organisational Action: An Introduction: and "Accounting and Organisational Action." Questions of a more explicitly social nature are addressed in the rather brief "Economics and the Regime of the Calculative," a paper that reflects my remaining worries about the unproblematic advance of calculative practices, whether they stem from economic or social rationales for action, and in "The Tale of a Committee that Never Reported: Disagreements on Intertwining Accounting with the Social" and "Accounting Research and Accounting Practice: The Ambiguous Relationship Between the Two." Recognizing the potential for the development of accounting in the public sector in the United Kingdom to illuminate some of the more general issues at stake in an organizational and social analysis of accounting, a number of papers have specifically sought to address this area in a tentative way. "Accounting and the Pursuit of Efficiency" and *Accounting and the Domain of the Public: Some Observations on Current Developments* are illustrative examples. Although based on quite extensive contacts with such public sector developments, such analyses nevertheless remain preliminary, not least because of my own equivocality about the role that economic calculation is called upon to play in the reform of organizations seeking to advance quite particular conceptions of the social.

The research perspective addressed in such writings is all too clearly an emergent one. Individually they provide specific illustrations of the issues at stake and the potential offered. Others attempt to sketch out some of the more general implications for social understanding of accounting practice. However, whilst undoubtedly preliminary, the themes developed in the papers hopefully also have a coherence, not least when contrasted with those evident in other organizational and economic perspectives.

Emphasis is placed on both the reflective and constitutive aspects of accounting. Recognizing that accounting is not an autonomous calculative practice, attention is directed towards improving our understanding, not only of how factors external to accounting can impinge upon and change it, but also of how such interminglings can occur and of how accounting can mediate and reflect other organizational and social circumstances. Equally, however, emphasis is placed on the enabling and productive properties of accounting. Explicitly seeking to recognize how accounting can create quite particular and partial patterns of visibility, the analyses hopefully start to provide at least one basis for understanding how accounting can at times disturb and disrupt other organizational and social circumstances. Emphasizing the specificities of the economic categories and linguistic distinctions that infuse accounting in practice, a basis is provided for appreciating some of the ways in which the calculative practices of accounting can permeate and shape patterns of organizational concerns, influencing conceptions of the problematic, the desirable, and the possible.

In these analyses increasing emphasis is placed on the ways in which accounting is implicated in the wider diffusion of economic priorities and concerns. Greater attention is being given to the organizational and social consequences of the calculative rationality that can be associated with the advance of accounting practices. Not unrelated, more attention is being given to the discursive and theoretical conceptions with which accounting is often implicated. Once again recognizing that the technical practices are not independent of notions of their functioning and rationales, although the relationship between them is neither direct nor uniform, some of the papers reflect a growing interest in the knowledges and understandings capable of being advanced and diffused by them.

In all cases the understanding offered of the dynamics of accounting change is quite a complex one. Simple notions of functionality are questioned. Accounting is not seen as being a mere reflection of unproblematic essences or imperatives. A detailed understanding of the specific contexts in which accounting change occurs demonstrates the diversity of influences that can impinge on accounting and its consequences, the often quite complex and shifting circumstances, issues, and practices with which accounting can be associated, and, of equal significance, the roles played by the unintentional and the unanticipated consequences of accounting change.

All too clearly such emerging understandings reflect a combination of theoretical and empirical interests. Increasingly they emerge from a commitment to grounded inquiry and a concern to address and understand the specificities of accounting in use. Consistent with such a view, I still attempt to invest a great deal of time in trying to observe accounting, always trying to maintain an interest in new accountings, major accounting changes and reforms, and pragmatic attempts to articulate new or expanded rationales for accounting practice. The nature of the research task is such that only a small amount of material emerges in public form, although much of the rest influences the intellectual agendas I maintain and develop. Equally the understandings I have of accounting reflect a view that such appreciations are not implicit in the circumstances being observed but reflect the use of an interpretative theoretical lens. There is little doubt that over the years I have attempted to be more theoretically conscious, equally investing an enormous amount of time trying to inform myself of at least some to the theoretical developments in the wider human and social sciences. I also have possibly become more conscious and careful of the criteria that I seek to impose on my own theorizing. Recognizing that such theorizing is a human endeavor, I have become increasingly aware that the particular understandings I seek to develop should attempt to be consistent with the more general notions of knowledge and theory they themselves articulate. I also often say that theorists should always be willing to be subject to their own theories! I am happy to stand by that test, although I know of many theories of the economic, organizational, and social nature of accounting that I, at least, would oppose being subjected to.

CONCLUSION

Trying to give coherence to a diversity of work is not an easy task. It is equally difficult trying to account for something that so obviously remains open-ended and emergent.

What uniformity there is in the papers that follow reflects a long-standing attempt to delve into accounting, to observe and explore its functioning, to construct a basis for interrogating it in use, and indeed, as I have sometimes said, to account for accounting itself. Rather than accepting accounting, seeking unproblematically to advance its functioning and improve its rationality, I have sought to understand accounting, to appreciate what it is, what it does, and how it does it. My position vis-à-vis accounting has therefore been a more questioning one, always striving to examine it from without rather than from within. Such a stance continues and it therefore still remains appropriate to entitle this collection of papers *Accounting from the Outside*.

REFERENCES

Dev,. S., *Accounting and the L.S.E. Tradition* (London School of Economics and Political Science, 1980).

Hopwood, A.G., *Accouting and Human Behavior* (Haymarket, 1975; Prentice Hall, 1976).

Hopwood, A.G., *An Accounting System and Managerial Behavior* (Saxon House, 1973).

Kassem, M.S., "Introduction: European versus American Organisation Theories," in G.H. Hofstede and M.S. Kassem, eds., *European Contributions to Organisation Theory* (Van Gorcum, 1976).

Getting Started: Exploring Accounting in Use

An Empirical Study of the Role of Accounting Data in Performance Evaluation

ANTHONY G. HOPWOOD*

2

Accounting systems are often the most important formal sources of information in industrial organizations. They are designed to provide all levels of management with timely and reasonably accurate information to help them make decisions which are in agreement with their organization's goals. It is therefore surprising to find reports that managers, in adapting to accounting systems, deliberately falsify the data and make decisions which may be detrimental to the long-term interests of the organization. Yet there are many such reports in the accounting literature.

Many of the documented examples of falsification and dysfunctional decision making were an outgrowth of attempts to make the accounting reports a more favorable reflection of the manager's or the worker's performance. Whyte has described the ingenious attempts of a group of workers to obtain easier standards when their payments included a bonus based on these standards.[1] Other investigators have noted the tendency of managers to pad their budgets either to make the reported variances more favorable or in anticipation of cuts by either superiors or accountants.[2] Perhaps of even more concern to accountants are the numerous examples in the literature of managers making decisions in response to the accounting system, even though the decisions are contrary to the goals of the

* Lecturer, Manchester Business School.

[1] W. F. Whyte, *Money and Motivation* (New York: Harper and Row, 1955).

[2] See, for instance, L. S. Rosen and R. E. Schneck, "Some Behavioural Consequences of Accounting Measurement Systems." *Cost and Management*, October (1967), pp. 6–16; A. E. Lowe and R. W. Shaw, "An Analysis of Managerial Biasing: Some Evidence from a Company's Budgeting Process," *Journal of Management Studies*, V (1968), 304–15; M. Schiff and A. Y. Lewin, "The Impact of People on Budgets," *The Accounting Review*, XLV (1970), 259–68.

organization.[3] Dearden has reported many such anecdotes in a series of publications.[4] For instance, he tells of a manager who was reluctant to replace equipment, even when it was in the company's economic interest, because of the heavy book losses which would be unfavorably reflected in his current performance reports.

There are many similar examples in the accounting literature, but unfortunately most of them are in the forms of anecdotes and, of more importance, little consideration has been given to the conditions under which such behavior is likely to occur. Yet this type of knowledge is important for accountants who are concerned with system design and change. In particular, it is important to know whether the dysfunctional behavior is a necessary consequence of using the accounting data in performance evaluation or at least of the imperfections in accounting systems or, rather, whether it is dependent upon the precise manner in which the accounting data are used. The issue is a significant one because the various alternative explanations suggest different remedies.

3

Some Problems with Accounting Measures of Performance

Although accounting data can reflect at least some of the important dimensions of managerial performance, accountants are faced with a series of major problems in designing information systems for this purpose. First, not all the relevant dimensions of managerial performance are included in accounting reports since neither accountants nor managers have developed comprehensive measures and standards.[5] Second, even considering the economic aspects of performance, an organization's economic cost function is rarely known with precision and an accounting system can only attempt to approximately represent its complexity. This is a particular problem with highly interdependent patterns of activities. Third, the accounting data are primarily concerned with representing

[3] For instance, F. J. Jasinski, "Use and Misuse of Efficiency Controls," *Harvard Business Review* (July–August, 1956), pp. 105–12; V. F. Ridgway, "Dysfunctional Consequences of Performance Measurements," *Administrative Science Quarterly,* I (1956), 240–47; A. Etzioni and E. W. Lehman, "Some Dangers in 'Valid' Social Measurement," *Annals of the American Academy of Political and Social Science,* CCCLXXIII (1967), 1–15.

[4] J. Dearden, "Problem in Decentralized Profit Responsibility," *Harvard Business Review* (May–June, 1960), pp. 72–80; B. D. Henderson and J. Dearden, "New System for Divisional Control," *Harvard Business Review* (Sept.–Oct., 1966), pp. 144–60.

[5] The development and utilization of human resources is one example, although some preliminary research is now being conducted into ways of measuring the value of human resources. For one line of thought on this issue, see R. L. Brummet, E. G. Flamholtz and W. C. Pyle, "Human Resource Measurement—A Challenge for Accountants," *The Accounting Review,* XLIII (1968), 217–24, and W. C. Pyle, "Monitoring Human Resources 'On Line,'" *Michigan Business Review,* XXII (1970), 19–32. The general topic of more inclusive measures of performance is discussed in the "Report of the Committee on Non-Financial Measures of Effectiveness," *The Accounting Review,* supplement to XLVI (1971), 165–212.

outcomes, while managerial activity is concerned with the detailed process giving rise to the final outcomes. If there are factors which constrain the reported efficiency of the process despite the quality of the manager's performance, the accounting data will be an inadequate reflection of his performance. For a fair evaluation, the controllable component of the reports should be isolated, yet this is a difficult, if not impossible, task.[6] Fourth, the main emphasis of accounting reports is on short-term performance indexes while the evaluation of managerial performance is often concerned with more long-term considerations.[7] Ultimately, of course, the very cost of providing the information is an important constraint on the accuracy and relevance of the data.

In addition, accounting systems are also trying to serve many purposes. Each purpose may ideally necessitate the preparation of a unique set of data, although accountants frequently try to produce general purpose reports which are of some value for at least some of these many purposes. However, in trying to satisfy a series of purposes, the reports may fail to
4 perfectly satisfy the requirements for any single purpose—the appraisal of managerial performance, for instance.

While it is frequently possible to improve an existing accounting performance measurement system, it is often, if not always, impossible to achieve the ideal system. The information provided by an accounting system must therefore usually be used with discretion when evaluations are made on the basis of it. Many accountants realize this and some act accordingly, but the accounting data are also used by other managers who may not use them in an appropriate manner. It was for this reason that the present research was undertaken, in the belief that an understanding of the way in which managers adapt to accounting systems depends upon a more detailed knowledge of how accounting data are used. Particular

---

[6] In a basic sense the problem may be insoluble. The determination of whether a budget variance, for instance, is due to a manager's efforts or uncontrollable factors in either the internal or external environments of the organization would require a model of the organization and its relationship to the environment. In this way we would certainly be able to measure the influence of a manager but is such a model possible in a world of uncertainty, and even if it existed, might not the role of the manager be radically changed? See K. J. Arrow, "Research in Management Controls: A Critical Synthesis," in *Management Controls: New Directions in Basic Research*, ed. C. P. Bonini, R. K. Jaedicke, and H. M. Wagner (New York: McGraw-Hill, 1964).

[7] Short-term accounting reports may look favorable because decisions have been made to postpone or cancel expenditures as part of a strict cost control program, although the final costs, which may not even be reflected in the cost center reports, may be higher than the cost, at the time, of postponement. This problem is illustrated by Likert's discussion of the more problematic long-term impact of cost control programs despite their apparent short-term success. Although there is the usual tendency to overgeneralize, there is sufficient evidence that the problem is an important one. See R. Likert, *New Patterns of Management* (New York: McGraw-Hill, 1961) and *The Human Organization: Its Management and Value* (New York: McGraw-Hill, 1967).

attention is given in the study to the use of accounting data in managerial performance evaluation, a topic which has been of some concern to both practicing and academic accountants.[8]

The Use of Accounting Data in Performance Evaluation

It is important to recognize that even standard accounting reports can be used in many different ways in performance evaluation. Within the human consciousness, while the accounting data are given, their interpretation and precise use is the outcome of a personal and social process which is sustained by the meanings, systems of belief, pressures and purposes that are brought to bear by the managers using the data. In of necessity providing the data with a personal significance and placing them in their own wider intellectual context, managers are able to use them, perhaps without reflection, in a variety of ways.

Such a process is recognized by many in the social sciences, although,
surprisingly, the problem of differential use has not been systematically 5
considered in the accounting literature. So far attention has been primarily focused on the technical design of performance measurement systems and the possibilities for reducing the unanticipated behavioral consequences by changing the indexes used. There is no doubt that this is a necessary concern. It reflects, however, only a partial viewpoint and it is just as necessary to develop a perspective which enables us to distinguish between the plurality of ways in which accounting data can be used to evaluate performance. To this we now turn.

The relative visibility of events within an organization is partly determined by accounting measures of managerial performance since they influence both individual perceptions and the process by which the expectations held by managers at all levels are formulated and revised. While they are designed to mobilize individual energies and motivations to increase the efficiency of an organization's operations, it is possible that at times their presence can lead to a transference of interest from the wider organizational purposes which they were designed to serve on to the specific behavior which is necessary to improve the indexes of performance. Merton has discussed this process in terms of a "displacement of goals" whereby "an instrumental value," in this case an index which is intended to identify areas for investigation and enquiry, "becomes a terminal value" sought for on its own accord.[9]

---

[8] One indication of recent interest in this topic is the symposium held at Ohio State University in 1968. See T. J. Burns, ed., *The Behavioral Aspects of Accounting Data for Performance Evaluation* (Columbus, Ohio: College of Administrative Sciences, Ohio State University, 1970).

[9] R. K. Merton, "The Unanticipated Consequences of Purposive Social Action," *American Sociological Review*, I (1936), 894–904, and *Social Theory and Social Structure* (New York: The Free Press, 1957), pp. 199–200.

The accounting measures of managerial performance are given a meaning and interpretation. In this paper these broad distinctions are used as the basis for distinguishing between ways in which accounting reports which show the actual and budgeted costs for a cost center, and the difference between them, can be used in evaluating the performance of the person responsible for the cost center. Three styles of evaluation which make distinctly different uses of the data are isolated and defined:

1. *Budget Constrained Style.* Despite the many problems in using accounting data as comprehensive measures of managerial performance, the evaluation is primarily based upon the cost center head's ability to continually meet the budget on a short-term basis. This criterion of performance is stressed at the expense of other valued and important criteria and a cost center head will tend to receive an unfavorable evaluation if his actual costs exceed the budgeted costs, regardless of other considerations.

2. *Profit Conscious Style.* The performance of the cost center head is evaluated on the basis of his ability to increase the general effectiveness
6 of his unit's operations in relation to the long-term purposes of the organization. One important aspect of this at the cost center level is his concern with the minimization of long-run costs.[10] For this purpose the accounting data must be used with some care in a rather flexible manner.

3. *Nonaccounting Style.* Accounting data play a relatively unimportant part in the supervisor's evaluation of the cost center head's performance.

While the accounting data clearly indicate whether a person has been successful in meeting the budget, they do not necessarily indicate whether he is behaving so as to minimize long-run costs, let alone influence other determinants of effectiveness. In order to assess this ability, the data may have to be used with discretion and, where necessary, supplemented with information from other sources. Unlike a Budget Constrained evaluation, a Profit Conscious evaluation is therefore concerned with the wider information content, or lack of it, of the accounting data, and not with just a rigid analysis of the direction and magnitude of the reported budget variances.

Responses to the Use of Accounting Data in Performance Evaluation

A study of the manipulations and other dysfunctional behaviors made in response to an accounting based evaluation poses a number of impor-

[10] The idea of cost minimization is overly simple because, in itself, it does not necessarily result in either profit maximization or the attainment of more wide-ranging definitions of organizational effectiveness. However, since production volume was not determined by the persons in charge of the cost centers in the subject company, the objective of minimizing the long-run costs for the specified volume of production is more likely to be congruous with profit maximization. More generally, the idea is used to reflect the direction of concern rather than a constraint.

tant methodological problems. We would expect to find differences between cost centers in both the opportunities for such behavior and its ease of detection. This means that it is difficult to study behavioral responses of this type by the use of survey or data analysis techniques across a large number of cost centers. Instead, they must be investigated through the intensive study of a smaller number of cost centers. However, in order to provide some basis for the selection of cost centers for such an investigation, as well as adding some validity to the findings, concern is given in the study to the specification of a series of concurrent conditions associated with such behavior. In this way a more thorough understanding will be gained of the behavioral responses to the various styles of evaluation.

If the accounting reports are used in a manner consistent with a Profit Conscious style of evaluation, problems associated with using the accounting data in performance evaluation are less important. It may be difficult to isolate the relevant aspects of the data, but the person making the evaluation will at least be aware of the problems. Perhaps of more 7
importance he will know that his own objective of long-term cost minimization is not necessarily consistent with a set of favorable short-term budget variances. Additional information sources must be used to supplement the accounting data.

However, in the case of a Budget Constrained evaluation, the implications for the cost center head are different. Due to the incomplete nature of the accounting data there will be disagreement and conflict between him and his supervisor over the dimensions, and their values, on which the job is described and evaluated. This is capable of resulting in some anxiety since performance evaluations are often an important aspect of the development and maintenance of a person's self-esteem.[11] The cost center head will not gain recognition for his accomplishments on dimensions which he views as important and relevant but which are not reflected in the accounting data, although he might well be evaluated on dimensions which he genuinely considers to be irrelevant.

Furthermore, even if the cost center head tries to improve his performance in terms of the accounting indexes, the behavior which is necessary to achieve this is not always clear if some of the reported costs are not under his control or if the standards are subject to error. His own efforts to improve the performance indexes may be overshadowed by the behavior of other persons who are able to influence his reports. He cannot be sure that a given action will result in a favorable evaluation—a further condition which can contribute to experience of tension and anxiety.[12]

---

[11] S. F. Miyamoto and S. M. Dornbusch, "A Test of Interactionist Hypotheses of Self-Conception," *American Journal of Sociology*, LXI (1956), 399–403.

[12] See, for instance, A. R. Cohen, "Situational Structure, Self-Esteem and Threat Oriented Reactions to Power," in *Studies in Social Power*, ed. D. Cartwright (Ann Arbor, Mich.: Institute for Social Research, University of Michigan, 1959), and R. L. Kahn, *et al., Organizational Stress: Studies in Role Conflict and Ambiguity* (New

The disagreement, biases and uncertainty introduced into the performance evaluation by a Budget Constrained style of evaluation are not only likely to be seen as unjust by the cost center head, but they will also be a source of conflict, tension and anxiety. As a consequence, he is less likely to be satisfied with the supervisor whose style of evaluation poses such a threat to his security.[13]

The cost center head can, however, attempt to relieve the tension associated with a Budget Constrained style of evaluation by engaging in various forms of coping behavior. First, he can try to blame other cost center heads for his own unfavorable variances. He can concentrate on the activities of his own unit, trying to improve the reported budget variances regardless of how this affects the performance of other units. Argyris found that there was the greatest rivalry and competition, and less friendship between colleagues in departments with the highest pressure from management controls.[14] In his earlier study of the budgetary system of four companies, he presents vivid evidence of interdepartmental strife,
8 department centeredness, and blaming other persons when things go wrong.[15] Behavior of this type is hypothesized to be a result of the competitive relationships between the cost center heads in a Budget Constrained department, and the consequent deterioration in their friendship ties, helpfulness and mutual respect.[16] The result is one which is not only uncomfortable for the cost center heads but also dysfunctional to the company since a certain amount of cooperation is essential for achieving

---

York: John Wiley, 1964), pp. 85–86. There is also evidence of a positive relationship between uncontrollability and feelings of tension and anxiety in the specific case where one organization subunit is interdependent with one or more other subunits, whether the interdependence is facilitative or hindering. See M. Deutsch, "An Experimental Study of the Effects of Cooperation and Competition upon Group Process," *Human Relations*, II (1949) 199–231, and E. J. Thomas, "Effects of Facilitative Role Interdependence on Group Functioning," *Human Relations*, X (1957), 347–66.

[13] E. Kay, H. H. Meyer, and J. R. P. French, Jr., "Effects of Threat in a Performance Appraisal Interview," *Journal of Applied Psychology*, XLIX (1956), 311–17. Kahn and his associates have also found that persons who receive conflicting and ambiguous role expectations are less likely to maintain favorable relationships with the persons sending the expectations. See Kahn *et al.*, *op. cit.*, p. 90.

[14] C. Argyris, *Understanding Organizational Behavior* (Homewood, Ill.: The Dorsey Press, 1960).

[15] C. Argyris, *The Impact of Budgets on People*, a study prepared for the Controllership Foundation (Cornell University, School of Business and Public Administration, 1952). H. White has also described a case of interdepartmental conflict due to the specific problems caused by the allocation of costs. See his "Management Conflict and Sociometric Choice," *American Journal of Sociology*, LXVIII (1961), 185–99.

[16] On the relationship between competition and the quality of interpersonal relationships, see Deutsch, *op. cit.*, Thomas, *op. cit.*, and E. Trist and K. Bamforth, "Some Social and Psychological Consequences of the Longwall Method of Goal Getting," *Human Relations*, IV (1951), 3–38.

efficient performance and allowing a flexible response to unusual circumstances.[17]

The cost center head can also attempt to achieve a favorable set of budget variances by manipulating the accounting data. He can falsify the accounting records and make decisions purely on the basis of their effect on the short-term budget reports even when the results are contrary to the long-term interests of the company. Blau found that a group of administrators behaved so as to improve their performance on the basis of the statistical indexes which were used in their evaluation, even if this behavior resulted in dysfunctional consequences for the organization.[18]

The above arguments can be expressed in the following hypotheses which are tested in the study:

> If a cost center head perceives that he is evaluated on the basis of a Budget Constrained style he is (a) more likely to experience job related tension; (b) more likely to report having poor relations with
> his supervisor; (c) more likely to report having poor relations with 9
> his peers; (d) more likely to engage in falsification of the accounting data and dysfunctional decision making, than if he perceives that he is evaluated on the basis of either a Profit Conscious or a Non-accounting style.

Research Site and Methodology

The study was conducted in one manufacturing division of a large Chicago-based company.[19] The division has a labor force in excess of 20,000 persons and has an annual revenue of several hundred million

[17] See, for instance, B. S. Georgopoulos and A. S. Tannenbaum, "A Study of Organizational Effectiveness." *American Sociological Review,* XX (1957), 534–40. It should be borne in mind, however, that the relationship between both personal and organizational conflict and organizational effectiveness is not straightforward, the outcome depending on the type of conflict, its context, the manner in which it handled one's personal values. See M. Deutsch, "Conflicts: Productive and Destructive," *Journal of Social Issues,* XXV (1969), 7–41.

[18] P. M. Blau, *The Dynamics of Bureaucracy* (University of Chicago Press, 1955), pp. 36–56. The study has been replicated by H. Cohen in his *The Demonics of Bureaucracy: Problems of Change in a Government Agency* (Ames, Iowa: Iowa State University Press, 1965).

[19] The division is divided into a series of areas, departments, and cost centers. Each area includes several departments, and each department is divided into a series of cost centers. There are nine major hierarchical levels in the division: (1) Vice President; (2) General Manager; (3) Assistant General Manager; (4) Area Manager; (5) Departmental Supervisor; (6) Assistant Departmental Supervisor; (7) General Foreman; (8) Foreman; (9) a blue-collar bargaining unit level. Cost centers are usually under the responsibility of a general foreman, although some foremen and assistant departmental supervisors are also in charge of cost centers. One person may be in charge of several cost centers; at the time this study was conducted, there were over 350 cost centers under the responsibility of 193 cost center heads.

dollars. It is a company whose senior management is justifiably proud of its record of good personnel relations and high employee satisfaction.

The division's accounting system, which is a fairly sophisticated one based on flexible budgets and standard costing techniques, was installed a decade ago, and it is now an accepted and important part of the work environment. Monthly reports comparing the actual and budgeted costs for cost centers are issued to all cost center heads and their departmental supervisors,[20] and these are supplemented by daily and weekly reports on such matters as production, labor and supplies, the nature and content of which vary between cost centers. All internal transfers of materials and services are made at a predetermined standard price which is based on the full cost of providing the material or service, and all the reports contain overhead costs allocated from other units in one division.

The study consisted of two phases, a questionnaire phase, the results of which receive primary attention in the present paper, and an interview phase. This research design was selected so as to enable a study of
10 manipulative behavior in a series of carefully selected cost centers, while allowing the other hypotheses to be tested by the use of survey techniques with a larger sample of subjects.

The analysis is based on questionnaires sent to all of the 193 persons in the division who were in charge of cost centers. Where a respondent failed to return the initial questionnaire, up to two follow-up letters were sent to him. The final response rate was very high, namely 87 percent (167 out of the 193). Once the questionnaires had been returned and the basic analysis completed, 20 cost center heads in four departments (two predominantly Budget Constrained, one Profit Conscious and one Nonaccounting) were selected as the focal persons for the interview phase of the study. The statistical analysis of the questionnaire responses is based on nonparametric statistics, namely Kendall's Tau and the Mann-Whitney U test.[21]

Measurement of the Variables

THE SUPERVISOR'S STYLE OF EVALUATION

Information on the supervisor's style of evaluation was obtained from each cost center head. Eight possible criteria of performance were in-

[20] Three monthly reports are prepared for the large production cost centers, namely a Performance Summary, an Operating Statement and a Processing Cost Statement The Performance Summary provides an analysis of the monthly variance and a summary of production data. The Operating Statement accounts for the materials charged to the cost center and the rejected output in both physical quantities and dollars. A statement of the related budget variances is included on the report. Finally, the Processing Cost Statement presents detailed budget and actual cost information on all elements of cost other than the cost of the principal materials. Only the Processing Cost Statement is prepared for the smaller production cost centers and the service cost centers.

[21] S. Siegel, *Nonparametric Statistics* (New York: McGraw-Hill, 1956).

cluded in the questionnaire. A Budget Constrained style of evaluation was represented by the criterion "meeting the budget" and a Profit Conscious style by "concern with costs." These phrases were selected to represent the two styles on the basis of observations made during a series of exploratory interviews on the research site. At the time, it was found that they were used by cost center heads to refer to distinct patterns of behavior which were in agreement with the distinctions described above.[22]

Two measures of the supervisor's style of evaluation were obtained from the questionnaire responses. The principal measure is based on the relative importance of the various criteria. Cost center heads were asked to rank order the three most important criteria in their evaluation. On the basis of the rankings, the following evaluative styles are defined. The number of respondents in each group is shown in parentheses:

(i) Budget Constrained style (BC): meeting the budget, but not concern with costs, ranked among the top three criteria (33).

(ii) Budget-Profit style (BP): both meeting the budget and concern with costs among the top three criteria (17). 11

(iii) Profit Conscious style (PC): concern with costs, but not meeting the budget, ranked among the top three criteria (43).

(iv) Nonaccounting style (NA): neither meeting the budget nor concern with costs ranked among the top three criteria (74).[23]

In addition to these measures based on the relative importance of the various criteria, another series of measures was based upon the cost center head's ratings of the absolute importance of each separate criterion. The ratings were given on a five-point scale varying from "of no importance" to "very important," and there is evidence of consistency between the rankings and the ratings.

THE DEPENDENT VARIABLES[24]

A 15-item index of job related tension, which has been used extensively in previous research, was used in the study.[25] In addition, a 3-item index

[22] The other performance criteria were cooperation with colleagues, getting along with the boss, effort put into the job, and concern with quality. Also, attitude towards the work and company, and ability to handle the men.

[23] The operational definition of the Nonaccounting style should be interpreted as implying a *low relative importance* to the accounting related criteria.

[24] A complete discussion of the operational definition and characteristics of the dependent variables is included in A. G. Hopwood, "An Accounting System and Managerial Behavior" (unpublished Ph.D. dissertation, University of Chicago, 1971).

[25] See Kahn *et al.*, *op. cit.*, pp. 424–27. In the present study, it is important to investigate the behavioral and attitudinal correlates of tension because in organizational studies, as in personality studies, it cannot be assumed that tension is necessarily dysfunctional to the individual or the organization. Indeed, there is evidence which suggests that certain amounts of tension can be functional to both the individual and the organization, and that the relationship between functional consequences and tension is more like a curvilinear one. See E. P. Torrance, "A Theory of Leadership and Interpersonal Behavior Under Stress," in *Leadership and*

of specific cost tension was developed concerned with the extent to which the cost center head worries about costs, meeting the budget, and feels that this interferes with the rest of his work. The index of specific cost tension is independent of the job related tension index (Tau = 0.07). So as to obtain a comprehensive picture of the state of interpersonal relations, eight indexes of the cost center head's relations with his supervisor and six of his relations with his peers were included in the questionnaire.[26]

Results

The first part of the analysis is based upon the evaluative styles defined in terms of the relative importance of the various performance criteria. An examination of Table 1 reveals that cost center heads who feel that they are being evaluated on the basis of a Budget Constrained style report a significantly higher level of job related tension than those who are evaluated on the basis of either a Profit Conscious or a Nonaccounting style.
12 There is also a tendency for this to be true even when an attempt is made to combine the Budget Constrained and Profit Conscious styles. However, all of the accounting related styles of evaluation result in a similar level of specific cost tension. A Profit Conscious style does lead to worrying about costs and the budget, but unlike the Budget Constrained style, this does not spread to more general features of the job.

When cost center heads are evaluated on the basis of their ability to continually avoid unfavorable budget variances, success in satisfying this criterion results in lower job related tension. For the combined Budget Constrained and Budget Profit evaluation groups, there is a small but significant negative relationship between the cost center head's success in

Interpersonal Behavior, ed. L. Petrullo and B. M. Bass (New York: Holt, Rinehart and Winston, 1961), pp. 100–117, and D. Sirota, "Some Effects of Promotional Frustration on Employees' Understanding of, and Attitudes Toward, Management," *Sociometry*, XXII (1959), 273–78. It is therefore of interest to note that previous studies have found that the index of job related tension used in the present study is correlated with role conflict and ambiguity, and the presence of mild neurotic symptoms. This provides evidence that the index is sensitive to at least some of the dysfunctional aspects of tension. See B. J. Indik, S. E. Seashore and J. Slesinger, "Demographic Correlates of Psychological Strain," *Journal of Abnormal and Social Psychology*, LXIX (1964), 26–38; Kahn *et al.*, *op. cit.*, and J. D. Snoek, "Role Strain in Diversified Role Sets," *American Journal of Sociology*, LXXI (1966), 363–70.

[26] The indexes of relations with the supervisor are trust in the supervisor; respect for the supervisor; the perception of the supervisor's understanding of job problems; the perceived reasonableness of the supervisor's expectations; satisfaction with the supervisor's technical knowledge; satisfaction with the supervisor's administrative ability; satisfaction with the supervisor's human relations skills; general satisfaction with the supervisor. The peer relations indexes are peer supportiveness-achievement; peer supportiveness-affiliation; peer agreement; peer helpfulness; respect for peers; peer friendship. The indexes were developed at the Institute for Social Research at the University of Michigan, and have been extensively used in various studies by members of the Institute.

meeting the budget in the six-month period before the receipt of the questionnaire,[27] and the job related tension which they experience (Tau = −0.17; $p < .05$). There is no similar reduction in cost tension (Tau = − 0.04). Past success is not, however, instrumental in reducing job related tension in either the Profit Conscious or Nonaccounting groups (Tau is 0.04 and 0.03 respectively), an important finding which increases our confidence in the construct validity of the operational definitions of the evaluative styles.[28]

A person who is subject to a Budget Constrained evaluation may have little control over the month-to-month variances, and as a result he is forced to devote a large part of his time and effort to frantic attempts to find some way out of the dilemma. One such cost center head described his difficulties in the following way:

> You have to get yourself out of the woods. It's a process of staying out of the red.
> You have to. It's true, it's true, and it makes a job so much more difficult, There'd
> be times when I could do a good job and save some money by spending a bit 13
> now. But no, the only thing I concentrate on is what I've got forthcoming that's
> going to put me in the red. I've got to concentrate to see . . . there's no more
> money to spend. God, it causes me some problems.

Sometimes it is almost impossible to make the short-term budget variances more favorable, as is the case for the cost center heads whose variances are highly dependent on production volume. "When I'm in the red I start cutting on manpower. Well, I should, but I can't. We've been down on manpower for sometime now. I just have to live on my budget, close to the bone, but you can't, you can't." These frantic and often unsuccessful attempts only result in more problems, more tension and more worry.

Cost center heads who are subject to a Profit Conscious evaluation are

---

[27] The index of past success in meeting the budget is based on the mean of the percentage ratios of budgeted to actual costs for the six months prior to the receipt of the questionnaire. This ratio is the principal form in which the monthly variances are reported in the subject company.

[28] L. J. Cronbach and P. E. Meehl, "Construct Validity in Psychological Tests," *Psychological Bulletin,* LII (1955), 281–302. The finding is important because it provides some independent evidence of the validity of the evaluative classifications. Furthermore, it is not subject to at least the danger of self-consistent responses when the cost center heads supply both the information on the evaluative styles and on some of the dependent variables. In this respect, it is important to note that although the level of general job satisfaction was significantly lower in the BC group than in the PC and NA groups, the overall level of satisfaction in all groups was rather high. With a possible range of 7 to 35, the range of responses on the index of job satisfaction was 18 to 35, with a mean of 30.2 and a standard deviation of 3.9. The level of job satisfaction in the BP group was not significantly different from that in the PC and NA groups. In addition, it is also important to note the subsequent evidence, some of which is based on an analysis of the accounting data, of different decision behaviors associated with the evaluative styles.

not, however, having an easy time, as is shown by the following quotation:[29]

> [The Profit Conscious supervisor] is always asking about costs—all the time. This is basically the heart of it. I guess, costs. Anytime we get together or whenever he gets you its costs, costs, costs. "See if we can cut down." "It's going pretty fast, we'd better talk about it." He's a little bit too strict really. I'm used to discipline, but he runs a tight ship. He does not like us to get sloppy; he gets hot under the collar. He tries to save whatever he can. He just likes to operate that way. He is just that type of person, but to be fair, he applies pressure where it is appropriate.

A Profit Conscious style is seen as a demanding style of evaluation but it is also seen as a fair one. Uncontrollable variances are either not queried or, even if they are queried, they can usually be explained. The cost center heads are able to justify actions which result in long-term cost savings even though they produce unfavorable current budget variances. Indeed it is the ability to explain which plays an important role in avoiding the
14 higher tension and anxiety associated with the Budget Constrained style, a style whose approach is "just don't do it, rather than asking for explanations."

The different uses of the accounting data in performance evaluation affect the cost center heads' perceptions of how justly their performance is evaluated.[30] In Table 2 it can be seen that when there is a tendency to use the accounting data in terms of a Budget Constrained style, the cost center heads feel that their evaluation is less just than those reporting either a Profit Conscious or Nonaccounting style.

The evidence on the effects of the styles of evaluation on relationships with the supervisor is in agreement with hypothesis (b). As can be seen in Table 3, there is a tendency for the cost center heads' perceptions of their relations with the supervisor to deteriorate if he is seen as using a Budget Constrained style or even if he attempts to combine the Budget Constrained and Profit Conscious styles. In contrast, if the supervisor uses a Profit Conscious style, there is a tendency, not sufficient however to reach statistical significance, for the cost center heads to report more favorable relations with him than with even a Nonaccounting supervisor.

A Budget Constrained style of evaluation also results in reports of less favorable relations with peers. The evidence presented in Table 4 is an

---

[29] There is additional evidence in the questionnaire responses which supports this statement. Cost center heads were asked to rank not only the top three criteria used in their evaluation, but also the three which they would prefer to be used. A comparison of these responses shows that 17 of the 43 (39.5%) respondents who reported that their supervisor used a Profit Conscious style thought that concern with costs should have a lower rank in their evaluation.

[30] Based on responses to the question "How justly do you think your performance is evaluated?" The responses were given on a 5-point scale ranging from "my performance is always evaluated justly" to "my performance is never evaluated justly," and the index has a possible range of 1 to 5.

agreement with hypothesis (c), with the worst reports of peer relationships occurring when the supervisor is perceived as using either a Budget Constrained or a Budget Profit style.[31] When someone is continually asked about budget variances over which he has little or no control, there is a tendency to try to pass on the responsibility by blaming other persons. This is known as "finger pointing" or "passing the buck." The practice is described by a cost center head in a Budget Constrained department:

> There's passing the buck when we're told to cut down, because we have no control. What good is it telling us to cut back. We don't have control. Occasionally there's a noncritical item that I could hold back but, in the main, most conditions of being in the red are things we have no control over. Yet we're still blamed for them. It's a tension reliever to pass it on to someone else.

Not only is there a definite tendency to blame other persons, but also, because each cost center head in this situation is anxiously devoted to the avoidance of unfavorable red variances, he concentrates solely on the 15
activities of his own cost center, failing to be concerned with how this affects the neighboring operations. This can have an important effect on the efficiency of the department's operations, since it results in a sluggish decision process and a constraint on innovation.[32] The arguments and

[31] The questionnaire responses cover only certain rather general aspects of the effects of the different evaluative styles on the network of interpersonal relations. In all cases the questions on peer relations, for instance, referred to "the people (or the man) at your level in the company with whom you have to deal in your job." The general reference, while locating important differences between the styles of evaluation, also obscured some of the detailed patterns of response. Some limited forms of task cooperation between cost center heads reporting a Budget Constrained evaluation were noted during the interview phase of the study. There was, however, a very definite preference for this cooperation to be with persons in charge of cost centers in departments other than one's own, particularly the central service units, or with persons in the same department who were in charge of noninterdependent units. The relationships were usually instrumental in nature, being formed for the purpose of mutually improving budget variances, the relationships forming part of a system of reciprocal obligations (see A. W. Gouldner, "The Norm of Reciprocity: A Preliminary Statement," *American Sociological Review*, XXV (1968), 161–78). The findings are similar to those reported by Roy in his "Efficiency and 'the Fix': Informal Intergroup Relations in a Piece Work Machine Shop," *American Journal of Sociology*, LX (1955), 255–66.

[32] The relationship between budgetary systems and innovation has been referred to in the research conducted as part of the Carnegie Project on the Behavioral Theory of the Firm. See R. M. Cyert and J. G. March, *A Behavioral Theory of the Firm* (Englewood Cliffs, N.J.: Prentice-Hall, 1963) and J. P. Crecine, *Governmental Problem Solving: A Computer Simulation of Municipal Budgeting* (Chicago: Rand McNally, 1969). The problem was also raised during the discussions reported in Burns, *op. cit.*, pp. 254–55. In those conference proceedings, Bedford notes, perhaps a little too strongly, the "... complete neglect of the influence of risk on innovation acceptance.... Clearly, any study of the behavioral response to accounting data should include consideration of different types of risks involved in making changes." Burns, *op. cit.*, p. 323.

conflicts in the Budget Constrained departments increase the difficulty of controlling important but highly interdependent aspects of the production process such as delay time. No one wants to take responsibility for a decision, just in case it costs too much or results in an unfavorable budget variance, as is illustrated by the following comments made by a cost center head in a Budget Constrained department:

> We sometimes have problems coming to an agreement. Well, it's the way we talk around here. Discussions can get pretty heated at times. Well, there was one item not too long ago. Whenever a buddy came up with an idea, no one's idea was the same and, as a consequence, we still haven't got it. "No, that wouldn't be worth a damn," that's what the others say. One guy wanted it this way, one guy that way, and as a consequence we still haven't got it. Sometimes there's disagreement on whether to do it at all. That's why I personally like to talk it over with the rest of them so that when it's finished and done they can't come back and say it's not worth a damn.
>
> What do you mean by coming back and saying 'it's not worth a damn'?
>
> 16 ...If the others were against it and it breaks down, then you're just left on your own because they say that it was no damn good to start with. Usually, the trouble is because it would cost too much, and then if it doesn't work 100 percent or if it costs a bit more than you thought, they say it was no damned good in the first place. Well, it's more difficult to blame anyone if you all agree first isn't it?
>
> So other people in the department blame each other for this type of thing?
>
> Yeah, there's finger pointing. Maybe not directly, but you hear about it in a round about way. It always comes back. They go to [the supervisor] on their own. "That's not my idea," that's what they tell him. "I didn't think a damn when it was put in. That was so and so's idea." But they wouldn't come directly and tell you themselves. There is a fair amount of this among the general foremen here, but it's done behind the scene.

On the basis of the intensive study of the selected series of cost centers, it was also found that cost center heads reporting a Budget Constrained style were more likely to engage in manipulative behavior than those evaluated in a Profit Conscious or Nonaccounting manner. The evidence is therefore supportive of hypothesis (d).[33] The manipulation in Budget Constrained departments was found to take three principal forms. First, cost center heads attempted to charge items of cost to other cost centers. This method, which took advantage of the cost center head's role in recording the basic accounting information, was done with some care so as to minimize the chance of detection. The practice was also more likely to occur when the cost center heads had recently received reports of unfavorable budget variances. It was the first frantic response to a stressful situation, and in some cases preceded the design and use of more sophisticated means of manipulation.

Cost over which the cost center heads were able to exercise some discretion as to their timing and amount represented an important focus

[33] A more complete description of the means of manipulation and their comparative incidence is given in Hopwood, *op. cit.*, pp. 118–58.

for manipulative attempts. In the subject company this was particularly true of repairs and maintenance expenditures. To minimize the total costs, including the opportunity costs of interrupted production, such expenditures should ideally be incurred at times of low production. The monthly repairs and maintenance budget, however, was determined on the basis of the month's production volume, resulting in a low budget when the costs should ideally be incurred. Both interview evidence and a statistical analysis of the cost data suggest that the cost center heads who are evaluated on the basis of a Budget Constrained style, unlike those evaluated on the basis of the other styles, tended to time the expenditures in the light of their effects on the short-term variances. They tended to ignore the more long-term implications and the elements of cost which are not reflected in the accounting system.

The correlations between monthly production and monthly expenditures on repairs and maintenance in 1969 were calculated for a series of cost centers.[34] In Table 5 the correlation coefficients are shown for the cost centers in two departments which have a similar technology. One depart- 17
ment is under a Budget Constrained supervisor; the other is under a Profit Conscious supervisor. Three of the six cost centers in the Budget Constrained department have a significantly positive correlation and, in addition, the value of one other coefficient (for cost center B4) approaches significance at the 10 percent level. There is therefore some tendency to do repair work at times of high production when the budget is available, and so avoid red variances. In contrast, none of the coefficients for the eight cost centers in the Profit Conscious department are significantly different from zero; decisions on the timing of repairs and maintenance expenditures are not made in the light of current production volume.

The next analysis is for a single department where the supervisor selectively uses a Budget Constrained style of evaluation. Four of the seven cost center heads in the department report that their supervisor uses this style, the other three reporting another style. In Table 6 it can be seen that for the five cost centers under the responsibility of persons who report a Budget Constrained style, one of the correlations is significantly

[34] The analysis presented a number of problems. First, some cost centers were closed down for a significant portion of the year. Second, repairs and maintenance expenditures are not separately identified for some cost centers. Both these sets of cost centers were excluded from the analysis. Third, different departments have different procedures for accounting for repairs and maintenance expenditures. In some departments such costs are separately charged to the cost center responsible for incurring the cost. In other departments, important portions of such costs are accumulated in a departmental account and then allocated to the separate cost centers on the basis of an engineering estimate of the average expenditures in a predetermined base period. Essentially the portion of the costs so allocated is beyond the control of the cost center head. In the analysis, the basic repairs and maintenance cost data are those directly controlled by the cost center heads; allocated costs are not included.

positive and another (S2) is close to significance at the 10 percent level. The correlations for the six cost centers under the responsibility for persons who did not report a Budget Constrained style are all negative, two reaching a statistically significant level. Again, there is some evidence that the cost center heads use a different decision rule.[35]

A third form of manipulation was available to relatively few persons. Some cost center heads did, however, attempt to influence the volume and type of production. Three ways of doing this were found:

(1) the creation of "pseudo-production" which only exists in the records;

(2) the maintenance of inventory buffers which gave the cost center head greater control over the volume and type of production in a period;[36]

(3) attempts to influence the production scheduling decision itself. Such attempts were instrumental in making the variances more favorable because of the insensitivity with which the accounting system reflected production changes and varying product mixes.

18 In summary, the evidence on the effects of a Budget Constrained style of evaluation, where this is interpreted as a high relative importance being given to a rigid use of the short-term accounting data in performance evaluation, has supported the hypotheses. The use of accounting data in terms of a Profit Conscious style does not, however, result in such unfavorable consequences.

The Effects of High Absolute Importance Being Attached to Meeting the Budget and Concern with Costs

We now discuss the effects of the absolute importance attached to the two accounting related criteria, where absolute importance is defined as the importance attached to a criterion independent of that attached to other criteria. The evidence is contrary to the hypotheses. As can be seen

[35] It is interesting to note one effect this type of manipulation can have on the usefulness of the accounting data for analytical work. As the initial step of a program concerned with achieving a more realistic separation of the fixed and variable elements of cost, members of the company's accounting department performed a statistical analysis of the monthly repairs and maintenance cost data for a series of departments. The analysis was inconclusive. Widely varying patterns of relationships with production volume were found. However, an examination of their findings on the basis of the evaluation groups established in this study suggested that the direction of the relationships with production volume was related to the dominant style of evaluation used in the department. There is a tendency for a Budget Constrained use of the accounting data to reinforce the assumptions built into the accounting system; if some elements of discretionary cost are accounted for as variable costs, a rigid use of the data will insure that they are incurred in this manner.

[36] Thompson has commented on the role of inventories in absorbing uncertainty in organizations. See J. D. Thompson, "Decision-Making, The Firm, and the Market," in *New Perspectives in Organization Research,* ed. W. W. Cooper, H. J. Leavitt, and M. W. Shelly (New York: John Wiley & Sons, 1964).

in Table 7, cost center heads who report that their supervisors attach high absolute importance to both meeting the budget and concern with costs are likely to experience relatively low job related tension, although they do tend to worry about specific matters affecting their costs and the budget.

There is also a positive relationship between the ratings of the absolute importance of the two criteria and the cost center heads' reports of their relations with their supervisors. An examination of Table 8 reveals that a high absolute importance of either criteria is associated with greater reported trust, respect and satisfaction with the supervisor. He is seen to be more understanding of the job problems. It would appear however, that the improvement in relations occurs without an easing of job expectations. A similar but weaker pattern of relationships is found for the indexes of peer relations reported in Table 9.

Hence it is only when meeting the budget becomes important in relation to other valued criteria of job performance that unfavorable consequences
occur. Of itself, concern with meeting the budget can result in quite 19
favorable consequences. This might reflect the fact that one purpose of a budget is to clearly set out the objectives for a cost center. While this certainly cannot be done with perfect accuracy, it is possible to carefully and cautiously use the budget for this purpose and thereby add an important element of structure and clarity to the job environment.[37] In Table 10 it can be seen that for the sample as a whole, the perceived absolute importance of meeting the budget is indeed associated with perceptions of greater goal clarity.[38] However, a more detailed examination of the data reveals that the concern with the budget has this effect only if it does not achieve high relative importance in performance evaluation. Significant positive relationships between the absolute importance of meeting the budget and goal clarity occur only in the Profit Conscious and Nonaccounting groups.

A Nonaccounting evaluation, in particular, might be made on the basis of rather vague criteria: attitudes, the way the cost center head handles

---

[37] French and his colleagues have commented on the advantage of specific job goals. See J. R. P. French, Jr., E. Kay and H. H. Meyer, "Participation and the Appraisal System," *Human Relations,* XIX (1966), 3–19. The literature on the relationship between goal specificity, and organizational and personal variables is reviewed by E. A. Locke, "Toward a Theory of Task Motivation and Incentives," *Organizational Behavior and Human Performance,* III (1968), 157–89, and T. F. Lyons, "Role Clarity, Satisfaction, Tension and Withdrawal," *Organizational Behavior and Human Performance,* VI (1971), 99–110.

[38] The index of perceived goal clarity is based on responses to the question: "Do you know what is expected of you in your job?" Respondents were asked to select one of four responses varying from "I am very sure of what is expected of me" to "I am not at all sure of what is expected of me." In the table, the Budget Constrained and Budget-Profit groups have been combined so as to increase the size of the group for analysis. This is done on the basis of the evidence which suggests that there is no significant difference between the two groups (see footnote 39 below).

his men, and effort. While such criteria are important, they are surrounded by a great deal of uncertainty. It is difficult to clearly specify what constitutes good and bad performance, and a supervisor might find it difficult to determine when improvement occurs. In these circumstances, the budgetary system offers one definite advantage. It attempts to express the units' objectives in a precise manner.

Discussion

The important management dilemma which provided the basis for the present study also serves to highlight the relevance of the findings. Although accounting data are often the most important formal sources of information in an organization, attempting to reflect matters which are of vital concern, they are usually incomplete and even biased indicators of managerial performance. A manager may want to make his subordinates aware of the relevant aspects of the data, and yet to use the data in their
20 appraisal is potentially inequitable, and may encourage defensive behavior which is contrary to the very goals of the organization the accounting system was designed to serve.

The study clearly demonstrates the real importance of the manner in which accounting data are used. Accounting data do not in of themselves pose a threat to members of an organization, and their imperfections need not necessarily be seen as unjust when they are used in performance evaluation. A manager is not therefore faced with a simple choice between using or not using the data in performance evaluation. Instead, he can reap many of the benefits of the accounting system by stressing factors which it attempts to measure without this resulting in either emotional costs for the persons being evaluated or defensive behavior which is dysfunctional for the organization. To do so, however, he must, in the terms of the study, use the accounting data in a manner consistent with a Profit Conscious style of evaluation rather than a Budget Constrained style.

The distinction between the two styles is a crucial one.[39] A concern with accounting data, which is often so vital for the efficiency of an organization, is accepted by the cost center heads so long as the data are used with care and the budget variances are not emphasized at the expense of other valued performance criteria. Cost center heads are satisfied with an in-

[39] The evidence suggests that the Budget Constrained and Profit Conscious styles are distinct and that it is not possible to successfully combine them. The Budget Constrained style dominates in the conflicting situation. Seventeen indexes of dependent variables have been presented in Tables 1 to 4. In all cases the values for the Budget Constrained group were not significantly different from the Budget-Profit group. In contrast, in 12 cases the values for this latter group were significantly different from those for the Profit Conscious group. One of the five cases where they did not significantly differ is for the cost tension index. It will be remembered that we noted that all the accounting related styles resulted in high cost tension.

creased absolute importance being attached to both their concern with costs and the extent to which they meet the budget, the latter possibly helping to clarify the job environment and goals. They are satisfied with the Profit Conscious style of evaluation even though it certainly does not result in easier job requirements. It is a demanding style and, as we have seen, produces a high level of cost tension, but it is accepted and respected, and results in significantly less tension, rivalry and ill feelings than the Budget Constrained style.

The Profit Conscious style appears to be one aspect of a problem solving style of management, as distinct from a style which attempts to impose a false measure of cognitive simplicity onto a complex and highly interdependent series of activities. The accounting system is seen as a valuable, although at times imperfect aid to management, and its reports are used in a creative manner, serving as a bias for inquiry and a source of ideas for change. "He throws 'if' into our cost statements. The cost is this or that, so throw an 'if' in and find the cost savings for the year and for a month." The data are not, however, automatically taken at their 21
face value. Rather, the Profit Conscious supervisor probes into their significance and meaning, supplementing them by many other sources of information, both formal and informal, so that the alternatives can be compared and the inconsistencies investigated. All these are processes which allow a continual test of the validity of the accounting data and which help to maintain the healthy, indeed essential element of skepticism in relation to the data.

In contrast, the Budget Constrained style is one in which the evaluation of performance is of primary importance, influencing all aspects of the supervisor's and the cost center head's behavior. Evaluation is not viewed as an ongoing part of the managerial process, interrelated with other important aspects of the job, and just one aspect of the process of influence. Rather, it is seen as a distinct and dominant activity, and the primary source of influence and control, overshadowing other vital elements of the process. The budget becomes not an aid to problem solving but a constraint on it, resulting in short time horizons and a sluggish and inflexible decision process. In the words of one interviewee:

> [A Budget Constrained supervisor] takes the budget to heart, while what [a Profit Conscious supervisor] does is accept it upon himself and if he doesn't agree with it then he'll reject the budget. He's a much tougher guy and it's difficult to argue with him. You have got to have some good arguments, but if he agrees with you then out goes the budget. [The Budget Constrained supervisor] can be stubborn. He aims to stay right on his budget, and that's that.

Although the study has illustrated a number of the important effects of these different ways of using accounting data in performance evaluation, it has not been directly concerned with the overall effects on the final efficiency of operations. This was partly because in the subject company, as in many organizations, the available indexes of efficiency are based on the accounting data and may therefore reflect both real efficiency and successful manipulation of the data. Nevertheless, the issue is both of immediate concern to the manager and of importance in placing the observed effects in a wider organizational context. Accordingly, while the need for further research is recognized, it is worthwhile to briefly review the available evidence which, although incomplete, is suggestive.

While both the Budget Constrained and Profit Conscious styles result in a concern with costs, only the Profit Conscious supervisor achieves this concern without the costly dysfunctional decision making and manipulation of the data. Examples were found of decisions taken in Budget Constrained departments which resulted in higher processing costs, less innovative behavior and a poorer quality service to the customer, and where the manipulation of the data reduced their usefulness for analytical purposes.[40] In addition, the climate of distrust and rivalry which is a consequence of the Budget Constrained style is also of importance because
22 it is known that in many situations such factors can influence long-term performance and success.[41] The presence of the type of tension and conflict observed between members of a Budget Constrained department can often impede the cooperation, mutual help and assistance which are so essential for controlling interdependent activities and maintaining a flexible response to unusual circumstances. These are problems which are nowhere near so prevalent with either a Profit Conscious or Nonaccounting style, a finding which should be borne in mind when the relative advantages and disadvantages of the latter style in particular are being considered.

The evidence is certainly suggestive that a Profit Conscious style is likely to result in a higher general level of efficiency than the Budget Constrained style. Nevertheless, the possibility does remain that it is still better to place at least some emphasis on the accounting data: in other words, some persons could indeed argue that the Budget Constrained style, despite its advantages, results in greater efficiency than the Nonaccounting style.

A number of the issues mentioned above are relevant to this important question, although there obviously remains a need for further research. While the cost associated with the difficulties of controlling interdependent operations, the short-time horizons, the manipulated accounting data and the climate of distrust are often important, their impact on the efficiency of operations will vary from situation to situation. The precise balance of costs and benefits may be different for the control of a stable, technologically simple situation than for the control of an uncertain and highly

[40] Some examples have been referred to above, but for a more complete discussion see Hopwood, *op. cit.*

[41] Georgopoulos and Tennenbaum, *op. cit.*

complex situation. Rather than trying to unnecessarily generalize at this early stage, it is essential that some further attempts be made to isolate the conditions influencing the relative advantages of the various styles of evaluation.

In addition, the Nonaccounting style has been regarded as a residual category in the present study and we have investigated neither its nature and variety nor the implicit assumption behind the design of many accounting systems that efficiency is dependent upon the rather direct use of accounting data in evaluation by supervisors.[42] Yet it is possible that in at least some of the so-called Nonaccounting evaluations, the accounting data may represent an important means of feedback to a cost center head, influencing his self-evaluation and subsequent behavior even though they are relatively unimportant in his superior's evaluation.

Some measure of subordinate defensiveness may be a reaction to all forms of evaluation by a superior. For instance, one group of researchers found that managers' attempts to assist subordinates by indicating areas for improvement were likely to be seen as a threat by the subordinates 23
and frequently resulted in defensiveness.[43] In which case, the present study has been concerned with differences in the level of threat, and it is possible that even the Profit Conscious style does not represent an optimal solution to the problem. Rather, a greater regard for the cost center head's self-motivation to be concerned with the accounting data may result in both efficient operations and an even lower level of threat.[44]

Such factors represent a significant and important direction for further research. More consideration needs to be given to the precise characteristics of the various styles, their implications for organizational effectiveness and the conditions influencing their relative advantages. While the research findings have suggested the outline of a perspective for viewing the differential use of accounting data in performance evaluation, our knowledge of the subject is still rudimentary. It can, however, best be advanced by further empirical research.

---

[42] E. H. Caplan, "Behavioral Assumptions of Management Accounting," *The Accounting Review,* XLI (1966), 496–509.

[43] E. Kay, H. H. Meyer and J. R. P. French, Jr., "Effects of Threat in a Performance Appraisal Interview," *Journal of Applied Psychology,* XLIX (1965), 311–17. Similar comments are made by N. R. F. Maier in his *The Appraisal Interview: Objectives, Methods and Skills* (New York: John Wiley & Sons, 1958).

[44] Bassett and Meyer found that a self-appraisal prepared by the subordinate resulted in less defensive behavior and a greater perceived improvement in performance than superior-review. See G. A. Bassett and H. H. Meyer, "Performance Appraisal Based on Self-Review," *Personnel Psychology,* XXI (1968), 421–30.

TABLE 1

The Effects of the Style of Evaluation on Job Related Tension and Specific Cost Tension

	Style of evaluation				Significance of paired comparisons[a]
	BC	BP	PC	NA	
Job related tension[b]	2.55	2.42	2.11	2.16	BC v. PC: $p < .01$ BC v. NA: $p < .05$ BP v. PC: $p < .05$
Cost tension[b]	2.81	2.78	2.81	2.42	BC v. NA: $p < .05$ BP v. NA: $p < .05$ PC v. NA: $p < .05$

[a] Significance tests are based on the Mann-Whitney *U* Test. Unless otherwise stated a paired comparison is not significant at the 5 percent level.

[b] Both indexes have been expressed as values on a 5-point scale ranging from 1 to 5.

TABLE 2

The Effects of the Style of Evaluation on the Perceived Justness of Evaluation

	Style of evaluation				Significance of paired comparisons[a]
	BC	BP	PC	NA	
Justness of evaluation[b]	3.30	3.63	4.17	4.00	BC v. PC: $p < .01$ BC v. NA: $p < .01$ BP v. PC: $p < .05$

[a] Significance tests are based on the Mann-Whitney *U* Test. Unless otherwise stated, a paired comparison is not significant at the 5 percent level.

[b] The index has a possible range of 1 to 5.

TABLE 3

The Effects of the Style of Evaluation on Reported Relations with the Supervisor

Index of relations with the supervisor[a]	Style of evaluation				Significance of paired comparisons[b]
	BC	BP	PC	NA	
Trust in supervisor	3.26	3.06	4.24	3.98	BC v. PC: $p < .01$ BC v. NA: $p < .05$ BP v. PC: $p < .01$ BP v. NA: $p < .01$
Respect for supervisor	3.67	3.82	4.60	4.33	BC v. PC: $p < .01$ BC v. NA: $p < .01$ BP v. PC: $p < .01$ BP v. NA: $p < .05$
Supervisor's understanding	3.27	3.18	4.09	3.89	BC v. PC: $p < .01$ BC v. NA: $p < .01$ BP v. PC: $p < .01$ BP v. NA: $p < .01$
Reasonableness of supervisor's expectations	3.12	3.13	3.44	3.49	BC v. NA: $p < .05$ BP v. NA: $p < .05$
Satisfaction with supervisor—administrative	3.36	3.53	4.40	4.11	BC v. PC: $p < .01$ BC v. NA: $p < .01$ BP v. PC: $p < .01$ BP v. NA: $p < .01$
Satisfaction—technical	3.42	3.75	4.42	4.21	BC v. PC: $p < .01$ BC v. NA: $p < .01$ BP v. PC: $p < .01$ BP v. NA: $p < .05$
Satisfaction—human relations	2.97	2.81	4.14	4.05	BC v. PC: $p < .01$ BC v. NA: $p < .01$ BP v. NA: $p < .01$ BP v. NA: $p < .01$
Satisfaction—general	3.33	3.47	4.58	4.38	BC v. PC: $p < .01$ BC v. PC: $p < .01$ BP v. PC: $p < .01$ BP v. NA: $p < .01$

[a] All the indexes have been coded on a scale of 1 to 5 for each case of comparison.

[b] Significance tests are based on the Mann-Whitney U Test. Unless otherwise stated, a paired comparison is not significant at the 5 percent level.

TABLE 4

The Effects of the Style of Evaluation on Reported Relations with Peers

Index of relations with peers[a]	Style of evaluation				Significance of paired comparisons[b]
	BC	BP	PC	NA	
Peer supportiveness—achievement	3.59	3.57	3.84	3.87	BC v. PC: $p < .05$ BP v. PC: $p < .05$ BP v. NA: $p < .05$
Peer supportiveness—affiliation	3.28	3.12	3.65	3.75	BC v. PC: $p < .05$ BC v. NA: $p < .01$ BP v. PC: $p < .01$ BP v. NA: $p < .01$
Peer agreement	3.36	3.35	3.72	3.76	BC v. PC: $p < .01$ BC v. NA: $p < .01$ BP v. PC: $p < .05$ BP v. NA: $p < .01$
26 Peer helpfulness	3.76	3.76	4.02	4.18	BC v. NA: $p < .01$ BP v. NA: $p < .05$
Respect for peers	3.73	4.00	4.10	4.14	BC v. PC: $p < .05$ BC v. NA: $p < .05$
Peer friendship	3.31	3.40	3.71	3.65	BC v. PC: $p < .05$

[a] All scales have been coded on a scale of 1 to 5 for ease of comparison.

[b] Significance tests are based on the Mann-Whitney U Test. Unless otherwise stated, a paired comparison is not significant at the 5 percent level.

TABLE 5

Correlations Between Monthly Production and Repairs and Maintenance Expenditures, 1969, for Two Departments

Budget Constrained department		Profit Conscious department	
Cost center code	Correlation between monthly production and R & M expenditures	Cost center code	Correlation between monthly production and R & M expenditures
B1	0.82*	NB1	0.21
B2	0.81*	NB2	0.13
B3	0.61*	NB3	0.12
B4	0.46	NB4	0.05
B5	0.28	NB5	−0.13
B6	0.02	NB6	−0.15
		NB7	−0.16
		NB8	−0.32

* Significant at $p < .05$.

TABLE 6

Correlations Between Monthly Production and Repairs and Maintenance Expenditures, 1969, for Cost Centers in a Department Where the Supervisor Selectively Uses a Budget Constrained Style of Evaluation

Cost centers where the cost center head reports that the supervisor uses a Budget Constrained style		Cost centers where the cost center head reports that the supervisor does not use a Budget Constrained style	
Cost center code	Correlation between monthly production and R & M expenditures	Cost center code	Correlation between monthly production and R & M expenditures
S1	0.52*	S6	−0.02
S2	0.49	S7	−0.26
S3	0.19	S8	−0.36
S4	0.01	S9	−0.39
S5	−0.01	S10	−0.54*
		S11	−0.59**

* Significant at $.05 < p < .10$.
** Significant at $p < .05$.

27

TABLE 7

The Relationship Between the Absolute Importance of Meeting the Budget and Concern with Costs, and Job Related Tension and Cost Tension (Kendall's Tau)

	The cost center heads' perceptions of the absolute importance of meeting the budget	The cost center heads' perceptions of the absolute importance of concern with costs
Job related tension	−0.18*	−0.29*
Cost tension	0.31*	0.31*

* Significant at $p < .01$.

TABLE 8

The Relationship Between the Absolute Importance of Meeting the Budget and Concern with Costs, and Reported Relations with the Supervisor (Kendall's Tau)

Index of relations with the supervisor	The cost center heads' perceptions of the absolute importance of meeting the budget	The cost center heads' perceptions of the absolute importance of concern with costs
Trust in supervisor	0.29*	0.27*
Respect for supervisor	0.30*	0.28*
Supervisor's understanding	0.23*	0.20*
Reasonableness of supervisor's expectations	−0.07	0.00
Satisfaction with supervisor—administrative	0.16*	0.16*
Satisfaction with supervisor—technical	0.30*	0.28*
Satisfaction with supervisor—human relations	0.28*	0.26*
Satisfaction with supervisor—general	0.18*	0.17*

* Significant at $p < .01$.

TABLE 9

The Relationship Between the Absolute Importance of Meeting the Budget and Concern with Costs, and Reported Relations with Peers (Kendall's Tau)

28

Index of the relations with peers	The cost center heads' perceptions of the absolute importance of meeting the budget	The cost center heads' perceptions of the absolute importance of concern with costs
Peer supportiveness—achievement	0.19**	0.14**
Peer supportiveness—affiliation	0.19**	0.14**
Peer agreement	0.13**	0.17**
Peer helpfulness	0.10*	0.14**
Respect for peers	0.02	0.08
Peer friendship	0.03	0.02

* Significant at $p < .05$.
** Significant at $p < .01$.

TABLE 10

Relationship Between the Absolute Importance of Meeting the Budget and Perceived Goal Clarity (Kendall's Tau)

	Total sample	Evaluation groups		
		BC & BP	PC	NA
Relationship between absolute importance of meeting the budget and goal clarity	0.17**	0.10	0.21*	0.22**

* Significant at $p < .05$.
** Significant at $p < .01$.

Leadership Climate and the Use of Accounting Data in Performance Evaluation

Anthony G. Hopwood

THE final effectiveness of any management accounting system is dependent not only upon its design and technical characteristics, but also upon the precise manner in which the resulting data are used. In the extreme, of course, a system contributes little or nothing to the efficiency of an organization's operations if the data are ignored. More generally, however, despite any amount of thought and consideration which may have gone into its design, no management accounting system ever achieves a perfect representation of the underlying structure of economic events. A careful use of the data is always essential to compensate for their many unavoidable inadequacies.

But it remains so much easier naively to acknowledge that the data should be used carefully than to specify what this entails in terms of managerial actions. Yet such an understanding is an essential prerequisite for the intelligent management of change and improvement. The present study was accordingly designed to investigate empirically some of the managerial factors which influence an accounting system's organizational and personal impacts. Particular consideration is given to the relationship between wider managerial behaviors and the use which is made of accounting data in performance evaluation.

DIFFERENT WAYS OF USING ACCOUNTING DATA IN PERFORMANCE EVALUATION 29

The investigation is based upon an analysis of the managerial determinants of the following three distinct styles of using budgeted and actual cost information in performance evaluation.

1. *A Budget Constrained Style.* Despite the many unavoidable problems in using accounting data as comprehensive measures of managerial performance, the manager's performance is primarily evaluated on the basis of his ability continually to meet the short-term budget.

2. *A Profit Conscious Style.* The manager's performance is evaluated on the basis of his ability to increase the long-term effectiveness of his unit in relation to the goals of the organization. The accounting data, although indicating whether the budget has been met, do not necessarily indicate whether long-term effectiveness is being attained. Therefore, while important, they are used with some care in a flexible and creative manner, and where

The author wishes to acknowledge the helpful comments and advice of Professor L. Richard Hoffman of the University of Chicago.

Anthony G. Hopwood is at the Administrative Staff College, Henley-on-Thames, England.

necessary, supplemented by alternative sources of information.

3. *A Nonaccounting Style.* Accounting data play a relatively unimportant part in the evaluation of the manager's performance.

Previous empirical research has demonstrated that these three ways of using accounting data have significantly different organizational and personal effects.[1] Although both the Budget Constrained and Profit Conscious styles resulted in a higher degree of involvement with costs than the Nonaccounting style, only the Profit Conscious style succeeded in attaining this without resulting in either emotional costs
30 for managers or defensive behavior which was dysfunctional for the organization. The Budget Constrained style resulted in a belief that the evaluation was unjust, in widespread tension and worry on the job, and in feelings of distrust and dissatisfaction with the supervisor. Not only were the managers who were evaluated in this way found to manipulate the accounting data and make decisions which resulted in higher long-term processing costs for the company as a whole, but the consequent conflict and rivalry between colleagues impeded the cooperation which was so essential for controlling their interdependent activities. In contrast, the Profit Consious style, while seen as very demanding, was accepted. It resulted in levels of tension and in satisfaction with the supervisor and colleague supportiveness similar to those which prevailed under a Nonaccounting evaluation.

Factors Influencing the Use Made of Accounting Data

As Argyris noted in this study of the personal impact of budgets in four industrial organizations, the way in which a manager uses budgetary data is only one aspect of his more general approach to the job.

> . . . It became obvious that the way people expressed their interest in budgets, and the way in which they described and used them, were directly related to the pattern of leadership in their daily industrial life.[2]

Many recent studies have made a distinction between the instrumental or task aspects and the socio-emotional aspects of managerial behavior. In this study, these two aspects of behavior are characterized in terms of the two dimensions of the Ohio State University Leadership Behavior Description Questionnaire (LBDQ), namely, Initiation of Structure and Consideration.[3] The Initiation of Structure dimension reflects the extent to which a manager defines both his own work role and those of his subordinates. A high score is indicative of clearly delineated roles and attempts to establish clear channels of communication, patterns of organization, and detailed job instructions. The Consideration dimension reflects the extent to which a manager is friendly, trusting, and respectful of his subordinates. A high score is indicative of a manager who is willing to explain his actions and who tries to maintain warm and personal relationships with his subordinates.

A manager who is seen as using a Budget Constrained style of evaluation is expected to have a leadership style characterized by a high score on the Initiation of Structure dimension of the LBDQ and a low score on the Consideration dimension. Because accounting data have an aura of objectivity and clarity, their use in a rather direct manner should appeal to a manager who is concerned with establish-

[1] A. G. Hopwood, "An Empirical Study of the Role of Accounting Data in Performance Evaluation," *Empirical Research in Accounting: Selected Studies, 1972,* Supplement to Vol. X, *Journal of Accounting Research.*

[2] C. Argyris, *The Impact of Budgets on People* (School of Business and Public Administration, Cornell University, 1952), p. 24.

[3] E. A. Fleishman, "A Leader Behavior Description for Industry," in *Leader Behavior: Its Description and Measurement,* edited by R. M. Stogdill and A. E. Coons (Bureau of Business Research, Ohio State University, 1957), pp. 120–33.

ing well-defined work procedures and means for evaluation.[4] To use the data in such a manner, however, the manager must also be relatively insensitive in his interpersonal relations, being more concerned with the task and goal attainment than with the maintenance of cordial and trusting relations with people. A more considerate supervisor is more likely to have that degree of empathy, and perhaps the open communications with his subordinates, which allow him to see the threat and the subsequent defenses which a rigid concern with the accounting data is capable of creating.[5]

It is, however, impossible to provide any adequate understanding of managerial evaluative behaviors without also considering the complex nature of the interrelationships between different levels of an organizational hierarchy. Since a manager himself is subject to an evaluation which may take on a similar form to those already described, it is necessary to look at the ways in which the demands and pressures are passed down from one level in the hierarchy to the next. In his simulation study of a firm's information and decision systems, Bonini[6] called such a process a "contagion effect," a term which is used in the present context to refer to any tendency for managers to evaluate their subordinates as they themselves are evaluated.

The contagion effect is particularly pertinent for a Budget Constrained style of evaluation because of the additive nature of accounting data. If a manager's superior pays attention to the extent to which the budget is met, the manager can satisfy this objective only by similarly paying attention to the budget variances of his own subordinates.

The above arguments can be summarized in terms of the following hypotheses which are discussed in this paper:

A manager is more likely to be seen as using a Budget Constrained style of evaluation if (a) he has a leadership style which is characterized by low Consideration and high Initiation of Structure; (b) he is himself evaluated on the basis of a Budget Constrained style.

Research Site

The manufacturing division of a Chicago-based company which served as the site for the study had a labor force in excess of 20,000 persons and an annual revenue of several hundred million dollars. The division's management accounting system had been in operation for over a decade and it was based on flexible budgets, standard costing techniques, and the allocation of certain overhead costs. All levels of management received monthly reports comparing their actual and budgeted costs; these were supplemented by daily and and weekly reports on such matters as production, labor, and supplies.

The division was organized on the basis of a series of areas, departments, and cost centers. Each area included several departments; and each department, a series of cost centers. A simplified organization chart is shown in Figure 1. The cost centers were usually under the responsibility of a general foreman, although some foremen and assistant departmental supervisors also had responsibilities at this level. One person could also be in charge of several cost centers. At the time the study was conducted, there were over 350 cost

[4] P. Weissenberg and L. Grunefeld, "Relationships Among Leadership Dimensions and Cognitive Style," *Journal of Applied Psychology* (October 1966), pp. 392–5.

[5] See E. A. Fleishman and J. A. Slater, "Humanizing Relationships in a Small Business: the Relationship Between the Leader's Behavior and His Empathy Toward Subordinates," *Advanced Management* (March 1961), pp. 18–20.

[6] C. P. Bonini, *Simulation of Information and Decision Systems in the Firm* (Prentice-Hall, 1963). Mann and Baumgartel provided some evidence that a manager's general attitude towards costs influenced his subordinates' concern with them: F. Mann and H. Baumgartel, *The Supervisor's Concern with Costs in an Electric Power Company* (Survey Research Center, Institute for Social Research, University of Michigan, 1953).

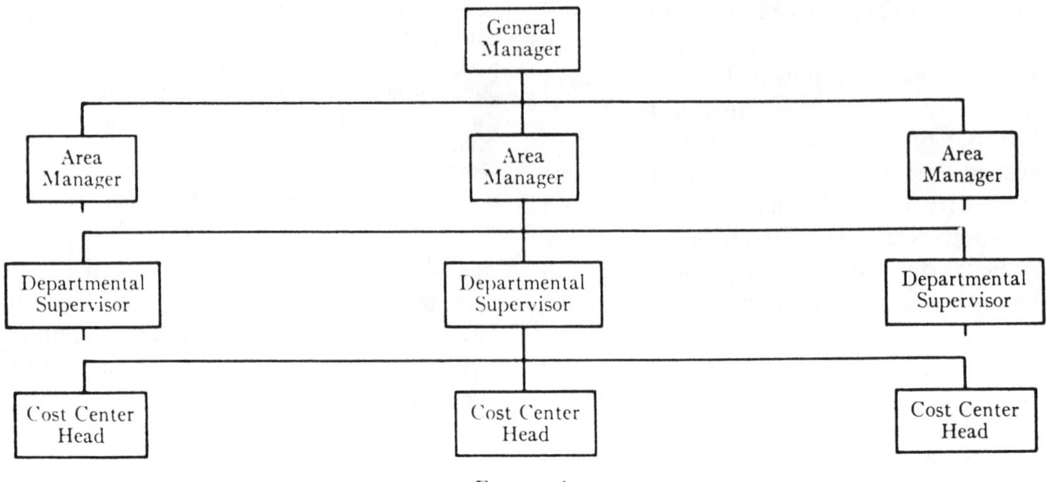

FIGURE 1

32 ORGANIZATION CHART FOR SUBJECT COMPANY

centers under the responsibility of 193 cost center heads.

Questionnaires were sent to 27 departmental supervisors and the 193 cost center heads. When a respondent failed to return the questionnaire two follow-up letters were sent to him. The final response rate was very high: 96% (26 out of 27) for the supervisors and 87% (167 out of 193) for the cost center heads.

MEASUREMENT OF THE VARIABLES

It was preferable to test for the presence of a contagion effect on the basis of independent reports from at least two levels in the organizational hierarchy so as to avoid any tendency for persons at just one level to report in a consistent manner. Therefore, the departmental supervisors were asked to report on the evaluative styles of the area managers and the cost center heads on the supervisors' styles.

The Area Manager's Style of Evaluation

The major methodological problem confronting the investigation concerned the means for empirically distinguishing among the different styles of using accounting data in performance evaluation. Although a broad set of behaviors had been isolated for each style, their operational definition necessitated an understanding of the meanings which the managers attached to these behaviors and the language which they used to describe them.

During a series of exploratory interviews, it was found that all levels of management referred to patterns of evaluative behaviors which were in agreement with the distinctions described above. In particular, a Budget Constrained orientation was referred to in terms of "meeting the budget" and a Profit Conscious orientation in terms of "concern with costs." These two phrases had distinct meanings which were known to all the managers interviewed, and therefore they were used as the basis for operationally defining the three styles of evaluation.

Each departmental supervisor was presented with a list of eight performance criteria which included both meeting the budget and concern with costs, as well as cooperation with colleagues, getting along with the boss, effort put into the job, concern with quality, attitude towards the work and company, and ability to handle the men. He was asked to rank-order the three factors which he saw as being most important in his own evaluation, and the following operational definitions of the evaluative styles were then defined on the basis of the rankings.[7] The number of respondents in each group is shown in parentheses.

1. *Budget Constrained Style* (BC): meeting the budget ranked among the top three criteria (6).[8]

2. *Profit Conscious Style* (PC): concern with costs, but not meeting the budget, ranked among the top three criteria (10).

3. *Nonaccounting Style* (NA): neither meeting the budget nor concern with costs ranked among the top three criteria (10).[9]

The Departmental Supervisors' Style of Evaluation

Although the 167 cost center heads completed an identical series of questions on their supervisors' styles of evaluation, the same operational definitions could obviously not be used because several subordinate cost center heads reported on the style of each of the 27 supervisors. Furthermore, in some departments, as is discussed subsequently, the cost center heads' perceptions were not in agreement. Some means of characterizing the *dominant* style reported by the cost center heads in each department was therefore required.

The following operational definitions of the supervisors' styles of evaluation are used in the study. The number of supervisors assigned to each style is shown in parentheses.

1. *Budget Constrained Style:* at least 40% of the cost center heads in a department reported that meeting the budget was one of the three most important criteria in their evaluation (12).

2. *Profit Conscious Style:* at least 40% of the cost center heads reported that concern with costs was one of the three most important criteria used in their evaluation, but less than 40% reported that meeting the budget was similarly important (7).

3. *Nonaccounting Style:* less than 40% of the cost center heads in a department reported that meeting the budget and concern with costs were amonst the three most important criteria in their evaluation (8).

Forty percent was selected since it was the median percentage for the relative importance of concern with costs, and although slightly above the median for the relative importance of meeting the budget, it took advantage of a break in the series.

The Departmental Supervisors' Leadership Style

The 48 items of the Ohio State Leadership Behavior Description Questionnaire 33
were included in the questionnaire sent to the cost center heads. The responses were coded to provide scores for the Consideration and Initiation of Structure dimensions of leadership behavior. The totals for all responding cost center heads under a departmental supervisor were then averaged to arrive at values of the dimensions for each supervisor. The range of the values of the Consideration dimension was found to be 50 to 92 (the possible range

[7] A discussion of the evidence on the validity of the operational procedures is given in Hopwood, "An Empirical Study of the Role of Accounting Data in Performance Evaluation."

[8] In an analysis of the cost center heads' perceptions of the departmental supervisors' styles of evaluation which was reported in the previous paper, a distinction was made between a Budget Constrained (BC) and a Budget-Profit (BP) style. The BC style referred to cases where meeting the budget, but not concern with costs, was ranked among the three most important criteria, and the BP style to cases where both the accounting-related criteria were in the top three. Subsequent analysis showed that the BC orientation dominated in the BP situation. There were no significant differences between the effects of the two styles, although the BP style did result in significantly different consequences than the pure PC style. In view of this evidence and the small size of the sample, the pure BC and BP styles are combined into a single Budget Constrained style in this analysis.

[9] The operational definition of the Nonaccounting style should be interpreted as implying a low *relative* importance to the accounting related criteria. It neither precludes some importance being attached to them nor their use for nonevaluative purposes.

TABLE 1

RELATIONSHIP BETWEEN THE REPORTED STYLE OF EVALUATION AND THE EXTENT TO WHICH THE COST CENTER HEADS MET THE BUDGET FOR DEPARTMENTS WITH DISAGREEMENT

Relationship Between Actual Costs and the Budget for 6-Month Period Prior to Receipt of Questionnaire	*Cost Center Head Reports a Budget Constrained Style of Evaluation*	*Cost Center Head Does Not Report a Budget Constrained Style of Evaluation*	*N*
On average at least met the budget	9	17	26
On average did not meet the budget	16	12	28
N	25	29	54

$\chi^2=2.69$; 1 d.f.; $P<0.11$.

was 0–112); the mean value, 75.6; and the standard deviation, 10.6. The range for the Initiation of Structure scores was 30 to 58 (with a possible range of 0–80); the mean value, 46.9; and the standard deviation, 7.0. The two dimensions were found to be independent (Kendall's Tau $=-0.04$).[10]

34

SELECTIVE USE OF A BUDGET CONSTRAINED STYLE

The cost center heads in some departments were not in agreement over whether or not their supervisors used a Budget Constrained style of evaluation. While at least two-thirds of the responding cost center heads in 19 of the 27 departments agreed that their supervisors either did or did not use this style, only 40% to 57% of the cost center heads in the remaining 8 departments reported that he did. Before proceeding with the main analysis, it was important first to investigate whether these differences in opinions were due to inaccurate perceptions or the insensitivity of the measurement procedures or a real selective use of this style by some supervisors. An analysis was therefore made of the factors influencing the style of evaluation reported by the 54 cost center heads employed in the 8 departments where there was substantial disagreement.

The analysis indicated that the cost center heads reporting a Budget Constrained style in these 8 departments tended to have been less successful in meeting their budget. In Table 1 the 54 cost center heads are divided on the basis of (1) whether or not they reported a Budget Constrained evaluation and (2) whether or not they had, on average, met their budget over the 6-month period prior to the receipt of the questionnaire. There is a difference between the two criterion groups, but the difference is only significant at the 11% level.[11]

Prevention might, however, have been seen as being preferable to cure. An analysis was therefore made to see whether the supervisors of these 8 departments focused their Budget Constrained approach on the large cost centers which had the greatest potential to influence the overall departmental results. The cost center heads were divided on the basis of whether or not they were responsible for a cost center or a series of cost centers which dealt with total annual costs above, equal to, or less than the departmental median. From Table 2 it can be seen that these supervisors were more likely to be seen as using a Budget Constrained style by per-

[10] A review of the relationships between the two dimensions of the LBDQ is given by P. Weissenberg and M. J. Kavanagh in "The Independence of Initiating Structure and Consideration: A Review of the Evidence," *Personnel Psychology* (Spring 1972), pp. 119–30.

[11] There was no significant difference between these two criterion groups when the analysis was based on the average performance in the 9-month period prior to the receipt of the questionnaire. For the remaining 19 departments where there was substantial agreement over whether or not the supervisor used a Budget Constrained style, there was no relationship between the reported style and performance in either the 6- or 9-month period.

TABLE 2

RELATIONSHIP BETWEEN THE REPORTED STYLE OF EVALUATION AND THE RELATIVE SIZE OF THE COST CENTERS FOR DEPARTMENTS WITH DISAGREEMENT

The Total Annual Costs of the Cost Center(s) in Relation to the Median Cost for Its Department	*Cost Center Head Reports a Budget Constrained Style of Evaluation*	*Cost Center Head Does Not Report a Budget Constrained Style of Evaluation*	*N*
Above the departmental median	16	10	26
Equal to or less than the departmental median	9	19	28
N	25	29	54

$\chi^2 = 5.23$; 1 d.f.; $P<0.05$.

TABLE 3

RELATIONSHIP BETWEEN LEADERSHIP STYLE AND THE SUPERVISORS' STYLE OF EVALUATION

Leadership Style	*The Cost Center Heads' Perception of the Supervisors' Dominant Style of Evaluation*			*Significance of Paired Comparison*[a]
	BC	*PC*	*NA*	
Mean Initiation of Structure	48.0	51.3	41.9	*BC:NA*: $p<0.01$ *PC:NA*: $p<0.05$
Mean Consideration	70.6	80.9	79.4	*BC:PC*: $p<0.05$ *BC:NA*: $p<0.05$
N	12	7	8	

[a] Significance of paired comparisons is based on the Mann-Whitney *U* Test. Unless otherwise stated, a paired comparison is not significant at the 5% level.

sons in charge of the *relatively* large cost centers in a department.[12]

The findings suggest that the supervisors of the 8 departments where there was substantial disagreement over their style of evaluation used the Budget Constrained style with discretion, emphasizing it where it was seen as likely to have the greatest impact on the departmental results. As such, the evidence is in agreement with other studies which have shown that managers do not necessarily use one personal style of management irrespective of their circumstances and subordinates.[13]

LEADERSHIP STYLE AND THE USE OF ACCOUNTING DATA

As can be seen from an examination of Table 3, both the Budget Constrained and Profit Conscious supervisors were seen as creating a structured job environment geared to the attainment of their perceptions of the organization's goals. The Budget Constrained supervisors, however, were seen as showing significantly less consideration for the feelings and opinions of their cost center heads than either their Profit Conscious or Nonaccounting colleagues. Yet without the maintenance of such a considerate managerial climate, the structured concern with the financial aspects of performance was seen in terms of

[12] There was no relationship between the reported style and the *absolute* size of the cost centers. Also no significant relationship was found between the reported style and either relative or absolute size in the nineteen departments with substantial agreement.

[13] See E. Kay and R. Hastman, *An Evaluation of Work Planning and Goal Setting Discussions* (General Electric Behavioral Research Service, 1966), and A. Lowin and J. R. Craig, "The Influence of Level of Performance on Managerial Style: An Experimental Object Lesson in the Ambiguity of Correlation Data," *Organizational Behavior and Human Performance* (November 1968), pp. 440–58.

a threatening emphasis on the accounting data in isolation of their organizational context. The findings are therefore supportive of hypothesis (a).

The Contagion Effect

The contagion effect was very strong for the Budget Constrained style of evaluation. With supervisors divided on the basis of whether or not their perceptions of the area managers' styles of evaluation were in agreement with their cost center heads' perceptions of their own dominant style, it can be seen in Table 4 that only one of the 6 supervisors who reported a Budget Constrained evaluation did not
36 pass down the same style to his cost center heads.[14] In contrast, there was no evidence of a contagion effect for either the Profit Conscious or Nonaccounting styles. For the Profit Conscious style, however, many of the supervisors maintained a concern with the accounting data, although the concern was just as likely to be rigidly tied to the short-term budget variances as it was to longer-term cost effectiveness. Four of the 10 supervisors who were evaluated on this basis evaluated their cost center heads in a Budget Constrained manner compared with the 3 who maintained the Profit Conscious style.

Table 4

Relationship Between the Area Managers' and the Departmental Supervisors' Styles of Evaluation

Relationship between the Cost Center Heads' Perception of the Supervisor's Dominant Style of Evaluation and the Supervisor's Perception of the Area Manager's Style	*Supervisor's Perception of the Area Manager's Style of Evaluation*			
	BC	*PC*	*NA*	*N*
Agreement	5	3	4	12
Disagreement	1	7	6	14
N	6	10	10	26

Supervisors were seen as passing on a Budget Constrained style even though they *intended* to do otherwise. All the departmental supervisors were asked to report how they thought that they evaluated their cost center heads, the responses being referred to as the supervisor's intended style of evaluation. It can be seen in Table 5 that only 2 of the 6 supervisors who reported being evaluated on the basis of a Budget Constrained style intended to evaluate their cost center heads in the same way. The other 4 supervisors intended to use a Profit Conscious style. In comparison, a majority of the supervisors who were evaluated on the basis of either a Profit Conscious or a Nonaccounting style intended to evaluate their cost center heads in the same manner, although they did not necessarily possess the requisite managerial abilities to put this into effect.[15]

The supervisors whose performance was evaluated upon the basis of their departments' short-term budget variances were in a conflict situation. It was easy for them to feel that it was necessary to evaluate similarly their cost center heads in order to obtain the desired results. Yet from their own experience they knew that this was an unfair evaluation which was likely

[14] While the Budget Constrained style might have been easier to resist if the departmental variances had been consistently favorable, the single supervisor who was the exception to the rule resisted the contagion effect despite having had unfavorable departmental variances for most of the fifteen months prior to the receipt of the questionnaire. His cost center heads saw him as having an average concern with a structured job environment (his Initiation of Structure score of 47 equals the median for the sample of supervisors), but an exceptionally high consideration for their feelings and opinions. His Consideration score of 89 was the second highest in the sample, and compared with the median of 79.

[15] Recent evidence relating self-reported leadership behavior to subordinate descriptions of behavior has also found that the two are not necessarily equivalent. See M. G. Evans, "Leadership Behavior: Demographic Factors and Agreement Between Subordinate and Self-Descriptions," *Personnel Psychology* (Winter 1972), pp. 649–53, and W. K. Graham and T. Olena, "Perceptions of Leader Behavior and Evaluation of Leaders Across Organizational Levels," *Experimental Publications System* (February 1970), p. 144A.

TABLE 5

RELATIONSHIP BETWEEN THE AREA MANAGERS' STYLE OF EVALUATION AND THE DEPARTMENTAL SUPERVISORS' INTENDED STYLE OF EVALUATION

Relationship Between the Supervisor's Perception of the Area Manager's Style and the Supervisor's Intended Style	*Supervisor's Perception of the Area Manager's Style of Evaluation*			
	BC	*PC*	*NA*	*N*
Agreement	2	7	7	16
Disagreement	4	3	3	10
N	6	10	10	26

to result in excessive tension and worry. One of them described his own experiences in the following way:

"When I'm in the red [the Area Manager] will always blame you. I'll get a black eye. Even if I'm not to blame, I'll still get a black eye. I like a good budget to shoot at but when you have obvious discrepancies in the budget, then it's difficult to show what you are doing. A good budget is a good thing, but a bad budget is a bad thing."

Yet he felt that he had to pass on the Budget Constrained style since his own superiors "will generally criticize me if I'm unfavorable, regardless of reason." So for some of his cost center heads, "if they're in the red, I'll probably know why, but I'll ask *them* why and I'll tarpoon [sic] a few things with them." He was, however, aware of the anxiety and undesirable behaviors which this could cause.

"The accounting numbers are a big thing for most of [the cost center heads]. It gets down to personalities; it's bound to. Generally [a cost center head] has to get a reasonable product to get a reasonable result. Well, he may want good relations with those who supply him with [his material], but then he wants to make himself look good, and to do that he makes others look poor."

With such problems in mind, he tried not to evaluate two of his cost center heads on the basis of their short-term budget variances because he thought that their highly skilled subordinates would react to the subsequent pressure by leaving the company. Since the two cost centers were also "low in real dollars," he was prepared to use a different style of evaluation.

All 5 of the superviors who were seen as passing down their own Budget Constrained evaluation used a similar means of resolving the conflict with which they were confronted. They were, in fact, responsible for 5 of the 8 departments where there was disagreement over this aspect of the supervisor's style of evaluation and in which, as we have already seen, the more rigid style was used for the larger cost centers and possibly those with a poor budget record.[16]

DISCUSSION

In supporting the hypotheses, the evidence allows the initial distinctions which were made among the three styles of using accounting data in performance evaluation to be placed in a wider managerial perspective. For the final impact of an accounting system on managerial behavior has been shown to depend on its interaction with the forms of social- and self-controls which are reflected within the various leadership climates and the personal motives and defenses which they activate.

In being responsive to the feelings and opinions of their cost center heads, the Profit Conscious supervisors recognized and responded to the threat which the financial concerns and structured job environment were capable of creating. But, in addition, the supportive organizational climate encouraged the cost center heads to discuss openly their budgetary problems with the supervisor.[17] This might, of

[16] The percentage of cost center heads in the 5 departments reporting a Budget Constrained style were: 40%, 50%, 50%, 50% and 57%.

[17] In a field study conducted in three major industrial organizations Read found that trust in the supervisor resulted in accurate upward communications. See W. H. Read, "Upward Communication in Industrial Hierarchies," *Human Relations* (February 1962), pp. 3–15.

course, be viewed as a means of avoiding responsibility, although this would be an inappropriate description of the situation in these departments. The Profit Conscious supervisors, while listening to explanations, certainly did not readily accept them. In the words of one cost center head:

> "[A Budget Constrained supervisor] takes the budget to heart, while what [a Profit Conscious supervisor] does is to accept it upon himself and if he doesn't agree with it, then he'll reject the budget. He's a real tough guy and it's difficult to argue with him. You have got to have some good arguments, but if he agrees with you, then out goes the budget. [The Budget Constrained supervisor] can be stubborn. He aims to stay right on his budget and that's it."

38

The budgetary pressures associated with the Profit Conscious style of evaluation were seen, in the words of another cost center head, as being applied "where they [were] appropriate." The cost center heads were aware of both the supervisors' willingness to listen and, in turn, explain the reasons for accepting and rejecting explanations. As a result, the supervisors were provided with the alternative sources of information which enabled them to test continually the validity of the accounting data and keep the job environment devoid of the rigidities of the Budget Constrained approach. In contrast, the cost center heads subject to a Budget Constrained evaluation hardly felt free to offer realistic explanations. One such cost center head described his supervisor's attitude in terms of "just don't do it, rather than asking for explanations."

Unfortunately the study did not directly investigate the relationship among the three styles of using accounting data and the overall effectiveness of operations.[18] The observed leadership style configurations are, however, of interest in this respect since studies using the LBDQ dimensions have found that, although the Initiation of Structure and Consideration scores were designed to be independent, supervisors who are rated high on both dimensions are considered to be more effective by their superiors, as well as favorably influencing their subordinates' morale and improving indices of productivity and labor turnover. Fleishman and Harris,[19] for instance, found that for production supervisors scoring high on both dimensions, the structured job environment was seen as less threatening and had little or no effect on grievances and turnover. That a number of other studies have come to similar conclusions[20] provides some indirect evidence on the potential benefits of the Profit Conscious style, although it should be stressed that such findings are no more than suggestive in the present context.

However, while recognizing the need for further research on the overall effects of the various styles, the findings do point to a number of implications for both accounting practice and the study of the behavioral impact of accounting data. At the very least, they serve to emphasize the importance of the accountant's educational function. With the increasing complexity of management accounting pro-

[18] A review of the evidence on the differential effects of the various styles did provide some basis for concluding that the Profit Conscious style was likely to be more effective than the Budget Constrained style in situations which required a careful consideration of a wide variety of information, a high degree of interunit coordination, a long time horizon, and an ability to respond in a flexible manner to unexpected circumstances: see the discussion in Hopwood, *op. cit.*

[19] E. A. Fleishman and E. F. Harris, "Patterns of Leadership Behavior Related to Employee Grievances and Turnover," *Personnel Psychology* (Spring 1962), pp. 43–56.

[20] E. A. Fleishman and J. Simmons, "Relationship Between Leadership Patterns and Effectiveness Ratings Among Israeli Foremen," *Personnel Psychology* (Summer 1970), pp. 169–72; A. W. Halpin, "The Leader Behavior and Effectiveness of Aircraft Commanders," in Stodgill and Coons; H. Oaklander and E. A. Fleishman, "Patterns of Leadership Related to Organizational Stress in Hospital Settings," *Administrative Science Quarterly* (March 1964), pp. 520–32. A survey of the relationship between the two dimensions of the LBQD and various criteria of organizational effectiveness is given in A. K. Korman, "'Consideration,' 'Initiating Structure' and Organizational Criteria—A Review," *Personnel Psychology* (Winter 1966), pp. 349–61.

cedures, it is unrealistic to expect managers to use the data in an appropriate manner without adequate preparation and training. But they need to be informed not only of the objectives and advantages of the accounting system, real though they may be, but also of the inadequacies of the data and the consequences of attaching too much importance to the short-term reports—a far more difficult task.

The different ways of using the data were not, however, simply based on ignorance. They were associated with much more widespread differences in managerial attitudes and behaviors, and for the Budget Constrained style, with the evaluative style of the superiors. Even the most carefully designed educational program is unlikely to provide an easy solution to the problem, and it would certainly require the active cooperation of specialists in organizational development. Hence, consideratio 1 needs to be given to how the use which is made of the data can be explicitly recognized as a factor in the design of accounting systems. This does not mean that accountants should immediately strive to stifle the undesirable responses by filling the obvious loopholes in their systems. Rather, there is a need for system designs to take account of the constraints and opportunities of their managerial environment in the manner that Wildavsky has contrived to design federal budgeting procedures which are congruent with the political process.[21]

Such a task requires both practical experimentation and systematic research. But, so far, many of the studies of the effects of accounting data on decision behavior have ignored their managerial context. They have all too often merely presented reports based on different accounting methods to samples of financial analysts, managers, and students, and observed whether their decision behaviors were dependent upon the type of data received. The present findings suggest, however, that the relationship between accounting data and decision behavior is moderated by the leadership style and social context of the decision maker. Much greater explicit consideration needs to be given to these factors in further research, although, in so doing, there may be a need to rely less on the abstractions of laboratory experimentation and more on the complexities of field research.[22]

[21] A. Wildavsky, *The Politics of the Budgetary Process* (Little, Brown, 1964) and *Toward a Radical Incrementalism: A Proposal to Aid Congress in Reform of the Budgetary Process* (American Institute for Public Policy Research, 1965).

[22] This is not to deny that some aspects of the problem can be studied in controlled experiments. Lowin and Craig showed the potential for simulating different leadership styles in the laboratory, and among others, Mock *et al.* have recently reported experiments on the effects of cognitive style on decision behavior: See T. J. Mock, T. L. Estrin, and M. A. Vasarhelyi, "Learning Patterns, Decision Approach, and Value of Information," *Journal of Accounting Research* (Spring 1972), pp. 129–53. Nevertheless, there are formidable difficulties in trying to simulate hierarchical patterns and organizational contexts within the analytical and time constraints of the experimental method.

PROBLEMS WITH USING ACCOUNTING INFORMATION IN PERFORMANCE EVALUATION

Anthony G. Hopwood, Lecturer in Management Accounting, Manchester Business School, Manchester, Great Britain

An Advancing Technical Sophistication . . .

The last few decades have witnessed an ever expanding basis of knowledge for the
design of effective management accounting systems. New areas of expertise have continually provided new insights, opportunities and challenges to the conventional ap- 41
proaches. Perspectives drawn from economic theory have provided a sound basis for selecting information relevant for decision making and the application of mathematical skills has added to our potential for rigorously analysing complex problems. Moreover the advances in computer technology have ensured the means for providing speedy information to the managers who need it. At least in philosophy, therefore, accounting for management needs no longer be seen as merely a reckoning of post events but as a function which has a vital and positive role in encouraging managers to learn from their past experiences and to anticipate the contingencies of their uncertain tasks.

. . . But a Neglect of Use?

These are signs of real progress. However, while a great deal of attention has been devoted to the different ways of designing management accounting systems, comparatively little consideration has been given to the different ways of using accounting information. Yet the final impact which any accounting system makes on managerial behaviour is dependent not only upon its design and technical characteristics but also upon the precise manner in which the resulting information is used.

In the extreme, of course, even the most sophisticated system can contribute little or nothing to the efficiency of a company's operations if the information is ignored[1]. More generally, however, despite any amount of care and consideration which may have gone into the design of an accounting system, its value may be questionable if managers use the information in an inappropriate manner, attributing either too much or too little validity to it or being unaware of its intended purposes. Few, if any, management accounting systems ever achieve a perfect representation of the underlying structure of economic and financial events, and a careful and considerate use of the information is always essential to compensate for the many unavoidable inadequacies of the system.

---

1 See R. Beresford Dew and K. P. Gee, "Managements' Use of Budgetary Information", *Management Accounting*, March, 1970, pp. 89—92.

However, any appreciation of the different ways of using accounting information must be based upon an understanding of the human context in which the use occurs. While the information might be given, its interpretation is the outcome of a personal and social process which is sustained by the meanings, beliefs, pressures and purposes that are brought to bear by the managers using the information. In of necessity providing it with a personal significance and placing it in their own wider context, managers are able to use the information, perhaps without reflection, in a variety of ways — appropriate and inappropriate.

Using Accounting Information In Managerial Performance Evaluation

Questions concerning appropriate use are particularly important when accounting information is used in managerial performance evaluation. The many documented examples of manipulation of accounting reports and undesirable decision making which were an outgrowth of attempts to make the reports a more favourable reflection of managerial performance suggest that we clearly have a number of problems in this area[2]. They are, however, problems which are easier to identify than to ensure the means for their solution.

Although many accounting systems do attempt to reflect at least some of the important dimensions of managerial performance, there are many difficulties in designing reporting systems for this purpose. The means for measuring vital social behaviours have yet to be devised and even the procedures used for measuring the narrowly economic aspects of behaviour are approximate and often biased. And it is impossible to close off all loopholes against manipulation. Sophisticated though present understandings may appear, the final reports are of necessity partial, often including uncontrollable factors and usually geared to reporting short-term outcomes rather than managerial efforts towards attaining longer-term effectiveness. In practice the problem becomes one of gaining the necessary social understandings to ensure the effective use of imperfect but nevertheless valuable information procedures.

Yet intriguing though all the many reports of manipulation and undesirable behaviour may be, they are often little more than anecdotal accounts of particularly inappropriate uses of accounting information. They do little to provide us with the essential understandings of the precise ways in which the information was used, their determinants and full effects. They do not give use the why's and the wherefore's. While the use which any manager makes of accounting information may well be in some senses unique, it is nevertheless necessary to spot uniformities in the patterns of use. As accountants, like other careful investigators, have found in other areas, only such informities provide the insights for appreciating the nature of a problem and the means for moving towards its diagnosis and solution. The present paper reports on a research study which attempted to move in this direction[3].

---

2 See the early reviews by F. J. Jasinski, "Use and Misuse of Efficiency Controls". *Harvard Business Review*, July-August, 1956, pp. 105—112, and V. F. Ridgway, "Dysfunctional Consequences of Performance Measurements", *Administrative Science Quarterly*, I (1956), 240—247.

3 A more detailed report of the methods, statistical analyses and findings is given in the author's *An Accounting System and Managerial Behaviour* (Farnborough: Saxon House, forthcoming).

Three Styles of Using Budgetary Information

Based upon a review of previous research findings and extensive interviews in one company, three distinct ways of using budgetary information in the evaluation of managerial performance were distinguished.

1. *Budget Constrained Style*
   Despite the many problems with using budgetary information as a comprehensive measure of managerial performance, the manager's performance is primarily evaluated upon the basis of his ability to continually meet the budget on a short-term basis. This criterion of performance is stressed at the expense of other valued and important criteria and the manager will receive unfavourable feedback from his superior if, for instance, his actual costs exceed the budgeted costs, regardless of other considerations.

2. *Profit Conscious Style*
   The manager's performance is evaluated on the basis of his ability to increase the general effectiveness of his unit's operations in relation to the long-term purposes of the organization. For instance, at the cost centre level, one important aspect of this ability concerns the attention which he devotes to reducing long-run costs. For this purpose, however, the budgetary information has to be used with great care in a rather flexible manner.

3. *Nonaccounting Style*
   The budgetary information plays a *relatively* unimportant part in the superior's evaluation of the manager's performance.

While the budgetary information obviously indicates whether or not a manager has succeeded in meeting his current budget, it does not necessarily indicate whether he is behaving in a manner which is consistent with achieving the organization's longer-term effectiveness. Current cost savings can, for instance, be made at longer term expense and some current cost overruns can also ensure lower cost operations in the future. There are many such problems and the budgetary information has not only to be used with care but also supplemented by information drawn from other sources in order to assess the manager's impact on future as well as current operations.

Unlike a Budget Constrained evaluation, a Profit Conscious evaluation is therefore concerned with the wider information content, or lack of it, of the budget reports and not with just a rigid analysis of the direction and magnitude of the reported budget variances. The budget is, in other words, seen as a means to an end rather than an end in itself.

Measuring the Styles

It is, however, easier to distinguish the styles in such a general sense than move towards defining them in an operational manner. But how are we to know whether any manager uses a Budget Constrained or Profit Conscious or Nonaccounting style? This is of course, the crucial methodological problem faced by all studies of how accounting information is actually used. In this instance, the problem was approached by probing into the meanings developed by a group of managers in one company. They certainly did not use my terms but they did distinguish between their colleagues and superiors on the basis of evaluative behaviours which were in basic agreement with those described above. And the language which *they* used to make such distinctions provided the means for operationally defining the three styles and in turn, determining the style used in the evaluation of each manager.

The Budget Constrained orientation was expressed in terms of "meeting the budget" and the Profit Conscious orientation by "concern with costs". The two phrases had distinctly different meanings. The managers were then asked to rank the three most important criteria used in their evaluation out of a list of eight which included these two accounting related criteria. If "meeting the budget" was included in the top three criteria, the manager was presumed to be subject to a Budget Constrained evaluation[4] and if "concern with costs" but not "meeting the budget" was in the top three, he was categorized as reporting a Profit Conscious evaluation. The remaining managers were defined as reporting a residual Nonaccounting evaluation.

The Research Site

The manufacturing division of a large Chicago based company served as the site for the study. The division had a labor force in excess of 20,000 persons and an annual revenue of several hundred million dollars. The accounting system was based on flexible budgets and standard costing techniques, and it was an accepted and important part of the work environment, having been installed for over a decade. Monthly reports comparing the actual and budgeted costs for cost centres were sent to all the responsible managers and their departmental supervisors. These were supplemented by daily and weekly reports on such matters as production, labour and supplies, the nature and content of which varied between cost centres.

The present discussion is based upon an analysis of items included in questionnaires which were sent to all the 193 managers in charge of cost centres and their 27 departmental supervisors. The final response was very high, being 87 % (167 out of 193) for the cost centre heads and 96 % (26 out of 27) for the supervisors. Subsequently, a series of intensive interviews were held with 45 managers at all levels in the division.

The Effects of the Three Styles

The empirical evidence, a summary of which follows, indicated that both the Budget Constrained and Profit Conscious styles resulted in a higher degree of involvement with costs than the Nonaccounting style. Only the Profit Conscious approach, however, succeeded in attaining this involvement without incurring either emotional costs for the managers in charge of the cost centres or defensive behaviour which was undesirable from the company's point of view.

The Budget Constrained style resulted in a belief that the evaluation was unjust and widespread tension and worry on the job. In the words of one manager:

> You have to get yourself out of the woods. It's a process of staying out of the red. You have to. It's true and it makes a job so much more difficult. They'd be

4 In the full analysis a distinction was made between a pure Budget Constrained style where "meeting the budget" but not "concern with costs" was ranked in the top three criteria and a combined Budget-Profit style where both of these criteria were given this high ranking. The empirical evidence indicated that the Budget Constrained orientation dominated the Profit Conscious orientation in the combined style, the pure and combined styles having very similar effects and determinants. Therefore in this report they are treated as one style.

> times when I could do a good job and save some money by spending a bit now. But no, the only thing I concentrate on is what I've got forthcoming that's going to put me in the red. I've got to concentrate to see . . . there's no more money to spend. God, it causes me some problems.

Sometimes it was almost impossible to make the short-term budget variances more favourable.

> When I'm in the red, I start cutting on manpower. Well, I should, but I can't. We've been down on manpower for some time now. I just have to live on my budget, close to the bone. But you can't, you can't.

Such frantic and at times unsuccessful attempts only resulted in more problems, more tension and more worry.

It was hardly surprising that such a single minded concern with the budget was met with manipulation of the accounting reports and even decisions which increased the total processing costs for the company as a whole. Costs were charged to incorrect accounts, repairs delayed until the money was available in the budget despite this resulting in higher costs and, in the words of one manager: 45

> Simply no one will take the decision to spend. Most people in this position try to make themselves look good. They don't want to see negative signs on their reports. They're aiming for promotion without worrying about the future. It's let's look good today, tomorrow I'll get promoted. It's someone else's problem then.

Manipulation and undesirable decision behaviour were not, however, the only means of relieving the tensions created by the Budget Constrained style. The managers' relationships with the Budget Constrained supervisors were allowed to deteriorate. But the rigid emphasis on the short-term budget results also served to highlight the interdependent nature of their tasks and the immediate instrumental concerns easily permeated the patterns of social relationships amongst colleagues in the same department. When the managers were continually asked about budget variances over which they often had little or no control they each went out to improve their own reports regardless of the detrimental effects for the organization of such a narrow parochalism, and if this failed, they then tried to pass on the responsibility by blaming their colleagues. Yet the ensuing rivalry and conflict often impeded the cooperation which was so essential for controlling their interdependent activities.

In contrast, the Profit Conscious style resulted in similar levels of tension, supervisor satisfaction and cooperation amongst colleagues as prevailed under a Nonaccounting style. And there was little or no fiddling of the reports. But while the style was accepted, even respected, it was certainly seen as very demanding. A Profit Conscious supervisor, according to one of the subordinates . . .

> . . . is always asking about costs — all the time. This is basically the heart of it, I guess, costs. Anytime we get together or whenever he gets you it's costs, costs, costs. "See if we can cut down." "It's going pretty fast, we'd better talk about it." He's a little bit too strict really. I'm used to discipline, but he runs a tight ship. He does not like us to get sloppy; he gets hot under the collar. He tries ta save whatever he can. He just likes to operate that way. He is just that type of person, but to be fair, he applies pressure where it is appropriate.

It was far from being an easy style to satisfy but the pressure was seen as being applied fairly rather than along the rigid lines of a Budget Constrained supervisor. The latter's approach was "just don't do it, rather than asking for explanations".

Table 1

A Summary of the Effects of the Three Styles of Evaluation

	Style of Evaluation		
	Budget Constrained	Profit Conscious	Nonaccounting
Involvement with costs	High	High	Low
Job Related Tension	High	Medium	Medium
Manipulation of the Accounting Reports	Extensive	Little	Little
Relations with the Supervisor	Poor	Good	Good
Relations with Colleagues	Poor	Good	Good

A summary of the effects of the three styles of evaluation is given in Table I. Unfortunately it was not possible to directly investigate the overall impact of the different styles on the effectiveness of operations. The presence of extensive manipulation in some cost centres made the accounting information unreliable for this purpose and given the subject of the research, it was difficult to revert to subjective assessments. The fiddling, short-time horizons, distrust, rivalry and parochial attitudes engendered by the Budget Constrained style are nevertheless vital considerations in all companies and the Profit Conscious style avoided these problems while at the same time ensuring an active involvement with the financial aspects of performance.

The costs associated with unreliable accounting records, short-time horizons and the difficulties of controlling interdependent operations will, however, vary from situation to situation. Therefore the precise balance of costs and benefits associated with the three styles might well be very different for the control of a stable technologically simple situation, for instance, than that of an uncertain and highly complex situation. It is essential that further attempts should be made to isolate the conditions influencing the relative advantages of the three styles[5].

A Choice of Uses?

It is always interesting to document the extent to which human initiative can be motivated to beat the most sophisticated of accouting systems, but many have done this before. What is of far greater significance than viewing the ingenious responses to the Budget Constrained style in isolation, however, is that the contrast between the Budget Constrained and Profit Conscious styles suggests that the accounting information did not in and of itself pose a threat to the managers of the company when it was used in performance evaluation. Both these styles resulted in some type of concern with financial consequences, however different these concerns might have been, although only the former also resulted in the questionable defensive responses. The threat came from the way in which the information was used.

5 Some recent research has addressed itself to closely related problems. See J. V. Baumler, "Defined Criteria of Performance in Organizational Control", *Administrative Science Quarterly*, XVI (1971), 340—350, and W. Murray, *Management Controls in Action*, Human Science in Industry — Study Number 6 (Dublin: Irish National Productivity Committee Development Division, 1970).

A manager is not faced with a simple choice of using or not using accounting information in evaluation and feedback. Instead it would appear that he can reap many of the benefits of an accounting system by stressing factors which it attempts to measure without this resulting in defensive behaviour. To do so, however, consideration must be given to the precise manner in which the information is used. But what are the various styles of evaluation related to? Certainly it is not sufficient to merely acknowledge their presence. It is also necessary to consider the factors determinig the styles because a systematic understanding of their nature is an essential prerequisite for the intelligent management of change and improvement.

The Determinants of the Styles

No doubt due to the arithmetical nature of accounting reports, the Budget Constrained style was difficult to resist passing down once it had been established at one level in the organizational hierarchy. If a manager was called upon to meet his budget, he could only ensure doing so by making his subordinates do likewise. All but one of the departmental supervisors who were themselves subject to a Budget Constrained evaluation assessed the performance of a significant proportion of their own subordinates on a similar basis.

Neither of the other two styles were passed down from one level to the next. For instance, while many of the supervisors maintained the concern with the budget reports expressed in their own Profit Conscious evaluation, whether this concern was interpreted in a flexible or rigid manner was dependent upon the second factor determining the styles, namely the manager's own capabilities.

The ways in which the accounting information was used were very clearly associated with much more widespread differences in managerial style. Using the well accepted dimensions of managerial style developed at Ohio State University, namely Initiation of Structure and Consideration[6], it was found that both the Budget Constrained and Profit Conscious supervisors, unlike those using a Nonaccounting style, were seen as trying to create a structured job environment. The Profit Conscious supervisors, however, were also seen as maintaining a warm and friendly atmosphere which was supportive and conducive for mutual trust and respect. In this regard they were similar to the Nonaccounting supervisors but very different from the Budget Constrained ones. Without the moderating effect of the considerate attitudes towards the subordinate managers, the concern for the budget reports was seen as threatening and stressful, and served as a trigger for defensive and often undesirable behaviour.

Problem Solving Versus Evaluative Approaches

The accounting information was one vehicle through which the managers were able to express their more general approaches to the job. The way in which it was used was often, in fact, a good enough indicator of the managerial philosophy and ethos which pervaded any section of the company. The Profit Conscious style, for instance, appeared to be only one aspect of a problem solving approach to management, as distinct

6 E. A. Fleishman, "The Description of Supervisory Behaviour", *Journal of Applied Psychology,* XXXVII (1953), 153—158, and "A Leader Behaviour Description for Industry", in *Leader Behaviour: Its Description and Measurement,* edited by R. M. Stogdill and A. E. Coons, (Columbus, Ohio: Bureau of Business Research, Ohio State University, 1957), pp. 120—133.

from an approach which attempted to impose a false measure of simplicity onto a complex and highly interdependent series of activities. The evaluation of performance was itself of primary importance with the Budget Constrained style, influencing all aspects of the managers' behaviours. Evaluation was not viewed as an ongoing part of the managerial process, interrelated with other important aspects of the job, and itself a problematic activity. Rather it was seen as a distinct and dominant activity, and the primary source of influence and control, overshadowing other vital elements of the process. The budget became not an aid to management but a constraint upon it.

Implications for the Operation of Accounting Systems

The study emphasizes the vital importance of considering the precise manner in which accounting information is *used* by line managers. It is never a simple matter of merely getting them to use the information in any manner. Budgets, like other management accounting procedures, are certainly quite capable of being important means for assessing achievement and helping to gain involvement and concern with the financial aspects of operations. But they also share with all the other procedures the problems of being partial and imprecise. The real challenge comes in trying to achieve an effective utilization of imperfect but nevertheless valuable procedures. Such a challenge is only just being acknowledged in many companies.

Understandably, it is easy for accountants to be defensive about any suggestion that their procedures are imprecise. Many would say that there are already enough problems in gaining the acceptance of accounting systems without adding any more. My comment is not, however, meant to be critical. While the imprecision and partiality may really reflect inadequate efforts in some situations, in many other cases, they simply reflect the current state of the art. Sophisticated though many procedures have become, they still have a long way to go. There is no need to be defensive if the full implications of the problem are recognized.

But one real danger comes in responding to many of the undesirable responses to accounting systems by immediately striving to improve the procedures. Work should indeed be devoted to this end but it must also be recognized that beyond some point, the search for technical perfection will achieve little in the foreseeable future. Of more importance, however, it can so easily lead to a diversion of effort from the identification and diagnosis of other central problems. In particular, the effectiveness of any management accounting system is not determined by its design alone. The design has to be actualized through the efforts of line managers. It has to be used appropriately.

At the very least accountants have an important educational function to serve. With the increasing complexity of management accounting procedures, it is unrealistic to expect managers at any level in a company to use the information in an appropriate manner without adequate preparation and training. But they need to be informed not only of the objectives and advantages of the accounting system, real though they may be, but also of the inadequacies of the information and the consequences of attaching too much importance to the short-term reports — a far more difficult task.

The different styles of using the information were not, however, simply based on ignorance. They were, as we have seen, associated with much more widespread differences in managerial attitudes and behaviours, and for the Budget Constrained style, with the evaluation style of superiors. Even the most carefully designed educational programme is therefore neither an easy nor the only solution to the problem.

The real need is for a view of accounting systems which sees them as a part of a much more complex process of influencing behaviour in organizations. They represent only one means of control and their final effectiveness is dependent upon how they interact with the other approaches to the problem. The behaviours so inadequately reflected within the dimensions of managerial style are, for instance, also trying to influence behaviour. And the effects of just these two approaches, let alone others, certainly do not occur in isolation. It is all too easy to concentrate on separate mechanisms for influencing behaviour, perhaps even achieving some satisfaction in the individual situations, but by not taking an integrated view of them as a whole, still fail to achieve their full potential.

Conclusion

The problems described in this paper point to the necessity of moving beyond questions of the design of management accounting systems, which have received the major share of attention to date, to gain a real and systematic understanding of this wider human and social factors which influence their effective use in large organizations. The systems are embedded in rich and varied organizational settings. They are designed to serve organizational purposes. Yet all too little is known about how they are used and function within organizations. However, while it is still an area where we have a lot to learn, the paper has tried to suggest that the potential benefits to be derived from empirical studies of the social context of accounting systems are great.

— Résumé —

Accounting in its Organisational Context

Accounting, Organizations and Society, Vol. 3, No. 1, pp. 3–13. 0361-3682/78/0301-0003$02.00/0

TOWARDS AN ORGANIZATIONAL PERSPECTIVE FOR THE STUDY OF ACCOUNTING AND INFORMATION SYSTEMS

ANTHONY G. HOPWOOD

Oxford Centre for Management Studies

Many might think that the introduction to a collected series of papers ought to reassure the reader, showing how each sheds light on the others and on the overall accumulation of knowledge, thereby guaranteeing the unity and coherence of the various contributions. Here, however, I believe that it would be unrealistic to attempt an introduction along such lines at this stage of conceptual development. Certainly the following papers, with one exception, were brought together for two workshops at a conference organized in late 1976[1] and all of them focus on the same topic – the relationships between the organization and its accounting and information systems. But the criteria employed in selecting the papers deliberately set out to provide a plurality of theoretical and empirical perspectives. So, it is important to point out right from the beginning that this diversity is not being concealed but, on the contrary, openly stated. It represents, in my opinion at least, not a pathological condition of inquiry into accounting and information systems, but quite the reverse. The diversity of conceptual and research strategies reflects scholarship in action. For understanding in any area of human inquiry has to be constructed through a process of debate, be it explicit or otherwise, between different conceptual systems, reasonings and analytical and methodological approaches. At the very least this collection of papers aims to illustrate the potentiality of such a debate for accounting (and information system) thought and practice.

PAST TRADITIONS AND CONCERNS

So many of the early studies of the way in which accounting systems operate, or might operate, in organizations have concentrated on gaining a rather static understanding of the more 53
psychological and social psychological aspects of the accounting process. A great deal of consideration, for instance, has been given to the way in which different accounting methods, configurations of data and modes of presentation influence the decision making behaviour and the decision outcomes of individual managers. And this tradition of research now provides the rationale, if not the intellectual basis, for today's increasingly influential and rigorous concerns with the way in which individuals process, interpret and use accounting information. However, it is now being recognized that this and other related research, has tended to study what are admittedly quite crucial aspects of the accounting process in isolation of the ongoing organizational context that provides the very *raison d'être* of the accounting function.

The relationship between individual responses to accounting information and other aspects of the dynamic functioning of the organizations in which individuals manifest their behaviour has rarely been regarded as explicitly problematic. And, in consequence, a great deal of the research on the human processing of accounting information has, of necessity, had to adopt a rather fragmented view of the organizational decision process and the

[1] The original versions of the papers by Bariff & Galbraith, den Hertog and Hedberg & Jönsson were presented at the Workshop on Designing Management Accounting Systems for Organizations in a Changing Environment organized by Anthony Hopwood at the November 10–12, 1976 meetings of the American Institute of Decision Sciences held in San Francisco. The paper by Waterhouse and Tiessen is a revised version of one presented at the Workshop on The Relevance of Modern Organization Theory for the Design of Accounting Systems organized and chaired by Vijay Sathe at the same meetings. A brief report of the latter workshop also appears in this issue.

role which information plays in this. Accordingly emphasis has had to be placed on understanding particular individual responses to particular presentations of information and little consideration has been given to either the more specific role that might be played by ongoing managerial learning, and the resulting shiftings of meanings and concerns, or the more general findings of those studies that have sought to investigate the way in which managers make decisions in organizations and the role that formal information systems, such as accounting systems, might or might not play in this process (March & Olsen, 1976; Mintzberg, 1973, 1975; Pettigrew, 1972, 1973, 1977). Although the resulting rather simple view of organizational, as distinct from individual, behaviour, with its emphasis on pro-active, goal directed behaviour in response to the discrete
54 presentation of information (Atkin, 1978), might be implicit rather than explicit, it is nevertheless real.

Even in cases where accounting has been studied in its organizational context, emphasis still has been placed on gaining a comparatively static understanding of the more individual, or at the most group, aspects of the process. So, for instance, the response of the individual manager or employee to different degrees of budget tightness has been studied, at one time, in a great deal of detail. However, this has been done without any consideration of the known social as well as individual influences on such responses, the effects of individual and organizational learning and of the possible relationship between different budget standards and formats and, for example, the distribution and management of organizational power and influence or alternative strategies for coping with uncertainty, even though it has been recognized that the managerial response to budgets might be as dependent, if not more so, on the organizational rather than the overt technical meanings attributed to them.

Studies of participation in the budgeting process, to cite another substantive body of the literature in this area, have also tended to focus on the static relationships between participation and such factors as managerial orientations to the budgeting system, extrinsic and intrinsic motivations to perform, levels of individual satisfaction and the propensity or not to engage in such protective strategies as 'padding' the budget and 'fiddling' the accounts rather than on attempting to gain an appreciation of the organizational process through which such results are achieved or of the relationship between budgeting and other organizational control structures and strategies. Indeed not only have accounting researchers not investigated such dynamic aspects of the process themselves but they have only made symbolic or little or no use of those pioneering studies by other social scientists that have focused on such matters (Argyris, 1952; Bower, 1970; Pettigrew, 1973; Roy, 1969; Whyte, 1955; Wildavsky, 1964). Related static and individualistic concerns are also evident in many of those studies that have focused on the way in which accounting information is actually used where factors such as managerial style and the characteristics of the manager–subordinate relationship have tended to dominate research perspectives.

After striving to identify the partiality of so much of the past research that has sought to understand the ways in which accounting systems operate it *must* be stated that an emerging area of research inquiry cannot hope to provide a comprehensive view, let alone appreciation, of all aspects of its problematic domain. Not only do choices have to be made, and the resulting partialities and incompleteness accepted, but it is more than likely that such choices should be made if enquiry is to be thorough and cumulative. Nevertheless, whilst respecting the inevitability of specialisation in such an embryonic area, it is still appropriate to retrospectively identify what choices have been made, particularly at a time when there are clear pressures for alternative approaches and domains of inquiry, and it is even more appropriate to ponder on those factors that might have influenced the direction of progress to date.

SOME INTELLECTUAL INFLUENCES

Firstly, it should be stated that the static and individualistic orientation of research on the behavioural aspects of accounting reflects much more general influences on the development of social science inquiry. Given that virtually all the pioneering studies in the area, and the vast majority of the subsequent work to date, has emanated from the U.S.A., or at least been strongly influenced by U.S. approaches and concerns, it should not be surprising that the conceptual and methodological approaches that characterise behavioural enquiries undertaken in the accounting area should be related to the dominant concerns in substantive areas of American social science. And this would appear to be the case. For although an adequate understanding of the complex social, political, institutional and philosophical factors that influence the development of social science knowledge remains to be achieved, numerous commentators (Hage, 1978; Karpik, 1978; Kassem, 1976; Lammers, 1976; Wilson, 1977) have pointed to the distinct and often divergent social science traditions and concerns in the U.S.A. and Europe, with the U.K. for this purpose at least, rather ambiguously having a foot on both sides of the intellectual Atlantic!

Such commentators, and particularly Kassem (1976) in his discussion of the contrasting perspectives brought to bear on the study of organizational behaviour, have tended to contrast the more micro American orientation, with its focus on organizational psychology, with the more macro European approaches focusing on questions of organizational sociology. Such comparisons have emphasized the centrality of U.S. concerns with the problems of the individual contributing to the organization, as reflected, for instance, in the human relations movement and the 'radical psychological individualists' (Whitley, 1974) and the consequent study of the organizational mechanisms for relating individual performance, and rewards, to organizational action and goal achievement, whether such mechanisms be seen as ways of increasing organizational rationality or as social and procedural means for managing commitment, motivation and hence achievement. Such pragmatic and functional U.S. concerns have been contrasted with more European interests in the structural and broader environmental influences on organizational processes and actions, which perhaps inevitably, because of the very breadth of the definition of the problematic, have been more oriented towards providing conceptual, interpretative and possibly critical appreciations of the historical and specific influences on organizational action (Hage, 1978; Sandberg, 1976, pp. 29–32).

Broad generalizations of this type are difficult to make for inevitably there are always exceptions, including, in this case, some rather influential ones. In the U.S., for instance, important sociological inquiries have been undertaken, not least the early studies associated with the Chicago School of Sociology, the work of Merton, Gouldner, Blau, Etzioni, Hage, Perrow and others and the more recent contingency formulations. And in Europe exceptions also abound. But the contrasts remain, in general terms, meaningful ones, and particularly in an accounting context if further consideration is given to the filtering processes inherent in the academic system itself. For in many of the major U.S. Business Schools the more micro psychological and social psychological perspectives have been even more dominant than in the social science community at large.

Perhaps related to the above broader intellectual concerns and perhaps, to some extent, independently building on them is another factor which also must be considered when analysing those factors that have influenced the development of research on how accounting systems operate. And this is the view taken of the broader purpose of the research task.

55

Research can seek to illuminate and elucidate, to provide, thereby, in the hermeneutic tradition (Taylor, 1971) a basis for interpreting and understanding the role played by accounting systems, and accountants, in organizational and social functioning. It can, however, have more pragmatic concerns, immediate or otherwise. Research can be oriented towards improving the functioning of accounting systems as we know them either by aiming to improve the effectiveness of present systems or by providing the basis for the design of accounting systems, possibly moving accounting a little nearer towards what Simon (1969) has called the 'sciences of the artificial'. And lest we forget it, given the present parsity of research, scholarly inquiry can also seek to provide a critical appreciation of the role played by current modes of accounting, questioning, in the process, the role they might play in furthering the influence of economic interests on organizational action, and possibly, on this basis, moving towards the design of alternative accountings.

Different research orientations, and clearly there are others, make very different demands on knowledge. Both the hermeneutic and critical perspectives require a broad appreciation of the social as well as organizational context of accounting, although clearly the critical approach also requires a more thorough insight into the relationship between accounting and social interests and the organizational knowledge that is so essential for any attempt to construct a design orientated perspective, critical or otherwise. Only when research accepts the present body of accounting knowledge as itself being unproblematic in broad outline, merely seeking to improve the effectiveness of present systems, are fewer demands made on knowledge. For with such a research orientation an appreciation of the organizational basis of accounting might be less crucial than understandings of the role played by the more detailed aspects of design, such as formats and modes of presentation, and of those psychological and social psychological processes which mediate the effects of any given system.

A view that as yet the research horizons of a great deal of accounting research might be (perhaps justifiably) constrained by an acceptance of the present functioning of accounting is supported by others (see Jensen, 1976) who have noted the relationship between research orientations and the demands on knowledge and the direction of scholarly inquiry in accounting. Indeed as other areas of accounting research have moved away from more limited research perspectives, shedding, in the process, some of the traditional constraints of accounting givens, in order to provide a basis for understanding the broader organizational, economic or socio-economic role played by accounting, one can witness the process in operation. This is certainly true for investigations into the role played by accounting information in the capital markets, the economic rationale for information and control system design and the more recent inquiries into the socio-political bases for accounting standard setting.

It is likely, however, that the effects of the broader intellectual traditions discussed above exert their influence on the research community indirectly through more specific and immediate aspects of the institutional context in which research takes place. We have, for example, already referred to the possible exaggeration of the individualistic orientation in the specific context of business schools. Research perspectives that orientate themselves more towards the production of immediately pragmatic and hopefully generalizable understandings, and are less questioning of existing approaches, will also be more acceptable in such contexts, as has already been demonstrated in the case of industrial psychology (Baritz, 1960). Then, as Kassem (1976) points out, the more micro organizational orientation to social research is more amenable to methodologies that are both compatible with the research traditions of academic peers in different disciplines and functional areas, and to the speedy production of research results. Both of these factors are important within the context of the reward structure of the academic community, influencing both individual advancement and what is acceptable to the established channels of communication.

CHANGING INTERESTS AND CONCERNS

However the approaches of a 'normal science' (Kuhn, 1970) carry within themselves the means for their own advancement and eventual succession. So although one can delineate some reasons why past research has focused on certain concerns to the detriment of others, such appreciations do not necessarily provide any basis for thinking that past concerns will continue into the future. Indeed the opposite is more likely to be the case in scientific endeavour. For whilst the institutional embodiment of research perspectives, in terms of reward structures for instance, can be a constraining influence, historical experience provides one with a basis for expecting that many, if not all, of such constraints will be overcome, sometimes with difficulty and delay, but often with amazing facility and speed.

At present there are indications of at least some pressures for change in the behavioural accounting research community. Some of these pressures eminate from within the present, advancing body of knowledge. Others stem from broader, ongoing changes in social science inquiry. Whilst yet other pressures come from the client community, broadly defined; some from the changing interests of existing clients in corporate management and others from the gradual recognition of the legitimacy of the interests of other social groups in accounting knowledge and research.

Certainly the gradual accumulation of psychological and social-psychological understandings of the way in which accounting systems operate in organizational settings has itself provided a basis for regarding more structural and organizational issues as being problematic. Hofstede's (1967) research on the social psychological dimensions of budgeting, for instance, pointed to the role that technological and organizational factors, as reflected in departmental and organizational cost structures, might play in mediating the effectiveness of budgetary procedures. And the comparative analysis of participation in the budgetary process undertaken by Swieringa & Moncur (1975) provided more direct evidence. Even social psychological studies undertaken in single organizational settings are no less suggestive when the differing results of individual studies are set side by side. So, for example, a comparison of the differences, and commonalities, in the findings of Hopwood (1973) and Otley (1978) points to the role that might be played by organizational level differences, particularly when the diverging results are set aside the comparative hypotheses and findings of Baumler (1971).

The presumption that ever more of such pointers will be discovered as empirical research progresses, and it should be remembered that we have precious little as yet, is supported by the findings of those studies that have been more consciously influenced by an organizational rather than an individualistic or group perspective. The early study of the organization of the accounting function undertaken by Simon and his colleagues (1954), which is so frequently cited by textbook writers for its analysis of the alternative modes of using accounting information but just as frequently ignored for its substantive findings, provided a clear indication of the relevance of such an appreciation. And the subsequent studies reported by Khandwalla (1972), Bruns & Waterhouse (1975), Watson (1975), Watson & Baumler (1975) and Hayes (1977), all much more directly influenced by advancing knowledge in the field of organizational behaviour, demonstrate not only the richness, relevance and potential of the approach but also the way in which the gradual development of behavioural accounting research is itself moving towards more explicitly recognizing the importance of understanding organizational questions.

Such an explicit recognition of developments in organizational behaviour research is itself of significance and no doubt we can expect many more explorations of this type. Certainly the emerging pattern of submissions to this and other journals, successful and otherwise, would support such a conclusion. Equally relevant, if not more so, is the growing interest that organizational researchers themselves are taking in questions related to the design and functioning of accounting and information systems. Whilst this is not a new phenomenon, as evidenced by the pioneering and influential studies undertaken by Agyris (1952) and Simon (1954) and the attention given to such issues by Roy (1969), Dalton (1959), Whyte (1955), Blau (1966) and Wildavsky (1964), amongst many others, there is some basis for believing that the critical role played by accounting and information systems in organizations is now being more generally recognized and studied by scholars of organizational behaviour (Pfeffer, 1977; Pettigrew, 1973; Pondy, 1970; Heydebrand, 1977; Connolly, 1977; etc.). If this is indeed the case then it can only add to our understanding of the area, most likely legitimising and encouraging, in the process, the adoption of similar research perspectives and methodologies by accounting scholars.

The pressures for change do not only eminate from within the research community however. For in business and public organizations there is, I think, and here one can only talk in a much more tentative way, drawing on one's own experiences and impressions, a growing appreciation of the need for a more organizational understanding. In part this reflects, inevitably perhaps, a greater awareness of the limitations of present pragmatic perspectives and approaches (Earl, 1978). More significantly, perhaps, it reflects an increasing recognition of the need for accounting and information system innovation and the role that new knowledge might play in this process.

Until recently the development of accounting and information systems was a very pragmatic affair, prodded, no doubt, by the recognition of the inadequacies of prevailing approaches and the possible relevance of known alternatives. Although change was often real and major (Chandler, 1962; 1977), one can only presume that it was guided by practical wisdom, and on occasions ignorance, and shaped by the rules of experience and the lessons of trial and error. Certainly there is little or no evidence of any systematic research being undertaken, least of all in an academic community.

The results of such processes constitute the substantive bulk of management accounting as we now know it (Gardner, 1954; Parker, 1969; Pollard, 1965). Critical as some researchers might be of it, and at least some of such criticism could be tempered by a greater appreciation of some of the radically innovative and seemingly modern marginal and oft forgotten developments made by our entrepreneurial predecessors, it nevertheless provides the basis on which today's more technical research on topics such as divisional performance measurement, costing methods and capital investment appraisal is conducted.

The increasing pace of change and the growing size and complexity of organizations have created a need for more rapid and more sophisticated accounting and information system developments however. And such increases in organizational complexity, in particular, have increased the relevance of and need for a more explicit understanding of the relationship between information (and accounting) systems and organizational design (Galbraith, 1973). Increasingly, therefore, business and public organizations have turned to outside consultants and researchers for help, sometimes also creating their own specialist developmental teams in the area. The growing sophistication of information system technology provides many examples of such a response, as do the increasing difficulties of costing and controlling both major, long term projects and of
58 deciding upon the production and commercial policies for products with increasingly short life cycles. Similarly, and perhaps more significantly, the complexities of designing the information and control systems, including accounting systems, for the massive modern aerospace and defence organizations have engaged the attention of researchers in both universities and specialized institutes such as the RAND Corporation (Chandler & Sayles, 1971). For in this area in particular the need for the joint design of organizational and information structures and processes was real and recognized.

That few accounting researchers *per se* might have been involved in such innovations does not detract from either their pragmatic or intellectual significance for the development of accounting and information system knowledge, although it might point to the isolation of main stream accounting researchers from matters of major organizational concern. But given that the design and functioning of accounting systems, like other information and control systems, are interrelated with wider aspects of organizational design, and that organizational designs have never been and are unlikely to be static, as witnessed, for example, by the growing relevance today of matrix (Knight, 1977), network and loosely coupled (Weick, 1976) organizations, past isolation by itself is unlikely to remove the continued pressures for new understandings of the organizational basis for accounting system design.

Broader social pressures are also likely to add to such pressures. For as recent research has illustrated (Braverman, 1974; Hales, 1974; Heydebrand, 1977; Marglin, 1974; Whitley, 1974), management practices and structures in organizations, including prevalent accounting and information systems (Mumford & Sackman, 1975), are reflections of wider social structures, institutions and ideologies. Although such aspects of our societies certainly do not change rapidly, there is already evidence of interest in the bases, and at times the reality, of alternative approaches as new social groups gain both power and an understanding of the relevance of managerial insights (Sandberg, 1976). For instance, in Europe research is already under way on the design of either more participative forms of information, accounting and control systems (Magnusson, 1974; Stymme, 1977) or even systems that explicitly aim to further the interests of labour rather than capital (Briefs, 1975; Nygaard & Bergo, 1975). And on both the sides of the Atlantic consideration is being given to the design of information and accounting systems that facilitate the management and assessment of new forms of work organization (Hopwood, forthcoming; Mirvis & Macy, 1976).

EMERGING POTENTIAL AND PROBLEMS

The pressures for a greater organizational appreciation of the way in which accounting systems operate are undoubtedly diverse but nonetheless real. Ranging from those that originate within the context of normal scientific development, through those arising out of the changing needs of existing salient interest groups, to those that stem from more questioning or even critical perspectives, all are slowly resulting in research endeavours and new understandings. At this stage, however, the diversity of approaches and concerns and the relative sparcity of findings, makes an overall assessment a precarious task, and such an assessment certainly is not attempted within the confines of this introductory essay. Already however, the developments do point to an emerging potential and, perhaps of equal importance, to some of the problems that might have to be met on the routes ahead.

The first and most obvious advantage is that an organizational perspective provides a way of building on research developments that are already in progress. As we have discussed, some scholars have laid a basis for exploring both the organizational processes through which accounting and other information systems effect, or not, the consciousness and actions of members of organizations and those organizational, and even wider environmental, factors that influence, shape and constrain the form that accounting and information systems take and the organizational roles that they perform. The papers by Waterhouse & Tiessen, and Wildavsky, and the report by Sathe, contained in the present issue all highlight such developments and their potential. Furthermore, implicit in such ongoing work, and possibly more explicitly in future concerns, might also be a basis for better understanding some of the differences and contrasts that are now evident when the findings of separate psychologically and social psychologically oriented studies are compared, some examples of which have been mentioned above.

Such developments are important for a number of reasons, not least of which is the potential for achieving an understanding of the accounting function that complements the complexities of accounting in action. Rather than being satisfied with an understanding of accounting that focuses on the generalizations that can be made across organizations, organizational researchers might be able to move towards an understanding that is able to cope with the heterogeneous and changing circumstances that shape the form, significance and effects of accounting in specific organizations and sections of organizations. And, in trying to articulate and substantiate such an understanding, it is also likely that consideration will have to be given to views of the accounting and information function that move beyond today's almost exclusive characterisation in terms of the particular combination of techniques, procedures and technologies in use. For whilst these certainly constitute an important part of the whole, and that part which is most obviously visible, the partiality of such a characterisation will be realised when consideration has to be given to those organizational structures and processes through which the technical aspects of accounting achieve their effect. As Simon and his colleagues sought to illustrate, the organization of the accounting function itself and those organizational linkages through which it relates to the rest of the organization are as essential as the techniques and procedures, and often more problematic in managerial terms. Yet our understanding of the organizational form and locus of the accounting function is minimal and both it and the derivation of a more heterogeneous basis for diagnosing and analysing the functioning of accounting systems can only be advanced if accounting research starts to draw on the perspectives and findings of organizational sociologists and theorists.

Such a closer relationship with wider developments in the social sciences, the potential of which already has been illustrated in other areas of accounting research, would enable the consideration of important topics known to be of significance but so far not systematically investigated.

At present the behavioural understandings so far gained by accounting researchers stand in rather stark contrast with the findings of those other social scientists who have strived to probe into their relationship to the dynamics of the organizational decision making process (Bonini, 59
1963; Bower, 1970; Crecine, 1971; Pettigrew, 1973; Whyte, 1955; Wildavsky, 1964). The emerging understandings of, for instance, feedback processes (Annett, 1969; Rosenthal & Weiss, 1966), the retrospective interpretations and rationalizations that accompany and shape prospective decision making (March & Olsen, 1976; Weick, 1969), the role of bargaining and negotiation in resource allocation (Bower, 1970; Pondy, 1970; Wildavsky, 1964), the way in which commitments develop and influence both the production and use of information (Bower, 1970; Staw & Ross, 1978) and the relationship between the design of information and accounting systems and the ways in which those with organizational power attempt to manage the attribution of meaning and significance in an organizational context (Jönsson & Lundin, 1977; March & Olsen, 1976; Pettigrew, 1977) are providing interesting and important leads to the understanding of accounting in action. And, as Bariff and Galbraith suggest in this issue, the reemergence of social science inquiry into power and conflict in organizations (Burns & Buckley, 1976; Pfeffer, 1977; Zald, 1970) has obvious relevance for the study of a subject that has overtly recognized its role in organizational control, influence and restrain.

One important aspect of the emerging organizational appreciation, and one that also relates to more immediate pragmatic concerns, is the consequent possibility it offers for moving towards a more explicit design orientation for accounting. For although accounting systems are organizational artifacts (Simon, 1969), consciously designed and adapted, the study of them has tended to focus on generalizable specifics more than either the nature of the design process, and the way in which design choices are constrained, or the manner in which systems are adapted to organizational circumstances. The foundations for a theory of accounting system design, if they do exist, currently remain within the experiential understandings of accounting practitioners and consultants.

But many of the pragmatic pressures for new accounting and information system knowledge require a more explicit appreciation of the factors that influence and constrain system design (Bjørn-Andersen & Hedberg, 1977). In days of moderate change, implicit understandings may suffice. However a more systematic and articulated
60 understanding becomes vital when organizational structures change with increasing regularity, when, as discussed by both den Hertog & Hedberg and Jönsson in the present issue, there is a growing realisation of the constraining influence of past designs and when ever more social interests attempt to influence design options and the design process.

Real though the potential of an organizational appreciation of the accounting function may be however, its achievement will not be unproblematic. For progress will be dependent not only on accounting researchers mastering new methodologies and theoretical perspectives, some, at least, of which will initially be at variance with those which are embodied and valued within the institutions in which such research takes place, but also on the research keeping pace with the evolving nature of organizational thought and research. It is tempting in all interdisciplinary research, to focus on those insights from the neighbouring disciplines that are thought to be firmly established rather than those that are still in the process of being established, or rejected. But however admirable such a tendency might be in theory, in the context of normal let alone revolutionary scientific progress (Kuhn, 1970) the resulting 'citation lag' will not only unnecessarily constrain the development of research but also do little to discourage it from focusing on findings and perspectives that were subsequently questioned, if not discredited. So, for instance, accounting research is starting to investigate the relevance of contingency theories at the very time when their empirical basis and present theoretical formulation is being questioned (Pennings & Tripathi, 1978; Aldrich & Mindlin, 1978; Weick, 1977).

A further difficulty facing organizational research in accounting relates to its very potential for changing our perceptions of the accounting function. Findings related to the relationship between accounting and the management of power and conflict in organizations will be challenging. Evidence of the contingent nature of the accounting system design process will be disturbing to technical universalists. And research oriented towards the specification of accountings that service new values will be regarded as threatening by existing interest groups.

However, even in having to cope with the latter problem as well as the problems stemming from the substantive nature of the research itself, accounting research will be dealing with difficulties that are endemic to most scientific progress.

CONCLUSION

Accounting and information systems play a vital role in organizational functioning. They have, as a result, responded, and still are responding to changing organizational and environmental circumstances and there is no reason whatsoever for thinking that the future will be different. New knowledge and insights are constantly needed and although research might not have played a major role in the past, it does have at least the potential to influence the future.

Research which is oriented towards understanding the organizational basis for the design and operation of accounting and information systems is particularly important in this respect. For despite the pioneering work that has been done, particularly on information systems *per se* where investigations may have advanced more readily in the absence of either such a well articulated set of techniques and procedures or their professional embodiment, we still have only the barest understanding of the factors which shape either the design of information systems or the processes through which they, in turn, influence the consciousness and actions of organizational participants. The challenge to understand accounting in action remains, in other words, a real one, although, as we have discussed, the pressures for change are equally evident.

Perhaps, outside of such a context, the differences between the articles in this issue of *Accounting, Organizations and Society* may appear more evident than any similarities. Certainly very different intellectual, social and pragmatic bases are evident. But in what might be very different ways they jointly illustrate how research on how accounting and information systems are designed and function is now responding to the challenge of organizational understandings and the pressures and circumstances of wider environmental change.

BIBLIOGRAPHY

Aldrich, H. & Mindlin, S., Uncertainty and Dependence: Two Perspectives on Environment, in Karpik, L., ed., *Organization and Environment Theory, Issues and Reality* (Sage, 1978).

Annett, J., *Feedback and Human Behaviour* (Penguin, 1969).

Argyris, C., *The Impact of Budgets on People* (School of Business and Public Administration, Cornell University, 1952).

Atkin, R. S., Review of *Information and Control in Organizations, Administrative Science Quarterly* (March, 1978), pp. 168–171.

Baritz, L., *The Servants of Power: A History of the Use of Social Science in American Industry* (Wesleyan University Press, 1960).

Baumler, J. V., Defined Criteria of Performance in Organizational Control, *Administrative Science Quarterly* (September, 1971), pp. 340–350.

Bjørn-Andersen, N., and Hedberg, B. L. T. Designing Information Systems in an Organizational Perspective, in Nystrom, P. C. & Starbuck, W. H., *Prescriptive Models in Organizations* (North-Holland, 1977), pp. 125–142.

Blau, P. M., *The Dynamics of Bureaucracy: A Study of Interpersonal Relations in Two Government Agencies* (Chicago University Press, 1966).

Bonini, C. P., *Simulation of Information and Decision Systems in the Firm* (Prentice-Hall, 1963).

Bower, J. L., *Managing the Resource Allocation Process* (Division of Research, Graduate School of Business Administration, Harvard University, 1970).

Braverman, H., *Labor and Monopoly Capital* (Monthly Review Press, 1974).

Briefs, U., The Role of Information Processing Systems in Employee Participation in Managerial Decision-Making, in Mumford, E. & Sackman, H., *Human Choice and Computers* (North-Holland, 1975).

Bruns, W. H. & Waterhouse, J. H., Budgetary Control and Organization Structure, *Journal of Accounting Research* (Autumn 1975), pp. 177–203.

Chandler, A. D., *Strategy and Structure* (MIT Press, 1962).

Chandler, A. D., *The Visible Hand: The Managerial Revolution in American Business* (Harvard University Press, 1977).

Chandler, M. R. & Sayles, L. R., *Managing Large Systems* (Harper & Row, 1971).

Connolly, T., Information Processing and Decision Making in Organizations, in Staw, B. M. and Salancik, G. R., eds., *New Directions in Organizational Behaviour* (St. Clair Press, 1977).

Crecine, J. P., Defense Budgeting: Organizational Adaptation to Environmental Constraints, in Byrne, R. F. *et al., Studied in Budgeting* (North-Holland, 1971), pp. 210–261.

Dalton, M., *Men who Manage* (Wiley, 1959).

Earl, M. J., Prototype Systems for Accounting Information and Control, *Accounting, Organizations and Society*, Vol. 3, No. 2 (1978).

Galbraith, J., *Designing Complex Organizations* (Addison-Wesley, 1973).

Gardner, S. P., *Evolution of Cost Accounting to 1925* (University of Alabama Press, 1954).

Hales, M., Management Science and the 'Second Industrial Revolution', *Radical Science Journal* (January, 1974), pp. 5–28.

Hage, J., Toward a Synthesis of the Dialectic Between Historical-Specific and Sociological-General Models of the Environment, in Karpik, L., ed., *Organization and Environment: Theory, Issues and Reality* (Sage, 1978).

Hayes, D. C., The Contingency Theory of Managerial Accounting, *The Accounting Review* (January, 1977), pp. 22–39.

Heydebrand, W., Organizational Contradictions in Public Bureaucracies, in Benson, J. K., ed., *Organizational Analysis: Critique and Innovation* (Sage, 1977).

Hofstede, G. H., *The Game of Budget Control* (Van Gorcum, 1967).

Hopwood, A. G., *An Accounting System and Managerial Behaviour* (Saxon House, 1973).

Hopwood, A. G., *Towards Assessing the Economic Costs and Benefits of New Forms of Work Organization* (ILO, forthcoming).

Jensen, M., Reflections on the State of Accounting Research and the Regulation of Accounting. Paper presented at the Stanford University Lectures in Accounting, May 1976.

Jönsson, S. A. & Lundin, R. A., Myths and Wishful Thinking as Management Tools, in Nystrom, P. C. & Starbuck, W. H., *Prescriptive Models of Organizations* (North-Holland, 1977).

Karpik, L., *Organization and Environment: Theory, Issues and Reality* (Sage, 1978).

Kassem, M. S., European versus American Organization Theories, in Hofstede, G. H. & Kassem, M. S., *European Contributions to Organization Theory* (Van Gorcum, 1976).

Khandwalla, P. N., The Effects of Different Types of Competition on the Use of Management Controls, *Journal of Accounting Research* (Autumn, 1972), pp. 275–285.

Knight, K., ed., *Matrix Management* (Gower Press, 1977).

Kuhn, T. S., *The Structure of Scientific Revolutions* (2nd edition: University of Chicago Press, 1970).

Lammers, C. J., Towards the Internationalization of the Organization Sciences, in Hofstede, G. H. & Kassem, M. S., *European Contributions to Organization Theory* (Van Gorcum, 1976).

Magnusson, A., Participation and the Company's Information and Decision Systems, Working Paper 6022, Economic Research Institute, Stockholm School of Economics, 1974.

March, J. G., and Olsen, J. P., *Ambiguity and Choice in Organizations* (Universitetforlaget, 1976).

Marglin, S. A., What Do Bosses Do? The Origins and Functions of Hierarchy in Capitalist Production, *Review of Radical Political Economics* (Summer, 1974), pp. 33–60.

Mintzberg, H., *The Nature of Managerial Work* (Harper & Row, 1973).

Mintzberg, H., *Impediments to the Use of Management Information* (N.A.A., 1975).

Mirvis, P. H. & Macy, B. A., Accounting for the Cost and Benefits of Human Resource Development Programs *Accounting, Organizations and Society*, Vol. 1, No. 2/3, (1976), pp. 179–194.

62 Mumford, E. & Sackman, H., *Human Choice and Computers* (North-Holland, 1975).

Nygaard, K. & Bergo, O. T., The Trade Unions – New Users of Research, *Personnel Review* (1975), pp. 5–10.

Otley, D. T., Budget Use and Managerial Performance, *Journal of Accounting Research* (forthcoming, 1978).

Parker, R. H., *Management Accounting: An Historical Perspective* (Macmillan, 1969).

Pennings, J. M. & Tripathi, R. C., The Organization–Environment Relationship: Dimensional Versus Typological Viewpoints, in Karpik, L., *Organization and Environment: Theory, Issues and Reality* (Sage, 1978).

Pettigrew, A. M., Information as a Power Resource, *Sociology* (1972), pp. 187–204.

Pettigrew, A. M., *The Politics of Organizational Decision Making* (Tavistock, 1973).

Pettigrew, A. M., The Creation of Organizational Cultures. Working Paper. European Institute for Advanced Studies in Management, Brussels, 1977.

Pfeffer, J., Power and Resource Allocation in Organizations, in Staw, B. M. & Salancik, G. R., *New Directions in Organizational Behaviour* (St. Clair Press, 1977).

Pfeffer, J. & Salancik, G. R., Organizational Decision Making as a Political Process: The Case of a University Budget, *Administrative Science Quarterly* (1976), pp. 227–245.

Pollard, S., *The Genesis of Modern Management* (Edward Arnold, 1965).

Pondy, L. R., Toward a Theory of Internal Resource-Allocation, in Zald, M., ed., *Power in Organizations* (Vanderbilt University Press, 1970).

Rosenthal, R. A. & Weiss, R. S., Problems of Organizational Feedback Processes, in Bauer, R. A., *Social Indicators* (MIT Press, 1966).

Roy, D., Making-Out: A Counter-System of Workers' Control of Work Situation and Relationships, in Burns, T., ed., *Industrial Man* (Penguin, 1969).

Sandberg, A., *The Limits to Democratic Planning* (LiberForlag, 1976).

Simon, H. A., *The Sciences of the Artificial* (MIT Press, 1969).

Simon, H. A., Guetzkow, H., Kozmetsky, G. & Tyndall, G., *Centralization Versus Decentralization in Organizing the Controller's Department* (Controllership Foundation, 1954).

Staw, B. M., and Ross, J., Commitment to a Policy Decision: A Multi-Theoretical Perspective, *Administrative Science Quarterly* (March, 1978), pp. 40–64.

Stymme, B., To Organize For Participation, Working Paper, Stockholm School of Economics, 1977.

Swieringa, R., and Moncur, R. H., *Some Effects of Participative Budgeting on Managerial Behaviour* (NAA, 1975).

Taylor, C., Interpretation and the Science of Man, *Review of Metaphysics* (1971), pp. 1–45.

Watson, D. J. H., The Structure of Project Teams Facing a Differentiated Environment: An Exploratory Study in Public Accounting Firms, *The Accounting Review* (April, 1975), pp. 259–273.

Watson, D. J. H. & Baumler, J. U., Transfer Pricing: A Behavioural Context, *The Accounting Review* (July 1975), pp. 466–474.

Weick, K. E., *The Social Psychology of Organizing* (Addison-Wesley, 1969).

Weick, K. E., Educational Organizations as Loosely Coupled Systems, *Administrative Science Quarterly* (March, 1976), pp. 1–19.

Weick, K. E., Enactment Processes in Organizations, in Staw, B. M. & Salancik, G. R., *New Directions in Organizational Behaviour* (St. Clair Press, 1977).

Whitley, R. D., Management Research: The Study and Improvement of Forms of Cooperation in changing Socio-Economic Structures, in Roberts, N., ed., *Information Sources in the Social Sciences* (Butterworth, 1974).

Whyte, W. F., *Money and Motivation* (Harper & Row, 1955).

Wildavsky, A., *The Politics of the Budgetary Process* (Little, Brown, 1964).

Wilson, H. T., *The American Ideology: Science, Technology and Organization as Modes of Rationality in Advanced Industrial Societies* (Routledge & Kegan Paul, 1977).

Zald, M., ed., *Power in Organizations* (Vanderbilt University Press, 1970).

11

The Organisational and Behavioural Aspects of Budgeting and Control

ANTHONY G HOPWOOD

Professor of Accounting and Financial Reporting,
London Graduate School of Business Studies 65

Introduction

In accounting texts, budgeting and other related procedures of financial control are portrayed as technical phenomena. Emphasis is placed on the rules and calculative procedures by which budgets are formulated and thereafter used to provide means for evaluating the adequacy of actual performance. Consideration is given to the identification of key budgetary constraints, to the alternative mechanisms for assembling and analysing the mass of expectations for the budgetary period, and to the technical possibilities for analysing the variances between budgeted and actual performance. Although such statements of the technical apparatus of budgeting and financial control invariably commence with appeals to the underlying organisational processes and roles which they serve, the detailed discussion of the technical means for their attainment invariably results in a distancing of the technical from the organisational – a distancing which once achieved is often difficult to reverse.

Unfortunately such an emphasis on the technical rather than the organisational has resulted in an appreciation of budgeting which is detached from the organisational setting in which it operates and the ways in which it is implicated in other organisational processes. Emphasis has been placed on the calculative procedures which give rise to 'the budget' and its subsequent comparison with actual performance, but not on the organisational processes through which budgetary pressures and demands emanate, and as a result of which budgeting achieves its organisational significance. Hardly any consideration has been given in traditional accounting sources to either the competing political processes within organisations which provide the bases for deliberations about an uncertain future, or those processes for organisational evaluation and review which provide the context within which budgetary comparisons are considered and used. Furthermore, in emphasising the calculative and procedural aspects of budgeting, attention has not been given to the ways in which budgeting

and other instruments of financial control themselves have shaped the structure and operation of the modern organisation. However, the organisational map of cost centres, profit centres, divisions and programme units, which underlies the structure of budgeting today, bears witness to the roles which mechanisms for financial planning and control have played in reconstituting and, indeed, creating what we now know as the modern organisation. In part, at least, the organisation is now defined in terms of the mechanisms which were introduced to further its control. Moreover, by facilitating the separation of planning and control from action, budgets and other mechanisms for financial control have played a key role in enabling the centralised managerial control of ever larger groupings of activities.

An organisational view of budgeting also highlights the social as well as economic and technical nature of budgetary outcomes, a fact that is well known to practitioners of the craft. 'The budget' is a reflection of the underlying political structure of the organisation, as well as economic constraints and opportunities and the technical procedures out of which it arose. It has a social as well as an economic significance, reflecting the outcomes of debates over organisational power and influence, the social location of uncertainties and constraints within the organisation, and the allocation of organisational resources.

Therefore, in the realm of accounting practice as distinct from that of the accounting textbook, it is difficult, if not impossible, to disentangle the organisational and the technical aspects of budgeting. Both shape each other. The technical components are designed to activate organisational processes, and can themselves help to shape participants' perceptions of the organisational domain. And budgeting, in turn, achieves its significance through those organisational processes which the techniques engender.

To further our understanding of the organisational nature of budgeting, we will consider the many and often conflicting purposes which it serves, the processes which give rise to the practice of budgeting, and the different ways in which budgetary information can be used. We conclude with some speculations on the possible relationships between financial practice and organisational performance.

Budgeting as a Multi-purpose Activity

Budgeting can serve a variety of roles and purposes, often simultaneously. Even several purposes can enter into the justification and implementation of a budgetary control system, as different managerial groups, or even individuals, emphasise different roles which it can serve. Those in the finance department, for instance, can have interests and needs in mind very different from those in production and marketing, let alone general management; and yet all might agree on the need for an extension of budgetary practice. And the purposes to which budgeting is put also can be very different from those which entered into its original justification. For, once installed, budgetary systems have some measure of autonomy. As the technical apparatus becomes intertwined with the activities of a wider array of organisational participants, it can be used to further a diverse and often conflicting array of organisational and personal ends.

Such a view of budgeting in action suggests that it would be a difficult and rather futile activity to list, in isolation from the organisational context in which they operate, the purposes which budgets and other mechanisms for financial control have come to serve. They are so diverse, and often so idiosyncratic, that very little of general value would be gained from the exercise. Instead, we shall try to understand some of the ways in which the practice of budgeting and financial control can arise out of the interplay of organisational processes, paying particular attention to how they are implicated in the processes of decision making.

Different Approaches to Organisational Decision Making

Decision making in organisations takes place in the context of uncertainty or disagreement over both the objectives and consequences of action. Different participant groups, both within and outside the organisation, have different views of both the desirable and the achievable. Whilst those with financial inclinations, for example, might seek to establish the
68 primacy of economic ends, those interested in the management of the organisation's technical resources might articulate concerns with either more immediate physical indicators of performance, or the organisation's longer-term innovative potential. These, in turn, might well be different from the interests emphasised by marketing and personnel management groups. For the organisation is rarely an assembly of the agreed. Debate and deliberation are almost inevitable features of organisational life. With different interests and perspectives coming together to constitute the organised endeavour, objectives, as such, are rarely pre-given, but rather emerge out of the interplay of organisational pressures, constraints and opportunities. At times there might be a temporary resolution with many, if not all, agreed on the primacy of particular overall concerns. Equally, there might be agreement over the aims of either particular organisational actions or the activities of particular organisational units. At other times, however, discord and debate might well be the only way of characterising the organisational mission.

Views over the consequences of particular organisational actions are subject to no less variation. Where there is considerable investment in past experience and where the environment for action is stable and known, relative certainty may prevail. Organisational participants may then be able to presume that particular sequences of actions are likely to result in certain patterns of consequences. On other occasions, however, the

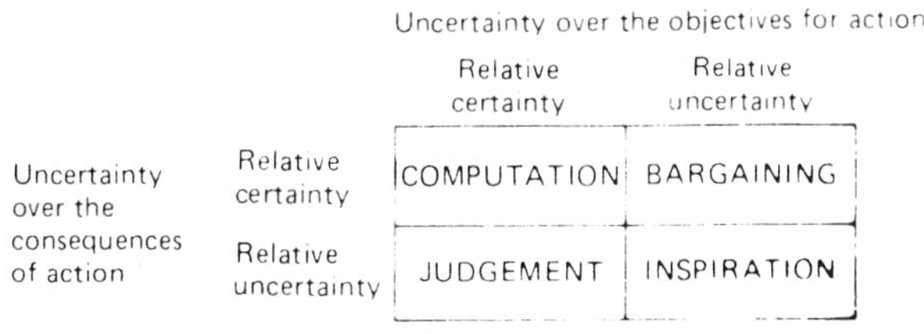

Figure 11.1 *Uncertainty and Decision Making Processes*

consequences of action may be far from predictable. With either limited experience or a volatile and poorly understood environment, they are likely to be subject to disagreement and debate. A whole range of possible consequences will then have to be considered at some stage in the decision making 69
process.

What are the consequences of acknowledging such a variety of uncertainties in decision making? If in any particular instance the objectives for action are clear and undisputed, and if the consequences of action can also be presumed to be known, decision making can then proceed in a computational manner, as illustrated in figure 11.1.[1] In such circumstances it is possible to compute whether the consequences of the action or set of actions being considered will, or will not, satisfy the objectives that have been unambiguously articulated beforehand. As the consequences of action become more uncertain, however, the potential for computation diminishes.

1. The discussion of organisational decision making is based on J.D. Thompson and A. Tuden, Strategies, structures and processes of organisational decision, in J.D. Thompson *et al.* (eds), *Comparative Studies in Administration*, University of Pittsburgh Press 1959. See also J.D. Thompson, *Organisations in Action*, McGraw-Hill 1967. Further discussions of the subsequent extension of this decision making framework to take account of the organisational roles of information and control systems are given in M.J. Earl and A.G. Hopwood, From management information to information management (a paper presented at the IFIP TC8 WG 8.2 Working Conference on the Information Systems Environment, Bonn 1979; to be published in *Organisational Dynamics*) and A.G. Hopwood, Information systems and organisational reality, Occasional Paper No. 5, Thames Valley Regional Management Centre 1980.

Decisions then have to be made in a judgmental manner, with organisational participants subjectively appraising the array of possible consequences in the light of the agreed objective or objectives. Just as the introduction of uncertainty into the specification of the consequences of action results in a different approach to decision making, so does the acknowledgement of debate or uncertainty over the objectives themselves. If the consequences of action are presumed to be known, disagreement or uncertainty over objectives results in a political, rather than a computational, rationale for action, as organisational participants seek to further their own particular objectives. A range of interests in action are articulated in such circumstances and decision making, as a result, tends to be characterised by bargaining and compromise. And when
70 even the consequences of action are in dispute, decision processes can be complex indeed, being rather positively characterised in figure 11.1 as of an inspirational nature! With so little known beforehand, rationales for action can emerge in the course of the decision making process itself.

Mechanisms for financial planning and control, like other information and control systems, invariably have been justified in terms of the contribution which they make to organisational decision making. In providing such rationales, the process of decision making has only rarely been considered in social terms, however. Emphasis has repeatedly been placed on the economic and the technical, rather than on the social and the political. If, in contrast, we do try to recognise, not only such a social context, but also the variety of approaches to decision making that can stem from the uncertainties that might be inherent in both the consequences of action and the objectives for action, what insights can we gain into the roles which such mechanisms serve? How, in other words, might interests in budgets and other financial procedures emerge out of organisational decision processes? And what different roles might they serve in the contexts of the computational, the judgmental, the political and the inspirational? To such questions let us now turn.

Accounting and Computational Practice

Given low uncertainty over both the consequences and the

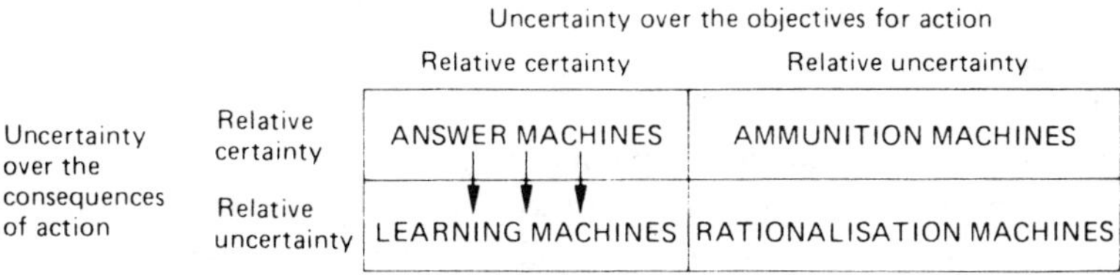

Figure 11.2 *Uncertainty, Decision Making and the Role of Information and Control Systems*

objectives of organisational action, we approach the management scientist's definition of certainty where algorithms, formulae and rules can be derived to solve problems by computation. Alternatively, this situation may represent what Herbert Simon[2] has called structured decision making, where the intelligence, design and choice phases are all specifiable and programmable. And in case you have not recognised it, this is also the organisational world presumed by many introductory management accounting textbooks!

In all cases a wide variety of management practices, including the mechanisms of financial planning and control, can serve as what in figure 11.2 are termed 'answer machine' aids to decision making. The techniques of budgeting and investment appraisal, for instance, can further the evaluation of proposed actions in the light of agreed financial objectives. By providing a way of comparing the achievable and the desirable, in a world of relative certainty, the computations introduce a powerful element of structure into the decision making process. Similarly, the practice of budgeting can facilitate the co-ordination and integration of organisational activities by computational means. Production and marketing operations can be synthesised, inventory policies evaluated and amended in the light of envisaged organisational circumstances, and the consequences for particular organisational resources, such as cash, calculated and evaluated.

Moreover, some, at least, of the certainties which enable the use of computational approaches can be created by managerial action, rather than having to be implicit within the organisational task. By a judicious management of inventory, for

2. H.A. Simon, *The New Science of Management Decision*, Harper and Row 1960.

instance, production operations can sometimes be temporarily buffered from the uncertainties inherent in the market place. The impact of other uncertainties can be isolated by the availability of surplus capacity and resources. And internal organisational boundaries can be drawn so that the more certain spheres of organisational endeavour can be managed in partial isolation from their more uncertain context. In ways such as these, the organisational and the technical can together create a particular decision making environment. With organisational strategies creating pockets of activities with higher predictability and surer ends, computational approaches to decision making can function and flourish in otherwise alien terrains.

72

Accounting and Organisational Learning

In the context of judgmental decision making, such 'answer machine' approaches are no longer of such direct value. Acknowledging the uncertainties that are inherent in action requires that they be confronted rather than managed.

Of course, many of the procedures created to serve 'answer machine' roles are still used in judgmental contexts. Often, however, this is in spite of, rather than because of, the underlying uncertainties over the consequences of organisational action! So in circumstances which cry out for information to stimulate managerial learning and the exercise of judgement, we find routine financial evaluation and control systems which often assume the very certainties which cannot be found. Indeed, as is illustrated by the arrows in figure 11.2, such procedures have been subjected to enormous increases in technical sophistication as various experts have sought to extend the boundaries of computational practice. The articulation of forms of risk and probabilistic analysis in a budgetary context bears witness to such tendencies.

Often, however, computational procedures are used in a judgmental context, but in very different ways. Rather than directly facilitating the search for answers, they are used to explore problems and to probe into assumptions and the range of possible implications. Serving to stimulate the human mind, they can be used to analyse the analysable before organisational participants finally resort to judgement. In figure 11.2 such approaches are referred to as 'learning machines', in order to emphasise the potential for a more active interplay between the technical and the cognitive.

Sensitivity analyses involving the multiple use of computational procedures are of this type, as is the use of simulation models in budgeting and planning. In both cases the procedures can help organisational participants to appreciate the nature of the decision environment in which they are working. And the iterations to and from departments and organisational levels which characterise the practice of budgeting point to a similar interrelationship between the computational and the judgmental. Indeed, one of the most frequently quoted purposes of budgeting, that of encouraging an active concern
with the future, focuses on the learning rather than the mere 73
calculative potential of the process.[3] When seen in this way, the procedures of budgeting can serve to emphasise the need to investigate, albeit if thereafter to constrain, the financial and wider organisational implications of possible future activities. By iteration and deliberation, the discipline and structure which are implicit in the budgetary process can stimulate organisational participants to reflect on at least some of the implications of what they are proposing; to test out their assumptions and estimates, and ascertain whether the necessary resources are likely to be available to the organisation as a whole and its constituent parts.

Accounting and Political Processes

Whilst the roles served by the procedures of financial planning and control in computational and judgmental decision situations have been explicitly discussed in the official literature of accounting, those which are served when the objectives of action are themselves subject to debate have not. In their writings, at least, accountants have tended to assume that the objectives of organised endeavour are given. By now you are all familiar with those seemingly unproblematic

3. A stimulating discussion of the role of planning in organisational and social learning is given in D. Michael, *On Learning to Plan and Planning to Learn*, Jossey-Bass 1973.

assertions that the objectives of a firm are '. . . to maximise profits', '. . . to maximise cash flow', '. . . to maximise shareholder wealth', or whatever. Fortunately or unfortunately, such assertions represent gross abstractions from organisational practice, useful for some purposes perhaps, but of limited value when trying to understand rather than influence the ways in which organised endeavour emerges out of coalitions of interests and concerns. For when objectives are themselves uncertain and decisions characterised by bargaining and debate, financial planning and control practices can arise out of the political processes which permeate organisational life, serving as (in the terminology of figure 11.2) 'ammunition machines' to articulate and promote particular interested positions and values. Rather than being reflective of agreed ends, the mechanisms of financial control seek to articulate and further particular ends.

Indeed, budgeting and other mechanisms for financial control most likely achieved a great deal of their present organisational significance because of the roles which they came to play in furthering the centralised, financially orientated, control of large organisations, whether public or private. In this context, however, it should be stated that financial practices cannot be operated independently of other management practices. They both reinforce and, in turn, enable to operate those practices which establish particular patterns of organisational segmentation: the procedures which delineate management responsibilities, the methods for the regular reporting of performance, and the practices, formal or otherwise, for the evaluation of managerial performance.[4] Seen in such terms, mechanisms for financial control are but one component of the battery of control practices which enabled and assisted the birth of the modern organisation.

In such a constellation of management practices, budgeting and other mechanisms for financial control nevertheless have a

4. For discussions of the organisational origins of management accounting and related practices see A. Chandler and H. Deams, Administrative co-ordination, allocation and monitoring: a comparative analysis of the emergence of accounting and organisation in the USA and Europe, *Accounting, Organisations and Society*, Vol. 4, Nos. 1 and 2, 1979.

number of vital roles to play. Out of the mass of organisational actions and their consequences, they can influence those which become relatively more visible and influential, particularly to senior management groups. And the visibility so established is invariably an asymmetric one: the powerful can observe the less powerful (but not vice versa), as a rather particular mode of surveillance is established. The centralised co-ordination of activities can thereby be facilitated. Equally, however, demands, requirements, pressures and influences can be more readily passed down through the organisation, particularly in the spheres of the financial and the economic, because of the disaggregative arithmetical properties of the accounting art. Budgeting and financial reporting practices together can provide the framework within which a measured and observed delegation of authority can take place. A pattern of expectations can be established, an organisational ethos articulated, and even motivations influenced, as the visibility which is created provides a basis for organisational rewards and sanctions. Moreover, by influencing the accepted language of negotiation and discourse, control and reporting systems can help to shape what is regarded as problematic, what can be deemed to be a credible solution and, perhaps most important of all, the criteria which ought to be used in the selection of a particular solution. Even the more ritualistic roles of budgeting are important in this context.[5] As one senior manager once commented: 'You will never understand the budgetary system in my company unless you realise that it is like a rosary bead: it quite simply makes sure that every manager says profit, cost, cash, working capital, etc. at least a thousand times a year!'

Accounting and the Rationalisation of Organisational Action

However, financial reporting practices are used not only to influence what is to be. Although the realms of the computational, the judgmental and the political can be important, in all organisations they are complemented by the inspirational,

5. An interesting discussion of the ritualistic and mythical roles of accounting is given in T. Gambling, Magic, accounting and morale, *Accounting, Organisations and Society*, Vol. 2, No. 2, 1977.

where actions arise out of the uncertainties of both aims and consequences. And even that particular variety of decision making provides a basis for roles which the mechanisms of financial planning and control can serve. In such circumstances, the roles are related to the justification and legitimation of what has been decided upon. In the terminology of figure 11.2, financial practices serve as 'rationalisation machines' in such a context.

The widespread use of capital budgeting procedures, for instance, has resulted in the availability of justification devices for proposals which have gained early commitment and support, as well as simply providing information (prior to decision making) on those proposals which remain problematic to the end.[6] Having decided on action, organisational parti-
76 cipants can consciously or otherwise manage the calculations which are used for its more official evaluation. Similarly, budgets and plans can be built around what is to be. Particularly in the context of large, complex and highly innovative decisions, organisational knowledge of the preconditions for action can be widely dispersed and plans can serve to provide a more general, albeit retrospectively created, rationale. Even quite complex procedures for evaluation and control can arise out of the need to marshall support for action. The emergent apparatus of social cost–benefit analysis served such purposes in the nineteenth century,[7] let alone today, and many more recent innovations in control system design have originated from the pressures to maintain an organisation's autonomy for action in the face of external pressures and influences.[8]

6. Further insights into the retrospective interpretation of action are given in K. Weick, *The Social Psychology of Organising*, 2nd edn, Addison-Wesley 1979.
7. G. Pringle, The early development of cost–benefit analysis, *Journal of Agricultural Economics*, January 1978, pp. 63–71. For a further discussion of the role of accounting in the rationalisation of action see S. Burchell, C. Clubb, A.G. Hopwood, J. Hughes and J. Nahapiet, The roles of accounting in organisations and society, *Accounting, Organisations and Society*, Vol. 4, No. 4, 1979.
8. See J. Meyer and B. Rowan, The structure of educational organisations, in M.W. Meyer *et al.* (eds), *Environments and Organisations*, Jossey-Bass 1978.

Pressures for the practices of financial planning and control therefore arise in many ways. Whilst accounting textbooks continue to emphasise those which reflect a particular computational rationality, other rationales are equally influential in organisational life. For, faced with the uncertainties and complexities of organised action, information is a vital resource. It can serve to constrain and influence in a political context, facilitate the exercise of judgement, and legitimise what has been done, as well as what might be. All such roles, including the computational, have provided organisational bases for the development of the technical practice of budgeting and financial control and, of equal importance, all continue to influence the use which is made of that practice, regardless of its specific organisational origins. Indeed, many of the complexities and dilemmas which characterise budgeting in action stem from the very diversity of the uses which have been, and are, made of it.

Budgeting and Organisational Action

With such diverse origins and uses, it is hardly surprising that the organisational practice of budgeting and financial control is complex, grounded as it is in the intricacies of organisational processes and politics. Unfortunately, however, all too little is systematically known about the organisational functioning of budgeting and other control practices. Whilst a wealth of experiential insights are potentially available, comparatively few attempts have been made to probe into the underlying organisational processes, the ways in which control practices do and do not interrelate with other management practices, and their significance for organisational performance.[9] Much

9. Some rich and interesting insights into the practice of budgeting in public organisations are given in A. Wildavsky, *The Politics of the Budgetary Process*, 2nd edn, Little, Brown 1974; A. Wildavsky, Policy analysis is what information systems are not, *Accounting, Organisations and Society*, Vol. 3, No. 1, 1978; and H. Heclo and A. Wildavsky, *The Private Government of Public Money*, Macmillan 1974. The last reference is based on British experience, whilst the others are based on US practice. Unfortunately there

of what is known contrasts with the rather stark computational and procedural rationality that has been codified in and propogated by accounting texts. Compared with the economic analytics of the latter, ongoing practice has been seen to be often characterised by bargaining, controversy and debate, and by a rather loose, indeed ill-defined and shifting, relationship with many other management practices; with its consequences being dependent upon the wider organisational processes in which it is embedded and which determine how it is used.

The Strategies of Budgeting

Assembling a budget for a large organisation is a massive as well as contentious endeavour. The persons engaged in the process have, of necessity, to use strategies to reduce both the uncertainty of the endeavour and the sheer burden of calculation, as well as to promote particular interests and aims. As a result the process is often an incremental activity. Emphasis is placed on the deviations which might be made from the firmer historical base of either past budgets or past performance. And because of, rather than in spite of, the complexity of the task, budgeting is an activity which is invariably characterised by the use of the simplest rules of thumb.

However, although such approaches reduce the burden of calculation and breadth of debate, these benefits are gained at the expense of focusing the remaining discussion on the areas of particular uncertainty and controversy, namely the changes from one year to the next. 'Is an increase justified?' 'And what of the over-spending on last year's budget?' 'Should this year's budget be the same or higher?' Careful analysis can, of course, provide some assistance, but since the basic problem involves the extrapolation of an uncertain past into an uncertain future, analysis alone cannot solve the problem. Lobbying, exhortation and an array of bargaining and simplifying strategies come into play.

---

are no similar descriptions of business practice, although the interested reader might consult the descriptive studies of capital budgeting reported in J. Bower, *Managing the Resource Allocation Process*, Graduate School of Business Administration, Harvard University 1970.

Where proposed activities are beyond the comprehension of budget officers and senior managers, the final decision may well depend on their impressions of factors which, although relatively minor, are nevertheless within the bounds of their own experience. Financial procedures themselves can also contribute to such simplifying processes, as they are used to force the debate along more predictable lines. Budgetary decisions can also be made within the context of a predetermined amount of resources which are to be allocated. 'How much can we afford?' then becomes more important than the objectives which might be attained, and organisational norms develop to guide the priority to be given to individual requests. A multitude of other similar simplifying strategies may be used; but in the end, if all else fails, the 'big meat-axe' approach (as it was called by one senior manager) may be used to 'just arbitrarily, without logic, dictate a cut of x% across the board'.[10]

Such strategies are a response, not only to the uncertainties and complexities which are inherent in the budgetary process, but also to the fact that budget demands reflect individual and group ambitions. Intertwining the logic of both economics and politics, the demands are strategies in an intensely serious game. The ability to estimate 'what will go' is a vital skill. Managers seek out facts and opinions, in order to arrive at an estimate of what they should ask for in the light of what they can expect to get and then, with due 'padding' to allow for anticipated cuts, they seek to market their budgetary demands. The support of others is actively canvassed and demands are packaged in the most appealing way. Tangible results can be given undue weight and complex activities described in either the simplest or the most complex of terms – but not the more understandable mean! Emphasis can be placed on the qualitative rather than the measurable advantages, the forthcoming rather than the current results, and the procedures to be gone through rather than the outcomes to be achieved. Points can be stretched a little, but never so far as can be

10. C.C. Schwarz, The behavioural aspects of accounting data for performance evaluations at industrial nucleonics, in T.J. Burns (ed.), *The Behavioural Aspects of Accounting Data for Performance Evaluation*, College of Administrative Science, The Ohio State University 1970, p. 101.

tested. If some cuts are seen to be inevitable, essential or popular activities can be pruned first, in anticipation of their subsequent restoration. It can even be pleaded that the smallest of cuts could damage an entire programme of activities. For new activities it is often beneficial to emphasise their relationship to the old, and sometimes it is best to demonstrate that they can either 'pay for themselves' or that it is a case of 'spending a bit now to save a lot later'.

The practice of budgeting provides a forum for organisational debate. It can influence what are regarded as viable organisational strategies, and the techniques of budgeting themselves can be used more actively to influence and constrain the political processes which constitute organisational life. In the last resort, however, the technical components of both budgeting and other mechanisms of financial control are only a part of a wider organisational process -- a process which combines the technical and the economic with the human and the political.

Using Budgetary Information

Very different approaches can be used to disseminate budgetary and other financial information through the organisation. Attempts can be made to ensure its widespread availability, or it can reside in the hands of a few. Many can participate in the processes from which it arises, or it can emanate from the higher realms of corporate authority. It can be integrated with other management practices, particularly those concerned with organisational evaluation and the provision of recognition and reward, or it can remain a rather detached endeavour, only loosely related to other aspects of organisational functioning. Because of such options, the practices of financial control have few automatic and obvious consequences. If there are consequences, they stem from the ways in which the financial controls intertwine with other organisational processes and from the managerial contexts which influence if, and how, they are used.

In the area of performance evaluation, for instance, comparisons of budgeted and actual performance can be used in very different ways. Even in large organisations noted for the

sophistication and rigour of their financial planning and control practices, the data provided by them may have little influence on managerial concerns, if they are seen as being the almost exclusive province of specialist financial experts who are detached from the mainstream of management practice. At the other extreme, a great deal of managerial emphasis can be placed on the data.[11] For instance, data may be taken at their face value and used to influence the distribution of organisational recognition and rewards. Such use, however, can result in explicit concern with the data as such, rather than with the underlying organisational transactions which they (imperfectly) reflect. In such ways perceptions of the intra-organisational boundaries which are implicit within the budgetary framework can be intensified, lateral as well as hierarchical conflicts thereby engendered, 81
and the budgets and accounts subjected to 'padding' and manipulation. In other contexts, however, the data can be used in more problem oriented ways, not being emphasised in their own right but evaluated, questioned and used alongside other pertinent information, both formal and informal.

An appreciation of the different ways in which financial planning and control practices are used in organisations must therefore be based on an understanding of the human and social contexts out of which their use arises. Technical understandings alone are not sufficient. The interpretation and use of the information provided by financial practices, although influenced by the technical characteristics of those practices, is also the outcome of personal and social processes which are sustained by the meanings, beliefs, pressures and purposes that are brought to bear by both organisational participants and external agents. It can be ultimately intertwined with the use of managerial power. External pressures and demands can create particular rationales for the economic and the financial. And in striving to facilitate the decision making process, its use can be influenced by the ways in which organisational participants clarify and define the problematic, the possible and the desirable. In placing the information in their own wider contexts, managers and employees provide

11. For a more comprehensive discussion see A.G. Hopwood, *An Accounting System and Managerial Behaviour*, Saxon House 1973.

the information with a personal and organisational significance. In this way the information can be, and is, used in a variety of ways – and with a variety of consequences.

Some Thoughts on the Consequences of Financial Control Practices

Budgeting and other practices of financial planning and control have been shown to have a complex relationship to organisational functioning. Although invariably introduced in the name of economic efficiency, their origins and functioning have been seen to have as much to do with political and social, as with economic, rationality. Whilst they can, and do, facilitate economic decision making, they can also be
 used to introduce a particular political order, reinforce patterns of organisational power and segmentation, and provide for the legitimacy and understanding of the organisational past as well as playing a role in the creation of the organisational future. Once introduced into an organisation, the use which is made of financial practices, and thereby the consequences which they have, is shaped by the ways in which they interrelate with other complex organisational processes. Capable of being influenced by a wide variety of pressures, practices and beliefs, they can have a range of possible consequences, only some of which would be deemed to be compatible with the furtherance of economic performance.

In fact, we know very little about the organisational consequences of the practices of financial planning and control. A great deal of their ultimate utility has been taken on faith, despite the all-too-evident differences in investment in them made by different, but apparently equally successful, organisations. Rather than probing into the ways in which they operate and the consequences which they have, analysts have been content to emphasise the adequacy of the economic logic inherent in their construction and technical design. However, as we have seen, the technical can have an ambiguous relationship with the organisational; and the ultimate consequences of even economic rationales can be determined in the spheres of the social and the political as well as the economic – interrelationships which are only partially understood at the organisational level.

Perhaps in the light of these observations it should not be surprising that what evidence is available, which is not very much, points to the rather equivocal relationship between organisational performance and the practices of financial planning and control.[12] On the positive side, there are some insights into the processes through which they can facilitate organisational choice and action by helping to shape patterns of organisational visibility, influencing thereby perceptions of both the problematic and the possible and reinforcing certain sequences of actions and constraining others. Some other evidence is potentially more questioning, however. In part, this might reflect very different approaches to the organisational dissemination of the practices: at least on
occasions, even potentially favourable consequences might not be exploited. And on other occasions, the evidence no doubt reflects the fact that poorly performing organisations tend to be the ones which systematically increase their investment in the practices of financial control as they seek, possibly with uncertain effect, to re-establish a particular economic order – a phenomenon which has been termed 'newly poor behaviour'. However, the evidence which remains is still consistent with the possibility that particularly heavy emphases on the rigours of financial planning and control can hinder, rather than facilitate, the achievement of economic ends. For organisations are complex artifacts, the survival and development of which are dependent on the mutual satisfaction of numerous and often conflicting demands, both internal and external to the organisation itself. To focus on any one, without due care, might result in the neglect of others, on which (paradoxically) the achievement of the focal concern can, in turn, depend.

If for no other reason, the equivocality of such findings

12. A very brief discussion of some of the evidence is given in A.G. Hopwood, Criteria of corporate effectiveness, in M. Brodie and R. Bennett (eds), *Perspectives on Managerial Effectiveness*, Thames Valley Regional Management Centre 1979, pp. 81–96.

points to the need for an organisational, as well as technical, appreciation of the financial craft.

Conclusion

In seeking to demonstrate both the breadth and potential of an organisational and behavioural understanding of the practices of financial planning and control, consideration has been given to how interests in such practices can arise out of organisational processes; and how those processes, in turn, can shape the use which is made of the practices and the consequences which they might have. Our explorations accordingly have taken us into realms that remain implicit
84 within accounting texts. Almost inevitably, many problems have been raised rather than answered. Indeed, even conflicting tendencies have been acknowledged. For rather than focusing on detailed understandings and research findings, emphasis has been placed on illuminating the range of issues where an organisational appreciation can provide not only new, but useful, insights. All too obviously, the arena for such a discussion is enormous, both in scope and potential. Many issues of importance have not been discussed, or have received only fleeting mention. Hopefully, however, those issues which have been considered will stimulate you to think and read about those which have not.[13]

13. A more comprehensive introduction to the area is provided by A.G. Hopwood, *Accounting and Human Behaviour*, Prentice-Hall 1974.

14 The design of information systems for matrix organisations

ANTHONY G. HOPWOOD

The design of appropriate information and control systems should be a crucial part of any attempt to develop and implement a matrix organisation. Matrix organisations, like any other management structures, require information to function effectively. Planning procedures, information for decision making and systematic ways of monitoring and controlling performance are an essential part of the management process. Indeed for matrix organisations the need may be all the greater. For the matrix 85
approach is invariably implanted within an existing organisation and there are usually innumerable forces that have the potential to frustrate its success. There is invariably a real need for carefully designed information and control systems that explicitly aim to support the matrix rather than neutralise or even destroy its potential. Yet, on so many occasions, the seemingly obvious need for appropriate information systems is not given the emphasis that it deserves, and matrix structures are left to exist alongside information and control systems orientated towards a previous functional management structure.

In part this reflects a much more general management problem. The complexities facing modern organisations, and their increasing size, have resulted in a fragmentation of not only the actual management task but also the evolving body of management expertise and knowledge. Once started, this fragmentation process develops its own momentum. Technical and functional boundaries become jealously guarded, and, with time, as different management groups respond to differing circumstances and the pressures of their increasingly separate environments, leads and lags, if not stark inconsistencies in managerial practices, become increasingly apparent.

Of course, matrix organisations are intended to provide one way of overcoming these very problems, but the same factors which provide the impetus for their development can also constrain their effective implementation. In no area is this more readily observable than in the design and use of complementary information systems. The technical concerns of the designers of information and control systems, and the behavioural and organisational assumptions that they implicitly make, can easily appear to be, and frequently are, very distant from the concerns and assumptions of those organisational designers who have fostered matrix approaches.

An illustrative example

That the fragmentation of expertise and efforts certainly has its attendant costs is illustrated by the endeavours of one major company that was experiencing tremendous difficulties in co-ordinating a complex set of highly interrelated activities. Recognising that co-ordination required both an appropriate organisation and more effective information systems, senior managers in the company proceeded to establish two high-level task forces in these areas. Both groups produced what appeared to be emin-
86 ently reasonable recommendations and, with comparatively few changes, these were speedily implemented. But no sooner had this been done than the underlying problems got even worse. For whilst the organisational group had recommended the use of project and product managers to strengthen the co-ordinating role of lateral relationships in the company, the emphasis that the information group placed on clarifying existing responsibilities and producing more comprehensive departmental performance information did little either to highlight the troublesome interdepartmental problems or to help with their solution. Indeed, with the new reports providing more detailed and comprehensive information on the activities within departments, existing departmental loyalties and the power of the vertical patterns of influence were strengthened. As each manager strove to improve the reported results of his own unit, conflict between the units intensified and co-ordination became ever more difficult.

The recommendations of the information group were firmly based on the doctrines of individual responsibility and accountability that are so influential in accounting thought and practice. The group had thought that the previous co-ordination problems were a result of the fact that responsibility for some crucial areas of management activity was far too diffused. From their point of view it appeared that many managers could not be held responsible for all the consequences of their own actions. Hence they had sought to extend the degree of individual accountability and to do this they recognised that an improved information system was an essential requirement. With more comprehensive departmental information systems, they thought that it would be possible to motivate individual managers to achieve specific objectives which were in the interests of the company as a whole and for which they could be held personally responsible.

Within the context of their own separate bodies of expertise, both sets of recommendations had looked reasonable enough, but their orientations and aims conflicted. One had focused on the activities of separate units and their aggregation through the management hierarchy whilst the other had focused on the relationships between units. By making those differences explicit, their combined implementation intensified rather than reduced the difficulties of co-ordinating the company's complex activities. Rather than supporting the move towards more influential lateral relationships, the new and highly visible information and control system helped to undermine both their affective and analytical bases. It strengthened existing departmental loyalties and provided little or no information to improve the quality of interdepartmental decision making.

If, however, the dominant concern is with the effectiveness of the 87
overall enterprise, both organisational structures and information and control systems need to be designed so that they reinforce each other's concerns with the wider ends rather than dissipate each other's potential in the creation of additional conflict. Both, in other words, need to be seen as part of an organisational design endeavour. For, as Galbraith (1973, pp. 4–6) has pointed out, both are means by which enterprises strive to cope with the uncertainties and complexities of the task which they manage. Although the approach in practice may depend on the ends to be fulfilled, the overall need is present whether the aim is to achieve better co-ordination, facilitate organisational responsiveness, promote participation and autonomy or emphasise the significance of organisational outcomes rather than just internal processes.

Some common problems

Given that there is a frequent tendency to maintain traditional information and control systems alongside a matrix organisation, or only to modify them marginally to deal with the most apparent inconsistencies, it is important to consider the nature of the problems that this can create. Many management information and control systems, and particularly responsibility accounting systems which are so influential in practice, concentrate on reporting the consequences of activities within particular sub-units of an enterprise and on the aggregation of the information vertically through the enterprise. In so doing they reflect not only the need to compile the aggregate information on the enterprise that is required by law, but also the evolving role that such information systems have come to play in facilitating the exercise of authority downwards through the enterprise. In contrast, however, matrix organisation structures frequently aim to facilitiate inter-unit co-ordination through a greater emphasis on lateral decision processes.

In reflecting vertically oriented conceptions of organisational control, such information systems can, if used rigidly, encourage managers to focus too narrowly on the operations internal to their own units to the detriment of their relationships with other interacting units. The structure of the information system can, in other words, itself encourage a fragmentation of managerial perceptions, and as this occurs, the attendant rivalries and conflicts can endanger the very lateral relationships that a matrix structure aims to facilitate.

The dominant role that so many of today's information systems play in
88 enforcing the influence of a vertically oriented power structure also means that they emphasise the production of information for the evaluation and control of subordinates rather than providing the information which is needed for decision making. This is a particularly important problem when traditional information system designs are implemented within matrix organisations. For whilst the need for decision information within the functional management units of the matrix remains, the project managers have additional needs for decision information that can facilitate co-ordination and integration and more generally contribute to the overall decentralisation of power and influence.

The above factors suggest that functionally oriented information and control systems have the potential to frustrate the aims of a matrix organisation. Similarly, however, the implementation of an integrative information and control system without a complementary change in the management structure can also be of no avail. If the underlying objectives of the matrix approach are to be realised, the management structure and the information and control systems must be mutually reinforcing.

Towards a framework for information systems design

One way of looking at both the problems and the potential of designing information and control systems for matrix organisations is to consider two fundamental dimensions underlying system design. The first dimension relates to whether the system emphasises decision or control information. Information for decision making is oriented towards facilitating the exercise of self control by managers, whilst information for control is oriented towards control by others, especially by hierarchical superiors. The second dimension relates to whether the information system is oriented towards facilitating the management of functional units, with an emphasis on the utilisation of resources, or towards the overall project or programme of activity to which these contribute, with an emphasis on end results. The two dimensions and the resultant information system categories are illustrated in Fig. 14.1.

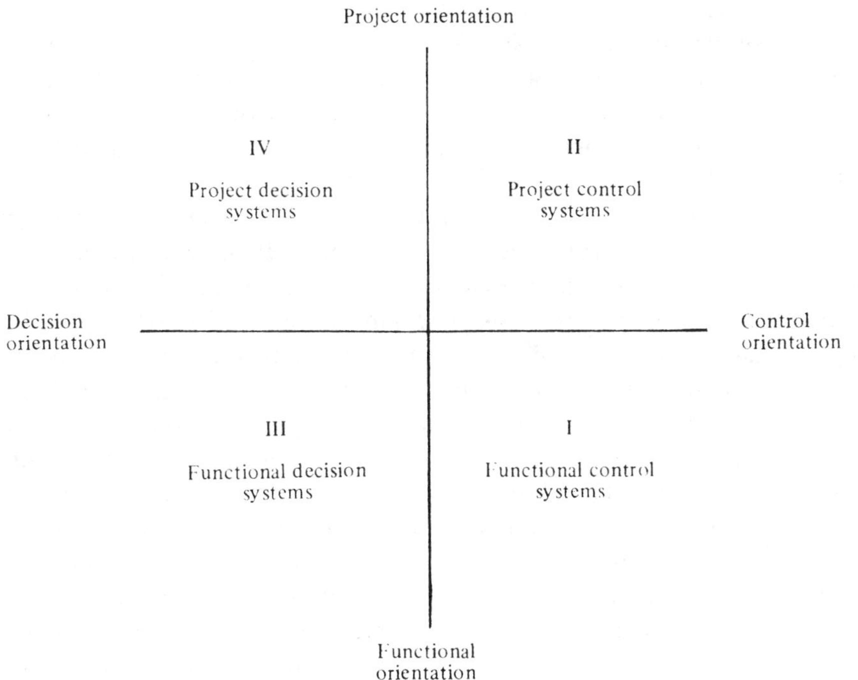

89

Fig. 14.1 A classification of information systems

Type I functional control systems are for monitoring the performance of functional management units. Many, if not most, of today's responsibility accounting systems, budgetary control systems and financial reporting procedures are of this type. Reporting on the utilisation of resources and the associated financial expenditures in areas of functional management responsibility, consideration is generally given to the relationship between financial inputs and outputs only at higher levels of the organisational hierarchy, and often then on a multi-product or project basis. Project control systems of the type II variety, on the other hand, are explicitly oriented towards monitoring the performance of the separate projects and programmes of the enterprise. In contrast with the primary input orientation of the type I systems, type II systems are goal oriented, aiming to reflect the relationship between inputs and outputs at all relevant organisational levels on an ongoing basis.

Information systems for the financial control of projects report on project costs and revenues irrespective of the functional management units in which these have been incurred or realised (Cleland and King, 1975). Engineering, production, distribution and marketing costs are, for instance, related to the anticipated or realised revenues of particular projects. Similar procedures are used for monitoring the performance of contracts in sectors such as the construction and heavy engineering industries. In both of these cases the collection of the information in this way can be used to facilitate the monitoring of progress against time budgets.

90 The ability to express project outcomes in financial terms eases the design of type II control systems. But in the public sector, and also in some increasingly important areas of private sector activity, it is often impossible to express outcomes in financial terms. Nevertheless, some progress has been made on the design and implementation of related programme planning and budgeting systems (Anthony and Herzlinger, 1975). Extending beyond traditional departmental boundaries, such systems aim to relate all expenditures (and other indicators of resource utilisation) on particular programmes of activity to both quantitative and qualitative indices of programme performance. In local government, for instance, attempts have been made to relate expenditures on community health activities incurred within public health, welfare, education, recreation and sanitation departments to an array of indicators of community health including the incidence of diseases, mortality rate and hospitalisation statistics. Control systems of this type are undoubtedly in their early days. Numerous conceptual and practical problems remain to be solved. But this is not to say that they are not useful. If used with appropriate care they can greatly assist the management of complex and important activities.

The basic aim of types III and IV information systems should be to improve the quality of decisions made by individual managers of the enterprise. The type III systems aim to do this for the managers of functional units whilst the type IV systems strive to facilitate the activities of the project managers who are concerned with overall co-ordination and integration. In both cases the information should focus on those aspects of the job where the manager has discretion to act. If the flow of raw materials, for instance, is beyond the control of a particular manager, information that aims to assist in their control is of no practical value to him. But where the flow is within a manager's discretion, information on the quantity, quality and timing of the flows and associated stocks, and more importantly, on the factors that influence these, is of potential value.

The fact that information systems of this type should reflect the nature of the job that they are aimed at assisting makes it difficult to generalise about the nature and scope of functional decision systems in particular. Different jobs have different information requirements and different management styles may also influence the demand for and use of information. Given these problems it should not be surprising that at this stage we know little about the general principles that might underlie such information systems. But this very ignorance is at least suggestive of the way in which they should be designed.

91

The basic question that should guide the design of functional decision systems should always be: what information do *you* need to do a better job? Any presumption that *we* know better should be viewed with some caution. Managers may have difficulty responding but the fact that so many do design and operate their own personal information systems suggests that the problem is mainly one of asking the right questions. Given that these systems aim to assist individual managers, their design should, as we consider again later, be of a participative nature, actively drawing on the resources and ideas of both information specialists and the ultimate users.

Project decision systems of the type IV variety should aim to facilitate the activities of the project managers who are concerned with overall project co-ordination and control. Although project managers should also be involved in the design of these systems, the integrative nature of the job suggests that type IV systems should at the very least provide two distinct types of information.

As is illustrated in Fig. 14.2, integrative information systems aim to facilitate the overall co-ordination of a project or programme. They place particular emphasis on the way in which the activities of separate management units jointly contribute to the desired outcome. PERT techniques (project evaluation review techniques) are of this type, as are contract, project and programme planning procedures (Cleland and King, 1975). Coupling information systems, on the other hand, aim to facilitate the co-ordination of particular management units. Whilst of necessity operating within the broader content established by the integrative planning systems, their orientation, scope and hence design can be very different. Many stock control procedures and interdepartmental scheduling procedures are of this type, as are information systems which help to co-ordinate the activities of such separate functions as production and marketing.

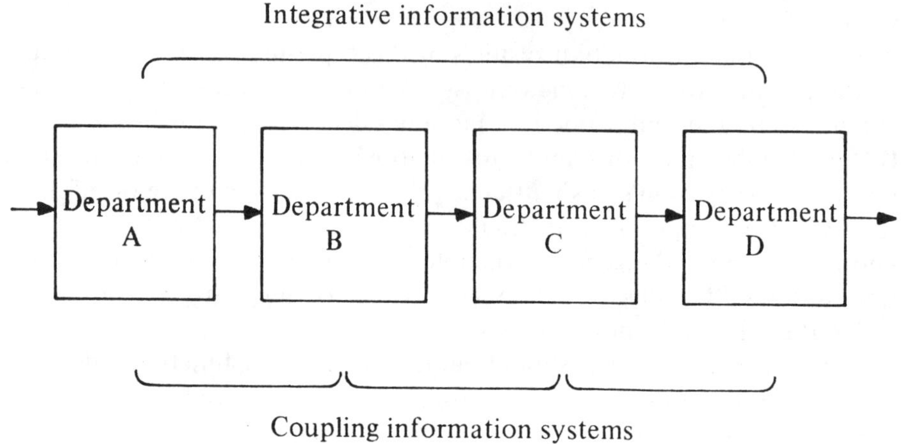

92

Fig. 14.2 Integrative and coupling information systems

Functionally organised enterprises tend to emphasise the need for type I information systems. There is less overt need for the type II and IV project systems, although increasingly it is being recognised that these can play a valuable role, and even functionally oriented information systems for decision making of the type III variety are often weakly developed at the official level. But what are the information system needs of the matrix organisation? What combination of systems is required to support the operation of a management structure that explicitly aims to integrate the often disparate activities of separate management units?

Information systems for the matrix organisation

It is tempting to think that there might be a single design strategy that would help to identify the information needs of a matrix organisation. Given the emphasis that has been placed on formulating the outline of such a strategy for the functionally managed organisation, surely something similar must be necessary for complementing a matrix structure? However such thinking is misguided. It is increasingly being realised that many of the norms underlying the systematic design of such information systems may not correspond to the realities of organisational life. Several recent investigations have found that high performing enterprises have complex, multi-faceted and even mutually conflicting information systems (Gordon and Miller, 1976; Grinyer and Norburn, 1975). Whilst a concern for simple information system design strategies might meet the designers' needs for clarity, order and tidiness, it is not so obviously related to ensuring organisational effectiveness.

The matrix organisation is complex and multi-faceted. The effectiveness of the whole organisation depends on achieving a continuous balance between vertical and lateral processes. It is this aspect of the matrix approach that provides the clue to its information needs. Rather than looking for a single integrated and tidy information system, it needs to be recognised that to survive and flourish the matrix requires a diversity of information systems. Just as there is a need for both decision and control
information, so both the vertical and lateral processes within the matrix 93
need to be provided with their information support. A matrix structure requires, in other words, types I, II, III and IV information systems.

Ways in which type I and II systems may be combined in an integrated control system for matrix organisation have been suggested by Vancil (1973) and Davis (1973), although little evidence of the actual effect of such strategies exists at present. One possibility is that of treating functional departments as cost centres, products or projects as profit centres, with separate controls on each. A second step is to use transfer pricing to allocate part of the profit to the functional managers and part to projects or products (though the frequent arbitrariness of price determination may engender its own forms of conflict). The third possibility is a system of double counting, with total costs or profits being calculated both vertically and horizontally in an accounting matrix which matches the organisational one (cf. Wilkinson, 1974). What evidence we have on the information and control systems that have been associated with the implementation of matrix organisations, and admittedly this is rather limited at present, tends to support the need for a multiple information system strategy.

In the National Aeronautics and Space Administration, surely one of the most complex of modern organisations, project and functional control systems functioned alongside one another. As Sayles and Chandler (1971, p. 307) comment:

> In the daily course of events, managers have to use, and be responsive to the use by others of, a variety of control measures. Some are

> consistent with, and critical to, . . . 'dispersed' responsibilities [where the emphasis is on an entire project, without regard to inter-personal, departmental or organisational boundaries]; others represent the more traditional concern with 'jurisdictional' responsibility (of a functional nature) . . . . In the real world of advanced technology implementation both types of controls are necessary.

However, although important, control information alone was not sufficient for the management of this complex enterprise.

> Unfortunately, most high- and low-level controls try to measure accomplishment: how actual costs, schedules, and performances compare with the original estimates. This can be misleading, in part because such controls assume rigid plans, compartmentalized jurisdictions and responsibilities. ('Our engineers are mesmerized by watching dollars when they should be watching technology and
> 94 people.')

The adaptability and responsiveness of the whole organisation depended on the use of more flexible sources of decision oriented information. Given the dominance of the overall mission of this agency, the managers themselves responded to this problem and provided their own sources of information (Sayles and Chandler, p. 314):

> Rather than emphasising regular reports, managers place importance on random organisational probes designed to identify co-ordination problems. Thus, each . . .. manager concentrates on monitoring the interfaces . . . . These include suppliers of components and subsystems, the next and preceding work-flow stage, test and control groups.

The initial self-designed information-for-decision systems were of an informal nature. With time, however, such pressing needs for information for decision making resulted in the design and official implementation of coupling information systems of the type IV variety, type IV integrative systems which 'direct the attention of . . . managers to the total system's requirements and to the breakdowns that threaten its performance', and, within the functional management units, supportive information systems of the type III variety.

The descriptions of matrix oriented information systems in other governmental agencies and departments also stress the complementary role of project and functional control systems. The very terminology of programme planning and budgeting systems serves to emphasise the recognised need for, if not the actual attainment of, project information systems which serve both decision making (planning) and control (budgeting) needs.

Within the context of the industrial research laboratory, Wilkinson (1974) outlines how functionally oriented financial control systems can be adapted to provide project and programme control information and also considers, albeit briefly, the need for type IV planning information within the matrix structure. Costs were planned and monitored on the basis of individual research projects and project groupings as well as in relation to overall cost type and functional location. Bergen (1975), on the other hand, discusses the construction and use of a type IV project planning system for new products which identifies resource and time requirements by project, function and specific managerial activity. Complementing the existing functional controls, this planning procedure also had the potential of providing the basis for a subsequent type II 95
project control system through which actual accomplishments could be compared with the original plan. In a comprehensive, even if not detailed, description of matrix support systems, Goggin (1974) outlines the multi-faceted management systems that are used to support Dow Corning's 'multi-dimensional' structure. MbO, profit reporting and personnel reviews provide the basis for both type I and II control systems whilst corporate planning, economic evaluation and a comprehensive new business planning system constitute systems of the type III and IV decision varieties.

These and the few other descriptions of practice in the area do provide an indication that a variety of information systems are in simultaneous use in matrix organisations. However, with the possible exception of the more thorough review of the National Aeronautics and Space Administration's experiences provided by Sayles and Chandler (1971), they give little indication of either the way in which the systems actually function as against how they are designed to function, or the relative or combined effectiveness of the various approaches. Yet in this area, as in functional organisations, actual practice can, and does, deviate substantially from what is both intended and claimed.

Problems and potential

Information systems in a matrix organisation should provide flows of information that support the conflicting yet ultimately interrelated pressures that constitute the matrix itself. Yet the very fact that the overall integration of the enterprise is achieved through the use of potentially conflicting means itself provides the basis for some common and important problems.

The different types of information system have different sources of organisational support and different patterns of growth and development. The functional control systems draw their strength from the vertical power hierarchy which they are designed to complement, whilst the use and final impact of the project oriented information systems and particularly the project decision systems depends on the often more fragile patterns of lateral relationships.

To be effective, project control systems need to be associated with an organisational structure and culture that stresses the overriding importance of the goals of the enterprise. Project controls without a project oriented management structure have little effect and whatever may be a particular enterprise's equivalent to 'getting a man on the moon' must be known, visible and well articulated. In order to survive, such systems must
96 be given their own separate existence. Whilst they can, and often should, share a common data base with the functional control systems, project control systems need to be much more than minor extensions of the functional controls. Product costs appended to functional reports or highly summarised project control information alongside detailed functional control information are not sufficient. To be effective, the project control information needs to be at least as visible and well articulated as the functional control information.

If these conditions are fulfilled, however, the use of the type II project control systems is capable of undermining the very different and equally valuable role that can be played by the type IV systems for project decision making. For the planning activities that the type IV systems aim to facilitate can easily be dominated by the anticipation of subsequent evaluation and control on the basis of the type II systems. Where a great deal of emphasis is placed on monitoring actual project performance against the original plans, the plans themselves may be formulated so as to provide easier targets rather than realistic guides to action. Rather than helping to identify potential problem areas, the project planning systems can become mere adjuncts of the control procedures. As the managers seek to establish plans that improve their own performance-potential in an interdependent organisation, the operation of the system can help to create rather than overcome inter-unit conflict.

What is needed is that the decision oriented information systems should become separate from and independent of evaluation oriented control systems, providing local information resources at the operating level (Hedberg, 1975). An increasing number of people are beginning to realise that the involvement of managers in the design of their own decision oriented information systems may be one way of attempting to achieve this. In this way, and particularly if priority is given to the establishment of the decision oriented information systems, both type III and type IV systems might be given a source of independent support. Rather than using the information of 'others' in decision making, managers might be able to establish a sense of ownership over the information that they use. This might provide not only a means of ensuring the viability of these types of information system, but also help to ensure their more effective utilisation.

Ultimately, of course, the final effectiveness of any type of information system or combination of information systems depends on its appropriate use (Hopwood, 1973). It is easy for complex information systems to be either rejected or taken at their face value. But, to have the appropriate effect, they must be used in a careful and considered manner, sometimes
being used but on other occasions being set aside in the light of alternative 97
evidence. How information is used reflects quite general managerial characteristics. To change these is difficult. Certainly educational programmes have a role to play if they aim to help managers understand the rationale, advantages *and* disadvantages of the systems rather than merely present a public relations version of the activities of the information specialists. But real progress might depend on trying to influence how managers actually use information. As information system designers try to do this, their efforts will be related directly to the organisational development activities of those organisational designers who strive to create the social environment in which a matrix structure can survive and flourish.

Conclusion

The design of information systems for matrix organisations remains an emerging area of concern. Many unknowns and doubts remain and, as yet, many of the early experiments have still to endure the test of practice. At this stage, however, there is reason to think that the appropriate systems will reflect the conflicting but mutually reinforcing pressures of the matrix itself. Rather than constraining the simultaneous exercising of vertical and horizontal influences, such information systems will provide both the means for these influences to function and some of the checks and balances that are so necessary for the enterprise as a whole to function effectively. However alien design principles of this type may be to those information system designers who look for orderliness and simplicity, they do offer the possibility of nurturing and supporting the vital organisational processes that the matrix approach seeks to promote.

Summary

The effectiveness of matrix organisation is often frustrated by the retention of inappropriate information and control systems based on a previous functional structure. An example is described in which a reorganisation aimed at strengthening lateral co-ordinating links was made ineffective by a new information system which placed greater emphasis on the vertical reporting patterns of separate departments.

To assist in the development of information systems which will support rather than hinder the operation of matrix structures a two-dimensional
98 classification of information systems is proposed, which distinguishes between control and decision oriented information and between functional emphasis on resource utilisation and project emphasis on end results. This results in four types of information system being distinguished. An examination of the needs of matrix organisations suggests that they require the simultaneous existence of all four types of system, rather than a single overriding design strategy. The little evidence which is available tends to support this view.

The danger that decision oriented project information systems may be distorted by being subordinated to evaluation oriented control systems may be avoidable by involving managers in the design of their own decision information systems. This might make it more likely that information systems will be used constructively to increase the effectiveness of matrix organisations.

5. CRITERIA OF CORPORATE EFFECTIVENESS*

Anthony Hopwood**

The idea of corporate effectiveness is an illusive, indeed curious one. Despite appearing to be pragmatic in orientation and intent, its all embracing scope makes it virtually impossible to operationalise in any satisfactory way, with its practical definition ranging from the narrowly technical to visionary depictions of corporate potential. It is also a concept that, until recently at least, has not entered into the discourse of corporate management itself. Concerns with survival, profit, growth and market penetration have certainly been articulated by practising managers. Consideration has also been given to product quality, innovative record, if not potential, consumer impact and even public image. And more recently we have heard of the seeming attractions of the socially responsible corporation with the attendent identification of such manifestations of corporate impact as the quality of working life, energy conservation and the contribution to employment, both regional and national. But effectiveness *per se* has rarely, if ever, been articulated as a management aim. Interest in that concept invariably has emanated from those outside the corporation who have or claim to have some interest in it.

Perhaps not too surprisingly the idea of effectiveness has entered

* I acknowledge the stimulation received from my colleagues Stuart Burchell, Colin Clubb and John Hughes at the London Business School and Janine Naphiet of the Oxford Centre for Management Studies.

** Professor of Accountancy and Financial Reporting at the London Graduate School of Business Studies and Professor of Management at the European Institute for Advanced Studies in Management, Brussels.

into the language of those who seek to change corporate actions and performance. Be they management consultants, facilitators or educators, they have readily adopted a concept which can be used to point to unexploited potential and — so some at least of the literature would have us believe — a constantly expanding horizon of the novel and the unknown. And that very same normative orientation has also appealed to an increasing number of both corporate critics and agents for corporate change. Indeed the very ambiguity of the concept has been attractive to those, be they in private interest groups or agencies of the state, who have sought or currently seek to create and legitimise their own interest in the corporation and the means for facilitating their interventionist concerns.

Such a view of corporate effectiveness implies that the idea is neither a self-sufficient nor a unitary one. Concerns with effectiveness presume, at the very least, an interest, a rationale or an intent
100 and often, albeit implicitly rather than explicitly, a particular conception of the nature and functioning of the corporation. Accordingly, there is, I would venture to suggest, no such thing as effectiveness *per se*. Concepts of corporate effectiveness are socially constructed, their meanings and roles stemming from the articulation of particular social concerns, interests and demands and the specific contexts in which the concepts operate. And, as such interests and contexts vary and change over time, so do the prevailing notions of effectiveness.

Indeed it may well be that the current interest in the concept of corporate effectiveness reflects just such underlying pressures for change. For whilst there always have been competing notions of effectiveness, more recent events have added a new dynamism to the debate. Past interests have been reassessed and new concerns have entered the corporate arena. The government, for instance, be it at a national or local level, has certainly been more influential, seeking both to further its own interests and concerns and to act as a more active agent of the public interest. The media and particularly more independent agencies for change have started to examine and question the consequences of corporate behaviour, the organisational processes from which they emanate and the mechanisms for external accountability and review. Thereby the interests of the consumer, for instance, have started to be recognised and endowed with a more substantive legal status and those of labour also have been articulated more clearly and forcefully. And within the corporation itself change has been underway. The emergence of the personnel function (Watson, 1977), in particular, and especially its recent concern with personnel and organisational development, has provided a basis on which long standing notions of economic and technical effectiveness can be and have been elaborated, if not challenged. In ways such as these, accepted notions of corporate effectiveness have been made problematic at the very least. What may have been taken for granted is now being questioned and reassessed.

Of course the social contexts of particular notions of effectiveness, be they new or longstanding, rarely enter into their articulation for invariably that would constrain their acceptance and use. Indeed, as the bases of at least some of our concerns with corporate effectiveness have come to be recognised, it has become even more important for the articulated criteria to appear self-evident and disinterested. As a consequence, in a world where an ever increasing number of interests are being expressed, we are being faced with an ever expanding array of criteria for judging corporate effectiveness, most of which are so stated as to appear universalistic and objective (Pfeffer and Salancik, 1974).

THE ROLE OF RESEARCH ON CORPORATE EFFECTIVENESS

Such a social view of the interest in corporate effectiveness increases the complexity of understanding the roles which research and scholarly inquiry have and can play. For if notions of effectiveness are socially constructed, the role of research cannot be seen in terms of a simple and unproblematic search for the real and the true or the ideal and the absolute. With concerns with effectiveness being seen as stemming from the articulation of interests and concerns, the relationship which research itself bears to such processes must also be recognised and considered.

Seen in such terms, research can play three main roles within the context of an interest in corporate effectiveness. First it can seek to facilitate the articulation of particular notions of effectiveness by improving their underlying conceptual frameworks, their empirical approximation or the processes through which they gain their organisational significance and impact. Such research may also help to promote those important elements of empirical objectification and contextual neutralisation, the growing need for which already has been mentioned. Secondly research can try to further our appreciation of the social nature of concerns with corporate effectiveness. An interest in effectiveness in such a research context will be seen as a problematic rather than a self-evident phenomenon. The research task then becomes one of understanding the social nature of such interests and the social processes through which they are articulated and change prevailing conceptions of what is or is not regarded as effective corporate performance. Finally research can play a role in increasing our understanding of the effects which particular notions of effectiveness have in organisational terms and the processes through which such impacts are or might be achieved.

To date most research on corporate effectiveness has emphasised the first role. Rather than seeking to establish the social and organisational nature of the interest in particular concepts of corporate effectiveness, researchers have tended to accept at least some basic notion of effectiveness as being unproblematic, trying on this basis to improve its conceptual clarity and its empirical assessment. However, there are now some indications that research interests are starting to expand. Some, at least, of the earlier concerns with the elucidation of universalistic and objective criteria of corporate effectiveness are being set aside, as researchers adopt a more complex view of organisational functioning (Scott, 1978) and the very observation of, if not involvement in, the many recent debates and even conflicts over possible criteria for appraising corporate action has itself encouraged a more questioning and analytical stance. How, some researchers are starting to ask, can we understand the
102 changing orientations? How do they come to be articulated? What meanings and consequences do they have? And through what organisational processes are these achieved?

Such concerns are being reinforced by a number of other research developments. Not least in importance might be the emergence of a more independent tradition of inquiry in organisational research which has started to investigate and even question the prevailing conventional wisdom of corporate action. New rationalities are emerging, for instance, which attach a different significance to goal setting and assessing processes and procedures in organisations (Cohen, March and Olsen, 1972; March and Olsen, 1976; March, 1978; Weick, 1969) and research is starting to inquire into the ways in which meanings in organisations become established and change (Pettigrew, 1977). Also, as research has come to recognise explicitly the pluralistic or even conflicting nature of corporate functioning (Fox, 1966), concerns with effectiveness are being seen in new ways (Benson, 1977; Tribe, Schelling and Voss, 1976; van Gunsteren, 1976), with some researchers, particularly in Scandinavia (Carlsson et al, 1979), trying to help very different groups articulate and assess their own interests and perspectives.

One consequence of such ongoing research developments is that a series of very different perspectives are now being brought to bear on the study of corporate effectiveness. Whilst this might be frustrating, if not challenging, to those who merely want simple answers and improved procedures, some at least of the emergent approaches do offer the possibility of providing a basis for understanding problems which are undoubtedly of real organisational and social significance. For the dominant interest in clarifying and assessing particular notions of corporate effectiveness has resulted in a neglect of the organisational processes through which change might be achieved.

And yet, as any one who has tried to implement a new approach can testify, such processes are far from being unproblematic. On so many occasions a concern with the new has been frustrated in part at least because of our unbalanced understanding of organisational action and achievement.

Some of the ways in which research is starting to throw light on such issues of orgaisational practice are discussed later. Before doing so, however, it is important to gain some further insights into the problematic nature of particular criteria of corporate effectiveness and some of the ways in which concerns with these have developed over time. We can start by focusing, albeit in far too brief a manner, on the recent debates on financial measures of corporate performance, the traditional concern of the accountant, and the more recent questioning both from within corporations and without of the dominance and adequacy of these. For however partial financial criteria measurements may be, there can be little doubt as to their 103
practical significance.

CORPORATE ACCOUNTING IN A CHANGING WORLD

Accounting in practice, in the past a seeming citadel of traditional orientations and concerns, has gone through, and indeed continues to go through, a period of turmoil in most industrial nations. Unease, at the very least, with many conventional accounting measures of corporate performance and position has been expressed by many traditional users of and commentators upon accounting reports. And, at the same time, a whole array of new social interests and associated perspectives have entered into accounting debates. Public policy issues in the area, for instance, have been articulated with increasing frequency by both state bureaucracies and legislative assemblies, and interest groups, once not concerned with accounting matters, including in many countries the organised labour movement, have started to isolate their own demands for the development of accounting practice and regulation. Moreover, at the same time as accounting debates have grown in both complexity and contentiousness, so many of the institutional mechanisms for considering and introducing change, if not a new order, into the accounting domain have entailed a search for more satisfactory frames of reference and modes of operation.

Such debates have gone a long way towards irreversibly changing the way in which accounting indicators of corporate economic performance are perceived and accounting discourse takes place. Rather than being seen as one of the more stable albeit partial components of an effectiveness repertoire, quite explicit attention has had to have been given to the sheer diversity of accounting procedures (Briloff, 1972) including some newly emergent alternatives, to the many and varied arguments that can be and are marshalled in support of a large number of them, and to the range of their impacts and consequences (May and Sundem, 1976). In the process, consideration also has had to be given to the origins of particular interests in the development of accounting measures of corporate performance and to the varied and often conflicting organisational and social roles that are served by forms of accounting practice.

Not too long ago, a profit was a profit was a profit. Accounting measurements were seen as rather neutral approximations to an underlying economic truth and the role and intent of both research and practice was to further such an empirical approximation. Of course the ultimate could never be achieved, but the potential for improvement was recognised. Either by abstracting from theoretical discourse or by inquiring into what were presumed to be the decision 'models' and economic information 'needs' of the users of account-
104 ing reports (Carsberg, Hope and Scapens, 1974) attempts were made to get ever closer to achieving the accounting ideal.

The impact of an inflationary economic environment resulted in such notions of truth being irreversibly set aside. In such an economic setting, interplay between the adaptive responses of corporate management, the actions of a profession struggling for its continued autonomy and those of a government moving towards discovering the significance of accounting policy for its own economic management concerns, resulted in a whole array of alternative accounting indicators of corporate economic performance entering into practical discourse. The progression, if that is the appropriate word, from the Accounting Standards Steering Committee's Current Purchasing Power Accounting, to Sandiland's Current Cost Accounting, to the Morpeth 'mix', to the Hyde Guidelines, to . . . is now familiar to all. Perhaps less familiar is the fact that as a result of such deliberations accounting has had to be recognised quite explicitly as a conceptual phenomenon, with alternative concepts increasingly having to be evaluated on the basis of both their internal logic and their practical consequences rather than on their approximation to some underlying notion of an economic truth.

Accounting research was strongly orientated towards the former logical task (Baxter, 1976; Chambers, 1966; Lee, 1974; Sterling, 1970). Practical discourse and debate continued to move on, however, as it emphasised the consequences of alternative modes of accounting that might arise in the specifics of a particular economic and social milieu rather than within the abstract confines of a theoretical framework. So some corporations were clearly concerned about the effects that might flow from a very low level of reported profits. Others focused on the dangers in the opposite direction. Yet others, including albeit in a tentative way some representatives of the labour movement, emphasised the fact that in an increasingly bureaucraticised world, where decisions are made by administrative rather than competitive means, accounting had become an even more influential medium. With, for example, allowable price and wage increases in both the private and public sectors and certain forms of government financial assistance being dependent in part on reported profit margins, alternative accountings could and did have different economic consequences. And with past accounts of the utilisation of economic resources so influencing their future availability, accounting debates became even more political in nature (Watts and Zimmerman, 1979). Interests in accounting had become clear and visible.

Once perceived as an approximation of an economic reality, accounting started to be recognised, perhaps implicitly more than explicitly, as a social phenomenon, grounded in the political economy of the nation and serving a variety of roles within the nexus that links the corporation, the capital markets and increasingly the state and an array of other social interests that relate to them. Indeed, the roles and modes of 'accounting' in such a context are still emergent. Many of the social, institutional and economic changes which are resulting in our changing appreciations of financially orientated modes of accounting are also stimulating an active and more fundamental questioning of the adequacy of financial representations of corporate performance and well-being. Both within the corporation and outside, notions of social accounting, social reporting and social auditing, of social cost-benefit analysis and of social calculation, are being articulated with increasing frequency and interest.

Within the corporation, for instance, factors such as the changing nature of the labour market, the growing power of trade unions and the increasing scope and significance of legal provisions and requirements in the industrial relations area have fostered the development of a more extensive form of internal corporate social administration, manifested in the growing significance of the personnel function in most corporations in recent years. The routine administrative concerns of such a function themselves resulted in the collection and compilation of a growing volume of social information on the activities of the corporation, at least some of which has provided the basis for more extensive developments in social information processing within the context of changing forms of work organisation (Jonson, Jönsson and Svensson, 1979) and the growing recognition of the need to report to employees and trade unions (Dekker, 1977; Page, 1978). And some corporations, particularly in the USA (Epstein, Flamholtz and McDonough, 1976) and Germany (Dierkes, 1978), have given attention to the internal development of wider forms of external reporting. Still varying tremendously in content, scope and form of presentation, the social account or report in the USA started as a response to the criticisms of the social role of the corporation that were a feature of the mid to late 1960s, their German parallels possibly being more attuned to the developing environmental concerns of the State.

Whilst to date internally initiated forms of social accounting have been almost completely absent from the United Kingdom, we have seen a proliferation of interest in and experimentation with broader and more critically orientated criteria of corporate impact by a whole range of external pressure and interest groups. The activities of the Public Interest Research Centre, one of the pioneers in the area, gave rise to the publication of the journal *Social Audit*, the conduct of a number of social audits of both public and private organisations (Medawar, 1976), including that of Avon Rubber
106 (1976), and, on the basis of such experiences, the articulation of a set of concerns and approaches that goes far beyond the group's original basis in the consumer movement (Frankel, 1978; Medawar, 1978). Related, if somewhat more radical concerns have also emanated from Counter-Information Services. The government sponsored Community Development Projects also forged their own approaches to the socio-economic assessment of public and private organisations within the context of urban and industrial change and decline (1974, 1975).

Such experiences have yet to be assessed and incorporated into wider public discourse. In the meantime, however, sections of the trade union movement have started to develop their own perspectives and empirical approaches (Coates, 1978). Often grounded in the specifics of redundancy and unemployment, some at least have nonetheless sought for an appreciation of their situation in terms of wider social and economic criteria. Sometimes this has added little to debates over policy options and alternatives. But on occasions, such as that provided by the Alternative Corporate Plan published by the Lucas Shop Stewards (Cooley, 1978), trade union groups have offered a challenge to all of those who claim to be interested in notions of corporate effectiveness. Just how, if at all, do strategies for, and evaluations of, corporate action based on concepts of value in use rather than value in exchange relate to prevailing concerns in the more conventional literature on corporate effectiveness?

Research, at least as conventionally defined as taking place within the confines of the academy or similar institutions, has played a rather limited role in the search for and assessment of wider, more socially orientated criteria for corporate effectiveness. For the vast majority of initiatives would appear to have been grounded in the development of ongoing practice, be that located within or without the corporation as such.

Internally to the corporation, innovation, where it has occurred, has resulted from the identification of problems which have arisen as management has sought to adapt to the changing nature of and constraints upon the management task. Often with an interest in maintaining an existing order, the specifics of new management practices have been created. Complex in concept and operation, these have necessitated the construction of new flows of information and often from these have stemmed more embracing concepts and methods for assessing aspects of corporate action.

External to the corporation, there has been a similar relationship between the new and the intended. Innovation, where it has occurred, has also been grounded in the specifics of organisational and social reality, often stemming from a desire to change. With an interest in the promotion of new social objectives, or at the very least patterns of social accountability and responsiveness, consideration has been given to the means by which present practice can be assessed, alternative aims articulated and new options suggested.

Indeed, to be honest, the roles that more traditional varieties of 'accounting' research can play in such a socio-political milieu are still emergent. On the one hand, some corporate practitioners and professional associations have started to recognise the tactical role that research can serve in the ongoing political forum of accounting discourse, and some representatives of other interests are now following this lead. All seek to elicit the support of research and the new bodies of knowledge which it can create, in the elaboration, articulation and objectification of their own particular notions of corporate performance and effectiveness. A few researchers, on the other hand, are becoming increasingly interested in trying to understand the complexities of just such accounting deliberations and changes (Moonitz, 1974; Watts and Zimmerman, 1978; 1979; Zeff, 1971). Seeing the former varieties of research as operating *within* a particular accounting context, these latter researchers see themselves as striving for an appreciation *of* accounting and the processes by which it adapts and changes.

Such uncertainties of the research role themselves emphasise the way in which our perceptions of accounting have changed. Here at least, an important component of almost any corporate effectiveness repertoire can be seen to be in a state of flux. Once seemingly grounded on the firm rock of economic reality, the shifting nature of its context and the emergence of new interests in it have shown accounting to be as problematic a form of practice as those which underlie the newer criteria of corporate effectiveness which people with different perspectives of organisational functioning have been trying to articulate. For many, of course, the loss of such a former certainty might be, and indeed will be, disturbing. In the context of the wider debates on corporate effectiveness, however, such a loss may have its advantages if it can point to a view of effectiveness which resides in the realm of ongoing organisational and social practice rather than in that of the ideal and the absolute.

CRITERIA OF EFFECTIVENESS AND ORGANISATIONAL FUNCTIONING

In fact the relationship between concerns with the measurement and reporting of particular notions of corporate effectiveness and organisational practice has been the focus of another developing body of research. Rather than seeking either to improve the measurements themselves or to explore the social conditions for their existence, such research has tried to inquire into how particular measurements of corporate effectiveness function in organisations, the range of their effects and the processes through which these are achieved. Albeit slowly and cautiously, the research has been building up a body of quite important insights, appreciations and perhaps for the practitioner all too open-ended questions.

Some such studies have explored the potential organisational significance of the identification and dissemination of particular indicators of corporate effectiveness. Conceiving the corporation as an arena where multitudinous activities take place, each having a range of consequences both theoretical and actual, such research has focused on the role that indicators of corporate performance and effectiveness play in creating a selective visibility for particular consequences (Becker and Neuhauser, 1975; Gordon, Tanon and Morse, 1977; Shortell, Becker and Neuhauser, 1977). Do the particular conceptions of effectiveness, which are reflected in the flows of information which permeate the corporation, influence perceptions of the problematic and the possible, and thereby, the patterns of actual achievement? Do they, in other words, succeed in infiltrating and influencing the specifics of organisational practice and action? Perhaps not too surprisingly, the answer provided by research has been a possible 'yes', with the possibility being dependent on the presence of organisational mechanisms and processes through which the particular visibility can be articulated and diffused. Even potentially similar organisations which have implemented different patterns of internal visibility have been shown to follow very different patterns of performance over time.

In a study of insurance companies, for instance, different patterns of visibility for the financial consequences of corporate action themselves explained the major portion of the observed variance in the ratio of profits to assets (Becker and Neuhauser, 1975). And a detailed study of American hospitals illustrated how investments in the measurement and reporting of either the economic or the medical components of performance could result in very different outcome consequences if they were disseminated through the relevant organisational communication and decision processes (Shortell, Becker and Neuhauser, 1977). With such dissemination, hospitals emphasising economic consequences were indeed cheaper whilst those emphasising medical consequences tended to be more innovative in the use of both medical technology and pharmaceuticals (Gordon and Tanon, 1974; Rosner, 1968).

The importance of the organisational utilisation of performance information has been suggested by other bodies of research findings. Recent studies of the use of management accounting information, for example, have demonstrated that the effects of such information are not dependent on either its mere existence or its technical characteristics (Hofstede, 1967; Hopwood, 1973a). The way in which information is used, particularly the way in which the social context of its use influences the meaning which is attributed to it, can and does exert a major influence on the roles which such information is seen as serving and the organisational effects which it has. As I have stated in a previous context (Hopwood, 1973b, p.84):

> 'while the information might be given, its interpretation is the outcome of a personal and social process which is sustained by the meanings, beliefs, pressures and purposes that are brought to bear by the managers using the information. In of necessity providing it with a personal significance and placing it in their own wider context, managers are able to use the information, perhaps without reflection, in a variety of ways — appropriate and inappropriate'.

Rigid uses of accounting information, for instance, can certainly stimulate an active concern with those characteristics of financial performance which are reflected within the reporting system. But such a concern is often achieved at the expense of high degrees of vertical and horizontal conflict in the corporation and the manipulation of the accounting data themselves (Hopwood, 1973a), both being consequences which can constrain organisational achievement more broadly conceived. However more flexible uses of the information can be realised. In a context where both the human and task components of the managerial job are valued and where information of any variety is not valued as an end in itself but as a means to a wider end, research has shown that it is possible to gain many of the advantages which can stem from the availability of a particular information system without this resulting in other damaging organisational consequences.

Other research also has started to demonstrate how particular organisational ends may not necessarily be achieved by a

concentration on their mere assessment. The evidence of the relationship between financial performance, to cite that area yet again, and the presence of detailed mechanisms for financial control and accountability is equivocal at the very best. The 'newly poor' (Olofsson and Svalander, 1975) are often those who invest heavily in the search for internal economic visibility, although often in so doing they may further dislocate themselves from their problematic external environments as they consciously or unconsciously succumb to the demands of their ever more visible internal environments. Financially efficient, they may in other words still walk to their economic grave! And the financially successful, on the other hand, tend, so some tentative research findings (Child, 1973, 1974, 1975; Rosner, 1968; Turcotte, 1974) would suggest, to avoid many of the rigors of contemplating ever further heights of financial effectiveness. Seemingly they revel and flourish within the context of
110 multiple and overlapping flows of information (Grinyer and Norburn, 1975), informal planning and assessment practices (Child, 1974) and continually renegotiated exchanges between organisational participants (Georgiou, 1973). Like the all too effective Japanese motor cycle manufacturers studied by the Boston Consulting Group (1975), which failed to use the detailed financial appraisals so beloved of their unsuccessful British competitors, concentrating instead on indicators of potential market penetration and overall corporate strategy, somehow they got there without too consciously trying to.

According to such studies, at least certain of the concerns with the articulation of criteria of corporate effectiveness would appear to be related to rather particular organisational rationalities and goal orientated, instrumental conceptions of the social functioning of organisations. By probing into the ways in which the interventionist strategies which can so readily emanate from such concerns can constrain rather than facilitate the action sequences which constitute organised endeavour, such research is starting to point to the rather uneasy relationship between our emerging knowledge of the social nature of organisational life and the organisational presumptions which underlie so many of the strategies for change.

Of course it would be pretentious to claim that the emerging body of research on the organisational dimensions of the measurement of corporate effectiveness has succeeded in untangling the complexities that reside in such relationships. It has not and will not for some considerable time to come. Already, however, it looks as though it is starting to move in that direction.

The emphasis which it has placed on the organisational processes through which and by which particular concerns with corporate effectiveness are or are not realised was much needed. By themselves criteria of effectiveness, of whatever variety, certainly have a potential to create particular meanings and understandings of corporate life and thereby influence action. But the realisation of that potentiality is far from being unproblematic. It is dependent on the way in which the articulated criteria interlink with complex and ongoing social and human processes, the functioning of which remains poorly understood in theory and practice. If, for the time being, the research can do no more than to introduce an element of caution and complexity into practice and of renewed vigor into research, it has certainly served its role.

CONCLUSION

Systematic research into criteria for assessing corporate effectiveness is recent in origin. Until now the vast majority of new perspectives and approaches have emanated from the development of practice. Whether stemming from the concerns of corporate management, or from those who seek to question if not challenge them, notions of effectiveness have been pragmatic in orientation, seeking either to guide and legitimise or to question and change ongoing practice and associated patterns of performance. Slowly, however, the role of research and inquiry has been recognised. Initially, it perhaps inevitably focused on the elaboration and operationalisation of particular notions of effectiveness. More recently, though, at least some research on the criteria of corporate effectiveness has adopted a more questioning and analytical stance, as it has started to delve into the complexities that influence their organisational roles and effects and the social processes of which they are themselves an outcome.

Generalisations from such an emergent body of research do not come easily. However, the above review has sought to emphasise the following points.

1. Criteria of corporate effectiveness are neither self-sufficient nor unitary in nature. Rather they are socially constructed, their roles and meanings stemming from social interests and concerns and the specific contexts in which they operate.
2. Financial criteria of effectiveness are as problematic as many others in both concept and operationalisation. Their dominance in practice is derived from the strength and resilience of the interests on which they rest, rather than from any superior claim to approximate the real and the true.
3. The practical significance of criteria of effectiveness does not stem from their mere existence. In and of themselves, criteria of any variety have little more than the potential to influence corporate action. The realisation of that potential is dependent, however, on the way in which articulated criteria interlink with

the complex social and organisational processes through which they are endowed with a particular meaning and relevance. For those concerned with corporate change, an understanding of such processes is at least as vital as that of the more technical aspects of criteria design and implementation.

4. Once grounded in the specifics of organisational practice, however, criteria of effectiveness can indeed influence organisational action. By helping to shape the patterns of organisational viability, they can influence perceptions of both the problematic and the possible, reinforcing certain sequences of actions and constraining the achievement of others.

5. Intriguingly, however, a predominant concern with a particular criterion of effectiveness may not necessarily result in its achievement. For organisations are complex artifacts, the
112 survival and development of which are dependent on the mutual satisfaction of numerous and often conflicting demands, both internal and external to the organisation itself. To focus on any one, without due care, may result in the neglect of others on which paradoxically the achievement of the focal criteria can in turn depend.

6. Finally, research is starting to explore the varied roles which criteria of effectiveness play in organisational functioning. Whilst acknowledging that in many instances the articulation of criteria precedes action, in other cases it is seeing how criteria can be derived from action itself, helping thereby retrospectively to create meanings and understandings of the dynamic sequence of events which constitutes organised activity. Seen in such terms, the effective organisation might well be the one which knows from whence it came!

Although undoubtedly preliminary in nature, such findings nonetheless constitute a rich and challenging agenda for both practical action and further research.

REFERENCES

Baxter, W.T. *Accounting Values and Inflation*. McGraw-Hill, 1975.

Becker, S.W. and Neuhauser, D. *The Efficient Organisation*. Elsevier, 1975.

Benson, J.K. (ed.) *Organisational Analysis: Critique and Innovation*. Sage, 1977.

Boston Consulting Group *Strategy Alternatives for the British Motor Cycle Industry*. HMSO, 1975.

Briloff, A.J. *Unaccountable Accounting*. Harper and Row, 1972.

Carlsson, J., Ehn, P., Erlander, B., Perby, M-L. and Sandberg, A. 'Planning and Control from the Perspective of Labour: A Short Presentation of the DEMOS Project', *Accounting, Organisations and Society* 1979, Vol. 3, No. 3/4.

Carsberg, B.V., Hope, A. and Scapens, R.W. 'The Objectives of Published Accounting Reports', *Accounting and Business Research*. Summer, 1974.

Chambers, R.J. *Accounting, Evaluation and Economic Behaviour*. Prentice-Hall, 1966.

Child, J. 'Strategies of Control and Organisation Behaviour', *Administrative Science Quarterly*, 1973, pp.1.17.

Child, J. 'Management and Organisational Factors Associated with Company Performance — Part I', *Journal of Management Studies*, 1974, pp.175-189.

Child, J. 'Managerial and Organisational Factors Associated with Company Performance — Part II', *Journal of Management Studies*. 1975, pp.12-27.

Coates, C., ed. *The Right to Useful Work*. Spokesman, 1978.

Cohen, M.D., March, J.G. and Olsen, J.P. 'A Garbage Can Model of Organisational Choice', *Administrative Science Quarterly*. 1972, pp.1-25.

Cooley, M. 'Design, Technology and Production for Social Needs', in Coates, 1978.

Community Development Project Intelligence and Information Unit *The National Community Development Project*. 1974.

Community Development Project Intelligence and Information Unit *National Community Development Project Forward Plan* 1975-6. 1975.

Dekker, C. 'Social Reporting in the Netherlands'. Paper presented at the INI Colloquium, Madrid, December, 1977.

Dierkes, M. 'Corporate Social Performance in Germany — Conceptual Developments, Practical Experience and Political Interests'. Paper presented at the Academy of Management Meetings, San Francisco, 1978.

Epstein, M., Flamholtz, E. and McDonough, J.J. 'Corporate Social Accounting in the USA: State of the Art and Future Prospects', *Accounting, Organisations and Society*. 1976, Vol. 1, No. 1, pp.23-42.

Fox, A. *Industrial Sociology and Industrial Relations*. HMSO, 1966.

Frankel, M. *The Social Audit Pollution Handbook*. Macmillan, 1978.

Georgiou, P. 'The Goal Paradigm and Notes Towards A Counter Paradigm', *Administrative Science Quarterly*. 1973, pp.291-310.

Gordon, G. and Tanon, C.P. 'Costs, Professional Power and Hospital Structure'. Paper presented to the American Sociological Association, Montreal, 1974.

Gordon, G., Tanon, C.P. and Morse, E.V. 'Decision-Making Criteria and Organisation Performance', in *Organisational Research in Hospitals*, ed. by S.M. Shortell. Blue Cross, 1977.

Grinyer, P. and Norburn, D. 'Planning for Existing Markets: Perceptions of Executives and Financial Performance', *Journal of the Royal Statistical Society*. Series A, 1975, pp.70-97.

Hofstede, G.H. *The Game of Budget Control*. Van Gorcum, 1967.

Hopwood, A.G. *An Accounting System and Managerial Behaviour*. Saxon House, 1973a.

Hopwood, A.G. 'Problems with Using Accounting Information in Performance Evaluation', *Management International Review*. 1973b, pp.83-91.

Jonson, L.C., Jönsson, B. and Svensson, G. 'The Application of Social Accounting to Absenteeism and Personnel Turnover', *Accounting, Organisations and Society*. 1979, Vol. 3, No. 3/4.

Lee, T.A. *Income and Value Measurement: Theory and Practice*. Nelson, 1974.

March, J.G. 'Bounded Rationality, Ambiguity and the Engineering of Choice', *The Bell Journal of Economics*. Autumn, 1978, pp.587-608.

March, J.G. and Olsen, J.P. *Ambiguity and Choice*. Oslo: Universitetsforlaget, 1976.

May, R.G. and Sundem, G.L. 'Research for Accounting Policy: an Overview', *The Accounting Review*. October, 1976, pp.747-763.

Medawar, C. 'The Social Audit: A Political Review', *Accounting, Organisations and Society*. 1976, Vol. 1, No. 4, pp.389-394.

Medawar, C. *The Social Audit Consumer Handbook*. Macmillan, 1978.

Moonitz, M. *Obtaining Agreement on Standards in the Accounting Profession*. American Accounting Association, 1974.

Olofsson, C. and Svalander, P.A. 'The Medical Services Change Over to a Poor Environment — "New Poor" Behaviour' Unpublished Working Paper, University of Linköping, 1975.

Page, G.T. *An Employer's Guide to Disclosure of Information*. Kogan Page, 1978.

Pettigrew, A. 'The Creation of Organisational Cultures', Working Paper, European Institute for Advanced Studies in Management, Brussels, 1977.

Pfeffer, J. and Salancik, G.R. 'Organisational Decision Making as a Political Process: The Case of a University Budget', *Administrative Science Quarterly*, 1974, pp.135-151.

Public Interest Research Group *Social Audit of Avon Rubber Co. Ltd.* 1976.

Rosner, M.M. 'Administrative Controls and Innovation', *Behavioural Science*, 1968, pp.36-43.

Scott, W.R. 'Effectiveness of Organisational Effectiveness Studies', in P.S. Goodman, J.N. Pennings and Associates, *New Perspectives on Organisational Effectiveness*, Jossey-Bass, 1977.

Shortell, S.M., Becker, S.W. and Neuhauser, D. 'The Effects of Management Practices on Hospital Efficiency and Quality of Care', in S.M. Shortell, ed., *Organisational Research in Hospitals*, Blue Cross, 1977.

114 **Sterling, R.** *Theory of the Measurement of the Business Enterprise*, University of Kansas Press, 1977.

Tribe, L.H., Schelling, C.S. and Voss, J. *When Values Conflict – Essays on Environment Analysis, Discourse and Decision*. Wiley, 1976.

Turcotte, W.E. 'Control Systems, Performance and Satisfaction in Two State Agencies', *Administrative Science Quarterly*, 1974, pp.60-73.

Van Gunsteren, H.R. *The Quest for Control*. Wiley, 1976.

Watson, T.J. *The Personnel Managers*. Routledge and Kegan Paul, 1977.

Watts, R. and Zimmerman, J.L. 'Towards a Positive Theory of the Determination of Accounting Standards', *The Accounting Review*, 1978, pp.112-134.

Watts, R. and Zimmerman, J.L. 'The Supply of and Demand for Accounting Theories: The Market for Excuses', *The Accounting Review*, 1979.

Weick, K. *The Social Psychology of Organising*. Addison-Wesley, 1969.

Zeff, S. *Forging Accounting Principles in Five Countries: A History and an Analysis*. Stripes, 1971.

116

Discussion of "Some Inner Contradictions in Management Information Systems" and "Behavioral Implications of Planning and Control Systems"

ANTHONY G. HOPWOOD

The study of the organizational and behavioral aspects of management accounting now has quite a long, albeit somewhat irregular, history. Stimulated in large part by Chris Argyris' initial study of the behavioral consequences of budgeting,[1] the area has since attracted the attention of both accounting scholars and an array of social psychologists, sociologists and political scientists who have been interested in exploring the part which accounting plays in organizational functioning and control. Although our knowledge must still be regarded as emergent, real understandings nevertheless have been achieved. Moreover the potential importance of the area is now acknowledged by a growing number of both scholars and practitioners, and the insights that are available are even starting to replace those gratuitous and often mythical genuflections to the human and organizational context of the craft that have graced so many management accounting texts.

[1]Chris Argyris, *The Impact of Budgets upon People* (New York: The Controllership Foundation, 1952).

Given the current stage of development of the area, the papers by Chris Argyris and Bob Swieringa together provide an interesting basis on which to consider the state of our knowledge of the organizational and behavioral aspects of accounting and the challenges which might lie ahead. To comment on their papers, I shall first briefly review the differing traditions of inquiry which have characterized the area to date. Thereafter, after considering the two papers themselves, I shall attempt to discuss some of the implications which they might have for the future direction of research.

TWO TRADITIONS OF INQUIRY

Our understandings of the organizational and behavioral aspects of management accounting systems have so far emanated from two rather different traditions of inquiry. On the one hand, a number of 117
sociologists, social psychologists, political scientists, and other scholars of the social have been fascinated, yet puzzled, by the organizational significance which accounting has achieved. Just what roles do management accounting systems play in organizations? How do they really function? And what consequences do they have? With no commitment to the prevailing procedures of the craft, they have sought to delve into the seeming mysteries of accounting in action, in the process providing us with a rich, illuminating and challenging array of insights into the accounting condition.[2] On the other hand, we have a growing number of inquiries undertaken by accounting researchers themselves. Although sometimes stimulated by the findings of their social science colleagues, the perspectives which have influenced their inquiries have often been very different, for rather than seeking to gain an appreciation of management accounting's wider organizational context and significance, until recently accountants have tended to adopt a more instrumental approach. How, they often have asked, can we overcome the resistance to the accounting craft? Which accountings are likely to have more impact? And just what roles can different organizational and behavioral approaches play? Accepting the preordained imperatives of the accounting mission and the conventional conceptions of the instrumentality of the craft, many accounting scholars of the behavioral have sought to increase its effectiveness by behavioral means. Rather than venturing to appreciate, let alone question, accounting in action, they have continued to seek new ways of influencing its outcomes.

[2]Particular note should be made of the works listed in Appendix A.

Hardly surprising, the two traditions of inquiry have remained rather detached. Many, although by no means all, of the social scientists who have been interested in the accounting endeavor have not chosen to use their understandings to influence the process of accounting itself. Equally, however, their studies have only rarely been cited in the accounting literature. Although occasionally used to legitimize an area of inquiry, until recently the substantive findings and perspectives have had little or no impact on the studies undertaken by accountants. Leads for further research have remained unexplored and accounting scholars have repeatedly failed to draw on either the theoretical or methodological contributions and insights.

With the traditions of the appreciative and the applied remaining so separate, accounting scholars of the behavioral have forged their
118 own separate lines of investigation. Rather than delving into the complexities of accounting as it is practised, so often they have preferred to rely on the possibilities of the psychological laboratory. Indeed it is difficult to name more than a handful of inquiries that have been undertaken within the factory gate—or even outside the college wall. The world of accounting as it is has been largely ignored. Seemingly questions of internal validity have been emphasized to the almost complete neglect of external validity. Almost invariably, emphasis has been placed on methodological rather than theoretial sophistication and on the rigors of hypothesis testing rather than theory generation.[3] So, few attempts have been made to analyze directly the processes of accounting development and change, the interplay between accounting and other features of organizational life, and the consequences which accounting might or might not have for organizational action. Apparently it has been deemed to be sufficient to theorize in the armchair, to borrow a neat theory here and there,[4] and to so construct a basis for a tightly controlled excursion into a specifically constructed unknown. The net result of such a tradition of inquiry is a rather fragmented set of insights, however, many of which have a largely unknown and possibly equivocal relationship to accounting in action.

The reasons for such a research tradition are numerous.[5] The intel-

[3]See C. Tomkins, D. Rosenberg, and I. Colville, "The Social Process of Research: Some Reflections on Developing a Multi-Disciplinary Accounting Project," *Accounting, Organizations and Society* (1980).

[4]R. E. Jense, "Empirical Evidence from the Behavioral Sciences: Fish Out of Water," *Accounting Review* (July 1970): 502-8.

[5]A. G. Hopwood, *An Accounting System and Managerial Behavior* (London: Saxon House, 1973); idem., "Towards an Organizational Perspective for the Study of Ac-

lectual traditions which have been deemed acceptable in schools of business no doubt have had a major role to play. So has an academic reward structure which has emphasized speedy, low-risk research having readily visible signs of rigorous inquiry. Also of importance, however, has been the accounting tradition itself, for while social scientists outside it have been prepared to take a less committed look at accounting as it is practiced, many accounting scholars of the behavioral have chosen to accept more readily the preordained canons of the accounting mission. Rather than trying to construct a view of what is, they have tried to shape what might be. Even when accountants have ventured into the world of practice, appreciative inquiries into the functioning of accounting have been rarer than attempts to provide more directly bases for improving the accounting endeavor. So while we have seen research oriented toward increasing accounting's motivational potential, analyses of the interplay be- 119
tween accounting and the political and the powerful have been rare indeed.

Such divergent research traditions of the past provide a fascinating context for considering the papers by Argyris and Swieringa, for to some extent the authors are seemingly engaged in a process of role reversal! Although Chris Argyris draws on a vast accumulation of insights into accounting and information systems as they are, he nevertheless seeks to provide some pointers as to how they might be. Bob Swieringa, on the other hand, not only critically points to the presumptions of the accounting past, but also seeks to draw upon and promote traditions of organizationally grounded inquiry which are oriented towards illuminating what is.

ORGANIZATIONAL CONTRADICTIONS AND THE ROLE OF MANAGEMENT INFORMATION SYSTEMS

I agree with many of the points raised by Chris Argyris. Like him, I also have been confronted repeatedly with the frustrations which managers, and other organizational participants, I might add, can experience as a result of trying to cope with conventional management information and accounting systems. In such circumstances I, like him, find it difficult not to be aware of the constraining and disabilitating consequences which they can have at the individual level, the organizational consequences of which must be real and profound. So I can not only sympathize but also join in with his

counting and Information Systems," *Accounting, Organizations and Society* (1978): 3-14; and Tomkins, Rosenberg, and Colville, "Accounting Project."

strong concluding plea for a body of knowledge on the basis of which we might be able to design information flows which can engender learning and adaptation rather than frustration and disillusionment at both the individual and organizational level.

In the course of his discussion, Argyris provides us with a rich insight into the relationships between the instruments of official management practice and the complexity of the social processes which influence how management information systems emerge, develop, and function, and the consequences which they can have. I particularly approve of the emphasis which he gives to the constraints which are placed on the ability of organizational participants to articulate and thereby learn from and build upon *their* knowledge of the reality of information practice. So much of that reality is taboo in today's organizations. The limitations of official practice are
120 known to many, as are the richness and relevance of the unofficial information underworld. Yet such perceptions of the world of action invariably must be distanced from the language of management. So often the existence of what invariably are essential parts of organizational functioning is officially denied. They do not enter into the language of management and, as a consequence, they cannot influence the possibilities for change and development. With what "might be" thereby being shaped by rather limited conceptions of "what is," official practice becomes ever more influenced by particular and highly abstract notions of both action and order.

Argyris points to the dynamic consequences of such a situation. On the one hand, we see the emergence of central pressures for further system elaboration and development. In the continual "quest for control,"[6] systems are "tightened," gaps are plugged so that the systems might become even more "tamper proof," and renewed searches are made for ever further precision. And although Argyris emphasizes the internal origins of such tendencies, we should not forget that pressures external to the organization also can give rise to the same phenomenon. Olafsson and Svalander have illustrated the interests which the "newly poor" have in control system elaboration in constrained economic circumstances,[7] and Meyer, among others, has pointed to the roles which management and information practices can play in the creation of a symbolic order between those within the organization and external parties, such as the State, which have an

[6]H. R. van Gunsteren, *The Quest for Control: A Critique of the Rational Central-Rule Approach in Public Affairs* (London: Wiley & Sons, 1976).

[7]C. Olafsson and P. A. Svalander, "The Medical Services Changeover to a Poor Environment—'New Poor' Behavior" (University of Linköping, 1975).

interest in it.[8] On the other hand, as Argyris points out, the refinement and yet further abstraction of the official and centralized information practices results in the development of a range of informal, ad hoc and often idiosyncratic modes of information processing—his local MIS. Organizational participants increase their investment in their own approaches to information processing. "Black books"[9] and "just-in-case files"[10] are elaborated, and the power and significance of more tacit ways of managing information increased.

The description which Argyris provides of such conflicting tendencies in information practice is a useful one. However, as Argyris recognizes by his own rather cautious and ambivalent discussion of the possibilities for change, care should be exercized in discussing the implications which such a state of affairs might have for both organizational and information system development and change. My
own grounds for emphasizing the need for such caution are both 121
organizational and social in nature.

At the organizational level, we should remember that it might well be that at least some of the tendencies which Argyris outlines are exaggerated by particular ways of using official management information systems, for despite a growing body of research on differential system use and its individual and organizational consequences,[11] comparatively little consideration has been given to its implications for organizational change. That, however, is a small point. More importantly, we need to explicitly recognize that complex and dynamic organizations require a vibrant mix of different approaches to information processing.[12] Official information systems do have limitations. They can only service particular needs for organizational learning and control, having constraints on their ability to con-

[8]J. Meyer, "Environmental and Internal Origins of Symbolic Structure in Organizations" (Paper presented at the Seminar on Organizations as Ideological Systems, Stockholm, 1979).

[9]Simon et al., *Centralization vs. Decentralization in Organizing the Controller's Department* (New York: The Controllership Foundation, 1954).

[10]Argyris, *The Impact of Budgets*.

[11]Becker and Newheuser, *Efficient Organization* (Amsterdam: North-Holland, 1975); C. Cammann, "Effects of the Use of Control Systems," *Accounting, Organizations and Society* (1976): 301-13; S. M. Shortell and M. Brown, eds., *Organizational Research in Hospitals* (Blue Cross, 1976); Hopwood, *Managerial Behavior*; and M. Rahman and A. M. McCash, "The Influence of Organizational and Personal Factors on the Use of Accounting Information: An Empirical Study," *Accounting, Organizations and Society* (1976): 339-55.

[12]M. E. Earl and A. G. Hopwood, "From Management Information to Information Management" (Paper presented at the IFIP TC8-WG8.2 Working Conference on the Information System Environment, Bonn, 1979); and J. Galbraith, *Designing Complex Organizations* (Reading, Mass.: Addison-Wesley, 1973).

tinually adapt to the novel and the new.[13] So while we can contrast the characteristics of local and central approaches to the management of information flows, such contrasts should not prevent us from seeing the very different roles which the different approaches might serve. Perhaps in today's organizations, the central cannot assume the characteristics of the local; perhaps very different "conceptions of order" should exist; perhaps, therefore, the local and the central need to coexist in the complex and changing organizations which we have today. Indeed, it may well be that the effectiveness of official management information systems depends on their ambiguous and questioned existence and use. In circumstances where the need for information is changing and cannot be completely anticipated, the systemic and the preplanned might need to have a "loosely coupled"[14] relationship to ongoing management practice. The of-

ficial and the central might need to be complemented by the unofficial and the local. Indeed, I think that we are now starting to realize the role which ambiguity and redundancy can play in organizational functioning. As a review of the development of innovative management practices in the National Aeronautics and Space Administration (NASA) indicated,[15] their effectiveness might well have been dependent upon the loose, entrepreneurial, and irreverent manner in which they were used. Although such a perspective undoubtedly increases the difficulty of system change and implementation, I think that we should recognize both that official information systems may need to be used, but not believed, and we should acknowledge the potential facilitating roles served by unofficial, local and other modes of information processing. I would have liked to have seen Argyris giving some consideration to this yet further set of organizational paradoxes and contradictions.

Our recognition of the difficulties of gaining improvement and change in the information system area might be even further increased if we consider in greater detail the organizational and social roles which they serve. Argyris emphasizes the learning potential of management information systems, quite rightly contrasting, however, the roles which they might play in self-learning with the roles which they do play in facilitating the learning of others. In this way, he places the design and use of management information systems

[13]W. H. Starbuck, "Information Systems in Organizations of the Future," in *Information Systems and Organizational Structure*, ed. E. Grochla and N. Szyperski (New York: de Gruyter, 1975).

[14]K. E. Weick, "Educational Organizations as Loosely Coupled Systems," *Administrative Science Quarterly* (1976): 1-19.

[15]R. L. Chapman, *Project Management in NASA* (NASA, 1973).

firmly within the context of the management of the modern hierarchical organization, seeing much of present information-system practice as being oriented towards increasing unilateral patterns of hierarchical control. However, having done that, I do not think that Argyris goes on to extract and discuss the full consequences and implications of such an organizational positioning, despite the fact that this could provide a host of further insights into the origins and consequences of the organizational contradictions on which he focuses his subsequent discussion.

To the extent that information systems are implicated in the management of the hierarchical relationships on which the modern organization is grounded, as Argyris himself points out, they are not and cannot be considered as being apart from the organization. Forming part of the micro apparatus of power on the basis of which organized activity is ordered, information systems, like other forms of 123
conventional management practice, are constitutive of the organization as we know it. In other words, not only are information systems influenced by the organization, but they, in turn, influence the form which the organization takes. Reflecting pressures that have been put on the organization as well as the processes of internal management and control, information systems are involved in both the definition of the organization itself and the constituent parts of it. They are implicated in the delineation of those who shall be considered within and without it, and vital processes of organizational segmentation and integration are based at least in part on the categories of organized endeavor reflected in the official flows of information. Providing mechanisms for planning and control, they not only facilitate but enable the separation of planning and control from the execution of the task—a key characteristic of the modern organization. Plans can be grounded on the specifics of organizational practice but thereafter readily aggregated to centralized decision making and control. Objectives for specific organizational activities can be distributed throughout the organization, with information systems then providing a selective pattern of organizational visibility on the basis of which achievement can be monitored at a distance and the distribution of organizational rewards attuned to particular forms of accomplishment. In ways such as these information systems create and propagate a particular form of organizational visibility and consciousness, they help to shape participants' views of the organization itself and what is to be regarded as both problematic and desirable, and they provide one basis on which power and influence can be gained and exercised. Today's information systems are, in other

words, centrally implicated in the creation and functioning of the hierarchical organization as we now know it.[16]

Such a view of the organizational and social context of information systems provides a rich basis on which to appreciate the full implications of the contradictions inherent in information system practice which are highlighted by Argyris' discussion. In such a context, "learning about others' performance in order to control their performance" may well "inhibit learning" by the subject of attention. Indeed, some even have gone so far as to suggest that this may often be the intention.[17] At the very least, an awareness of the roles which official information systems play in the separation of planning and control from the execution of the task helps us to appreciate just what might be at stake in the contradictions which Argyris emphasizes. Equally a more critical social insight into the organizational bases of
124 information systems functioning places us in a better position to appreciate the difference between "a map for understanding" and "a map for taking action" and how the use of information flows in order to manage "a system" under control can "create conditions of injustice," for such concerns point to the very real possibility that the practices of information management rest upon the surer bases of concerns with the direction of organizational power and influence. However, Argyris' suggestion that the "tightening up" (of) MIS in order to "get a performance under control" may inhibit the achievement of this objective more directly suggests that such contradictions are not "inner" to the condition of management information systems themselves but are reflective of more basic contradictions which characterize modern organizational and social life. Equally suggestive in this respect is his statement that "Model 1 theories-in-use do not make it possible for people to have problem solving skills that question the governing values of theories-in-use."

When viewed in such a way, one can well appreciate why so much

[16]Indeed M. Foucalt, in *Discipline and Punish* (London: Allen Lane, 1975), would maintain that information systems now constitute a key feature of the "disciplinary mode of domination" which is characteristic of much organized endeavor today. For at the centre of such a mode of domination or control "lies a distinctive organization of observation. Discipline is based on the perpetual surveillance of its subjects, as well as on its own administrators: on a surveillance that is public in the sense that everyone knows of their constant subjection to its gaze; on a surveillance that is non-reciprocal, in that its subjects can neither know nor influence when they are being observed, or what the content and effect of their observation is; on a surveillance that is asymetrical, in that its subjects are not in a position themselves to survey their surveyors." B. Fine, "Struggles against Discipline: The Theory and Politics of Michael Facault," *Capital and Class* (1979): 75-96.

[17]H. Braverman, *Labor and Monoply Capital* (New York: Monthly Review Press, 1974).

of the reality of information practice in organizations might remain taboo. Its revelation would be threatening to both the powerful and the controlled, for in such a contested context, to illuminate the multiplicity of information worlds which characterize organizational life would illustrate the partiality of official practice and might stimulate changes in it over which the providers of any insights might have little or no influence.

Illustrative of both the search for control and the resistances to it, the management of information flows can never stand in isolation of more all-embracing and thereby contentious questions of organizational design and influence. The creation of patterns of organizational visibility, be they official or otherwise, is inextricably bound up with the formation of modes of organizational operation and control, and the propagation of organizational rationales. Information system change, therefore, is a complex and difficult endeavor. 125
Certainly there are most likely few occasions on which information flows can be changed without influencing other aspects of organizational functioning. The informational invariably intersects with the organizational. And because of such interrelationships, it may well be that the radical information system changes which Argyris points to in his paper will require complementary organizational changes of an equally profound nature.

By emphasizing the relevance and interconnectedness of such issues, Argyris' paper serves an important purpose: it provides a basis for a questioning appreciation of the information and management accounting system craft. Equally, however, it, like my own comments, illustrates the extent of what is not known about the roles and operation of management information systems. For although we have a whole array of insights into the technical possibilities for information and accounting system design and at least some appreciation of the social nature of the modern organization, we still have comparatively little appreciation of the interrelationship between the two and the ways in which one might serve the other. One can only hope that it stimulates others to contribute to that broader basis for the design and operation of management information systems which is so central to Chris Argyris' concerns.

ORGANIZATIONAL AMBIGUITY AND THE STUDY OF ACCOUNTING IN ACTION

Bob Swieringa provides us with a rather different appreciation of the management accounting (and implicitly, the MIS) craft. Emphasizing the complexity of illuminating "what is," he explicitly avoids any consideration of the accounting that "might be." Nevertheless Bob's is a valuable paper. Unlike so many in the behavioral accounting repertoire, it focuses on at least some of the moving frontiers of organizational thought. More significantly perhaps, he chooses not to prioritize a particular conception of the organizational world, but rather illustrates a number of organizational perspectives, including that which is implicit in the management accounting texts with which we are all so familiar.

The result of Swieringa's multiple analysis of the Birch Paper case is illuminating and rich in possibilities, not least because it begins to focus our attention on some elements of the social construction of organizational observation and the implications which that can have for the appreciation of the accounting craft. The analyses illustrate the relationship between theory and observation. They point to the
126 possibility of diverse conceptions of the real, even within an organization itself. By together emphasizing the multiple, overlapping, and possibly inconsistent uses to which accounting is both put and seen to be put, they illustrate the heterogeneous nature of the ways in which accounting enters into organizational discourse and debate, and even some of the ways in which the contradictions noted by Chris Argyris might emerge. In these respects, Swieringa's contribution is both useful and important providing a basis in the management accounting area for moving beyond those rather simple searches for the real and the true which have tended to dominate many of our inquiries to date.[18]

At what is undoubtedly an early stage in the recognition of the importance of such issues, we should not be too concerned about the fact that Swieringa has sought to describe and utilize a number of alternative theoretical perspectives on organizational functioning rather than to critically evaluate them either in terms of their general theoretical status or their potential relevance for illuminating particular aspects of the accounting craft. Hopefuly, however, subsequent scholars will attempt to provide that more critical review.

[18]Similar questionings of the nature of accounting knowledge and practice have been evident in the financial accounting domain for sometime now. See for example, R. Watts and J. L. Zimmerman, "The Demand for and the Supply of Accounting Theories: The Market for Excuses," *Accounting Review* (April 1979): 273-305. No doubt stimulated by both the theoretical diversity and political contentiousness of recent policy debates, they are resulting in a more appreciative and critical analysis of financial accounting deliberation and practice. Unlike some of his financial accounting colleagues however, Swieringa chooses not to prioritize a particular conception of the true on the basis of which to politize the status of alternative and competing conceptions.

However useful the behavioral theory of the firm, for instance, might be, we should remember that it provides a relatively static appreciation of the organizational world. Accepting so much of the social and organizational context as given, it provides a rather constrained view of the processes of organizational change and those conflicts for power and influence which underlie the contradictions of information and organizational practice which were emphasized by Argyris. In other words, the behavioral theory, and many of the theoretical perspectives which have been derived from it, tell us little about either how organizations and the information and accounting systems which function within them have come to be what they are or how they might change. Equally, we should remember that the apparently more challenging conceptions inherent in the garbage can and organizing models also tend to be based on rather micro and short-
term analyses of organized endeavor. While they can illuminate some 127
of the paradoxes and contradictions of organizational life, they too provide only limited insights into the processes of organizational change, taking as given many of the constraints, relationships, and filters which currently influence what organizations are.

Swieringa has drawn on only some of the available understandings of organizational behavior, emphasizing the insights which can be derived from theories which tend to accept the organizational context as we now know it. As such, his analyses consider micro rather than macro processes of change and individual and organizational as distinct from social influences on behavior. Let me make it clear that I do not criticize him for this; there are very real limits on what can be done within the confines of a single paper, theoretical preferences also vary, and what has been done is illuminating, useful, and important. However, I think that the partiality of the analyses should be pointed out so that others might be encouraged both to explore other competing views of the organizational world and to be both conscious and critical of the status, potential, and limitations of the perspectives which are or might become available.

Another implication of Swieringa's selective utilization of organizational theories is that he has emphasized the need to understand accounting as it is, rather than as it has become and as it might be. However, I still find myself intrigued as to what he might see as being the implications which his analyses hold for the practice as well as the study of the accounting craft. One personal reason for this is that I have my own uncertainties (rather than doubts) about the practical directions in which the garbage can and organizing theories might take us! By providing such illuminating and provocative insights

into the complexities of what is, do they also encourage us to accept that status quo? More particularly, if it is useful to conceive of organizations as "organized anarchies,"[19] are we to resign ourselves to the fact that information and accounting practice might have to focus on the organizing elements while other practices stimulate the anarchical? Are we really to lose out on all the fun? Or are there real possibilities for "designing" (in an anarchical and loosely coupling manner, of course!) information flows which can promote the anarchical as well as the organized, and the loose as well as the tightly coupled? Can we really think in terms of designing "semi-confusing information systems"[20] and "foolish" information technologies?[21] And if we can, just who is to set the parameters for confusion and foolishness? Who, in other words, is to do the fooling, and who is to be fooled? Admittedly, such questions are posed in a jocular manner.
128 However, I think that they point to serious issues underlying any attempt to relate the appreciative to the applied, particularly when the appreciative does relatively little to explicate the underlying presumptions of organizational and social life that may be implicit within it.[22]

Such concerns set an agenda for the future, however. In the meantime, the radical questioning of the "tenets of the (accounting) faith" which is so central a part of Swieringa's paper must be welcomed. For so long, such imperatives of the accounting mission have remained supreme, all be they amazingly detached from the practice of accounting in action. By discussing how the uses to which accounting is put can be emergent rather than pregiven, how accounting practice can further be diverse and far from consistent ends, and how the rationalities implicit in action can be shaped by the accounting craft as well as influencing the impacts which it in turn has, Swieringa has provided a useful stimulus for further inquiry. One can only hope that other scholars will be encouraged to delve further into the issues which he raises. Hopefully, such inquiries will also shed some light on the equally intriguing question of why those

[19]M. D. Cohen and J. G. March, *Leadership and Ambiguity: The American College President* (New York: McGraw-Hill, 1974).
[20]B. Hedberg and S. Jönsson, "Designing Semi-Confusing Information Systems for Organizations in Changing Environments," *Accounting, Organizations and Society* (1978): 47-64.
[21]J. G. March, "The Technology of Foolishness," in *Ambiguity and Choice in Organizations*, ed. J. G. March and J. P. Olsen (Bergen: Universitetsforlaget, 1976).
[22]What may be at stake with such concerns can be illustrated by the comment made by one of my students after he had read a number of works by one of the authors cited in Swieringa's paper: "This guy is really serious about foolishness!"

tenets of the accounting faith have remained so unquestioned and supreme for so long.[23]

SOME IMPLICATIONS FOR FURTHER INQUIRY

Both Chris Argyris and Bob Swieringa point to the complex ways in which management information and accounting systems are implicated in organizational functioning. While as accountants many of us continue to propogate the absolute virtues of the craft, the analyses of Argyris and Swieringa illustrate that the consequences and impacts which it has in practice are the result of the ways in which the calculative technologies intersect with a diverse variety of other organizational practices and processes. Considerations of organizational power and influence, the ways in which the organization as we now know it has emerged, and the processes underlying organiza- 129
tional action and change all have a profound effect on what management accounting is perceived to be and the consequences which it does and might have. As both papers repeatedly demonstrate, albeit in very different ways, management accounting is a phenomenon which needs to be understood in organizational terms.

However, both papers also demonstrate how little we currently know of the organizational aspects of the management accounting and information system crafts. Argyris concludes his analysis with a plea for an alternative body of knowledge on the basis of which we might seek to change at least some of their individual and organizational consequences; and Swieringa explicitly seeks to demonstrate the potential of alternative organizational perspectives which as yet have not been applied within the accounting arena. Albeit in different ways, both point to the need for further inquiry. However, just what type of research is now required in the so-called behavioral accounting area? What perspectives and approaches are most likely to enrich our understandings of accounting both as it is and as it might be?

Put quite simply, my own view is that accounting researchers need

[23] In the meantime, inquiries into the latter question could well commence within the academy itself. In his paper Swieringa notes that so much of the teaching of management accounting continues to propagate the tenets of the faith, in the process often denying the relevance of the rich appreciation of organizational functioning and accounting in action that might be present in the student body. Indeed on occasions students are encouraged to deny their own perceptions of that richer reality. As the introduction to a "solution" in the instructor's guide for an accounting text stated: "Students will often want to emphasise the organizational aspects of this case. This should be discouraged. This should start by focusing on the accounting alternatives. . . !"

to get inside the factory gate or the office door. There is, I think, an urgent need for observational studies of accounting in action, and I think that this would be the opinion of both Argyris and Swieringa. We need to study how accounting systems function, how accounting information is and is not used, how accounting does or does not permeate other organizational processes, and the consequences which accounting does or does not have at both the individual and the organizational level. We need to ascertain just what the relevant variables for understanding the accounting craft are, rather than presuming them beforehand, and we need to ascertain precisely how different organizational perspectives can enrich our understandings of accounting as it is. In fact, I find myself repeatedly amazed that such work has not been done. Surely, one tends to think, and many of my nonaccounting colleagues do think, scholars with such applied
130 instincts as accountants would revel in the complexities of accounting in action. Well, revel they might; but apparently they have not, for we have so few studies of the organizational functioning of accounting. Just what have been the pressures for accounting change? Have they emanated from within the organization or without? What organizational significances have been attributed to the craft, and in what circumstances? What have been the relationships between accounting and other forms of organizational practice? Just what roles has accounting played in the emergence of the modern hierarchical organization? When, for instance, have organizations invested heavily in accounting? And of equal significance, when have they continued to function quite adequately without the assistance of such sophisticated forms of control?

Such latter forms of inquiry also point to the need for inquiries into alternative forms of accounting and accounting as it might be. What accountings, for instance, have been associated with organizations claiming to have very different modes of operation and forms of governance? Are there ways of reducing rather than increasing an organization's dependence on the craft? Just why do some organizations seem so peculiarly accounting intensive while others invest in alternative modes of control? Rather than so readily presuming any functional imperative for the accounting craft as we now know it, I think that we, as researchers, should be prepared to take a less committed stance, on occasions seeking to problematize "what is" so that we might gain some rather different appreciations of "what might be."

Such organizational and historical investigations would be very different from what is now done in the name of management accounting research, even be it of an organizational and behavioral variety. For that reason alone, there are a host of reasons why such studies will not be done. Yet that should not delude us from recognizing that if we are to build on the richness of Argyris' and Swieringa's insights, very different research perspectives and strategies will be required in the management information and accounting system area.

APPENDIX A

Argyris, Chris. "Management Information Systems: The Challenge to Rationality and Emotionality." *Management Science* (1971): B275-92; idem., "Organizational Learning and Management Information Systems." *Accounting, Organizations and Society* (1977): 113-23; Simon, H. et al. *Centralization Versus Decentralization in Organizing the Controller's Department.* New York: The Controllership Foundation, 1954; Whyte, W. F. *Money and* 131
Motivation. New York: Harper and Row, 1955; Ray, D. "Efficiency and 'The Fix': Information Intergroup Relations in a Piecework Machine Shop." *American Journal of Sociology* (1955): 255-66; Dalton, M. *Men Who Manage.* New York: Wiley, 1959; and P. M. Blau. *The Dynamics of Bureaucracy.* Chicago: University of Chicago Press, 1955. For the contributions of the Carnegie Project on the Behavioral Theory of the Firm, see Cyert, R. M. and March, J. G. *A Behavioral Theory of the Firm.* Englewood Cliffs, N.J.: Prentice-Hall, 1963; Bonini, C. P. *Simulation of the Information and Decision Systems in the Firm.* Englewood Cliffs, N.J.: Prentice-Hall, 1963; Clarkson, G. P. *Portfolio Selection: A Simulation of Trust Investment.* Englewood Cliffs, N.J.: Prentice-Hall, 1962; Crecine, J. P. "Defense Budgeting: Organizational Adaptation to Environmental Constraints." in *Studies in Budgeting*, ed. R. F. Byrne et al. Amsterdam: North-Holland, 1971; idem. *Governmental Problem Solving: A Computer Simulation of Municipal Budgeting.* Chicago: Rand McNally, 1969; and Williamson, D. E. *The Economics of Discretionary Behavior.* Englewood Cliffs, N.J.: Prentice-Hall, 1964. Also refer to Wilkavsky, A. *The Politics of the Budgetary Process.* Boston: Little, Brown, 1964; idem. "Policy Analysis Is What Information Systems Are Not." *Accounting, Organizations and Society* (1978): 77-88; idem. and Hammand, A. "Comprehensive Versus Incremental Budgeting in the Department of Agriculture." *Administrative Science Quarterly* (1965): 321-46; Heclo, H. and Wildavsky, A. *The Private Government of Public Money.* London: Macmillan, 1974; Hofstede, G. H., "People and Techniques in Budgeting." in *Quantitative Methods in Budgeting*, ed. C. B. Tilanus. Leiden: Martinus Nijhoff, 1976; idem., *The Game of Budget Control.* Van Gorcum, 1967; Bower, J. *Managing the Resource Allocation Process.* Graduate School of Business, Harvard University, 1970; Ackerman, R. W. "Influence of Integration and Diversity on the Investment Process." *Administrative Science Quarterly* (1970): 341-52; Pettigrew, A. M. *The Politics of Organizational Decision Making.* London: Tavistock, 1973; and Michael, D. *On Learning to Plan and Planning to Learn.* London: Jossey-Bass, 1973. At a more organizational level of analysis, see the work of Chandler, A. *Strategy and Structure.* Cambridge, Mass.: MIT Press, 1963; idem. and Deams, H.

"Administrative Co-ordination, Allocation and Monitoring: A Comparative Analysis of the Emergence of Accounting and Organization in the USA and Europe." *Accounting, Organizations and Society* (1979): 3-20; Litterer, J. A. "Systematic Management: The Search for Order and Integration." *Business History Review* (1961); and idem. "Systematic Management: Design for Organizational Recoupling in American Manufactauring Firms." *Business History Review* (1963): 369-91; and Galbraith, J. *Designing Complex Organizations.* Reading, Mass.: Addison-Wesley, 1973. The interest of social scientists in information and accounting systems continue in the work of Becker, S. W. and Neuheuser, D. *The Efficient Organization.* Amsterdam: North-Holland, 1975; Shortell, S. M. and Brown, M., eds. *Organizational Research in Hospitals.* Blue Cross, 1976; Ouchi, W. G. "The Transmission of Control through Organizational Hierarchy." *Academy of Management Journal* (1978): 173-92; Pfeffer, J. "Power and Resource Allocation in Organizations," in *New Directions in Organizational Behavior*, ed. B. M. Shaw and G. R. Salancik. Chicago: St. Clair Press, 1977; idem. *Organiza-
132 tional Design.* Arlington Heights, Ill.: AHM Publishing, 1978; Salancik, G. R. and Pfeffer, J. "Organizational Decision Making as a Political Process: The Case of a University Budget." *Administrative Science Quarterly* (1974): 135-51; and Fox, F. V. and Staw, B. M. "The Trapped Administrator: Effects of Job Insecurity and Policy Resistance on Commitment to a Course of Action." *Administrative Science Quarterly* (1979): 449-71.

The Information Systems Environment
Lucas, Land, Lincoln, Supper (Editors)
North-Holland Publishing Company

FROM MANAGEMENT INFORMATION TO INFORMATION MANAGEMENT

Michael J. Earl
Oxford Centre for Management Studies

and

Anthony G. Hopwood
London Graduate School of Business Studies

Systems designers, managers and researchers increasingly recognize that there are problems in the development and operation of MIS. Frequently lack of management support and involvement are cited as causes of inadequate MIS and calls are made for managing information as a resource.

In this paper the authors argue that a new perspective is required, from a concern with management information as a technical phenomenon to a concern with information management as a substantive organizational phenomenon. Such a re-direction may depend on new metaphors, language and frameworks being derived first.

Among both researchers and managers there is an increasing realization of problems in the management information area. A recurring theme in the literature is that MIS have been disappointing in so far as they commonly have failed to meet expectations (Argyris 1977). In management courses, sessions on MIS rarely want for lively discussion, heated debate and general concern. Managers frequently complain of information overload on the one hand and an information gap on the other. The professional information providers - systems analysts, accountants and management scientists - proudly describe their achievements and earnestly explain their current plans. The information users listen with mixed feelings ranging from hope to scepticism, from commitment to antagonism and from understanding to incomprehension. There are problems in the current state of MIS.

Meanwhile substantial sums of money continue to be spent on information processing. Companies commonly claim that their data processing budgets consume 2% of sales turnover. One major multinational company has estimated that 10% of its world-wide corporate turnover is spent on information processing. Ten percent of net assets on world-wide balance sheets are thought to be explained by hardware investment and a UK multinational's data processing budget is currently growing by 30% per annum compound. Top management understandably is becoming concerned with "value for money".

Gibson and Nolan (1974) have suggested that DP budgets follow an S-shaped curve characterized by increasing management attention to planning and control of the computer resource. Concern with efficiency of information processing is expressed by productivity audits, performance monitoring and proliferation of controls. Effectiveness is emphasized by the introduction of steering committees, attempts at cost benefit analyses and charging for computer services. Maturity, they suggest, is reached only when the computer resource is fully integrated into everyday management practice and thinking. Our evidence would suggest that such a maturity has yet to be achieved however. While continual thinking and concern may be evident, it would appear that we are a long way from gaining the full integration of the computer resource into management practice.

Meanwhile information processing technology continues to advance. Mainframes and mass storage continue to approximate to Grosch's Law providing more power for less money. Minicomputers, and now microcomputers, threaten to change the shape of data-processing and perhaps of MIS. "Convergence" of computing, data communication and word processing will extend the scope of formal information processing. Managers and specialists are both excited and alarmed. The specialist contemplates new techniques and new applications. The DP manager sees new options and new anxieties. Managers wonder whether an opportunity has arrived to regain control or, more frequently perhaps, whether the technology will finally leave them stranded.

Yet despite some of the fundamental questions posed by these trends, investment in formal MIS continues. With the persuasiveness of so many interested parties, particularly the information providers, the appeal of sophisticated technology and the felt need to keep up with others, it is easy to justify ever more information systems. There is always an information need, the system always needs improving and incremental growth is generally invisible. Indeed MIS perpetuate themselves: they are necessary because they are there. Professions and disciplines such as accounting, computer science and cybernetics are built around them. Other seemingly successful organizations have MIS and publicize them. Yet in transferring systems from other organizations we fail to examine the context in which they originally operated, often implementing misfits as a result. Finally, we seek spin-offs, trying to satisfy management information needs on the basis of existing data-orientated systems (Zani 1970). In short, MIS are assumed to be good for us. After all, or so it is frequently claimed, is not information the raw material of decision making, the *sine qua non* of planning and control and the life blood of organizations?

Increasingly however the existence of any *a priori* relationship between formal MIS as commonly conceived and effective organizational performance is being questioned. In a planning context, for instance, Grinyer and Norburn (1975) found no significant relationship between formal information systems and financial performance. Instead they found use of both informal channels of communication and informal decision-making processes was associated with success. Lorsch and Allen (1973) found that complexity of management control information systems facilitated upward information flows, but not downward flows. However both downward and upward flows were found to be associated with favorable financial performance with alternatives to formal MIS appearing to be essential.

Indeed it is the "newly poor" (Olofsson and Svalander, 1975) that invest heavily in additional mechanisms for internal visibility and control, although often in so doing they may further dislocate themselves from their problematic external environments as they consciously or unconsciously succumb to the demands of their ever more visible internal environments. Financially efficient, they may still walk to their economic grave (Hopwood, 1979). And the financially successful, on the other hand, tend to avoid many of the rigors of ever more sophisticated information and control systems (Child, 1973, 1974, 1975; Rosner, 1968; Turcotte, 1974). Seemingly they revel and flourish within the context of informal planning and assessment practices (Child, 1974), multiple and overlapping flows of information (Grinyer and Norburn, 1975) and continually renegotiated exchanges between organizational participants (Georgiou, 1973). Indeed the hearsay evidence of many managers suggests that the information they use in critical decisions does not emanate from the formal MIS. As Mintzberg (1972) discovered, top managers select and prefer informal information processing in most of their work.

Thus with the past disappointments with information systems which explicitly have claimed to facilitate the process of management, the growth of expenditure on information processing and the newly emergent technological developments, pressures on both MIS designers and users are undoubtedly increasing. Concerns and dissatisfactions are being expressed and at least some are starting to probe for alternatives.

The theme of our paper is that a major constraint on both current practice and the delineation of alternatives is that information processing is viewed in too narrow and technical a manner. Information is still seen as a technical phenomenon, a "thing" that has a seemingly problematic relationship to the intricacies of organizational processes and practices. And, as a consequence, our underlying information concepts and language tend to encourage the formalization, bureaucratization, standardization and mechanization of information processes - the very things which the recent studies quoted above suggest neither fit nor suit the realities of organizational activity. If this is the case, and we think that it is, then the alternatives to present practice may not be recognized because our existing MIS perspectives are outdated and not descriptive of even present organizational practice.

In this paper we argue for a new perspective, from a concern with management information as a technical phenomenon to a concern with information management as a substantive organizational phenomenon. Our theme is not just a play on words or a mere evangelical call to put management back into information systems. The perspective which we seek is one that is concerned with a broader appreciation of information processing in organizations. We are urgently in need of some new and very different metaphors for considering the roles which information does, can and might play in organizational functioning. To illustrate this we start by examining the variety of ways in which organizations process information.

THE INFORMATION PROCESSING MIX IN ORGANIZATIONS

Despite the emphasis which has been placed on MIS, organizations have invested and continually do invest in a multitude of ways of processing information. One way of looking at the variety of approaches used in practice is to distinguish between routine and non-routine and official and unofficial modes of information processing. The resulting array of information possibilities is depicted in Figure 1.

	Routine	Non-Routine
Official	MIS Management Accounting Systems; Production Control Systems	Access Facilities; Task Forces; Liaison Roles
Unofficial	Black-books; Just in Case Files	The Grape Vine; Lunch Table Chats

Figure 1. The Information Processing Mix

The official, routine information processing box contains the MIS which have been emphasized so much. They are often the operational systems upon which our organizations depend from day to day. In some businesses they have even become a substantial part of the business itself; for example air-line reservation systems, production control systems in the engineering sector and transactions systems in banking.

The unofficial, routine category of information processing contains systems which serve local needs. In some cases these strive to compensate for the inadequacies of the routine systems; in other cases they are maintained as defensive information against attack from superiors and peers. It is evident from research (Hopwood

1973; Simon et al., 1954) and from discussions with managers that such informal, but nonetheless routine, approaches to information processing are ubiquitous. Hedberg and Johnson (1978) saw them as having value in creating and maintaining subcultures to question and challenge the status quo and stability. Also they suggested that they often provide more flexibility and discretion to managers than the official counterparts. Argyris (1977) suggests that unofficial, routine systems often represent actuality, provide concrete descriptions of unique situations, indicate true causality and provide private and tacit views. Earl (1978a) suggests that they may be attractive because they are simple and may serve as unofficial prototypes for subsequent official routinization.

The non-routine, official category includes purposive approaches to facilitating the processing of information such as investments in the capability to provide ad hoc information and mechanisms for furthering access to information. Also included in this category are those structural approaches to information processing which are effective because they are based on managerial actions and interpersonal activities through which "things get done" and by which we can learn from experience. Such structural mechanisms provide means for crossing intra-organizational boundaries, for transcending levels of authority and influencing others by discourse and persuasion. Meetings, conferences and task forces provide channels of lateral and downward communication when often the routine MIS are predominantly upward. By being less formal and structured, non-routine and official "information systems" may also help achieve "control with" rather than "control over". They may perhaps offer top management a means of keeping "in touch", when the formal and official MIS no longer represent the reality they once measured. Finally they can often be created quickly and then killed when their purpose has been satisfied. Conversely the routine, official forms of information processing take a long time to create and may never die.

The unofficial, non-routine category comprises many of the informal information systems upon which managers depend. These devices carry news quickly, convey nuances, and can process qualitative information. To discover what is important, one joins the grape-vine. To influence some-one or break down the system one sits at the right lunch-table. To try and make sense of complexity we share the problem and construct our organization and world through and with each other. These forms of information processing are personal and private and accordingly fulfill purposes which the official or routine system could never attempt.

The reality of information processing in organizations is the vibrant and varied mix depicted by this framework. Organizations both have and require a balance of complementary information processing forms, including the more personal and structural varieties. However it seems to us that so much of this reality does not influence or enter into legitimate professional discourse in the MIS area, and this may well be a major constraint on organizational adaptation or change. Investing heavily in routine, official MIS we often forget and exclude investment in, and development of, competing, counter-balancing, overlapping and reinforcing information flows and processes. Just why does the emphasis on the formal and routine continue? What is at stake with the development of MIS as we now know them? What organizational roles do they really serve? To address such questions, let us consider further a key aspect of the interface between information and organization, namely the roles which information plays in decision-making. How is the development of MIS implicated in the very different types of decision-making processes which constitute organizational life?

INFORMATION AND DECISION

Many writers have seen MIS as servants of decision making and several authorities have devised decision-orientated strategies for MIS design (Ackoff 1967; Zani 1970; Mason 1969). The relationship between information and decision making has been an influential basis for the analysis, development and articulation of normative MIS "solutions". Indeed some have even described MIS as Decision Support

Systems (Gorry and Scott-Morton 1971).

However, one problem with the use of the decision-making perspective for the analysis of both information needs and information systems is that the relationship between information and decision has rarely been critically examined. The link has, in other words, been presumed rather than described and analyzed. A particular view of human rationality and the attendant relationship between information and decision-making has been uncritically adopted. We have tended to presume, for instance, that the specification and analysis of information preceeds decision-making, that the roles played by information in decision-making are invariate across a multitude of different decision situations. Information is there to facilitate and ease rather than more actively influence, if indeed not frustrate, the decision-making process. Such presumptions are however little more than abstractions from the complex reality of information processing in organizations. While they might simplify the information system design process, their relationship to the realities of organizational life is questionable.

One way of looking at the relationship between information and decision-making in more detail can be based on the analysis of Thompson and Tuden (1959) which adds to the traditional view of the link between decision-making and uncertainty by classifying various states of uncertainty and different types of decision-making processes. As can be seen in Figure 2, they distinguish between uncertainty (or disagreement, for that is the same at the organizational level) over organizational objectives and the uncertainty over the cause and effect relationships which are embodied in particular organizational actions. When objectives are clear and undisputed, and cause and effect certain, Thompson and Tuden highlighted the potential for decision-making by computation. As cause and effect relationships become uncertain, however,that potential diminishes and decisions start to be made in a judgemental manner. If the focus of uncertainty resides in the specification of objectives, however, decisions tend to be the result of compromise when cause and effect relationships are certain, and of a more "inspirational" nature when even that clarity disappears.

		Uncertainty of Objectives	
		Low	High
Uncertainty of Cause and Effect	Low	Decision by Computation	Decision by Compromise
	High	Decision by Judgement	Decision by Inspiration

Figure 2. Decision-Making and Uncertainty

By being based on a more detailed characterization of the ways in which uncertainties are perceived and located in organizations, we believe that such an array of decision possibilities is of real significance in trying to understand the emergence and functioning of information systems in organizations. Moreover the framework relates to the views of those who have seen information processing as a means of uncertainty reduction (Galbraith, 1973) and information value as the degree to which uncertainty is reduced. However rather than presuming the link between information and uncertainty, let us consider the roles which information processing and information systems might and do play in the different decision situations described by Thompson and Tuden.

First we strive to articulate a normative view. Using an all too unsatisfactory "machine" analogy, Figure 3 outlines the orientations which information systems perhaps might adopt in the best of all possible worlds. Given low uncertainty on each dimension, we approach the management scientists' definition of certainty, where algorithms, formulae and rules can be derived to solve the problem by computation. Alternatively it may represent Simon's structured decisions (1960) where the intelligence, design and choice phases are all programmable. In either case stock control systems, credit control routines and linear programming models are all examples of what we call "answer machines".

		Uncertainty about Objectives	
		Low	High
Uncertainty of Cause and Effect	Low	Answer Machines	Dialogue Machines
	High	Learning Machines	Idea Machines

Figure 3. A Normative View of the Relationship Between Information Systems and Uncertainty

Given clear objectives but uncertain causation, we need to explore problems, ask questions, analyze the analyzable and finally resort to judgement. Here MIS cannot provide the answer but they can go part of the way, providing assistance through what Gorry and Scott-Morton (1971) would call decision support systems, Mason and Mitroff (1973) might call dialectical systems and Churchman (1971) calls inquiring systems. Examples of what we refer to as "learning machines" are enquiry facilities, sensitivity analysis and what-if models.

Given uncertainty or disagreement over objectives but relative certainty on causation, then values, principles, perspectives and interests conflict. In a rapidly changing economic, social and political environment, such bargaining situations may be increasing. Here political processes are important where often the vital tasks include discussion, intelligence and problem-sharing to gather different points of view, seek conflict resolution or just keep talking. Examples of relevant information processing here might include 'think-tanks', information centers, consultative and participative processes, retreats and the like - all examples of what we refer to as "dialogue machines". The orientation is towards freeing channels of opinion and communication and toward polemics and debate, with the value of information being measured by the number of consistent points of view that can be persuasively argued with the data and within the context provided by the information system (Boland 1979).

Finally given uncertainty in both dimensions, or decision by inspiration, we seek "idea machines". Here the formal MIS may provide multiple streams of thought which Koestler (1964) suggests triggers creativity. Other information processing forms may include the semi-confusing information systems suggested by Hedberg and Jonsson (1978) and the use of creativity techniques, such as Delphi processes or brainstorming. They will also include experience sharing and contact with other organizations or related thinkers. Certainly fluid or organismic organization design will be advantageous, encouraging boundaries to be crossed and the fertilization of ideas (Burns and Stalker, 1961).

Most people will not argue with this exposition. When presented in such terms they are prepared to acknowledge the variety of roles which information systems might serve and even the consequent variety of approaches to information system design and operation. However although the analysis may be acceptable, it describes, we would venture to suggest, a set of circumstances which is very different than the reality of the relationship between information and decision-making which exists in many organizations. That reality which is so fundamental to our argument is illustrated in Figure 4.

		Uncertainty about Objectives	
		Low	High
Uncertainty of Cause and Effect	Low	Answer Machines	Ammunition Machines
	High	Answer Machines	Rationalization Machines

Figure 4. Uncertainty Decision-Making and the Roles of Information Systems

On the whole we have learned how to develop MIS for decision by computation. While some problems may remain, quite successful "answer machines" are in widespread use. Thereafter, however, organizational reality starts to diverge from the normative and all too appealing set of circumstances outlined in Figure 3. Rather than using "learning machines" to confront the uncertainties inherent in cause and effect relationships, information system designers have sought to reduce or even camouflage them. Uncertainty, it would appear, is seen as a threatening rather than inevitable state of the world, which rather than being exploited for what it is, needs to be masked by an enormous investment in tidy minded systems and in pushing down the boundaries of computational practice. So in circumstances which cry out for information which can stimulate learning and the exercise of judgement, we find routine MIS which often assume the very certainties which cannot be found.

The management scientist seeks to develop optimizing models where descriptive models can only be appropriate. The same specialist promotes the use of probability models and modes of risk analysis where a sensitive use of deterministic models may better facilitate the exercise of judgement. The systems analyst prescribes enquiry systems which have specified answers rather than interrogation facilities for the user to select and develop, and the modeller seeks solutions as answers rather than frameworks for decision-making. All the above assume a certainty which the user has never readily experienced. Designers simply forget how much prior knowledge and insight their procedures require, or impute, and by so doing they are rarely, if ever, able to come to terms with the "wicked" (Mason and Mitroff 1973) problems which constitute an important part of management practice.

In emphasising the more technical mechanisms for the improvement of information, designers so often ignore the complementary but equally essential investments which need to be made in interpretative and decision skills. In other words our parent disciplines of computing, accounting and management science have sought for answers where they cannot always be specified, aiming for technocratic solutions regardless of the context of either the user or the organizational environment.

Such approaches result in the presumption of states of quasi-certainty which do not exist and the use of particular forms of economic and scientific rationality which bear little or no relationship to those which are implicit in the processes of management decision-making.

Then as we also suggest in Figure 4, far from creating a basis for dialogue and interchange, MIS tend to be used as "ammunition machines" in decisions by compromise. By the use of this perhaps emotive term, we wish to point to the ways in which information systems serve to promote and articulate particular interested positions and values. Political processes in organizations give rise to the emergence and elaboration of information systems as one party or interested group seeks to influence others. For as Bariff and Galbraith (1978) point out, information systems may be used to perpetuate or modify decision-making processes and social structures. By influencing the accepted language of negotiation, such systems can help to shape what is regarded as problematic, what can be deemed to be a credible solution and, most important of all, the criteria which are used in their selection. In ways such as these, traditional management accounting systems and mechanisms for financial appraisal can be used to reduce the complexity of a decision environment into a simple uni-goal economic system that has a life of its own divorced from the broader realities of organizational functioning. As one

manager put it: "given a sensitive strategic decision (for example divestment) the information on the table is generally financial. Once the decision is made and we discuss its implementation other information is used, such as engineering, marketing or personnel considerations".

The "idea machine" we suggested for decision by inspiration may appear to be the only contribution that MIS can make in the context of such extreme uncertainty. However we suspect that that very uncertainty creates the need for other roles which they can and do serve. Rather than seeking to promote the creativity, inspiration and entrepreneurship which is so vital in such strategic contexts, MIS may more often than not operate as "rationalization machines" seeking to legitimize and justify actions that have been decided upon. As Bower (1970) discovered, and as many managers have described to us, the widespread adoption of capital budgeting procedures has resulted in the availability of justification devices rather than the simple and unproblematic provision of information for, and prior to, decision-making.

We do not seek the question the necessity for rationalization machines, for organizations require mechanisms through which they can legitimize what is to be done and retrospectively create a rationale for action. What we do suggest is that the information processing which is typical of such procedures be recognized for what it is, and that more active acknowledgement be given to the fact that the creativity and inspiration, which are so necessary in such contexts, are more likely to spring out of socially interactive forms of information processing.

By introducing our rather strong metaphors for information and decision, we are calling for a re-orientation away from the exclusive emphasis on technocratic and bureaucratic forms of information processing which is so characteristic of today's information system practice. There is, we think, an urgent need to acknowledge the reality of information practice in its full diversity; to see, in other words, the processes which create the roles for information processing and give rise to information systems in their wider organizational context. Such metaphors point to both the present existence of, and extended future possibilities for, MIS designs which acknowledge the uncertainties of organizational life. Hedberg and Jonsson (1978) in prescribing semi-confusing information systems called for a similar re-orientation. Like them, we advocate a move to a process view of MIS rather than the structured view which has been prevalent hitherto. Such a view would be dynamic rather than static, emphasizing the roles which information processing plays on the actions and interactions through which and by which managers make sense of their environments and cope with uncertainty.

TOWARDS INFORMATION MANAGEMENT

In summary, we can state that many MIS specialists adopt a partial and rather idiosyncratic view of the role which information processing does and can serve in organizations. Emphasizing the importance of formal and systemic approaches, they invest heavily in a perspective and approach which can be, and often is, radically at variance with the way in which managers in their own organizations engage in the active and influential processing of information. Indeed we frequently get the impression that the MIS function is increasingly operating in a rather isolated, albeit comfortable, organizational niche. That is not to say that it lacks influence. Isolated though it may sometimes be from the more active processing of information in organizations, it can nonetheless have an important influence on the delineation of the desirable and the possible. However that influence stems not from the appropriateness of the MIS designs, but from the way in which the resultant information is taken up and used by those managers who strive to personally influence ongoing processes of organizational control. So, in the last resort, it may well be that it is the managers, or at least some of them, who put the management into MIS!

If these claims are valid, it becomes apparent that information management which emphasizes the development of conventional MIS in isolation from their organizational context will only at best yield marginal gain. At worst it might be dysfunctional for it can perpetuate and strengthen information processing forms which neither represent the social reality of organizations nor the real complexity and uncertainty of the organization and its environment. Indeed it is by no menas unlikely that such a limited view of information processing may be impairing organizational performance and threatening organizational survival.

However, we should not overlook the fact that today's organizations do contain a mix of vibrant and varied information flows and processes. The routine co-exists with the non-routine, the official with the unofficial and despite the massive investment in formal MIS and the application of limited information-decision concepts, the undercurrents of the non-routine and unofficial have survived. Indeed we would like at least to acknowledge the possibility that their survival is the result of under-emphasis and inattention. It could well be that if we attempt to plan, organize and control them too much, we may kill the very spontaneity, flexibility and informality on which their effectiveness depends. This is indeed a real possibility. Nevertheless we are still convinced that if information management is to offer something of real benefit to organizations, it has to have a framework that can at least place the formal within its wider context. Otherwise a continued focus on the narrow, technical aspects of information processing may not only ultimately drive out these very necessary complements and counterparts, but also we may fail to fully exploit the real possibilities for the organizational processing of information which emerging technologies may offer (Earl, 1978b).

The wider, alternative and complementary forms of information processing which currently co-exist in organizations must therefore start to enter into the discourse of MIS designers, managers and even users. Indeed a vital task of information management needs to be the explication of a broader framework for the consideration of information processing in organizations and an understanding of its implications for MIS analysis and design.

We can summarize our own, albeit tentative, suggestions for the outline of such a framework in the following way:

* New frameworks and metaphors are required to re-orient our information thinking.

* A major goal of such frameworks and metaphors is to explicate social reality and challenge technocratic wisdoms.

* Information problems do not necessarily require information systems; alternative forms of information processing can, do and should exist in organizations.

* Investment in organizational processes and structural forms of information processing are required to complement the MIS.

* We need to improve our understanding of how organizational decision-making and control is achieved, before major advances in MIS will be possible.

* Many MIS will need to generate frameworks rather than providing mere solutions.

With such a broader organizational perspective, tasks and responsibilities of <u>information management</u> will take on a very different form.

With the technical so explicitly linked to the organizational, no one management function can be, or should be, responsible for the whole of information processing. The role of the information specialist therefore will need to become that of a catalyst for change. The user in contrast will need to have the confidence to
142 explicate and describe his own information environment, processing and problems. In such a context progress in information management therefore will depend on <u>us</u>, as managers and users as much as, if not more than, on <u>them</u> as specialists.

REFERENCES

(1) Ackoff, R.L., Management Misinformation Systems, Management Science, Dec. (1967), 147-156.

(2) Argyris, C., Organisational Learning and Management Information Systems. Accounting, Organisations and Society, Vol.2. No.2. (1977), 113-123.

(3) Bariff, M.L., and Galbraith, J.R., Intraorganisational Power Considerations for Designing Information Systems. Accounting, Organisations and Society, Vol.3. No.1. (1978), 15-28.

(4) Boland, R.J., Control, Causality and Information System Requirements, Accounting, Organisations and Society, Vol. 4. No.4. (1979), forthcoming.

(5) Bower, J., Managing the Resource Allocation Process (Division of Research, Graduate School of Business Administration, Harvard University, 1970).

(6) Burns, T., and Stalker, G.M., The Management of Innovation. (London, Tavistock, 1961).

(7) Child, J., Strategies of Control and Organisation Behaviour. Administrative Science Quarterly, (1973), 1-17.

(8) Child, J., Management and Organisational Factors Associated with Company Performance, Part 1. Journal of Management Studies (1974), 175-189.

(9) Child, J., Managerial and Organisational Factors Associated with Company Performance - Part 2. Journal of Management Studies, (1975), 12-27.

(10) Churchman, W., The Design of Inquiring Systems. (Basic Books, New York, 1971).

(11) Earl, M.J., Prototype Systems for Accounting, Information and Control, Accounting, Orgnisations and Society, Vol.3. No.2. (1978a), 168-172.

(12) Earl, M.J., What Microprocessors Mean. Management Today, December (1978b), 67-74.

(13) Galbraith, J., Designing Complex Organisations (Addison-Wesley, 1973).

(14) Gibson, C.F., and Nolan, R.L., Managing the Four Stages of EDP Growth. Harvard Business Review, (Jan.-Feb. 1974), 76-88.

(15) Gorry, G.A., and Scott-Morton, M.S., A Framework for Management Information Systems, Sloan Management Review, (Fall, 1971), 56-70.

(16) Georgiou, P., The Goal Paradigm and Notes Towards a Counter Paradigm. Administrative Science Quarterly. (1973), 291-310.

(17) Grinyer, P., and Norburn, D., Planning for Existing Markets: Perceptions of Executives and Financial Performance. Journal of the Royal Statistical Society, Series A, (1975), 70-97.

(18) Hedberg, B., and Jonsson, S., Designing Semi-Confusing Information Systems for Organisations in Changing Environments, Accounting, Organisations and Society, Vol. 3., No.1 (1978), 47-64.

(19) Hopwood, A.G., Criteria of Corporate Effectiveness, in Brodie, M., and Bennet, R., (Eds.) Managerial Effectiveness, (Thames Valley Regional Management Centre, 1979). 143

(20) Hopwood, A.G., An Accounting System and Managerial Behaviour, (Saxon House, 1973).

(21) Koestler, A., The Act of Creation, (Hutchinson,London, 1964).

(22) Lorsch, J., and Allen, S., III, Managing Diversity and Independence, (Division of Research, Graduate School of Business, Harvard University, 1973).

(23) Mason, R.O., Basic Concepts for Designing Management Information Systems, (AIS Research Paper No. 8. Graduate School of Business Administration, University of California, Los Angeles, October, 1969).

(24) Mason, R.O., and Mitroff, I.M., A Program for Research on MIS. Management Science, (Jan. 1973), 475-487.

(25) Mintzberg, H., The Myths of MIS. California Management Review. (Fall, 1972) 92-97.

(26) Oloffson, C. and Svalander, P.A., The Medical Services Change Over to a Poor Environment - "New Poor" Behaviour. Unpublished Working Paper, University of Linkoping. (1975).

(27) Simon, H.A., Guetzkow, G., Kozmetsky, G., and Tyndall, G., Centralisation v. Decentralisation in Organising the Controller's Department. (New York, Controllership Foundation Inc. 1954).

(28) Thompson, J.D., and Tuden, A., Strategies, Structures and Processes of Organisational Decision, in Thompson, J.D., et.al. (Eds.), Comparative Studies in Administration, (University of Pittsburgh Press, 1959).

(29) Turcotte, W.E., Control Systems, Performance and Satisfaction in Two State Agencies. Administrative Science Quarterly, (1974), 60-73.

(30) Zani, W.M., Blueprint for MIS. Harvard Business Review, (Nov.-Dec.1970), 95-100.

CHAPTER 2: EVALUATING THE REAL BENEFITS

Anthony G. Hopwood

INTRODUCTION

Computer-based information systems can have pervasive effects on organizational life, including many which do not enter into the original justification of the system. They not only have the potential to alter the nature of work, employment levels, cost structures and the efficiency of 145
operations directly, but can also have major indirect impacts on the whole functioning and performance of the organization over a long period of time.

The remainder of this book examines in detail the consequences of information-system changes for individuals and organizations. This chapter uses many practical examples to provide an overview of key problem areas that have been encountered during such changes. It illustrates the narrow scope and short time focus that often characterizes evaluations of information systems, and suggests a basis for making wider, more strategic assessments that take into account the political nature of the decision-making processes involved.

THE ROLE OF INFORMATION IN ORGANIZATIONAL LIFE

The evaluation of computer-based information systems is a complex endeavour because information plays a key role in most activities in modern organizations. Information is gathered and analyzed to make decisions at all levels. Information delineates organizational structures, the responsibilities of particular units, the nature of managerial authority and associated spheres of discretion and influence. Flows of information disseminate organizational goals and missions, forge the linkages between organizational units and assist the co-ordination and integration of the complicated interactions between specialized tasks.

Information therefore creates perceptions of organizational reality and is actively involved in supporting and effecting work activities. It is neither a static nor a self-contained phenomenon but permeates all functions. A new information system can influence and sometimes radically alter the environments that need to be managed. Yet many computer-based information systems are introduced on the basis of limited administrative, economic and technical analyses and expectations.

Organizational flexibility

An information system can hinder or help an organization's ability to adapt to meet new challenges. For example[1], after introducing the extensive use of automated control processes and robotics, a large motor manufacturer realized that it had successfully automated the traditional concept of an assembly line, building in all the rigidities of the old process.
146 About the same time, a key competitor had introduced new systems only after a more fundamental evaluation of the potential of information technologies which questioned the need to maintain the previous manufacturing rigidities. The competitor's resultant system was much more flexible, even though it employed similar technological components. This flexibility gave the competitor considerable strategic and economic advantage when the automobile market became volatile and unpredictable.

Similarly, an insurance company planned to introduce a new type of policy. To promote it, the company wanted to identify all of their existing policy-holders, between certain ages, who did not have the relevant cover. This is an ideal task for an integrated computerized database management system but the relevant information within the company was on different files. While these files were being integrated, at great expense and with difficulty, a competitor launched a similar policy. 'We lost out because our information systems had just about set like concrete,' commented the Managing Director.

Organizational control

Information systems reinforce or change relationships between central authorities and local departments and agents. A manufacturing company operating through subsidiaries around the world, for example, reinforced centralized control by introducing a global computerized system which gave direct, updated reports on cash and fund flows directly to corporate headquarters. This provided a mechanism to implement effectively the management policy of having each subsidiary responsible for generating profits against an annual plan and contributing to an annual dividend in cash to corporate funds.

On the other hand, a government department used an information system to devolve management control, by introducing new office technology to facilitate the collection of information in its geographically remote regions. This enabled regional managers to have more direct control over local costs. It also implied a passing of authority to the regions to initiate actions which previously required central sanction. This led to a backlash from some officers at the centre who felt their authority and status had been eroded.

Indirect impacts

The implications of a new information system often extend into areas outside the context for which they were initially introduced. For example, a central information system implemented by a credit card company changed the company's marketing strategy. Previously, advertising had to be selective and upmarket as a means of controlling who was allowed to use its card. However, the new information system could provide up-to-date monitoring of the transactions made by card holders as a means of management control. The advertising policy could therefore be changed to be less selective.

Labour relations are often brought into the development and operation of new information systems (see Chapter 9). For example, when a retail chain installed new 'point of sale' equipment at checkouts, the union asked for the operators' jobs to be upgraded because they were now responsible for providing input into corporate systems. In a British company, the union asked for access to personnel records, which they were entitled to under collective bargaining legislation. From this, the union could tell the labour rates at various plants, which influenced its bargaining position.

A computer-based system can change job functions, which makes a significant difference to an individual's motivation and job satisfaction (see Chapters 8 and 11). For example, when a bank computerized its local branch operations, the main aim was to automate the cashier's work. It also altered the manager's function by shifting much of the accounting and control of branch operations to the head office. As a result, many managers complained that they had become merely 'salesmen' selling central services rather than influential figures in the local business community.

MISTAKES IN EVALUATING COMPUTER-BASED INFORMATION SYSTEMS

Computer-based information technology has the potential to improve many processes involved in managing information. In practice, however, many problems have been encountered in trying to fulfil that potential. The techniques which have traditionally been used to set objectives have tended to look at mainly technical and short-term quantifiable economic criteria. This has been satisfactory for identifying the technical problems that arise from the rapid rate of innovation, but it is inadequate as a means of pinpointing and managing the broader — and crucial — human and organizational aspects.

148 Despite the massive growth in routine information provision by computer-based systems, many organizations have found that demands for information are still unmet, particularly when faced with newly turbulent environments. Systems based on formal organizational procedures (see Chapter 6) reflect the problems and crises of the past rather than the present 'need-to-know'; unfortunately, such formal systems are the bases for many computer-based information services.

Different evaluation strategies are needed to relate new office technology developments to the whole spectrum of real-world requirements. It must remain important to consider technical, administrative and quantifiable economic elements which have been emphasized in the past. The relationships which information flows have to other aspects of organizational functioning suggest, however, that consideration of these factors is insufficient to comprehend the complexities of the information problems of today's organizations. The main mistakes that have been made in setting objectives and evaluating implementations have been:

— Placing the primary emphasis on short-term economic consequences;

— Evaluating the information system in isolation from organizational functions which they serve — often ignoring human and social consequences or, when they are considered, placing an overemphasis on individualistic needs and physical ergonomics;

— Failing to relate economic and social perspectives;

— Recognizing uncertainties in the future but not giving sufficient priority to providing flexibility in the system to adapt to changes;

—Viewing information in a partial way;

—Taking a limited view of the roles served by information systems in organizations.

The following sections examine the experiences which have brought these problems to light.

Too much short-term economics

When considering investments in new information systems, there is a tendency, as in other investment decisions, to emphasize the relationship between the initial capital costs of the project and the net operating savings. Instead of giving high priority to *value-added* aims, the ways in which the new system can add value to various organizational activities, a dominant position is given to the *cost-substitution* assessment. This calculates savings in personnel costs and financial gains from improved operational activities, such as more efficient inventory control and speedier decisions. The savings are compared to the costs of the new system's capital, operational and development expenditure and related personnel training. In most cases, the primary problems confronted are of a technical and forecasting nature. The image of the change process created by this concentration on short-term economics invariably requires that little consideration is given to other closely related aspects of organizational functioning and to longer-term economic aspects. Attention is focused on those economic factors which can be identified at the time the decision is taken to introduce a new system. This in itself is a complex process and has sometimes missed important practical considerations, such as the support and maintenance costs for the equipment.

Even when care has been taken to try and look deeper than straight cost-substitution analysis, mistakes have been made. A leading European car manufacturer, for example, introduced a vehicle inventory recording system throughout its network of main dealers, enabling each dealer as well as the company to know the location of all stock via immediate direct computing access to the data. A thorough economic appraisal of the system seemed to demonstrate that it could be cost effective, assisting dealers' sales efforts and giving more efficient management of the manufacturer's inventories. Unfortunately, the major economic consequence of the system was not anticipated: the ease of access to inventory information inadvertently induced dealers to reduce their own stocks. Why keep large stocks of cars, they asked, when they could satisfy customers' needs by finding the nearest location of a suitable model at the press of a button? This meant that the manufacturer had to increase its own stocks, which significantly added to its costs.

Another manufacturing company was faced with a sudden increase in competitive pressures. It ordered a complete review of its information systems strategies after finding that the information produced by the computer was mainly oriented towards internal, short-term problems whereas the company's real problems were external and long-term.

Isolating the information system

The calculation and acceptance of short-term economic criteria are simplified if the information system is regarded as a self-contained entity. Growing technological complexities and the increasing influence of technical professionals has meant that such false simplifications have
150 often caused the information function to become isolated from other organizational activities. Lip-service may be paid to concepts like 'information as a corporate resource' but, in practice, information systems can become an almost autonomous development.

The characteristics of the information itself and the information system are emphasized rather than the consequences that these might have. What is needed is a more detailed charting of the specific implications for key activities such as marketing strategies, production options, labour relations and financial structures. In the next chapter, Peter Keen recommends a strategy to handle new office technology products which effectively integrates all aspects.

An example of what can go wrong is the experience of a large oil company which had a sophisticated long-range plan for computer developments. Unfortunately, the strategy had been created separately from product and market development plans and was not updated in phase with changes in the business environment. Eventually, a crisis occurred when there was a fundamental shift in marketing policy. 'We are tending to revert to manual systems to meet the urgent, rapid changes in data needs,' the Chief Executive commented ruefully.

The inward-looking nature of many information systems institutionalize internal management processes and perceptions at a time when increasingly interdependent and volatile world economic, industrial and technological activities mean that more problems come from external sources. The Marketing Director of a major European consumer electronics firm, for example, succeeded in initiating a major review of corporate information system after discovering that it could not cope adequately with changes in the life cycles of products. The average product life cycle had been cut from 7 to 8 years to 1.5 to 2 years. A major management problem was therefore to develop strategies which would span across life cycles but the information system was optimized to handle within-life-cycle performance.

Inadequate attention to human and social consequences

During the first phase of commercial computing in the 1960s and early 1970s, hardly any attention was given to the human and social consequences of computing. Most users of the systems were given special training to handle generally complex and difficult-to-use systems. When microelectronics caused computing to come closer to real working environments, such as the office, increasing attention was paid to the individual's use of systems (see Chapters 10 and 11).

Research was carried out, particularly into the physical ergonomic design of systems to make them safe, comfortable and easy to use. The nature of the software interaction between user and system and the impact of the system on individuals' motivation and productivity also began to be regarded by managers as a significant factor in information system changes. This concern was sharpened by laws on ergonomics introduced in some West European countries and by pressure from trade unions (see Chapter 9). The interest in these aspects was a step in the right direction but its partial nature should be noted. The emphasis has been individualistic rather than on the broader organizational ramifications.

The emphasis on individualistic and ergonomic aspects can be made compatible with the narrow short-term economic and technical perspectives discussed above. The advocates of ergonomics usually regard themselves as being in a more 'human' tradition than the rationalist school of 'scientific management' which dominated production-line automation (see Enid Mumford's comparison of Taylorism and socio-technical techniques in Chapter 4). Somewhat paradoxically, however, quantifiable ergonomic standards have often been used by management to reinforce a scientific management approach that would be opposed by many who are sympathetic to the ergonomic approach.

Failing to relate social and economic perspectives

Given that social issues themselves have generally been treated in a partial and haphazard way, it is not surprising that it has been rare for social and economic evaluations to be related. It has also been rare for a social analysis to be used as a way of determining the nature of the economic goals or for economics to be used explicitly to constrain the assessment of the social environment. Prevailing practices have maintained the autonomy of these two aspects despite the fact that repeated evaluations of information system changes illustrate the limitation of doing this.

The kind of problems which result from this separation were highlighted by the experience of a major North American manufacturing company. It invested in a massive centralized computer-based information service to support key decisions and facilitate planning and scheduling of marketing and production. The same information, however, was also used to set targets to motivate managers. Being aware of its evaluative uses, the managers biased many of the key information flows. The resultant optimistic forecasts led to increased expenditures on unnecessarily high inventories and production line work-in-progress and made for a lack of
152 flexibility in co-ordinating marketing and production activities.

Inability to adapt to the future

When evaluating the consequences of information systems attention is usually given to the improvement of forecasting methods, probabilistic assessments and other techniques which try to decipher future uncertainties. It is less common for recognition and priority to be given to the more fundamental, unpredictable discontinuities which characterize the future. Despite a theoretical genuflection towards the need for information systems to respond to the unexpected, in practice emphasis has usually been placed on the need to identify the most efficient way of responding to what is perceived as a known future.

As the quotation from the Managing Director of the insurance company indicated, the result is that many systems have been 'set in concrete'. Little attention has been given to creating systems which are flexible, responsive and adaptive. In addition to the earlier examples given of the inflexibility of some computer-based systems, an evaluation exercise by an important manufacturing company highlights the far-reaching negative impact of an over-shortsighted design. The company found that its information system had detracted from, rather than enhanced, its operational flexibility, management processes had been made more complex and time consuming, investment in rapid access to *ad-hoc* information had been neglected and management defensiveness had increased.

Over-emphasizing formal information flows

There has been a tendency to stress the official routine flows of information when designing computer-based systems, despite the fact that many studies of the way organizations work stress the significance of the diversity of other information channels[2]. A summary of the main type of information flows is given in Figure 2.1. Computer-based systems have provided an explosion of 'official-routine' information in activities such as personnel, materials management, inventory control, production control and many other management and administrative functions. This is supplemented by unofficial but still routine information kept in 'black books' or 'in the desk drawer', which individuals feel they need to make decisions. 'Just-in-case' files contain routine but unofficial information, which an individual feels could be used in defence of decisions and actions.

	Routine	Non-routine
Official	Computer-based information systems	*Ad hoc* queries Direct access to data Task forces
Unofficial	Black books Just-in-case files	The 'grapevine' Lunch-table chats

Figures 2.1. Types of information flow

Informal information flows play an important role in all organizations. These are passed via the grapevines and *ad hoc* chats which permeate managerial, office and shop floor circles and are facilitated by close personal proximity or by membership of clubs and outside organizations. Even official computer-based systems can be used to provide non-routine *ad hoc* enquiries or to give direct access to a database. Structural changes are also made in the organization, such as the setting up of task forces to improve communications channels.

Computer-based systems are primarily used in — and emphasize — official information routines, although the unofficial, alternative information flows are known to play strategic roles in organizational activities. These important unofficial communications can be endangered unless the partial role played by official information is recognized and active steps taken to understand and cater for the complex informal sources of information which contribute to organizational performance.

The dangers of failing to investigate the organizational impact of unofficial information was dramatically illustrated by the experiences of a

British company. It had emerged as the only large company in its sector to survive a turbulent period, although it was in a lean and financially insecure state. Management initiated rationalizations, including the dispersal of two-thirds of head office staff to a suburban site, and expansion of the existing computer-based system to provide 'better information on management efficiency'. Shortly before implementing these plans, a consultant undertook a survey of information flows, which led to the abandonment of the move. The consultant found that the company had survived the crisis that had hit the industry primarily because of the close physical proximity of key organizational members. This enabled messages from the volatile outside world to be transmitted through the company and acted on very quickly. That role had not been recognized in the original plan.

154 Another example of the problems with partial information occurred in a hospital which intended to introduce new office technology. One aim was to 'rationalize' the information flows, which had been shown to include a substantial amount of 'redundant' information which was either duplicated or unused. Instead of producing the expected cost savings, the change was a painful process, with many key organizational processes grinding to a halt. The reason was that no consideration had been given to the important role of the 'redundant' information in assisting staff motivation and the co-ordination of activities. Although it did not help senior management to monitor lower level performance, it did help local managers to understand what was going on in their own areas. Eventually that so-called redundant information had to be provided again, at a higher cost than with the original system.

Ignoring the political role of information

Most evaluations of computer-based information systems give primacy to the 'rational' role which such systems are deemed to service, such as 'facilitating decision making, providing 'quicker, more accurate and relevant' information or assisting in the 'efficient' allocation of resources. Participants in the organization, however, realize that this is a limited view of the real role of information.

Information system requirements are closely related to organizational power and emerge from essentially political processes which characterize organizational life[4]. Although official evaluations attempt to suggest that new systems are neutral technical artifacts, there is strong grassroots awareness that this 'rational' perception is a very partial representation of reality. Based on the work of two American sociologists, Michael Earl and I have categorized the different roles that the same information system can take within an organization (see Figure 2.2)[3]. The important elements, which they believe determine the role of the information system, are the degree of certainty/uncertainty that applies to the objectives of actions and to the cause and effect relationships underlying organizational processes.

		Objectives	
		Certain	Uncertain
Cause and effect relationships	Certain	Answer Machine	Ammunition Machine
	Uncertain	Learning Machine	Rationalization Machine

Figure 2.2. Various roles of information systems

When the cause and effect and objectives are both certain, decisions tend to be made in a computational manner, using the information system as a mechanistic 'answer machine', within a highly structured and well understood decision-making process. With increasing uncertainty of the cause and effect relationship, the information system can assist the decision-maker to exercise subjective judgements. It acts as a 'learning machine', which helps the user to understand the context in which he or she is operating and to find out about some of the uncertainties involved.

Where there is uncertainty about objectives but the underlying cause and effects of decisions are certain, demands for information arise from the process of managing an environment characterized by conflict and bargaining. Information systems in this context serve as 'ammunition machines' used to support a particular case or to shape a picture of 'reality'. If all certainty disappears, 'inspirational' decision-making has to be used. In this case, information is marshalled by a retrospective 'rationalization machine' to legitimate actions already taken.

The roles of information systems as answering or learning machines are the main substance of official computer system designs and evaluations. Information specialists are reluctant to be associated with the more 'political' roles because it is threatening to them. They like to use the traditional and partial approaches criticized earlier in this chapter to provide partial and short-term ammunition and rationalizations to defend their supposedly neutral technology.

EVALUATION AS A SOCIAL PROCESS

This chapter has illustrated some of the mistakes in making narrow and shortsighted evaluations of computer-based information systems. It is possible, however, to extend the horizons of economic assessments to include, at least in qualitative form, organizational considerations of a more strategic nature. The remainder of this book examines methods of implementing such broader perspectives, in particular by explicitly integrating human, organizational and social consequences with technical and economic considerations.

Such techniques, however, will merely serve to provide better and more refined 'answer' and 'learning machines' unless there is a recognition of the political context in which the information system has a key role. Evaluations should take into account the political interests of various groups with different interests and concerns. This would sharpen the perceptions of problems, influence the options available for action and assist in adapting the resultant system to real requirements. There is no magic formula, however, which can solve what is intrinsically a complex and unpredictable task. As Rob Kling analyzes in Chapter 13, information system planning and design must satisfy pluralistic and often conflicting demands. Issues that need to be decided range far beyond purely technical considerations or factors which can be simplified in terms of isolated applications of the technology. Typical questions that arise include: Should decision processes be centralized or decentralized? Will changes create more or less social interaction? Will organizational flexibility be lost or will information systems enable the organization to cope more effectively with a volatile environment? Does the system increase the efficiency of social surveillance and control? Can computer-based systems replicate the subtle, informal, personal communications on which all organizations depend? How can society in general cope with the employment and training implications of information technology?

Technical and short-term economic aspects cannot be separated from the social dimensions of these impacts. The only way to resolve questions such as these is explicitly to recognize the political aspects of decision making. One way of doing this has been for some interest groups to press for legislation and to negotiate agreements which provide staff with rights to participate in taking decisions which influence the direction of technological change. Generally, however, the technically-oriented approach has predominated because it is based on relatively well-developed methodologies (although there are many difficult unsolved technical problems) and tends to reinforce the existing and well established power structures.

Both the technical and political perspectives of new office technology require a great deal of live practical experience before they can provide a mature understanding of exactly how to manage the total process of technological change to take account of the multiplicity of interactions and implications. A first step in that direction is at least to recognize that evaluations of information systems should face up to the whole spectrum of human and organizational aspects which has been highlighted in this chapter and is further examined in the rest of the book.

RECOMMENDATIONS

1 Acknowledge that the setting of goals and evaluation of information systems is a political process involving many groups and individuals with vested interests.

2 Seek to illuminate the various interests and their consequence for the eventual evaluation process.

3 Examine the mechanisms for the representation of different interests, the institutional means by which divergent evaluations can be discussed and the ability of different groups to have access to informed opinion and relevant data regarding the options available.

4 Recognize that evaluations can take place from different perspectives — the individual, the group, the organization and the social.

5 Give active consideration to the ways in which new information systems will influence the diversity of official and unofficial information flows.

6 Never evaluate an information system in isolation from its organizational context and consider the ramifications of information system developments for the operation, performance and integration of various functions in the organization.

7 Consider the importance of ensuring that the information system is

flexible and adaptive, particularly in a world characterized by uncertainty and the occurrence of the unexpected.

8 Avoid evaluations that divorce social aspects from economic factors.

9 Question the apparent certainties of short-term evaluative exercises and probe the assumptions of simple, short-term cost-benefit justifications of new systems.

10 Be aware that the evaluation exercise is itself a complex information processing activity, subject to all the problems and opportunities which characterize this area.

REFERENCES

1 Examples in this chapter are taken from a number of sources, including Tricker, R.I., *Effective Information Management*, Beaumont Executive Press, Oxford, UK, 1982.

2 Minzberg, H., *How Managers Manage*, Harper & Row, New York, 1974.

3 Earl, M., Hopwood, A.G., 'From Management Information to Information Management' in Lucas, H.F. *et al* (eds) *'The Information System Environment,* North-Holland, Amsterdam, 1980.

4 Burchell, S., Clubb, C., Hopwood, A.G., Hughes, J., Nahapet, J., 'The Role of Accounting in Organizations and Society', *Accounting, Organizations and Society*, Vol 5, No 2, 1980.

Accounting, Organizations and Society, Vol. 8, No. 2/3, pp. 287–305, 1983. 0361–3682/83 $3.00 + .00
Printed in Great Britain. Pergamon Press Ltd.

ON TRYING TO STUDY ACCOUNTING IN THE CONTEXTS IN WHICH IT OPERATES

ANTHONY G. HOPWOOD
London Graduate School of Business Studies

Accounting has come to be seen as playing a key role in organizational functioning. Concerned, as it now is, with such activities as assessing the costs and benefits of organizational actions, the setting of financial standards and norms, the representation and reporting of organizational performance, and financial planning and control, accounting has been used to cast important aspects of the functioning of the modern organization into economic terms. By offering particular economic representations of organizational activities and outcomes to both internal participants and interested external parties, it has come to be involved in the creation of a quite specific organizational order and mission. Accounting is now associated with particular ways of seeing and trying to shape organizational processes and actions, with the maintenance of certain forms of organizational segmentation, hierarchy and control, and with the furtherance of an economic rationale for action (Batstone, 1979). Indeed in many cases the forms taken by decision processes, the structuring of organizational activities and even the specification of an organizational boundary are not independent of the accounting representation of them. Modes of accounting have become not only important and valued management practices but also ones whose existence and consequences are difficult to disentangle from the functioning of organizations as we know them. Accounting, in other words, has become centrally implicated in the modern form of organizing.

With accounting so intertwined with organizational functioning it is surprising that so little is known of the organizational nature of accounting practice. That, however, is the case. Although early studies of accounting in action focused on trying to understand its organizational roles and consequences, many more recent investigations have detached accounting from its organizational setting, preferring instead to study the consequences which it has at the individual rather than the organizational level.[1] Admittedly such studies are providing us with many interesting and useful insights into both the interpretation of accounting information and ways of trying to facilitate its use in decision making situations. Be that as it may, they do not explicitly aim to help us to understand what is at stake in the organizational

[1] Some of the reasons for this are discussed elsewhere (Hopwood, 1976; 1978). An interesting discussion of the general problem is given in Gowler & Legge (1981). Given the relative recency of research into the behavioural and organizational aspects of accounting, the latter's citation of Platt (1976, p. 42) is particularly interesting:

> . . . there are strong insitutional forces pulling people towards distinct disciplinary approaches; the pressure to disciplinary conformity is probably particularly strongly felt by younger people who do not yet have a securely established base or identity in a particular field. To the extent that this is so, the effects of different patterns of intellectual training and socialisation are reinforced by personal needs . . .

I think that a case could be made that such a situation has prevailed in the behavioural study of accounting, the assessment becoming even more appealing when the situation in management accounting is contrasted with that prevailing in the financial accounting area where legitimacy has been provided to institutional (i.e. market) rather than individual level studies.

practice of accounting, even though it is the latter which provides so many of the rationales for the accounting craft. Studies at the individual level can neither illuminate the ways in which accounting intersects with other organizational practices, decision processes and power structures nor the factors which both give rise to the accounting phenomenon and induce it to change.[2]

Together the papers collected here aim to provide some perspectives on accounting in an organizational context. As such, they aim to build upon earlier collections (see, for example, *Accounting, Organizations and Society*, Vol. 3, No. 1 (1976)) and contributions to show both the potential of an organizational perspective for the study of accounting practice and some of the range of

approaches which might be included within it. However, before trying to summarise some of the key concerns of the papers and the more informal discussions which they stimulated, it is useful to attempt to delineate both some of the distinguishing features of an organizational level interest in accounting and the reasons for its significance.

SOME RATIONALES FOR AN ORGANIZATIONAL FOCUS

Individual level studies of accounting invariably take the accounting phenomenon for granted. Accounting, as such, is not the problematic issue. The primary concerns are with understanding and improving the interpretations which are made of it, with these insights frequently being seen as providing a basis for fine tuning rather than more fundamentally reforming the practice and technology of accounting. Moreover in the vast majority of such studies this emphasis enables accounting to be detached from both its organizational setting and other organizational practices. Accounting is seen to be a relatively independent art, having its roles and consequences primarily moderated by the cognitive properties of its immediate users rather than the setting in which it is placed. Indeed on many occasions the exclusive focus on the cognitive mediation of accounting justifies transferring the settings in which this can be studied to the college classroom and the psychological laboratory.

A more organizational approach would not deny the significance of such cognitive mediation. Indeed, the ways in which accounting influences individual action are a central part of its concern. However, rather than detaching accounting from its organizational setting, organizational researchers aim to understand the meanings which are given to accounting in particular settings, emphasising not the interpretation of an accounting given but the more active ways in which a particular account can shape, mould and even play a role in constructing the setting of which it forms a part. Accounting, to the organizational theorist, cannot be isolated from the processes which give rise either to its presence or to its present significance, be those within or without the particular setting or even organization in which it plays a role.

For the cognitive theorist accounting is primarily an independent variable, although, on the basis of the understandings which are gained from observing the responses to it, he or she also might seek to change, indeed to improve, the accounting representation of what is seen as being an independent organizational reality. The organizational theorist, on the other hand, can see accounting as both a dependent and an independent phenomenon. Some organizational scholars of accounting seek to emphasise the contingent nature of the accounting craft, aiming to provide an understanding of how particular accountings emerge from organizational and social settings. Such theorists do not necessarily remain content with offering an explanation of a particular accounting manifestation, however. Together with those other scholars of the organizational who place primary emphasis on the ways in which accounting both influences and is constrained by the meanings given to the organizational setting in which it operates, they seek to explore the social processes through which accounts of organizational action influence both the meanings and actions which constitute

[2] For interesting discussions of these and similar points see the papers by Connolly, March & Shapira, Cummings, Pondy and Weick in Ungson and Braunstein (1982).

organizational life.

Such distinctions, however, provide only a relatively superficial view of an organizational level interest in accounting. Given the significance of the contrast, not least in the context of the present studies, it is worthwhile to explore in some more detail the ways in which an organizational perspective might view the accounting phenomenon, appealing both to the studies which are collected here and others which are now available.

Accounting repeatedly becomes what it was not

Accounting is neither a static nor a homogeneous phenomenon. Over time, all forms of accounting have changed, repeatedly becoming what they were not. Accounting, moreover, is not a homogeneous craft. Both management and financial accounts are characterised by an amazing diversity, both within a national culture and even more so across different national contexts (Horovitz, 1980). All too apparently accounting is a phenomenon which is what it isn't and can become what it wasn't!

Unfortunately we have a very limited understanding of the forces that either influence accounting change or help to shape the different forms that the accounting craft can take. Although a great deal of work has been done on the history of accounting, many of the studies that are available have adopted a rather technical perspective, seeking not only to emphasise the developments that have occurred rather than also probing into the rationales for them (Hopwood *et al.*, 1980) but also, even when raising questions about the underlying forces at work, all too readily presuming a functionalist and even progressive interest. Indeed, until recently, both historical and comparative analyses of the accounting phenomenon have adopted a most atheoretical stance, only rarely seeking to relate their insights to broader understandings of the development of the corporate form, its social and economic setting, and the roles which organizational accounts might have played in the emergence of both the organization as we know it now and the relationships which it has to other bodies and interests.

These questions are now starting to be addressed by accounting and other scholars however, as the papers and comments by Johnson (1983), D. Flamholtz (1983), Meyer (1983) and Tiessen & Waterhouse (1983) illustrate.

On the historical side, studies of accounting development are beginning to utilise more theoretical analyses of the emergence of the corporate form and the particular roles which procedures for both internal control and the maintenance of external legitimacy have played. Interestingly, scholars from other social science disciplines also have started to be intrigued by the processes underlying the growing significance of the accounting craft and the roles which it may have served in the emergence of modern institutional forms. Consideration has been given to the roles played by economic record keeping in the construction of forms of organizational visibility 161
which can further particular organizational interests, to the ways in which accounting and other forms of management practices became implicated in the resolution of the conflicts which characterised the emergence of today's organizational forms, and to the contribution which accounting has made to the articulation and propagation of a legitimate myth of disinterested administrative rationality and order.

From an organizational perspective, studies of accounting diversity have drawn on the precarious but nevertheless useful understandings available from contingency theory (Otley, 1980). Consideration has been given to the implications which organizational environments, technologies and tasks and management structures have had for the development of accounting practice. Illuminating though such perspectives have been, however, there is now an increasing recognition of the need to move beyond the restrictive static and often functionalist presumptions which have characterised past forms of contingent analysis. More direct interest is now being expressed in trying to understand the nature of the organizational processes through which accounting becomes what it was not. Albeit slowly, there are signs that consideration is being given to appreciating the ways in which both other management practices and external phenomenon intersect with accounting practices to create pressures for change and the difficulties raised by attempts to understand the

implications for accounting of the multiple contingencies which characterise organizational life. Attention is also slowly being given to how accounting can be changed in the context of organizational and social conflicts and debates in order to create different but still persuasive images of organizational aims and achievements. Not least in significance, there are signs that the roles which accounting plays in shaping its own development also are being recognised, be these seen in terms of the implications stemming from the professionalisation of the body of knowledge that has emerged around the practice of the craft or of the ways in which accounting actively shapes the perception of and salience attached to some of the very phenomena which are supposed to put
162 pressures on it to change.

Interestingly, questions related to the emergence of organizational forms and the controls which go with them now attract the attention of the economist as well. Rather than being content to view the organization as an unproblematic "black box", economists have started to explore some of the rationales that may be implicit in prevailing organizational forms, appealing to both the comparative advantages of markets, hierarchies and other organizational forms, and the ways in which modes of organization can moderate and further patterns of economic interest and accountability. As Johnson (1983), Tiessen & Waterhouse (1983) and others (Baiman, 1982; Spicer & Bellew, 1983) illustrate, both of these perspectives emphasise the important roles that procedures for monitoring and control can play, helping, thereby, to cast some light on some of the origins of the accounting function. As of yet, however, most of this work has emphasised the role of technical and economic interests. In contrast to historical and organizational inquiries, economists, to date, have given little or no attention to either the ways in which the economic intersects with the social and the political or the more particular questions involved in how accounting itself may have come to be involved in the very specification of those economic interests in the name of which it is changed.

At present all such explorations of the rationales that might be implicit in the accounting craft remain at an early stage of development. The perspectives of the historical, the organizational and the economic remain largely independent, each tending to offer relatively self-contained explanations of the emergence of organizational accountings and the pressures for them to change, and few studies have been made of the emergence and development of particular modes of accounting practice. Nevertheless such attempts to understand the processes of accounting change are of significance, not least because of their potential to provide us with a very different perspective, or more likely, series of perspectives, for understanding what might be at stake in the accounting endeavour.

Conventional understandings of accounting view it from a relatively unproblematic technical perspective. It is presumed that accountings are there to facilitate organizational and social action (see Burchell *et al.*, 1980 for a further discussion of this point). Only rarely, if ever, is the nature of that facilitation and the ends that might be so served examined. Although notions of cost, profit and other indices of financial performance may not be seen as being unproblematic, the difficulties which they give rise to stem, according to such a conventional view, from the problems of operationalizing pre-given aspects of organizational and social reality and achievement. Accounting, so conceived, is essentially a revelatory endeavour, aiming merely to reflect rather than more actively to construct a view of organizational reality and ends. Seeking, albeit often with difficulty, to explicate and make visible an unproblematic view of the means for organizational achievement, accounting is seen as a phenomenon divorced from the social, as distinct from technical, struggles and innovations that have resulted in its emergence.

All too clearly alternative views of the accounting endeavour will not be appealing to those who have invested in articulating and propagating such a conventional perspective. However for those who are willing to consider them, they offer at least the potential of a way of understanding accounting and its problems that is consonant with the historical conditions which have resulted in its emergence and development and those current organizational forces which contribute to its significance.

Accounting and organizational action

Accounting gains much of its contemporary significance from the ways in which it helps to shape and guide organizational processes and actions. However although accounting texts, pronouncements and recommendations repeatedly emphasise the ways in which it contributes to organizational efficiency, the improvement of managerial and employee motivation and performance, and the more effective allocation of resources, little is known of if and how such ends are achieved. Compared with the extent of the technical ediface of accounting, very little is known of the organizational processes which this seeks to activate and through which the technical achieves its potential.

What roles does accounting play in the construction of organizational participants' views of the desirable and the possible? Does accounting get implicated in the creation of particular conceptions of organizational time? And if so, with what effects? How and when do accountings of organizational performance provide an incentive for action? How does accounting contribute to the articulation of an organizational mission and through what means do the particular and very partial patterns of organizational visibility that accounting creates facilitate the achievement of control within the organization, be that seen in either social or technical terms? How does the routinized provision of information which accounting emphasises relate to the multitude of informal decision arenas which characterise organizational life? Just how, in other words, does accounting achieve and maintain a position of organizational significance?

Such questioning could be extended. For although a great deal of effort has been invested in extending and refining the technical basis of accounting in the name of its organizational roles and consequences, very little is known about the ways in which the potential which is claimed on behalf of accounting is realised. For some, at least, that is a paradoxical situation for a craft that has continually sought to emphasise the pragmatic organizational implications of its technical endeavours.

An organizational view of accounting has enormous potential to illuminate some of the more problematic aspects of the accounting craft. For instance, it could help us to understand the roles which accounting plays in the creation of particular patterns of organizational segmentation and the consequences which this has, not least in those circumstances where the requirements of the task point to the provision of lateral flows of information which are at variance with the vertical ones which accounting more usually emphasises. Equally, greater insights into the ways in which accounts of organizational performance provide particular mappings of both the organizational environment and its internal processes and outcomes could help those concerned with the design of more effective information provision in times of change and discontinuity. Many also would find it helpful to understand the roles which different, and often conflicting, assessments of organizational performance, both past and prospective, play in the determination of decisions and the allocation of scarce resources. Just how does accounting's emphasis on the economic relate to the interests and practices of those who seek to extend the visibility of the technical, the human and the wider environmental characterisation of organizational performance? And how does accounting's commitment to the detached, analytical consideration of the new relate to the need to generate the commitment which may play a determining role in the realisation of the actual? Together insights of this nature could provide at least a basis for trying to ground the technical apparatus of the accounting craft in the specifics of organizational action, thereby hopefully trying to realise the pragmatic potential that is so frequently claimed on accounting's behalf. At present, however, such insights reside in the realm of experience, only rarely being set aside the abstract and highly generalised claims that grace the manuals of technical accounting practice.

Accounting and the achievement of the accounting mission

Conventional discussions of accounting invariably presume that the craft is capable of achieving the claims that are made on its behalf. Accounting, so we are told, is capable of enhancing organizational efficiency and performance (forgetting, of course, the role that it also plays in the definition of the very ends it is trying to further). It can play a positive role in increasing managerial and employee motivations to perform. And accounting can provide the type of information that can facilitate managerial decision making, not least in environments characterised by uncertainty and doubt.

Increasingly, however, some, at least, of such highly generalised claims are being compared with the more equivocal impressions emerging from both research and pratice.

164 There is a long tradition of scholarly inquiry which has sought to illuminate the dysfunctional as well as functional consequences, both latent and manifest, of the accounting craft. More recently, there have been studies which at least have pointed to the ways in which accountings appear to proliferate amidst concerns with organizational crisis and decline rather than in the less problematic days of growth and success. Sometimes such research even has pointed to the ways in which the consequent desire for greater control can result in organizational procedures which detract from rather than enhance the flexibility of managerial response in such conditions.

Such concerns with the actual rather than the claimed achievements of accounting now have started to be articulated by some of the practitioners of the accounting craft. Faced with economic restraint and often with increased competitive pressures, such practitioners have started to become concerned about the limitations of the routinized flows of information which accounting so often provides.

Sometimes seeing how accountings of the present reflect crises of the past, such practitioners have come to appreciate the need for new understandings of how accounting systems emerge in practice rather than in theory and the potential, or otherwise, which they offer for managerial decision making. Although such worries, let alone their causes, have yet to be systematically documented, it is not unusual for such people to express their concerns over the rigidities which routinized controls endow to organizational processes and the contracted time horizons which conventional accountings can often instil. Many also are worried about the problems which result from accounting's almost exclusive emphasis on the economic and the financial, and it is not unusual to hear even quite conventional practitioners articulate their concern for the inefficiencies which might have been legitimised by repeated annual cycles of budgetary reveiw and authorisation. At a more general level, there are now some organizations that are starting to express concern over the full range of implications that might have stemmed from the ways in which accounting and other control practices have resulted in an abstract process of control removed and often distanced from the practice of the task that is being controlled.

All too clearly such concerns are not the worry of the average practitioner. Whilst often concentrated in large organizations, an era of very real economic restraint nevertheless has resulted in at least some accounting practitioners and their managerial colleagues probing into what their investment in accounting has and has not achieved. Although rarely, if ever, expressed in ways other than the immediate set of implications for their own organizations, such questionings have resulted in a new awareness of the interdependency between the technology of the accounting craft and the human and social processes through which the objectives which are set for it are achieved. Moreover that awareness is often expressed in much more subtle terms than those used by the academic practitioners of accounting who have come to see behavioural and organizational studies as providing only a base for their more esoteric colleagues who only deem it worthwhile to worry about the icing on top of the accounting cake.

Unfortunately research on the organizational aspects of accounting is presently not in a position to fully address such practitioner worries. What studies are available have tended to focus on particular aspects of the accounting domain, often seeking to further the missions of accounting as conventionally defined rather than provide a more questioning account of accounting's consequences. Only rarely has research on the behavioural and organizational aspects of accounting concerned itself with investigating those wider linkages between accounting and other organizational processes and practices that provide the basis for some, at least, of the concerns currently emanating from practice.

Be that as it may, an organizational perspective can provide a basis for appreciating the practitioners' worries. It can contrast, for instance, the conventional organizational rationales for accounting which are detached from other organizational processes and concerns with a much more interactive view of organizational life (Ashton, 1976). From the latter perspective, the consequences of interventions in the name of one practice can be seen to be dependent on factors other than the intentions and means of organizational action which are consciously articulated and mobilised. It can be seen that actual outcomes also depend on the practical capacity of accounting procedures to encapsulate, penetrate and then influence the complex fabric of modern organizations, on the ways in which they intersect with both other organizational practices and the wider aims and actions of organizational participants, and, in the latter respect, on the resistances which specific attempts to mobilise one set of organizational practices induce. When seen in such terms there is at least the potential for the aims of any particular intervention in organizational life, be it of an accounting or any other nature, to remain partly or even totally unfulfilled (indeed even resulting in consequences which were wholly unanticipated) since the eventual outcomes are influenced by phenomena which did not enter into its original justification (Merton, 1936; Boudon, 1982). In the words of Hindess (1982, p. 498):

> Outcomes . . . may or may not conform to the intentions or objectives of any of the agents concerned. They are produced in the course of practices which take place under definite conditions and which confront definite obstacles, including the practices of others.[3]

Perhaps when seen in such a light it is not surprising that some consideration is now starting to be given to the circumstances under which accounting does and does not realise the aims that are articulated on behalf of it. The organizationally detached discourses that permeate accounting texts and manuals are being compared with the ways in which accounting has to relate to the practices and underlying bodies of knowledge of other approaches to organizational control. Accounting is being related to questions of organizational design and consideration is being given to how it functions alongside the interrelated practices of production, personnel and even financial management. Finally the resistances to accounting also are now being investigated, be they seen in terms of the behavioural processes which determine the actual use of the accounting craft or the social struggles within the organization in which accounting becomes intertwined. Be that as it may, it must be recognised that an organizational view of accounting in action is still emergent. There remains a very real need for further reflection and inquiry if we are to understand those processes through which accounting achieves the consequences which it both seeks to have and does in fact have.

AN ORGANIZATIONAL AGENDA

No doubt numerous other rationales could have been provided for an interest in the organizational nature of accounting practice. More emphasis could have been placed on the ways in which accounting becomes implicated in the construction of prevailing conceptions of organizational power and the furtherance of particular organizational interests. Greater consideration could have been given to the nature of the organizational order

[3] Hindess (1982) goes on to argue that "the securing of outcomes should always be seen as problematic, that it is subject to definite and specifiable conditions in at least two respects. First, the means of action of agents are dependent on conditions that are not in their hands. Secondly, the deployment of these means of action invariably confronts obstacles, which often include the opposing practices of others. Success in overcoming those obstacles cannot in general be guaranteed" (p. 501). He concludes his argument by suggesting the need to take "seriously the particular conditions in which these practices and struggles take place and in which their outcomes are produced" (p. 509).

which accounting attempts to maintain and the roles which it plays in creating a particular pattern of economic and financial visibility within the enterprise. Equally, more stress could have been placed on the need for organizationally orientated accounting research to facilitate the decision roles of information within the organization, with consideration even being given to the need to construct new organizational accounts which can positively illuminate different aspects of organizational functioning. In part, at least, such additional factors have been alluded to. More importantly, the discussion of the organizational nature of accounting has sought only to provide a basis for a different view of the accounting craft. Even though it may be partial, it nevertheless has hopefully outlined an area that is of some significance to all interested in the accounting endeavour and an area that is in urgent need of further study and inquiry. Indeed the conference itself was designed to help pursue this latter aim.

The papers presented at the conference focused on a number of different issues, drawing, in the process, on a range of very different organizational perspectives. Rather than striving to attempt to present *an* organizational view, a conscious aim of the conference was to provide an opportunity for the presentation and discussion of a number of different ways of analysing and trying to understand the organizational world in which accounting is embedded.

Together Johnson (1983), D. Flamholtz (1983), as discussant and Tiessen & Waterhouse (1983) provided a number of different perspectives on the processes by which accounting has become what it now is. Attempting to relate both social and economic views of the organization, they provided some bases for appreciating how accounting has become implicated in the construction of the modern business organization and how, in so doing, accounting has provided one means by which the organization can be related to wider economic and social interests, including, in the context of D. Flamholtz's remarks, those of the State. However, although the aims might be related, the approaches adopted by Johnson and Tiessen & Waterhouse are very different. Johnson presents a historical view of the ways in which accounting contributed to the emergence of the modern business enterprise. In part, at least, such a historical perspective provides us with an opportunity for seeing how accounting is both influenced by and in turn shapes the organizational form adopted by the enterprise. Tiessen & Waterhouse, in contrast, attempt to build upon a contingent view of management accounting by seeking to understand how accounting is used to construct a calculative interface between organizational management and those outside the enterprise who seek to pursue an interest in it. By appealing to economic conceptions of organizational rationality, they show how accounting plays a role by making visible a particular view of economic order. Johnson, on the other hand, at least points to the possibility that the resultant order is as much constructed as it is revealed by accounting means. From such a perspective it is possible to see the internally controlled domain of opportunities that is the firm as being a product of both the historical struggles out of which such domains emerged and the present as well as past use of management practices, such as accounting, for their preservation and development.

The papers by Birnberg *et al.* (1983), E. Flamholtz (1983) (and his discussant Kerr, 1983), Boland & Pondy (1983), Markus & Pfeffer (1983) and Hayes (1983) focus on ways of trying to understand how accounting is implicated in the ongoing processes of organizational functioning. In some respects this group of papers is notable for its diversity rather than for its convergence on any single viewpoint or issue. Indeed Hayes explicitly aims to present a number of different ways of accounting for the organizational significance of the accounting phenomenon. However beneath the seeming diversity a number of themes emerge.

Albeit in very different ways, both E. Flamholtz and Markus & Pfeffer discuss accounting's relationship to the bases of organizational power. Indeed in both papers not only the fact of that relationship but also the legitimacy of the present mode of articulation is accepted. With Flamholtz, however, accounting's contribution to mobilizing the powerful and power based organization is accepted implicitly, this seemingly being an unproblematic part of the accounting task. The challenge is to forge sufficient organizational linkages for the power potential of accounting to be realised. Whilst appearing to accept the ways in which accounting (and other forms of information and control systems) further particular conceptions of organizational power, Markus & Pfeffer explicitly discuss, although do little to appraise, the plurality of the bases of power in organizations, the ways in which accountings relate to the exercise of power and the strategies which an explicit recognition of this suggests for the design and implementation of new accounting and information and control systems. So although the organization is seen as having some aspects of a "contested terraine" (Edwards, 1979), strategies seemingly are available to further the contribution which accounting can make to the exercise of a particular powerful interest. Both papers therefore recognise that the accounting endeavour cannot be seen in purely technical terms. Equally, both suggest how the organizational might be mobilized in the name of the technical.

The tension between the technical and the organizational bases of the accounting task is a theme which pervades other papers. Birnberg and his colleagues contrast the stated aims of accounting with some aspects of its organizational achievements. Hayes seeks to ground the artifacts of accounting in the context of the symbolic, linguistic and legitimising roles which they serve. A more direct discussion is provided by Boland & Pondy, however, in terms of the perspectives of the rational and the natural, the former being related to the technical view of an objective accounting that permeates conventional discussions of the subject whilst the latter focuses on the ways in which accountings arise out of processes of social interaction, both reflecting and creating the symbolic structures that give meaning and significance to organizational life. Although outlining two very different views of how accounting is implicated in organizational functioning, Boland & Pondy nevertheless seek to demonstrate the utility of both perspectives. They consciously aim to illustrate how the rational provides a framework for the natural and how the natural can serve as a basis for the emergence and elaboration of the rational. Indeed, by so doing, they focus quite explicitly on the very real tensions that can be created by the juxtaposition of the two; tensions which create the very basis for the development of the accounting craft and the attribution of meanings to it.

Reflecting on such discussions, both Meyer (1983) and Cooper (1983) point to some of the wider issues involved. Meyer focuses on the symbolic domain that is created by accounting fictions, a domain that is important for creating the type of legitimate and seemingly coherent entities that are demanded by the agencies of the modern world. Although acknowledging the ways in which the rational domain so constructed is sometimes only loosely related to the ongoing processes of organizational life, Meyer nevertheless emphasises how the abstract fictions that permeate the accounting craft can nevertheless have a very real impact on organizational decision making and action. Not only does the symbolic define the real, but the reality so created can be and often is changed in the name of the symbolic. With what might initially appear to be the loosely coupled thereby having a very real possibility of becoming quite tightly coupled, Meyer therefore not only asks for a greater understanding of the processes through which this takes place but also suggests the very real need for a greater appreciation of the broader social and ideological factors that are implicated in these processes. Cooper also emphasises this latter point. He too is aware that the technical and the rational can come to be seen as natural; that, in other words, a new view of a seemingly natural order can be created in the name of the technical. However to Cooper, and indeed increasingly to others, such new organizational orders are neither unproblematic nor fully understandable in terms of the technical. Like Meyer, Cooper emphasises how important it is for accounting research both to recognise the wider social nature of the technical and the organizational world that it can in part create. He asks us to analyse much more consciously and systematically than has been the case in the past the social, institutional and ideological factors that are implicated in the emergence of particular conceptions of the technical and the rational, and the implications which they have for organizational and social functioning.

Although such wider debates only had an indirect relationship to the final group of papers presented at the conference, the interests of both Mirvis & Lawler (1983) and Mitroff & Mason (1983) were in part at least mobilised by their dissatisfaction with both the prevailing rationalities incorporated into the accounting craft and some of the organizational consequences of today's accounts. Mitroff & Mason emphasise the dilemmas facing the designers of information and accounting systems in an increasingly complex and uncertain world. Unhappy with the unitary logic which structures today's accounts of organizational action and performance, they argue for an approach to system design which more consciously

attempts to map the contradictions, tensions and dilemmas which characterise organizational life. Like Mirvis & Lawler, however, they recognise the resistance which seemingly faces their new organizational order. For Mitroff & Mason such resistance resides in the realms of the cultural, the psychological and the social, all sources, apparently, of an irrational response to the different rationality which they seek to instil. Mirvis & Lawler, on the other hand, at least start to probe into the wider organizational forces which might be implicated in the resilience of the old organizational order which they initially sought to reform – the very same resilience which provided the basis for the wider questionings of both Meyer and Cooper.

By any stretch of the imagination the papers presented at the conference on "Accounting in Its Organizational Context" provided a rich insight into some of the issues that might be at stake in analysing the accounting phenomenon from an organizational perspective. Given this, in the above remarks I have not attempted to provide an overview of all that was said or even the most important things that were on the agenda. I merely have sought to emphasise some similarities, differences, trends and implications from a personal point of view. The task of conducting a detailed assessment remains in the hands of the reader.

SOME EMERGENT ISSUES

The value of almost any conference rests not only on the papers that are formally prepared and presented but also on the informal discussions which these stimulate. This conference was no exception. It therefore might be useful to conclude with a brief presentation of some of the issues, worries, concerns and possibilities that emerged during the course of the conference deliberations.

Accounting as a changing phenomenon

Repeatedly consideration was given to how accounting had become what it now is and to the strategies that might be used for changing it. Stimulated no doubt by the historical perspectives offered by both Johnson (1983) and D. Flamholtz (1983), and by the socio-economic approach of Tiessen & Waterhouse (1983), the conference discussions often tended to focus on the changing nature of both the accounting domain and the accounting craft – on both what was accounted for and the means through which that was achieved. There was an ever conscious awareness of the fact that accounting changes: it becomes what it was not. Equally, however, there was a recognition of the paucity of our understandings of the processes through which this takes place, the broader issues that might be at stake and the consequences of the changes that do occur. Not only was the latter seen in terms of our own inadequate basis for accounting as we now know it, but also, and more generally, the discussions often emphasised our present inability to confront what might be at stake, both in terms of its antecedents and its consequences, in the seemingly ever increasing pervasiveness of the accounting phenomenon.

Dissatisfaction was voiced over the ability of conventional analyses of accounting history to address such questions. Seemingly it was more concerned with documenting the changing accounting phenomenon and the technologies that are at its deployment than providing an insight into the underlying social, institutional, economic and political forces at work. Indeed it was recognised that a great deal of research into accounting history had adopted, consciously or otherwise, a very atheoretical stance, ignoring, in the process, the problems involved in trying to provide an adequate social understanding of the accounting craft. The roles of accounting had been seen in relatively unproblematic and often very contemporary terms. The juxtaposition of accounting innovations in the *nexi* of relationships between the organization, the markets for both labour and capital, and the State had not been emphasised. And accounting scholars of the historical had seemingly distanced themselves from the concerns of both social theorists of the corporation and the corporate state and more recent theoretical advances in historical inquiry.

Equally, dissatisfaction was expressed with organizational attempts to account for accounting change. Although it was recognised that contingency approaches had provided some insights into the nature of accounting diversity, the relatively static and functionalist presumptions of such perspectives also were discussed. Contingency theory had difficulty confronting the dynamics of organizational and accounting change. In adopting a narrowly organizational perspective, it restricted the range of factors which it could consider in its pursuit of the origins of both difference and change. And its concern with more unitary conceptions of organizational aims and achievement foreclosed too many possibilities for inquiring into how organizational accounts emerged from political processes endemic to the organization rather than from the dictates of a more rational economic order.

In criticising the efforts of the past, and it should be said, the present as well, conference participants were aware of the very real conceptual and empirical difficulties involved in trying to provide more adequate and illuminating insights into the processes of accounting change. Indeed it was quite explicitly recognised that the issues involved reside at the frontiers of scholarly inquiries in the social sciences generally. Even so, although aware that research into accounting was not necessarily backward or too far behind that in other social science disciplines, it nevertheless was thought that much could be gained if accounting scholars were prepared to recognise more explicitly the organizational and social issues at stake and the range of theoretical perspectives that are at least available. It was thought that at the very least such a reorientation in perspective might encourage them to undertake a more sustained series of analyses of the emergence and development of accounting systems and practices. These, in turn, might provide a richer empirical basis for reflecting on those factors that might be implicated in accounting change and the processes through which this takes place.

Accounting as a heterogeneous phenomenon

Similar discussions also focused on the diverse nature of the accounting craft, particularly in respect of the practices of management accounting. Not only was there an awareness of the enormous range of technical practices in use (summarised by one participant in the terms of "you name it; somebody is using it!") but also consideration was given to the diversity of those organizational linkages which ground accounting and other information and control systems into the ongoing processes of organizational life. Accounting and control departments are variously organized. Planning, budgeting and performance monitoring procedures operate at different organizational levels, are subject to different degrees of participation, have different expectations and practices for their revision, and even can consider very different time periods. Accounting systems also serve to establish very different patterns of organizational segmentation and relate to the practices for the management of organizational interdependence in a variety of ways. From these and many other viewpoints the accounting domain was seen to exhibit a diversity that seemingly was at odds with the myth of a more generalised phenomenon that permeates accounting texts and those manuals that seek to guide accounting change and reform.

Yet again consideration was given to the inadequate state of our understanding of not only the factors underlying such diversity but also the implications that this might, and perhaps should, have for both the evaluation and change of accounting practice.

Perhaps in this context more sympathy was expressed with at least the aims of contingency approaches. In discussions of the heterogeneous accounting domain at least the contingent nature of the practices was recognised. The roles played by differing technologies, environments, management structures, corporate cultures and other factors were all alluded to. However it was recognised that not only had research from this perspective not progressed as far as it might but also that not sufficient consideration had been given to some of those difficulties of contingent approaches which already have been discussed. The problems raised by multiple contingencies were seen to be important; concern was expressed about the rather deterministic nature of present contingency theories; attention was focused on the need to understand the interplay between management choices and whatever constraints might be deemed to be imposed by the organizational context; and some, at least, wanted research to address more directly the interactive nature of the accounting craft by recognising not only how accounting might be shaped by its context but also how at least some aspects of that very same context might in turn be shaped by accounting itself.

More generally it was recognised that research which could provide insights into both accounting diversity and change had a very real potential to illuminate many key problems of accounting in practice. For the issues which such questions raise about the relationship of accounting to the context in which it operates are ones that are high on the problem agendas of accounting practitioners and consultants. By trying to disentangle the processes by which particular accountings arise, function and change, such research offers the potential to relate knowledge to the specifics of the accounting condition with which such practitioners have to deal.

Competing accounts of the organizational terrain

Albeit less explicitly, consideration nevertheless was given to the diverse accounts which seek to characterise organizational life and its outcomes. At the individual level, all organizational participants construct their own maps of the organizational terrain, delineating the significant, the problematic and the possible, accounting in their own terms for significant organizational boundaries, what they see to be the centres of power and influence, and those rationales which they think do and ought to influence choices and actions. Even in the sphere of rationalised systems of information and management, a multitude of accounts pervade organizational life. Physical and technical mappings are provided by engineers and production management; their systems also seek to shape and influence the physical reality of the organization in terms of volumes, flows, qualities, stocks and tolerances for performance. The personnel, marketing, financial and distribution functions (and others) also all impose their own accounts on the organization. Like the accountant, these practitioners also have invested in complex procedures for delineating the organizational world which they seek to manage and change, for recording those attributes which they have assigned to it and for influencing the cognitions and social behaviours of other organizational participants. Therefore the accountant's *Account* is merely one of many that attempt to make visible and salient particular aspects of organizational life and the constraints that are deemed to apply to it. Rather than existing in isolation, *Accounting* was seen as being in a state of tension with the multitude of other organizational accounts, seeking to impose a particular perspective, order and mission on a domain that is characterised not by the absence of maps for its exploration and explitation but rather by the sheer richness of the competing surveys of its problematic terrain.

When the accounting phenomenon was seen in such terms it invariably raised questions about the means through which a particular account had become enshrined as *Accounting* practice. Questions also were asked about the interplay of the diverse accountings, those factors that might have influenced their relative power, their differential consequences and the relationship which the mobilisation of particular accounts had to the patterns of organizational choice and action over time.

To date accounting research has adopted all too parochial a perspective. A very special significance has been attached to the economic and financial mappings provided by the professionalised practitioners of the accounting craft. As a result, a particular account has been accepted as *the Account*. Whilst there are good reasons for some specialisation of interest (not least in a world characterised by increasing system diversity, complexity and technical sophistication), the unproblematic acceptance of the priority accorded to such a partial ordering of organizational life undoubtedly has not only restricted the nature of the inquiries undertaken into the organizational nature of accounting practice and the problems which it faces but also, and perhaps more fundamentally, prevented people from exploring the organizational and the wider social factors which have resulted in one account being attributed with so much significance and power – in the world of action as well as in that of scholarly inquiry. It was thought that at least some investigations of the latter set of issues might help to illuminate some key aspects of the accounting condition, those organizational roles which accounting is expected to serve and the tensions which its implementation and use so often engender.

The tension between organizational order and disorder

Such a perspective of competing organizational accounts helped to focus attention on the often precarious nature of the organizational order which accounting seeks to create. Only rarely, if ever, is accounting elaboration and change an unproblematic endeavour of charting an organization anew. More frequently, organizational participants already hold their own views of the significant and the desirable, and usually these have been shaped by the practices of other practitioners who have sought to change the organization in the name of their own particular missions and aims. Accounting, accordingly, enters into a disputed terrain. Its consequences have to be achieved by contesting the dominance of pre-existing conceptions of organizational order and purpose. Accounting therefore can be characterised not only in terms of the aims that are attributed to it but also in terms of the resistances which it engenders. Indeed it is just such resistances which already have stimulated behavioural inquiries and the concerns and worries of those practitioners of the accounting craft who have reflected on the consequences which it has not achieved as well as those which it has achieved but which did not enter into its original justification.

The organizational world in which accounting operates therefore can be seen in terms of the order which accounting seeks to implement and the disorder which its implementation both confronts and, in part, engenders. Moreover both dimensions of such a perspective can be elaborated in terms of what might over simplistically be called the vertical and the horizontal axes of organizational action. Operating vertically, accounting seeks to reinforce a particular conception of organizational power. It aims to create a partial but influential pattern of visibility which can facilitate the operation of the organizational hierarchy by creating a form of organizational segmentation, by channelling down through that an objective for action and subsequently by monitoring actual performance. Seen in such terms, accounting is a tool in the hands of the powerful. Viewed horizontally, accounting also can be seen as being implicated in the propogation of a financial and economic rationale for action, seeking either to contest those alternative conceptions of organizational mission that can be advanced in the name of the technical, the market, the social and whatever or to serve as a means for converting (and invariably modifying in the process) such aims into the language of the economic. On both axes of organizational life accounting can be seen as trying to create a particular conception of organizational order. Equally, however, on both axes that conception of order is invariably contested and challenged, albeit with differing degrees of effectiveness.

In emphasising only the order which accounting seeks to advance rather than the contexts in which it operates there is an ever present danger that accounting scholars of the behavioural merely seek to expose the defects in the present apparatus of accounting and move towards its reform without appreciating the diverse and contested nature of the organizational regime in which accounting operates.

Perhaps somewhat paradoxically, attention also was focused on those circumstances in which accounting had succeeded in imposing its own particular order. Rather than greeting this achievement with acclamation, however, at least some conference participants were concerned with the organizational consequences which might result, with the latter seen in terms of both more general notions of organizational effectiveness and the particular regimes of power that accounting serves to reinforce.

Concerns were expressed about the potential problems which might stem from trying to guide and manage a complex and diverse organization on the basis of a single perspective. In part such worries reflected an awareness of the dangers of the bureaucratic rigidity which could result from a singular emphasis on the routinised procedures for inducing a particular organizational visibility which are so often associated with the accounting craft. In addition, however, the discussions of the organizational context in which accounting operates had resulted in a recognition of the need
172 for a diversity of accounts to map into the organization the very different but equally salient aspects of both its external and internal environments. Even an approximation towards a singular informational order was seen as too narrowly restricting the messages, the options and, thereby, the actions that were available to organizational members. Thought therefore was given to the need for a more organizationally grounded view of accounting that would be compatible with a role as a complementary rather than over-reaching information and control system – a view that would be content with the disorders as well as with the ordering of organizational life.

Of course the concerns with the power potential of accounting also questioned such notions of a unitary organizational order. Accounting, when seen from such a perspective, was centrally implicated in the construction of particular notions of organizational ends and achievements. Rather than merely reflecting in a neutral manner the constraints and imperatives that impinge on organizations as we now know them, accounting was seen as being involved in the specification and articulation of a specific organizational mission. As such, it could not be seen as a disinterested endeavour. Accounting was at least related to the propogation of a particular set of interests, even though that relationship may be moderated by some aspects of the autonomous nature of the craft, the complex of institutional structures in which its practice is embedded and the diverse agents which call upon its practices and procedures. According to this view a questioning of accounting would necessitate an examination of the interests in the name of which it is mobilised, its effectiveness to serve these ends and the strategies that might be available if other interests wished either to challenge or themselves to utilise the accounting craft.

Conceptions of order and disorder therefore were seen to be far from unproblematic terms, appealing both to views of organizational achievement and those political regimes which might underlie accounting practice. Different though they may be, however, it was recognised that both viewpoints had had little impact on accounting inquiry.

The reflective and constitutive role of accounting

To date organizational research in accounting has emphasised the ways in which accounting systems reflect other aspects of the environments in which they are embedded. As has been indicated already, consideration has been given to the impact which technologies and markets have on accounting, to the relationship between organizational structure and the design and use of accounting systems, and some initial interest has been expressed in examining the broader cultural influences on the form taken by accounting and other types of control systems. In such ways accounting has been shown to be a contingent phenomenon, designed and used in the context of other important features of the organizational environment.

Although concern has been expressed about the adequacy of our present conceptual and empirical skills for handling such contingent relationships, the general notion of an interdependent accounting has not been contested. At the conference it was seen to be a partial view however. For although accounting plays a role in mapping into the organization other salient aspects of the managerial, task and external environments, it also has the power to shape and influence organizational life on its own accord.

The environments that are mapped into the organization can become defined in accounting terms. They can become "profitable" or "costly", "cash cows" or "rising stars". Similarly the organization structures which impinge on accounting practice invariably do not have a manifestation that is completely independent of their accounting reflection. Modes of organizational decentralization are defined in terms of cost, profit and investment centres; organizational units have accounting as well as managerial boundaries; and accounting mechanisms for the monitoring of subunit performance help to make real the powerful potential that is reflected within the organization chart. Equally, accounting plays a role not only in shaping the visible map of what is known of organizational functioning but also in expressing and thereby influencing the objectives that are stated for organized action. An operational definition of profit has been a particularly powerful notion. However consideration must also be given to the mobilising potential of concepts such as cash, working capital, assets and, not least, cost. All provide illustrations of where accounting has made operational, and therefore powerful, more abstract notions of economic discourse.

In ways such as these accounting has come to play a positive role in creating our present conceptions of organized endeavour. Whilst in part reflecting many other parameters of organizational life, accounting also has played a more active role in constructing the organizational world in which it is now embedded, shaping views of both the constraints on organized action and the ends which it seeks to serve. There is, in other words, a complex interplay between the reflective and the constitutive roles of accounting,[4] the former serving to create accounting's dependency on the organizations in which it is embedded and the latter often constraining organizations in the name of the possibilities and potentialities of the accounting craft.

The external origins of internal accounts

The conference had explicitly aimed to focus on the organizational nature of the accounting craft. The objective had been to provide some bases for appreciating how accounting was implicated with other aspects of organizational functioning.

At an early stage in the proceedings, however, such an aim was seen to be a partial one. Just as accounting could not be disentangled from the organizational, so the organizational could not be disassociated from the wider social context in which it in turn was embedded. Accounting, thereby, increasingly came to be seen as a phenomenon subject to the influences of both the particular organization and the wider social fabric in which it functioned.

Many of the organizational influences on accounting were seen to be specific manifestations of social influences, pressures and tensions. The State, for instance, in trying to further its own missions had repeatedly provided a basis for the elaboration of calculative endeavours within the enterprise. Its strategies for the control of prices and wages had resulted in the furtherance of those accounting procedures which sought to define, examine, restrain and plan within the organization those phenomenon which had a macro-economic significance at the national level. In the name of both economic crisis and growth the State had sought to further a regime of economic awareness within both organizations and those constituencies, such as the labour movement, which were deemed to have an interest in them. Calling upon conceptions of economic efficiency and effectiveness (and more recently "value for money"), the State repeatedly had tried to reform both its own administrative apparatus and the management practices of those organizations which were thought to play a significant role in the national economy.

Wider social agencies, including those of the State, the media and the professional institutions of the accounting craft, also could play a significant role in establishing a view of both the prevailing technical state of the accounting art and those managerial practices which were regarded as legitimate and in order. A view of the current, the modern, the desirable and the achievable could be propogated with some autonomy from the particular needs and histories of specific organizations. Accounting, particularly when professionalised,

---

[4] A further discussion of the reflective and constitutive roles of accounting is contained in Burchell *et al.* (forthcoming).

could achieve, and indeed had achieved, some degree of independent action. Solutions could indeed hunt for problems. The craft itself could influence the organizational. Equally significantly, organizations seeking to respond to the pressures of their environments could seek to utilise particular accounting and management practices in the name of the external legitimacy they could endow rather than on the basis of any presumed internal consequences. Indeed with the social thereby becoming the organizational, management might even uncouple their internal procedures and actions from the externally orientated practices of a rational management regime. So although influenced by the social, the organizational might even live in a state of flux with it.

The internal tensions and conflicts within organizations also cannot be detached from broader social movements. Concerns with the humanization of management practices in particular organizations have rarely existed in isolation of social movements which have provided a basis for their rhetoric and aims. The emphasis on the social in accounting itself has been a manifestation of the broader mobilisation of attempts to construct the organization in different terms. Equally, the ways in which accounting has sought to further a particular hierarchical order within organizations cannot be seen outside of the context of the conflicts between different social groups. In this sense accounting has both mirrored the context in which it has operated and enabled it to function in the ways it has. Only certain phenomenon have been regarded as costly. Particular conceptions of time have been emphasised. The benefits that have been incorporated into accounting calculations have not occurred in isolation of the socio-economic fabric to which they seek to relate. Accounting, in other words, has played a not insignificant role in embedding the social into the organizational. Accordingly its practice can never be seen in purely organizational terms.

Such a conclusion is a paradoxical one to emerge from a conference dedicated to exploring the organizational nature of the accounting craft. It reflects, however, the highly interdependent nature of our social world and the complex ways in which accounting has come to be embedded in our everyday lives. The social is not and cannot be isolated from the organizational. Indeed, in part at least, the social is manifest in the organizational and the organizational, in turn, constitutes a significant part of the social. It might even be useful to see the social as passing through the organizational, with both wider and more localised concerns calling upon practices such as accounting to create an ambiguous but nevertheless tethered conception of reality.

The methodologies of accounting research

The paucity of empirical studies of accounting in action was a major constraint on the conference deliberations. Repeatedly it had to be recognised how little was known of the accounting endeavour.

Our organizational colleagues had assumed that accounting researchers would be applied social scientists, committed to exploring the intricacies of accounting in practice. They had presumed that by now behavioural and organizational enquiries would have resulted in a mass of insights into the ways in which accounting was related to the fabric of organizational life. Indeed they had come to be illuminated on the relationship of accounting to the organizational, the strategic and the social. Those expectations could not be met however. The simple fact is that accounting research has tended to isolate itself from accounting in practice, if not accounting practice. The vast majority of efforts have been devoted to furthering the technical ediface of the accounting craft rather than seeking to illuminate the ways in which accounting intersects with the organizational and comes to have the significance it now has.

All too clearly if accounting researchers are to advance our understanding of the accounting context very different methodological perspectives will be required. There is a very real need for theoretically informed studies of both the use and design of accounting systems. Much more needs to be known of the ways in which accounting reflects, reinforces or even constrains the strategic postures adopted by particular organizations and of the ways in which accounting relates to the structures that are created for ensuring a coherent and vertically responsible organization. Studies of accounting changes also could do much to illustrate the nature of the diverse forces, both internal and external to the organization, that are operating on the accounting craft. Such studies also might help to cast some light on the ways in which the ambiguities that so often pervade accounting practice might play a positive role on bridging different, if not conflicting, pressures on accounting to change.

Of course all such investigations require the very commitment that is missing in accounting research to-date – a commitment to study, analyse and interpret accounting in the contexts in which it operates. The fact that so little of this work has been done suggests that change will not be easy. The constraints on organizational empirical inquiry must be very real indeed. To-date the difficulties of access and the inexperience of accounting researchers have been important factors. More significant, however, may be those pressures of the academic reward structure which push for speedy and voluminous research, the very low legitimacy which somewhat paradoxically has been given to grounded empirical inquiry, and the marginal commitment which many academic accountants have to the research endeavour. Unfortunate though these constraints may be, they nevertheless are very real ones. Accordingly change will not occur by mere ennunciation. Demonstration is a much more likely route. We can only hope that slowly, but surely, new precedents can be established by adventurous researchers seeking to explore what lies behind today's accounting condition.

CONCLUSION

Organizational inquiry remains a new area of investigation for accounting research. Despite accounting being given an organizational rationale, we have few insights into the factors which influence accounting systems in the contexts in which they operate.

When one reviews the organizational research on accounting that has been undertaken to-date, it is clear that much of it has been limited in scope, fragmentary and essentially atheoretical. The primary concerns often have tended to be the the laudable but nevertheless constraining ones of exposing defects in the accounting craft and seeking a basis for the reform of prevailing practice. Useful though such inquiries often may be, there nevertheless is a very real danger that if too fragmentary in nature they can serve to perpetuate or even to foster myths about the organizational practice of accounting. What is needed are more substantive investigations orientated towards providing bases for understanding or explaining the workings of accounting in action. Yet it is precisely such studies that have been neglected to-date.

However, as the studies collected in this issue illustrate, there are signs of an emergence of interest in the organizational nature of accounting. The origins of this are diverse, spanning economics, organization theory and sociology. Frequently non-accountants have taken the lead. Economists, for instance, have started to probe into the roles served by accounting in the construction of modern organizational forms and their links to external agents. Organization theorists recetly have become much more interested in questions of information and control, in the process exploring into not only the taken for granted roles which such practices are presumed to serve but also the symbolic and even political aspects of organizational life with which they can become intertwined. And sociologists too have started to recognise the research potential offered by the accounting craft, asking questions about how accounting might be related to the more general elaboration of calculative practices in modern society, the ways in which accounts have provided a powerful calculus for forging a new visibility which can facilitate specific modes of control within the business enterprise in particular, and the more legitimising functions of the accounting craft.

Most of these influences are reflected in the present collection. The result is an impression of an area in motion. Together the papers (and the discussant's remarks) provide both a useful insight into research in progress and a helpful agenda for future inquiries.

BIBLIOGRAPHY

Ashton, R. H., Deviation-Amplifying Feedback and Unintended Consequences of Management Accounting Systems, *Accounting, Organizations and Society* (1976) pp. 289–300.

Baiman, S., Agency Theory in Management Accounting: A Survey, *Journal of Accounting Literature* (Spring 1982) pp. 154–213.

Batstone, E., Systems of Domination, Accommodation, and Industrial Democracy, in Burns, T.R., Karlsson, L.E. & Rus, V. (eds.) *Work and Power: The Liberation of Work and Control of Political Power*, pp. 249–272 (London: Sage, 1979).

Birnberg, J. C., Turpolec, L. & Young, S. M., The Organizational Context of Accounting, *Accounting, Organizations and Society* (1983) pp. 111–129.

Boland, R. J. & Pondy, L. R., Accounting In Organizations: A Union of Natural and Rational Perspectives, *Accounting, Organizations and Society* (1983) pp. 223–224.

Burchell, S., Clubb, C., Hopwood, A., Hughes, J. & Nahapiet, J., The Roles of Accounting in Organizations and Society, *Accounting, Organizations and Society* (1980) pp. 5–27.

Burchell, S., Hopwood, A. G. & Clubb, C., Accounting in its Social Context: Towards a History of Value Added in the UK, *Accounting, Organizations and Society* (forthcoming).

Connolly, T., On Taking Action Seriously: Cognitive Fixation in Behavioural Decision Theory, in
176 Ungson, G. R. & Braunstein, D. N. (eds.) *Decision Making: An Interdisciplinary Inquiry* pp. 42–47 (Kent, 1982).

Cooper, D., Tidiness, Muddle and Things: Commonalities and Divergencies in Two Approaches to Management Accounting Research, *Accounting, Organizations and Society* (1983) pp. 269–286.

Cummings, L. L., A Framework for Decision Analysis and Critique, in Ungson, G. R. & Braunstein, D. N. (eds.) *Decision Making: An Interdisciplinary Inquiry* pp. 298–308 (Kent, 1982).

Edwards, R., Contested Terrain: *The Transformation of the Workplace in the Twentieth Century* (New York: Basic Books, 1979).

Flamholtz, D., The Markets and Hierarchies Framework: A Critique of the Models Applicability to Accounting and Economic Development, *Accounting, Organizations and Society* (1983) pp. 147–151.

Flamholtz, E., Accounting, Budgeting and Control Systems in Their Organizational Context: Theoretical and Empirical Perspectives, *Accounting, Organizations and Society* (1983) pp. 153–169.

Gowler, D. & Legge, K., The Integration of Disciplinary Perspectives and Levels of Analysis in Problem Oriented Organizational Research, Working Paper 81/3, Oxford Centre for Management Studies (1981).

Hayes, D. C., Accounting for Accounting: A Story about Managerial Accounting, *Accounting, Organizations and Society* (1983) pp. 241–249.

Hindess, B., Power, Interests and the Outcomes of Struggles, *Sociology* (November 1982) pp. 498–511.

Hopwood, A. G., The Path Ahead, *Accounting, Organizations and Society* (1976) pp. 1–4.

Hopwood, A. G., Towards an Organizational Perspective for the Study of Accounting and Information Systems, *Accounting, Organizations and Society* (1978) pp. 3–13.

Hopwood, A. G., Burchell, S. & Clubb, C., The Development of Accounting in Its International Context: Past Concerns and Emergent Issues, in Roberts, A. (ed.) *A Historical and Contemporary Review of the Development of International Accounting* (Georgia State University, 1980).

Horovitz, J. H., *Top Management Control in Europe* (London: Macmillan, 1980).

Johnson, T., The Search for Gain in Markets and Firms: A Review of the Historical Emergence of Management Accounting Systems, *Accounting, Organizations and Society* (1983) pp. 139–146.

Kerr, S., Accounting, Budgeting and Control Systems in Their Organizational Context: Comments by The Discussant, *Accounting, Organizations and Society* (1983) pp. 171–174.

March, J. G. & Shapra, Z., Behavioural Decision Theory and Organizational Decision Theory, in Ungson, G. R. & Braunstein, D. N. (eds.) *Decision Making: An Interdisciplinary Inquiry*, pp. 92–115 (Kent, 1982).

Markus, M. L. & Pfeffer, J., Power and the Design and Implementation of Accounting and Control Systems, *Accounting, Organizations and Society* (1983) pp. 205–218.

Merton, R., The Unanticipated Consequences of Purposive Social Action, *American Sociological Review* (1936) pp. 894–904.

Meyer, J. W., On the Celebration of Rationality: Some Comments on Boland and Pondy, *Accounting, Organizations and Society* (1983) pp. 235–240.

Mirvis, P. H. & Lauter, E. E. III, Systems are not Solutions: Issues in Creating Information Systems that Account for the Human Organization, *Accounting, Organizations and Society* (1983) pp. 175–190.

Mitroff, I. I. & Mason, R. O., Can We Design Systems for Managing Messes? Or, Why So Many Management Information Systems are Uninformative, *Accounting, Organizations and Society* (1983) pp. 195–203.

Otley, D. T., The Contingency Theory of Management Accounting: Achievements and Prognosis, *Accounting, Organizations and Society* (1980) pp. 413–428.

Platt, J., *Realities of Social Research: An Empirical Study of British Sociologists* (London: Sussex University Press and Chatto and Windus, 1976).

Pondy, L., On Real Decisions, in Ungson, G. R. & Braunstein, D. N. (eds.) *Decision Making: An Interdisciplinary Inquiry*, pp. 309–311 (Kent, 1982).

Spicer, B. H. & Ballew, V., Management Accounting Systems and the Economics of Internal Organization, *Accounting, Organizations and Society* (1983) pp. 73–96.

Tiessen, P. & Waterhouse, J. H., Towards a Descriptive Theory of Management Accounting, *Accounting, Organizations and Society* (1983) pp. 251–267.

Weick, K. E., Rethinking Research on Decision Making, in Ungson, G. R. & Braunstein, D. N. (eds.) *Decision Making: An Interdisciplinary Inquiry*, pp. 325–332 (Kent, 1982).

Commentary
The Growth of "Worrying" about Management Accounting

Anthony G. Hopwood

Until recently it has been rare for accounting to be interrogated in the name of either its organizational functioning or its precise organizational effects. Accounting discourse has remained a purely technical one. Little effort has been invested in exploring the ways in which it intersects with other organizational processes, the actual consequences which it has, and the implications of these for organizational performance. The justifications given for accounting practice, both contemporary and prospective, not only have continued to reside in the technical domain but also have been content to draw on presumptions of its organizational desirability rather than a more pragmatic concern with its actual effects. The result is that accounting, although undoubtedly an influential part of organizational practice, nevertheless has remained an isolated craft, with its normative presuppositions only rarely tested against the very practical contexts that its practitioners somewhat paradoxically continue to emphasize.

Now, however, there are some encouraging signs that these manifestations of the accounting past are slowly starting to change in both the worlds of academic inquiry and practice.

Professor Kaplan's chapter is both symptomatic of, and a significant contribution to, the changes that are taking place in management accounting research. Rather than being content with designing, at a distance, ever more sophisticated technical procedures that seemingly have the potential to improve organizational decision making and control, researchers increasingly have become more interested in understanding management accounting as it is, the factors that influence the forms it takes and the organizational consequences it actually has. Albeit slowly, management accounting research is starting to confront management accounting practice.

Of course, this development is manifested in many and various ways. Accounting practice is being interrogated from a number of very different perspectives. There are those who seek to understand its economic rationality in organizational terms. Others place the emphasis directly on the organizational or social or even political nature of accounting practice. More significantly, perhaps, even the newer variety of management accounting researchers seemingly are content to remain theorists of the accounting craft. Despite the growing concern with confronting practice that is implicit in a number of the new approaches, very few have sought to directly observe management accounting in practice. Kaplan is one of these few and, because of this, his contribution is even more significant.

Kaplan's arguments also are interesting because they are reflective of a growing realization that management accounting not only is not what it should be but also might even be having effects that it
180 shouldn't have. Of course the later realization that practice is subject to unanticipated dysfunctional consequences certainly is not a new one, not least in the research community. Until recently, however, it is fair to say that it has been possible to presume that, although present, the undesirable "side effects" did not prevent the achievement of the main management accounting task. The icing, in other words, was perhaps starting to deteriorate but the cake itself was still regarded as wholesome. Such a presumption, however, is now being questioned. A more radical view that something "might," but only might, be more fundamentally astray with the management accounting craft interestingly started to emerge in the corporation rather than in the academy and Kaplan has provided the first research statement of this growing focus of "corporate worrying."

The history of the development of worrying about management accounting has not been documented as yet. Indeed I sense that much of it has been masked as corporations have simply introduced other management strategies and techniques that complement the increasingly limited and rigid practices of accounting. Other control techniques have been made to operate alongside management accounting, as Kaplan notes. Lateral overlays of information have been introduced to provide the integration that has become more important in organizations segmented by the vertically oriented influence of accounting practice. Other management disciplines even have started to confront the problems involved in the control of cost structures very different from those that both accompanied management accounting's birth and underlie many of the pronouncements made in the textbooks and manuals of the craft. However, despite these important complementary developments, there nevertheless is now a more direct history of practical worrying about management accounting.

The organizational rigidities that were furthered by many management accounting practices were of concern to those who sought to implement more flexible forms of work organization in the late 1960s and early 1970s. The limited notions of costliness incorporated into traditional systems were clearly identified at the same time. At a more general level, a number of major manufacturing organizations started to realize how their existing management information and control systems, including the management accounting systems, might be implicated in the narrowing of management attention onto the purely economic; in the construction of far too short conceptions in time; in a rigidity of organizational structures that was clearly dysfunctional in an era of uncertainty and change; and in a costly regime of suboptimal decision making. 181

In the early 1970s Philips was one of the earliest corporations to specifically identify this disease. In subsequent years other major corporations came to a similar realization, particularly as a result of an intensification in their competitive environment which highlighted the organizational costliness of their cost accounting systems. The rise of strategic notions of corporate management only served to further the perception of a problem as management strategists grappled with the difficulty of relating traditional short-term, accounting-based oriented management information systems to the needs of a more aggressive formulation and monitoring of corporate strategy.

The net result of these developments was a slowly growing corporate awareness of the types of problems discussed in Kaplan's chapter. Some organizations established working parties and study groups in the area. One even restricted any changes in its financial control systems until it had a better idea of where it was going. The Ford "After Japan" ("AJ") program was seen to have implications for their massive existing commitment to financial control systems. In numerous other organizations the traditional accounting information flows are being supplemented, particularly in the name of the vocabulary of "strategy."

Still, however, traditional notions of the management accounting craft are firmly entrenched, as Kaplan's chapter makes clear. As someone from the United Kingdom, surely one of the most accounting-intensive countries in the Western world, I have to agree with his view that accounting is still about accounting. In most of its manifestations it appears to remain an organizational practice rather loosely connected with changes occurring in other organizational arenas. Its emphasis is still on the narrowly financial, the short term, and the organizationally constraining. Although there are some signs of change, these are slow to emerge, contained within relatively few organizations and very poorly known and understood.

Kaplan seeks to account for the seeming permanence of the old in terms of organizational lag and traditionalism. Again, coming from the United Kingdom, I cannot disagree with many of the points he makes in this respect. Management accounting as we now know it did arise amidst the very specific cost structures and control problems that characterized manufacturing organizations of the past. Accounting system reform does appear to be an unknown art. Financial accounting has had a dominant influence, and one that might still be increasing. Textbooks, in particular, and the accounting education process, more
182 generally, are still firmly grounded in the traditions of the past. Until recently, information processing technologies have provided a very constraining influence. And few, if any, alternative conceptions of accounting have been, or even are now being articulated. Accounting still is accounting.

However, although I share Kaplan's view that these factors are implicated to a significant extent in the conservatism that pervades accounting practice, I am far less convinced that together they give an adequate account of accounting as it is. I admit the problems of articulating alternative explanations: Accounting practice is an inadequately researched domain. It is even difficult to isolate the full variety of forms that it takes, let alone outline the factors that lie behind its development and the linkages that it has with other organizational practices. Be that as it may, other considerations are involved in accounting as it is. Some of them, at least, might help us to understand why senior corporate management has not sought to grapple with the problems of accounting practice in the ways that Kaplan might have expected.

The first such factor relates to some of the diverse and conflicting influences that have an impact on accounting practice. Kaplan emphasizes the needs of new manufacturing processes, their attendant cost structures and control needs, and a more competitive environment. But the very same competitive environment that has highlighted the importance of flexibility, noneconomic competitive advantages, and the significance of a more strategic, longer term perspective, also have reinforced the relevance of the immediate and the traditionally economic. Budgets have not only been tightened but revised much more frequently. Standards have been cut. Cash controls have been introduced to complement cost controls. A renewed emphasis has been placed on financial responsibility, accountability, and control. In many organizations these complementary factors have resulted in a vast increase in the regime of economic calculation that pervades organizational life.

So, not only is accounting alive and well, but so is a concern with many of its traditional emphases. The short term has been of significance alongside the longer term. The economic has been emphasized alongside the noneconomic. The very real requirements for flexibility have had to compete with a renewed interest in the constraining and the specific. In other words, all the accoutrements of what has been provocatively called "newly poor behavior" (Olofsson and Svalander 1975), in which accounting traditionally has been implicated, have been very actively competing for organizational space, visibility, and significance with what might be seen as the very different manage- 183
ment practices associated with the rise of the strategic and its less direct concerns with the economic. And no doubt a lot of the balancing of these competing pressures has been done by practitioners firmly grounded in the concerns of the past.

It would have been illuminating if Kaplan had specifically sought to identify the positive interests that there might have been in the accountings of the past rather than just confronting the difficulties faced by the emergence of the new. Further research most definitely needs to confront the variety of current organizational forces influencing accounting. Accounting needs to be seen as emerging and functioning in a conflicting domain with divergent interests, needs, and perspectives seeking to attach themselves to its technical procedures.

A second factor lying behind accounting practice as it is might reside in the diversity of roles that accounting serves in organizations. In part, Kaplan points to this when he contrasts the needs of the new with management accounting's present domination by the dictates of an increasingly regulated corporate financial accounting. Of course the two need not be so tightly coupled. They were not in the past and they are not in some other national contexts. However, one would like to know more about what is at stake in the intertwining that we see today. Rather than too readily labeling it as a manifestation of lag or ignorance or both, one might probe more into the roles that perhaps are being asked of accounting practice in organizations.

In saying this I draw on a view of the roles that accounting serves that go beyond the directly decision-facilitating ones that are implicit not only in Kaplan's paper but in much of the contemporary accounting literature (Burchell et al. 1980). Although the reformist rationales that underlie that decision-facilitating role are valuable, they should be complemented with a much more explicit appreciation of how accounting has been involved in the construction and furtherance of organizational power structures, in the creation and propagation of the goals of organized endeavors, and in the establishment of a dominant pattern of economic visibility that pervades the organization.

When seen in such terms, accounting is involved with much more than directly facilitating managerial action. It is concerned with making visible and thereby governable the detailed work processes of an organization. It provides for both aggregating and disaggregating organizational actions and outcomes—a powerful tool in the hands of organizational managers. It is involved with the establishment of a language of organizational motive, with rendering into the domain of the economic important aspects of the physical and task reality of the
184 organization. And it is quite centrally involved in the construction of operational concepts of accountability, responsibility, and even performance which play a significant role in the creation of a manageable organizational regime.

Such wider organizational roles provide an important basis for understanding not only the development and present functioning of accounting but also the paradoxes and seeming inadequacies of its practice which Kaplan so acutely observes. Although accounting's involvement with facilitating operational decision making is important, not least in the management of change and improvement, that alone cannot provide anywhere near a complete basis for appreciating accounting as it is, the conflicting nature of the organizational pressures on it, and the effects that it actually has. The language of motives, power, and control must be utilized alongside that of decision making. Accounting has to be seen as an influential organizational ritual and an instrument of control and governance as well as a decision aid. The metaphors of acccounting as an "ammunication" and "rationalization machine" need to complement those of the "answer" and "learning machines" that characterize so much of official accounting discourse (Burchell et al. 1980).

A third factor lying behind the present practice of accounting is the professional competition that pervades the management arena. Organizations may need to be managed and controlled, but that can be done in a multiplicity of different ways. Different organizations have invested in different regimes of control. Control practices and emphases have changed over time. And of particular importance in the present context, different occupational and professional groups have competed for the right to control the corporate arena (Armstrong, 1985).

When seen in such terms, a reliance on accounting controls cannot be dissociated from the rise to power of the corporate accountant and financial manager as compared with, for instance, the engineer or the personnel manager. This is not the place to discuss what might have been at stake in the growing significance of industrial accountants and the techniques and procedures that they brought into the organizational arena. Suffice it to say that the conflict for control of the management of the corporation has been resolved in different ways in different contexts. The accountant as a corporate manager is very much a phenomenon of the Atlantic fringe countries of the United States, the United Kingdom and, possibly, the Netherlands—all countries that are playing a leading role in the worrying that is taking place over the adequacy of management accounting practice. As
Horovitz (1980) makes clear in his comparative study of management control practices in European countries, not only are financial management practices less well developed in continental European countries but also a much greater investment has been made in the creation of alternative visibilities in the organization. There appears to be a more active competition for management attention between the visibilities of the technical, the human, the financial, and the marketplace.

Comparative and historical studies may play an important role in helping us understand the factors implicated in the accounting practices of today. Equally, but somewhat more provocatively, they might well show how the imperatives and justifications that are so often associated with different management practices emerge from, as well as result in, the practices that we observe today.

One final factor is of importance in understanding management accounting as it is. Most justifications and indeed studies of accounting practice emphasize its internal organizational roles. Kaplan's chapter has adopted this viewpoint, as has this commentary so far. However, further insights into both the practice and functioning of accounting, not least in manufacturing organizations, can be gained from an appreciation of how it came to be involved in the social as well as the organizational management of the corporation.

The discussion so far has been suggestive of this point. This commentary has emphasized the potential of accounting for furthering particular conceptions of organizational power. Attention has been given to the regime of economic visibility created by accounting practices. Accounting's involvement in the construction of governable organizations has been highlighted. And accounting's dependency on a significant professionalized body of practitioners has at least been considered. All of these points provide a basis for understanding the significant linkages between the organizational and the social practice of accounting.

Accounting, when seen in such terms, is more than a mere technical organizational practice oriented to the furtherance of pregiven conceptions of organizational efficiency and achievement. It is a practice that has come to play a significant role in the very articulation and furtherance of the concepts on which it is grounded. Operating, as it does, in organizations where the elucidation of both the ends and the means of organized endeavor resides in a contested domain rather than in one that is subject to the dictates of a pregiven rationale, accounting can be seen as having the characteristics of an interested practice that is
186 concerned with creating and quite actively mobilizing, rather than merely facilitating, the context that it is used to regulate.

Such a perspective is particularly useful when comparative understandings are needed of accounting practice—not an insignificant stimulus for the present questioning. In some contexts the corporation may have been a less significant site for social control. Organizational participants may have already been inculcated into the norms appropriate for the operation of a manageable organizational regime. Accounting then may well have been able to concentrate on its organizational roles. Elsewhere, however, any such presumption may not have been in order. With the corporation itself being a very active site for social action, investments were made in organizational practices that sought to create a more disciplined and controllable work force, an economic vocabulary of organizational motive, and a legitimacy for organizational authority and influence as well as an effective management process. In many Western countries accounting was created and often still functions at just such an intersection of the organizational and the social. It is doubtful whether its development, present functioning, effects, and the contradictions to which it is subjected can be understood outside of this context.

On this basis I therefore conclude these comments by emphasizing that a recognition of accounting as being such a multifaceted practice is important for understanding many of the problems with today's practices. Residing in the realms of both the organizational and the social, they are subjected to both the demands of control and decision making. While undoubtedly influenced by the dictates of traditionalism, accounting also has been shaped by occupational competition, very diverse organizational demands, and even conflicting contemporary pressures. So although often treated as an isolated and purely technical organizational phenomenon, the history of the emergence of accounting as we now know it, its present organizational functioning, and its specific consequences and effects, cannot be understood in such isolated terms. Any accounting of accounting, be it to use the accounting language, historical or current, must be based on a wider appreciation of the contexts in which it emerged and the very diverse expectations that are held of it.

Such a perspective is helpful for understanding the dilemmas, undesirable effects, and even lags identified by Kaplan. It can provide a way of understanding the contradictions currently faced by accounting practice. It can illuminate the factors that both mobilize and constrain accounting developments. And it can provide a basis for appreciating the changing pressures that are impinging on accounting as we know
it. For the corporate arena is not a stable one. The salience of past 187
needs can change. The expectations that are held of particular management practices can be volatile, and different occupational groups can seek to renegotiate the interests and influence they have in corporate control.

When seen in such terms, Kaplan has provided us with some significant insights. His chapter provides us with a rich, provocative, and illuminating start on a wider exploration of the accounting craft. His contribution has served to problematize the accounting craft. That has not been done so succinctly and pertinently before. Not only has Kaplan usefully questioned the effects that accounting has, but he has also highlighted the very real need for research to confront the specifics of accounting as it is. I share Bob Kaplan's view of a new, more organizationally grounded appreciation of accounting. Equally, however, I share his view of the sheer magnitude of the steps that are needed to create a different accounting future. A considerable organizational and intellectual distance still needs to be traversed.

References

Armstrong, Peter. "Changing Management Control Strategies: The Role of Competition Between Accountancy and Other Organizational Professions." *Accounting, Organizations and Society*, 1985.

Burchell, Stuart, Colin Clubb, Anthony Hopwood, John Hughes, and Janine Naphapiet. "The Roles of Accounting in Organizations and Society." *Accounting, Organizations and Society*, 1980, 5–27.

Horovitz, Jacques H. *Top Management Control in Europe*. London: Macmillan, 1980.

Olofsson, C., and P. A. Svalander. "The Medical Services Change Over to a Poor Environment." University of Linkoping Working Paper, 1975.

1 Management accounting and organizational action: an introduction

Anthony G. Hopwood
London School of Economics and Political Science

Now is an opportune time to appraise the state of management accounting research. Some important aspects of the technical practice of the subject are in the process of being re-examined by practitioners and, for somewhat different reasons, research perspectives are also starting to be questioned and slowly changed. A body of knowledge that until recently seemed adequate is now entering into a period of flux. The taken-for-granted is starting to be seen as more problematic; organizational assumptions, linkages and consequences that for long have remained implicit in the design and functioning of management accounting systems are now being made explicit; and, as a result, a very different array of questions are being asked of both management accounting concepts and practice.

Such a re-examination partly reflects the fact that accounting practices designed to serve the organizations of the past are now in the process of confronting the different contingencies of the present. Different approaches to organizational structuring are creating different information needs for decision-making and control. Greater emphasis is being placed on the need to service both local and central management needs for information (Hopwood, 1982); the roles which accounting information can play in facilitating co-ordination in integrated organizations are becoming more important (Galbraith, 1973; Hopwood, 1977); and the more diverse information needs of semi-autonomous business units being created within the framework of larger organizations are now recognized. The language of strategy has entered into the managerial vocabulary, providing, in the process, a different basis on which to appraise the adequacy of present information flows and a different perspective for shaping the accounting practices of the future (Goold, 1986; Simmonds, 1983). Accounting is also being called upon to play a quite explicit role in the mobilization of organizational change. No longer seen as a mere passive reckoning of the economics of the past, accounting systems are now being implicated in the design of different approaches to the management of organizational visibility and different incentives for organizational action. And although there are those who wish for still further change, accounting is already starting to become much more involved with the articulation of more economic-orientated vocabularies of managerial concerns. Related to the latter, the advance of an economic rationale for action into different sectors of society than those traditionally subject to a regime of economic calculation is also creating new pressures for the elaboration and reform of accounting practice. Most obviously, accounting is being used as one means to infuse the public sector with the language, organizational practices and managerial concerns of the private (Hopwood, 1984a; Plowden, 1986). At the same time, changing task technologies in organizations are starting to create different economic structures for which to account (Kaplan, 1983, 1986) and developments in information-processing technology are creating a seemingly ever expanding array of new possibilities for designing, structuring and managing the information flows of the present and the future (Kaplan, 1986; McCosh, 1986).

All of these changes are now in the process of adding to the body of management accounting practice and knowledge. However, current developments are also more directly undermining the adequacy of the management accounting practices of the past. Although many traditional concerns with the economic control of the organization continue, a more turbulent, competitive
190 and changing environment has placed an ever greater premium on the need for relevant information, rapidly available and expressed in terms which are compatible with increasingly strategic conceptions of management. As a result, past emphases on the provision of routine, short-term information are starting to be appraised in different terms. The demand for *ad hoc* decision-specific information is growing (Earl and Hopwood, 1980). The wider organizational implications of rigid information structures are being recognized and a flexibility of information response is now at a premium. More active consideration is being given to the incorporation into accounting practice of models which can provide a more sympathetic and useful mapping of the contingencies and uncertainties of the present business world. And, for very similar reasons, attention is also being given to the ways in which accounting can constrain management perceptions of time. The debilitating effects of a continual emphasis on the short term are now seen to be problematic.

Although often having only an ambiguous relationship to the practice of the management accounting craft (Hopwood, 1984b), research in the area is also starting to go through a process of re-examination. Not only is it slowly starting to be influenced by the changing agenda of practice (Kaplan, 1983) but it is also independently adopting different perspectives from which to investigate the management accounting domain (Scapens and Arnold, 1986; Dent, 1986). Rather than being content merely to further the technical rationality of the craft, rather belatedly the research community is in the process of adopting a more appreciative stance. A diverse set of questions are now being asked of the organizational rationales for economic information flows (Aiken and Covaleski, 1986; Baiman, 1982; Burchell *et al.*, 1980; Cooper, 1981; Meyer, 1986), the ways in which management accounts permeate and modify organizational processes for decision-making and control (Dent, 1986; Hopwood, 1986), and, once again, the precise organizational consequences which stem from the use of the craft. No longer taking for granted either management accounting as it is or the roles which traditionally have been attributed to it, consideration is being given to the

organizational origins of accounting as we now know it (Johnson, 1986), to the ways in which its emergence has been enmeshed with the design and development of other approaches to the governance of the enterprise and to how such other strategies for organizational regulation and control have both impacted upon and, in turn, been themselves enabled by the developments in the regime of internal economic visibility that has been created by management accounting systems. Although such approaches remain preliminary and diverse (contrast, for example, Scapens and Arnold (1986), and Birnberg and Sadhu (1986), Dent (1986) and Johnson (1986)), much more attention nevertheless is being given to management accounting as it is and designs for its reform are starting to be moderated by an awareness of the practicalities of accounting in action. Management accounting is now starting to be questioned, examined and interrogated in the name of its organizational functioning. Members of the research community are becoming more interested in what organizations are doing and the rationales that might be implicit in this. An account of accounting
is beginning to be compiled. In the USA, the UK and continental Europe the
specificities, complexities and actual rather than envisaged consequences of the craft are now in the process of becoming the foci of research.[1]

It is these processes of both conceptual and practical re-examination which provide the context for the present book. The subsequent chapters focus on some of the changes occurring in the sphere of management accounting practice, the changing nature of research in the area and a number of significant current pressures for continued change.

After Horngren's introductory review of the changes that have occurred, and are still occurring, in management accounting research, Allen and Kirwan provide two views of the area from the perspective of practice, one from the viewpoint of a senior corporate financial executive and the other drawing on the experiences of a leading management consultant in the area. Thereafter, the detailed research reviews are organized around the contributions made by different disciplinary perspectives.

Johnson focuses on the changing nature of historical inquiries in the area, emphasizing how they are starting to throw more light on the emerging organizational roles played by cost and management accounting systems rather than merely document a story of isolated technical elaboration and advancement. The organizational embeddedness of accounting is also emphasized in Scapens and Arnold's discussion of the developments taking place in economic

1 Although there are examples of prior investigations into the organizational functioning of accounting by other social scientists (e.g. Argyris, 1952; Simon *et al.*, 1954; Whyte, 1955; Wildavsky, 1964), the concern of US accounting researchers with organizationally grounded inquiry is relatively recent (see Kaplan, 1983, 1986; Merchant and Simons, 1985). Interest in the UK and northern Europe emerged somewhat earlier (for the UK see the reviews of Colville (1981), Cooper (1977, 1981), Hopwood (1978), Hopwood and Bromwich (1984) and Otley (1984); discussions of the relevant Scandinavian literature appear in Lukka *et al.* (1984), Madsen and Polesie (1984), Ostman (1984), Samuelson (1986) and Hagg *et al.*, (1983)). For a more general discussion of differences in North American and European research in a closely allied discipline see Hofstede and Kassem (1976).

research. Contrasting an earlier emphasis on exploring and improving the economic rationality of technical accounting practices with more recent research on the economic roles served by management accounting systems in organizational monitoring and control, they show how such research is starting to provide a more adequate appreciation of the current state of practice and some of the factors that can induce it to change. Kaplan's review of the quantitative tradition of research also documents a process of re-examination and change. Aware of the rather equivocal relationship between practice and the technical sophistication of past quantitative research, he discusses some of the practical pressures which are questioning existing research emphases and creating new agendas for investigation.

Research into the organizational practice of the management accounting craft is explicitly discussed by Birnberg and Sadhu, and Dent. Concentrating on the growing body of research on the psychological and social-psychological aspects of the functioning of management accounting in action, Birnberg and Sadhu demonstrate how it is increasingly relating to issues of some significance for both understanding and improving the practical effectiveness of the craft. Dent thereafter reviews more recent research conducted into the organizational nature and functioning of accounting. He shows how a research perspective is emerging that is striving to relate management accounting systems to their wider organizational context. The relationships which they have to important aspects of organizational structure, strategy and process are reviewed from the perspective of current research and particular emphasis is given to the nature of the new research agenda that is starting to be created in this area.

In the final group of chapters consideration is given to some of the continuing pressures for management accounting change. Goold discusses the different needs for information which arise from a more strategic conception of management decision-making. The consequences of changes in information technology are discussed by McCosh and a British perspective on the developing interest in accounting for the public sector, a phenomenon evident in many countries at the present time, is provided by Plowden.

As Bromwich makes clear in his final review, together the contributions provide a view of an area in motion with the realms of both the practical and the scholarly being in the process of re-examining what hitherto has been taken for granted. By way of a preface to these contributions, the subsequent discussion aims to identify a number of issues which are relevant for an appreciation of the present context of management accounting. Consideration is given to some of the factors implicated in the development and current functioning of the craft, those of their consequences which have provided the basis for the current questioning of practice, and the implications which changing conceptions of management accounting might have for the conduct of research in the area.

The creation of management accounting as it is

Management accounting has not had a regular path of development. Born amidst the organizing upheavals which accompanied the emergence of the industrial system, from what we can gather, in the early days accounting within the enterprise was unevenly practised (Pollard, 1965). Identifying a strategic need for information, some entrepreneurs developed the rudiments of systems for costing and internal control (see Johnson, 1984, 1986, for a review). In such contexts a basis was started to be created for internal accountings to be related to the control and restructuring of the manufacturing process, the provision of economic incentives for action, and pricing and output decisions (Hopwood, 1987). Elsewhere, however, other firms relied on a market calculus and perceived no reason to devise elaborate accounting procedures.

The subsequent development of internal accountings demonstrated the importance of the mutual relationship between accounting and modes of organizing – a factor also of some significance when trying to appreciate the different patterns of development in the USA and the UK. In the USA the advance of management accounting seems to have been influenced by the rise of large vertically integrated and geographically dispersed enterprises which could no longer rely on market prices or external rules to guide economic action (Chandler, 1962, 1977; Chandler and Daems, 1979; Johnson, 1983). Accounting systems were devised and elaborated in order to provide a basis for internal processes of control and decision-making. Alongside the rise of a specialized managerial cadre, accounting appears to have created one of the important prerequisites for a managed internal economy within the enterprise. Even more extensive developments accompanied the rise of an interest in organizational efficiency and the role which what were seen as more scientific forms of management could play in this (Epstein, 1978; Wells, 1978). In the UK, in contrast, manufacturing enterprises were smaller, there were many fewer examples of mass production, and the process of rationalizing production was much slower (Hannah, 1976). The British class structure was not so conducive to the emergence of a new middle class of management professionals who would encourage such developments (Merkle, 1980), and industrial partnerships and family-owned firms remained the typical bases of organization and ownership in most types of manufacturing (Hannah, 1976). As a consequence, conditions in the UK were much less favourable to the widespread development of elaborated systems of cost accounting and internal financial control. Even so, some developments did occur. With growing international competition, a prolonged period of recession and increasing industrial concentration, a basis was provided for asking more precise questions of the economic functioning of the enterprise. An increasingly turbulent work force also enhanced the significance of obtaining economic control of the labour process (Littler, 1982) and articulating a more explicit economic rationale for action that could permeate into the inner workings of the enterprise (Batstone, 1979). Albeit slowly, the language and practices of costs and costliness did start to gain a greater managerial significance. However, it was the interventionist activities of a wartime government concerned with economic regulation and the control of prices and profits that provided a much more explicit incentive for the advancement of a more comprehensive regime of internal economic calculation in the UK (Loft, 1986). In the context of the First World War not only was a relevance created for advances in cost accounting but also the practice of the craft was endowed with a wider legitimacy. That and continued economic restraint appears to have provided an influential basis for the subsequent expansion of the craft in the UK (Armstrong, 1985, forthcoming).

Albeit in a number of different ways, a mutual relationship between internal accounting and modern modes of organizing, and social, as well as economic, management, nevertheless was born. In part, at least, the business enterprise started to be managed and controlled on the basis of the accounts of it. A particular regime of internal visibility started to become influential. Accounting developments, in turn, not only reflected the continuing paths of organizing

developments but also started to play a much more active role in facilitating and enabling these to take place. The modern interrelationship of accounting and the management of the enterprise was in the process of being forged.

Although there are enormous dangers in abstracting from the specific contexts of management accounting's emergence, it nevertheless is useful to consider some of the more general processes implicated in the rise of management accounting systems as we now know them. Recognizing that these always functioned in the diverse contexts of particular organizations and were always influenced by their specific contingencies and trajectories of development, there are still advantages to be gained from more critically examining some of the organizational tendencies underlying the advance of the craft and the ways in which it has come to function within organizations.

The penetrating accounting eye

Accounting provides a way of making visible the internal functioning of an organizational economy. It enables management to probe into the inner workings of the organization, to observe the processes of work, to assign to the physical nature of the organization an economic significance, and to both aggregate and, thereafter, again disaggregate in economic terms the mass of separate events which constitute organizational life. Where physical distance or architectural forms constrain managerial observation, an accounting system can provide a silent means of seeing. The otherwise unknown can be translated into an organizational record. The specific and the diverse can be generalized into economic terms. The accounting eye, although often itself unseen, can nevertheless render the organizational terrain not only visible but also, because of that, manageable and potentially controllable.

The visibility so created by accounting is not, however, a mere recording of what is otherwise there. The facts which enter into the organizational accounting are not merely collected but more actively created by the accounting craft

(Crawford, 1984). The categories of cost, profit, efficiency and capital are imposed onto the physical flows which constitute the organization. The activities of the human being are transformed into the language of the human resource. Organizational diversity is reduced and rendered meaningful in economic terms by its assimilation into accounting's categories. Rather than being merely revealed, a coherent organizational economy is a creation of the accounting craft. Not obviously flowing from the specifics of the organization as it is, the more standardized facts of organizational life are forged by the accounting of it.

The facts so created provide only a partial portrayal of organizational functioning, however. Their significance stems not only from what they emphasize and endow with a significance and an impression of reality but also from what they thereby exclude from the organizational record (Foucault, 1971). For in understanding the management accounting craft, it is as important to seek to appreciate where the accounting eye does not penetrate as it is to understand where it does. What organizational processes remain in the dark? What consequences of organized endeavour never enter into the organizational records? And with what effects? What concerns can be furthered by their incorporation into the archive? Equally, what is not transposed into the domain of the economic? What concerns must remain implicit, unknown and perhaps even illicit, remaining, as they do, unrecognized in the world of organizational facts?

So wrenching a partial domain of the observable from the complexities of organizational life, accounting provides an influential means for the governance and control of the enterprise. Rules, regulations and incentives can be mobilized around the domain of the purported factual. The detail of organizational action can be rendered meaningful in terms of overall organizational objectives and goals. The specific can thereby start to be more precisely reformed in the name of the general. The organization can become not only a less opaque concern but also one that can be more actively regulated, planned and controlled.

The will to know (Sheridan, 1980) in accounting terms has had numerous origins. Faced with the contingencies of an uncertain environment, management has striven to influence the inner workings of the enterprise (Hopwood, 1987). As questions have been asked of both the organizational actual and possible, investments have been made in rendering visible a particular and legitimate organizational terrain. Equally, the desire to regulate and control the internal labour process of the organization has also provided an influential incentive to penetrate into the organization, making visible the detailed workings of its technical core (Clawson, 1980). Human performance thereby has been brought into the domain of facts, enabling economics to become intertwined with the personal. And, finally, as is discussed below, agents external to the organization have also had an influential role to play in the expansion of the accounting eye. Whether they be agents of the state or the capital markets, their regulatory intentions and requests for information have served to expand significantly the activities which are enshrined within the organizational record.

By whatever means they arise, the facts of organizational life quickly become abstracted from the detailed functioning of the organization. The organizational record is physically, linguistically and managerially detached from the context from which it emerged and, as a result, the organization can come to be seen, known and managed in the name of the facts so established. They develop a significance and autonomy of their own. Rather than being seen as having a complex and often ambiguous relationship to the processes which they seek to represent, organizational accounts and records start to constitute a new truth, in the name of which the organization can itself be changed and reformed. The accounting eye can thereby start to be seen as the organization itself, providing a new reality on which to base organizational management and control.

Management accounting and the celebration of the present

The facts created by management accounting enable the organizational past to be continually brought into the organizational present (Crawford, 1984). Often divorced from the contingencies and uncertainties which were implicated in the circumstances from which they arose, a specific and a precise past can always be rendered into the here and now. With accounting, an organizational record is available for accessing. A more orderly past can thus be interrogated, analysed and compared. The immediate can be contrasted with the distant. A whole new reality of averages, ranks and relationships can be created. So detached from the specifics which gave it an original meaning, the stark factual past can more readily be endowed with a contemporary significance.

The techniques of accounting enable an active intervention in the processes of time. Indeed, their application can create a temporal fluidity as the practices of accounting for the past are also applied to bring forward the future into the present. So abstracted from its own temporal domain, the future can be examined as if it were a greater certainty in the present. By way of budgets and plans, what-might-be is given a current significance, being examined, analysed and decided upon as if it is. The future, thereby, like the past, can be made to be always with us.

Not only can managerial perceptions of uncertainty thereby be radically transformed but also the clinical act of assessing the future as if it were the present frequently ignores the power of human agency which is required to forge and create that future. As is now starting to be realized in a practical context, by focusing exclusively on its contemporary analysis, such a technology for managing the future does little to create the organizational conditions and processes out of which that future can be realized.

Nowhere is this more readily observable than in the area of investment analysis. The accounting telescope not only gazes into the future but also, by using the technology of discounting, wrenches it into the present for analysis and decision. Being so largely detached from the contingencies which will inevitably accompany it, the future-in-the-present can be subjected to detailed and detached analysis and evaluation. Desirable as this at times may be, it nevertheless ignores the role which such an orchestrated process of organizational detachment might play in constraining the mobilization of the very commitments and enthusiasms out of which a future can be made.

Accounting's celebration of the present is still a far too little appreciated but immensely important aspect of its functioning. Deriving, as it does, from its ability to create a domain of the factual which is divorced from the contexts out of which it either arises or will arise, it is one which can play a very significant role in organizational management, enabling the control of not only the immediate but also of both conceptions of the past and intentions for the future.

A normative intent

Management accounting is not only implicated in creating observations. Its practices also enable a more pro-active management of the organizational world. Arising initially out of the power of accounting to provide a basis for comparing and analysing across both time and space, the selective facts of organizational life instilled a concern with differences and with strategies for normalization (Foucault, 1977). The unproductive could be identified by its comparison with the productive, the inefficient with the efficient, the costly with the less costly, and the profitable with the loss-making. A whole new domain of organizational reality thereby emerged and one which stimulated an active search for strategies to eliminate the inferior and to enhance the superior. Not only could lessons be learnt from favourable circumstances but the requirements of the latter could start to be imposed upon the organization as a whole. Organizational life could not only be observed but accounting could also be implicated in strategies for its improvement. The organization could start to be mobilized in a much more detailed way. Standards, budgets and plans could be established in ways which could penetrate the specifics of the organization. The world of what is could thereby be constantly compared with what could and should be (Miller and O'Leary, 1987).

Such strategies of normalization are now a prevalent feature of organizations. Management accounting has become a dual activity. Bringing the facts of the past into the present to be compared with the norms which had been set in the past for the future which is today, it provides a powerful basis for the mobilization of the specifics of the organization in the name of the general. At one and the same time accounting can impose a normalizing intention upon the organization while bringing to attention the individual differences which are identified by that (Foucault, 1977).

Management accounting and the creation of an organizational order

Accounting is involved with the creation of a more orderly and manageable organization in a number of very different ways.

Organizational hierarchies are endowed with a greater significance and force by the delineation of responsibilities which accompany the use of the accounting craft and the subsequent processes of monitoring and performance review. The exercising of management authority thereafter can be more constrained, more legitimate and more effective. Formal managerial expectations can be more readily diffused through the organizational hierarchy. Performance can be subjected to a more meticulous review. Questioning can be related to prior plans. The use of power need no longer be general and diffuse as it focuses on the detailed representation of organizational activities which is cast in the accounts. A new enabling force can be given to the vertical mobilization of the organization.

Accounting is no less significant for facilitating the ordering and control of the spatial dimensions of organizational life. Implicated in the mapping of the organization into a more managerial space, it helps to give a very particular meaning to the patterns of segmentation which are imposed on the organizational terrain. Cost centres, profit centres, investment centres, strategic business units and subsidiaries all receive much of their significance from the accounting representation of them. Organizational events are thereby more easily attributed to particular managerial responsibilities. Recognized sequences of consequences are more readily confined within the intra-organizational boundaries. Accounting helps to isolate a realm of manageable organizational spaces.

Moreover, management accounting is also involved with the integration of the lateral and vertical orderings of the organization. Through budgets, plans and the subsequent processes of monitoring and review, one can be related to the other. A powerful basis for task co-ordination is created. Of equal significance, the local can be mobilized in the name of the whole. By the transformation of the diverse details of organizational activities by aggregated and subsequently disaggregated information, a powerful ability in itself, the specific can be related to overall objectives and plans. The language, categories and concerns of a financial motive can thereby infuse and change the detailed operational and technical functioning of the organization. A basis for a new economic order can be created.

The ordering potential of accounting also impacts upon the temporal dimension of organizational life. Time is not only made into a more fluid and seemingly more manageable factor in organizational functioning, as has already been discussed, but it itself is also ordered into distinct periods. Although stemming from wider social forces and involving other technologies (Landes, 1983), accounting nevertheless powerfully reinforces the salience of the year, the month and the day. Through accounting, moreover, time can be re-ordered as the temporality of financial transactions is related to different schemes of organizational events. And rather than facing an open-ended future, by plans, budgets and performance reports the organization can be made to focus on specific periods of time. Opportunities can be created for management to come to the end of one period of time before considering the activities associated with another.

The external origins of internal accounts

Management accounting has arisen to satisfy more than the internal task needs of management. The activities of external agencies and wider social movements have also left a significant impact on the flow of economic information which now pervades organizational life.

The regulatory activities of the state have been particularly influential in this respect. The emergence of corporate taxation served to increase both the regime of economic calculation within the enterprise and the cadre of organizational specialists associated with it. Wartime control of prices and profits has been equally influential, not only implanting in organizations more detailed systems of costing but also endowing these and the specialists associated with them with a greater social legitimacy and acceptability (Crawford, 1984; Loft, 1986). In more recent times, national strategies for macro-economic management have left important residues in the management accounting systems of organizations (Hopwood *et al.*, 1980). Policies for price control have reinforced the salience of cost information. Attempts to regulate profits have even resulted in a recognition of the revenue-enhancing potential of legitimate financial information. Wage-control policies have served to extend further the sphere of detailed economic calculation around the human resource (Burchell *et al.*, 1985). More generally, the state has frequently been a more direct catalyst for management accounting change, particularly in the UK (Armstrong, forthcoming). Associating the presence and use of accounting systems and procedures for the economic evaluation of investment opportunities with a competitive and profitable organizational stance, the furtherance of such systems has often been explicitly incorporated into national economic policies.

Managerial accounting also has been implicated in the control of wider social forces passing through the organization. Attempts to discipline and regulate a newly industrialized work force resulted in the development of management regulatory practices, including those of accounting. The growth of an organized labour movement provided an important incentive for a managerial interest in making visible the detailed work process of the organization, standardizing patterns of work behaviour, and using information systems to try to instil an economic incentive for action. Even more recently, changes in the relative power of the labour movement at times have resulted in an expansion of the domain of economic calculation in the enterprise. Accounting information has been more widely diffused to employees and their trade union representatives. More directly related to conventional views of management accounting, attempts have been made to relate internal modes of financial reporting to more detailed representation of the economic functioning of the production process through the use of categories such as value added (Burchell *et al.*, 1985). On occasions, experiments have also been made to provide a more comprehensive account of the employment relationship (Flamholtz, 1974; European Foundation for the Improvement of Living and Working Conditions, 1982; Hopwood, 1979a).

Management accounting has also been involved with the creation of a wider external legitimacy for the enterprise. As systems of budgeting, planning and financial performances assessment have become associated with organizational efficiency and effectiveness, at times they have been implemented because of the greater organizational legitimacy which such functional claims might be able to create.[2] Rather than being directly advanced in the name of internal management processes, management accounting has come to be seen as a cultural rather than a purely technical symbol of modernity and rational organizational functioning (Meyer and Rowan, 1977; Meyer, 1983; DiMaggio and Powell, 1983). Although management accountings having such origins can still become internally significant, not least because of the new interior visibility and management linkages which they create, the relationship which they have to the functioning of the organization is a question for empirical assessment rather than automatic presumption.

So, although invariably justified in terms of their internal management roles, management accounting systems can also reflect the wider social and environmental contexts in which they operate. While technically functioning within the organization, both their orientation and consequences can be external as well as internal.

200

Accounting and the practitioners of the accounting craft

One final tendency is worth explicit consideration. Along with the development and expansion of the management accounting domain a cadre of practitioners of the craft has arisen. Indeed, sometimes the activity has resulted in a distinct occupation (Loft, 1986), a factor which itself can introduce a new dynamic into the patterns of management accounting changes.

International comparisons suggest that such developments should not be endowed with any presumption of necessity, however. Different occupational claims to the area and different patterns of occupational specialization have emerged in different countries. When seen in such terms, it needs to be recognized that organizational control is itself a sphere for occupational competition (Armstrong, 1985), with accountants only sometimes becoming more influential than other control practitioners. The procedures of the management accounting craft can be and are designed, implemented and operated by business economists and analysts, industrial engineers and information system technologists, as well as by accountants *per se*. Indeed, this is an area where change is currently taking place as new bodies of management knowledge emerge, new management occupational groups arise and new demands are made for different organizational linkages between economic information systems and other aspects of organizational functioning.

2 Management accounting systems can also be involved with the direct management of external interests. Such uses might not be unusual in nationalized enterprises in the UK where, until recently, at least, planning and financial reporting procedures may have been orientated as much toward sponsoring civil service departments and political constituencies as to internal management operations. See Berry *et al.* (1985).

The organizational practice of management accounting

The path of management accounting's development has been neither a simple nor a linear one. A diverse array of factors have impinged on the domain of organizational economic calculation. Moreover, by playing a positive role in actively shaping the organizational forms we now know, management accounting has also provided some of the preconditions for its own subsequent development, often in ways that were not anticipated in the original formulation of any particular system. Indeed, the rise and growing recognition of such unanticipated consequences is one of the main elements in the contemporary development of 'worrying about management accounting' (Hopwood, 1985). We now turn to a consideration of some of these important implications of the underlying organizational tendencies associated with management accounting.

A diverse craft

The varied circumstances which have impinged on management accounting's development have resulted in a very diverse set of practices in the area. Not only are there significant national differences (Horovitz, 1980) but, within any single country, management accounting practices also vary from company to company, even within the same industrial or commercial sector (Dent, 1986). Seemingly, the state of practice reflects not only environmental, market and technological factors, which one might expect to result in some uniformity within a sector, but also the vagaries of particular organizational cultures, patterns of power and influence, and the specifics of the company history. Furthermore, within a single enterprise, the so-called management accounting system usually consists of only a partially integrated set of practices and procedures, many of which, to the rational observer, might appear to be in conflict with one another. Often reflecting the different historical junctures at which they were implemented, the different managerial and other interests prevailing upon them, and the changing fashions of the managerial world, as well as a poorly articulated body of accounting knowledge, the world of management accounting in practice often appears to be at odds with the myth of a more coherent and integrated phenomenon that permeates accounting texts and those manuals that seek to guide accounting change and reform.

Diversity also pervades the organizational linkages which ground accounting and other information and control systems into the processes of organizational life. Accounting and control departments are variously organized. Planning, budgeting and performance monitoring procedures operate at different organizational levels, are subject to different degrees of participation, have different expectations associated with them and different practices for their revision, and can even consider very different time periods. Accounting systems also serve to establish very different patterns of organizational segmentation and relate to the practices for the management of organizational interdependence in a variety of ways.

All told, the management accounting area is diverse, complex and even messy. At the very least, the state of practice bears only a loose relationship to the more generalized body of knowledge that seeks to embrace it. Although that might be an understandable implication of the varied factors that have impinged on the development of practices in the area, it nevertheless represents a significant problem for both practitioners and scholars who aim to have some more adequate appreciation of management accounting as it is.

A constitutive accounting

Although management accounting plays a significant role in mapping salient aspects of both the managerial task and the external environment into the organization, it also has the power to shape and influence organizational life on its own.

The environments that are mapped into the organization can become defined
 in accounting terms. From a positive point of view they can become 'profitable' or 'costly', 'cash cows' or 'rising stars'. More negatively perceived, the accounting mappings are only partial ones, with the accounting representations being as significant for what they exclude as for what they include for managerial attention.

Similarly, the organization structures which impinge on accounting practice do not have a manifestation that is independent of their accounting representation. Modes of organizational decentralization are defined in terms of cost, profit and investment centres; organizational units have accounting as well as management boundaries; and accounting mechanisms for the monitoring of subunit performance help to make real the powerful potential that is implicit within the organization chart. Equally, as we have discussed, accounting plays a significant role not only in shaping the visible map of what is known of organizational functioning but also in expressing and thereby influencing the objectives that are stated for organized action. An operational definition of profit has been a particularly powerful notion and consideration must also be given to the mobilizing potential of concepts such as cash, working capital, assets and, not least, cost. All provide illustrations of where accounting has made operational and therefore powerful within the organization more abstract notions of economic discourse. Finally, as we have seen, salient notions of time in organizations are invariably influenced by the accounting of them (Cooley, 1985).

In ways such as these accounting has come to play a positive role in creating our present conceptions of organized endeavour. While in part reflecting many other parameters of organizational life, accounting has also played a more active role in constructing the organizational world in which it is now embedded, shaping views of the constraints on organized action, the ends which it seeks to serve and the pragmatic means through which these can be achieved. There is, in other words, a complex interplay between the reflective and constitutive roles of accounting (Burchell *et al.*, 1985; Hopwood, 1985), the former serving to create accounting's dependency on the organizations in which it is embedded and the latter often constraining organizations in the name of the possibilities and potentialities of the accounting craft.

Such an interplay presents dilemmas to both the practitioner and the scholar. For the latter, the process of understanding the pattern of management accounting's development and its current functioning within the organization becomes a much more complex one, requiring more subtle frameworks for appreciating the practice of the craft. For the practitioner, the interplay can constrain the process of management accounting development. As accounting can both reflect and create the contexts in which it operates, it not only plays some role in shaping the preconditions for its own developments but also results in organizations which are not independent of, and therefore dependent upon, the accounting of the organizational past (Hopwood, 1987). In such circumstances management accounting change becomes a much more complex art – a factor that is now recognized by those worried about the adequacy of their present accountings.

Management accounting and that which happens in its name[3]

Conventional discussions of management accounting invariably presume that the craft is capable of achieving the claims that are made on its behalf. Management accounting, so we are told, is capable of enhancing organizational efficiency and performance. It can play a positive role in increasing managerial and employee motivations to perform. And management accounting can provide the type of information that can facilitate managerial decision-making, not least in environments characterized by uncertainty and doubt.

Increasingly, however, some, at least, of such highly generalized claims are being compared with the more equivocal impressions emerging from both research and practice.

A long tradition of scholarly inquiry has sought to illustrate the dysfunctional as well as functional consequences, both latent and manifest, of the management accounting craft (Argyris, 1952; Hayes and Abernathy, 1980; Hopwood, 1973, 1979b; Jasinski, 1956; Merchant, 1985; Ridgway, 1956). There have also been studies which have pointed to the ways in which accountings appear to proliferate amidst concerns with organizational crisis and decline rather than in the less problematic days of growth and success (Khandwalla, 1978; Olofsson and Svalander, 1975). Sometimes such research has even suggested ways in which the consequent desire for greater control can result in organizational practices which detract from rather than enhance the flexibility of managerial responses in such conditions (Starbuck *et al.*, 1978).

As we have already discussed, not unrelated concerns with the actual rather than the claimed achievements of accounting have now started to be articulated by some practitioners. Faced with economic restraint and often with increased competitive pressures, such practitioners have started to become concerned about the limitations of the routinized flows of information which accounting so often provides. Although rarely, if ever, expressed in ways other than the immediate set of implications for their own organizations, such questionings have resulted in a new awareness of the interdependency between management accounting and the human and social processes through which the objectives which are set for it are achieved.

Some of the factors implicated in such questioning can be appreciated in terms of the tendencies underlying the development of the craft that have been outlined above. The creation of a partial visibility can be seen to be problematic when organizational circumstances change. Management accounting's celebration of the present at times can be seen to constrain the development of a more future responsive stance. The diverse organizational and social roles served by the craft can be seen as being capable of resulting in organizational disorder rather than order as they become intertwined with the exercising of power and influence. The organizational rigidities which can follow from the constitutive roles of
204 management accounting can be better understood. It can be appreciated that the consequences of interventions in the organization in the name of management accounting are dependent on factors other than the intentions and means of organizational action which are specifically mobilized. A recognition can develop that actual outcomes also depend on the practical capacity of management accounting systems to encapsulate, penetrate and then influence the complex fabric of modern organizations, on the ways in which they intersect with both other organizational practices and the wider aims and actions of organizational participants, and, in the latter respect, on the resistances which specific attempts to mobilize one set of organizational practices induce.

When seen in such terms, there is at least the potential for the aims of management accounting to remain partially or even totally unfilled. Indeed, they can even result in consequences which were wholly unanticipated, since eventual outcomes are influenced by phenomena which did not enter into the original system specification or justification.

It is not surprising therefore that more research consideration is now starting to be given to the actual practice of management accounting. Questions are being asked of the circumstances under which it does or does not realize the aims that are articulated on behalf of it. In such ways the organizationally detached discourses that permeate accounting texts and manuals are slowly being compared with the ways in which management accounting relates to the functioning of actual organizations and the practices and underlying bodies of knowledge of other approaches to organizational control.

The agenda for research

Such emergent concerns are evident in all of the contributions to this book, be they by academics or practitioners. From the latter perspective, both Allen and Kirwan portray a body of practical knowledge that is currently in motion, trying to adapt to the pressures of new demands that are being made on it. The research surveys are possibly even more suggestive of the changes underway, however. All of them illustrate in their own very different ways the changing foci of management accounting research discussed by Horngren. As Johnson makes clear, historical inquiry is becoming much more concerned with understanding the interdependency between management accounting and other organizational practices, and the factors which induce accounting systems to change. According to Scapens and Arnold, and Kaplan, both economic and quantitative traditions of research in the area are now becoming increasingly concerned with explicitly addressing questions of organizational complexity, with understanding the organizational functions and implications of practice, with adopting a richer view of economic and technical rationality, and with adopting a more cautious and organizationally grounded approach to technical change. The rise of a behavioural and organizational research interest in management accounting was itself an early reflection of the changing perspectives on the craft. Although progress to date has been slow, both Birnberg and Sadhu, and Dent illustrate how the research agendas in the behavioural and organizational areas have changed so as to illuminate the actual functioning of management accounting systems. Not surprisingly, given their remit to focus on some important current pressures for change, the final three chapters by Goold, McCosh and Plowden further reinforce the salience of the new practical and research agendas.

Such emergent concerns are encouraging. For, at present, relatively little is systematically known of the practice of management accounting. Its contours and parameters have not been documented. The pressures for it to change are not well understood. Albeit that present research is being conducted from a variety of different and, indeed, conflicting perspectives, at the very least it can help to illustrate technical diversity, highlight the particular and varying features of specific kinds of management accounting systems and their patterns of change, and thereby hopefully enrich our appreciation of management accounting as an organizational and social practice. If nothing else, research of this type can play an important role in stimulating the asking of new questions and the search for alternative ways of conceiving the management accounting craft. What is more, such research, if well conducted, can at least start to provide a view of the management accounting domain as one that is not subject to a unified *a priori* pattern of rational development or a set of procedures reflecting some abstract essence of the craft. Instead, a better understanding might be gained of how organizations have chosen, or even stumbled into, varying patterns of accounting development in the past and how such earlier choices, in turn, both limit and open up alternative possibilities for further change. Such research at least has the possibility of helping us to make better sense of the unfolding of unintended as well as intended consequences of the management accounting craft.

However, as such an outline should make clear, description *per se* is only a part of the process of gaining more adequate understanding of management accounting in action. Although a positive role can be played by attempts to document management accounting as it is, it must be recognized that all description involves a process of categorization, labelling and analysis. If not done explicitly, the resultant descriptions are almost invariably conducted within the implicit framework of existing notions of management accounting, imposing traditional technical rationalities, functional claims and wider organizational presumptions onto the seemingly purely technical account. These still might provide useful stimuli to other researchers, but in and of themselves they can offer few possibilities for appreciating the contextual and dynamic aspects of management accounting in action that have provided the rationales for the new agenda of both scholarly inquiry and practical action.

When seen in such terms, the challenge for the research community resides in the need to develop new conceptual appreciations of management accounting as it functions. While the technical aspects of the craft must not be ignored, for that is one of the ultimate rationales for accounting research, perspectives are needed which can ground the technical in wider organizational and social processes and
 patterns of transformation. For only through such conceptual and theoretical developments can sense be made of both the technical and organizational contradictions and paradoxes which are a prevalent and now much more frequently recognized feature of the craft.

Although the contributions to this book suggest that some progress is now starting to be made, they also point to the significance of the research agenda remaining for the future. For not only is further progress needed if sense is to be made of existing understandings of the craft but that progress is also a vital precondition for any attempt to improve, from whatever interest or perspective, the practice of the craft in ways that are sympathetic to the human, organizational and social contexts in which it operates.

References

Aiken, M. and Covaleski, M., 'Accounting and Theories of Organizations: Some Preliminary Considerations', *Accounting, Organizations and Society* (1986).

Argyris, C., *The Impact of Budgets on People*, The Controllership Foundation (1952).

Armstrong, P., 'Changing Management Control Strategies: The Role of Competition Between Accounting and Other Organizational Professions', *Accounting, Organizations and Society* (1985), pp. 129–148.

Armstrong, P., 'The Rise of Accounting Controls in British Capitalist Enterprises', *Accounting, Organizations and Society* (forthcoming).

Baiman, S., 'Agency Research in Management Accounting: A Survey', *Journal of Accounting Literature* (1982), pp. 154–213.

Batstone, E., 'Systems of Domination, Accommodation, and Industrial Democracy', in T. R. Burns, L. E. Karlsson and V. Rus (eds), *Work and Power: The Liberation of Work and the Control of Political Power*, Sage (1979).

Berry, A. J., Capps, T., Cooper, D., Ferguson, P., Hopper, T. and Lowe, E. A., 'Management Control in an Area of the NCB: Rationales of Accounting Practice in a Public Enterprise', *Accounting, Organizations and Society* (1985), pp. 3–28.

Birnberg, J. G. and Sadhu, K., 'The Contribution of Psychological and Cognitive Research to Managerial Accounting', in M. Bromwich and A. G. Hopwood (eds), *Research and Current Issues in Management Accounting*, Pitman (1986).

Burchell, S., Clubb, C., Hopwood, A., Hughes, J. and Nahapiet, J., 'The Roles of Accounting in Organizations and Society', *Accounting, Organizations and Society* (1980), pp. 5–27.

Burchell, S., Clubb, C. and Hopwood, A. G., 'Accounting in Its Social Context: Towards a History of Value Added in the United Kingdom', *Accounting, Organizations and Society* (1985), pp. 381–413.

Chandler, A., *Strategy and Structure*, MIT Press (1962).

Chandler, A., *The Visible Hand: The Management Revolution in American Business*, Harvard University Press (1977).

Chandler, A. and Daems, H., 'Administrative Co-ordination, Allocation and Monitoring: A Comparative Analysis of the Emergence of Accounting and Organization in the USA and Europe', *Accounting, Organizations and Society* (1979), pp. 3–20.

Clawson, D., *Bureaucracy and the Labour Process*, Monthly Review Press (1980).

Colville, I., 'Reconstructing "Behavioural Accounting"', *Accounting, Organizations and Society* (1981), pp. 119–132.

Cooley, M., 'Work and Time', in C. Rawlence (ed.), *About Time*, Jonathan Cape (1985).

Cooper, D., 'Organizational Aspects of Budgetary Control', in J. E. Lewis and G. Dickinson (eds), *Handbook of Financial Management*, Kluwer-Harrap (1977).

Cooper, D., 'A Social and Organizational View of Management Accounting', in M. Bromwich and A. G. Hopwood (eds), *Essays in British Accounting Research*, Pitman (1981).

Crawford, A., 'Cost Accounting, Work Control and the Development of Cost Accounting in Britain 1914–1925', paper presented to the Congress of the European Accounting Association, St Gallen, Switzerland (1984).

Dent, J., 'Organizational Research in Accounting: Perspectives, Issues and a Commentary', in M. Bromwich and A. G. Hopwood (eds), *Research and Current Issues in Management Accounting*, Pitman (1986).

DiMaggio, P. J. and Powell, W. W., 'The Iron Cage Revisited: Institutional Isomorphism and Collective Rationality in Organizational Fields', *American Sociological Review* (1983), pp. 147–160.

Earl, M. J. and Hopwood, A. G., 'From Management Information to Information Management', in H. C. Lucas, E. F. Land, T. J. Lincoln and K. Supper (eds), *The Information Systems Environment*, North-Holland (1980).

Epstein, M. J., *The Effect of Scientific Management on the Development of the Standard Cost System*, Arno Press (1978).

European Foundation for the Improvement of Living and Working Conditions, *Economic and Working Conditions: Methodological Aspects*, EFIL&WC (1982).

Flamholtz, E., *Human Resource Accounting*, Dickenson Publishing (1974).

Foucault, M., 'Orders of Discourse', *Social Science Information* (1971), pp. 7–30.

Foucault, M., *Discipline and Punish: The Birth of the Prison*, Allen Lane (1977).

Galbraith, J., *Designing Complex Organizations*, Addison-Wesley (1973).

Goold, M., 'Accounting and Strategy', in M. Bromwich and A. G. Hopwood (eds), *Research and Current Issues in Management Accounting*, Pitman (1986).

Hagg, I., Magnuson, A. and Samuelson, L. A., 'Research in Budgeting in the Nordic Countries – A Survey', unpublished Working Paper, University of Stockholm (1983).

Hannah, L., *The Rise of the Corporate Economy*, Methuen (1976).

Hayes, R. H. and Abernathy, W. J., 'Managing Our Way Out of Economic Decline', *Harvard Business Review* (1980), pp. 67–77.

Hofstede, G. and Kassem, M. S., (eds), *European Contributions to Organization Theory*, Van Gorcum (1976).

Hopwood, A. G., *An Accounting System and Management Behaviour*, Saxon House (1973).

Hopwood, A. G., 'Information Systems for Matrix Organizations', in K. Knight (ed.), *Matrix Management*, Saxon House (1977).

Hopwood, A. G., 'Towards an Organizational Perspective for the Study of Accounting and Information Systems', *Accounting, Organizations and Society* (1978), pp. 3–14.

Hopwood, A. G., 'Economic Costs and Benefits of New Forms of Work Organization', in *New Forms of Work Organizations*, Vol. 2, International Labour Office (1979a).

Hopwood, A. G., 'Criteria of Corporate Effectiveness', in M. Brodie and R. Bennett (eds), *Perspectives on Management Effectiveness*, Thames Valley Regional Management Centre (1979b).

Hopwood, A. G., 'Some Thoughts on Information and the Structural Organization of Companies', *Proceedings of the 5th Annual Conference of the Association of Information Officers in the Pharmaceutical Industry* (1982).

Hopwood, A. G., 'On Trying to Study Accounting in the Contexts in Which It Operates', *Accounting, Organizations and Society* (1983), pp. 287–305.

Hopwood, A. G., 'Accounting and the Pursuit of Efficiency', in A. G. Hopwood and C. Tomkins (eds), *Issues in Public Sector Accounting*, Philip Allan (1984a).

Hopwood, A. G., 'Accounting Research and Accounting Practice: The Ambiguous Relationship Between the Two', a paper presented at the Conference on New Challenges to Management Research, Leuven (1984b).

Hopwood, A. G., 'The Tale of a Committee that Never Reported: Disagreements on Intertwining Accounting with the Social', *Accounting, Organizations and Society* (1985), pp. 361–377.

Hopwood, A. G., 'The Archaeology of Accounting Systems', *Accounting, Organizations and Society* (1987).

Hopwood, A. G., 'The Development of "Worrying" About Management Accounting', in K. B. Clark, R. H. Hayes and C. Lorenz (eds), *The Uneasy Alliance: Managing the Productivity—Technology Dilemma*, Harvard Business School Press (1985).

Hopwood, A. G. and Bromwich, M., 'Accounting Research in the United Kingdom', in A. G. Hopwood and H. Schreuder (eds), *European Contributions to Accounting Research: The Achievements of the Last Decade*, Free University of Amsterdam Press (1984).

Hopwood, A. G., Burchell, S. and Clubb, C., 'The Development of Accounting in Its International Context: Past Concerns and Emergent Issues', in A. Roberts (ed.), *A Historical and Contemporary Review of the Development of International Accounting*, Georgia State University (1980).

Horovitz, J. H., *Top Management Control in Europe*, Macmillan (1980).

Jasinski, E. J., 'Use and Misuse of Efficiency Controls', *Harvard Business Review* (1956), pp. 105–112.

Johnson, H. T., 'The Search for Gain in Markets and Firms: A Review of the Historical Emergence of Management Accounting', *Accounting, Organizations and Society* (1983), pp. 139–146.

Johnson, H. T., *The Role of Accounting History in the Education of Prospective Accountants*, University of Glasgow (1984).

Johnson, H. T., 'The Organizational Awakening in Management Accounting History', in M. Bromwich and A. G. Hopwood (eds), *Research and Current Issues in Management Accounting*, Pitman (1986).

Kaplan, R. S., 'Measuring Manufacturing Performance: A New Challenge for Managerial Accounting Research', *The Accounting Review* (1983), pp. 686–705.

Kaplan, R. S., 'Quantitative Models for Management Accounting in Today's Production Environment', in M. Bromwich and A. G. Hopwood (eds), *Research and Current Issues in Management Accounting*, Pitman (1986).

Khandwalla, P. N., 'Crisis Responses of Competing Versus Noncompeting Organizations', *Journal of Business Administration* (1978), pp. 151–178.

Landes, D. S., *Revolution in Time: Clocks and the Making of the Modern World*, Harvard University Press (1983).

Littler, C. R., *The Development of the Labour Process in Capitalist Societies*, Heinemann Educational (1982).

Loft, A., 'Towards a Critical Understanding of Accounting: The Case of Cost Accounting in the UK, 1914–1925', *Accounting, Organizations and Society* (1986).

Lukka, K., Majala, R., Paasio, A. and Pihlanto, P., 'Accounting Research in Finland', in 209
A. G. Hopwood and H. Schreuder (eds), *European Contributions to Accounting Research: The Achievements of the Last Decade*, Free University of Amsterdam Press (1984).

McCosh, A. M., 'Management Accounting in the I.T. Age', in M. Bromwich and A. G. Hopwood (eds), *Research and Current Issues in Management Accounting*, Pitman (1986).

Madsen, V. and Polesie, T., *Human Factors in Budgeting: Judgement and Evaluation*, Pitman (1981).

Merchant, K. A., 'On the Incidence and Cause of Dysfunctional Side Effects of Control Systems', unpublished Working Paper, Graduate School of Business Administration, Harvard University (1985).

Merchant, K. A. and Simons, R., 'Research on Control in Complex Organizations: An Overview', unpublished Working Paper, Graduate School of Business Administration, Harvard University (1985).

Merkle, J. A., *Management and Ideology: The Legacy of the International Scientific Management Movement*, University of California Press (1980).

Meyer, J. W., 'On the Celebration of Rationality: Some Comments on Boland and Pondy', *Accounting, Organizations and Society* (1983), pp. 235–240.

Meyer, J. W., 'Social Environments and Organizational Accounting', *Accounting, Organizations and Society* (1986).

Meyer, J. W. and Rowan, B., 'Institutionalized Organizations: Formal Structures as Myth and Ceremony', *American Journal of Sociology* (1977), pp. 340–363.

Miller, P. and O'Leary, T., 'Accounting and the Construction of the Governable Person', *Accounting, Organizations and Society* (1987).

Olofsson, C. and Svalander, P. A., 'The Medical Services Change Over to a Poor Environment – "New Poor" Behaviour', unpublished Working Paper, University of Linkoping (1975).

Ostman, L., 'Some Impressions of Accounting Research in Scandinavia During the 1970s', in A. G. Hopwood and H. Schreuder (eds), *European Contributions to Accounting Research: The Achievements of the Last Decade*, Free University of Amsterdam Press (1984).

Otley, D., 'Management Accounting and Organization Theory: A Review of Their

Interrelationship', in R. Lister, D. Otley and R. W. Scapens (eds), *Management Accounting, Organizational Behaviour and Capital Budgeting*, Macmillan (1984).

Plowden, F., 'Management Accounting: Pressures for Changes in the Public Sector', in M. Bromwich and A. G. Hopwood (eds), *Research and Current Issues in Management Accounting*, Pitman (1986).

Pollard, S., *The Genesis of Modern Management*, Edward Arnold (1965).

Ridgway, V. F., 'Dysfunctional Consequences of Performance Measurements', *Administrative Science Quarterly* (1956), pp. 240–247.

Samuelson, L. A., 'Discrepancies Between the Roles of Budgeting', *Accounting, Organizations and Society* (1986), pp. 35–46.

Scapens, R. W. and Arnold, J. A., 'Economics and Management Accounting Research', in M. Bromwich and A. G. Hopwood (eds), *Research and Current Issues in Management Accounting*, Pitman (1986).

Sheridan, A., *Michel Foucault: The Will to Truth*, Tavistock (1980).

Simmonds, K., 'Strategic Management Accounting', in D. Fanning (ed.), *Handbook of Management Accounting*, Gower Press (1983).

Simon, H. A., Kozmetsky, G., Guetzkow, H., and Tyndall, G., *Centralization v. Decentralization in Organizing the Controller's Department*, The Controllership Foundation (1954).

Starbuck, W. H., Greve, A. and Hedberg, B. L. T., 'Responding to Crisis', *Journal of Business Administration* (1978), pp. 111–137.

Wells, M. C., *Accounting for Common Costs*, International Center for Accounting Education and Research, University of Illinois (1978).

Whyte, W. F., *Money and Motivation*, Harper and Row (1955).

Wildvasky, A., *The Politics of the Budgetary Process*, Little, Brown and Company (1964).

ACCOUNTING AND ORGANISATIONAL ACTION

Anthony G. Hopwood

Management accounting is a diverse craft. It seemingly takes different forms in not only different sectors, and even different enterprises within a sector, but also shows a diversity of arrangements and emphases across both time and space. Different historical junctures have had their different accounting priorities. Interestingly, in the context of a consideration of the cultural aspects of accounting, different cultural configurations appear to make different appeals to the accounting art, endowing it with different roles and different significances [Birnberg and Snodgrass, 1986; Horovitz,
212 1980].

However, accounting diversity, and the factors that lie behind it, largely remain hidden from the contemporary view. Educational texts and manuals of consulting practice invest heavily in the articulation of a quite homogeneous technical domain. They attribute homogeneous rationales to the accounting craft. The multitude of ways in which accounting becomes embedded in organisational forms, the diverse ways in which it can become intertwined with organisational action, and even the actual consequences of the technical art are all virtually ignored by contemporary commentaries on the accounting craft. For the rhetoric of accounting has tended to be one of intention. Emphasis has been placed on the accounts that organisations need and the technical accounting configurations that they must have. Pragmatic necessities, normative intentions, and even conceptual imperatives have mobilised the ways in which accounting is conceived and talked of in its organisational context. The actual practice of the craft, the ways in which it does, rather than might, become intertwined with organisational functioning, the actual contexts in which appeals to accounting are made, and the ways in which it becomes related to organisational action, have all tended to be ignored, seemingly confined to the domain of the uninteresting and thereby the unknown. The mission and the potential rather than the actuality of accounting have tended to monopolise attention.

Of course others have been concerned with this state of affairs. Even a few of our intellectual ancestors, like DR Scott (1931), sought to understand the wider societal pressures that put accounting into motion and that shaped not only the technical form that accounting took but also the social and organisational functions which it was called upon to serve. However, Scott's was a lonely voice, then and now, compared with the pronouncements of those who preferred to try to make accounting what it was not.

Anthony G. Hopwood is Arthur Young Professor of International Accounting and Financial Management, London School of Economics and Political Science.

I am grateful for the helpful comments of Jake Birnberg and Tony Tinker.

Subsequently a whole series of major intellects tried to interrogate the accounting actuality, to delve into its involvement with the organisational condition, and to illuminate, however partially and problematically, the organisational consequences of the imperatives that seemingly drive the application of accounting techniques. Such names as Chris Argyris [1952; 1977], Melville Dalton [1959], William Whyte [1955], and Aaron Wildavsky [1964; 1978] come to mind. Both individually and collectively they provide a rich and provocative account of the accounting condition, an account that many might have thought would have stirred the accounting imagination into investigating and accounting for its own condition. But very little of that occurred. The rhetoric of a dominant accounting mission and potential was seemingly too strong, too focused, and too embedded in the social fabric of both accounting intellectual life and its practice for such pleas and such exemplars to encourage accounting to account for itself.

Perhaps there is a little more reason to be optimistic of some small change of direction at the present time. Kaplan's pleas for us to address the actuality of the accounting condition are not going unnoticed [Kaplan, 1983]. I and others seem not to be talking in a wilderness when we seek to explicate, albeit in different ways, some of the means by which we can advance our capability to interrogate the accounting 213
condition and strive to appreciate its involvement with organisational, economic, and social affairs [Burchell et al., 1980; Burchell et al., 1985; Hopwood, 1983; 1985a]. Moreover, although I will subsequently distance myself from its conventional epistomological stance, the rise of an interest in empiricism, even if not its expression in terms of an umproblematic philosophy of positivism, has already achieved some reformulation of our conceptions of the accounting condition [Watts and Zimmerman, 1986]. If nothing else, such investigations have placed accounting in a more interdependent position with respect to other forms of information processing and wider institutional arrangements for the governance and regulation of the enterprise. They have even provided at least some basis for appreciating the institutional preconditions for some forms of accounting theorising [Watts and Zimmerman, 1979], although not, as will subsequently become clear, of the bases that might underlie theorising about accounting theorising.

It is such attempts to appreciate, explore, and indeed account for accounting that I wish to build upon and develop in the argument that follows. My remarks of necessity have to be brief. However, they will draw upon my own recent inquiries into both the factors that are implicated in accounting change [Burchell et al., 1985; Hopwood, 1987], that, in my words, make accounting what it was not, and the rationales which are associated with such mobilisations of the accounting craft [Burchell et al., 1980]. The aim in so doing is to inquire into accounting as it has come to function, to ask questions of it, indeed to interrogate it, with a view not to appreciating its technicalities in isolation but rather to appreciate its organisational functioning. Indeed my remarks constitute what one of my friends, on hearing the text, described as a "paper about understanding ourselves." I also hope that it will help some to understand both accounting and the possibilities for accounting research. For in the analysis, I seek to characterise accounting in ways that are not part of the discipline's conventional wisdom. I use conceptual frameworks and languages that do not form a part of the normal accounting discourse. I seek to probe into a few rationales for accounting development that are not a part of accounting's account of itself. In so doing I try to suggest the powerful role that knowledge plays in accounting change and I aim to provide a characterisation of some of the many ways in which accounting can become intimately involved in organisational action.

MANAGEMENT ACCOUNTING AND THE DIVERSITY OF INFLUENCES UPON IT

Management accounting, as we now know it, bears the mark of many influences, only some of which form a part of the conventional wisdom that is associated with it.

In the United Kingdom, for instance, the government regulation of prices and profits during World War I resulted not only in a considerable increase in the accounting calculus implanted in the enterprise but also the enhanced social acceptance and legitimacy of the accounting craft and its practitioners [Loft, 1986]. And that legitimacy was to serve accounting well in the subsequent occupational struggles that were to determine which practitioners had an influential position in the control of the enterprise [Armstrong, 1985] – struggles that were resolved in very different ways in different countries. In subsequent years very different interests appealed to accounting within the enterprise. During the crisis years of the Depression it was advanced as a sign of efficient management that was acceptable in the eyes of the financial establishment [Armstrong, 1987]. The State strove to inculcate the accounting art as part of its strategy to restructure British manufacturing industry, both immediately
214 after the Second World War and thereafter. Indeed, in the context of continued economic difficulties, the economic management policies of the State continued to advance the regime of accounting calculation within enterprises. Price controls resulted in a plethora of more detailed and sophisticated costings. Wage controls resulted in the advance of accounting for productivity, for value added, and for a wider dissemination of financial information within the firm as accounting sought to transform economic motivations and orientations prevailing within the enterprise [Burchell et al., 1985].

So although management accounting conventionally is given an internal rationale, many of the residues of economic calculation that reside within the enterprise have external origins. And such a phenomenon is in no way an idiosyncrasy of the British. Early American regulatory attempts also transformed the forms of economic calculation utilised within the enterprise. Wider social and political transformations associated with the efficiency movement [Haber, 1964] and the quest for enhanced enterprise accountability [Hays, 1959] changed the bases of legitimacy underlying management practices and resulted in an enhanced concern with what came to be regarded as rational approaches to management, including forms of accounting and financial management. As in the United Kingdom, the crises of legitimacy engendered by the Depression and the Great Crash resulted in regulatory attempts that utilised accounting and provided means by which external conceptions of economic calculation could inculcate internal accounting – something that only now is starting to be made more problematic by Kaplan and others. And also, as in the UK, war, the cold war, and defence contracting have all played a role in implanting within the enterprise particular forms of economic calculation.

Although it may be difficult for those accustomed to the present practice of management accounting to disentangle such external origins from the internal rationales which are now attributed to the resultant practices, the same forces can be observed at work in other management areas, and perhaps it is easier to recognise their significance there. Consider, for example, the present condition of human resource information systems in U.S. enterprises. No longer do they merely reflect the internally recognised needs for information. In the main they reflect a mass of federal and state regulatory provisions regarding employment, plus the demands of fiscal, insurance, and all manner of other agencies. Here the external origins of the internal information flows are clearer to see. Here too, as with financial information, external circumstances not only create a demand for information but also leave an information residue that has the potential to shift and disturb internal patterns of visibility and knowledge. A potential thereby is created for a more disruptive effect.

Management accounting also has been appealed to in order to help regulate social forces which pass through the organisation rather than remain at the door. In both the United States and the United Kingdom the rise of internal economic calculation and costing was associated with the regulation of the labour force and the rise of the labour movement. Management was not faced with a disciplined, orderly work force which was tolerant of management authority and accepting of economic rationales for action. Rather, the discipline and order in the factory had to be constructed by an array of architectural forms, management practices, and organisational controls on the utilisation and specification of time. A domain for economic action had to be laboriously constructed – often, as numerous authors have illustrated [Burawoy, 1979, 1986; Clawson, 1980; Edwards, 1979], in the midst of resistances and strategies for counter-control. In striving for the control of the enterprise, management had to address both problems of social and organisational control. Accounting was appealed to for both inseparable reasons. The accounting eye provided a means for penetrating into the inner workings of the organisation, constructing a strategic visibility of the economic. The aims of management could be diffused throughout the enterprise in a powerful way, economic rewards could start to become related to action, and the detailed workings of the newly visible corporate economy could be exposed to those in positions of power and authority. Not only could the enterprise thereby attempt to confront the forces of the social through accounting and other means, but also the newly ordered enterprise could itself contribute to the different functioning of the social – and it did. Seen in such terms, caution must be exercised in imposing a boundary between the enterprise and society. Society passes through the enterprise and is often transformed in the process, sometimes by accounting means.

Of course such mobilising rationales do not enter into conventional accounting dialogue, and, of course, that is my reason for emphasising them. Management accounting, as conventionally seen, is an internal organisational phenomenon. Many of the factors implicated in its emergence have been forgotten. And, as a result, there is now little appreciation of the ways in which external influences have transformed internal accounts, of the ways in which the factual residues those forces created have transformed the internal economy, and of the ways in which a selectivity thereby has entered into explanations of the accounting craft.

Be that as it may, such alternative views are extremely useful for appreciating the ways in which the accounting craft comes to occupy a different place and hold a different significance in different national cultures. Different regulatory practices of the State can make different appeals to economic calculation and result in different implantations of economic visibility in the enterprise – a phenomenon of particular importance in the U.S.A. Different appeals by the State to the practitioners of economic calculation, especially accountants, can endow them with different social legitimacies and recognition, and thereby shift some of the preconditions for the interoccupational competition for the control of the enterprise. For certainly we know from the work of Horovitz [1980] and Armstrong [1985; 1987] that there is no general approach to either enterprise control or visibility that prevails across national boundaries. Different configurations of practices are observed, different emphases are given, and different strategies are used to interrelate the economic with the noneconomic – all differences that are at least suggestive of the ways in which the cultural environment and different national institutional structures and strategies pass through enterprises and their accountings, transforming them in the process.

Perhaps even more significantly, an awareness of the wider social origins of the accounting craft can alert us to the possible ways in which both the form and significance of organisational accountings can be dependent on the precise configurations of practices oriented towards enhancing social rather than organisational control. Where the instilling of an acceptance of the legitimacy of order, discipline, and perhaps even an economic rationale for action is effectively achieved by the institutions of the family, the educational system, and the community, the factory can focus on accounting for the organisation. That prior investment in socialisation certainly could not be taken for granted in the formative days of accounting in the United States and the United Kingdom, however, and possibly still cannot. The enterprise had to address issues of both organisational and social control. An organisational order had to be explicitly forged out of the social fabric through the use of well-articulated management structures, information and control practices, and associated discourses which enhanced both their organisational and social legitimacy. Questions of discipline and the organisational management of time equally gave rise to innovations in organ-
216 isational rather than just external social practices. And the mobilisation of an economic rationale for action resulted in an ever more penetrating accounting eye as investments were made in constructing rather than merely revealing a conception of economic reality that could infuse much of organisational life.

Hardly surprisingly, in those countries where the enterprise had to address questions of both organisational and social control, there is a tendency to find more elaborated information, control, and accounting systems which have a greater significance and legitimacy. For accounting, by linking economic and social conditions, is a phenomenon that arises out of the social fabric, is infused by it, and contributes to its transformation.

THE DIVERSE FUNCTIONS OF THE MANAGEMENT ACCOUNTING CRAFT

Already I hope to have disturbed at least some of the conceptions of a narrow functionality and instrumentality that are implicit in conventional accounting discourses. However, I do not want to ignore the very real mobilising potential that more frequently cited rationales for accounting have had. Accounting is invoked to provide an informational bridge between markets and production. It is used to orchestrate an economic rationality within the enterprise. And it is used to mobilise and monitor organisational members dispersed across hierarchical levels. My aim, however, is not to be comprehensive but rather to open up for a wider consideration the instrumentality of the accounting craft and to emphasise some of the diverse but influential arenas which have given rise to accounting as it is.

For notions of functionality are all too frequently conceived too narrowly in the accounting literature, ignoring both the wider rationales that can mobilise accounting change, and, as I briefly discuss later, the often equivocal relationship between the rationales that infuse accounting rhetoric and the actual consequences of accounting in action.

Consider for a moment the functionality of the clothes in which I stand. They not only provide a way of cushioning me from the elements in a way that is cognisant of the prevailing climatic conditions, but also they reflect cultural notions of the way in which the male body should be attired [Barthes, 1985] – and how extensively it should be attired. All too clearly, the latter notions have changed over time. Indeed I come to you attired in the garb of the 1980s and I hope that I would be reluctant to expose myself to you in the clothes of the 1950s, or '60s, or '70s. For clothes are also a cultural and symbolic phenomenon, conveying a whole host of messages about my wider relationship to the world and it to me. Although at times they have a more particular functionality – for instance, when I go climbing or hiking, or expose myself either to the heat of the southwest or the winters of the midwest – they also are involved in the management of appearances, in the creation of a symbolic conception of Hopwood, and in my occasional attempts to purchase a particular legitimacy with a particular audience.

Accounting too has a range of functionalities, many of which are also symbolic and cultural in nature, and only some of which enter into the official discourses of the craft. The techniques of accounting can be implicated in the creation and propagation of a particular significance, in the furtherance of strategic changes in language, in the articulation of a set of categories and codes that enable the wider dissemination of other information as well as accounting information itself, in the construction of quite particular conceptions of time, and, not least in significance, in attempts to enhance enterprise and organisational legitimacy [Meyer, 1986].

As far as the latter is concerned, to refer to the concerns with social accounting and 217
auditing in the socially turbulent days of the 1960s and 1970s is a little too obvious, and too distanced from the conventional practice of the accounting craft. Rather we should ponder on the impacts on accounting, particularly in the public or not-for-profit sphere, of the changes in political practice and rhetoric that accompanied the emergence of the Reagan administration in the U.S.A. and the Thatcher government in the U.K. With such sudden changes in the legitimacy of particular actions and interests, new means for justifying action were needed, new ways of demonstrating conformity to prevailing values were required, and public organisations had to clothe themselves in the newly legitimate practices of economic action and what was regarded as efficient management. As we know from the work of John Meyer of Stanford, at times such as this accounting can be endowed with a symbolic significance, helping to shape the organisation in ways that are consistent with the symbolic structures prevailing in its environment [Meyer, 1983; 1986]. Although at least initially loosely coupled to patterns of ongoing action in the organisation, and thereby facilitating the speedy consulting change assignments that so many of us have witnessed, these legitimising strategies nevertheless leave an informational residue and shift the patterns of significance and concern in the organisation. Worries start to be talked about in different ways. New experts can enter the organisational power structure. A newly created domain of economic facts can confront the politically and socially vague and nebulous. In these and other ways, the symbolic can disturb the status quo, allowing accounting sometimes to function as an agent for wider organisational transformations in the name of externally mobilised rhetorics [Hopwood, 1984].

THE POWER OF BOTH ACCOUNTING KNOWLEDGE AND ACCOUNTING ITSELF

Hopefully I have at least created some conception of not only a diverse accounting craft but also one that is implicated in diverse rationalities and functions. Hopefully I also have created a conception of the craft that stands in some contrast to the ones that are enshrined in the texts that we use. For although some element of technical fragmentation pervades such works, they nevertheless substitute an abstract conception of accounting in the organisation for the diversity of accounting's links to organisational functioning. They also impose a very particular selectivity on the rationales that are articulated for accounting action, indeed using what rationales are given to construct a coherence for management accounting. A unity thereby is created within their pages that stands in stark contrast to the diversity of accounting in action.

Be that as it may, the world of textbook accounting is of great significance both in itself and for the wider forces that it reflects. For such texts are exemplars of our ability to talk and write accounting rather than merely to do it. They are one reflection of the enormous growth of knowledge that has occurred around accounting – a knowledge that has emerged amidst professional regulation, educational practices, enterprise standardisation and specification, state regulatory initiatives, the development of competitive consulting practices, and only more recently, academic research. As a result of developments in all of these areas we can now talk rather than merely do accounting. And we should recognise that accounting-speak can have an autonomy from accounting practice. Very different factors can influence it. It can become intertwined with other very different bodies of knowledge, such as economics, organisational behaviour, and mathematics. But even though it can change independently of accounting practice, accounting talk – accounting knowledge – can still be brought to bear to question, assess, and indeed change accounting practice. The level
218 of abstraction implicit in accounting talk facilitates just that. At times the doing of accounting can be confronted by our ability to talk accounting, and changed as a result. Indeed, although the contribution of formal research to accounting talk is relatively recent, I nevertheless think that both accounting academics and practitioners massively underestimate the impact that accounting ideas have had.

Costing practice can now be confronted with abstract notions of costliness, and changed as a result. Investments have even been made in specialised institutions for talking accounting. Bodies like the Financial Accounting Standards Board and the Accounting Standards Committee both consume and produce vast amounts of knowledge and operate on the practice of the craft by their ability to appeal to and advance discursive notions of it. In management accounting generally, the role of knowledge has been no less great. The fragmented practices can now be addressed in terms of notions of management responsibility and functions. Accounting now can be powerfully related to cognitive conceptions of decision making. The diversity of practice can be orchestrated by appeals to notions of management and organisational control that not only impose a unity on the diversity but also give priority to particular conceptions of the rationales that have made management accounting what it is.

Seen in such terms, it is accounting knowledge rather than accounting itself that has made much of my earlier conception of accounting in action a somewhat alien and unfamiliar one. For so great is the impact of our investment in quite particular accounting knowledge that we now see and understand accounting in quite specific ways; ways, moreover, whose patterns of emergence and intellectual preconditions are lost amidst the seeming obviousness of accounting as it is. Accounting no longer is just accounting. It is a more rationalised, more coherent, and apparently less social phenomenon that is observed, analysed, and changed through a lens, the making and components of which are no longer remembered.

When seen in this way, it can be appreciated that accounting knowledge has played a role in making accounting what it was not. It has not merely reflected the world in any simple positivistic sense. It has changed it. In this sense, though, it is like accounting itself. For although we conventionally think of accounting as reflecting organisational notions of control, decision making, and strategy; of reflecting the production, technological, organisational, and market circumstances of the enterprise; in fact accounting itself (along with other organisational practices, of course) has had the power to play a role in mobilising and creating the enterprise as we now know it.

Through its intertwining with notions of accountability and responsibility, accounting has played a role in the reconstitution of organisational agents and actors, enabling different configurations of organisational arrangements to exist. By extending the range of influence patterns within the enterprise, by creating different patterns of interaction and interdependence, and by enabling new forms of organisational segmentation to exist, accounting has played a positive role in both shifting the preconditions for organisational change and influencing its outcomes. By its routinisation of information flows and the ways in which it imposes a spatialisation on time, it has changed conceptions of the past, the present, and the future, contributing different saliences to each, which in turn have moderated temporal preferences and emphases, and thereby, organisational actions. Creating quite particular objectifications of the otherwise vague and abstract and particular conceptions of economic facts, accounting also has created not only a context in which the conditions exist for other organisational practices to change, but also a means by which a particular organisational visibility can either compete for or be imposed upon managerial attention; and, if such strategies succeed, perhaps even eventually exclude the visibility and significance of other ways of characterising the organisational terrain. Moreover, as such developments occur, the transformational potential of accounting is 219
only enhanced further, as the facts created by the craft give rise to an influential language and set of categories for conceiving and changing the organisation in economic terms.

So not only am I describing a diverse accounting that serves many roles, many of which are not accounted for in accounting's account of itself – an accounting whose practice and our conceptions of it are infused by knowledge in many more ways than is conventionally appreciated – but also an accounting and a knowledge of it that does not merely sit in the enterprise, reflecting other organisational pressures and constraints, but one that has a more active potential to transform the enterprise, to make it what it was not. Accounting, from such a view, at times can be much more influential than is often presumed.

ACCOUNTING IN ACTION

It is useful to see some of these forces in operation in a specific accounting area. For this purpose let us consider financial methods of investment appraisal – capital budgeting and the methodology of discounted cash-flow analysis.

Capital budgeting is interesting because it owes its more widespread implantation into the enterprise to the very development of financial and accounting knowledge that has just been discussed, and, in the United Kingdom at least, to the concerns of the State with the national need for efficient business management and a form of economic calculation that could recognise the financial interdependence between the enterprise and the State. Seen in such terms, it is a technique which bases its rationale on a formal and abstract economic rationality rather than on empirical appeals to its effectiveness in shaping patterns of investment in different and more strategic ways. It is grounded in an external logical obviousness rather than being infused by any understanding of organisational process and action and the ways in which it might intersect with other organisational processes and practices.

Yet even within the context of economic reasoning, possibilities exist for different ways of infusing economic investment rationalities into the enterprise. If, for example, we assume highly competitive markets, as most economic and financial theorists do, then our expectation should be that the acceptable project should have a zero net present value. Few such projects enter our texts, however, so we can only presume that the authors implicitly are assuming that particular competitive advantages prevail, if only temporarily. But if it is competitive advantage that is the source of profitability, an alternative mode of economic evaluation would be to first analyse in strategic, marketing, manufacturing, technological, or whatever terms the nature of that advantage and the means for its possible furtherance. Once such analyses had isolated any advantages, the role of a formal financial analysis would be more minimal – to check on the arithmetic, to assure that everything had been done to increase the efficiency of the project, and to ensure a compatibility with the enterprise's overall financial policies.

From what we can gather, just such an approach characterises Japanese approaches to investment analysis. A temporal priority is given to strategic rather than financial assessment. Both, of course, are compatible with a formal economic reasoning. But the two approaches can call on different bodies of knowledge, give priority to different modes of analysis, call on different experts, and create different organisational linkages and interdependencies during the evaluation process. And because of these differences, rather than their formal logical similarities, the two approaches can become intertwined with other aspects of organisational action in different ways and thereby
220 have at least the potential to have a different impact on the enterprise.

Such different intertwinings of economic rationality and organisational action are ignored by dominant bodies of knowledge, however. Despite being oriented towards changing organisational processes and consequences, they nevertheless conceive of the organisation as a vacuum, as a phenomenon that seemingly has no possibilities for more proactively influencing the investment process. Moreover, dominant views also ignore how and when evaluative technologies are used. The ways in which assessment procedures become involved with organisational politics are not considered. Yet when they function as what I have called "ammunition machines" [Earl and Hopwood, 1980], the orientation of the methods can radically change. They no longer provide an evaluation within an agreed framework but rather form part of a strategy for forging agreements on aims and objectives, striving to construct that hopefully agreed-upon framework. The organisational processes and actions associated with such different uses can be very different indeed; as can those stemming from the use of evaluative procedures which follow, rather than form, a part of the decision process, particularly for complex, uncertain, and multiple-person decision processes. In such circumstances formal evaluation is less a proactive instrument of choice than a means for rationalisation, for the construction of legitimate rationales for action, and for the mobilisation of support – all very necessary and very important processes, but ones which do not enter into the formal bodies of knowledge which give rise to the techniques that are utilised in these ways.

Such wider organisational processes are emphasised, albeit all too briefly, because they are an important part of the context in which abstract rationales for intervention in the organisation become interconnected with organisational action and they therefore play a role in shaping the ultimate instrumentalilty of the practices themselves. There is no obvious and automatic relationship between an abstract accounting or financial rhetoric and an intervention in the organisation in the name of it. Rather than being presumed, that relationship has to be painstakingly constructed, as all practitioners know but few rationalisers of practice admit. Nowhere is this clearer than in the cognitive emphasis given to investment appraisal methodologies. The stress is placed on making the right decision. Assuming that the realm of the future lies ahead, the methods serve as a telescope for observing its characteristics – and wrenching it into the present via discounting so as to enable a decision to be made as to whether the enterprise wishes to occupy that future space. But such an approach, however dominant in our formal bodies of knowledge, is partial because it ignores the action processes through which that future must be created rather than passively occupied. Perhaps that partiality is less problematic if organisational cognitions and actions are relatively independent [Brunsson, 1982]. But they might not be. The very detail of an evaluation might influence perceptions of uncertainty and risk, and thereby action. Clinical and analytical approaches to evaluation might do nothing to engender, if not more negatively disturb, the processes of commitment and enthusiasm out of which the future might be created. In these and many other ways there are very real possibilities for an interdependency between cognitions and actions, possibilities which further disturb the obviousness of the relationship between abstract rationalities and organisational praxis, and possibilities which provide further insights into the nature of the relationship between the knowledge through which we have come to know accounting and the contexts in which accounting functions.

Once again I have pointed to the partiality of emphases implicit in accounting knowledge, to the selective rationales for action, and to the under-accounting for both accounting as it is and for the ways in which it has its effects. Once again I have
emphasised the extent to which very partial concerns with "shoulds" and with "oughts" 221
monopolise imagination outside of any appreciation of organisational praxis. For people who claim to be practical, applied, and pragmatic – indeed who see themselves as practical agents for change and improvement – such partialities ought to be profoundly worrying. I think it is profoundly worrying that they are not.

SOME IMPLICATIONS FOR RESEARCH AND PRACTICE

Although the implications of my remarks for both research and practice are great, to some extent they are consistent with some current directions for change. I too look for greater concern with accounting as it is practised – a view articulated by Kaplan [1986], amongst others. I therefore am sympathetic with many aspects of empiricism within the accounting research community. We do need to observe, survey, and delve into accounting as it was and as it is. But as I hope should be clear from the emphases that I have given, I think that observation and analysis are tasks that are inevitably, of necessity, theoretically grounded and driven. We have to think as we observe. And it is that joint theoretical and empirical task that lies behind my concern to advance not just our knowledge of the bits and pieces of the accounting craft, but our understanding and appreciation of accounting as it has come to be, as it now functions, and as it might come to be. It is the emphasis on understanding, appreciation, and simple human intelligibility that I seek to stress.

From this perspective, we simply cannot just observe the world as it is. Observation is of itself a theoretical exercise. To observe we must of necessity appeal to categories, languages, conceptual interrelationships, and theories. As of now it is not just our observations that are inadequate; it is our theories also. We have pitifully few at our disposal that allow us to interrogate, question, and understand accounting in the contexts in which it operates. Our theories or the implicit bodies of knowledge that serve in their place actively mask and reduce the salience and significance of so much accounting as it is. In seeing what we think, we not only have a view that is partial but we also have few insights into its partiality.

Characterising the problem in this way, I think it is a pity that accounting is having to witness a rise of interest in positivism [Watts and Zimmerman, 1986], an epistemological stance that denies the interdependence of theory and observation, at the very time when it has been rejected by most of the human and social sciences. So many of the greatest intellects of the nineteenth and twentieth centuries have articulated philosophies that undermine the pretensions of positivism and provide alternative epistemological frameworks for guiding the human task of understanding the world in which we live. Even Popper [1976, pp. 87-88], whose strategies of falsification are appealed to in order to buttress the positivistic framework in accounting, has felt compelled not only to ask "Who killed . . . positivism?" but also to answer "I fear I must admit responsibility." Not knowing of accounting developments, Popper even went on to note that "Everyone knows nowadays that...positivism is dead."

Dead may it be, positivism has seemingly come to haunt accounting research, along with a number of other theoretical ghosts that seem to have little relationship to the wider patterns of intellectual life in many other human and social sciences.

I do not want to overemphasise this point because I am most sympathetic with the empirical questioning of accounting that has resulted from such a stance. Even so, I think that it is a pity that at the very time when accounting needs to appreciate the complexity, the social nature, and the wider consequences of the act of theorising, it seemingly moves towards adopting a perspective that is less conducive to grappling
222 with such issues. And the same could be said for that strongly articulated functionalism that pervades accounting research – a view that assumes that what is, is what should be – and our seeming inability to deal with dynamics, with process, and with action, something that is heavily reinforced by the ahistorical nature of most accounting theoretical stances.

What is needed is a much more open approach to theorising and research in general. In accounting we need to reflect more on patterns of theorising in other fields of intellectual endeavour rather than the present approach that seemingly only allows a few to innovate theoretically and that is even reluctant to allow younger researchers to push at the boundaries of our knowledge; something that would be inconceivable in most other disciplines. Research is something that is still relatively new to accounting. We are still unsure of research, unsure of intellectual questioning rather than technical propagation, and possibly because of this, invest the research life with a whole series of social and institutional constraints. Equally, and possibly because of it, we are reluctant to admit the social nature of our theorising. Research is seen as residing in a purely technical domain, like accounting itself. We are hesitant to admit its human and social bases, even the humane nature of the drive for intelligibility and understanding that lies behind it.

If only we could do more to set at least some of these constraints aside, be more self-conscious about research, be more at ease with the research life, be more appreciative of the human activity of understanding, and be more willing to see it in human terms rather than mask it in a mantle of epistemological privilege, we could start to address the prerequisites for good and sound theorising more effectively. And for me, one of those prerequisites should be a theoretical reflexivity. We should be willing to apply our own theories to ourselves. Theorists of accounting theories should be willing to at least entertain the implications of their views for their own condition. Those appealing to the primacy of supply and demand should reflect on the constraints which prevent those forces applying to their own act of theorising, so destabilising the epistemological claims of any temporary theoretical equilibrium.

I choose to emphasise these points, rather than many others which I also see as important for research progress, because I think that above all else a more self-conscious awareness of the research endeavour is a prerequisite for any significant change in accounting's ability to account for itself. If we are to see and perceive accounting differently, if we are to see it in the contexts in which it operates rather than as an exercise in formal logic, and if we are to appreciate both the diversity of the craft itself and the diversity of the rationales and forces that mobilise it, major advances in our conceptual understanding and ability to theorise are required.

For at a more practical level, what is at stake with a view that seeks to ground accounting in the organisational and social contexts out of which it emerges and in which it functions is a more adequate way for appreciating accounting as it is and as it might become. Such a view can provide an improved basis for understanding the ways in which accounting intersects with other organisational processes and practices, for appreciating how it can actively shape the organisational fabric, and for sensitising us to at least some of the ways in which accounting fails to have the consequences which were anticipated for it and has consequences which were not anticipated – all vital factors lying behind the current development of worrying about management accounting [Hopwood, 1985b], and all factors stimulating some practitioners to look at accounting in ways that increasingly are different from those used by many of their academic colleagues.

From an educational point of view, an organisationally grounded accounting could provide a basis on which management accounting textbooks could become more than 223
the bricklaying or plumbing manuals of the accounting craft. It could enable a more explicit design approach to accounting education to emerge, one that helps students to relate technique to circumstance, one that strives to encourage them to consider and appreciate the wider organisational consequences of their acts, and one that moves towards an architecture, albeit a landscape or community-oriented architecture, of accounting system design.

All too clearly a great deal more work is required before such educational, practical, and research objectives can be realised. To me, however, that work is of the greatest importance. Put simply, I think that the enhanced ability of accounting to account for itself is an essential prerequisite for our ability to direct accounting so that it might better serve organisations, and indeed society, as a whole.

REFERENCES

Argyris, C., *The Impact of Budgets on People* (New York: The Controllership Foundation, 1952).

———, "Organizational Learning and Management Information Systems," *Accounting, Organizations and Society*, *2* (1977), pp. 113-123.

Armstrong, P., "Changing Management Control Strategies: The Role of Competition Between Accountancy and Other Organizational Professions," *Accounting, Organizations and Society*, *10* (1985), pp. 129-148.

———, "The Rise of Accounting Controls in British Capitalist Enterprises," *Accounting, Organizations and Society*, *12* (1987).

Barthes, R., *The Fashion System* (London: Jonathan Cape, 1985).

Birnberg, J.G., and C. Snodgrass, "Culture and Control," Unpublished working paper (Graduate School of Business, University of Pittsburgh, 1986).

Brunsson, N., "The Irrationality of Action and Action Rationality: Decisions, Ideologies and Organizational Actions," *Journal of Management Studies* (January 1982), pp. 29-44.

Burawoy, M., *Manufacturing Consent: Changes in the Labor Process Under Monopoly Capitalism* (Chicago: University of Chicago Press, 1979).

———, *The Politics of Production* (London: Verso, 1986).

Burchell, S., C. Clubb, and A.G. Hopwood, "Accounting in its Social Context: Towards a History of Value Added in the United Kingdom," *Accounting, Organizations and Society, 10* (1985), pp. 381-413.

———, ———, ———, J. Hughes, and J. Nahapiet, "The Roles of Accounting in Organizations and Society," *Accounting, Organizations and Society, 5* (1980), pp. 5-27.

Clawson, D., *Bureaucracy and the Labour Process* (New York: Monthly Review Press, 1980).

Dalton, M., *Men Who Manage* (New York: John Wiley & Sons, 1959).

Earl, M., and A.G. Hopwood, "From Management Information to Information Management," in H.C. Lucas, F.F. Land, T.J. Lincoln and K. Supper (Eds.), *The Information Systems Environment* (New York: North-Holland, 1980).

Edwards, R., *Contested Terrain: The Transformation of the Workplace in the Twentieth Century* (New York: Basic Books, 1979).

Haber, S., *Efficiency and Uplift: Scientific Management in the Progressive Era 1890-1920* (Chicago: University of Chicago Press, 1964).

224 Hays, S.P., *Conservation and the Gospel of Efficiency: The Progressive Conservation Movement 1890-1920* (Boston: Harvard University Press, 1959).

Hopwood, A.G., "On Trying to Study Accounting in the Contexts in Which it Operates," *Accounting, Organizations and Society, 8* (1983), pp. 287-305.

———, "Accounting and the Pursuit of Efficiency," in A.G. Hopwood and C. Tomkins (Eds.), *Issues in Public Sector Accounting* (Oxford: Philip Allan, 1984).

———, "The Tale of a Committee that Never Reported: Disagreements on Intertwining Accounting with the Social," *Accounting, Organizations and Society, 10* (1985a), pp. 361-377.

———, "The Development of 'Worrying' About Management Accounting," in K.B. Clark, R.H. Hayes, and C. Lorenz (Eds.), *The Uneasy Alliance: Managing The Productivity - Technology Dilemma* (Boston: Harvard Business School Press, 1985b).

———, "The Archaeology of Accounting Systems," *Accounting, Organizations and Society, 12* (1987, in press).

Horovitz, J., *Top Management Control in Europe* (London: Macmillan, 1980).

Kaplan, R.S., "Measuring Manufacturing Performance: A New Challenge for Managerial Accounting Research," *The Accounting Review* (October 1983), pp. 686-705.

———, "The Role for Empirical Research in Management Accounting," *Accounting, Organizations and Society, 11* (1986), pp. 429-452.

Loft, A., "Towards a Critical Understanding of Accounting: The Case of Cost Accounting in the U.K., 1914-1925," *Accounting, Organizations and Society, 11* (1986), pp. 137-169.

Meyer, J.W., "On the Celebration of Rationality: Some Comments on Boland and Pondy," *Accounting, Organizations and Society, 8* (1983), pp. 235-240.

———, "Social Environments and Organizational Accounting," *Accounting, Organizations and Society, 11* (1986), pp. 345-356.

Popper, K., *Unended Quest: An Intellectual Autobiography* (London: Collins, 1976).

Scott, DR, *The Cultural Significance of Accounts* (New York: H. Holt, 1931; Reprinted, Houston: Scholars Book Co., 1973).

Watts, R.L. and J.L. Zimmerman, "The Demand for and Supply of Accounting Theories: The Market for Excuses," *The Accounting Review* (April 1979), pp. 273-305.

———, and ———, *Positive Accounting Theory* (Englewood Cliffs, NJ: Prentice-Hall, 1986).

Whyte, W.F., *Money and Motivation* (New York: Harper & Row, 1955).

Wildavsky, A., *The Politics of the Budgetary Process* (Boston: Little, Brown & Co., 1964).

———, "Policy Analysis is What Information Systems are Not," *Accounting, Organizations and Society, 3* (1978), pp. 77-88.

Accounting and the Transformation of the Public Sector

Value For Money: Practice In Other Countries

ANTHONY G. HOPWOOD
Professor of Accounting and Financial Reporting, London Graduate School of Business Studies; Professor of Management, European Institute for Advanced Studies in Management, Brussels; American Accounting Association Distinguished International Visiting Professor in the USA 1981.

Although a great deal of attention is being given to the need for value for money auditing in the United Kingdom, far less consideration is being paid to the lessons that can be learnt from the practical exercises that have been undertaken so far, both here and elsewhere. As in so many other areas of management debate, apparently it is much easier to discuss what should be and how it should be done than what is being done, why it is being done and, perhaps most important of all, the practical consequences that have followed from it. Indeed in this area, as in others, even the most practical of people often appear reluctant to engage themselves with the intricacies of practice, preferring instead to conduct their discussions in the realms of what might be rather than in the world that is. Such preferences can have, and indeed have had, many unfortunate consequences however, not least because even the best intentions often give rise to a set of consequences that are very different from those hoped for or expected. If for no other reason than this, I think that it is of great importance to complement our discussions of what should be done in the value for money area with at least some consideration of the lessons that can be learnt from what has been done.

With such an objective in mind it is only natural that I should focus my attention on those situations where I have some first hand knowledge of current practice. Athough often useful, so much of the literature in the area nevertheless places more emphasis on the intentions lying behind action than on what actually has been achieved. For this reason alone I will concentrate my comments on developments in the USA, Canada and Sweden, ignoring the perhaps equally important experiments elsewhere. First of all, however, it is useful to consider briefly a number of the important generic issues lying behind the current discussions of value for money auditing in the UK.

SOME ISSUES UNDERLYING THE PRESENT DEBATE

Just why has there been such a sudden emergence of interest in the concept of VFM auditing in the UK? Not too long ago it would have appeared alien to the British political scene — an imported notion from realms where management processes have a more explicit and perhaps rapidly changing vocabulary. Now, however, the idea is widely discussed. No doubt many factors are implicated in that change. I think three are of particular significance however; two of them in a more positive sense and the third playing a somewhat negative role.

First, the last few years undoubtedly have seen a growing questioning of the legitimacy of the state in both the UK and elsewhere. Increasingly both the authority of the state to intervene in certain areas of economic and social life and the adequacy of such interventions are being debated and re-examined. Rather than that authority being taken for granted, demands are growing for both a greater visibility of governmental processes and a more systematic examination of actions and achievements. The VFM debate is merely a part of this more general development.

When seen in this way it is perhaps not surprising that government audit operations are most highly developed in those countries, such as the USA, where there has been a longer tradition of suspicion of government activities, and least developed in those countries, possibly such as France and Germany, where the machinery of government has had a greater historical legitimacy. In the past the UK has occupied an intermediary position. It would appear,
230 however, that there have been pressures recently for that position to change.

Such tendencies have been reinforced by current economic circumstances, not least in respect of the pressures for economy in governmental operations and the associated demands not only for greater accountability in general but also for a greater investment in accounting, more specifically defined. For although the UK has made one of the greatest investments in accounting expertise and its practitioners, both have had relatively little involvement with the operations of central government, at least until recently. Even these current pressures are best seen in a longer historical perspective however, for accounting has tended to flourish and develop in the UK during periods of major economic difficulty. The auditing profession as we now know it was born amidst the bankruptcies that came with the great depression that characterized the latter part of the nineteenth century and auditors made their entry into the financial administration of industrial companies during the troubled times of the 1930s. Even now the intricacies of accounting do not give rise to such extensive management practices in the financial sector or central government, although the last few years have seen demands for the latter to change.

A third factor underlying the present debate is a more curious one. For despite the current pressures to change, both central and local government in the UK already have a considerable investment in and experience of financial and economic evaluation, review and audit, although only rarely has this been associated with the body of professionalized accounting practice. Be that as it may, let us not forget that the UK has pioneered in the social cost-benefit analysis of government projects and that economic analyses of policies, both proposed and realized, are not an infrequent aspect of administrative life. Moreover both the Exchequer and Audit Department and the District Audit Service have a distinguished tradition of thorough and innovative work in their respective areas. Indeed today there could well be more experience of operational and VFM audits in those organizations, in terms of both their potential and practical achievements and problems, than in the private audit sector, where notions of management and operational audit have been peculiarly slow to develop. That might well come as a surprise to many. If nothing else however, that surprise should make us realize that governmental auditors in the UK have been reluctant to discuss their activities in any meaningful way and, unlike many of their overseas colleagues, have not graced their activities with a new technical jargon. Although the absence of the latter might be very desirable, I nevertheless think that we should be given many more opportunities to examine the approaches used by those who seek to make visible the actions of others. If for no other reason than to enhance the processes of accountability in the public domain, the nature of these examinations and the standard of their scrutiny should be more widely known. The contrast with American practice is particularly striking in this respect.

SOME COMPARATIVE EXPERIENCES

Practice in the United States 231

A wider concern with the efficiency and effectiveness of government operations has been a part of the administrative process in the USA for much of the post-war era. Although its origins may have had more to do with assuring the political support necessary for the implementation of new and controversial programmes than with the desire for an unbiased evaluation of their consequences, repeated legislative provisions for the monitoring of achievements nevertheless have resulted in the creation of a large body of expertise in the area of policy review or 'evaluation research', as it is now known. Initially such reviews were separate from the financial compliance audits undertaken by the General Accounting Office (GAO), the US equivalent of the Exchequer and Audit Department. However with the appointment of Elmer Staats as Comptroller and Auditor General attempts started to be made at integrating compliance audits with VFM and effectiveness reviews.

To this end Staats announced a ten year programme for transforming the professional expertise of his department, aiming to supplement the traditional emphasis on accounting skills with the employment of economists, technologists, sociologists, educationalists and others who could enhance the GAO's ability to comment on both the aims and the achievements of government policy. Today almost a half of the professional staff of the GAO are non-accountants – a paradoxical result for those in the UK who expect VFM concerns to result in an enhancement of the accounting perspective!

Before commenting further on what such a reorientation of the audit task might have achieved, it is important to emphasize a number of basic differences between the UK and American contexts. First, the GAO is a part of the legislative branch of government. The Comptroller and Auditor General is an officer of Congress and a significant amount of the investigatory work undertaken by the GAO is done at the request of Congress. Second, the reorientation undertaken by the GAO was only a part of a wider attempt to increase the visibility and scrutiny of governmental operations in the USA. At the time the reforms were being introduced into the audit area, freedom of information provisions were enacted and 'sunshine' and 'sunset' legislation also strived to make governmental activities more amenable to wider observation and review. Finally, no doubt reflecting such wider concerns, the GAO itself has invested a lot of effort into making its assessments available to a wider audience. Freely available to all, the mass of reports produced are written in a popular style with titles that owe more to journalistic flair than a more cautious administrative mind.

However, the fact that all the above points differentiate the American context from that prevailing in the UK should not be used as a basis for suggesting that we cannot learn from their experiences to date. Although it might be true that wholesale copying is not in order — it rarely is — I nevertheless think that some important lessons can be gained at a more general level.

To me, by far the most significant one relates to the lack of investment by the Americans in new and explicit routines for the wider review of government operatives. Despite the length of time that they have been engaged in VFM

reviews, their approaches have remained diverse and non-standardized. The origins of their inquiries are diverse, reflecting both congressional, and thereby political interests and the agency's own longer term strategies for areas in need of audit and assessment. The disciplines, perspectives and approaches used in their investigations also are characterized by diversity. There is neither a uniform methodology nor a standard way in which their findings are reported or taken-up. Rather than bureaucratising its concerns with efficiency and effectiveness, the GAO has provided a continual series of informed, multidisciplinary and — dare one say it — ad hoc investigations into topics of concern. For me at least however, in that very ad-hocracy resides one of the most crucial bases of the agency's effectiveness. By emphasizing an informed diversity rather than attempting to routinize its concerns with efficiency and effectiveness the GAO might have enabled more of its messages to penetrate the walls of officialdom. However difficult it might be to justify such an approach in conceptual terms, it could well be that at a practical level government officials are simply less skilled at deflecting a series of sharp, well-informed but diverse assessments, than the more predictable findings of a standardized 'audit cannon'.

It should be remembered, however, that such an ad-hocracy can only work if the reviews emanate from a respected and professional source. With few routines and technical means to provide a legitimate basis for commentary, an agency using such an approach must rely heavily on the legitimacy of its institutional origins and present nexus of relationships, and the professional expertise in which it has invested so much. If for any reason these are questioned, the approach can very quickly become quite problematic.

Despite in my view achieving a great deal, the GAO nevertheless has not been immune from criticism. For one thing, it has proved difficult to maintain the legitimacy of its basis for action. With reviews of programme effectiveness almost inevitably becoming intertwined with the political questioning of the desirability of particular policies, some have accused the agency of encroaching into the political domain. Somewhat paradoxically, faced with such criticisms, immediately prior to his retirement as Comptroller and Auditor General, Elmer Staats established an institute within the GAO which has the task of improving the professional basis of, and possibly introducing some element of standardization into its evaluative approaches. However, if nothing else, such an initiative should serve to demonstrate just how elusive such methodologies are. After so much experience in the area, practice to date has remained grounded in professional skill rather than in the mysteries of technique. Perhaps more significantly, the GAO also has been accused of neglecting its more traditional audit responsibilities in the area of financial compliance and regularity.

Although such accusations undoubtedly reflect some element of political concern with the extent of 'waste, fraud and abuse' rather than 'economy and efficiency' in the executive function, they nevertheless should alert us to the fact that auditing is and must remain a multi-faceted endeavour. Although the perspectives of the past might be in need of extension, their replacement is not in order.

The Situation in Canada

The wider review of governmental activities is a more recent concern in Canada. As in so many other countries, it has stemmed from the questionings of the accountability of public sector organizations that were articulated during the 1960s and 1970s. Unlike in the UK however, that debate resulted in quite a number of institutional innovations, of which the reform of the audit function was only one. In Canada the enactment of freedom of information legislation and the provision of numerous other mechanisms for wider public participation in the political process have resulted in a much more general enhancement of the means available for observing the state than has occurred in the UK.

Be that as it may, the wider brief given to the Auditor General's Department in relation to all three aspects of economy, efficiency and effectiveness is still of interest. In respect of economy and efficiency the brief is a direct one. The Auditor General's Department is itself responsible for appraising the adequacy of governmental operations in relation to these, albeit quite general, criteria. The brief in respect of effectiveness is an indirect one however. Being aware of the potential overlap between a questioning of effectiveness and the political consideration of policies, the enabling legislation for the department provides it with a responsibility for monitoring the adequacy of departmental and agency systems and approaches for monitoring and reviewing their own effectiveness. Unlike in the other two areas, in this one the primary emphasis is still placed on self-evaluation and democratic debate.

Both the direct and indirect responsibilities given to the Auditor General's Department have resulted in a programme of considerable change and reform – a programme that is still in process. Indeed after several years of experience, officials still speak of the 'experiment' that is 'underway'. Despite recruiting a new cadre of professional auditors from the accounting profession and elsewhere, it has taken much longer than expected to mobilize the organization so that it can serve its new objectives, to recruit and to train the relevant staff and, not least, to establish both expertise and respect in relation to its new mission. For however simple and attractive notions such as economy and efficiency, let alone effectiveness, might initially have appeared, their translation into practical terms and operational procedures has been a task of genuine and unanticipated complexity and difficulty — a lesson that should not be lost on British observers.

As might be expected, the indirect brief given to the Auditor General's Department in respect of effectiveness already is resulting in an approach very different from that adopted in the USA. Unable to investigate directly, emphasis is having to be placed on the review of system effectiveness, albeit quite widely defined. In such a context the ad-hocracy that has characterized the activities of the GAO hardly appears appropriate. In its place is developing a concern for the specification of those standards for agency management processes and procedures that it is thought are, or perhaps more accurately, should be associated with effective management.

It is too early to judge whether such an emphasis on ensuring that the use of the standard routines of efficient and effective management will result in
234 the realization of greater efficiency and effectiveness. However even at this stage I would have some personal concerns. Evidence from elsewhere suggests that the relationship between such routines and organizational performance is far more equivocal than is being presumed. Not only does their own effectiveness depend on the existence of far more subtle organizational processes than can be encapsulated in organizational manuals and reports, but also such procedures invariably have consequences that are unanticipated as well as anticipated, particularly in times of political and environmental change. In addition to influencing the direct management of the task, organizational systems and procedures can affect factors such as the locus of visibility in the organization, the perception of risk and uncertainty, the distribution of power and influence, and not least in significance at the present time, the organization's ability to respond to the new and unexpected. Although it might be possible for such questions of organizational rather than purely system design to be addressed by those guiding the administration of the Department's indirect brief, I suspect that it will take much more time, effort and not least, the lessons of experience. To be fair however, there already are some officials within the Department that share such concerns.

Experiments in Sweden

The situation in Sweden is much more difficult to characterize not least because of the ambiguous role which government auditing plays. On the one hand, at least until recently, the machinery of the state had a high degree of social legitimacy. Athough audit was still of significance, perhaps less was expected of it as a mechanism for scrutiny and review. On the other hand, there exist numerous other ways of observing the state, not least in importance being the rights for citizens to access public information that were enshrined within the constitutional provisions of the eighteenth century state. In such a context, so different from that prevailing in the UK, it hardly is surprising that the audit task has been seen as an ambiguous one.

Nevertheless the Swedish situation is still of some interest, if only because of their traditional openness to administrative innovation and reform. Compared with many other countries, the Swedes have at least experimented with numerous technical and organizational ways of approaching the wider review of governmental activities. Equally, however, they have failed to find any easy solutions. As a result they are now investing much more effort into understanding the organizational processes of questioning and debate which an audit should stimulate rather than seeing the problem in terms of administrative technique alone.

SOME IMPLICATIONS

Despite the importance of the VFM debate, I would venture to suggest that practical progress in the area will be slow.

One reason for this stems from the very ambiguity of the phrase, a characteristic that we should remember has a very positive value in the political arena. Everyone can agree with the need for it without knowing what they might be getting! However that very characteristic is guaranteed to make the
transition from political rhetoric to administrative practice far from an easy one.

More significantly in the present context, comparative experiences in the area are suggestive of a number of other implications:

(a) At present there is no readily available technology for VFM auditing. Despite the wealth of their experience, the American situation suggests that it is an area where the routinization of practice is difficult. Moreover the length and difficulty of the Canadian experimental stage confirms this observation. Although such a view contrasts with the claims of those who see it as not only 'necessary' and 'needed' but also 'straight forward' and 'obvious', perhaps the difficulties can best be appreciated by saying that it is more than likely that the evaluation of any task has at least some relationship to the simplicity or complexity of the task itself. To the extent that the relevant governmental activities are simple (which some are), we can expect speedy progress in the audit area. However, where the underlying tasks cannot be so characterized, the audit task will start to assume some of the difficulties which are inherent in the activities and policies that are being evaluated.

(b) Familiarity with experiences elsewhere should instill a greater realization of the differences between what should be done and what is said to be done, and what is done and what might be done. Unfortunately much of the literature in the area is full of normative imperatives and technical analyses. Far less attention has been given to documenting, let alone understanding, either the underlying organizational processes that sometimes enable the claims of the technical to be realized or the organizational consequences which arise when greater emphasis is placed on evaluative activities.

Such organizational analyses will not be of direct assistance to all however. Although they offer some potential to understand the processes which shape how evaluative activities are implemented and the consequences which they give rise to, they also can shed some light on the origins of the interest in new forms of organizational review. To further appreciate that evaluations can improve processes of policy formulation and decision making will not be contentious. But understandings of political interests in evaluation and the ways in which evaluations of the past can arise from conceptions of the future might be more provocative. Be that as it may, we are starting to appreciate some of the many processes by which an interest in evaluation can arise and such understandings will make it increasingly difficult to discuss the technical bases for evaluation in isolation of the nature of the interests in them — as some of the present debates already demonstrate.

(c) Both the size of the developmental task and the observed disparity between aims and achievements suggest that value for money auditing is an area where experimentation is needed. Rather than presuming what can be done, a series of specific initiatives should be encouraged and every effort made to monitor their achievements
236 and consequences. The latter point needs particular emphasis, not only because of the pervasiveness of the unexpected but also because experience also suggests that those who seek to review the activities of others only rarely invest in monitoring themselves. Although feedback may be said to be important, we should not forget the resistances to it!

(d) One final implication is worth emphasizing. In so many of the countries where VFM auditing is underway, its emergence often has been associated with the development of other mechanisms for increasing the visibility of governmental processes and the extent to which they are subjected to public scrutiny and review. In the UK however, attempts to gain greater value for money have been related to a very different set of political issues. Rather than being part of a debate on the democratic accountability of public institutions, British discussions have adopted a more economic stance, placing more emphasis on the need for economy rather than on accountability *per se* and on the roles which experts rather than the public might be able to play. When trying to understand the different national contexts in which auditing mechanisms operate, this difference must be borne in mind.

All too clearly the lessons which can be learnt from experiments with VFM auditing in other countries do not only reside in the technical domain. It undoubtedly is useful to contrast the insights into the complexity of the task with the often simplistic statements of what can readily be achieved. Equally significantly, however, reflections on experiences elsewhere should serve to emphasize that an interest in audit and review cannot be isolated from wider interests in the dynamics of the political process and the organizational means for their fulfillment. The technical problems in the area are real and important but the suggestions for their solution must be considered in a wider context.

9
Accounting and the Pursuit of Efficiency

ANTHONY HOPWOOD

'Every society keeps the records most relevant for its major values.' (Lazarsfeld, 1959, p. 108)

Accounting for the public sector has become a major issue for both discussion and action. In the last few years both the language and the practices of accounting have entered much more frequently and forcefully into debates about the efficiency, accountability and even scope of public sector activities. Appeals are now being made to the apparent inefficiency, lack of cost effectiveness, unprofitability and waste associated with the public sector. Referring to the existing economic calculus, it is being said that we are now 'living beyond our means', supporting that which is not 'economically viable', and either unable or unwilling, to face 'the facts of economic reality'. Although there is a long history of investing in accounting mechanisms for recording, planning, controlling and making visible public sector activities, within a very short period of time indeed recent pressures for change have succeeded in challenging the adequacy of existing public accounts and management accounting practices. New demands are now being made for the practices of accounting to become even more implicated in public sector management.

Where have these pressures for change come from? What form do they take? And what are their implications? How, in other words, can we not only better understand the forces at work but also attempt to gain a more adequate appreciation of their consequences for both the technical practice of accounting and the conduct of business within the public sector?

Before focusing on these questions, however, it is useful to consider some of the ways in which existing accounting practices have become intertwined with quite substantive issues of public policy. For, like today, much of the power of the public accountings of the past derived from their ability to move beyond merely facilitating the operation of pregiven and relatively unproblematic forms of economic and financial management. Accounting has already been implicated in a more positive shaping and influencing of that which is regarded as problematic, the forms
238 which public debates take and the options seemingly available for management and public action.

Accounting and Public Policy

Accounting records provide a way of freezing the decisions of the past (Bahmueller, 1981, p.193). What was problematic and debated can become lost within the accounting archive. 'Facts' can thereby be created out of dissent and disagreement. An aura of the obvious and the unchallengeable can and does emerge out of the residues of past actions which accounting presents.

The significance of the ability of accounting to forge a domain of the factual in this way can be seen in the patterns of both relative and absolute performance of many public sector bodies. Past subsidies, allowances and provisions, decisions on transfer prices and payments, and the specific means used for their financing, play a significant role now in determining where current costs are incurred, continuing subsidies required and profits and losses both generated and shown. The relationships between past policies in the areas of defence, industrial development and regional support, all have current impacts of this type. Examples abound in the interplay between taxation, economic and social policies. For the National Coal Board, British Rail, London Transport and the Central Electricity Generating Board the patterns of present financial performance emerge out of a complex array of decisions of a social and political, as well as purely economic, nature. But those decisions give rise to accounting residues which can be and are used independently of the contexts out of which they emerged. Being 'profitable' or 'unprofitable', 'subsidised' or 'a drain on the Exchequer', can have a powerful contemporary significance. In this way accounting seems to provide a means of judiciously selecting the time-scale for comment and debate. The compelling obviousness of the present can overwhelm the contingencies of the past.

The fact that accounting, as we know it, provides a partial record of organisational choices and actions has also been of enormous importance. Organisational accounts both reflect and, in turn, influence the emphases that are given in public debates. Consequently, the economic has undoubtedly been made more visible than the social and the political, in many spheres of public life. Now, however, the imperatives of those economic 'facts' can be contrasted with the more questionable dictates of political ideology and social preference, illustrating, in the process, the powerful influence that the recording tools of the public domain can have.

In fact, organisational accounts laid down to orientate management action to wider ends can themselves come to serve as statements of the ends to be achieved (Ridgeway, 1956). Much of the apparatus of national income accounting emerged to aid the management of a constrained wartime economy (Seers (1976), Tomlinson (1981, pp. 129–132)). In the postwar discussions on the desirability of economic growth, however, GNP started to take on many of the attributes of being an end in itself and, in the process, had a more widespread influence on other governmental policies. The imagery of profitability and self-sufficiency has been subject to the same transformation. And, in more recent times, we have seen how actions have come to be taken in the name of such indicators as the Public Sector Borrowing Requirement—a complex and ambiguous indicator that emerged in the context of attempts to manage a constrained economy.

Accounting has also become implicated in the development of the institutional structures and linkages which today characterise the public sector. Particular forms of accounts have been used to buffer certain organisations from the dictates of government policy and intervention. 'Losses', for instance, have served as a pretext for price increases which have provided subsequent investment autonomy, sometimes on a very large scale; profits, similarly, have been used as evidence of both the granting of greater autonomy and its positive achievements. More frequently, accountings have served to tighten the relationships between different parts of the public sector. They have been used as a means of restraint; to constrain expenditures, actions and policies. The selective visibility created by organisational accountings has served to further the salience of imposed patterns of standardisation and uniformity. The information which they produce is used to monitor and evaluate the actions of others, and more frequent plans, budgets and reports can facilitate centralised control at the expense of local discretion.

All told, accounting is already centrally implicated in the institutional frameworks, language and patterns of power and influence that characterise the public sector. As a means of collecting and reporting selective patterns of information it has played a not insignificant role in the construction of public organisations and policies as we now know them. There are, however, yet further pressures for public sector accounting not only to change but also to expand its sphere of influence.

Pressures for Public Sector Accounting to Change

The pressures for the expansion and reform of public sector accounting are numerous, diverse and even conflicting in nature. Moreover, the emphasis given to particular factors can change remarkably over time, as recent decades have illustrated. In what follows, an attempt is made to outline only some of the main forces at work in recent debates in the area.

Changing Conceptions of the State

One of the major factors behind the current interest in public sector accounting is the changing view of the State that has entered political discourse in recent times. The legitimacy and value of at least some State actions and prerogatives are now being questioned from the perspective of a very different ideological stance. Indeed, a new way of examining and managing the State is emerging, and accounting is being implicated in that process.

Agencies of the State are now being asked to account for their aims, actions and achievements. Many more of their activities are coming to be seen in quite explicit economic terms. Cost and efficiency rather than effectiveness are being highlighted and debated. Information on economic consequences is being demanded. 'Value for money' has now entered the vocabulary of government.

In a whole series of ways the practices of accounting are increasingly being used to infiltrate and change, rather than merely record, the activities of the State. A new economic visibility is being forged to emphasise what was previously ignored and to challenge what was previously taken for granted. Economic calculations are now being seen as a way not only of reforming the management of the State but also of influencing the priorities which are given in policy determination and decision making. Accounting is quite explicitly becoming implicated in the construction of different views of the problematic, the desirable and the possible.

Accounting and Economic Restraint

Organisations tend to increase their investment in economic calculation and visibility during periods of restraint. In what has become known as 'newly poor behaviour' (Olofsson and Svalander, 1975), the constrained organisation places a renewed emphasis on costs, financial information and the calculus of economic decision making. Mechanisms for enhancing economic visibility extend further into the organisation. Financial standards, budgets and plans become both more detailed and more subject to change. The organisation overall becomes more economically orientated, more influenced by economic calculation and, somewhat paradoxically (given that very frequently the economic difficulties emanate from without rather than from within), more orientated towards the seeming dictates of its own internal economic circumstances rather than the pressures of the world at large.

Accounting in the United Kingdom has tended to flourish during just such periods of economic difficulty. The auditing profession emerged during the great depression of the latter part of the nineteenth century, and was, in many senses, a product of attempts to reform the practice of bankruptcy administration. (Only later did the profession gain the legal requirement for an audit and the

legal monopoly in its practice that together provide the basis for the auditing profession today.) At the same time, cost accounting and the elementary practices of financial control started to play a more important role in manufacturing organisations faced with a rising real cost of labour at a time of general deflation and recession. In the depression of the 1920s, cost accounting seems to have been used aggressively as a way of getting at the 'facts' of economic difficulty. Similarly, the slump of the 1930s saw a dramatic rise in the role and status of accountants in industry as members of the auditing profession started to enter the upper echelons of manufacturing industry. Accounting has also been called upon in other times of economic restraint. The practice of costing was much
242 utilised and developed in the munitions factories of the First World War. The Second World War saw investment in an internal economic calculus for government that was to provide the basis for national income accounting as we now know it. And, in the post-war period of economic restraint, it was the government that attempted to further the practices of economic management in industry in the name of enhanced international competitiveness.

During periods of economic difficulty, accounting and accountants have consistently expanded their sphere of influence in the UK. However, the relatively large British investment in the profession remains quite localised in its influence, having, until recently, much less of a presence in the service, financial and governmental sectors than in the area of manufacturing industry. Now, it seems, the current recession is providing a pretext for that to change, at least for the public sector. As the economic receives more emphasis in government, and as economic decision making itself becomes more constrained, more and more demands are being made for the type of economic calculations that accounting provides.

The Search for Greater Efficiency

Continued economic restraint has given a new urgency to demands to improve the efficiency of management in the public sector. More and more accusations of waste, maladministration and inefficiency have been made. High staffing levels have been pointed out. The traditionalism and sluggishness of decision processes in the public sector is noted repeatedly. Although it is sometimes realised that the demands of public accountability and decision making in a political context can serve to limit the extent to which concepts of efficiency derived from the private sector can be applied uncritically in the public domain, there nevertheless remains a feeling that much could be done to improve resource utilisation. Efficiency remains a very real and persuasive dream.

To this end, there is a renewed interest in importing into the public sector management practices developed in the private sector. Reference is made to the valuable roles that might be served by more adequate instruments for management planning and control. Appeals are made to the potential offered by improved costing procedures, more specific criteria for resource allocation, improved management information systems, investigations of administrative efficiency and better audits (which compare actual accomplishments with both original intentions and experience elsewhere). Such improved management practices, including those related to accounting itself, are seen as being able to assist in locating the inefficiencies of the past and ensuring that better performance is achieved in the future, not least by making public sector management and employees accountable for their actions and decisions.

Accounting and the Demand for Accountability

Appeals to the concept of accountability pervade many discussions concerned with the advance of accounting practice in the public sector. Accounting is seen as a way of both making visible and disciplining performance so that accountability can be demanded, policed and enforced.

A major impetus to the development of financial accounting in the private sector occurred when a separate cadre of managers came to be recognised as being accountable for their actions and performance to shareholders, the legally recognised owners of business. Since then, periodic crises of confidence have resulted first, in more and more elaborate and detailed accountings of both organisational aims and achievements being demanded; and second, in the supply of such accountings by managers who have tried to maintain respect for their ability to manage the assets of others. Equally, in the public sector, accounting has been implicated with the development of notions of stewardship and accountability. Accounting information has flowed from agencies of the State to Parliament and the public at large in recognition of the emerging constitutional requirement for the former to provide an account to the latter.

In the 1960s and early 1970s there were, in many Western countries, quite major pressures to expand the concept of accountability. In the name of social performance, environmental impact and the quality of working life, attempts were made to redefine the basis of organisational accountability to include aspects of performance broader than the purely economic. Related efforts were orientated towards expanding the information provided by the organisation in order to enable assessments to be
244 made of its performance in new areas of concern. Notions of social, environmental and energy accounting and auditing were discussed and experimented upon. In the public sphere not unrelated developments were underway. Wider audiences started to demand the right to question the actions of the State. Not only was the State increasingly being asked to account for its actions and achievements, but greater demands were also being made for the right to assess public information, attend public meetings and more generally observe and interrogate the machinery of the State so that others might construct their own accounts of its performance. Concepts such as 'freedom of information' and 'the right to information' started to enter the language of political negotiation and debate.

However, in retrospect, it is interesting to note that most of these developments were much less significant in the UK than elsewhere. Here they did not result in any appreciable questioning of, let alone change in, our concepts of either accountability or accounting. Ideas of wider accountings of the social remained peripheral to UK concerns. Nor was the traditional secrecy of the State effectively challenged in the name of wider rights to public information. Accounting maintained its emphasis on the economic, and disclosure, rather than access, remained the vehicle by which information flowed. The reasons for this relative lack of debate and change in the UK are little understood. However, it is possible to point to the continual dominance of the economic over the social in the UK, the emphasis that all sides of the political spectrum have put on the primacy of the ownership of assets (be they in private or public hands), rather than on other strategies for regulating their deployment and use, and the long history of constraints on the dissemination of information which still pervade our legal, administrative and constitutional systems.

From such a perspective perhaps we should not be surprised that recent discussions of the advance of public sector accounting in the UK continue to emphasise the narrowly economic. Efficiency and value for money, rather than effectiveness, are the focuses of attention. Equally, we can note how little attention continues to be given to strategies for the wider dissemination and use of information, accounting or otherwise. Although demands for more accounting are still permeated with the rhetoric of accountability, the latter continues to have quite a constrained meaning. Indeed, many recent discussions appear to emphasise the role that account- 245
ing can serve in advancing accountability within the machinery of the State, rather than between it and the public at large. Administrative rather than public accountability appears to be the problem at issue.

No doubt other factors have played a role in mobilising current concern with the state of public sector accounting in the UK. On the supply side, for instance, attention could have been drawn to the increasing interest of the accountancy profession in expanding its sphere of influence and activity in all areas of the public sector. However, hopefully, sufficient has been said to demonstrate that the interest in public sector accounting is not purely a technical one. Accounting is explicitly implicated in the development of quite strategic interests and concerns. Rather than emanating from the specifics of particular accountings, deficient or otherwise, current pressures for change have stemmed from views of the role which the particular might play in mobilising more general strategic arguments.

However, such strategic interests in accounting are now attempting to grapple with questions of the particular and the specific. A rhetoric of economy, efficiency and value for money is now being used to call for a detailed concern with the specific accounting innovations that can service these wider ends.

The direction of change, from the general to the specific, has important implications for those interested in understanding and directing the practical process of accounting reform in the public sector. The generality, and indeed ambiguity, of notions such as efficiency and value for money must be recognised. For, although

the ideas appeal to the comparison of inputs and outputs, and financial resources with their consequences, the delineation of those inputs, outputs, resources and consequences remains both a practically and conceptually difficult endeavour, not least in organisations which are complex, have little tradition of financial administration and economic record keeping, and where outputs and consequences repeatedly arise in organisations different from those initiating the developments. In fact, very little is known about not only the practice of the new public accountings but also the wider impacts which might stem from such an intensification of economic visibility in the public domain. To date, accountings for efficiency and value for money have been advanced in the name of
246 their presumed potential rather than their practical possibility or actual consequences.

On Examining the Practices of Accounting

In order to facilitate an examination of the practical consequences of public sector accounting developments, we now consider some of the ways of examining and questioning proposals for such accounting changes. Attention is directed towards the technical practices of accounting themselves, the ways in which they are embedded in organisations, and the wider issues to which extensions of accounting give prominence and significance.

Accounting as Technique

Given the ambiguity which pervades such notions as 'efficiency' and 'value for money' when used in public debate, it is always important to analyse proposals for the practical assessment of these concerns carefully and precisely. Only rarely can it be presumed that there will be a direct and unproblematic relationship between the issues of concern and their measurement in practice. More frequently, there will be a gap between the policies which mobilised interest and the specific accounting practices that result from them. Accounting, in practice, invariably requires a specification of detail and a reliance on other organisational practices and procedures that make the final assessments arrived at only partially dependent on the initial interest in them. When subsequently taken up and used in decision making and policy formulation, practical accountings can, and do, have the potential to result in consequences very different from those originally envisaged for them.

Discretion often exists as to what inputs are deemed to be relevant, the costs that are assigned to the resources used, the outputs that are seen to flow from them, and their assessment in both financial and other terms. Issues of organisational interdependency will invariably arise, questions of presumed patterns of causal relationships will need to be debated, and proposals for specific valuations, weightings and assignments of priority will rarely be straightforward and unproblematic. Indeed, the difficulties of accounting in practice are such that it is often easy to arrive at a whole array of costs, efficiencies and value-for-money assessments. Many of these never see the light of day, however. Some are buried as a result of seemingly technical accounting choices; others fail to be recognised because of the dominance of particular organisational emphases and favoured theories of the determination of outcomes and consequences; and still others never emerge from internal discussions of 'the message to be presented'.

The ambiguous relationship between the general and the specific in the accounting area is such that attention needs to be directed to the assumptions, choices and practices that enter into the process of making practical what was previously rhetorical. Proposals for accounting change should always be interrogated in the name of the technical; for if this is not done, the consequences that such accountings have may bear only a loose relationship to those which explicitly entered into their justification and development.

Accounting and the Process of Organising

Accounting has the potential to have organisational consequences beyond merely facilitating, in a technical manner, the processes of decision making and policy formulation. By making visible what was previously unknown, it can open up different areas of the organisation for examination and debate. That visibility can also transcend different levels of the organisational hierarchy. What is accounted for can thereby shape the patterns of power and

influence both within the organisation and without. Those with the power to determine what enters into the organisational accounts have the means to articulate and diffuse their values and concerns, and subsequently to monitor, observe and regulate the actions of those that are now accounted for. An expanded flow of information on organisational resources, capabilities and achievements can enable the monitoring, control and planning of organisational actions to be more readily abstracted from their execution. Management, in other words, can become more centralised. New linkages can be drawn both within and between organisations. Different and more abstract criteria can be used for resource allocation. And opportunities can be created for new specialists to
248 enter into the processes of decision making and policy formulation.

The process of organising is not invariant to the accounting of it. Different investments in accounting do have the potential to enable different decisions to be made by different people in different parts of the organisation. Only rarely, however, does an organisational questioning accompany proposals for accounting change. Without it though, an ambiguous rhetoric can enable a partially independent accounting to shape quite important features of organisational life in ways which might not have entered into its original justification.

Accounting and the Creation of the Significant

The selective visibility which accounting gives to organisational actions and outcomes can play an important role in influencing what comes to be seen as problematic, possible, desirable and significant. Neither organisational participants, nor interested parties outside, can ever know the whole extent of organisational life. Direct observation can play a vital role in determining what is seen and valued. However, in organisational hierarchies and in those circumstances where geographical distance and organisational boundaries restrict what is directly visible, observation is soon supplemented and often superseded by that which is recorded. 'Information', both accounting and otherwise, then comes to play a significant role in determining what is known of the organisation and what is expected of it.

In such circumstances, those who influence what enters into the organisational accounts have a powerful and influential role. Some organisational disturbances are more likely to be seen as problematic than others. Some organisational options for change will be able to appeal more readily to supportive information and facts than others. Some criteria for the evaluation of change will likewise find it easier to relate to the partial mappings of the organisation that are incorporated into the accounting system. In these and other ways, not only can the emphasis given to different aspects of the organisation be changed, but also different values can more readily enter into decision processes and appeals can be made to different legitimacies for action. The economic, for instance, can be given more attention than the social. The internal workings of the organisation can be emphasised rather than its external context. The immediate can be given priority rather than the longer term. Accounting, by shaping the realm of the visible, can have a major impact on the significance that is attached to both organisational life as it is and the directions of change which are considered desirable. Both the organisational landscapes of the present and the future are in part, at least, a creation of the accountings that are given of them.

A very conscious attempt has been made to emphasise the need to interrogate and understand proposals for accounting change in terms different and wider than those in which they are usually presented. The ambiguity and generality of the accounting desirable needs to be confronted by an insight into the specificity of actual accounting practice. This needs to be done in terms of its precise operationalisation, the impacts that it has on organisational functioning and the emphasis that it creates in discussions and debates. Just as accounting is called upon to serve more than the merely technical, so it needs to be evaluated in commensurate terms.

Accounting for Accounting

It is possible to examine developments in public sector accounting on numerous grounds and from a variety of different perspectives. In the discussion which follows, emphasis will be placed on just a few axes for questioning which, nevertheless, raise issues of quite widespread significance. Stemming from an appreciation of how the technical practice of accounting intermingles with the fabric of political and organisational life, the aim is to identify some issues which are worthy of consideration by a much wider audience than they attract at present.

Accounting, Technical Practice and the Realm of Politics

Accounting has the potential to create 'facts' out of the uncertain world of the past and even, in a planning context, the future. What was, and still is, debated and challenged can give rise to a residue of accounting calculations of what is costly, beneficial and of value. A
250 world of the seemingly precise, specific and quantitative can, in this way, emerge out of that of the contentious and the uncertain.

A calculative priority can be given to the economic rather than the social. Costs, consequences and benefits can come to be divided into the defined and known, and the imprecise and intangible. In such ways accounting can create very different maps of organisational and social functioning. Particular emphases are given. Only certain chains of reaction are made visible. Only some consequences of actions enter into the world of the precise, the known and even the knowable. In part, at least, what comes to be known of organisational reality starts to be created by the accountings of it. A different view of what is central, and what is residual and peripheral, can start to be reinforced by the ways in which the calculations of accounting intertwine with the complex functionings of organisations as we know them.

Such changes in the visible are accompanied by other changes in organisational life. Expertise in the creation of particular organisational realities starts to emerge and be rewarded. Different legitimacies can come to be attached to arguments and viewpoints, depending on the extent to which they appeal to the domain of the newly factual. Quite specific calculative procedures for decision making and resource allocation can come to be used in contexts where underlying disagreements remain.

Accounting, in other words, can become implicated in the creation of a domain where technical expertise can come to dominate political debate. By appealing to the centrality of the newly visible, be it the economic or whatever, an imperative for technical action can more readily be justified. What were previously seen to be problems of political priority can now start to be seen as requiring management guidance and expertise. We must now face the facts of the newly emerged reality. Rather than debating and arguing, we must appeal to those with expertise in the technical. Politics must stay at the door of public organisations. Within them, so it is said, planning, decision making, resource allocation and the evaluation of performance must come to be seen in management terms. The emerging domain of the technically factual and necessary must be given priority over the domain of the political.

Such attempts to restructure the sphere of legitimate political debate and action have profound consequences for the nature of the society in which we live. Is it necessary, one wonders, for politics to be thus confronted by the domain of the technical? From what political strategies does this itself emerge? And what are the wider consequences for political and social life? Just what might be at stake in such a juxtaposition of the rhetoric of efficiency with that of democracy? Is it really necessary, one wonders, for the enhancement of the legitimacy of the technical to be gained at the expense of the legitimacy of politics?

Of course, not all changes in public sector accounting raise such fundamental questions. Indeed, accounting itself can be used to mobilise political arguments and debates. The ambiguity of technical accounting practice is such that it often has an uncertain relationship to political practice. Nevertheless, both some specific proposals for accounting change and the general emphasis which together they place on the managerial and the economic, suggest that, at times, accounting developments do need to be seen in such wider terms. Although often masked by the language of the technical and the procedural, accountings can have quite profound consequences in the political sphere.

Accounting, Organisational Visibility and the Centralisation of Authority

Accounting can also become implicated in the creation of very different patterns of organisational influence and control. The selective patterns of visibility which it creates can enable the local to become known to the centre. Institutional boundaries can be made less opaque. Different patterns of local behaviour can come to be seen, compared and more readily labelled as conforming to, or deviating from, the dictates of the centre. Equally, the preferences of the centre can more easily become known to the local. Procedures for planning, budgeting and performance assessment can serve to both disseminate and make real the demands of the centre. Constraints on local behaviour can be imposed on the basis of the calculative visibility created by accounting systems. Specific behaviours can be monitored and more readily restrained. The local can, in this way, come to be managed as a part of the centre. Organisational interrelationships can become tighter. Discretion can more readily be specified and monitored. Indeed, the local can start to enter into the plans, policies and strategies of the centre so

that the meaning of the distinction between the local and the centre can be radically changed.

Yet again, accounting can become implicated in the attainment of a set of consequences which extend far beyond the merely technical. Questions, therefore, can be, and perhaps should be, asked of the organisational and wider consequences of accounting developments.

Just who is made visible to whom? Are the patterns of visibility symmetrical or otherwise? Can only the centre observe the local? Or can the local also observe the centre? Equally, what emphasis is placed on the forging of a visibility within the system of public administration, as compared with the creation of an external account? In other words, just what concepts of accountability (as distinct from accounting) are implicated in the process of accounting change?

Accounting and the Enhancement of Organisational Legitimacy

Accounting can also provide quite a direct basis for enhancing organisational legitimacy. Investments in rational organisational accounts and technical management procedures can be used to demonstrate to others that the organisation accepts the legitimacy of economic and technical bases for action and is seeking to further these ends. Accounts, plans, budgets and the practices of efficient management then become symbols of the organisation's commitment to efficiency both as an aim and a particular strategy of rational governance and management.

The manifestation of such accounting symbols need not result in their coupling to organisational action however (Meyer, (1979), Meyer and Rowan (1977)). The display of the rational accounts may be orientated to those who ask questions of the organisation and seek to probe into its affairs from without, rather than to those who determine from within the organisation's course of events. So, somewhat paradoxically, if the investment in accounting provides sufficient evidence of the organisation's commitment to the course of rational economic and technical action, the discretion so gained might be used to uncouple organisational actions from the accounts which are made of them. Accounting might, in such circumstances, provide the freedom for the organisation to be unaccountable. By successfully appealing to the symbols of legitimate action, accounting might enable the internal affairs of the organisation to have a looser relationship to the external accounts of them.

Accounting and the Routinisation of Concern

Thus, the practices of accounting can come to be valued independently of the precise ways in which they intermingle with other organisational practices to influence the course of practical events. In any event, accounting, often stemming from more wide-ranging and ambiguous concerns, can have difficulty reflecting the specificity of both particular mobilising concerns and particular organisational phenomena, not least in the public sector. In addition, accounting can also come to function as a specialist area of activity in its own right. Technical questions of accounting can arise independently of the contexts in which it functions; accounting can be changed in the name of its own organisational bases and management rather than the wider concerns of the organisations in which it operates.

Such tendencies serve to detach accounting from the organisations in which it functions and the concerns in the name of which it was mobilised. Efficiency, for instance, can lose its force as the basis for accounting changes, to be replaced by a more procedural concern for accounting for efficiency. Similarly, plans can become more important than planning; budgets than the process of budgeting; and costing than the ascertainment of costs. A routine emphasis on accounting as procedure and technique can, at times, supersede accounting's initial concern for the issues in the name of which it was introduced and reformed.

Such a displacement of concern does not always take place. There is no imperative in this direction. Care, diligence and continual attention can result in the routines of accounting maintaining their orientation towards the purposes which they were established to serve. Accounting can continue to penetrate the organisation and change it in the name of more strategic ends.

However, the tendency for accounting over time to emphasise the procedural and the routine, to the detriment of the managerial and the strategic, has recently been recognised as a problem in the industrial sector (Kaplan, 1983). There accounting's routine
254 emphasis on the short-term economic has been seen to constrain the organisation's strategic vision and posture (Simmonds, 1983). Concerns have been expressed about the rigidity of the information and control practices which accounting has traditionally advanced. Accounting has been seen to emphasise the proliferation of routine techniques in the absence of a concern with the specific managerial consequences which they have. And quite active attempts are now being made in some parts of the private sector to reform accounting in the name of what it should be doing rather than what some now see as what it has done.

Accounting and Its Use

Accounting developments do not always lose contact with either the organisations or the missions which they seek to serve. Similarly, accounting does not have any automatic relationship to shifts in organisational legitimacy, the location of social power and influence, and what are seen to be legitimate or illegitimate bases for political action. Moreover, even when accountings of organisational actions and achievements do become intertwined with such substantive concerns, they do not necessarily have any automatic effects. Accountings can counter accountings: those provided by one organisation can confront those made by others. The routinisation of accounting can even limit the changes in organisational power that might stem from accounting developments. The legitimacy that a particular accounting helps to establish at the organisational boundary can protect rather than necessarily disrupt the internal political processes of decision making.

The consequences of accounting are multiple, often conflicting and far from automatic. There is no imperative intrinsic to the accounting mission (Burchell *et al.*, 1980). Although accounting can have very real consequences, those consequences are created in the specific contexts in which it is made to operate. The effects of accounting are determined by the uses that are made of it, the organisational and social roles which it is made to serve, the ways in which it intersects with other organisational and social processes and practices, and the resistances which its use engenders. Rather than being either a unitary or automatic phenomenon, accounting comes to function in a variety of very different ways in very different settings. And it is those ways and settings which influence the effects that it comes to have.

However, such a contingent view of accounting and its consequences does not deny that accounting can raise quite legitimate and significant questions at levels far beyond the purely technical. If for no other reason than this, accounting developments should be examined in a wider forum. Attempts should be made in this way to account even for accounting itself.

Accounting and That Which Happens in its Name

Throughout this discussion an attempt has been made to demonstrate that the consequences of accounting do not necessarily have a close and automatic relationship with the aims in the name of which it is introduced and changed. For one thing, the aims that are expressed on behalf of accounting are general and often ambiguous. Stemming from political and managerial rhetoric, they are rarely expressed in terms of the specific operational and pragmatic questions which accounting must address before it can give rise to its technical procedures and practices. However, that gap between the general and the specific can be a very large one. As a result, the precise operationalisation of accounting's aims can introduce quite significant elements of technical autonomy into the accounting process. These elements serve to distance the specific from the general to which it seeks to appeal. Equally significantly, accounting practices come to be enmeshed in wider organisational processes and concerns. The domain of the factual, that they create, gives rise to a visibility, emphasis and basis for governability that can enable the consequences of accounting to become both more pervasive and more independent of the original aims which might have been advanced on its behalf.

It is, therefore, always legitimate to seek to confront accounting with an analysis of the specific consequences which it has had. What has been changed in the name of accounting both within the organisation and without? What effects have attempts to increase efficiency actually had? What precisely has happened to costs, resources and outcomes? What organisational actions have been curtailed or expanded? What changes, if any, have been introduced
256 into the power structure of the organisation and its processes of management and governance? And how do any such precise consequences of specific accountings relate to the missions and rationales which mobilised them in the first place?

Although such an examination should not be alien to the accounting perspective, accounting itself has only rarely been accounted for. The furtherance of accounting in the public sector could, however, provide an ideal context in which to ask questions of accounting; for its use in this sector can raise questions of a wider organisational, social and even political nature. Given this, perhaps we should use the current pressures for change as a basis for starting to account for accounting and to ask questions about what is actually achieved in the pursuit of efficiency.

References

Bahmueller, C. E. (1981) *The National Charity Company: Jeremy Bentham's Silent Revolution*, University of California Press.

Burchell, S., Clubb, C., Hopwood, A., Hughes, J. and Nahapiet, J. (1980) 'The roles of accounting in organisations and society', *Accounting, Organisations and Society*, pp. 5–27.

Kaplan, R. S. (1983) 'Measuring manufacturing performance: A new challenge for management accounting research', *The Accounting Review*, October.

Lazarsfeld, P. F. (1959) 'Sociological reflections on business: consumers and managers', in R. A. Dahl, M. Haire and P. F. Lazarsfeld (eds), *Social Science Research on Business: Product and Potential*, Columbia University Press.

Meyer, J. (1979) *Environmental and Internal Origins of Symbolic Structure in Organisations,* Paper presented at the Seminar on Organisations as Ideological Systems, Stockholm.

Meyer, J. and Rowan, B. (1977) 'Institutionalised organisations: formal structure as myth and ceremony', *American Journal of Sociology*, September, pp. 340–363.

Olofsson, C. and Svalander, P. A. (1975) *The Medical Services Change Over to a Poor Environment*, Unpublished Working Paper, University of Linköping.

Ridgeway, V. F. (1956) 'Dysfunctional consequences of performance measurements', *Administrative Science Quarterly*, Vol. 1, pp. 240–247.

Seers, D. (1976) 'The political economy of national accounting', in A. Cairncross and M. Pur (eds), *Employment, Income Distribution and Development Strategy*, Macmillan.

Simmonds, K. (1983) 'Strategic management accounting', in D. Fanning (ed.), *Handbook of Management Accounting*, Gower Press.

Tomlinson, J. (1981) *Problems of British Economic Policy 1870–1945*, Methuen.

Accounting and the Domain of the Public: Some Observations on Current Developments

ANTHONY G HOPWOOD

ACCOUNTING in the public sector has become a topic of widespread interest and debate. In the last few years both the language and the practice of accounting have entered much more frequently and forcefully into debates about the management, accountability and even scope of public sector activities. Appeals have been made to the apparent inefficiency, lack of cost effectiveness, and unprofitability associated with activities that reside within the public sector. Referring to the existing economic calculus, it has been said that we are 'living beyond our means', supporting that which is not 'economically viable' and either unable or unwilling to face 'the facts of economic reality'. Although there is a long history of investing in accounting mechanisms for recording, planning, controlling and making visible public sector activities, within a very short period of time recent pressures for change have succeeded in challenging the adequacy of existing public accounts and management accounting practices. New demands have been made for the practices and practitioners of accounting to become ever more implicated in public sector management.

Recognizing these developments, I nevertheless have been perplexed by the form that they have taken, the rhetoric with which they have so often been associated and, not least, the inadequacy of our means for appreciating both the factors at stake in such transformations and their implications for organizational, social and political action. Although I have been both an observer and an active participant in the area, I still have found it difficult to come to a personal view of the developments under way in public sector accounting. At times I indeed have recognized the need for a more adequate economic calculus in public sector organizations, for ways of enhancing the visibility of consequences within the public domain, and for better means of planning and control. In some instances it would be difficult not to do so. At the same time, however, I also have been aware of both the wider patterns of transformation with which the calls for enhanced accountings have been associated and the ways in which the apparently managerially specific can be associated with a wider and legitimately debatable rhetoric of economic and political change. Equally, as a person interested in the organizational and social aspects of accounting and related forms of economic calculation, I have been aware of the problematic relationship between the justifications which are often provided for accounting developments and their actual organizational and social consequences. So although I have sometimes recognized the need for change and, on occasions, participated in it, my view of current developments in public sector accounting remains a questioning and ambivalent one.

That unease and uncertainty is reflected in the title for this lecture – 'Accounting and the Domain of the Public'. It is quite deliberately a complex and ambiguous one. For although I have already referred to public sector accounting, and will continue to do so, I wanted a title that would enable me to make the area somewhat more problematic than is usually the case and in ways that also might not be the usual ones.

The title is designed to acknowledge that there is a legitimate debate over what should be regarded as public and what should be regarded as private. In part, such debates arise out of very long term processes of social development. As historians and sociologists have documented, there has been an ever growing tendency to create private spaces and private realms out of communal life. Barrington Moore (1984), for example, has provided a rich analysis of both the social location of private concerns and some of the factors involved in the emergence of public authority. Elias (1978; 1983) vividly illustrates the articulation of the sphere of the private during the Medieval and subsequent periods, illuminating in the process the ways in which such patterns of transformation created a new vision of the self. In more recent times, not least in the nineteenth and twentieth centuries, whilst the sphere of the private continued to expand, debates about the appropriate responsibilities and activities of the State have also intensified, creating, in the process, a tension between the realms of both the private and the communal and that of the public. The frontiers between them, although rarely stated, have nevertheless appeared to be in an almost continual state of flux. And, as Hirschman has documented in his fascinating volume on *Shifting Involvements: Private Interests and Public Action*, those debates have themselves been subject to a cyclical process of ebb and flow, as the public has been promoted over the private, only to be reversed and reversed again and again – a process that strikes us as a very real one as we sit in the midst of the dynamics of attempts to achieve just such a reversal.

Fascinating though such processes are, some may question their relevance for an understanding of accounting. I want to argue to the contrary, however. I want to advance the view that accounting, as an activity that is implicated in the creation of both visibilities and their boundaries, is one of the ways, but only one, in which the private is demarcated from the public, in which the concerns of the public attempt to permeate the sphere of the private, and in which private emphases can be brought to bear on public concerns. It acts as an information frontier but one which has dynamic properties, allowing some of the visibilities of one sphere of action to be known to the other, and, by so doing, enabling the practice of each to be partially reconstituted in the name of the other.

Just consider the paradox that private sector financial accounts are one of the ways in which Public Limited Companies are enabled to remain in the private sector. Consider also the outcome of the debates on the appropriate mode of accounting for public private sector companies in the nineteenth century. Resulting in a calculative schema which deducted dividends after the declaration of profit, the accounting portrayal of enterprise financial performance was seemingly compatible with a view which located the shareholders, the legal owners of the enterprise, outside of the organizational boundary. Finally consider the numerous ways in which accounting has been used to permeate the boundaries of private sector companies in the name of public interests and concerns. Taxation is an obvious example. In Sweden enterprise accounting is quite explicitly used as a calculative basis for facilitating the management of counter cyclical macro-economic policies. Even in the United Kingdom, however, the economic calculus of accounting has been used, and often transformed in the process of such usage, in order to mobilize private sector organizations to act in ways which are deemed to be in the public interest. Accounting has served as an important basis for price controls in both times of war and peace, with such a use often providing both an incentive for an expansion of the regime of detailed economic calculation in the enterprise and a basis for its wider legitimacy (Loft, 1986). Wage controls and national incomes policies also have utilized the accounting craft and provided a context for a more pervasive calculus of productivity within many enterprises (Burchell et al, 1985). Not least in significance, public concerns with the inadequacy of national economic performance have been used to encourage the more widespread use of economically rational means of investment appraisal within private enterprises. Indeed such strategies of calculative penetration are still seen to be effective by both politicians of the left and the right. On the one hand, we have concerns with social accounting and the means for a wider calculation and revelation of the costs of employment and unemployment in order to infuse the concerns of the public into the sphere of the private. On the other hand, there is a belief in the advantages that can flow from infusing economic calculations into spheres where such managerial strategies have traditionally not been emphasized. Indeed it is just such a concern that provides the context for the present discussion.

So not only is there a fluidity in our notions of the public and private but, of particular importance for the present argument, accounting has some role to play in both establishing a calculative boundary between the two at any point in time and facilitating any process of transformation as the position and legitimacy of such boundaries change over time. Given such a contribution, it is particularly appropriate to consider such issues at the present time when the legitimacy of prevailing conceptions of the public and the private is being debated and when accounting is being brought into the conduct of such debates.

From such a perspective my unease with current developments in public sector accounting becomes more understandable. For although I recognize the value which particular accounting innovations and applications can make, I nevertheless have difficulty in drawing any line between accounting as a mere facilitator of organizational action and the role which it can play in the furtherance of broader social and political initiatives, between its contribution to managing economic resources to other ends and its positive furtherance of the priority of the economic itself. Indeed I sense that no such line can be drawn. Whatever the reasoning that might lie behind even a small, incremental and seemingly technical extension of the accounting craft, it can contribute to the creation of a new visibility and establish a new economic linkage between seemingly disparate organizational actions. Even if such aims had not entered into their original justification, seemingly minor amendments to the accounting regime can, at times, nevertheless play some role in the articulation of a new organizational and social significance.

One of the important ways in which accounting can have such effects stems from its potential to create 'facts' out of the uncertain world of the past and even, in a planning context, the future. What was and still is debated and challenged can give rise to a residue of accounting calculations of what is costly, beneficial and of value. A world of the seemingly precise, specific and quantitative can in this way emerge out of that of the contentious and the uncertain. A calculative priority can be given to the economic rather than the social. Costs, consequences and benefits can come to be divided into the defined and seemingly known and the imprecise and intangible. In such ways accounting, often by a slow process of change, can and does create very different ways of organizational and social functioning. Particular emphases are given. Only certain chains of reaction are made visible. Only some consequences of action enter into the world of the precise, the known, and even, what is considered to be knowable. In part, at least, what comes to be known of organizational reality starts to be created by the accountings of it. A different view of what is central and what is peripheral can start to be reinforced by the ways in which the calculations of accounting intertwine with the complex functionings of organizations as we know them.

Such changes in visibility can sometimes be accompanied by other changes in organizational life. Expertise in the creation of particular organizational realities starts to emerge and be rewarded. Different legitimacies can come to be attached to arguments and viewpoints depending on the extent to which they appeal to the domain of the newly factual. Quite specific calculative procedures for decision making and resource allocation can come to be used in contexts where underlying disagreements remain.

Accounting, in other words, can become implicated in the creation of a domain where technical expertise can come to dominate political debate. By appealing to the centrality of the newly visible, an imperative for technical action can more readily be justified. What were previously seen to be problems of political priority can now start to be seen as requiring management guidance and expertise. We must now face the facts of the reality newly emergent. Rather than debating and arguing, we must appeal to those with expertise in the technical. Politics seemingly must stay at the door of public organizations. Within them, so it is said, planning, decision making, resource allocation and the evaluation of performance must come to be seen in technical and managerial terms. The emerging domain of the technically factual can start to claim a priority over the domain of the political, sometimes restructuring in the process what is seen to be the sphere for legitimate political debate and action.

Of course not all changes in public sector accounting raise such fundamental questions. And, as we will see, the ambiguity of accounting practices can be such that it often has an uncertain relationship to political practice. Nevertheless both some specific proposals for accounting change and the general emphasis which together they place on the managerial and the economic suggest that at times accounting developments do need to be seen in such wider terms. Although often masked by the language and rationality of the technical and the procedural, accounting can and does have quite profound consequences in the political sphere. Because of this it is always as important to consider the context of accounting use and the factors both impinging and likely to impinge upon it as it is to analyse the technical bases of any new accounting proposals. All are important for making an informed assessment.

Seen in such terms, some of my other uncertainties about the current pace of developments in the area of public sector accounting might become more understandable. For instance, I still have difficulty understanding the complex organizational and social dynamics which result in specific public sector accounting initiatives. As an outsider I have often found it difficult, and indeed still do so, to distinguish between the advance of accounting for ritualistic, legitimizing and rationalizing reasons and its advance out of a belief that it can and should engage with the detail of organizational process, to change and hopefully to improve the organization rather than to justify its status quo. Another concern is not unrelated to this. For although I am interested in the provision of intelligent information on the use of economic resources, I nevertheless do have some more fundamental worries about the appeals that so frequently seem to be made to the bureaucracy of systems and to the formality rather than the actuality of planning and organizational control and decision making. Not only can such initiatives sometimes mask either a more explicitly political or legitimizing intent to change the structures of language, meaning and significance either within the organization or without, but also, even when they strive more directly for some form of organizational improvement, they seem to ignore what I see as the very real dangers that can stem from a bureaucratization of concern rather than a more informed and nuanced attempt to disturb and redirect the factors that mobilize action within organizations.

One last concern, possibly one that may well be implicit in those already mentioned, relates to the very real degree of ambiguity that is present in many debates in the area of public sector accounting. The concept of efficiency illustrates this well. Just what is efficiency? At best it is a concept that can be subject to a wide variety of interpretations. Although it is possible to change the world in the name of efficiency, there are very real problems in relating the generality of the concept to the specific operational procedures, let alone their specific consequences in organizations, that can flow from its articulation and use. Of course that very ambiguity is a very positive factor in political discourse. It is difficult to disagree with a concern with efficiency. Who wants to be inefficient? Be that as it may, the indeterminacy of the concept can be much more problematic at the level of its organizational implementation. While not wishing to dissent from the rhetoric, I may well object to what is done in the name of it in any specific instance, either in terms of organizational procedures and practices or their organizational and social consequences. As with efficiency, the ambiguity of so many of the concepts that are appealed to as mobilizing concerns in recent debates in the public domain seemingly enables an uncoupling of the general from that which happens in its name. To me this is something worthy of very genuine debate.

At this stage in my argument I would like to extend my comments on just two of my concerns with recent developments. First, I turn to the intermingling of accounting and politics. Second, I will discuss in a little more detail some of the implications which I see as flowing from the complexity of the organizational processes associated with the advancement of both abstract concepts of efficiency and specific organizational practices, such as accounting, that go along with them.

As far as the political dimensions of accounting are concerned, I do not want to be interpreted as implying that the intermingling of accounting with political affairs is a new phenomenon. Accounting's role in creating a strategic visibility of the economic has ensured it a long history of involvement in the political area.

The very rise of notions of political accountability in the public sector resulted in the advance of both audit and accounting. Long before there was a legislative requirement for the audit of private accounts, we should remember that the municipal reform movements of the 1830s resulted in the establishment of the District Audit Service, thereby giving the public sector a longer history of expert financial scrutiny. Moreover the political debate and modernization movements that gave rise to the present central civil service also concerned themselves with questions of financial control and accountability, creating the Exchequer and Audit Department and the post of Comptroller and Auditor General.

Neither is the appeal to efficiency a new phenomenon in the public realm. In the 1870s Joseph Chamberlain justified his municipal policies not only on the grounds of pubic welfare but also on the basis of the argument that there were economies to be made by efficient municipal management which could in turn produce profits with which to subsidize rate-borne expenditures (Gyford, 1985). Later the Fabians also came to advocate both a concern with efficiency and the roles which modern methods of administration, including accounting, could play to this end. Addressing his fellow members of the Fabian Society, H G Wells said that those who would municipalize activities must also 'develop the most efficient bodies possible' (Wells (1959), quoted in Gyford, 1985). For Wells and others of his political persuasion the advance of efficiency and the utilization of the techniques associated with it were related to the achievement of an overall social efficiency rather than a concept that was orientated solely towards private gain. Perhaps in this context it should not be surprising that the authors of the first British text on cost accounting – Garkle and Fells – were founding members of the Fabian Society.

Around the turn of the century, in the midst of a period of national questioning and debate, there developed a more widespread efficiency movement that encapsulated concerns with the body and its health and reproduction and the mind and its education and training as well as the organization and its management (Searle, 1971). But although the wider ramifications of the use of the efficiency concept were to have a profound impact on social consciousness, institutions and policies, by the 1940s the concept had become increasingly associated with the realm of the economic, where it provided a basis for an interest in the achievement of economies of scale, once again considered from the perspective of national needs rather than private gains. On this basis some of the arguments for the advent of Public Corporations as the vehicles for nationalization and even the creation of the National Health Service were mobilized. Efficiency had come to infuse and influence the language of political debate and the arguments appealed to for the rationalization of action.

Even at that time, however, such concerns were not seen as unproblematic by some. Building on the essential ambiguity of the concept of efficiency, Wright Robinson, a former Lord Mayor of Manchester, said in 1948 (Robinson (1948), quoted in Gyford, 1985):

> Many . . . feel that a point has been reached in this drive when technical efficiency is being pursued without sufficient consideration being given to the long term effect on the democratic efficiency of a human society.

Such doubts did not prevent the forward march of the concern with efficiency, either at that time or subsequently. Striving to promote the efficiency of the private sector, the State advocated the increasing use of management accounting techniques and other practices of rational management. In subsequent times institutions were established to restructure the corporate economy in the name of increased efficiency and enhanced competitiveness. Mergers were seen as a means of ensuring economies of scale rather than monopoly power. Focusing increasingly on the purely economic rationale for investment, agencies of the State sought to promote the use of modern methods of economic investment appraisal.

A not dissimilar rhetoric still permeates political debate. But rather than the public trying to promote the efficiency of the private, the public realm is now itself the focus of deliberation as the practices associated with the private sector (many of which had previously been the target of public promotion) are advocated as a means of increasing the efficiency of the use made of scarce economic resources in public sector organizations.

Admittedly such an historical survey is all too brief and many significant episodes have been ignored. However, I hope that it has nevertheless illustrated how the concept of efficiency and the techniques and practices that are presumed to be associated with it have not only been intertwined with the pursuit of politics but also have been advanced from a number of very different political perspectives. So perceived, accounting can be appreciated as a phenomenon that has been caught up with and related to a wide variety of social, political and economic movements and concerns, only some of which have been articulated in the course of its furtherance and transformation. If nothing else, such an awareness should help to instill a concern with both the ambiguous and changing nature of the concept of efficiency and, thereby, an appreciation of the important role played by the management practices, such as accounting, that serve to provide a precise operationalization of its meaning and significance at any particular point in time. In some senses it is through such specific manifestations of the wider phenomenon, and their actual consequences, that we come to know in more concrete and visible terms the issues that are actually at stake.

The ambiguities associated with accounting's use also inform my difficulties in understanding the organizational dynamics which can result in public sector accounting change. To illustrate this difficulty, let me initially refer to an experience I had a number of years ago (see Hopwood, 1984).

After being privy to a series of meetings which one major public sector corporation held to evaluate and reform its management accounting systems, I became fascinated by the highly abstract notion of managerial process which underlay accounting change. Participants in the exercise dissociated themselves personally from the imperatives which they saw pushing for change. They were not so unhappy with the old information. They did not want the new information. They, it seems, accessed a wide and rich variety of formal and informal information already. They already knew what was going on. Still, however, change was contemplated and eventually agreed, not in the name of any specific practical use or user but rather in the name of a 'person' whom I came to see as residing in the (empty) middle of the table, a 'person' of some considerable significance whom I later came to describe as the person on the Clapham Omnibus. Rather than explicitly acknowledging the operative interests in a centralization of influence, an information flow that would increase the salience of economic factors and a central concern for increasing the structured component of the managerial task, the participants repeatedly referred to the decision needs of a 'person' whom they admitted had very different information desires than themselves. As a result of this experience I became fascinated with the practical interest in seemingly abstract conceptions of information use and the ways in which a rhetoric of facilitating rational decision making can mask a variety of other interests in accounting change.

Building on this example, I would like to extend my arguments relating to the ways in which accounting relates to organizational action.

As the example itself illustrates, although accounting can be appealed to in times of economic restraint, such as now, to provide information to help allocate scarce economic resources, potentially, to a variety of ends wider than the economic itself, I do not think that such a conception of the role of accounting in and of itself gives a full and fair – one might say true and fair – account of the factors implicated in the advance of accounting and the achievement of its consequences. For accounting is appealed to for reasons much wider than its particular technical enabling roles, important though at times these may be. The visibilities which it creates can play a role in mobilizing power and influence both within organizations and without.

Accounting can also play more symbolic, but none the less significant, roles. It can help to shift the patterns of organizational significance. It can facilitate the articulation of new structures of meaning. It can help to demonstrate a concern with the economic at times when economic priorities and ideologies are dominant, such as now.

Having such a diversity of origins and roles, the relationship which accounting has to action is not surprisingly subject to some degree of indeterminacy. Moreover, as organizational participants respond to new pressures and concerns, the organizational accounts are rarely completely transformed. Accountings accumulate in organizations, reflecting both the crises of the past and the concerns of the present, and those stemming from the former, creating, as they do, their own visibilities and emphases, are only rarely inconsequential. A singular rationality is almost never in play in the accounting domain. Competing rationalities and purposes, diverse visibilities and a variety of interpretative schemas serve to disrupt any singularity that might be promulgated as an accounting mission. And, if only because of this, the organizational and social actions that rise from accounting inventions are positively and often surprisingly enacted rather than being mere reflections of any predetermined intent.

Accounting does not always achieve what it sets out to achieve. Indeed in a complex organizational setting, a concern with only the economic can never do justice to the mobilization of the diverse emphases, resources and concerns that are required to create even particular economic outcomes. Abstract notions of economic rationality have difficulty engaging with the multidimensional characteristics of organizational life. The technical, the social and the environmental need more direct management even for the fulfilment of economic aims. The time scales implicit in the conventional economic calculus often do not relate to those underlying the rhythms of competitive and technological change. And the modes of formal organization and patterns of influence engendered by the visibilities which accounting often creates might not be compatible with the responsiveness and capacity to adapt and change that modern circumstances require. The static categorizations and the normative standardizations that are implicit in the conventional accounting craft may relate uneasily to the turbulence of a particular organizational setting.

Indeed such concerns have provided the basis for the recent development of a widespread 'worrying about management accounting' in the corporate sector (Hopwood, 1985), not least in the USA. Often initiated by enterprises faced with a more competitive environment, even senior financial executives have been encouraged to ponder on the adequacy of their own craft in the name of wider corporate objectives. Studies and investigations have been commissioned. More probing questions have been posed of the accounting mentality. Attempts have been made to extend the range of organizational visibility. The accounting craft has been complemented by information on other significant aspects of organizational performance. More explicitly related to longer-term planning, accounting has been given a more strategic posture. Ad-hoc analyses and interpretations are now starting to be emphasized alongside the routinization of concern that so far has tended to characterize the accounting craft.

There are indeed some signs that accounting itself is in the process of being brought to account. It undoubtedly remains an important and influential form of organizational practice, but the obviousness of its functionality is at least starting to be questioned from a wider managerial perspective. Economic calculation is coming to be seen in more problematic terms. Accounting is increasingly being seen as something that needs to be much more proactively mobilized and consciously related to the functioning of other organizational practices if enterprise objectives are to be met.

Returning to the consideration of current developments in public sector accounting, it might appear paradoxical that so much of the conventional wisdom of accounting of the past seemingly is being transferred unproblematically to the public realm at the very time when it is being subjected to more questioning in the private sector. Of course, in part this reflects the relative lack of prior investment in quite rudimentary procedures in some public organizations. Be that as it may, the development of a wider and more questioning discourse around accounting has encouraged some people to look further than concerns with organizational level economic rationality for explanations of the upsurge in the appeals to public accounting, in fact to explanations which place less emphasis on the direct technical rationality of the craft and more on its symbolic and politically strategic properties. Indeed at the present time it is tempting to place at least some emphasis on the role of accounting in reflecting a conformity to dominant economic values and political priorities. However, although such an explanation certainly should not be dismissed, in and of itself it provides only a partial account of the symbolic nature of the appeals being made to accounting practice. Not only does it not do justice to the history of the involvement of accounting and economic conceptions of efficiency in diverse political arenas but also it fails to consider the ways in which accounting might be seen as a sign of a wider notion of sound and effective management – a long-standing and peculiarly important concern in the United Kingdom.

To enable me to take this part of my argument further, I would like to offer some elements of a short, albeit idiosyncratic Hopwoodian account of accounting in the United Kingdom – an account that some might consider consists of a number of provocative (and certainly debatable) statements and the drawing of a number of very tentative conclusions.

I am not sure how widely it is realized that the United Kingdom has one of the highest national investments in accounting in the western world. Although there admittedly are problems of definition, I nevertheless think that it can be argued that we have one of the highest, if not the highest, accountant per capita ratios of any industrialized nation. And that investment shows every sign of growing before our very eyes, consuming an ever larger proportion of our skilled human resources. In a country where only a modest proportion of the relevant age group enter higher education, over 10 per cent of all university graduates (in all subjects) have been entering the accountancy profession in recent years.

Despite such facts, we have incredibly little understanding of the factors behind the long-standing and still developing British investment in accounting expertise. The nature of our capital markets is most likely involved in this, as is their role in the structuring of British industry through mergers and acquisition – a role which could well have implemented a distinct financial rather than business logic in the governance structures of the resultant enterprises. However, I sense that other factors are also involved, and to a brief consideration of these I now turn.

There is reason to think that economic, social and political circumstances in the United Kingdom have stimulated our urge to account. On the economic side, the country has a long history of economic problems and restraint, albeit one peppered with periods of prosperity and growth. Economic resources have been at a premium, particularly in the manufacturing sector, and pennies have been seen as having to be counted. Indeed it is in such a 'newly poor' environment (Olofsson and Svalander, 1975) that extensive investments in economic visibility and calculation take place, albeit, in this case, repeatedly so, even though it is now sensed that the resultant internal financial visibility may have an equivocal relationship, at best, to the external circumstances which lie behind the economic difficulties. Be that as it may, the urge to economize provides a fruitful environment for the growth of accounting systems and the wider acknowledgement of the expertise of the practitioners associated with them. In all probability social circumstances may have reinforced such concerns. A contentious society with continued debates over the priority to be given to the economic has resulted in a national investment in the articulation of economic rationales for action and a conception of a determining economic reality.

Enterprise management has not been able to presume the existence of a disciplined, orderly and economically orientated work force. The factory and the office have had to invest in strategies and practices for socio-economic as well as organizational control, and the means for their legitimation, and the regimes of economic visibility and calculation that accounting systems create have been tied up with such attempts to gain mastery over the social, the economic and the organizational infrastructure of the enterprise. Their effectiveness in so doing perhaps has been more problematic, however, a factor that paradoxically might well be implicated in the continued appeals for investment in the accounting craft.

Partly because of the significance of the economic and social problems endemic to Britain, there also has been a long history of direct and indirect government intervention in the economy, which continues to the present day. Having often to rely on surrogates of the corporate economy and its components, such political strategies also have utilized the economic visibility provided by accounting systems. This is true of concerns with taxation and its strategic fine-tuning, with wartime attempts to control prices and profits in the name of social equity, with the pursuit of macro-economic policies orientatated to the control of wages and prices, 271
and with the operational development of micro-economic policies of industrial investment, industrial restructuring and regional development, and the re-orientation of management in the public sector.

Indeed we should recognize that the accountancy profession in the United Kingdom was born in the context of government regulation of and intervention in the economy, and has continued to flourish in that context. Difficulties associated with the administration of the bankruptcy laws of the State provided a powerful incentive for the formation of a professional institute. Thereafter the profession developed in the context of a market for audit services that was to become legally required, and eventually gained a legal monopoly in its provision. The role which accountants played in price and profit control during the First World War not only enhanced the legitimacy of costing, a task that previously had been deemed to be the province of clerks rather than professionals (Loft, 1986), but also increased the social prestige of accounting practitioners. Subsequently accountants were active in governmental attempts to restructure the economy in the 1920s and 1930s and in the post-war reconstruction served as agents of the State's concern with improving management expertise and practices in the private sector. Today that active involvement on the axis between State and the private sector continues. So much of the work of professional accountants resides within the interstices of State interventionist policies, not only in areas such as taxation and corporate restructuring, but also in their capacity as applied economic consultants, specialists in the compilation of economic data and intelligence.

Even though it is difficult to understand the contemporary significance of the accountancy profession in the United Kingdom without appreciating its mutual intertwining with the modern conception of the State, the profession itself also has adopted a most entrepreneurial stance. It has repeatedly done what it has not done before. It moved into industrial accounting and administration after having seen such work as too lowly. It has been an innovator in the application of office equipment and information technology. Now it is moving into general management consultancy and, of particular significance in the context of the present argument, the public sector. Such an entrepreneurial posture has no doubt been enabled by the absence of any effective competition. Lawyers in the United Kingdom have, until recently, stayed with the law. And unlike the USA or continental Europe, Britain has tended not to invest in university trained experts in economic praxis.

So accounting has continued to march forward in the United Kingdom for a variety of quite diverse reasons. Interestingly, however, our high national investment in the area has been extremely unevenly distributed, a

phenomenon which is itself little understood. Outside of immediate professional circles, accountants have tended to be concentrated in British manufacturing industry and, to some extent, local government. Until recently there were relatively few in the financial sector, not a high proportion in the service sector and a very small number indeed in central government and its agencies.

Any account of accounting needs to probe into this uneven distribution. I sense that an investigation might reveal many of the same factors operating that lay behind the expansion of accounting *per se*. Economic difficulties have been particularly severe in the manufacturing sector. State intervention also has traditionally been orientated towards manufacturing and local government. And the contention about the priority to be given to the economic has been a phenomenon associated with the manufacturing enterprise, as is illustrated by the rise of an interest in costing and economic calculation alongside the rise of a more active shop steward movement. However, I sense that even more might be at stake, not least at the present time.

So pursuing my investigation of the factors implicated in accounting elaboration and change in the public sector, I would like to advance the proposition that one significant (albeit partial) factor involved in an organization's desire to account can be a questioning of its legitimacy. When the bases of organizational action are being challenged, when prevailing views of organizational purpose are being undermined, when significant groups start to interrogate and question the organization on grounds different from those involved in its current functioning and when questions are asked of either the adequacy or appropriateness of its modes of operation, there is a tendency both for the organization to account for itself by offering a more detailed and strategically directed explanation of its rationales, modes of functioning and consequences, and, where possible, for it to invest in the symbols and practices of the newly emergent rationality, seeking at least to conform outwardly to the newly articulated expectations for its behaviour and mode of operation.

Such appeals to legitimating strategies are not unfamiliar to the accounting profession both in the United Kingdom and the USA, and no doubt elsewhere. At times when its institutions for accounting regulation have no longer had sufficient authority and legitimacy, and yet do not wish to appeal directly to the democratic mandate of the State, they have invested in the bases of alternative legitimacies. Although not becoming part of the apparatus of government, they nevertheless have tended to incorporate some of the procedural rules associated with democratic institutions, including, in the American context, a concern with due process. Recognizing the singular interest base of existing bodies, the profession has sought to widen the representative nature of the regulatory agencies, once again appealing to political notions of the legitimate bases for authority. Not least 273
in significance, being aware of the traditional nature of professional claims to expertise, professional regulatory agencies have started to commission more modern rational analyses of the accounting craft and the technical options on their agendas.

Similar shifts in the bases of legitimacy have confronted a multitude of other organizations. Further investigation might reveal, for instance, that accounting and accountants were so appealed to by manufacturing concerns amidst the economic crises of the 1920s and 1930s and in the midst of their subsequent reconstruction. More significantly in the present context, we can today witness the questioning and probing that faces organizations in the public sector, not least on economic grounds. Questions are being asked not only of their right to exist and their rationales for action but also of the appropriateness of their organizational forms and both the efficiency and the effectiveness of their management functioning. No longer is it sufficient to claim a social, political or even macro-economic rationale. The language of political economic discourse has been brought to bear on the rationales underlying their existence within the public domain and the most detailed aspects of their functioning. As a result, many organizations are now having to account for themselves or at least shift the basis of their accounting. Rationales have to be articulated and newly stated in the emergent vocabulary. Their performance on economic grounds has to be made known. And there has to be a public demonstration of their commitment to the new ethos by an investment in the apparatus of economic management.

Hardly surprisingly, accounting itself has been appealed to in the process of such transformations, not only as a means of giving a direct account, a way of satisfying the will to disclose, but also more indirectly as a way of demonstrating a commitment to the now accepted and legitimate modes of economic functioning. As such, accounting has been appealed to as much, if not more so, for what it is rather than for what it might help the organization to become. Accounting seemingly has been seen as a manifestation of sound economic management, of appropriate organizational arrangements and of a commitment to the objective of efficiency. In the midst of the urgency to change, accounting has been provided with a symbolic rather than a technically instrumental role. It has been implicated in the management of appearances – a peculiarly important phenomenon in the British scene.

Cast in such terms it is possible to appreciate not only the haste with which new accountings have been implanted into organizations of amazing diversity but also the very possibility of so doing in such incredibly short periods of time. Although a consulting boom has been based on such speedy transformations, a phenomenon that might itself further change the nature of the accountancy profession, the speed of implementation contrasts sharply with the slow and often agonizing process of change confronting those who have sought to instil a conception of economic reasoning into the detailed management functioning of very similar organizations.

Accounting, it would appear, is being appealed to as an indicator of good management, independently of the means through which it engages with and becomes coupled to the detailed processes of organizational functioning. Within the prevailing political discourse, a value and legitimacy is seemingly being set on accounting itself. This is a phenomenon of some interest in its own right. However research has yet to confront the perplexing question of how, in the United Kingdom, what are seen to be organizational practices of the private sector, and particularly industry, can be seen to instil a legitimacy for the managerial functioning of public bodies, being drawn, as they are, from an organizational sector that itself has an equivocal record of economic performance.

The mystery is further increased when one looks at some of the more specific appeals that are being made to both accounting in particular and economic calculation in general. Once again, a paradox emerges. At few times in the past have more appeals been made to 'facts', 'economic reality' and 'the imperative of economic circumstances'. Yet it is difficult to remember a time when those very same facts and realities have been more open to management and manipulation. The unemployment statistics have been a floating phenomenon. Attempts have been made to recast the measurement of inflation and the Public Sector Borrowing Requirement, despite both seemingly having a significance as real objects for policy initiatives. Local government accounting has become a site for artistic creation and the preprivatization accounts of some of the nationalized industries have served as a source of amazement for those interested in the finer aspects of the accountant's skill. One could go on. The facts, accounts and economic statistics to which policy appeals are made seem to be increasingly seen as moveable and manageable phenomena, possibly more so than ever before. Apparently the facts are not the facts.

It would seem that in the 1980s this can be done even if people know that it is being done. Whilst newspaper headlines proclaim 'When in doubt fix the index' (*Guardian*, 21 June, 1985), 'It just goes to show that one man's statistics are another's lies' (*Guardian*, 16 October, 1985), 'How Ministers fiddle figures' (*New Society*, 28 February, 1986) and 'When people are right and statistics are wrong' (*New Statesman*, 23 May, 1986), a fact can still be used as a fact. Unlike the days of the 1970s when investments had to be made in conceptually different measurement schemas with externally accepted logics and rationales, such as inflation accounting and value added, to change conceptions of economic reality, a more direct and seemingly more confident approach is in order today at the very time when the language of the factual has become a more dominant feature of political discourse. It is almost as if some claim to know a reality hidden by the facts.

Although research has yet to grapple with all the factors implicated in the diverse and often paradoxical pressures impacting on the public sector and its accountings, their consequences are evident for all to see. The National Health Service, one of the cheapest vehicles for health care provision in the industrialized world, is under pressure to invest in more legitimate instruments of management, many of which have difficulty becoming connected with the complexities and subtleties of its specific management processes. In local government, accounting has been used as an instrument to further the influence of central government, in the process stimulating such a display of creative accounting that even the *New Statesman* (30 August, 1985) could proclaim the virtues of council accountants for their efforts in maintaining an informational buffer between the local and the central. Universities are being encouraged to adopt abstract management regimes that seemingly have little relationship to either the educational task and the generation of knowledge, or the very real changes that are needed if British higher education is to adapt to a modern era. The nationalized industries have invested in externally orientated management systems to manage their relationship with Whitehall, and when accounting started to be politicized in the National Coal Board, the official response was speedy and forceful, all too obviously, recognizing the role which a legitimate account plays in creating the pretence of a dividing line between management and politics, between the private and the public.

So although accounting has important symbolic properties and is implicated in the management of changes in legitimacy in society at large, such examples illustrate that it is more than a mere symbol. Accounting can penetrate into organizational functioning. It can create a particular visibility. It can facilitate the construction of a specific significance. It can shape the ways in which arguments can be mobilized and the information and bodies of expertise which are deemed to be relevant for their resolution. It can serve as a means for transferring power and influence, allowing what was hidden to be observed and enabling constraints to be imposed on economic action. Accounting can be an enabling craft. It can result in organizational change. Through such processes even symbolic accountings can have their effects. What might initially have been uncoupled to organizational process can start to play a more proactive role. Accounting can and does have its effects, although often ones that did not enter into its original justification.

276 Indeed much more effort should be devoted to knowing accounting through its effects. Rather than focusing on general rationales, more attention needs to be placed on the specific manifestations of accounting in specific organizations. The generality of the practice needs to be questioned. Instead we should become interested in the ways in which it interacts with specific decision making and control processes, its particular consequences for resource allocation and through these effects, the ways in which over time it moderates organizational action and its consequences. Accounting, in other words, should be accounted for. It should be known for what it does rather than for what it might be able to do.

That represents the main message with which I would like to conclude the analysis. It might appear simple. Indeed it is. However I think that it is one of great importance. Accounting needs to be recognized for what it is – a useful but imperfect craft that operates in highly localized and specific contexts. Compared with the abstract and highly generalized notions accompanying accounting in the past, we want more adequate ways of appreciating accounting in the specific contexts in which it operates.

Adequately formulated, such knowledge would help us to recognize the wider pressures impacting on accounting and the accountancy profession. It would help us to disentangle the conflicting pressures that I am sure will be of greater intensity and concern in the years ahead. By looking at accounting in action, such a way of appreciating accounting will not blind us to the broader organizational, social and political consequences of the craft. Rather, the insights into the uses made of it, the ways in which it relates to organizational action and the means through which it moderates organizational processes and structures, and has its effects, will help us to see accounting as it is rather than as it often accounts for itself.

It is my view that such understandings are necessary if the positive enabling properties of accounting are to be realized. For although they have not been emphasized in this analysis, the values of appropriate and intelligently assembled economic information can be enormous. The realization of that potential needs, however, a means for grounding it in particular contexts, unless, that is, we too want to defend an organization from external pressures. In that context the generality of the appeal is of extreme utility, but, of course, such a use would represent a quite explicit political act.

REFERENCES

Burchell, S, Clubb, C and Hopwood, A G, Accounting in its Social Context: Towards a History of Value Added in the United Kingdom, *Accounting, Organisations and Society* (1985), pp 381–413.

Elias, N, *The Civilising Process: The History of Manners*, Basil Blackwell, 1978.

Elias, N, *The Court Society*, Basil Blackwell, 1983.

Gyford, J, *The Politics of Local Socialism*, George Allen and Unwin, 1985.

Hirschman, A, *Shifting Involvements: Private Interest and Public Action*, Princeton University Press, 1982.

Hopwood, A G, Accounting Research and Accounting Practice: The Ambiguous Relationships Between the Two. A paper presented at the Conference on New Challenges to Management Research, Leuven, 1984.

Hopwood, A G, The Development of 'Worrying' About Management Accounting, in K B Clark, R H Hayes and C Lorenz, eds, *The Uneasy Alliance: Managing the Productivity–Technology Dilemma*, Harvard Business School, 1985.

Loft, A, Towards a Critical Understanding of Accounting: The Case of Cost Accounting in the UK, 1914–1925, *Accounting Organisations and Society* (1986), pp 137–170.

Moore, B, *Privacy: Studies in Social and Cultural History*, M E Sharpe, 1984.

Olofsson, C, and Svalander, P A, The Medical Services Change Over to a Poor Environment – 'New Poor' Behaviour. Unpublished working paper, University of Linköping, 1975.

Robinson, W, Labour and Local Government, in H Tracey, ed, *The British Labour Party*, Caxton, 1948, Vol II, pp 177–190.

Searle, G R, *The Quest for National Efficiency*, Basil Blackwell, 1971.

Wells, H G, A Paper on Administrative Areas Read Before the Fabian Society, reprinted in A Maas, ed, *Area and Power*, The Free Press, 1959, pp 206–221.

Social Accounting and the Social Significance of Accounts

SOCIAL ACCOUNTING – THE WAY AHEAD?*

Anthony G. Hopwood, Oxford Centre for Management Studies.

The idea of a social accounting has captivated the imagination of a large number of people in a comparatively short period of time. Experiments are apace; articles are being printed in both professional and research journals; even books on the subject are starting to pour from the presses in many Western countries, and in Japan; and conferences are being held – of which this is the first in the United Kingdom.

For someone accustomed to the rather slow pace of development in accounting this is itself a surprising phenomenon. But the diversity of interested parties is equally surprising. Few concepts, and social accounting must still be considered at the conceptual level since the practicalities for the most part remain embryonic, have ever before had such an apparent appeal to both the critics of our present enterprises and organisations and numerous senior managers in these same institutions. Social accounting, however, is being 281
discussed, and in some cases used, by such diverse agencies. Although first articulated by those concerned with establishing, and monitoring, the wider accountability of the enterprise and the public organisation, as presently formulated and perceived the concept also appeals to those who seek to reinforce the legitimacy of the constitution and social role of the enterprise as we now know it.

The very diversity of appeal and the embryonic stage of development make it difficult to outline a future path, or even paths, for the development of social accounting. Yet this is my appointed task on this occasion. So, before proceeding to tackle my brief, I must state that my comments are only, and can only be, based on my role as an interested observer of the accounting scene. Neither by temperament nor training do I make any claim to be a futurologist, least of all in the accounting area.

IS THERE A WAY AHEAD?

Even a fleeting acquaintance with recent developments in accounting must introduce an element of caution into anyone's predictions for the way ahead. Surely no one could have forecast the accounting turmoils of the late 1960's, the ensuing institutional innovations and the subsequent meanderings and conflicts in the 1970's! So much seems to have happened in such a short period of time.

In retrospect, however, such developments are now starting to be considered in a wider perspective. Whilst it was, and still is, difficult to appreciate the speedy movement of events in a purely accounting context, when considered in the light of the changing structure of the economy, emergent social and

* The author acknowledges the financial support of the Anglo-German Foundation for the Study of Industrial Society for the research project on which this paper is based.

political changes, changing expectations of enterprise and institutional behaviour, the more general demystification of professional expertise and status, and the conserving role of the present institutional embodiment of accounting thought and practice, the changes and the consequent conflicts and uncertainties, become more amenable to interpretation.

It is only because of such a growing appreciation of the wider forces that shape the development of accounting that we have any possibility for meaningfully discussing the emergent nature of social accounting. Social accounting must be considered, in other words, not merely as a potential new addition to the accountant's ever expanding array of techniques, important as this may be, but rather in the light of if and how it relates to wider patterns of social and economic development.

In the present discussion of the potential for social accounting I therefore emphasise the social nature of **all** accounting thought and practice, providing thereby the possibility for seeing social accounting as a particular manifestation of accounting as social. Thereafter consideration is given to the growing international experience in the area, using this, in part, as a basis for considering some of the factors that presently are influencing the social roles played by social accounting.

Accounting as Social

All too often accounting has been seen as a rather static and purely technical phenomenon. Perhaps because of only recently having emerged from a long period of comparative stability in the accounting domain, reflecting, in part, no doubt, the conserving role of professional interests, it is easy to have a view of accounting as accounting as accounting. But nothing could be further from the truth. Any familiarity with the history of accounting, let alone with the all too obvious recent developments, suggests that the purposes, processes and techniques of accounting and its human, organisational and social roles have never been stated. The distinctions drawn by accountants, and the methods which they use, can be seen in historical perspective to be creations of the human intellect, reflecting social as well as economic evaluations. They have evolved, are evolving and no doubt will continue to evolve in relation to changes in the economic, social, technological and political environments of organisations.

The recent inflationary era has provided one vivid illustration of the pressures for accounting methods to respond, and in some countries to respond quite quickly, to an important change in the economic environment. But although the impetus for change was economic, we are all well aware of how the ensuing debate on the topic has been influenced by the changing nature of today's institutional and social environment. The government, both directly through the agency of a committee of inquiry and indirectly through the presentation of its evidence and concerns and the establishment of its own interdepartmental committees, has had a much more important role to play.

This, in turn, has brought to bear a wider array of social, economic and political influences on accounting thought and practice. And the inflation accounting debate also illustrates how the primacy of the professional bodies interests in the development of accounting has been questioned by the organised interests of industrialists and industrial accountants and by the media.

In the midst of all the consequent discussions and debates it was all too easy to focus on the disarray and the need to re-establish institutional legitimacy and control. But however important the latter, in particular, may have been and indeed still may be, the opportunity should not be lost to reflect on the implications of the experience for the changing nature of accounting debate. For inflation accounting, albeit a phenomenon in the economic rather than the social domain, provides us with an important illustration of how the more general nature of the world in which we live can and is influencing the pattern of accounting discourse and its outcomes.

But of course at the present time there are many other equally significant economic, social and institutional changes which have the potential to have important implications for the development of accounting thought and practice. And in many areas this potential already is being realised.

Social pressures have influenced the disclosure requirements delineated in company and other legislation and government plans show that these influences continue. Economic problems and the changing structure of this economy have influenced government concerns with productivity and investment, and their taxation and subsidy policies, and these in turn have had major implications for accounting and accountants. At the same time trade union demands for greater disclosure of and access to information have also introduced new requirements and concerns.

One could go on and on. Accountancy practices and problems, and the extent of the accounting domain, are reflections of wider social concerns. And although such a view does not provide us with a basis for anticipating whether or not social accounting, as presently conceived, will become a more prominent part of the accounting domain, it does suggest that we should expect that accounting, broadly defined, will continue to respond to those changes in the social and political environments of both public and private organisations of which we are all increasingly aware. Whether, however, these changes will be perceived to lie in the main stream of accounting development, or some alternative to it, will depend, in part, on the institutional responsiveness of accountants and the accountancy profession.

The Comparative Experience

Merely to itemise the extent of the interest in, and the development of, social accounting does not necessarily provide a basis for predicting developments in the UK in the area. However the present volume and dispersion of interest in the topic in industrialised nations, and the increasing institutionalised form that this is taking, does suggest that the interest is more than merely the latest, and temporary, technical fashion or fad in the accounting area.

In France, for instance, social reports must now be prepared and published by all enterprises employing over 700 people. And the latest information suggests that over a third of all major companies are already experimenting in the area. Interest is also real in Germany and Holland, with major experiments and a growing if early interest in standardisation in the former and over 100 companies preparing reports on the internal social circumstances of their organisation in the latter. In Sweden the publication of the first social report has taken place and several other companies are paying particular attention to the development of internal social accounting formats, one even going so far as to advertise for the first "social accountant". Experiments are also underway in Spain, and outside Europe, companies and other organisations in both Japan and the USA have been discussing the topic and experimenting for some time. In the USA, for instance, 'several major reports on social
284 accounting have now been issued by organisations such as the American Institute of Certified Public Accountants, the National Association of Accountants and the American Accounting Association.

The widespread experimentation with social accounting does suggest that it is a response to social and institutional changes in many industralised nations. Even if the comparative experiences are not seen as a basis for expecting similar developments in the United Kingdom, which might legitimately be the case, at the very least we should have a better appreciation of why this is so.

Social Accounting and the Social Role of Accounting

Most of the discussions of social accounting stress its relationship to emerging pressures for the wider accountability of business and public organisations. Indeed such a relationship was quite explicit in many of the early experiments in social accounting and social auditing undertaken by such independent organisations as the Public Interest Research Centre in the UK and the Council on Economic Priorities in the USA. However although the pressures for greater accountability might continue, they do not provide the only rationale for social accounting, not necessarily the one which has resulted in the proliferation of corporate experiments in the USA and continental Europe. For social accounting also provides a way in which existing corporate interests can attempt to reinforce and extend their social legitimacy.

Faced with a multitude of pressures for change, managers of business and public organisations have turned to a variety of ways of articulating and promoting their existing rationales and demonstrating the extent of their existing involvement in wider concerns. And forms of social accounting certainly have been used in this way. By describing corporate exployment policies, attitudes towards industrial health and safety, policies towards the environment and expenditures on pollution control, and broader patterns of social involvement, the social reports have strived to provide a new and broader legitimacy for the organisation, extending beyond the confines of that implicit in the present modes of corporate reporting.

Real though the demands for broader channels of accountability may be and real though the potential of social accounting might be in the provision of these, in the shorter term, at least, the role that social accounting can play in the supply of social legitimacy might well be the rationale which will provide the basis for extended interest and experimentation in the area in the UK, as elsewhere. For whilst the relationship of social accounting to accountability might depend, in all probability, on the simultaneous existence of other innovative institutions for social discourse and decision making, its ability to articulate the social dimensions of existing actions is more readily available.

So, in the light of both our own and international experiences, there are reasons for expecting a greater interest in the social dimensions of accounting, in general, and in forms of social accounting in particular. I am tempted, therefore, to respond with a certain "yes" to the question as to whether there is a way ahead for some form of broader social accounting. Whether the emerging interest will be related to current approaches to social accounting remains to be established, however, for, as we will now discuss, alternative accountings and indeed alternative approaches to the social processing of information most certainly do exist.

SOCIAL ACCOUNTING AND THE SOCIAL PROCESSING OF INFORMATION*

Accounting represents one way of providing information for the social control of business and public organisations. It can play, as the early advocates of social accounting knew so well, a vital role in defining what is organisationally significant and, through the provision of information structured on this basis, strive to provide a means for the evaluation, review and, as demonstrated by later concerns, the justification of organisational performance. However, given the social and organisational importance of these roles, the extent of the accounting function and its social significance cannot be considered in isolation of other social processes and institutions. For the form that accounting takes and the roles which it plays are dependent, as illustrated in Figure 1, on both the other ways in which societies, and groups within them, attempt to exercise control over organisational actions and performance and the alternative approaches to the social processing of information that are available.

For instance, varying degrees and forms of government control over business enterprises certainly have had, as we are all so well aware, quite important implications for the social processing of information, in general, and for accounting in particular. Similarly different social constitutions for the enterprise, with their different implications for the distribution of power, influence and control, also generate very different needs for management

* An extended discussion of the material presented in this section is forthcoming in A. G. Hopwood, **Accounting and Social Change** *(Pitman)*.

information, for information with which to respond to the different demands for accountability and, given the consequent differences in the definition and roles of stakeholders, for information that helps to ensure continued legitimacy and support.

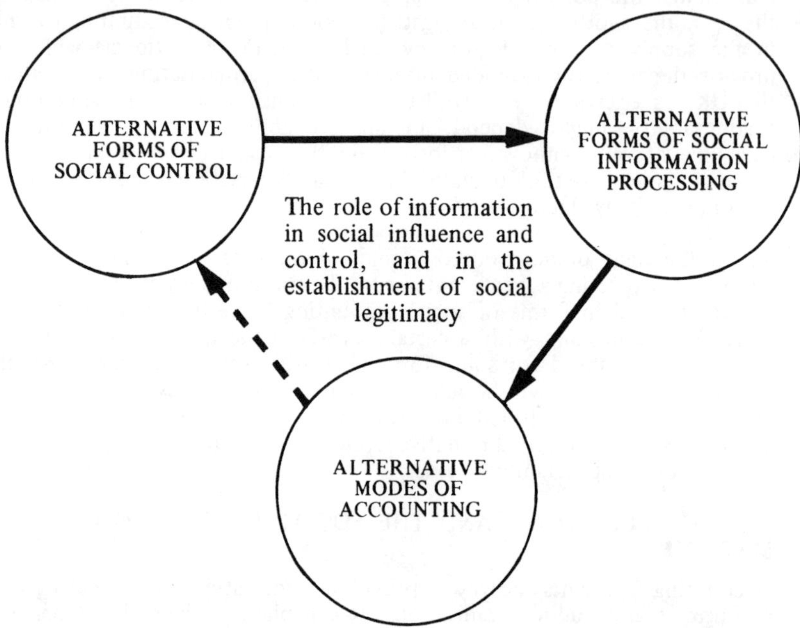

Figure 1 – The Accounting Context

So, given that the provision of information can play a role, albeit a far from costless one, in meeting the demands for greater control over the actions of organisations, what forms can this provision take? What options are available, in other words, and what role might accounting play in this? In considering these questions it is useful to distinguish between approaches which strive to reduce the constraints on the availability and use of existing sources of information and those which are dependent on the production and dissemination of "new" information, as is illustrated in Figure 2.

As evidenced by the outcome of many recent discussions of the social performance of a particular enterprise, societies invest in numerous means for constraining the availability and use of existing sources of information. Many of these take a legal form, including for instance, the laws of libel, slander, blasphemy, patent and copyright. And whilst change in all of these might be slow, and indeed difficult, at least the potentiality of so doing is illustrated by the differences in the scope and restrictiveness of such constraints from one country to another. Similar differences are also evident in national provisions for rights of access to existing sources of information, particularly in the public domain. The constraining influence of the Official Secrets Act in the United Kingdom, for instance, which has been subject to much discussion recently, contrasts with the constitutional provisions for citizen access to public information made in the eighteenth and nineteenth centuries in most of the Scandinavian countries and the similar, although more recent, provision of the US Freedom of Information Act. And although a right of access generally applies to public rather than private organisations, its application to the private sector is starting to emerge even in the UK in some of the recent industrial relations and health and safety legislation and in Sweden is incorporated in a more substantive form in the recent co-determination legislation.

1. Reduce the constraints on the availability and use of existing sources of information.
   i) Change the legal constraints on the use of information.
   ii) Provide access to information.
2. The provision of "new" information.
   i) Reporting and disclosure of further information.
   ii) Invest in "information intermediaries".

Figure 2 – Alternative Strategies for the Social Processing of Information

However threatening the provision of rights of access to information may be to the existing powerful, there is no doubt that this approach to the provision of information is being discussed, debated and even developed in most industrial countries. In the UK, for instance, one only has to think of recent parliamentary initiatives and debates, the use made by some national newspapers of the provision of the US Freedom of Information Act, the deliberations of the Outer Circle Policy Group and other organisations, even the preliminary drafting of similar laws for the UK, and, of course, the government's guarded response to these and other initiatives. But lest anyone should think that the provision of rights of access of information is a panacea for all the problems in the area, further consideration should be given to at least one of the problems associated with it. For there is reason to believe that the granting of access to information can, in the absence of other provisions, result in an exaggeration rather than reduction of information inequalities in society as those already having some access to information use this as a basis for appreciating the relevance of more.

Nevertheless the provision of greater information does not necessarily have to result in the production of more information. Yet, as every accountant knows so well, very often it does because there is either a reluctance to reduce the constraints on existing sources of information, or an inability to do this. So, yet again as we all know so well, a basis is set for ever greater disclosure and the provision of ever more reports to ever more groups and individuals as attempts are made to respond to the pressures for more and more socially relevant information.

But even if society aims to produce and disseminate more information, traditional disclosure and reporting modes are not the only way of doing this. As an alternative, groups within society themselves have established organisations which strive to collect, analyse and disseminate information. I term these "information intermediaries". The press and other sections of the media have always performed this role, sometimes serving, in the process, as an important voice for social accountability. More recently, however, in response to the very same social pressures which stimulated the interest in social accounting, we have seen the creation of numerous other organisations with such a function, ranging from the underground press, including, perhaps, Private Eye, in this category, to such bodies as the Consumers' Association, with its consumer audits, the Friends of the Earth, with, amongst other things, their use of energy accounting, and the Public Interest Research Centre, the originator of social auditing in the UK.

It is important to consider the alternative means for social information processing not only to place social accounting in context but also to stimulate a more extensive consideration of the roles played by the different approaches and their relative strengths and weaknesses as assessed from different points of view. From what sources have existing expressions of social concern emanated? What role has reporting **per se** played? And which interests might be interested in furthering the various alternatives and for what reasons? Whilst there is not the time here to consider such issues, they nevertheless represent vital aspects of any more thorough appraisal of the potential of social accounting.

However even though the role that might be played by increased disclosure and reporting, including that of social accounting must be seen as partial when considered from such a wider perspective, it is nevertheless an important one. For as present methods of accounting demonstrate so well, what is reported and disclosed is capable of having an important influence on social consciousness and action.

Just as we considered the alternative forms for social information processing, it is important to consider alternative modes of accounting. We do this by identifying two sets of important social assumptions underlying the design of any accounting system. The first focusses on the organisation's concern with and openness to wider social and environmental influences, distinguishing between accounting for an organisation in isolation of its environment.

and accounting for an organisation's relationship to, and effects on, its social environment; and the second assumption focusses on the management of conflict within the organisation, again, for the purpose of simplicity, distinguishing between a unitary or dominated organisation and a pluralistic or conflictful organisation. Whilst unitary and dominated organisations most certainly differ, from an accounting point of view, they share the property of requiring an accounting for a single set of interest, be these shared or imposed. In contrast the pluralistic or conflictful organisations requires accountings for differing interests. The four broad types of accounting systems stemming from these assumptions are illustrated in Figure 3.

	Unitary or Dominated Organisation	Pluralistic or Conflictful Organisation
Enterprise in Isolation	e.g. Profit and Loss Accounting e.g. MIS	e.g. Multiple Surplus Accounting e.g. SMIS WIS and MIS
Enterprise in Society	e.g. Social Cost Benefit Analysis	e.g. Social Audit

Figure 3 – Social Assumptions and Alternative Modes of Accounting

Present private sector modes of profit and loss accounting, with their internal MIS manifestations, are shown as emanating from a unitary or dominance perspective where the implications of an enterprise's relationship to a wider social environment are not specifically accounted for. Social cost benefit analysis, however, as developed by economists, strives, albeit problematically, to provide an accounting for the wider social consequences of the enterprise, whilst maintaining a unitary perspective.

Explicit accountings based on pluralistic or conflictful assumptions are more difficult since the aim is not to produce the final account that is conceivable, if not possible, in a unitary situation. Rather the aim is to service, with the provision of information, the divergent interests that are presumed to be present in the organisation and, if possible, to give an account of how each has contributed to the functioning of the organisation and shared in its outcomes. Of course such accountings exist informally in all enterprises. The calculating mechanisms and justificatory procedures used by production department are often very different from those used by marketing and finance department. Those of the latter, however, constitute **the** Accounting, whilst, perhaps unfortunately, the others are officially ignored. But in addition to such ongoing experiences with multiple accountings, more recent efforts have been made in Sweden, for instance, to design Self Management Information Systems (SMIS) that complement more participatory approaches to decision making and, in the case of both Sweden and Germany, to design Workers' Information Systems (WIS) to set alongside the existing MIS. Such accountings, for that is what they are, illustrate, as did the social audit activities in the UK, the possibilities for designing accounting systems posited on very different assumptions of the management and social conditions of the enterprise.

However many of the more recent developments in accounting, including some forms of social accounting, are not considered in the above perspective. For, in my opinion at least, they often represent a response to uncertainty or ambiguity over the social conditions of the enterprise. In such conditions, where the legitimacy of existing institutional forms might be questioned, it is tempting to adapt existing modes of accounting so that might serve the emerging, but still uncertain, social demands for accounting information. The process is illustrated in Figure 4 where the experiments with human resource accounting, various forms of socio-economic calculations and some types of corporate social accounting are shown as the respective elaborations of existing forms of profit and loss accounting, management accounting and social cost benefit analysis.

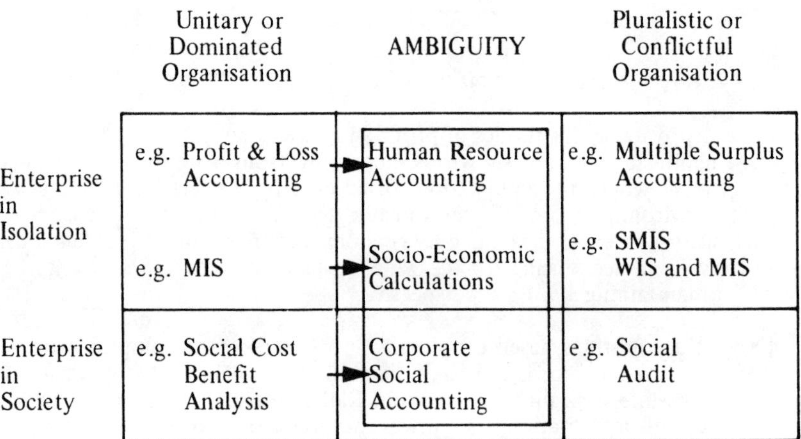

Figure 4 – Social Change and the Elaboration of Accounting Methods

Admittedly the longer term status of at least some of the present elaborations must be regarded as problematic when they are seen as responses to the uncertainties rather than the certainties of the social world. But even such adaptations serve to emphasise the social nature of accounting thought and practice. From this point of view alone we should continue to be interested in these and other forms of experimentation, recognising, in the process, the complexity of the factors that have influenced, are influencing, and more importantly, will continue to influence the definition of the accounting domain and the social as well as technical status of particular approaches and procedures.

SOME SIGNPOSTS TO THE WAY AHEAD

In the light of the above discussion it would be inappropriate for me to offer a detailed prescription for developments in the social accounting area. For social accounting, like all other forms of accounting, is a creation of the world in which we live. Developments, if they do occur, will be influenced not only by the changing nature of social values, institutions and power structures, but also, as we have seen, by the role that accounting strives to and is able to play in social information processing.

So easy answers are not available. I think, however, that some important messages, albeit quite general ones, do emerge from the perspectives that have been discussed in this paper. And to these we now turn.

The first concerns the importance of fully recognising and understanding that the interest in social accounting is a reflection of the changing nature of the world in which we live rather than mere fascination with some new piece of technical gadgetry. For at a purely technical level it most likely is possible to invent a million and one ways of social accounting. Indeed a fair number of these are already with us! Unless, however, they are designed in the light of an appreciating of the changing patterns of social influence and control and those factors that are shaping the social roles which information is serving, they are likely to have a rather limited social significance.

I think, in fact, that it should be emphasised that it is unlikely that purely technical and methodological difficulties will constitute a major barrier to action in the area. For at present a great deal of the relevant information is available within, and outside, organisations and much of it already is disclosed to regulatory agencies and other interested parties. So whilst the possibilities for improvement are ever present, an amazing amount can be done with current information flows and technical capabilities, **if there is the will to act**.

Nevertheless this is still an area where the accountant has a role to play, although not an exclusive one. His or her skills in quantifying, analysing, appraising and reporting information have much to offer. Increasingly, however, the accountant will have to recognise the role of not only other means for processing social information, some of which are going to be debated with greater urgency in the years ahead, but also that of other management colleagues in the social accounting area itself. For many of the relevant understandings will not emanate from within the confines of a single discipline or professional body of knowledge.

The procedents for collaborative endeavour in the accounting area are not as great as they might be. In part this reflects, I think, the tendency of many accountants to define their expertise in terms of the prevailing technical answers rather than their ability to respond to the demands of a problem.

This might be called the "I can do this rather than help you do that" syndrome. There are, however, signs of improvement, not least of which are those stemming from recent attempts to respond to the demands of organisational and social change. And, as a result of such endeavours, I think that there is a growing appreciation that progress in many of the more problematic areas of accounting is dependent on collaborative action.

Such endeavours would be encouraged if we could create in this area at least a climate of real experimentation and learning. Research, for instance, needs to be supported in both the academic and professional communities, and recognising that even at present so much is being done that is not generally known, for once a real effort should be made to disseminate information on the full variety of new initiatives. We should, in other words, be looking at this stage for an array of new approaches and procedures rather than for authoritative statements of what is required.

I emphasise the latter recognising that the temptation to promulgate rules in such an area might well be great. In France, for instance, this route already has been taken and in Germany there is real interest in self-regulation at the corporate level. The very uncertainties, both social and technical, which should argue against the early imposition of order and control can, as these examples illustrate, result in their achievement. Ultimately, of course, rules might be required, if only to ensure comparability and thereby ease the interpretation and use of the information. But, in the early stages at least, the short and turbulent history of rule making in the traditional areas of accounting, where we thought we knew what we were doing, should encourage us to exercise caution and restraint.

Finally let us recognise that social accounting, of all forms of accounting, should be allowed to develop through social processes of consultation and participation. Employees, trade unions, central and local governments and other interested parties should be involved in the design processes. For if the rationale of social accounting is that it should result in greater openness and responsiveness to wider social interests, the social philosophies inherent in the design of the approaches and procedures should not be at variance with the underlying rationale.

SOCIAL ACCOUNTING

294 SOCIAL ACCOUNTING: 1

'The idea of social accounting remains an illusive one'

Anthony Hopwood, *Professor of Accounting and Financial Reporting at the London Business School and* **Stuart Burchell,** *Senior Research Officer, introduce this feature with an explanation of the scope, intentions and practical applications of this new discipline*

THE IDEA of a social accounting has entered into public debate with increasing frequency. Surely, it is claimed, the days when we can reply on only financial indicators for assessing the performance of an organisation are numbered. With greater public emphasis being placed on the wider consequences of organisational activities, be they in the social, political or economic domain, it has been argued that some form of wider accounting must emerge to complement the more narrowly focused financial accountings of the past.

However, despite the increasing interest in social accounting, the idea remains an illusive one. Just what is implied by it? And however fine it might be in theory, how might social accounting be undertaken in practice?

Real concerns

Such concerns are very real ones. For although many might agree on the need for social accounting, there is much less understanding of, let alone agreement on, how it might be done. Admittedly, underlying virtually all of the demands for social accounting are concerns with the wider social responsibility of organisations, be they in the public or the private sector,and the need for greater corporate accountability.

'Social responsibility' and 'accountability' are themselves illusive and contentious concepts, however. Indeed, if we are honest, we must recognise that much of the social accounting debate is about their very definition rather than their simple operationalisation.

Different arguments

Given this, it should not be surprising that the advocates of social accounting have argued in very different ways for what might seemingly appear to be the same thing. In this area the apparent similarity of the technical demands often masks a much more fundamental and contentious debate.

So, for instance, some commentators have argued for social accountings to complement the quite explicit responsibilities for performance beyond the narrowly economic that already have been given to some organisations, particularly in the public sector. In the UK such arguments have been advanced in respect of both the nationalised industries and local authorities.

Other commentators, however, have appealed to social accounting as a way of increasing the legitimacy and significance of new concerns with the wider consequences of organisational action. Quite explicitly seeking to extend what objectives are recognised and acted upon, environmentalists, consumerists and local trade union and community organisations have seen social accounting as a way of establishing a new pattern of corporate visibility which might help to further their concerns.

Finally, and perhaps somewhat paradoxically, social accountings also have been used by those who seek to establish the legitimacy of the *status quo*. Seeking to gain recognition of the present reality of their concern with the wider consequences of organisational actions, they too sometimes have sought to forge a new visibility which attempts to illuminate that which previously might have been invisible.

All too obviously the social accounting concept has appealed to a number of very diverse and often conflicting groups. Indeed so varied are the array of interests in it that we need to recognise quite explicitly the plurality of social accountings that are both debated and implemented. At the present time there simply is not a social accounting. What practice there is has emerged in different contexts, to fulfil the different needs of different social interests.

Experience to date

The early social accounting experiments originated in the United States. In the context of the political debates of the 1960s, 'social responsibility' emerged as a key issue, the adequacy of existing modes of corporate governance and accountability were debated, and demands were made for greater openness and access to information. This was the era of Nader and his 'Raiders', the student movement and the campaigns against the Vietnam war, when many of the tenets of the American institutional structure were being reexamined, if not challenged.

Interestingly, however, social accountings tended not to be demanded

The concept of 'social accounting' is particularly applicable to the public sector, which is publicly underwritten and claims to be acting in the public interest. As pressure grows for decisions to be based upon quantified non-financial data, and the community demands more comprehensive reporting from those bodies financed by public money, **PFA** *examines this emergent science and its possible applications.*

In this major feature, we look at social accounting as a science with some of its potential implications; how the concept could be applied to British Rail; and how social factors influenced the Leeds/Bradford airport inquiry.

by the critics themselves. Their major demands were for the further regulation of the corporate sector, for different modes of corporate governance and, in the information area, for greater access to information rather than to regular reporting of it – a very different phenomenon. Rather than being demanded, social accountings tended to be a responsive strategy of corporate management.

Voluntary disclosure

Striving to demonstrate their existing commitment to such issues are the control of environmental pollution, racial and sexual equality and urban renewal, organisations like the Bank of America, General Motors, Quaker Oats and ITT voluntarily disclosed information on their 'social activities', in many cases preparing specific social reports for both their shareholders and other interested parties.

The public sector in the US was not exempt from such pressures, although many of the experiments with the formal processing of social information had originated with earlier concerns with the control, even on a more narrow economic basis, of rapidly growing governmental expenditures. However, existing modes of programme budgeting and cost effectiveness analysis, and concerns with the social as well as the economic monitoring of performance, were used to respond to the new pressures even if they had not stemmed from them.

Perhaps more significantly, the social pressures of the 1960s also resulted in a rather different set of responses in the American public sector. At least some attempts were made to respond more directly to the demands for greater openness. Access to information rather than the regular reporting of it lay behind the institutional innovations which were embedded in the 'Sun Shine' legislation and the Freedom of Information Act.

However it was the more formal social accounting initiatives in the corporate sector which were conveyed to the European setting. That setting was a very different one, however. Whilst many of the American social debates surrounding the corporation had focused on environmental, racial and community concerns, European debates had given a much higher priority to questions relating to the status, role and position of labour in the enterprise. This difference was to make a profound impact on the development of the social accounting debate in Europe.

So, for instance, although many of the early social accounting experiments in Germany were made by enterprises in the chemical and energy industries concerned with responding to environmental debates and subsequent governmental initiatives, the focus was almost immediately broadened to include matters of employment policy and the distribution of enterprise resources to the various stakeholders. Moreover when attempts were made by the pioneering organisations to standardise social accounting practice as much emphasis was put on the value added statement, showing the social distribution of enterprise financial resources, as on the statements of expenditures which were deemed to be of a 'social' nature and of the qualitative impacts which these and other social policies had made.

Critical role

The critical role played by the trade unions in Germany further illlustrates the very different European context for the social extension of accounting practice. Initially they adopted a very negative stance, seeing management initiated social accounts as being little more than propaganda. Now they are prepared to take a more positive view however, recognising the potential value of the wider provision of information for their own analytical and bargaining purposes.

Rather than automatically rejecting the information, they are analysing and criticising it. For one company (BASF) the unions even prepared an extensive 'counter' social report, disputing the partiality and adequacy of the information provided. More generally, the unions have argued about the technical form of value added accounting and are now working on proposals for a trade union orientated form of social accounting.

Not dissimilar trends are observable elsewhere. In France, the only country which legally requires enterprises to issue a social report, emphasis is placed on the internal social state of the enterprise rather than its wider external impacts. Accordingly voluminous information has to be reported on accidents, occupational health, absenteeism, turnover, unionisation and other aspects of personnel and employment policy.

Also in the Netherlands, much of what is now called social accounting has many of the characteristics of employee reporting in the UK. Although more attention has been given to the provision of social as well as economic information, the reports nevertheless have been orientated primarily towards employees and the members of works councils, with relatively little consideration being given to wider 'societal' matters.

Research experiments

And in Sweden, although there have been a few comprehensive corporate social reports, these have usually been research experiments rather than fully fledged management initiatives. Most of the management activity again has focused on the internal provision of personnel information and on ways of providing a calculative link between the realms of social and economic decision making. Volvo, for example, has experimented with ways of evaluating the economic consequences of new forms of socially organising work.

Elsewhere in Sweden, with trade unions now having legal rights of access to corporate information under the new industrial democracy legislation, social accounting has been called upon to play a role in employee education programmes and in the construction of lower level participative information systems.

And what of the UK? Certainly in the last decade the adequacy of present modes of accounting, disclosure and organisational assessment have been debated in both the public and private sectors. With greater attention being given to corporate accountability, disclosures have been increased by legislative and voluntary means.

Albeit slowly, social information is starting to be reported alongside the economic. Social pressures also have resulted in efforts to standardise accounting rules and formats and in the

Environmental issues have frequently taken second place in the UK.

public sector, at least, consideration has been given to the means for ensuring greater openness. Moreover, as elsewhere in Europe, employees and trade unions have been recognised to be the legitimate recipients of information.

All told, accounting has certainly become recognised as a valid phenomenon for social debate in the UK. Perhaps surprisingly however, there have been few, if any, comprehensive corporate social accounting initiatives. Although rumour has it that some large enterprises have conducted experiments, the resultant reports have remained locked in filing cabinets rather than being made publicly available. Why should this have been so? Just why, given all the effort which has been devoted to debating accounting in a wider social context, should social accounting *per se* have received so little management attention?

Many factors have played a role. A key one, however, is that recent public debates in the UK have focused for all too obvious reasons on the state of the economy and of our industrial relations practices rather than on environmental, consumer, racial and sexual issues. As a result, many of the social pressures for accounting innovation have given rise to an expansion of the sope of traditional accountings rather than the provision of alternative means for assessment.

Accordingly inflation accounting, renewed efforts to assess and improve productivity and efficiency and, in the same context, concerns with the disclosure of financial information to employees and trade unions have monopolised our attention to date. Even in the public sector, demands for greater 'value for money' would appear to be resulting in the provision of further traditional means for economic assessment rather than on the possibility of any new modes of evaluation and management.

Another factor which has most likely influenced developments in the UK is that unlike elsewhere, the idea of social accounting was appropriated at an early stage by critical rather than managerial groups. 'Social audits', for instance, were first attempted by consumer and public interest groups and resulted in managerial attacks rather than enthusiasm.

Political

Subsequently, with social accounting entering into the political domain, a mass of further experiments have been made by trade union and community groups in the context of redundancy and closure proposals stemming from those very same economic problems which might have constrained official developments. Such unofficial social audits, accounts and reports often have been designed to fundamentally challenge rather than merely elaborate upon the rationality of conventional managerial assessments.

Developments in the UK therefore have tended to take a different course than elsewhere. In an era of economic uncertainty, official social accountings have found it difficult to take root. Somewhat paradoxically however, unofficial varieties have prospered in the context of the social questionings that have been and still are being generated by the very same economic difficulties. The net result is that whilst there are undoubtedly renewed demands for the wider availability of information on organisational performance, as yet there are few official precedents for action.

Some observations

Reflecting on such a brief but varied set of experiences is far from easy. However we would suggest that the following observations can be made:

- Social accounting is not a homogenous phenomenon. Both proposals for action and actual experiments have taken many different and even conflicting forms.
- Social accountings have reflected the contexts, issues and problems which gave rise to them. The emphasis on the problematic status of labour in Europe has resulted in very different approaches to those observed in the USA, and even within Europe, different institutional, legal and economic contexts have had major impacts.
- Social accounting has as much, if not more, to do with the search for an adequate definition of the social nature of organisations as with its simple operationalisation. Given that the social roles of organisations are still contentious, at this stage many of the concerns with wider accountings reflect very preliminary attempts to recognise and incorporate into the management of the organisation new social interests and concerns.
- In many situations, but less obviously in the UK, social accountings have been provided rather than demanded. Compared with the managerial response of disclosure, many of the demands of critical groups have been for greater openness and access to information rather than the routine reporting of it.
- Finally, the social accounting debate is best regarded as only a part of a growing recognition of the wider social significance of the accounting function. As many of the wider debates on accounting standard setting and financial disclosure have illustrated, accounting is no longer regarded as an unproblematic technical phenomenon. All accountings have been seen to have implications for social and political as well as economic action, and it must be recognised that concerns with particular forms of social accounting have arisen in such a wider context.

Conclusion

Looking to the future, there are no reasons for believing that there will be any lessening of the demands for wider corporate accountability and responsibility. Although past pressures have arisen in very different ways in very different contexts, it has to be recognised that at a fundamental level organisations now are being viewed in a more critical manner and that there are very real pressures for both more responsive modes of governance and the greater availability of information.

As far as the public sector in the UK is concerned, it is likely that we will see renewed emphasis being given to the provision of wider accountings. Already many nationalised industries are using alternative accountings to emphasise their wider statutory responsibilities.

Some local authorities also are starting to explore ways of making more visible both their own roles in the community and those played by other major institutions, such as large local employers – present, threatened and potential. And although the applicability of the wider governmental accountings and audits undertaken in the USA and Sweden may still be questioned, real consideration nevertheless is being given to reforming our own more traditional practices.

Admittedly the incentives for action at the present time are both social and economic. Attempts to respond to the pressures for greater accountability and openness are being intertwined with the desire to establish a wider legitimacy in an era of economic restraint and cutbacks.

New precedents

Be that as it may, the resultant experiments and developments undoubtedly are creating new precedents, professional commitments and public expectations. Over time it may well be these institutional consequences, rather than either the initial technical experiments themselves or the particular pressures which gave rise to them, that will provide the basis for future developments in the social accounting sphere.

A useful overview of social accounting is contained in a booklet entitled *Social Accounting* that is published by CIPFA. More detailed reviews of the developments in other countries are published periodically in the international research journal, *Accounting, Organizations and Society*. The situation in the USA was discussed in an article by Epstein, Flamholtz and McDonough in Vol 1, No 1 (1976), pp 23-42.

Swedish developments were discussed by Grojer and Stark in Vol 2, No 4 (1977), pp 349-385 and Jonson, Jonsson and Svensson in Vol 3, No 3/4 (1978), pp 261-268. Finally, a very comprehensive assessment of the current situation in Germany was provided in a series of articles by Brockhoff, Dierkes, Schreuder and Ullmann which appeared in Vol 4, No 1/2 (1979), pp 77-133. *Accounting, Organizations and Society* is published by Pergamon Press Ltd.

by Stuart Burchell, Colin Clubb
and Anthony Hopwood

'A message from Mars'—and other reminiscences from the past

Where has the value added concept come from? Why the sudden interest in it?

The value added concept is now a recognised part of the accountant's repertoire. After attracting more and more attention in the last few years, it appears to have established a reasonably secure position for itself in both external and management reporting.

In the UK, 'The Corporate Report' played a key role in triggering this recent
298 interest. Following its publication in 1979, an increasing number of companies started to provide value added statements in their annual reports. In 1975-6, the *Annual Survey of Published Accounts* reported that 14 companies presented such statements: by 1977-78, 1978-79 and 1979-80 the numbers were 67, 84 and 90 respectively. No doubt aware of this phenomenon, the English and Scottish Institutes and the Association, have all published research reports on the use of value added in external reporting.

Value added has also been associated with the extension of corporate reporting to a wider array of stakeholders, and particularly with the preparation of reports destined for employees and trade unions. In addition to this use of the concept in the context of employee communication schemes and the preparation of simplified financial statements, it has also been used within the enterprise as a means of measuring economic performance and calculating financial remuneration.

In these areas there has also been a proliferation of both research reports and more pragmatic guides for action issued by bodies such as the British Institute of Management, the Engineering Employer's Federation, the Engineering Industrial Training Board, the Institute of Cost and Management Accountants, the Trade Union Research Unit and a host of independent commentators and consultants. Moreover the value added phenomenon has not been unique to the UK. Elsewhere in Europe there has been a similar growth of interest (Mcleay, 1980).

Athough some alternative and more critical concerns are sometimes articulated by others (Hird, 1978; Stolliday and Attwood, 1978; Labour Research, 1978), it seems fair to say that in an amazingly short period of time a large measure of agreement has been reached in the accountancy profession on the positive contributions which the value concept might make to financial reporting, both within and without the enterprise.

Where, however, has the value added concept come from? Why did the interest in it appear to emerge so rapidly? How, for example, did the concept surface so suddenly in 'The Corporate Report'? And why has it permeated both financial and management accounting practices so quickly? Just why should the apparent consensus on its rationale have crystallised so readily when this process has taken so long in other debates in the accounting?

Indeed, given the speed of its emergence into recent accounting debates, is the interest in value added really just a mere temporary fashion or fad? Or are there more substantive issues underlying its emergence, an understanding of which might throw some useful light on both the processes of accounting change and the options available for policy making in the area?

Already, in fact, a number of commentators have pointed to the role which more basic issues might have played in the value added debate. Writing in *The Financial Times*, for example, Barry Riley suggested that value added might have 'been seized upon by public relations men as a way of glossing over the problems of profit'. And even Vickers da Costa, the stockbrokers, have commented that most of the available value added statements are so orientated to showing 'how much of the "value added" goes to the employees themselves, how much the Government absorbs, and how little the shareholder receives' that there is a danger of them losing their analytical value, particularly for comparative purposes.

Such questionings of what might be at stake in the value added debate point to the importance of having a more thorough understanding of the factors which have resulted in this particular accounting change. With the aim of gaining some appreciation of how the technical debate over value added has related to wider institutional and social concerns, we seek to provide at least a partial insight into the historical background to the interest in value added, paying particular attention to the interest shown in the concept in the UK during the 1940s and 1950s. Hopefully, such experiences of the past might help to illuminate at least some of the debates and concerns of the present.

A past reincarnation. In the late 1940s and early 1950s then, as now, there was a tremendous interest in employee communication and information disclosure.

Stuart Burchell BSc MSc (top) is at preser researching the organisational aspects c accounting systems. **Colin Clubb** BA (Econ (centre) is a research officer. Both are at th London Business School. **Professor Anthon Hopwood** BSc (Econ) MBA PhD is the Institute' Professor of Accounting and Financial Report ing at the London Business School and is th year's American Accounting Association Dis tinguished International Visiting Professor.

Indeed, this was a period when the reade of professional journals could be greeted b headlines such as 'Telling workers th facts'; 'Scottish firm tells the worke "What and Why" '; 'More firms who sa where the money goes'; 'The facts abo

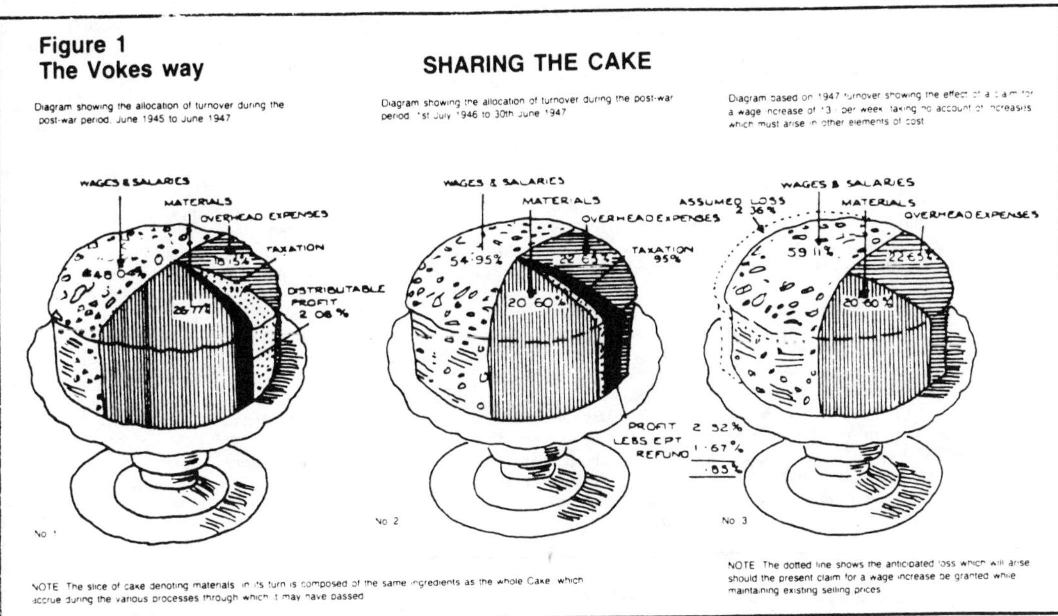
SHARING THE CAKE
Diagram showing the allocation of turnover during the post-war period. June 1945 to June 1947
Diagram showing the allocation of turnover during the post-war period 1st July 1946 to 30th June 1947
Diagram based on 1947 turnover showing the effect of a claim for a wage increase of 13/- per week taking no account of increases which must arise in other elements of cost
WAGES & SALARIES
MATERIALS
OVERHEAD EXPENSES
TAXATION
DISTRIBUTABLE PROFIT 2 08%
48 0%
26 77%
18 15%
54 95%
20 60%
22 63%
TAXATION 95%
PROFIT 2 32%
LESS EPT REFUND 1 67%
·65%
ASSUMED LOSS 2 36%
59 11%
20 60%
22 63%
No 1
No 2
No 3
NOTE The slice of cake denoting materials, in its turn is composed of the same ingredients as the whole Cake, which accrue during the various processes through which it may have passed
NOTE The dotted line shows the anticipated loss which will arise should the present claim for a wage increase be granted while maintaining existing selling prices

Figure 1
The Vokes way

299

factory economics' and even 'Workers had all the facts – up went efficiency'.

In 1948, an official Board of Trade publication commented that: 'There is undoubtedly widespread misapprehension among working men and women upon the subject of wages and profits. The points made by the Chancellor of the Exchequer . . . at the recent Trades Union Congress need further elaboration and emphasis. The subject must be dealt with fully and frankly if workers generally are to be satisfied on the issues involved . . . the workers, who suspect that the shareholders are reaping large rewards while he, the man who produces the goods, is denied his dues, should be given the facts. More often than not a full and frank explanation will remove such misconceptions . . . if we are going to stand on our own feet by the time American aid comes to an end – by 1952 at the latest – we must concentrate on productivity . . . if workers can be made to feel that they really are partners in this all-out effort to put this country of ours on its feet again, they are surely entitled to the full facts?'

Accounting was quickly mobilised to play its role in these endeavours. A growing number of companies started to introduce employee communication schemes, often giving particular emphasis to how each pound of revenue received is paid out to the various costs of manufacture or remain as profits. Indeed, in June 1948 *The Economist* noted the pioneering endeavours of companies like Ford, Vauxhall, United Steel, Courtaulds, Whitbread, Doulton and ICI in this area. These experiments, according to *The Economist*, clearly demonstrated that the rewards of equity capital are the marginal item.

Vokes Limited, a manufacturer of filtration equipment, was one of the many companies which received publicity for its experiments in this area. Management there introduced a system of informing the workers how turnover was disposed of, and what happened to profits. 'Only by being quite open with employees', claimed a Vokes manager, 'can we hope to get the fullest cooperative spirit'. To this end, the Vokes 'industry cake' was introduced. Quite explicitly modelled on the phrase 'You can't have your cake and eat it', the diagram aimed to tell the employees 'the true story of where the money went'. Vokes claimed that their policy of 'keeping nothing back from the workers' . . . helped considerably in their understanding of the business, besides showing what a tremendous part increases in overheads played in stepping up prices' – Figure 1.

Mars was another company which claimed to have 'a 100% determination that every one of the 750 employees . . . shall know the aims and policy of the business'. As part of its 'Tell the workers' policy of enlightenment, the firm's own product was used as an organising principle, information was given on distributions to suppliers, employees, distributions and other cost categories within the firm, with a remaining surplus available for reserves and taxation, development and dividends, 'if any'. (See Figure 2.)

Value added as the concept is now used did enter the employee communication practices of the Metal Box Company, however. In a way which almost completely anticipates the current approach of Sir Hector Laing of United Biscuits, the company produced a full colour booklet entitled *Added Value*. Written by Sir Robert Barlow, the company's chairman, *Added Value* was issued at the same time as the annual company accounts. 'In spite of paper difficulties', a copy was sent to every man and woman on the monthly and weekly staff, and to hourly-paid workers in certain long-service grades.

Writing in the booklet, Sir Robert commented that: 'There is . . . a great deal of misconception about profits, or, as they might properly be called, earnings. There is even a danger that they may be regarded as evil in themselves – hence that those who earn them are engaged in anti-social activities.

'Writing from the standpoint of productive industry, we say that this is the opposite of truth; that a profit which arises from the efficient working of a worthwhile enterprise is legitimate, desirable and necessary. For the alternative to a profit is a loss, and who, may it be asked, will be the better for that? Not the shareholders, not the employees, not the management, nor the State, for all of these benefit from a profit and would suffer from a loss. Least of all, perhaps, the customer; for no enterprise, operating at a loss, can supply him with what he will need in a market competitive in quality and price.

'The object of this booklet is to demonstrate this from facts; to go further and to show that from the operations of an industrial concern there arises an added value which is shared by all. For when a man performs a useful piece of work he creates wealth in its real sense. Once a body of men are actuated to perform their part of a common task in a better than normal way, and when from their efforts there flows a continually expanding activity, wealth is created to a considerably increased degree. Profit ceases to be, if indeed it ever has been, the dominating motive, and pride in work and an ensuing sense of responsibility takes its place.'

In the name of such ideals, Metal Box

introduced a whole array of strategies and practices to communicate the facts of business life to the workers – 'to explain the significance of . . . various points, their impact on the company, what the organisation as a whole and the men and women who make it work, can do to help.' Through information and communication, every effort was made to instil an ethic of partnership and productivity.

In the immediate post-war period, there was an acute awareness of the need for productivity and efficiency at the national level. To this end, all manner of attempts were made to propagate the value of more systematic management practices. However, a powerful element of the concerns expressed at the time was the need to mesh together the perceived imperatives of the economy with the imagery of co-operative endeavour. It was in this context that communication and the need to disclose information was seen to be significant and accounting too was called on to play a role in 'the national effort'.

Returning to today. The context of the 1940s and the 1950s was very different from that prevailing today, both generally and in terms of its implications for accounting policy making. More recently the concerns of accounting standardisation, the detailed formulation and conduct of Government incomes policies and the debates and experiments that have taken place in connection with the issue of industrial democracy have all been significant for accounting development and in particular for the recent upsurge of interest in value added (Burchell and Hopwood, 1981).

Be that as it may, observing value added accounting of the past can illuminate present concerns and debates. If such an exercise does nothing else it indicates the diverse sources of, and forces for, accounting change and hence the organic character of accounting development.

Although all accounting practices have a range of technical characteristics which can be described, debated and changed, at any particular time those practices adopted reflect wider interests and concerns. In th case of value added and other forms distributional accounting in the 1940s ar 1950s, we have seen how they functione as a part of a worker participati orientation towards the management economic performance. And as such the fate became tied up with that of tho same concerns. As their significan waxes and wanes, so does that of val added.

With us during the economic crises of t immediate post-war era, the value add statement disappeared during the prospe ous years of the 1950s and 1960s, only return, albeit with little or no consideratio as to what might have been its earli effectiveness, when similar strategic pos ures were adopted towards the manag ment of the economy in the mid-1970s.

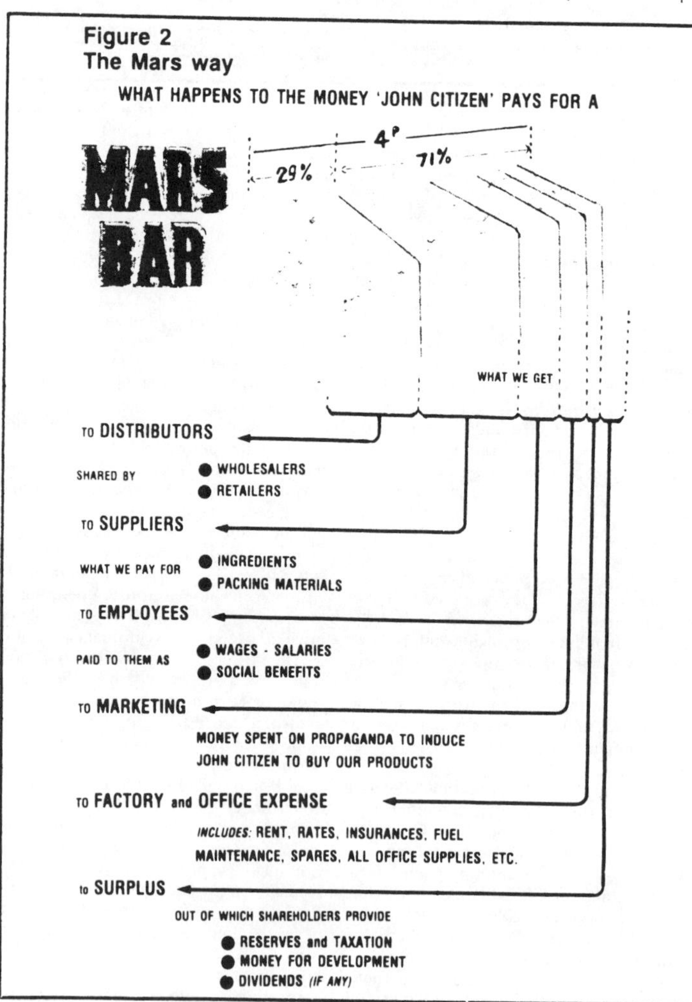

Figure 2
The Mars way

Conclusions. There are two major implic tions which follow from the above observ tions. First, there is the very pragma consideration that value added could qui possibly lose its signficance once again as result of shifts in our socio-political lan scape. However, so often the technic deliberations of accountants tend to insensitive to the conditions under whi they take place. Once an item has been p on the agenda as the result of one set circumstances there is a tendency for t subsequent debates surrounding, for exar ple its standardisation, to continue lo after those initial circumstances ha changed. Indeed, it has been argued that is precisely this feature of the accounti discipline that has obscured some of t major problems confronting the standa setting process and which in America least is now being challenged. There pe ple are now starting to speak about t social and economic consequences accounting (Zeff, 1978).

Second, if accountants are to assess t wider economic and social consequences accounting procedures and to become mo sensitive to the broader issues that evitably feed into their own debates th the knowledge base of accounti thought must be enriched by a far grea awareness of the ways in which accour ing performs and changes in practice. present there is no shortage of theor about how accounting *should* chang However, we would argue that there is very real shortage of studies showing h accounting *does* change.

References

Burchell S. and Hopwood A. G. (1981). 'Soc Accounting: Developments in the UK', paper present at the 'I Jornadas de Estudio Sobre Economia Socieded', Madrid.

Hird C. (1978). 'Beware of Added Value'. N *Statesman*, 4 August.

Labour Research (1978). 'Value Added – Mislead the Workers', February.

Mcleay S. (1980). 'Value Added Statements: A Com rative Study', paper presented to the Third Congress the European Accounting Association.

Stolliday I. and Attwood M. (1978). 'Financial Indu ment and Productivity Bargaining'. *Industrial Commercial Training*, Vol 10, No 6.

Zeff S.A. (1978) 'The rise of economic consequenc The Journal of Accountancy, December.

ECONOMIC COSTS AND BENEFITS OF NEW FORMS OF WORK ORGANISATION

Anthony G. Hopwood*

301

Recent decades have witnessed a growing concern with the consequences of the routine, repetitive and bureaucratically organised work which characterises so much of employment in a modern industrial society. With changing social and political values and an increasing awareness of the range of possibilities available, it is now realised that a great deal of modern work, whether in the factory or the office, offers little scope for exercising individual initiative and responsibility. People working on these jobs often see their tasks as boring and meaningless; and the effects of this view are now seen as extending far beyond the confines of the individual mind or even of the undertaking which provides employment. The nature of work can and does have wide-ranging implications for the effectiveness of the individual, the enterprise as a whole and the quality of life in society at large.

For a long time it had been assumed that the human and social consequences of work were an inevitable, even if unfortunate, result of modern production methods and the size and complexity of contemporary organisations. According to this view, little could be done to make work more satisfying. However, it is now becoming clear that it is possible to redesign the organisation of work so as to provide greater personal fulfilment without necessarily having to loose the advantages of modern technology.

The realisation that the organisation of work and its consequences are shaped by social as well as technological factors has led to an awareness of the various possible ways of organising work. From the 1950s, and particularly during the 1960s and 1970s, an increasing number of people both in Europe and in the United States started to experiment with different approaches to work organisation (Klein, 1976; Work in America, 1972), ranging from relatively modest rearrangements of the elements of individual jobs to a fundamental restructuring of those patterns of influence and control in organisations that help to determine the selection and use of technology. However diverse they may be, these various approaches all offer some possibility of relating the advances of

* Oxford Centre for Management Studies.

modern technology with the achievement of human needs and aspirations. Taken together, they are now starting to play a significant role in shaping our conceptions of the possibilities for the organisation, management and performance of an undertaking.

An emerging interest in evaluation

As was inevitable, many of the early experiments were concerned primarily with practical feasibility. At that stage the most vital point to establish was that different approaches to the social organisation of work could be designed and followed. General claims were made about the over-all effectiveness of such approaches, but their actual existence was important in its own right.

Subsequently a growing body of experience made a more detailed appreciation of the operation and effect of the different forms of work organisation more important. Beyond some point—one that is generally agreed to have been reached, if not passed—further learning and progress become increasingly dependent on understanding the factors that promote or hinder the achievement of the potential offered by the new approaches. The real magnitude and scope of that potential also needs to be delineated; and with an increasing range of possible approaches it becomes important to consider in a reasoned manner their relative strengths and weaknesses and the circumstances in which they are most effective.

Such concerns helped to promote an interest in evaluating the social effectiveness of the new forms of work organisation. Many of the early evaluative attempts were crude and simplistic, but more recently a great deal of effort has been devoted to monitoring the social nature of the change process itself and its human consequences in a more systematic manner. Although numerous problems undoubtedly remain, significant progress has been made. Undertakings now have at their disposal useful and convenient instruments for appraising the effect of different forms of work organisation on individual attitudes and forms of social behaviour (Biderman and Drury, 1976; Portigal, 1974; Portigal, 1976; Seashore, 1976); and an increasing number of undertakings are doing just this.

In contrast, however, the assessment of the economic costs and benefits of programmes designed to improve the quality of working life has been relatively neglected. There has been a tendency for both social innovators and persons professionally concerned with economic measurement to see financial performance and the fulfilment of human needs as two separate areas of concern. Instead of choosing to emphasise the interplay of social, technical and economic forces which itself constitutes an undertaking, these different groups of people have often chosen, albeit implicitly, to emphasise the divergent value bases which might underlie the differing views of an undertaking's effectiveness. Professionals in economic measurement have accordingly emphasised the dominance of existing financial criteria, and in consequence they have often viewed social innovations in an unduly narrow perspective. Conversely, and with few exceptions (Likert, 1967), social innovators have tended to interpret expressions of concern over economic consequences as improper attempts to reinforce past perspectives, options and influences rather than facilitate the process of change.

Accordingly it is not difficult to appreciate why, until recently, there has been little demand for—let alone supply of—appropriate methodologies for economic assessment. What concern there has been with the economic consequences of different forms of work organisation has reflected a desire to legitimise rather than to either assess or learn (Klein, 1976, p. 47).

For these reasons the potential magnitude of the economic consequences of programmes designed to improve the quality of working life is only just being realised. So far both their costs and benefits have invariably been lost within the mass of detailed calculations which give rise to the aggregate assessment of financial outcomes.

However, real and genuine interest is now shown in evaluating the economic consequences of different forms of work organisation. That interest stems from a number of factors. First, there is a growing realisation that the economic aspects of change, or of not changing for that matter, are important. To cite only one example, it is now realised that the replacement of the 100,000 workers leaving the Bell telephone system every year costs over $100 million (Gustafson, 1974). 303
When seen in such terms, it is not only right that programmes directed towards improving the social fabric of the undertaking should be considered alongside programmes concerned with technological, market and financial change; they also need to be analysed in a comparable manner, because they also represent vital ways in which the profitability of the undertaking can be improved. Secondly, it is realised that if changes in work organisation are not analysed in a comparable manner, there is a danger that they may be seen as purely resource-consuming activities rather than potential resource-generating activities; and in those circumstances technological and marketing changes are likely to be given preference over equally profitable programmes concerned with improving the quality of working life. At no time is this more likely to happen than when resources are severely limited, as at present. When there are strong pressures to economise, potentially successful social initiatives can easily be either rejected or abandoned on the ground that they will not pay for themselves.

One such instance has been documented by Weir (1976, pp. 27-29). Despite known improvements in throughput, the amount of work in progress, quality, absenteeism and labour turnover, and greater flexibility of the production process, an autonomous working group experiment in a clothing manufacturing company was abandoned in mid-course. As the general economic situation worsened, a highly visible and immediate increase in unit costs was emphasised at the expense of the other improvements, even though the increase might have reflected the peculiarities of the products being processed at the time and the idiosyncracies as well as partialities of the cost accounting system. In the absence of any attempt to evaluate systematically the over-all economic consequences of the experiment, the influential though partial returns produced by the existing accounting system had a decisive effect on policy.

The need for more general awareness of the economic implications of social change is of fundamental importance. Current programmes for work reorganisation have been based on a concern for moving beyond the damaging fragmentation of perception and understanding which had become so characteristic of our intellectual tradition. Possibilities of overcoming the constraints inherent in modern production technology were created by explicitly considering the relationship between the technological and social structures of enterprises. Further progress might be encouraged by recognising that the domains of economic and social action can never be satisfactorily separated. Our economic structures, perspectives and methodologies have always reflected emerging social values and possibilities. Instead of imposing stronger economic constraints on social progress, an awareness of the interplay between social and economic advances within the undertaking can generate further suggestions for future progress (Likert, 1967; Vanek, 1970, 1971). Today's difficult economic conditions only serve to increase the need for and potential of such a wider approach.

Costs and benefits classified

It is useful to classify the economic costs and benefits of work reorganisation
304 programmes into three broad categories: the operational, the systemic and the societal.

Operational

The concept of operational consequences covers the effect that the organisation of work has on the regular operating flows of an enterprise. The differing requirements for personnel and materials, the financial implications of these, including the effect on wage levels and the costs associated with different levels of absenteeism and labour turnover, and the effect on such organisational costs as supervision and maintenance, are all included in this category, as are interest costs and overheads. Such operational consequences have been investigated in a number of work reorganisation experiments, and increasing consideration is being given to assessing them in a more systematic manner, as will be seen below.

Systemic

The consideration of systemic consequences, on the other hand, goes beyond matters of ongoing efficiency to focus on the effect that a work reorganisation programme has on the undertaking's capacity to adapt to the requirements of its environment in the longer term. As such it includes the costs involved in initially committing scarce resources to the reorganisation effort. The costs of additional plant, space and stocks, of covering any initial dip in internal efficiency, and of pursuing the initial, often time-consuming consultations, are included in this category. Conversely the potential benefits to be derived from thus improving the undertaking's over-all ability to respond to changing market and production circumstances are also included in this category, as are the possible advantages of having improved customer relations and, even if over a substantially longer period of time, an organisation more consonant with the changing nature of the social environment. Although the precise economic benefits of such systemic advantages must inevitably remain embodied within over-all financial performance, this should not prevent their separate acknowledgement and consideration: experience is now beginning to suggest that in some cases at least such systemic benefits are real enough.

The way in which more flexible forms of work organisation now improve the responsiveness of production operations to unforeseen market and technological changes has been noted in reports from IBM (Sirota and Wolfson, 1972), Saab (Norstedt and Agurén, 1974), Atlas (Björk, 1975), General Time (Weir, 1976), Pye (Manufacturing Management, 1972) and Volvo (Agurén, Hansson and Karlsson, 1976) amongst many others. The advantages of this kind of work design have been emphasised particularly by enterprises with complex and changing product mixes (Staehle, 1979) and those facing rapidly developing technological environments. Butera (1975, pp. 186-187), in commenting on the experiences of Olivetti, stresses this point:

> To achieve production flexibility, demanded by the increasing complexity of the model mix . . . , the organization had to be such that it would not be necessary to redesign and re-balance the assembly lines every time a variation occurred. The ideal solution was a "cellular" organization that could provide the increase and variety of 305
> production merely by adding new organizational units, rather than by making the assembly line longer or shorter.
>
> Complexity of performance demands and the dynamics of competition make the market life of a product . . . short: . . . What is more, in such a short life cycle, the product does not stay unchanged but undergoes continuous technical modifications, partly stemming from technological evolution and partly from customers' new performance requirements. The time available for implementing a series of operations to simplify, rationalize, and organize the work . . . is therefore extremely limited. This generates a series of temporal and economic restrictions and, as a result, it is no longer feasible to determine a detailed division of labor and work content; the only possible solution is to provide the organizational units and roles with greater autonomy, contrary to the (Taylor) scientific management tradition.

In conditions of discontinuity, which many believe to be more prevalent today, the form of work organisation itself becomes a resource of major importance. Recent research in other areas of management (Burns and Stalker, 1961; Lawrence and Lorsch, 1967) is starting to assess the benefits to be derived from having forms of organisation that can cope with uncertainty and change. Although the benefits may not be quantifiable in precise economic terms, a flexible and responsive organisation of work can undoubtedly contribute to the economic viability of the enterprise as a whole. It is interesting to note that the awareness of such benefits is far from recent. Adam Smith, who did so much to legitimise dominant forms of the division of labour, expressed his own concerns and doubts in the following way:

> In the progress of the division of labour, the employment of the far greater part of those who live by labour, that is, of the great body of the people, comes to be confined to a few very simple operations; frequently to one or two. But the understandings of the greater part of men are . . . formed by their ordinary employments. The man whose life is spent in performing a few simple operations, of which the effects . . . are, perhaps, always the same, or very nearly the same, has no occasion to exert his understanding, or to exercise his invention in finding out expedients for removing difficulties which never occur. He naturally loses, therefore, the habit of such exertion, and generally becomes as stupid and ignorant as it is possible for a human creature to become. . . .
>
> It is otherwise in the barbarous societies, as they are commonly called, of hunters, of shepherds, and even of husbandmen in that rude state of husbandry which precedes the

> improvement of manufactures . . . In such societies the varied occupations of every man oblige every man to exert his capacity, and to invent expedients for removing difficulties which are continually occurring. Invention is kept alive, and the mind is not suffered to fall into that drowsy stupidity, which, in a civilised society, seems to benumb the understanding of almost all the inferior ranks of people (Smith, Book V, Chapter 1, Part III, Article II, "Of the expense of the institutions for the education of youth").

Societal

The societal consequences of work organisation are the costs and benefits which, although real and significant, are borne or received by society as a whole rather than by the enterprise from which they emanate. The effects of stress at work on health and on family life (Kornhauser, 1965), for instance, are included in this category, as are the consequences of shift work on the individual and on the cultural life of the community (Mott, 1975) and the wider implications of mechanisation, automation and computerisation themselves and of the patterns of social and work organisation which sustain them. Such societal implications are
306 as diverse as they are profound. Increasing attention is being given to them, particularly in cases in which systemic or operational benefits for the enterprise are clearly associated with societal costs, as when work reorganisation results in lower personnel requirements for the undertaking but higher levels of unemployment in society as a whole. Despite the undoubted and growing importance of societal consequences, and of cases in which there are clear conflicts between social and enterprise objectives, no attempt is made in this paper to review such issues or to consider the evidence to date.

Evidence available

For a more detailed examination of the scope and magnitude of the economic consequences of work organisation at the level of the undertaking consideration must be given to some of the rapidly growing number of reports on individual initiatives and experiments. Regrettably, however, it must be noted that many such reports are not an ideal source of information: there is quite clearly a reporting bias; experiments regarded as being successful have a much higher probability of being the subject of reports available to the public (Cummings and Salipante, 1976), despite the invaluable role that reports of nil and negative results can serve in guiding subsequent endeavours. So any conclusions that may be drawn must be tentative.

In this review two main sources of evidence are considered. First the conclusions of some previous more socially orientated surveys of the published material are presented. Thereafter consideration is given to the more detailed economic effects of a wide variety of work organisation experiments.

General surveys

One of the most systematic analyses of the published results of work reorganisation experiments has been conducted by Srivastva and his colleagues (1975). They identified 57 innovative experiments in which aspects of the work environment had been systematically changed and in which attempts had been made to determine the subsequent effects. An analysis of those experiments revealed that the changes in the work environment had focused on the following nine factors:

(a) pay and reward systems;

(b) autonomy and discretion;

(c) the organisation of support services;

(d) training;

(e) organisational structure;

(f) technology;

(g) task variety;

(h) information and feedback; and

(i) interpersonal and group processes.

Further examination of the experiments revealed, however, that these factors were changed in identifiable combinations. This made it possible to identify four major types of emphasis in work reorganisation: 307

(1) The establishment of socio-technical groups, work being restructured around self-regulating work groups that performed relatively complete tasks.

(2) The restructuring of jobs, including the expansion of individual jobs both horizontally and vertically.

(3) The introduction of more participation by workers in decisions that directly affected their work lives.

(4) Organisational changes which involved the modification of the formal structure of the organisation and of the information and feedback systems.

On the basis of this classification Srivastva and his colleagues isolated 16 socio-technical experiments, 27 cases of job restructuring, 7 participative management experiments and 7 instances of organisational change.

The analysis considered whether the four types of work reorganisation had a reported positive effect on five outcome factors, namely costs, productivity, quality, withdrawal behaviour, and attitudes. Although the study considered the direction rather than the magnitude of the consequences, it did reveal, as can be seen in table 1, an overwhelming number of positive results in a wide variety of organisational settings, including results that have direct economic consequences: there tended to be improvements in respect of costs, productivity, quality, absenteeism and labour turnover. Both this review and a similar examination of the findings of non-experimental correlation studies of different styles of supervision and work content (Srivastva et al., 1975) forcefully illustrate the potential economic significance of programmes that increase work autonomy, variety and feedback in particular.

Other slightly more comprehensive reviews of work reorganisation experiments have been undertaken, although in a desire to be comprehensive, the authors of such reviews have very often included studies which showed little evidence either of sustained experimentation or of adequate evaluation of its consequences. The mere fact of introducing a change is apparently still regarded as being of some significance. However, another review which deliberately aimed

Table 1. Summary of 57 experimental studies

Particular features	Main thrust of the 57 experiments			
	Establishment of socio-technical or autonomous groups (16 experiments)	Job restructuring (27 experiments)	Participative management (7 experiments)	Organisational change (7 experiments)
Percentage of experiments in which the following features of work organisation were adjusted:				
Pay or reward systems	*56*	*14*	. . .	*29*
Autonomy and discretion	*88*	*92*	*100*	*43*
Support	*31*	*22*	. . .	*43*
Training	*44*	*33*	*14*	*43*
Organisational structure	*19*	*14*	*14*	*100*
Technical and physical conditions	*63*	*22*	. . .	*29*
Task variety	*63*	*79*	. . .	*14*
Information and feedback	*63*	*45*	. . .	*71*
Interpersonal relations or group consciousness	*75*	*4*	. . .	*43*
Results				
Number of experiments in which results were reported in terms of—				
Costs	8	10	1	2
Productivity	15	20	7	4
Quality	7	17	1	2
Withdrawal behaviour	7	7	5	3
Attitudes	10	21	5	6
Percentage of foregoing cases in which results were wholly positive:				
Costs	*88*	*90*	*100*	*50*
Productivity	*93*	*75*	*57*	*100*
Quality	*86*	*100*	*100*	*100*
Withdrawal behaviour	*73*	*86*	*80*	*67*
Attitudes	*70*	*76*	*80*	*50*

Source: S. Srivastva et al.: *Productivity, industrial organization and job satisfaction: Policy developement and implementation*, Report to the National Science Foundation (Case Western Reserve University, 1975).

to exclude cases of the latter kind is reported by Taylor (1977). He found that the vast majority of work organisation experiments were at least reported as being non-negative, and usually as being positive, in their outcomes, although not quite as overwhelmingly positive as those covered in the survey undertaken by Srivastva and his colleagues. The most frequently reported measures of outcome were productivity, output or quantity. The vagueness and diversity of terminology in these and other respects illustrates the difficulties of systematic review and comparison. In 48 per cent of the cases covered some effect on these variables was reported. The second most frequent result was in respect of "job satisfaction", "morale" or just "favourable attitudes", effects on this set of variables being reported in 40 per cent of the cases. Effects on costs were next in order of importance, some improvement, or at least maintenance of cost performance, being reported in 36 per cent of cases. Improvements in quality of output were noted in 20 per cent of the cases and changes in the levels of absenteeism and labour turnover were mentioned in 23 per cent and 17 per cent of the cases respectively. Grievances, safety and accidents, changes in manpower requirements and improved system flexibility were each reported in less than 10 per cent of the cases analysed by Taylor.

The conclusion from this and other surveys (Butteriss and Murdoch, 1975; Butteriss and Murdoch, 1976; Lawler, 1970; Schoderbeck and Rief, 1969; Work in America, 1972) remains that work reorganisation programmes have significant economic potential. Although improvements in job satisfaction and autonomy are important in their own right, their achievement does not stand in isolation. The social and economic aspects of the activities of an enterprise are inextricably intertwined, and work reorganisation can, and often does, improve the economic performance of the enterprise as a whole. For this reason alone the economic dimensions of these experiments would demand specific consideration.

Reports on particular cases 309

Greater insight into the scope and magnitude of particular economic consequences must come from an examination of some of the rapidly growing number of reports on individual experiments. As has already been noted, these reports are not an ideal source of information. They tend to place much greater emphasis on the human and social consequences of the experiments than on their economic costs and benefits. Indeed in many cases economic data had not been collected at all, and where they had been the reporting was usually far from systematic. Obvious reasons of commercial and industrial relations policy largely account for restrictions on the release of such information; and at least until recently, the publication of economic results has also been restricted by the reluctance of social innovators to be seen as trying to justify social change in economic terms. Despite such problems, however, the reports on individual experiments are useful in two respects. In conjunction they provide a framework for considering the broad range of potential economic consequences: in other words they enable the observer to construct at least a tentative map of the economic linkages that can be affected by changes in the organisation of work. In addition they provide some insight into the potential magnitude of the economic effects; for the latter purpose the individual results, varying as enormously as they do, are less significant than the aggregate picture that is starting to emerge.

Particular costs and benefits

The following discussion of the economic costs and benefits of work reorganisation is first directed to systemic costs, i.e. the initial investment requirements in terms of plant, inventories and training. Thereafter consideration is given to the operational consequences for manpower, materials, output and the over-all efficiency of operations.

Initial investment in plant and machinery

Most of the new forms of work organisation entail higher investment costs for machinery and tools, and for construction costs in the case of new factories designed in accordance with advanced work organisation knowledge.

A number of authorities have estimated that the additional investment in
machinery required for doing small-volume assembly work in groups instead of
on a flow line is at least 10 per cent for tasks that are labour-intensive and 30 per
cent for those that are capital-intensive. In practice the proportion varies
enormously, however, depending not only on the specifics of the machinery in
question but also on the effect that the reorganisation itself has on machine
utilisation. If no improved utilisation is to be expected, investment costs can be at
least 50 per cent higher for group and individual working than for line. However,
numerous authorities have emphasised the favourable effect that different forms
of work organisation can have on the average utilisation of machinery. There is
certainly a real possibility of such improved machine utilisation. A recent survey
of British experience found that average machine utilisation was only about 50
per cent, with all but 5 per cent of the idle time being the responsibility of
management (Midlands Tomorrow, 1975). The fact that new forms of work
organisation can capture the potential is demonstrated by at least the early
310 experiences of the Volvo Kalmar plant (Agurén, Hansson and Karlsson, 1976,
p. 36) and an experiment in a plastic package manufacturing plant in the United
States which resulted in a 50 per cent increase in the actual run time capacity
(Taylor et al., 1972).

Similar differences are reflected in the reports of floor space requirements. Generally the establishment of group and individual working places requires greater floor space for machinery, buffer stocks and amenity areas. Additional requirements of between 10 and 25 per cent have been noted for electrical component manufacturing firms (den Hertog, 1976; Manufacturing Management, 1972). For the production of particularly bulky objects, increases of up to 100 per cent at Saab-Scania have been described (Norstedt and Agurén, 1973). In some cases, however, group working can reduce the floor space requirements: in a case of group assembly of typewriters total floor space requirements fell, despite the fact that "social areas" were provided adjacent to each of the reorganised lines (Birchall and Wild, 1974). And in the Langston Company in the United States, manufacturers of heavy machinery for the paper industries, floor space requirements fell by 23 per cent (Williamson, 1972, p. 157). With very few exceptions the additional construction costs of new factories in which all of the latest aspects of job design are incorporated remain shrouded in a great deal of secrecy. It has been estimated, however, that the cost for the Volvo Kalmar plant might be 10 per cent above that of a conventional assembly line plant (Agurén, Hansson and Karlsson, 1976). The additional expenditure in this case was probably the result of the space needed for the group workshop areas and the very generous amenities provided.

Investment in stocks

Again the evidence on the effects of new methods of work organisation on the level of stocks of materials and components is conflicting. The establishment of group and individual working places undoubtedly requires additional stocks (den Hertog, 1976, pp. 90-96), as do less innovative but still modified forms of flow line. However it would appear that this increase in immediate buffer stocks need not result in increases over-all. In large part this is the result of the effect that the new forms of work organisation have on the speed of production.

In many forms of production there is considerable scope for increasing the amount of material processed in a given time (throughput). For batch production, for instance, Williamson (1972, p. 142) estimates that the ratio of actual processing time to total cycle time is unlikely to exceed 1 per cent in many cases, with the high proportion of idle component time resulting in high and costly stocks of work in progress. It was found in a recent British survey of 137 manufacturing plants that the proportion of the production lead time (i.e. the interval between the placing of an order and its delivery) that was spent in processing was less than half in 83 per cent of the plants, and in 45 per cent of them less than a fifth (New, 1976). Moreover, these results related to companies in the flow type industries, in which much higher throughput efficiency can be expected. Although the situation in other countries may be better, it still leaves substantial room for improvement. In the United States, for instance, the proportion of manufacturing plants using less than half the lead time for processing was still 69 per cent in the 1960s (Green, 1970).

It has now been repeatedly demonstrated that different forms of work organisation can improve throughput efficiency and thereby reduce the size of the stocks required: falls of from 25 to 65 per cent in component stocks have been noted in a light engineering works (Kenton, 1973) and of 30 per cent in work in progress at Platt International (Spooner, 1973); the establishment of group working reduced stocks by a factor of six for electron tube assembly at Philips (den Hertog, 1976, p. 112) and by a factor of eight at Ferodo (Williamson, 1972, p. 157). Such differences, and the potential that they point to, suggest that careful planning, estimating and monitoring is required in this respect.

Training and initial consultations

All reports agree that all new forms of work organisation require more money to be spent in training personnel to perform more complex duties. There is also agreement that the additional need for training does not increase in proportion to the complexity of the new task. In the case of Olivetti, for instance, experience suggested that a man "takes considerably less time to learn a whole meaningful job than he does to learn the different factions of the same job" (Butera, 1975, p. 193).

Work reorganisation can also entail a substantial commitment of resources to initial consultations and discussions. These costs include both the cost of external consultants and the use of the time of operating and management personnel. With few exceptions (Mirvis and Macy, 1976), however, these costs are not separately identified, although the exceptions can illustrate their potential magnitude.

Initial dip in productivity

It was found in a survey of experience in Western Europe (Wilkinson, 1970) that an initial commitment of resources was commonly required to cover the fall in productivity that was often an immediate, even if short-term, consequence of work reorganisation. As people learn their new jobs and as the organisation adjusts to the changes, output may fall off at first. But to the extent that the learning is achieved, or the change reinforced, improvements will eventually occur. In a radio assembly plant in the United Kingdom the dip in output lasted from the 10th to the 23rd week of the experiment (Cox and Sharp, 1951).

Wage costs

Owing to the upgrading of tasks, work reorganisation tends to increase the wages of operative workers. There are frequent reports of increases of up to about 10 per cent (Work in America, 1972), some of increases of up to 20 per cent (Taylor, 1977) and a few reports of even higher increases (Butteriss and Murdoch, 1975). The restructuring can also result in higher bonus payments if there are productivity gains and linked incentive payments: reported bonus increases range from 12 to 60 per cent (Donnelly, 1971; Taylor, 1977). In many
312 cases, however, wage costs per unit of production fall because of productivity improvements, and the effect of increases in personnel costs on the cost of products and services is moderated by any effect that the change has on over-all personnel requirements. If it is successful from a management point of view, the reorganisation of work can lead to reductions in operating personnel, and the need for overtime and the use of temporary personnel can also be substantially reduced (British Oxygen Company Ltd., 1971; Kenton, 1973), if not eliminated (Walters, 1975). Direct gains in production efficiency and a reduction in the need to provide for high levels of absenteeism and labour turnover are partly responsible for this, as are the improvements stemming from the higher throughput efficiency that can be derived from group working (New, 1976). When production levels remain more or less static, possibly owing to the state of the market, the absolute number of operating personnel can fall.

Reports note experiments resulting in reductions ranging from 11 to 40 per cent (Butteriss and Murdoch, 1975; Hepworth and Osbaldeston, 1975; Huse and Beer, 1971; Tuggle, 1969; Walton, 1972; Work in America, 1972). With production increases, on the other hand, the personnel savings are reflected in less than proportionate increases in personnel.

Supervisory personnel requirements

The greater autonomy given to working groups can also result in reductions in supervisory personnel. Larger parts of the tasks of assigning work, training new employees, administering materials and checking on production quality tend to be done by the operating personnel themselves. Supervision was reduced, for example, by 50 per cent after the introduction of semi-autonomous working groups in a plastic package manufacturing plant in the United States (Taylor et al., 1972). Group working in aircraft maintenance at Air Canada (Chartrand, 1976) resulted in reductions of up to 75 per cent in supervision time. A job enlargement scheme in an engineering department of the American Telephone and Telegraph company reduced the number of management jobs at various levels and produced cost savings of $250,000 annually (Taylor, 1977). Similar results have been reported for Volvo (Agurén, Hansson and Karlsson, 1976) and Imperial Chemical Industries (Cotgrove, Dunham and Vamplew, 1971).

Furthermore the combination of quality improvements and the relocation of the inspection function within the work group can result in large reductions in quality and other control personnel. In the United Kingdom side of the Shell firm, testing in one department fell by 75 per cent (Hill, 1972). A work reorganisation programme in the quality control function of an International Business Machines plant in the United States resulted in a 50 per cent reduction in inspection, with the number of inspectors falling from 48 to 28 (Mahel, Overbagh, Palmer and Piersol, 1970).

Absenteeism and labour turnover

There are innumerable reports of work reorganisation programmes resulting in lower absenteeism and labour turnover (Locke, 1976). Until recently, however, there have been very few attempts to estimate the resulting economic gains. The
difficulties are great: even the concepts of absenteeism, and especially labour 313
turnover, are imprecise and subject to varying definitions and forms of statistical calculation (Latham and Pursell, 1975; Price, 1973; Van der Merwe and Miller, 1971). Yet even if some of the all too real societal consequences are ignored, reductions in absenteeism and labour turnover can clearly offer direct economic benefits to an enterprise, for recruiting costs are real enough. Personnel department costs can be affected directly and economic gains will certainly accrue if losses in production can be prevented, overtime working reduced and manpower requirements cut. Moreover high levels of absenteeism and labour turnover can jeopardise the productive capacity of a whole group of workers. These consequences have long been recognised, and in many cases have provided the impetus for organisational change; but few attempts have been made to calculate them precisely.

An early impetus for many of the endeavours to quantify the economic consequences of various forms of withdrawal behaviour was provided by Likert (1967). His plea for "human resource accounting" captured the imagination and energies of a small but enthusiastic group of scholars and practioners. A great deal of theoretical and practical development has been undertaken since that time (Flamholtz, 1974) and, if used with care, some of the ideas that have been developed might provide some guidelines for action. Working with insurance company employees, for instance, Flamholtz estimated that the replacement costs for claims personnel ranged from US$6,000 for a claims investigator to US$24,000 for a field examiner and those for sales personnel from US$31,600 for salesmen with below-average performance to US$185,100 for a sales manager.

Unfortunately, however, a great deal of the work on human resource accounting has been more notable for its technical sophistication than for its relationship to management concerns. Yet in one company human resource accounting information was used to identify the total investment cost of changing an assembly operation from flow-line to group working. Estimates made of the orientation, training, familiarisation and dislocation costs demonstrated that the "human resource costs" of the change-over amounted to almost four times the physical capital cost (Woodruff, 1974, pp. 16-17). And in the light of this surprising finding the company developed and used a regular financial report on human resources costs for management purposes.

Research and development work on more systematic methods of costing the consequences of personnel turnover is currently in progress in a number of organisations (Gustafson, 1974; Jonson, Jönsson and Svenson, 1979). Moreover, to assess the economic benefits of reductions in absenteeism and labour turnover stemming from programmes designed to improve the quality of working life, Herrick (1975) and more particularly Macy and Mirvis (1976) are developing methodologies suitable for more general application. This approach relies on an intensive analysis of the range of possible organisational responses to absenteeism and labour turnover, and of their financial implications in terms of direct, indirect and opportunity costs. The accompanying figure illustrates how the responses to absenteeism were mapped and costed. Using this approach Macy and Mirvis found that the average cost of one day's absenteeism in an assembly plant in the
314 United States was $55.36 in 1972-73, including downtime costs of $10.03, fringe benefits paid to the missing employee of $5.12, replacement workforce costs of $6.29 and under-absorbed fixed costs of $33.92. The average cost per "incident of turnover" was $120.59 in 1972-73, rising to $150.69 in 1974-75. These methods can be criticised for the assumptions they make, the methods they employ (under-absorbed overheads indeed!), their complexity of calculation and their pseudo-precision; but they should not be dismissed out of hand: at the very least they emphasise the potential management significance of the economic consequences of withdrawal behaviour and, in so doing, the inadequacies of traditional accounting methods.

While research in this field proceeds, management should not ignore the issue. The crude estimates of economic effect now being used by a few companies (Taylor, 1973; Weir, 1976) might well be preferable to ignoring the real effects that absenteeism and labour turnover can have on the financial and social performance of the enterprise.

Quality of output and reduction of waste

Many attempts to reorganise the working environment have resulted in an improvement in the quality of the work done. Scrap, reject and error rates have fallen. Rejects, for instance, fell by 80 per cent as a result of an autonomous working group design at the Topeka plant of General Foods (Work in America, 1972); Philips have reported falls of from 9 to 5 per cent and from 7 to 3 per cent in rejects (den Hertog, 1974; Jenkins, 1974); and in a continuous weld pipe mill in California, group working resulted in a fall from 39 to 9 per cent in spoilage. Several companies have by now estimated the economic advantages of these improvements. A simple approach involving estimates of the cost of scrap, customer returns and re-work, and the gains from recoveries, is outlined by Macy and Mirvis (1976).

Similar improvements have also been found with clerical jobs. Job enrichment at Imperial Chemical Industries resulted in reports of higher quality (Paul and Robertson, 1970), and the use of self-governing work groups in the motor

Measuring the costs of absenteeism

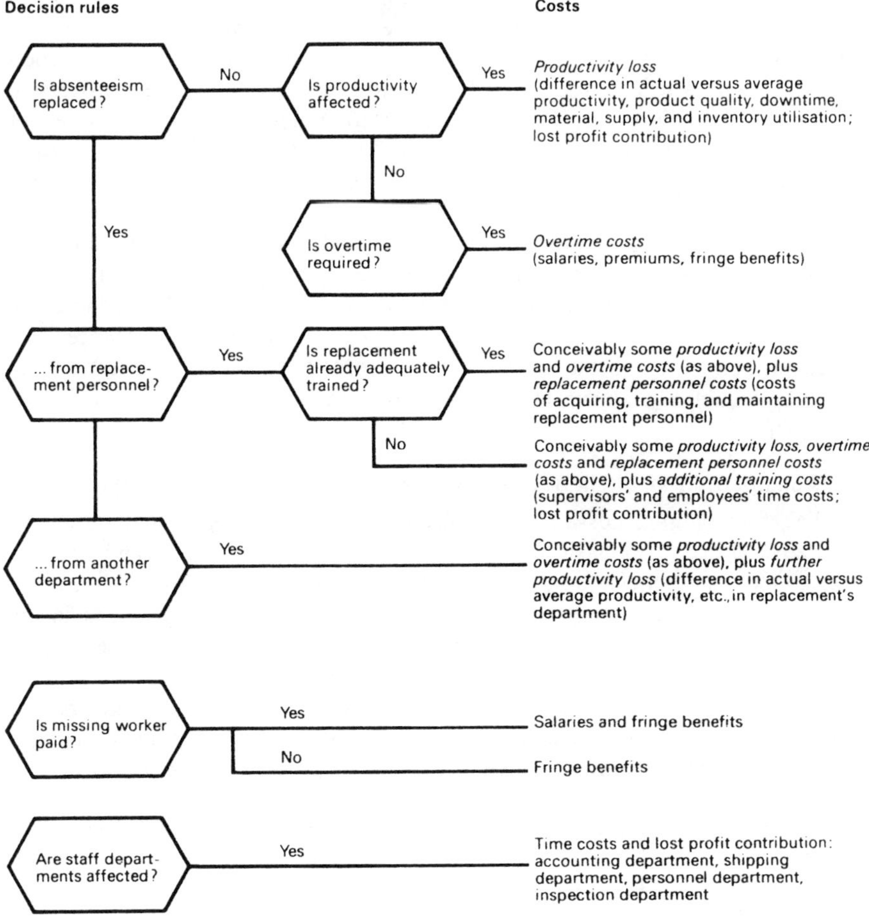

(Source: Barry A. Macy and Philip H. Mirvis: "A methodology for assessment of quality of work life and organizational effectiveness in behavioral-economic terms", in *Administrative Science Quarterly*, June 1976, p. 226.)

insurance office at Skandia cut the number of misplaced documents from 1,200 to 7 in the first four months of the new system (Hepworth and Osbaldeston, 1975). A more controlled experiment in the accounting office of a United States insurance company found that group work resulted in a fall in error rates of 35 per cent by comparison with returns from a control group (Ulich, 1974). Such gains are unlikely to be amenable to economic assessment, however.

It would appear that improvements in quality have been achieved principally where an individual or a group has taken responsibility for quality control. An increased sense of responsibility is, in part, responsible for the findings, although the clearer delineation of responsibility and the shorter feedback time also promotes more learning on the job.

Organisational costs

Work reorganisation programmes can also affect the overhead or organisational costs of an enterprise. As a result of the reduction in supervisory and control personnel there can be other related cost reductions. The introduction of autonomous working groups in Proctor and Gamble's Lima, Ohio, processing plant resulted, for instance, in falls of from 10 to 50 per cent in a wide variety of overhead costs (Jenkins, 1973). There can also be cost reductions stemming from the higher safety standards that can, on occasions, be associated with new forms of work organisation. Macy and Mirvis (1976) present a tentative way of gaining some insight into the possible immediate economic implications of such standards. Maintenance costs can also be affected, positively or negatively: on the one hand the shift of some maintenance functions to a group, and their increased responsibility for the plant in their care, can result in maintenance cost reductions; however, to the extent that the reorganisation results in a need for more production equipment, maintenance costs can increase. Evidence varies on
316 this point.

Over-all operational efficiency of resource utilisation

The foregoing discussion has reflected the rather fragmented nature of evaluative efforts. Emphasis has been placed on particular costs and benefits. Taken individually they tend to give a rather narrow and partial view of the effect of work reorganisation programmes, although in conjunction they do provide an indication of the broad range of potential over-all economic consequences. However, the assessment of over-all efficiency is notoriously difficult. Nevertheless, it has attracted the interest of many scholars and practitioners over many decades. The reasons for this are clear enough. In the undertaking a diversity of resources are employed in the production of a common group of products and services. Although it is useful for management to have indicators of the performance of separate resources at its disposal, it is also desirable that it should have some indication of their joint operation. However, the rationale for having indicators of over-all efficiency itself indicates their limitations. The problems of equating diverse resources are real (Salter, 1969), and even if they are surmounted the making of comparisons across enterprises, and even across functions and departments within a single enterprise, can be a difficult if not impossible task.

Productivity and throughput, the two common measures of over-all results, can provide useful, albeit crude, indicators of the immediate effect of work reorganisation programmes, and they are used for that purpose in numerous reports. However, such measurements need to be used with care. They give only a partial reflection of many of the economic gains derived from organisational changes, and fail to reflect many of the longer-term benefits. Also, as commonly defined, they do not enable any distinction to be made between the returns to the social reorganisation of work itself and to the higher capital investment which often accompanies such reorganisation. Some effort has been devoted to isolating the contributions of separate factors. The French research and experimentation on surplus accounts is particularly interesting in this respect (Lemaine, 1977;

Maître, 1979; and Templé, 1971). On the other hand, some authorities might now see the crudeness of productivity and throughput indicators as a potential advantage, focusing the attention of the observer on the over-all result instead of on the contributions of separate factors. In short, such over-all indicators of performance are useful, and throughput measurements, in particular, help to emphasise the relevance of time. But as means of assessing the economic consequences of a work reorganisation programme they cannot and should not stand on their own. Whilst they reflect in a simple manner some aspects of the over-all balance of gains and losses, and in so doing relate to the routine measurements of operational performance made in many enterprises, other vital consequences are ignored. Accordingly they can, with care, be used to supplement a consideration of the full range of economic consequences, but not as a substitute for it.

Fortunately some of the more recent attempts to move towards more comprehensive assessment have borne such considerations in mind. An instance is the economic assessment of the group technology programme introduced by 317
Serck Audco Valves Ltd., manufacturers of taper plug valves (Williamson, 1972). In the early 1960s Serck Audco had experienced difficulties in meeting delivery dates on export orders. An examination of the flow of products through the manufacturing process showed that the traditional methods of production were resulting in materials spending an average of 80 per cent of their total time in the factory in queues waiting for the completion of other components and the necessary adjustment and resetting of the machine tools. In the light of this examination the company developed the idea of cellular manufacture, a comprehensive socio-technical approach to the organisation of work which involved every function of the company (see Vol. 1 of the present publication, pp. 117-121). Between 1961-62 and 1966-67 the manufacturing time for products declined from 12 weeks to two-and-a-half. This contributed to a 44 per cent reduction in stocks during the same period and a consequent fall in the ratio of stocks to sales from 52 to 22 per cent. Indeed the initial capital invested in the conversion to group technology was recovered four times over by the stock reduction alone.

Recently a number of attempts have been made to provide a more comprehensive assessment of programmes designed to improve the quality of working life in both social and economic terms. The recent reports on the Volvo Kalmar plant made by Volvo itself and the Swedish Rationalisation Council (Agurén, Hansson and Karlsson, 1976) are indicative of the trend, as are the economic and social evaluations conducted elsewhere by Volvo and by Philips (den Hertog, 1976; Jonson, Jönsson and Svensson, 1979). The outline of the approach used by Saab-Scania has also been published (Norstedt and Agurén, 1973, pp. 39-40). Numerous other assessments of varying detail, scope and sophistication are being made, although few are available to the public.

By far the most comprehensive approach to assessment to date is contained in the work of Herrick (1975) and Macy and Mirvis (1976). The latter authors in particular are developing and applying a social and economic methodology for defining, measuring and costing the forms of behaviour on the job that are likely to be influenced by the reorganisation of work. These authors provide three criteria for the inclusion of a form of behaviour in their measurement scheme:

(a) it has to be defined so that it is significantly affected by the work structure;

(b) it has to be measurable and convertible to significant costs to the organisation; and

(c) the measures and costs of the behaviour variables have to be mutually exclusive.

On these bases the emergent methodology focuses on determining the economic and social consequences of ten types of variables in two broad categories, namely participation and membership behaviour (e.g. absenteeism, labour turnover and strikes) and job performance behaviour (e.g. production under standard, grievances, quality under standard, accidents, unscheduled downtime and machine repair, and material utilisation and inventory shrinkage). In all cases the standard measures of the costs of these variables were derived from accepted
318 organisational and accounting practice. Distinctions were made between initial outlay costs and time costs, and also between variable or direct costs, fixed or indirect costs and the opportunity costs associated with lost potential. The approach has now been used to assess the costs and benefits of a number of work reorganisation programmes. An example based on experience in a manufacturing and assembly plant is illustrated in tables 2 and 3. Table 2 reports the cost per incident and the total estimated organisational costs for each variable at the site during the baseline period (1972-73) and the first two stages of the reorganisation. These figures are cast into a cost-benefit framework in table 3, where the costs of the reorganisation programme are compared with the year-to-year changes in the cost of counter-productive behaviour. In this instance the over-all outcome at the end of the whole biennium remains negative. The total direct costs of $303,588 are associated with an indirect cost of $227,240, giving an over-all economic cost of $530,828.

However, measurement problems abound, and the organisational relevance and social implications of such comprehensive approaches to evaluation have still to be assessed. However, these approaches should not be ignored, since they do, at the very least, reflect a sincere desire to learn and inform. Although existing approaches are bound to be superseded in the course of the advancement of knowledge (see, for example, the ongoing work of Epple, Fidler and Goodman), the early efforts indicate an emerging desire to integrate social and economic forms of assessment, so that they can together provide a basis for more detailed and specific knowledge of the organisation of work.

Some influences on the economic effects of the reorganisation of work

The review of the detailed reports of particular operational consequences stemming from work reorganisation programmes, together with the earlier discussion of the possibilities for achieving real systemic gains, points to the economic potential of organisational changes of this type at the level of the undertaking. It would appear that they can indeed generate as well as consume economic resources, as traditionally defined, and so contribute to the economic

Table 2. Estimated costs of various aspects of worker behaviour at a plant in the United States, 1972-75 (In US dollars)

Type of incident	1972-73		1973-74		1974-75[1]	
	Cost per incident	Total cost	*Cost per incident*	Total cost	*Cost per incident*	Total cost
Absenteeism[2]						
Leave days	. . .	. . .	*55.04*	687 229	*61.64*	821 795
Other	*55.36*	286 360	*53.15*	510 453	*62.49*	431 494
Accidents[2]						
Reportable[3]	*727.39*	194 213	*698.31*	229 046	*1 106.52*	240 115
Minor[3]	*6.64*	21 122	*5.71*	38 331	*6.45*	35 856
Re-visits to plant first-aid facilities	*6.64*	11 992	*5.71*	14 018	*6.45*	13 081
Late arrival at work[2, 4]	*4.86*	56 920	. . .	. . .	. . .	. . .
Labour turnover (cessations of employment)[2]						
Voluntary resignation	*120.59*	18 089	*131.68*	33 973	*150.69*	18 083
Other	*120.59*	14 230	*131.68*	21 859	*150.69*	18 686
Submission of grievance[5]	*32.48*	1 851	*34.44*	1 378	*56.10*	2 300
Product quality below standard[6]	*19 517*	663 589	*19 517*	573 800	*19 517*	409 857
Labour productivity below standard[7]	*22 236*	266 838	*22 236*	335 764	*22 236*	255 714
Totals[8, 9]		1 535 204		2 445 851		2 246 971

[1] Costs associated with absenteeism, accidents, labour turnover and grievances during the last four months of this year are projections. The figures for product quality and labour productivity below standard are actual costs. [2] Rates and costs for salaried personnel are assumed to be the same as those for hourly paid workers (1972-73: salaried absence costs, $41,669; salaried accident costs, $11,638; salary costs of late arrivals, $9,641; salaried labour turnover costs, $1,829). [3] Under Section 8(*c*)(2) of the Occupational Safety and Health Act of 1970 (ILO: *Legislative Series*, 1970—USA 1), the Secretary of Labor, in co-operation with the Secretary of Health, Education, and Welfare, issues regulations requiring employers to report on "work-related deaths, injuries and illnesses other than minor injuries requiring only first-aid treatment and which do not involve medical treatment, loss of consciousness, restriction of work or motion, or transfer to another job". [4] The "tardiness" concept measured here in fact covered each absence or illness lasting less than 4 hours; the average was 27 minutes. [5] In writing in accordance with the labour-management contract. [6] For 1972-73 the costs of rejects and scrap was 3.4 per cent of total sales. Each reduction of 1 per thousand is valued at $19,517 per incident. In 1973-74 costs were 2.94 per cent of total sales; in 1974-75, 2.1 per cent. A constant dollar equivalence of $19,517 was used in 1973-74 and 1974-75 to discount inflation. The non-discounted cost of quality below standard in 1973-74 was $667,015 ($23,028 per incident); in 1974-75 the non-discounted cost was $613,970 ($29,237 per incident). [7] In 1972-73 plant productivity was 88 per cent of standard. The production below standard rate is 12 per cent; accordingly a reduction of 1 per cent is valued at $22,236 per incident. Plant productivity in 1973-74 and 1974-75 was 84.9 per cent and 88.5 per cent of standard respectively. A constant dollar equivalence of $22,236 was used to discount inflation in 1973-74 and 1974-75. The non-discounted cost of production below standard was $400,567 ($26,528 per incident) in 1973-74 and $290,938 ($25,299 per incident) in 1974-75. [8] The total cost in 1972-73 is $1,470,427 for hourly paid personnel, and $64,777 for salaried personnel. [9] The total cost is reflected in standard labour dollars. The estimated cost in real dollar equivalents in 1972-73: $1,688,724, or 10.4 per cent of sales; in 1973-74: $2,690,436, or 8.45 per cent of sales; in 1974-75: $2,471,668, or 10.61 per cent of sales.

Source: Barry A. Macy and Philip H. Mirvis: "A methodology for assessment of quality of work life and organizational effectiveness in behavioural-economic terms", in *Administrative Science Quarterly*, June 1976, p. 219.

Table 3. Financial cost-benefit analysis of a human resource development project at a plant in the United States, 1973-75
(In US dollars; differences from base year 1972-73)

Item	Initial year (May 1973-April 1974)	Second year (May 1974-April 1975)	Whole biennium
Direct costs			
Consultant fees, expenses, etc.[1]	225 000	61 600	
Site employee time, training activities, earned idle time, etc.[2]	2 403	14 585	
Totals	227 403	76 185	303 588
Indirect benefits (or costs)[3]			
Absenteeism	(224 093)	(145 134)	
Leave days	. . .	. . .	
Accidents			
320 Reportable	(34 833)	(45 902)	
Minor	(17 209)	(14 734)	
Re-visits	(2 026)	(1 089)	
Late arrival at work	. . .	. . .	
Labour turnover (cessations of employment)			
Voluntary resignation	(15 884)	6	
Other	(7 629)	(4 456)	
Submission of grievances	473	(449)	
Product quality in relation to standard	89 789	253 732	
Labour productivity in relation to standard	(68 926)	11 124	
Totals	(280 338)	53 098	(227 240)

[1] Nine different organisations and funding agencies made financial contributions to the project. In addition, three organisations provided office space and services. These contributions are excluded from the analysis. [2] Estimates of actual costs are low because only personnel paid by the hour are included. [3] For definitions see table 2, from which all estimates of indirect benefits or costs are derived.

and social vitality of the enterprise. Of course such potential is not always achieved. Regardless of the difficulties of recording and monitoring accomplishment, particular experiments can fail to exploit the full possibilities that are seemingly available and others, although initially achieving some positive economic results, do not maintain them over time.

The reasons for such failures are many and complex. The nature of the change process itself is often an important factor, as are the precise mode of implementation, the implications of the change for the structure of power and influence in the organisation and the congruity or otherwise of the change with the social values and norms prevailing in the enterprise. But whilst undoubtedly important, the roles that might be played by such social and organisational factors are discussed elsewhere (Davis and Cherns, 1975; and particularly Mirvis and Berg, 1978). Here, emphasis will be placed on the way in which the framework for considering the economic costs and benefits of work reorganisation programmes that has been outlined above can help to identify some further factors that can influence the over-all economic effect of a change programme.

An analysis of the framework points to the ways in which a number of structural characteristics of the undertaking can influence the extent to which the social implications of an organisational change programme affect its over-all economic results. The capital intensity of the enterprise, for instance, is capable of influencing both the level of the initial systemic costs for a programme of work reorganisation and at least some elements of operational advantage. The capital investment needed to bring about a change can often be high, but for a capital-intensive enterprise the benefits stemming from higher throughput, and particularly those associated with reductions in absenteeism and turnover, can be correspondingly great. Not only can many of the costs of lost production time be avoided, but the undertaking can also gain from greater flexibility of operation.

Similarly an economic perspective highlights the relevance of considering the cost structure of the product or service. That structure provides the weights for assessing the relative economic significance of any operational costs and benefits 321
in the fields of personnel, material and organisational (or overhead) costs (New, 1976). For example, the costs of producing products or services with a low added value will be lowered by work reorganisation programmes which result in gains on the utilisation of materials; products or services with a high personnel content will more readily benefit economically from programmes that result in reduced labour requirements or substantial improvements with regard to absenteeism or labour turnover; and enterprises with high organisational complexity, having a great deal of vertical and horizontal differentiation of tasks, have greater opportunities to reduce the resources devoted to supervision and other forms of hierarchical control.

Other things being equal, product models or particular services that are produced for a longer period also offer greater possibilities for reaping the potential benefits of work reorganisation programmes, for the longer the period the greater is the likelihood of achieving a positive ratio of the operational benefits gained to the initial investment of resources. Moreover, the sooner work is reorganised during the period of production of a particular model or service, the greater the economic benefits (den Hertog, 1976, pp. 147-148). It should be borne in mind in this connection that new forms of work organisation can reduce the costs incurred by an enterprise as it seeks to adjust to the shorter model lives that are a characteristic of the modern industrial era, as was illustrated by the experience of Olivetti discussed above (Butera, 1975). For by comparison with enterprises operating in a stable environment, those that have to cope with continuing uncertainty can gain more from the systemic benefits that can stem from more flexible forms of work organisation. Indeed the experience of Bosch and Siemens (Staehle, 1974), Olivetti (Butera, 1975) and others illustrates how the desire to reap the potential systemic benefits of different forms of work organisation can itself promote change.

At this stage in the development of knowledge of the economic consequences of programmes designed to improve the quality of working life it might be useful to pay special attention to such structural factors as the capital intensity of the enterprise, its organisational complexity, the length of model life, the uncertainty of the task environment and the market, and the cost structure of the product or service. It might be admitted that the factors listed are not the basic ones. The technological environment of an undertaking, for instance, may be a major determinant of many economic consequences; but factors such as these do have the advantage of providing a pragmatic way of considering in broad terms the over-all significance of the many separate economic effects.

Performance of different forms of organisation

The emerging interest in the economic effectiveness of more radically different forms of organisation and management may also afford some insight into the economic viability of new approaches to work organisation. Co-operative and self-managed undertakings certainly have many characteristics that go beyond the changes envisaged in the designs for most programmes aiming to improve the quality of working life in conventionally managed enterprises. On the other hand
322 some of the objectives are not dissimilar, nor are some of the means through which they are achieved.

Melman's study of the comparative performance of traditionally managed undertakings and co-operative societies in Israel is interesting in this respect (Melman, 1970-71). Comparing a paired sample of enterprises in the tool, instruments, diecasting, plastics, machining and canning industries, he found that over-all the co-operative societies showed higher labour productivity (26 per cent), higher capital productivity (67 per cent), larger net profit per production worker (115 per cent) and lower administrative costs (13 per cent). Certainly the more democratic mode of decision-making in these co-operative undertakings was at least as efficient, and probably more efficient, than the more hierarchical forms of decision-making practised in a comparable set of managerially controlled firms.

An even more relevant study was based on a comparison of productivity in worker-managed and conventional firms in the United States plywood industry (Berman, 1976). The opportunity to make this comparison revolves around several intriguing court cases in the United States that sought to determine whether co-operative societies pay higher wages (which are not taxed as company profits). In one case a co-operative society producing plywood in the North-West was able to satisfy the courts that one hour of its members' time was worth 30 to 50 per cent more than that of workers doing the same work in conventional firms. After ensuing audits of several other undertakings, the United States tax authorities have accepted the 30 per cent higher productivity figure as valid. The studies undertaken by consultants on behalf of the tax authorities demonstrated that the higher productivity in the co-operative societies was due to the fact that they had fewer foremen, that workers maintained their own machinery and that the members learned more jobs and were thus able to rotate jobs when needed. In many cases the workers also performed what elsewhere would be classified as executive-level jobs without additional pay. According to the author of the report the higher performance in the co-operative societies was due to the fact that they had used many of the approaches that are now being explored by conventional firms, such as autonomous working groups, participative approaches to decision-making and a greater disclosure of information.

As yet, the results of such studies are only indicative. They suggest, however, that a more detailed consideration of the economic performance of different forms of management might be able to provide some further insights into the potential of new forms of work organisation. Some other intriguing evidence on the economic aspects of work organisation is provided by studies conducted on comparable firms in France and the Federal Republic of Germany collected by the Laboratoire d'Economie et de Sociologie du Travail at Aix-en-Provence (Brossard and Maurice, 1976; Lutz, 1976; and also Fitzroy and Hiller, 1978). French firms appeared to be more stratified, hierarchical and centralised. The administrative workforce was larger and better paid at higher levels in France, while production workers were better trained and paid in the Federal Republic, where the division of labour was less pronounced and screening by formal education less prevalent. More recent research puts the United Kingdom in an intermediary position (Maurice, Sorge and Warner, 1978). Such results at least 323
point to the practical possibility of theoretical options, particularly since the firms in France and the Federal Republic of Germany, at least, appeared to be similar in respect of their profitability and total labour costs.

Future possibilities and needs

The foregoing review of past experience and insights has amply illustrated the economic potential of programmes designed to improve the quality of working life. It would appear that although directed to social ends, such programmes not only consume economic resources but can create further economic resources and add to the longer-term economic and social viability of the enterprise. When seen in these terms, the need for economic and social assessment is real enough: a great deal of fundamental and, in the best sense of the word, challenging experimentation is needed in this field. In the meantime, however, the subject cannot and should not be ignored. Enterprises trying to reorganise their work environment should be encouraged to concern themselves with the economic and the social consequences of so doing.

Much of the information required for any such analysis can be obtained without too much difficulty from existing accounting systems. Certainly the necessary information on the initial costs of a work reorganisation programme can be obtained in this way. Details of changing requirements for both operational and supervisory personnel, and the associated costs, will be an integral part of any standard accounting system. So will details of the changing investment in stocks and work in progress and the effect on organisational costs and overheads. A good indication of the benefits of improved product quality can be obtained from savings on the costs of scrap, customer returns and re-working. The only difficulty in all of these cases is to compile and present the information in a way that emphasises the effect of a programme, is instructive, and provides a basis for decision. Past experience in this and other fields of accounting suggests, however, that it will not be easy to meet these requirements. In addition, there are major difficulties in two particular fields. The first relates to the assessment of economic costs and benefits in service and clerical organisations, in which accounting systems are generally not so well developed. Although most such systems should give a useful indication of initial costs, changing personnel costs and the effects on organisational overheads, there will be enormous and in most cases insurmountable problems in estimating the economic implications of work of higher quality. If those implications are considered important, it will usually be necessary to rely on broad indicators of the changing nature of the task rather than on precise economic calculations.

The other exceptionally difficult task is the assessment of the economic consequences of changes in such matters as grievances, absenteeism, labour turnover and accidents and the calculation of the longer-term systemic benefits that were outlined above. However difficult it may be, some effort should be made to calculate these more subtle economic implications of an improved work environment, to which in many cases the major benefits may be due. Lower absenteeism and labour turnover, for instance, can contribute to the financial
324 performance of an enterprise. Productivity losses can be prevented, overtime and the use of temporary personnel can be reduced, savings can be made in the organisational costs associated with replacement, and on occasion over-all personnel requirements can be cut. It is common knowledge that traditional accounting systems are not designed to provide a ready assessment of such gains. The necessary data are in many cases collected but then lost in the mass of calculations which give rise to the measurement of over-all financial performance. With imagination and perseverance, however, what has been so lost can often be found. A few enterprises are now starting to demonstrate that such estimates can be made. Absenteeism is being related to lost production and overtime. Similar estimates of productivity losses, higher personnel costs and the often high costs of replacement are being related to labour turnover. Whilst often imprecise and partial, such indicators can be useful. Even if only collected irregularly, they can highlight the significant relationship between the social and the economic environment of the enterprise. The more sophisticated endeavours of Herrick (1975) and Macy and Mirvis (1976) may not, at this stage, be suitable for general use. But they do suggest the need for more practical but rigorous research in this field, and indicate its potential.

When the economic consequences of programmes designed to improve the quality of working life are being evaluated, primary emphasis should be placed on examining the over-all costs and benefits of a programme rather than on calculating ratios merely of productive performance and efficiency. Such ratios have their uses, but they can give only a partial and short-term indication of the over-all effect. To be instructive and provide an adequate basis for action, a delineation and assessment of systemic and operational costs and benefits must involve the computation and analysis of a whole range of indicators. Only in this way can the more subtle long-term influences of work reorganisation programmes be recognised and considered. Consideration should be given in particular to placing greater emphasis on the concept of value added (sales less purchases of raw materials and supplies) when reporting on both the over-all consequences of work reorganisation programmes and their particular effect on productivity ratios. By comparison with other indicators of financial performance, value added is particularly dependent on the joint role that capital and labour play in the creation of wealth. Without lending support to the assumption that the use of some resources, such as labour, gives rise to "costs" whilst others, such as capital, are properly rewarded by the distribution of profit, the calculation of value added focuses attention on the proportion of the total wealth created in the enterprise not only by the different parties but also over time. Wages and salaries, interest and dividends, and taxes can, in that way, be compared with the resources that have been set aside for ensuring the longer-term existence, viability and growth of the enterprise.

Unless special care is taken, economic assessments can all too readily focus attention on the calculation of short-term gains rather than longer-term systemic benefits. Hence consideration needs to be given to the joint use of social and economic indicators that can help to suggest whether programmes designed to improve the quality of working life are or are not giving rise to the systemic benefits discussed above. The aim should be to consider not the partial or 325
immediate effect of a programme but its over-all long-term effect. An initial investment might have to be made in work in progress and raw material stocks, for instance, to provide buffers for group and individual working. In time, however, if a reorganisation programme has a favourable effect on throughput, these investments may pay for themselves. Similarly, many reorganisation programmes result in a higher wage and salary bill. Again, however, if a programme improves productivity, the personnel component of product costs will not increase in the same proportion. Care should be taken to include estimates of the initial dip in productivity when calculating the initial costs of a programme. The costs associated with consultation and training should also be included. In many cases these can be as high as the costs of physical capital and inventories, if not higher (Woodruff, 1974). However, even higher costs of training for each worker need not necessarily result in higher total training costs. Volkswagen, for example, found that the lower rate of labour turnover resulting from a work reorganisation programme led to a reduction in the total cost of training new workers (Lindestad and Kvist, 1975). Numerous other instances of such secondary effects could be cited. However, the foregoing examples are sufficient to explain why an attempt should be made to cover secondary effects when assessing economic consequences.

The broad approach to the assessment of economic costs and benefits that has been outlined above aims to be useful and convenient. In most respects it should be relatively easy to follow in most undertakings. Matters such as the effects of "withdrawal behaviour" (absenteeism and high labour turnover) and longer-term systemic benefits are more difficult to handle. They should not be forgotten, however. There is a need for pragmatic experimentation in enterprises with the aim of producing a range of convenient, short-term solutions, and facilities for the exchange of experience in this respect could usefully be established. At the same time, more fundamental research should be encouraged with the objective of producing acceptable, usable and low cost means of long-term assessment.

Organisational role of economic assessment

In trying to assess economic consequences consideration must be given to the process by which the indicators are designed. For it would be paradoxical indeed if methods of economic measurement were applied without discrimination to a new social and technological structure the very existence of which may reflect broader conceptions of the social nature of the design process. With few exceptions, however, recommendations for new methods of economic assessment tend to be designed either by a small group of internal specialists or by outside consultants (Edstrom, 1976; Powers, 1972; Swanson, 1974). The designers invariably try to follow a path of seeming technical objectivity, appealing to the "obvious" needs of the enterprise "as a whole". But in so doing they often ignore many of the wider organisational factors that determine the potential use and final effect of their recommendations. This state of affairs may well explain present apprehensions and lack of progress in the economic assessment of new forms of work organisation.

326 Specialist skills are undeniably needed in designing means of economic assessment, but it should always be remembered that the method finally adopted reflects social as well as economic values. At the very least the specification of the organisational purpose to be served and the principles that should govern the design and use of the method should be discussed and challenged by a wider circle. Wherever possible, the whole design process should be on a participatory basis, for if that is not done new methods of work organisation will be assessed on the basis of procedures that neglect the fundamental tenets of what they are supposed to assess.

Most discussions of economic assessment tend to emphasis the technical aspects of evaluative methodologies rather than the organisational purposes which they can serve and the context in which they are to be used. Yet broader organisational issues can play a key role in determining not only whether a methodology is accepted and used but also the precise nature of its effect on decisions and action. Indeed many of the most difficult problems in the assessment of the economic costs and benefits of new approaches to work organisation are likely to result from apprehensions and anxieties over the context in which such an assessment will be used and the purpose it will serve. Will the new approaches be used, like so many other information and assessment systems, to support existing structures of hierarchical control? Or can they encourage a wider organisational interest and involvement in the possibilities and effects of change? Who, in other words, will be able to use the new calculations rather than be subjected to them? And are they truly capable of helping to change people's outlook, as some of their advocates claim? Or might they merely bring about greater organisational rigidity as people strive to satisfy their more immediate requirements rather than the broader ends which are the proclaimed intention of the designers?

A concern with further economic assessment can also engender anxieties because it can be seen as implying, albeit in a disguised form, a challenge to the value of social progress. Galbraith (1974, p. 7) notes that the "contribution of economics to the exercise of power . . . [is] instrumental in that it serves not the understanding or improvement of the economic system but the goals of those who have power in the system". However, although the stereotype of the "dismal science" can all too readily encourage a concern with the visible hand of economic restraint, in the present context it is important to state that such a concern is not necessarily justified. All depends on the context in which the information is used.

Whilst the distinction between economic and social assessment has its uses, it should not be carried too far. There are few social ends that do not require the use of economic resources, and economic progress, in turn, can often create significant social change. Instead of continuing to enforce an artificial distinction between the social and the economic, progress requires "the development of a comprehensive set of criteria that will take account of both economic and social considerations, not by forcing the one into the mould of the other, but by integrating them at a higher level of abstraction" (United Nations, 1965, p. 10). Assessment is always a complex social as well as technical activity. The organisational roles which it can and does serve extend well beyond those that are 327
used to justify it. Although some of these roles may not be readily acknowledged by the organisations themselves, they can none the less exert influence on the acceptance and use of new approaches. Accordingly, change in this respect must of necessity be seen as a difficult and demanding activity. Instead of being ignored, the organisational and social dimensions increasingly need to be seen as an essential part of the whole problem of bringing about change.

Conclusion

This survey has shown that new forms of work organisation and programmes designed to improve the quality of working life can make a positive contribution to the over-all economic performance of an organisation. They are often costly, but the resulting benefits can not only improve operational functioning but also contribute to an organisation's capacity to adjust to changing needs and circumstances. Longer-term systemic gains can, in other words, often supplement the more visible operational savings in personnel, material and organisational costs.

Many troublesome measurement problems remain, however. Although much can be learnt from an informed use of existing flows of enterprise-level financial information, that information is usually collected to serve a particular purpose of the organisation itself rather than to shed light on the possible need for a change in the form of the organisation of work. So many social assumptions underlie the prevailing forms of evaluation that invariably more tends to be known about current effects of new forms of work organisation than about their possible value in the longer term. However, as social values continue to change and as society's conceptions of the social nature and roles of the enterprise evolve along with them, more attention is being devoted to methods of economic assessment and appraisal. Although current approaches to social accounting and social audit may be crude and embryonic, they are nevertheless significant reflections of our changing conceptions of the accountability of the enterprise. Greater attention also is being paid to the interests of labour: not only has there been an increasing concern with the problems of disclosing information to workers and trade unions, but all over Europe interest is now being expressed in broader definitions of economic surplus and in forms of reporting that give different accounts of workplace behaviour and achievements. Such developments could have major implications for the economic assessment of programmes designed to improve the quality of working life. If they do succeed in challenging prevailing notions of enterprise performance, the current searchings and experiments may provide the basis for a broader and more vital portrayal of life in the enterprise as a whole.

References

Agurén, Stefán; Hansson, Reine; and Karlsson, K. G. *The Volvo Kalmar plant: The impact of new design on work organization.* Stockholm, Rationalization Council SAF-LO, 1976.

Berman, K. V. *Comparative productivity in worker-managed co-operative plywood plants and conventionally run plants.* Unpublished paper. Washington State University, 1976.

Biderman, A. D., and Drury, T. F. *Measuring work quality for social reporting.* Halsted Press, 1976.

Birchall, D., and Wild, R. "Autonomous work groups". *Journal of General Management,* Autumn 1974, pp. 36-43.

Björk, Lars E. "An experiment in work satisfaction". *Scientific American,* Mar. 1975, pp. 17-23.

Blauner, Robert. *Alienation and freedom: The factory worker and his industry.* University of Chicago Press, 1964.

Brossard, M., and Maurice, M. "Is there a universal model of organization structure?" *International Studies of Management and Organization* (1976), pp. 11-45.

British Oxygen Company Ltd. Unpublished paper by the Manpower Development Unit, 1971.

Burns, Tom, and Stalker, G. M. *The management of innovation.* London, Tavistock Publications, 1961.

Butera, F. "Environmental factors in job and organization design: The case of Olivetti". In L. E. Davis and A. B. Cherns (eds.): *The quality of working life* (The Free Press, 1975), Vol. 2.

Butteriss, M., and Murdoch, R. D. *Work restructuring projects and experiments in the United Kingdom,* Report No. 2, Work Research Unit, United Kingdom Department of Employment, 1975.

— *Work restructuring projects and experiments in the United States of America,* Report No. 3, Work Research Unit, United Kingdom Department of Employment, 1976.

Chartrand, Phillip J. "The impact of organization on labour relations at Air Canada". *The Canadian Personnel and Industrial Relations Journal,* Jan. 1976, pp. 22-26.

Cotgrove, Stephen; Dunham, Jack; and Namplew, Clive. *The nylon spinners: A case study in productivity bargaining and job enlargement.* London, Allen and Unwin, 1971.

Cox, David, and Sharp, K. M. Dyce. "Research on the unit of work". *Occupational Psychology.* Apr. 1951, pp. 90-108.

Cummings, T. G., and Salipante, P. F. "Research-based strategies for improving work life". In P. Warr (ed.): *Personal goals and work design* (Wiley, 1976), pp. 31-41.

Davis, L. E. "Toward a theory of job design". *Journal of Industrial Engineering,* Sep.-Oct. 1957, pp. 305-307.

Davis, L. E., and Cherns, A. B. (eds.). *The quality of working life.* The Free Press, 1975.

Donnelly, J. F. "Increasing productivity by involving people in their total job". *Personnel Administrator,* Sep.-Oct. 1971.

Edstrom, A. *User influence on the development of MIS: A contingency approach.* Unpublished working paper, European Institute for Advanced Studies in Management, Brussels, 1976.

Edwards, G. A. B. *Readings in group technology.* The Machinery Publishing Co., 1971.

Epple, D.; Fidler, E.; and Goodman, P. *Estimating economic consequences in organizational effectiveness experiments.* Unpublished working paper, Carnegie-Mellon University, Pittsburgh, n.d.

Fitzroy, F. R., and Hiller, J. R. *Efficiency and motivation in productive organizations.* Discussion paper, International Institute of Management, Berlin, 1978.

Flamholtz, E. G. *Human asset accounting.* Dickenson, 1974.

Galbraith, John Kenneth. *Economics and the public purpose.* Boston, Houghton Mifflin, 1973.

Green, J. M. (ed.). *Production and inventory control handbook.* McGraw-Hill, 1970.

Gustafson, H. W. *Force-loss cost analysis.* Paper presented to the AWV-Fachseminar: "Das Humankapital der Unternehmen", Bonn, September 1974.

Hepworth, A., and Osbaldeston, M. *Restructuring the motor insurance section.* Ashridge Management College Research Unit, 1975.

Herrick, N. Q. *The quality of work and its outcomes: Estimating potential increases in labor productivity.* Academy for Contemporary Problems, Ohio, 1975.

den Hertog, J. F. *Work structuring.* Eindhoven, Philips, 1974.

— *Work system design: Experiences with alternative production organizations.* Eindhoven, Philips, 1976.

Hill, Paul. *Towards a new philosophy of management: The company development programme of Shell UK Limited.* London, Gower Press, 1971.

Huse, Edgar F., and Beer, Michael. "Eclectic approach to organizational development". *Harvard Business Review,* Sep.-Oct. 1971, pp. 103-112.

Jenkins, David. *Job power: Blue and white collar democracy.* New York, Doubleday, 1973.

— *Industrial democracy in Europe* Business International, 1974.

Jonson, L. C.; Jönsson, B.; and Svensson, G. "The application of social accounting to absenteeism and personnel turnover". *Accounting, Organisations and Society,* Vol. 3 (1979), Nos. 3-4.

Kenton, Leslie. "The seven year switch". *Industrial Management* (London), May 1973. pp. 14-19.

Klein, Lisl. *New forms of work organization.* Cambridge University Press, 1976.

Kornhauser, A. *Mental health of the industrial worker.* New York, John Miller Press, 1965.

Latham, G. P., and Pursell, E. D. "Measuring absenteeism from the opposite side of the coin". *Journal of Applied Psychology,* 1975, pp. 369-371.

Lawler, Edward E., III. "Job design and employee motivation". *Personnel Psychology,* Vol. 22, 1969, pp. 426-435. Reprinted in Victor H. Vroom and Edward L. Deci (eds.): *Management and motivation,* selected readings (Harmondsworth, Middlesex, Penguin Books, 1970), pp. 160-169.

— *Measuring the human organization.* Unpublished paper presented to the Human Resource Accounting Seminar, Bonn, 1974.

— "Conference review: Issues of understanding". In P. Warry (ed.): *Personal goals and work design* (Wiley, 1976), pp. 225-234.

Lawrence, Paul [illegible] Lorsch, Jay W. *Organization and environment: Managing differentiation and integr*[illegible]ton, Graduate School of Business Administration, Harvard University, 1967.

Lemaire, B. "Comptes de surplus et économie de transition". *Revue Française de Gestion,* Sep. 1977, pp. 18-23.

Likert, Rensis. *The human organization: Its management and value.* New York, McGraw-Hill, 1967.

Lindestad, H., and Kvist, A. *The Volkswagen Report.* Swedish Employers' Confederation, 1975.

Locke, E. A. "The nature and causes of job satisfaction". In M. D. Dunnette (ed.): *Handbook of industrial and organizational psychology* (Rand-McNally, 1976).

Lutz, B. "Bildungssystem und Beschäftigungsstruktur in Deutschland und Frankreich". In H. G. Mendivs et. al.: *Betrieb-Arbeitsmarkt-Qualifikation,* 1 (Frankfurt, Aspekte Verlag, 1976).

Macy, Barry A., and Mirvis, Philip H. "A methodology for assessment of quality of work life and organizational effectiveness in behaviorial-economic terms". *Administrative Science Quarterly,* June 1976, pp. 212-226.

Maher, John; Overbagh, Wayne; Palmer, Gerald; and Piersol, Darrell. "Enriched jobs improve inspection". *Work Study and Management Services,* Oct. 1970, pp. 821-824.

Maître, P. "The measurement of the creation and distribution of wealth in a firm by the method of surplus accounts". *Accounting, Organizations and Society,* Vol. 3 (1979), Nos. 3-4.

Manufacturing Management, December 1972. "Work teams at Pye beat production line problems".

Maurice, M.; Sorge, A.; and Warner, M. *Societal differences in organizing manufacturing units: A comparison of France, West Germany and Great Britain.* Paper presented to the Ninth Congress of Sociology, Upsala, 1978.

Melman, S. "Managerial versus co-operative decision making in Israel". *Studies in Comparative International Development,* Vol. VI (1970-71), No. 3, pp. 47-58.

Midlands Tomorrow (West Midlands Economic Planning Council), No. 8, 1975. "Industrial productivity: Scope for improvement".

Mirvis, Philip H., and Berg, D. N. *Failures in organization development and change: Cases and essays for learning.* Wiley, 1978.

Mirvis, Philip H., and Edward E. Lawler III. "Measuring the financial impact of employee attitudes". *Journal of Applied Psychology,* Vol. 62, No. 1, 1977, pp. 1-8.

Mirvis, Philip H., and Macy, Barry A. "Accounting for the costs and benefits of human resource development programs: An interdisciplinary approach". *Accounting, Organizations and Society,* Vol. 1, Nos. 2-3, pp. 179-194.

330 Mott, P. E. *Shift work: The social, psychological and physical consequences.* Ann Arbor, Michigan, Institute for Social Research, 1975.

National Economic Development Office (United Kingdom). *Why group technology?* 1975.

New, C. C. *Managing manufacturing operations: A survey of current practice in 186 plants.* British Institute of Management, 1976.

Norstedt, Jan-Peder, and Agurén, Stefán. *The Saab-Scania report: Experiment with modified work organizations and work forms: Final report.* Stockholm, Swedish Employers' Confederation, 1973.

Paul, W. J., and Robertson, C. B. *Job enrichment and employee motivation.* Gower Press, 1970.

Portigal, A. H. (ed.). *Measuring the quality of working life.* Information Canada, 1974.

— *Towards the measurement of work satisfaction.* OECD Social Indicator Development Programme Special Studies No. 1. Paris, Organisation for Economic Co-operation and Development, 1976.

Powers, R. *An empirical investigation of selected hypotheses related to the success of management information system projects.* Unpublished Ph.D. dissertation, University of Minnesota, 1972.

Price, J. L. *The correlates of turnover.* Department of Sociology, University of Iowa, Working Paper No. 73-1.

Ranson, G. H. *Group technology.* McGraw-Hill, 1972.

Salter, W. E. G. *Productivity and technical change.* Cambridge University Press, Second edition, 1969.

Schoderbeck, P., and Rief, W. *Job enlargement.* Ann Arbor, Michigan, University of Michigan Press, 1969.

Schon, Donald A. *Beyond the stable state: Public and private learning in a changing society.* Temple Smith, 1971.

Seashore, S. E. "Assessing the quality of working life". *Labour and Society,* Apr. 1976, pp. 69-80.

Sirota, David, and Wolfson, Alan D. "Job enrichment". *Personnel* (Saranac Lake, New York, American Management Association), May-June 1972, pp. 8-17, and July-Aug. 1972, pp. 8-19.

Smith, Adam. *Wealth of nations.*

Spooner, P. "Group technology gives Platt a smoother run". *Business Administration,* Apr. 1973.

Srivastva, S., et al. *Productivity, industrial organization and job satisfaction: Policy development and implementation.* Report to the National Science Foundation. Case Western Reserve University, 1975.

Staehle, Wolfgang H. "Federal Republic of Germany". In Vol. 1 of the present work, pp. 77-106.

Swanson, B. "Management information systems: Appreciation and involvement". *Management Science,* 1974.

Taylor, J. C., et al. *The quality of working life: An annotated bibliography, 1957-1972.* Center for Organizational Studies, Graduate School of Management, University of California, Los Angeles, 1972.

Taylor, J. C. "Experiments in work system design: Economic and human results". *Personel Review,* Summer 1977, pp. 21-34, and Autumn 1977, pp. 21-42.

Taylor, L. K. *Not for bread alone: An appreciation of job enrichment.* Business Books, Second edition, 1973.

— *A fairer slice of the cake: The task ahead.* Business Books, 1975.

Templé, P. "La méthode des surplus: Un essai d'application aux comptes des entreprises, 1959-1967". *Economie et Statistique,* 1971, pp. 33-50.

Tuggle, G. "Job enlargement: An assault on assembly line inefficiencies". *Industrial Engineering,* Feb. 1969, pp. 26-31.

Ulich, E. "Die Erweitung des Handlungsspielraumes in der betrieblichen Praxis". *Industrielle Organisation,* Vol. 43 (1974), No. 1.

United Nations. *Methods of determining social allocations.* Report of the Secretary-General to the Sixteenth Session of the Social Commission of the Economic and Social Council. United Nations document E/CN.5/387, 31 Mar. 1965.

Van Der Merwe, R., and Miller, Sylvia. "The measurement of labour turnover: A critical appraisal and a suggested new approach". *Human Relations,* June 1971, pp. 233-253.

Vanek, Jaroslav. *The general theory of labor-managed economies.* Ithaca, New York, Cornell University Press, 1970. 331

— *The participatory economy: An evolutionary hypothesis and a strategy for development.* Ithaca, New York, Cornell University Press, 1971.

Walters, R. *Job enrichment for results.* Addison-Wesley, 1975.

Walton, R. E. *Workplace alteration and the need for major innovation.* Unpublished paper, 1972.

Weil, Reinhold. *Alternative forms of work organisation: Improvements of labour conditions and productivity in Western Europe.* International Institute for Labour Studies, Research Series, No. 4. Geneva, 1976.

Weir, M. *Redesigning jobs in Scotland: A survey.* Work Research Unit Report No. 5. United Kingdom Department of Employment, 1976.

Wilkinson, A. *A survey of some Western European experiments in motivation.* Institute of Work Study Practitioners, 1970.

Williamson, D. T. N. "The anachronistic factory". *Proceedings of the Royal Society,* Series A, 1972, pp. 139-160.

Woodruff, R. L. *Accounting for human research costs.* Paper presented at the AWV-Fachseminar on "Das Humankapital der Unternehmen", Bonn, 1974.

Work in America. Report of a special task force to the Secretary of Health, Education and Welfare, prepared under the auspices of the W. E. Upjohn Institute for Employment Research. Cambridge, Massachusetts, MIT Press, 1972.

ECONOMICS AND THE REGIME OF THE CALCULATIVE

'There is an enormous difference between economic principle and a regime of economic practice. Economic practice requires an intersection with the specifics of economic institutions and actors which is rarely considered by theorists of almost any variety. Even the most critical seemingly are content to accept much of economic practice as we know it. Indeed in economics the world of the practical only rarely has been made problematic.

That realm of the practical in economics calls upon a detailed regime of technical economic calculations. Practice cannot be reformed without a means to actualise the potential implicit in economic conceptions. And, as everyone knows, economic calculations play a significant part in the process. They serve to make visible, salient and actionable the realm of the economic. In practical affairs the calculative apparatus of the economic makes real what otherwise would reside in the realm of the discursive. It provides an objective, precise status to phenomena which otherwise would be vague and tenuous.

Such statements have a particular significance under the present political administration. No government has placed more emphasis not only on the economic but also on economic calculation. Policies have even been formulated in the name of economic calculations. The Public Sector Borrowing Requirement, for instance, has been made into an important symbol of the economically significant. It is difficult to conceive of an admistration that has made more of the significance or, as they would see it, the realities of cash limits. And few administrations in modern history have invested more in influencing, indeed amending, the stories that might be created in the name of economic calculations.
334 Unemployment, inflation and indices of the extent of the pervasiveness, potential or actual, of the penetration of the 'public' into the realm of the 'private' have never previously been so subject to influence and change. Economic policy-making has been a calculative endeavour in all senses of that term.

Be that as it may, the significance of economic calculation has not been subject to very much examination and criticism. Economics, per se, has been a contested phenomenon. But the means for operationalising the economic has not. Economic calculation has been seen as a by-product, a *mere* means to a wider end. Even those who would denounce what is being done in the name of the economic have not regarded economic calculation as a significant and important area. Economic abstractions seemingly have triumphed over economic practice from a diversity of perspectives.

Perhaps because of this very little consideration has been given to alternative practices and approaches. Regrettable as it is, few have invested in thinking about how alternative conceptions of the economic and the social might be realised. Ends have been seen as more important than mere means. The significance of the practical has not been recognised.

In the light of such a series of arguments it is tempting to think in terms of an alternative calculative regime of the social. What was ignored must be prioritised. What was invisible under the regime of the economic must be emphasised under the regime of the social. Social calculations at the very least must be set aside those of the economic. Social reports, audits and calculations must be given a new significance, a new priority, a new means for making the possible, the probable, the necessary into the actual and the real.

But while there is virtue in such an argument, it should only be accepted with great care. For:

(1) All calculations, social or economic, new or traditional, play a role in creating an objective domain of the seemingly factual that often can have an uneasy relationship with the contested, the uncertain and the imprecise. Social calculations may be useful but they are rarely adequate. That needs to be continually emphasised.

(2) The factual domains created by extensions of calculative practices are often conducive to management by new expert groups. When things can be known, ordered, regulated, ranked and controlled, a regime of expert administration can very easily develop. We have seen this happen repeatedly, including in areas of the social. Increasingly, however, there is a growing awareness of the different 335
patterns of dependency, and power associated with the advance of facts and expertise. That sceptical awareness needs to be maintained. We must continue to ask questions of what is actually done in the name of the calculative rather than being content to argue only in terms of its future potential.

(3) Related to the above, we need to be much more conscious of the relationships between calculations and political process. We need to see how calculations can emerge from politics, how they can facilitate the exercise of certain political strategies and how their potential to further the culture of the expert might even limit those areas of everyday life where political process is seen to be legitimate. Calculation can, in other words, be politically enabling and politically restrictive. That needs to be recognised.

The advance of social calculation therefore is an equivocal one. It can undoubtedly help to increase the visibility of the social. The economic can more readily be made to confront its consequences. Social action can be legitimised by appealing to the calculus of the economic. All these are advantages. But, on the negative side, we nevertheless must be aware of the ways in which an extended calculative regime, advanced for the best of reasons, can serve to further an administrative regime where experts confront politicians, where 'facts' have greater legitimacy than preferences and where concepts such as efficiency and rationality take priority over social value and need. Some of the latter possibilities are very real ones; so advocacy of a new calculative regime of the social must be 'contingent, tactical and rather cautious'.[2]

NOTES

2. Extract from Professor Anthony Hopwood's Paper to the Seminar on 28 February 1984 (with very minor editorial changes).

Accounting, Organizations and Society, Vol. 10, No. 3, pp. 361–377, 1985.
Printed in Great Britain

0361–3682/85 $3.00+.00
Pergamon Press Ltd.

THE TALE OF A COMMITTEE THAT NEVER REPORTED : DISAGREEMENTS ON INTERTWINING ACCOUNTING WITH THE SOCIAL*

ANTHONY G. HOPWOOD
London Business School

Abstract

The efforts of a committee which never finally reported provided an interesting insight into the problems involved in a social analysis of the accounting craft. In this tale of the deliberations of this committee both its mobilising concerns and bases for disagreement are emphasised. The latter are shown to be of wider significance to the accounting research community, related as they are to substantive debates in the social sciences generally.

"Accounting is a practice and discipline of study without an agreed and widely understood subject matter". So started the draft report of a committee that never finally reported. Established in 1977 by the then Social Science Research Council[1] in the United Kingdom to explore the need and potential for research on the social and political aspects of accounting, the committee had been set up as a direct result of a report on national research needs in the accounting area prepared by R. I. Tricker (1975).

After emphasising the changing nature of the pressures on accountancy practice, Tricker (1975) had highlighted the need for research orientated towards improving the understanding of "accounting . . . as a social-political process" and "the use of information about the enterprise by external parties". In the latter connection, Tricker again emphasised the changing social context of accounting by noting the growing significance of both governmental and trade union involvement in accounting affairs. Going on to recognise that "accounting theory is a product of western, capitalist, industrial societies" (Tricker, 1975, quoting Gambling, 1971), Tricker had noted that:

> Research into methods and effects of reporting in non-traditional patterns to a variety of interested parties has scarcely begun. Although most accountants in practice would claim objectivity and that they report facts, the truth is that the form and content of accountancy reports represents a series of value statements.

And, to reinforce the relevance of such a perspective for even the traditional spheres of accounting practice, Tricker concurred with the view that:

---

* The author served as a member of the committee whose activities are reported in this paper. Although not its chairperson, for a number of institutional reasons the official contract for the funding of the committee was issued in my name. Accordingly, when the committee itself failed to produce a final report, I was called upon to provide an accountability statement. The present paper is based on that statement. The comments made on a previous draft by Rob Bryer and David Cooper are gratefully acknowledged.

[1] In 1984 the name of the Social Science Research Council was changed to the Economic and Social Research Council. This was done on the explicit instruction of the Secretary of State for Education in order to emphasise that studies of the social and the economic had no *a priori* claim to scientific status.

> Despite much evidence to the contrary, many commentators and professionals still appear to consider the setting of accounting standards as a purely technical activity. That the equally important social, political and institutional factors are both usually ignored and certainly not well understood places real limits on a thorough apparaisal of the current activities and future potential.

In order to encourage further research on these topics Tricker recommended the establishment of a research seminar group "involving the younger accountancy teacher, informed practitioner, and non-accounting academic, as well as established figures".

The time was ripe for the Social Science Research Council to accept such a recommendation. Accounting practice had been recognised as being substantially implicated with significant national policy debates in the context of discussions on inflation accounting (see Whittington, 1983; Tweedie & Whittington, 1984). *The Corporate Report* (1975), a publication of the then Accounting Standards Steering Committee, had consciously articulated the need to broaden the scope and nature of corporate reporting in the social and political climate of the 1970's. Moreover the government had accepted many of its more controversial recommendations (Department of Trade, 1976; *The Future of Company Reports*, 1977), much to the concern of the leadership of the accountancy profession[2]. The need for and means of reporting to employees and trade unions also were being actively debated (for a review see Jackson-Cox *et al.*, 1984). And the concept of social accounting had entered into accounting discourse. Not only was there some awareness of the growing interest in this embryonic activity in both the U.S.A. and continental Europe, but an indigenous variety of social auditing had been developed and utilised in the United Kingdom itself (Medawar, 1976). In all of these ways accounting had been seen to be in the process of becoming more visibly intertwined with the social context in which it operated. A view was emerging that it no longer should be seen as an isolated technical endeavour.

The means for observing and changing accounting in the name of the social[3] were little understood, however. Because of this, the Social Science Research Council accepted the Tricker recommendation and set up a committee to investigate and report on research needs in the area. The group so established was both diverse and distinguished. Only six of the eleven members were (or had been) accountancy academics. An explicit attempt was made to include experts on sociology, organizational behaviour and industrial relations as well as representatives of the trade unions, the accountancy profession and the "public interest".

The committee so established was active and conscientious. Not only were there numerous full meetings of the group but also several more informal subgroup meetings were held and the committee co-sponsored a research workshop on Accounting in a Changing Social and Political Environment. In addition, the members of the group succeeded in generating an impressive number of working papers, research proposals and discussion notes. They also were prolific correspondents, writing at length on each other's ideas, proposals and counter proposals. This level of activity continued until the latter days of the formal existence of the group, and

---

[2] A quite innovative document, *The Corporate Report* had been hurriedly prepared by a sub-committee of the Accounting Standards Steering Committee in anticipation of the forthcoming government report on inflation accounting (Stamp, 1985). As such, it had not been approved by the leadership of the accountancy profession. Subsequent events demonstrated that such approval was not forthcoming.

[3] "The social" is used to refer to the "space of intelligibility" (Donzelot, 1979, p. xxvi) where social (and, in this instance, political) as distinct from economic aspects of human life are enacted, changed and reformed. Although itself an abstract category, it is seen as being mobilised by quite specific and changing problems, practices and strategies of intervention. Accounting can be, indeed has been and still is being, implicated in both the creation of the space that constitutes the social and the means by which it is constituted and changed (Burchell *et al.*, forthcoming).

indeed beyond. A great deal of effort was put into drafting a final report for the committee by several of its members, and by one in particular. Indeed a draft but incomplete "final" report was prepared but never finished or published.

The activities of the committee came to a rather sudden halt when it proved impossible to draft a version of the final report which could attract the unanimous support of all the members. Despite several attempts to do so and a deep concern on the part of some members with the dangers involved in what was seen to be the "suppression of an academic report", the task eventually was set aside because of the irreconcilable views on the fundamental nature and content of the report. As the last draft of the final report had ominously warned, accounting is indeed "a practice and discipline of study without an agreed and widely understood subject matter".

Although providing an interesting story, such a saga of incomplete action would constitute nothing more than a very minor disturbance on the path of development of accounting research were it not for the fact that the issues which prevented agreement were of a substantive rather than purely personal nature. Although cast in personal terms, the debates which took place in the committee reached deep into the heart of both accounting and accounting research as we now know them. Accounting at times was interrogated from the perspective of the social. Its social assumptions, functioning and consequences were questioned. Equally, great unease was expressed about existing traditions of research inquiry. The paradigms on which most current accounting research is based were explicitly examined and appraised. Their adequacy for enabling an examination of their social practice of the craft was reviewed, and found wanting by many members of the committee. So, although operating in a quite specific context, the committee nevertheless provided an arena in which the problems facing attempts to mobilise and understand accounting in the name of the social were articulated and confronted. For this reason alone, the experiences of the committee are not without a wider significance.

AN AGENDA OF CONCERN

From the start, the committee had dual aspirations: to advance the understanding of the social and political nature of accounting and to advance the social relevance and usefulness of accounting practice. The precise distinction between the two sometimes generated heated conflict; at other times, the two together provided a mobilising mission for virtually all members of the group. Always, however, the interdependent nature of the two aspirations was recognised. Although one aspiration seemingly resided in the realms of the intellectual whilst the other was apparently embedded in the realms of the practical, it always was recognised that a social understanding of accounting could never be independent of its practice and that practice, in turn, was founded and reformed on the basis of abstract views of its content, functioning and potential.

A central concern on the more pragmatic side of the deliberations focussed on the relationship between accounting and accountability. As Moore (n.d.) said in a paper prepared for the committee:

> . . . there have been pressures developing within companies which challenge and undermine the adequacy of conventional accounting principles and procedures, which require reconsideration of the forms and directions of accountability, and which represent the assertion of a re-ordering of social and economic values both within the company and in its relations with society generally and with particular geographic and functional interest groups within society. The enhancement of corporate decision-making's control as a result of increased size with multinational dimensions and the amplification of the effects of such decision-making as a consequence of accelerated technological change and geographical . . . concentration considerations, have led to the assertion of "rights to know" by organised labour, community and functional interest groups, as well as by the state itself. The repercussions of both positive (investment, employment, energy conservation take-overs, and mergers, exports) and negative (closures, liquidations, redundancies, energy wastage, pollution and other environmental debits, job [deskilling] and imports) results of chosen corporate strategies and development policies weigh so heavily upon communities and employees that the minimal annual provision to shareholders of a balance sheet, profit and loss account and director's report begin to

> appear, by way of historical analogy, as the twentieth century equivalent of an autocrat resorting to the divine right of kings in face of populist dissatisfaction with his administration, to justify his status and performance.

Acknowledging such pressures on accounting to change, the draft final report commented that:

> Our case for research into the social and political aspects of accounting arises, in the first instance, from our and others' perception of the need to widen the range of interest groups to whom accounting information should be reported beyond the traditional investor group. This perception has filtered through to both the accounting profession . . . and the government . . . . It is now widely recognised that (in particular) employee and consumer groups have legitimate rights to information about both governmental and corporate activities, and we accept the pluralist and democratic values which underlies it.

The draft also recognised, however, the controversial nature of such a view, not least in the accountancy community, for it went on to add:

> These values are, however, not widely accepted by either the accounting profession or academics of accounting, if their research interests and outlooks are taken as a guide. We shall need therefore, in setting the context for our general case and detailed research proposals, to highlight this bias.

The social pressures on accounting therefore were only seen as "*potential* harbingers of change". To emphasise this point the draft report noted that "they are only potential . . . and not actual, because of countervailing forces at work both within the accounting profession and the academic community".

Not surprisingly, the discussions of accounting practice which followed from these concerns were controversial. To whom, if anyone, was the present practice of accounting accountable? What interests did it represent and promote? Not only what roles did accounting play in enhancing the accountability of organizations in both the public and private sectors but also how can accounting serve to further that accountability? Or could this be done more effectively by alternative institutional mechanisms? What roles can be served by alternative non-professional, interest based accountings? In all these discussions the committee served as a microcosm of the wider community.

There were those who thought that:

> Accounting claims to produce useful information and, therefore, if it is to come of age as a scientifically respectable activity it must conform to the oldest canon of science and *publicly* demonstrate the usefulness of the information which it produces and provides. If the use of accounting information is socially and politically conditioned attention must be focussed on these aspects (emphasis in original) (Bryer, n.d.).

On the other hand, there were others who thought that:

> In recognising that we have a changing society it must also be recognised that accountants are not the missionaries of social and political change. What they do has social and political implications, which we should be able to elaborate more extensively; what they do and how they do it can affect the direction of the rate of the change but the impetus for the change has to come from society expressed through the usual social and political processes (Flint, n.d.).

One implication of the latter perspective was that "the nature and structure of the accountancy profession . . . with its peculiar characteristics is a subject for separate research."

On the pragmatic side, however, despite such basic disagreements, all members of the committee were agreed that priority should not be placed on the role which research could play in the technical development of new forms of "social accounting" which were receiving some attention in the media at the time. Initially it had been thought that this might have been a major area of concern for the committee and because of this a survey was commissioned of current practical developments in France, Germany and the Netherlands (Schreuder, 1978; a revised version of this survey was subsequently published as Schreuder, 1979). However that survey and discussions of developments in the area in the U.S.A. convinced all members of the committee that it would be premature for such developments to be tackled in technical isolation. Rather the committee emphasised the need for action research strategies to be conducted with the full cooperation and involvement of the concerned user groups and other interested parties. Social accountings, if they were to be, were seen as needing to be emergent in social settings. Indeed if the committee had agreed on a final report a recommendation of that document would have been the commissioning of an experimental series of such action research projects. The aim would have been to learn by doing.

More theoretical questions also were raised about the nature of the new accounting technologies being proposed. Seeing them as particular manifestations of the pressures on accounting to change, at an early stage in its deliberations the committee agreed on the need to further the understanding of the nature of accounting change, the ways in which broader social, political and economic concerns are implicated in such change processes, the influences that are brought to bear on these processes and their amenability to change and reform, and the wider implications of changes in accounting practice.

What, for example, are the social forces underlying an interest in social accounting? Through what processes can the social so intertwine itself with the calculative? And why did social accounting seemingly attract managerial interest in Germany and the U.S.A. while in France it has been a concern of the state and in the U.K. of the labour and public interest movements? What, in other words, is the nature of the social interest in social and indeed other forms of accounting?

Such questionings illustrate the permeability of the committee's distinction between the practical and the intellectual. Indeed it was the questioning of the social significance of social accounting that started to provide the basis for an intellectual agenda at an early stage of the committee's deliberations. Thereafter much attention was given to both defining and exploring these emergent issues. As was stated in the draft report:

> We believe that accounting properly understood, is fundamentally a social and political activity and that research designed to make its products more useful will only be fully effective if this is understood and acted upon.

However it was the attempt to realise this agreed project that produced the conflicts which resulted in the committee's inability to agree on a final report. Although it would be a difficult, if not impossible, task to summarise the nature of these extended deliberations in any complete and coherent manner, it is useful to consider at least some of the key mobilising concerns and those issues which gave rise to major disagreements.

The need for a historical appreciation

Given the concern with accounting change, the committee expessed an early interest in the historical development of accounting practice (Tomkins, n.d.). How had accounting become what it now is? How can we understand the processes of change? How have wider issues and concerns impacted on accounting practice? Given these agreed concerns, the draft report could, on this occasion, confidently state that there is a need to "look at the major changes which have taken place in accounting practices over a broad expanse of time and gain some impression of what gave rise to such changes".

Although aware of the considerable amount of work that already has been done on accounting history in the U.K., continental Europe and the U.S.A. (see, for example, Parker, 1981), and indeed the current re-emergence of interest in the area, most members of the committee nevertheless were dissatisfied with not only the present state of knowledge in the area but also the current directions of historical research. There has been a tendency for technical histories of accounting to be written in isolation of their social, economic and institutional contexts. Accounting seemingly has been abstracted from its social domain with many of the understandings that are available tending to present a view of the autonomous and unproblematic development of the technical. Where efforts have been made to offer alternative perspectives teleological, evolutionary or progressive notions of change have often been implicit in the understandings presented. Aware of both the criticisms of such notions of history in the social sciences (Burke, 1980; Carr, 1961; Hobsbawn, 1971; Johnson, 1978; Johnson *et al.*, 1982; Jones, 1972; La Capra, 1983; McLennan, 1979, 1981; Samuel, 1981; Thomas, 1963) and the availability of other, albeit often conflicting, appreciations of the dynamics of historical change, many members of the committee were concerned about the partial, uncritical, atheoretical and intellectually isolated nature of much historical work in the accounting area.

It was the view of the committee that much could be done to improve the understanding of the socio-political history of accounting. Indeed,

it was thought that this should be considered a priority area for further research not only because of its own intrinsic interest but also because of the role which such appreciations might play in casting light on what might be at stake in current pressures of accounting to change. How had the social been intertwined with the accountings of the past and the present? What factors had been forceful mobilisers of accounting change? And what roles had accounting played in both the construction and realisation of the domains of the social and the political?

However the committee recognised that the emergence of an improved social history of accounting could not be created by the mere provision of additional support for existing historical inquiries. An investment would need to be made in enhancing the theoretical and epistemological understandings of historical researchers in the area, possibly by the commissioning of a detailed consideration of the issues at stake or by the support of a few carefully selected studies which made explicit attempts to draw on the best of contemporary historical research.

The need for an explicit recognition of accounting as a social phenomenon

Members of the committee were concerned that prevailing discussions of social accounting might create a view of the social nature of such new accountings which contrasted with an uncritical acceptance of the asocial and purely technical nature of existing modes of accounting practice. They were concerned to articulate a view of the social nature, origins, functioning and consequences of *all* accounting practice.

One explicit statement of this view was provided by Bryer (n.d.).

> We should make it clear . . . that we believe that research should be funded which will elaborate and extend a new *paradigm* for accounting research. The alternative view of our task . . . is to make the claim that research into the social and political dimensions of accounting is an important new *specialism* . . . . There are several ways of explicating [a] vision of the nature of the paradigm within which accounting research should be undertaken . . . . We can take the issue head-on by confronting the existing paradigm — which is describable in terms of the intellectual traditions of economic research where the emphasis is on the technical control problems faced by individuals pursuing their given goals; this view makes accounting research a predominantly puzzle-solving activity whose output is the provision of "correct" information, definable partly in terms of "environmental" constraints — with an alternative paradigm which questions the "givens" presupposed in the existing one within a largely sociological framework. The case for a new paradigm can be made within a call for a *sociology of accounting* which focusses on the *actual use* of accounting data within social and political contexts. Like other "sociologies", the sociology of accounting should be a critical activity in the sense that it should be directed (through theoretical and empirical analyses) at the taken-for-granted "objective" contexts of the production and use of accounting data which are, in fact, socially constructed and sustained . . . Parallels can and should be drawn between this kind of accounting research and that which has been undertaken in other areas of professional activity, particularly those of law, medicine and education. Another very useful way of making the case for a paradigm shift in favour of a sociological perspective is in terms of arguing for the development of a sociology of the profession of accounting. The task here would be to make links between the development of the profession within its social and political contexts and the production and use of accounting information. This approach is complementary to the other as the focus is biased towards the production of information and away from its use.

The further development of such a perspective was not an easy undertaking for the committee, however. Not only did attempts to move in this direction expose rather fundamental differences in ideological persuasion and commitments to the social bases of present practice but also it was soon recognised that the offering of even a tentative, preliminary view of accounting as social at this time would require a major investment in new conceptual thinking. Indeed many members of the committee recognised that the very substance of any discussion of such issues in fact constituted the basis for further inquiry and research. Nevertheless most members recognised that accounting scholarship could not and should not be separated from other branches of social investigation. Although relatively little explicit study had been made of the social nature of accounting, understandings gained in other areas of social science did not only cast light on accounting issues but also provided a range of viable perspectives for pursuing social inquiries into accounting practices. Other modes of calculating practice had been the subject of scholarly investigation, for example (Gould, 1981; Hacking, 1981; Kamin, 1981; Kula, 1976; Mackenzie, 1981; Rose, 1979; Suther-land, 1977). Studies of the emergence of prevailing modes of institutional control in business (Bendix, 1956; Braverman, 1974; Edwards, 1979; Friedman, 1977; Herman, 1981; Vogel, 1978) and other organisations were available and serious consideration needed to be given to the social roles served by rationalised systems of administration (Callaghan, 1962; Hayes, 1980; Kaufman, 1977; Jacoby, 1973; Meyer, 1983; Meyer & Rowan, 1977, 1978; Wynne, 1982). Finally, the sociological study of professions was an area where quite considerable, albeit often conflicting (Saks, 1983), insights were available (Dingwall & Lewis, 1983; Larson, 1977).

The need to see accounting as an interested activity

The discussions of the social nature of accounting provided a context in which questions could be raised about the relationship of accounting to different social interests. Perhaps not surprisingly, these discussions did not result in a unanimous view on either the way in which accounting's relationship to such interests might be described and understood or on how our understandings in this area might be advanced.

On the one hand, there were those who emphasised the facilitating roles which accounting did and might play vis-a-vis a range of social interests. For these members of the group, it was possible to think of enhancing the range of accountings to different interests, for example by reporting to trade unions as well as investors. Such developments were not seen as impinging on the technical integrity of accounting itself however. Although usually remaining implicit in the discussions, such a view of accounting's development tended to see accounting as having the potential for a basic technical neutrality, a potential which was seen as being protected by an overriding professional interest.

As Flint (n.d.) put it:

> Accounting of itself cannot be the vehicle of social and political change although knowledge and understanding of the financial data which accounting can produce may well be vitally important both to those who wish change and those who wish to resist it; but accounting as a discipline cannot take sides although those who use it may well do so.

In contrast, other members of the committee offered a more explicit view of the relationship which accounting has to social interests by rejecting any notion of technical or even professional neutrality. Accounting, from this perspective, did not merely facilitate the articulation of particular interests but it emerged from the active pursuit of interested endeavours. It was to be seen, in other words, as an interested activity. The origin of specific accounts resided in the articulation of particular interests, in the creation of a legitimacy for them and in the construction of a calculative and administrative apparatus which would further those interests. According to this latter perspective, questions could, and indeed should, be asked about not only whether accounting could be made to serve particular new interests but also about the interests which accounting currently serves.

Some of the research implications of such an interested perspective were considered. As Bryer and Pettigrew (1978) expressed it:

> A deliberate choice should be made [by those intending to do research in accounting] on the objective which the

> knowledge produced is intended to serve. Should the objective of research in accounting be to improve prediction and control, to further an understanding of accounting as a social practice or to change and improve accounting as a form of social practice?

Developing this point of view, they went on to add:

> The use(s) to which the knowledge generated by research into accounting is to be put has a strong conditioning effect upon the approach to the research, and hence the type of knowledge which is produced. Just as there are many potential uses of knowledge, so there are many types of knowledge. An implication of this is that calling knowledge that pursues certain objectives "scientific" while calling all other types of knowledge "unscientific", is an obviously unsupportable value-judgement. A convenient classification of objectives for the uses of knowledge and the associated types of knowledge has been provided by Jürgen Habermas (1971)....
>
> Habermas analysed both the forms of human knowledge and the social conditions under which they first arise to arrive at a typology of human knowledge. Firstly, there are the empirical-analytical (natural) sciences which attempt to generate law-like hypotheses and predictions concerning the necessary behaviour of (predominantly natural) phenomena. These sciences, Habermas says, have a specific "cognitive interest" (objective for the use of the knowledge) in the phenomena they analyse: technical control over objectified processes. Secondly, there are the "hermeneutic-historical" (social) sciences. Here theories are not deductive and experience is not organised to promote prediction and control. The cognitive interest of the hermeneutic sciences lies in the extension of consensual understanding within a social tradition. Finally, Habermas distinguishes the "critical social sciences" which are concerned with distinguishing between genuine invariances in social life and those which only appear to be, but in fact are not, natural constraints. The cognitive interest here is "emancipatory". Critical science produces knowledge to *change* social relationships by assisting in the development of critical self-reflection on social practices.
>
> Research in Accounting could legitimately adopt any of these cognitive interests (emphasis in original).

Bryer and Pettigrew (1978) then noted the paucity of hermeneutic research in accounting and the virtual non existence of research orientated towards an emancipatory interest. Within the frame of reference provided by Habermas' schema, it was their view that "the massive amounts of research ... which has been (and still is being) devoted to the interest of technical control ... seems disproportionate."

As the above arguments suggest, considerable effort was devoted to outlining a coherent intellectual basis for research which explicitly recognised the interested nature of the accounting craft. Relatively less attention was given to advancing specific understandings of how calculative practices became intertwined with the articulation of particular interests. And more substantive theoretical issues also remained unresolved. For some members of the committee were content to see accounting as being both purposeful and purposive in the context of its orientation to the pursuit of social interests while others recognised a more fluid and equivocal relationship between the ends which accounting is used to serve and the consequences which accounting is seen to have.

In contrast, however, the advocates of the potential for calculative and professional neutrality had a more difficult task mobilising a substantive argument in support of their stance. They appealed to the authority of the profession and the claims which were made on its behalf. But, as others pointed out, such a view did not confront the interested nature of the profession itself. Nor did it seek to provide a justification grounded in the specifics of the emergence of particular accounting practices, the professional institutions and their activities, or the claims made on the latter's behalf.

All too clearly this was an area where further reflection and research was required. However I doubt if such inquiries will resolve the rather fundamental differences between the conflicting perspectives. For such differences are endemic to all aspects of social inquiry. From other areas of social investigation we know of the differences between those who seek to illuminate and thereby demystify the taken for granted practices of everyday life and those who merely seek to facilitate their continued operation. The latter see the former as engaged in a political activity, introducing ideology into social inquiry and debate. The former, however, see the uncritical inquiries of the latter as themselves constituting a political statement, with their inquiries not only being subservient to prevailing dominant interests but also having at least the potential to contribute to the maintenance of the ideologies which sustain them.

The need to explore the professional interest

One important aspect of the discussions of the relationship of accounting to social interests concerned the nature of the professional interest embedded in the prevailing institutions of a professional accountancy. Although only rarely articulated explicitly during the committee's formal deliberations, I think that it was an important part of the informal agenda, serving, in the end, to constrain the preparation of any agreed statement of accounting's relationship to the social.

On the one side, there were those who wanted to explore into the professional relationship with other social interests, not being content to accept the avowed statements of professional service to "the public interest". The metaphor of the corporate patron (Johnson, 1972) was sometimes used in this respect. Consideration also was given to the need to investigate the interested nature of the professional embodiment of accounting practice itself. On the other side of the debate were those who were content with prevailing dominant conceptions of the nature of the professional interest, seeking to develop these further in relation to new social groups rather than more critically exploring the nature of the professional licence.

More generally, however, it was recognised that there was a paucity of research in this significant area. Rhetorical generalizations are more prevalent than either empirical or theoretical insights. As Batstone (n.d.) put it in a paper prepared for the committee:

> . . . future research needs to be able to specify in some detail the influence of the profession upon actual accounting practice and its development. In other words it needs to be made more specific and go beyond simply assessing professional claims and statements. At the same time, such an approach has to assess not merely the aspirations of the profession but also how these are formulated and the extent to which these aspirations are actually achieved.

Consistent with such a perspective, consideration was given to the need "to look at how decisions are identified and made within the profession itself (and how particular issues are never taken up) and . . . the relative power and influence of the profession more generally" (Batstone, n.d.). Recognising the wider ramifications of a professionalised accounting, "investigation is required of the extent to which 'the profession' really does impinge upon its members' activities" (Batstone, n.d.). Equally, however, it was thought that there also was a need to consider "the extent to which patrons and clients may dominate the professional bodies". As Batstone went on to add:

> This may occur both directly — through, for example, their range of sanctions — or indirectly through their employees dominating the key posts within the profession. Here historical studies seeking to investigate relationships between changing industrial structure, and changing acounting tasks, on the one hand, and changes in the professional elite and its decisions would be of interest.

During its deliberations the committee repeatedly noted the importance of better understanding the relationship between the accounting profession and the State. Once again, Batstone articulates well some of the committee's interests in this area:

> [One] area of importance concerns the relationship between professional bodies and another significant long term trend, namely the increasing role of the State. . . . Two . . . aspects may . . . be selected as being of especial significance: the relationship between state and profession in terms of monopoly rights to practice, and the role of the professional bodies as expert advisers to state decision-making bodies.
>
> The first of these may be seen as fairly straightforward, but nevertheless of importance. One might encourage research, for example, into the nature of the claims by the profession for a monopoly and the conditions which facilitate the achievement of this desired end. One might similarly seek to assess changes in the behaviour of the professional bodies once this desired end has been achieved.
>
> The second question raised in relation to the state is more complex. Along with the greater involvement of the state there has been a growing pattern of discussions, at a variety of levels and by a range of methods, between

> the state and interested parties .... This pattern of discussion and agreement has been termed by some commentators "corporatism" .... It would seem that professional bodies may play an important role in this process in a number of ways which deserve attention: these include self-policing and professional recommendations (as a substitute for legislation) and providing expert opinions which may constitute an important element in legislation or codes of practice, etc. In other words, not only may the state play a mediating role between the profession and its clients/patrons, but also the profession may play a role as expert mediator between the state and industry and commerce. Again, areas particularly worthy of note here would be to see how this process has developed, the real influence of the professions, and the directions and implications of their professional advice.

Such notions are not unfamiliar to other social scientists, not least to those engaged in the development of the sociology of professions (Dingwall & Lewis, 1983; Johnson, 1977; Larson, 1977; Rueschemeyer, 1983). As yet, however, no explicit discussion of this debate has appeared in an accounting context. In retrospect, it is a pity that the deliberations of the committee did not succeed in achieving this.

The need for alternative research paradigms and methodologies

Despite the differences in many substantive areas, the committee did achieve more of a consensus on the need for accounting research to draw on a wider array of research perspectives and methodologies. As Bryer & Pettigrew (1978) expressed it:

> ... is research in accounting to be "contextual" or "context-free"? We [argue that it] should further an understanding and improvement of accounting as a social practice by adopting a contextual paradigm within which to make research choices ... it is only in this way that we can progress towards an understanding of the social and political aspects of accounting.

The agreed concern for the need to study accounting in the contexts in which it operates (Hopwood, 1983) was expressed in a number of different ways, ranging from criticism of the prevailing dominance of positivistic perspectives in the accounting research community, through the need to stimulate more theoretically informed empirical explorations of the accounting domain, to a concern with the need for more action based research in the accounting area, particularly with respect to attempts to relate extensions in accounting practice to the furtherance of a different range of social interests.

The need for an improved understanding of accounting's consequences

Aware of the claims made on behalf of both present and prospective accounting practices, the committee was united in its concern about the paucity of empirical evidence on the consequences which accounting has for both organizational and social functioning. Relatively little is known of either the effectiveness of the articulated consequences of the craft or the range of its unanticipated effects. Nor do we have much insight into those roles of accounting which provide it with the basis for a broad social significance, such as its relationship to the establishment of organizational accountability and legitimacy.

The committee recognised that a start had been made on the exploration of these issues, not least in the context of the developing research interest in both the behavioural and organizational aspects of accounting (Hopwood, 1978, 1979) and economic analyses of the implications which accounting disclosures have for capital market performance (see Zeff, 1978; Chow, 1983). However, at the time the committee was meeting (and possibly still [Hopwood, 1983]), the former interest had resulted in very few investigations of accounting in action in actual organizations, seemingly preferring either armchair theorizing or the construction of experimental environments. The latter economic interests also were perceived as having major limitations from the perspective of the social, not least because of the failure to confront questions concerning the aggregation of behaviours in the market place and the singularity of the theoretical perspectives which had guided the investigations (Bryer & Pettigrew, 1978).

It was the view of the committee that work orientated towards understanding, enhancing or changing the social practice of accounting would be facilitated by improved understandings of the processes by which accounting was brought to bear on organizational and social decision making. As Pettigrew (1977) noted in the context of studies of the role of accounting in organizational decision making:

> . . . accounting represents a mode of thinking for defining organizational problems. The accounting frame of reference like other such mental frames and their associated methodologies are in no sense neutral systems of dividing up and categorising the world. Accounting represents one of several often competing rationalities used to define problem situations. [Research should] aim to empirically define the accounting frame of reference as it is used by professional practitioners and others and to sketch out the competitive pull of this frame of reference in situations where there are other frames of reference seeking to influence the strategy formulation process.

Such a perspective was seen as useful by the committee whether the research problem related to the specifics of improved accounting disclosure to a particular interest or more general concerns about if and how such forms of disclosure increased organizational accountability. The former problem area was repeatedly illustrated by the relatively small amount of research that had been done on information disclosure to trade unions, not least by that undertaken on behalf of the Social Science Research Council by the Trade Union Research Unit at Ruskin College, Oxford (Gold *et al.*, 1979; Moore, 1977). The significance of the more general organizational and social questions was at least suggested by those sociological studies which pointed to the legitimising roles played by enhanced forms of rationalised disclosure (Meyer & Rowan, 1977) and those preliminary analyses which concerned themselves with whether enhanced access to information increased rather than reduced information inequalities.

Without an improvement in our knowledge of such processes and consequences it was thought that many policy decisions in the accounting area would continue to be taken in a vacuum, oriented towards improving the conceivable rather than the actual. It also was felt that an improved understanding of accounting's consequences — what one member termed an accounting of accounting — could facilitiate the extent to which particular interests might be served by accounting actions.

The need for an accountable accounting

Although expressed in different ways, all members of the committee expressed their concern that both accounting practice *and* research should explicitly recognise their social consequences and thereby, responsibilities. Some members of the committee expressed this in terms of the primacy of conceptions of accountability over particular modes of accounting. Others appealed to the bases of professional authority and responsibility. However members shared a general concern about the need for relevant research inquiry which was related to the constituents of accounting practice, however these be conceived. To this end, an enormous amount of time was spent discussing the relationship between research and practice (and vice versa), exploring the nature of the present linkages and considering ways in which these could be improved.

THE BASES FOR DISAGREEMENT

Although the seven issues outlined above aim to provide some insights into the mobilising concerns of the committee, they also provide some bases for understanding the nature of the disagreements which ultimately prevented the drafting of an agreed final report. For, as has already been indicated, the issues which characterised the committee's discussions were all quite general ones. Not only was there a recognised shortage of both empirical and theoretical understandings of the intersection of accounting and the social but also the issues themselves were of a sufficient level of generality to allow fundamental differences of opinion as to their meaning, significance and implications. In practice this was as true for the particular concerns with improving the methodological basis of research as it was for probing the interested nature of accounting in general and its professional manifestation in particular.

Characterising the precise nature of the differences in opinion which prevented the committee reporting to the Social Science Research Council as a group is not an easy endeavour. In part, I think this reflects the fact that many of the fundamental differences in outlook remained implicit. However basic they may have been, the committee was composed of polite people! In addition, the final statements of the irreconcilable differences occurred after the last formal meeting of the committee when the draft report was circulated for comment. This resulted in no extended and precise discussion of the different positions. Indeed many of the key concerns were not even articulated in writing since the gap was perceived to be so great by some members of the committee that they preferred merely to say "I beg to differ". And even if more detailed information had been at hand a problem of interpretation would have remained since only the manifest differences would have been articulated. The equally, if not more, important latent ones were likely to have remained implicit.

What follows therefore can only be a personal interpretation. Because of this, the discussion is relatively brief. Nevertheless, I think that the raising of at least the outline of the points of disagreement is of some importance because the differences do reflect more basic concerns rather than the personal idiosyncracies of the members of the committee.

It is my view that one of the fundamental difficulties concerned the extent to which it was thought possible and desirable to probe into and thereby question the basic nature of accounting. Was one role of the committee to make accounting a more problematic social phenomenon or were the existence and functions of accounting to be taken for granted? Was, in addition, the history of accounting to be seen in terms of an unfolding of technical progress — a progress which facilitated the achievement of a common social goal through the enhancement of accepted notions of organizational efficiency, effectiveness and accountability? Or was accounting to be seen as emerging and changing in the context of very specific configurations of social and institutional relations? Whilst the former perspective would tend to see accounting activities as both illuminating and enhancing a broadly pre-given set of notions of corporate performance and accountability, the latter view results in more strategic social and indeed political roles being attributed to the accounting craft. Elsewhere this difference has been discussed in terms of the distinction between theories *in* and *of* accounting (Hopwood, 1978). Rather than seeking merely to enhance and elaborate what are seen as relatively unproblematic conceptions of organizational functioning and performance, theories *of* accounting aim to provide an understanding of the way in which the craft is implicated in the social construction of particular views of organizational legitimacy and the strategies for the management of power relationships both within and between organizations. In fact such a view would see accounting as being at least one of the ways in which a problematic rather than self-evident social reality was constructed rather than merely being a means for its reflection and representation.

Not too surprisingly such broad differences in perspective had a number of implications. To these we now turn.

Different meanings

Committee members tended to hold rather different notions of both accounting in particular and accountability more generally. As Flint (1979) put it:

> Accounting and accountability have different meanings for members of the [committee] and are used in different senses at different places in the [draft] report, sometimes in relation to the activities, the skills and the knowledge of the accountancy profession and at other times in a wider sociological sense in relation to the responsibilities of organizations; in this last sense the responsibilities are not necessarily the concern of those whose capabilities are primarily financial skills. The confusion of meaning and the attribution of responsibilities to "accountants" must lead to confusion of the recipient of the report.

A neutral craft?

As might be expected, members of the committee also held very different views of the potential for and the desirability of the social neutrality of accounting. While not accepting a crude deterministic view of accounting's social functions, those members of the committee concerned with illuminating the social nature of the accounting craft did see accounting as having the possibility of playing rather strategic social roles which were not compatible with prevailing notions of social neutrality. Given this, some members of the committee placed a particular emphasis on the need to mobilise accounting, albeit defined in broader terms than were then prevalent, towards fulfilling a very different set of social roles that once again would not be compatible with any accepted view of social neutrality. Other members of the committee adopted a very different posture however. In part, they were concerned with the interpretation that could be given to the concept "political", commenting, in the words of Flint (1979), that "recognition of the fact that accounting is a political process is not carried through to recognition of the issues which arise from state intervention with the danger of accounting becoming a party political process". From such a perspective, "accounting as a discipline cannot take sides although those who use it may well do so". The distinction between political "danger" and "reality" thereby proved to be an insurmountable one.

Levels of analysis

Such different perspectives also resulted in concerns with the need for very different levels of analysis of the accounting phenomenon. Those more interested in theories *of* accounting tended to emphasise the need for sociological analyses. They wanted to see how accounting was emergent at its intersection with other social practices and issues. In contrast, those more concerned with the elaboration of theories *in* accounting, to use once again that relatively simplistic but useful distinction, emphasised the need for more social-psychological and behavioural studies of accounting as it is rather than as it has become. To quote one of the members of the committee who adopted the latter approach:

> Only some of the .... issues are recognised .... The behavioural and organizational behavioural issues are hardly touched on, for example, the interaction of systems with organization structure or management styles. On the other hand some of the major research issues which are raised are primarily for industrial sociologists with accounting expertise rather than for accountants, even with assistance.

Institutional allegiances

Another difference in perspective which is worthy of mention is more difficult to disentangle from the only implicit consideration given to it. However I do think that the question of the institutional allegiance of accounting research and accounting researchers did have some role to play in the discussions of the committee, particularly in the latter days of its existence. Just what was the significance for accounting of the present professional embodiment of accounting practice? Indeed, was accounting to be seen in terms of its present institutional as well as substantive representation or could alternative conceptions be entertained? Could ideas of alternative accounts and alternative institutional locii for them not only be formulated but also positively mobilise "accounting" research?

Accounting allegiances

Finally, and somewhat paradoxically, the allegiance of committee members to accounting itself could have provided a rich basis for disagreement, although this issue only rarely emerged during the course of the committee's deliberations even though it was to be more evident at the end. For some of even the most questioning analyses of accounting still accepted the need to reform accounting in the name of the social. Accounting was seen as having a very real social role to play and research was needed to facilitate that, both by exposing the intertwinings of the social with the accountings of the present and by helping to enable and direct the different accountings that could characterise the future. Other members of the committee adopted, or sometimes moved towards adopting, a more critical perspective vis-a-vis accounting itself however. While acknowledging the roles that it currently serves, they saw accounting as having no inherent monopoly of these. Other means of information processing were available. Other institutional mechanisms could further organizational accountability and reform. An account of accounting might show accounting to be wanting. The view of the future so seen might be one in which there could be fewer accountings rather than merely different ones.

The idea of accounting's alternatives had figured in the very early deliberations of the committee. The possibilities for the accessing rather than reporting of information had been mentioned as a topic worthy of further consideration. In this respect the U.S. Freedom of Infor-
350 mation Act was referred to alongside recent Swedish co-determination legislation which gave employees and their trade unions rights of access to corporate information. And comparative experiences in the U.K. also were expected to provide some insights into the relative effectiveness of different approaches to the provision of accountability. As Stymne (n.d.) noted in an early statement of purpose:

> Many of the questions which in the private sector are handled under the label of accounting are handled under other labels in the public sector. These questions are related to rights to information and claims from different groups that a certain agency is accountable to them. Since there is less of a mediating technology in the public sector to handle these questions their implications in social terms and in terms of power and resistance can be studied more easily. Since the nature of the problems are related, the public sector may function as a distant laboratory for research on future demands on accounting.

Unfortunately such leads were never pursued. It was not that the committee explicitly rejected any consideration of alternative social and institutional processes to accounting. That did not happen. Instead the problems of understanding accounting from a social perspective were themselves so great that accounting tended to monopolise attention. The deliberations implicitly became accounting oriented and the alternatives to the craft were not investigated.

That resulted in one interesting area for disagreement being ignored, however. As Medawar (1979) was later to say:

> . . . there is a screw missing in the implied argument that:
> (i) accounting explains economic data;
> (ii) employees and others need such data;
> (iii) therefore employees and others need accounting skills (i.e. an extension of existing ones).
> I have the instinct that we are investing far too heavily in tramway companies, when the internal combustion engine is nearly upon us. We seem to be turning to acountants because they are there and because what they are supposed to be doing is as close to what we want them to be doing as anything we can imagine. But we endlessly beg the question of whether they are actually capable of doing the job. The implied argument here is comparable to the reasoning "we have boats, therefore they must sail on useful trade routes". The fact is that the boats we have were designed for anything but the purposes we have in mind for them. New boats might be needed, or new forms of travel.

At times during the committee's discussions several members articulated the possibility of specific alternatives to accounting, but these were only rarely taken up in the subsequent discussion. Mention was made of the granting of rights of access to information, the role of inspection, external audit committees composed of representatives of relevant social interests and changes in the governance structure of organizations so that they might be more permeable to outside pressures and needs. Again Medawar (1979) offers a useful summary of these all too occasional inputs into the discussions:

> . . . there is a big question mark . . . about accountancy as an appropriate mechanism for accountability. For example, if consumers want to know about consumer practices, why not leave it to the trading standards officers; if employees want to know about the health and safety, what about factory inspectors; or if the polluted want help, why not the Alkali Inspectorate? Why accounts?? The case is not considered . . . clearly consideration needs to be given to the limits between what accounting and other mechanisms might be relied on to do.

Going on to argue that "the limitations of accounting" needed more explicit consideration, Medawar continued by noting:

> I'm trying hard to get away from accountants as agents of this so-called public interest . . . I think accountants, the

> professionals, are somewhat dead horses. Beyond that, I think that flogging is not simply unnecessary and inhumane. It will also guarantee an increased resistance by the profession to the notion of social accounting, which could set back the cause of social accounting (and already has to some extent) a long way.

Despite the passage of time, the alternatives to accounting still remain on the agenda for future research.

Other factors

Although the set of issues discussed above played a key role in both the committee's deliberations and its final inability to produce an agreed report, other factors also were of some significance. For instance, very different views were held of how action research projects could and should be organized, with some members of the committee seeing as consultancy assignments what others saw as a legitimate way of enhancing knowledge. There also were very different views on the relevance and accuracy of the historical sections of the draft report and the nature of the links between the academic and professional accounting communities that were going to be discussed in the report. However I think that it is fair to say that such more specific concerns were reflections of the more fundamental differences outlined above.

CONCLUSION

At all times the members of the committee spoke for themselves alone. The composition of the committee also was a very particular one. No one had attempted to make it a mirror image of anything other than itself. Be that as it may, I do not think that the concerns which divided the committee can be and should be readily set aside. Any knowledge of the social sciences more generally suggests that they were not idiosyncracies of a particular group of individuals. Indeed the very opposite is the case. The substantive issues which divided the group have similar, although usually more rigorously developed manifestations, in all other areas of social inquiry. So much so that some might even see their emergence in an accounting context as a sign of its growing intellectual maturity. Equally, however, I admit that there are others who would prefer an interpretation expressed in terms of the agonies of infancy! Regardless of such competing interpretations, there are signs in both Europe and the U.S.A. that other researchers in the accounting area are beginning to explore the very issues which divided this particular committee. Although this work is being undertaken from a number of very different perspectives, I think that the fact that it is being done by able and serious people suggests that the concerns of the committee cannot be and indeed will not be set aside. That, however, is very different than saying that this committee made any contribution to the debate. If it did, that will only be known through the subsequent inquiries of those who participated in its deliberations.

Of course the committee met at a time when the social was more visible and legitimate. Explicit attempts were being made to produce new intersections of accounting and the social. Effort was being devoted to reforming accounting in the name of the social. All too clearly the situation is very different today. The legitimacy of the social apparently is not so great. The economic has once again monopolized attention and action. The issues debated by the committee are no less significant as a result of that, however. The specific mobilisations of the technical in the name of the social were not of central significance to it. Rather, emphasis was placed on the social underpinnings and consequences of all accountings, and those issues are as alive today as they were then.

Although earlier there were appeals to accounting to help in transforming the economic into the social, now accounting is being implicated in converting the social into the economic. Accounting is becoming more prevalent in more sectors of society than ever before. The public sector increasingly is utilising the accountings of the private sector. Cost, efficiency, economy and effectiveness have entered into political discourse. Organizations are being reformed in the name of the accountings of them. Accounting thereby still remains an active and significant instrument of social and political as well as economic mobilisation.

The committee that never reported therefore left not only an unfinished agenda but also one that remains significant and underexplored.

BIBLIOGRAPHY

Accounting Standards Steering Committee, *The Corporate Report* (ASSC, 1975).

Batstone, E., The Sociology of the Profession, Unpublished paper prepared for the committee (n.d.).

Bendix, R., *Work and Authority in Industry* (University of California Press, 1956).

Braverman, H., *Labor and Monopoly Capital* (Monthly Review Press, 1974).

Bryer, R. A., Social and Political Aspects of Accounting, Unpublished paper prepared for the committee (n.d.).

Bryer, R. A. & Pettigrew, A. M., Paradigms and Intellectual Traditions in Accounting Research: Some Dimensions of Choice in Research Planning, Unpublished paper prepared for the committee (1978).

Burchell, S., Clubb, C. & Hopwood, A. G., Accounting in Its Social Context: Towards a History of Value Added in the United Kingdom, *Accounting, Organizations and Society* (forthcoming).

Burke, P., *Sociology and History* (George, Allen & Unwin, 1980).

Callahan, R. E., *Education and the Cult of Efficiency* (University of Chicago Press, 1962).

352 Carr, E. H., *What is History?* (Vintage Books, 1961).

Chow, C. W., Empirical Studies of the Economic Effects of Accounting Regulation on Secutiry Prices: Findings, Problems, and Prospects, *Journal of Accounting Literature* (1983) pp. 73–109.

Department of Trade, *Aims and Scope of Company Reports* (London: Department of Trade, 1976).

Dingwall, R. & Lewis, P., *The Sociology of the Professions* (Macmillan, 1983).

Donzelot, J., *The Policing of Families* (New York: Pantheon Books, 1979).

Edwards, R., *Contested Terrain: The Transformation of the Workplace in the Twentieth Century* (Basic Books, 1979).

Flint, D., Research on the Social and Political Aspects of Accounting, unpublished note prepared for the committee (n.d.).

The Future of Company Reports (London: H.M.S.O., 1977).

Gambling, T., Culture, Personality and Accounting Theory, Discussion Paper No. 25, Series B, Department of Accounting, University of Birmingham, 1971.

Gold, M., Levie, H. & Moore, R., *The Shop Stewards' Guide to the Use of Company Information* (Spokesman Books, 1979).

Gould, S. J., *The MisMeasurement of Man*.

Habermas, J., *Knowledge and Human Interests* (Beacon Press, 1971).

Hacking, I., How Should We Do The History of Statistics?, *Ideology and Consciousness* (Spring, 1981) pp. 15–26.

Hayes, S. P., *Conservation and the Gospel of Efficiency* (Atheneum, 1980).

Herman, E. S., *Corporate Control, Corporate Power* (Cambridge University Press, 1981).

Hobsbawm, E. J., From Social History to the History of Society, *Daedalus (1971)*.

Hopwood, A. G., Towards an Organizational Perspective for the Study of Accounting and Information Systems, Accounting, Organizations and Society (1978) pp. 3–14.

Hopwood, A. G., Criteria of Corporate Effectiveness, in Brodie, M. and Bennett, R. (eds.) *Managerial Effectiveness* (Thames Valley Regional Management Centre, 1979).

Hopwood, A. G., On Trying to Study Accounting on the Contexts in Which it Operates, *Accounting, Organizations and Society* (1983) pp. 287–305.

Jackson-Cox, J., Thirkell, J. E. M. & McQueeney, J., The Disclosure of Company Information to Trade Unions: The Relevance of the ACAS Code of Practice on Disclosure, *Accounting, Organizations and Society* (1984) pp. 253–274.

Jacoby, H., *The Bureaucratization of the World* (University of California Press, 1973).

Johnson, R., Thompson, Genovese and Socialist-Humanist History, *History Workshop Journal* (Autumn, 1978).

Johnson, R., McLennan, G., Schwarz, B. & Sutton, D., *Making Histories: Studies in History-Writing and Politics* (Hutchinson, 1982).

Johnson, T. J., Professions and Power (Macmillan, 1972).

Johnson, T. J., The Professions in a Class Structure, in Sease, R. (ed.) *Industrial Society: Class, Clevage and*

Control (Allen and Unwin, 1977).
Jones, G. S., History: The Poverty of Empiricism, in Blackburn, R. *Ideology in Social Science* (Fontana, 1972).
Kamin, L. J., *The Science and Politics of IQ* (Penguine, 1977).
Kaufman, H., *Red Tape: Its Origins, Uses and Abuses* (Brookings Institution, 1977).
Kula, W., *An Economic Theory of the Feudal System* (New Left Books, 1976).
LaCapra, D., *Rethinking Intellectual History: Texts, Contexts, Language* (Cornell University Press, 1983).
Larson, M. S., *The Rise of Professionalism: A Sociological Analysis* (University of California Press, 1977).
MacKenzie, D. A., *Statistics in Britain 1865–1930* (University of Edinburgh Press, 1981).
McLennan, G., The Historian's Craft: Unravelling the Logic of Process, *Literature and History* (1979).
McLennan, G., *Marxism and the Methodologies of History* (Verson, 1981).
Medawar, C., The Social Audit: A Political View, *Accounting, Organizations and Society* (1976) pp. 389–394.
Medawar, C., Private communication (1979).
Meyer, J., On the Celebration of Rationality: Some Comments on Boland and Pondy, *Accounting, Organizations and Society* (1983) pp. 235–240.
Meyer, J., and Rowan, B., Institutionalized Organizations: Formal Structure as Myth and Ceremony, *American Journal of Sociology* (September 1977) pp. 340–363.
Meyer, J., and Rowan, B., The Structure of Education Organizations in Meyer, M. (ed.) *Environment and Organizations* pp. 78–109. (Jossey-Bass, 1978).
Moore, R., The Acquisition and Use of Company Information By Trade Unions: Final Report for the SSRC (Oxford: Ruskin College, 1977).
Moore, R., Accounting as a Field of Social Study, Unpublished paper prepared for the committee (n.d.).
Parker, R. H., The Study of Accounting History in Bromwich, M. and Hopwood, A. G., *Essays in British Accounting Research* (Pitman, 1981).
Pettigrew, A., The Accounting Frame of Reference and the Process of Strategy Formulation, unpublished note prepared for the committee (1977).
Rose, N., The Psychological Complex: Mental Measurement and Social Administration, *Ideology and Consciousness* (Spring 1979) pp. 5–68.
Rueschemeyer, D., Professional Autonomy and the Social Control of Expertise, in Dingwall, R. and Lewis, P. (eds.) *The Sociology of the Professions* (Macmillan, 1983).
Saks, M., Removing the Blinkers? A Critique of Recent Contributions to the Sociology of Professions, *Sociology* (1983) pp. 1–21.
Samuel, R., History and Theory, in Samuel, R. (ed.) *People's History and Socialist Theory* (Routledge and Kegan Paul, 1981).
Schreuder, H., *Facts and Speculations on Corporate Social Reporting in France, Germany and Holland* (Free University of Amsterdam, 1978).
Schreuder, H., Corporate Social Reporting in the Federal Republic of Germany: An Overview, *Accounting, Organizations and Society* (1979) pp. 109–122.
Stamp, E., The Politics of Professional Accounting Research: Some Personal Reflections, *Accounting, Organizations and Society* (1985) pp. 111–123.
Stymne, B., Accounting as a Field of Social Study, Unpublished paper prepared for the committee (n.d.).
Sutherland, G., The Magic of Measurement: Mental Testing and English Education 1900–1940, *Transactions of the Royal Historial Society,* 5th Series (1977) pp. 135–153.
Thomas, K., History and Anthropology, *Past and Present* (1963).
Tomkins, C., The Development of Accounting: An Historical and Sociological Perspective, unpublished paper prepared for the committee (n.d.).
Tricker, R. I., *Research in Accountancy — A Strategy for Further Work* (Social Science Research Council, 1975).
Tweedie, D. & Whittington, G., *The Debate on Inflation Accounting* (Cambridge University Press, forthcoming).
Vogel, D., *Lobbying of the Corporation* (Basic Books, 1978).
Whittington, G., *Inflation Accounting: An Introduction to the Debate* (Cambridge University Press, 1983).
Wynne, B., *Rationality and Ritual: The Windscale Inquiry and Nuclear Decisions in Britain* (The British Society for the History of Science, 1982).
Zeff, S., The Rise of Economic Consequences, *Journal of Accountancy* (December 1978) pp. 56–63.

Differing Rationalities and the Dynamics of Accounting Change

Accounting, Organizations and Society. Vol. 5, No. 1, pp. 5–27.
Pergamon Press Ltd, 1980. Printed in Great Britain.

THE ROLES OF ACCOUNTING IN ORGANIZATIONS AND SOCIETY*

STUART BURCHELL, COLIN CLUBB, ANTHONY HOPWOOD, JOHN HUGHES

London Graduate School of Business Studies

and

JANINE NAHAPIET

Oxford Centre for Management Studies

Abstract

The paper seeks to contrast the roles that have been claimed on behalf of accounting with the ways in which accounting functions in practice. It starts by examining the context in which rationales for practice are articulated and the adequacy of such claims. Thereafter consideration is given to how accounting is implicated in both organizational and social practice. The paper concludes with a discussion of the implications for accounting research.

Accounting has come to occupy an ever more significant position in the functioning of modern industrial societies. Emerging from the management practices of the estate, the trader and the embryonic corporation (Chatfield, 1977), it has developed into an influential component of modern organizational and social management. Within the organization, be it in the private or the public sector, accounting developments now are seen as being increasingly associated not only with the management of financial resources but also with the creation of particular patterns of organizational visibility (Becker & Neuheuser, 1975), the articulation of forms of management structure and organizational segmentation (Chandler & Daems, 1979) and the reinforcement or indeed creation of particular patterns of power and influence (Bariff & Galbraith, 1978; Heydebrand, 1977). What is accounted for can shape organizational participants' views of what is important, with the categories of dominant economic discourse and organizational functioning that are implicit within the accounting framework helping to create a particular conception of organizational reality. At a broader social level, accounting has become no less influential as it has come to function in a multitude of different and ever changing institutional areas. The emergence of the modern state has been particularly important in this respect. The economic calculations provided by enterprise level accounting systems have come to be used not only as a basis for government taxation but also as a means for enabling the more general economic management

*We would like to acknowledge the financial support of the Anglo-German Foundation for the Study of Industrial Society and the Foundation for Management Education.

policies of the state to grow in significance and impact (Hopwood, *et al.*, 1979; Kendrick, 1970; and Studentski, 1958). Accounting data are now used in the derivation and implementation of policies for economic stabilization, price and wage control, the regulation of particular industrial and commercial sectors and the planning of national economic resources in conditions of war and peace and prosperity and depression. Indeed in its continuing search for greater economic and social efficiency (Bowe, 1977; Haber, 1964; Hays, 1959; and Searle, 1971) the state has been an active agent both for the continued development of accounting systems in industrial and commercial enterprises (Hopwood, *et al.*, 1979) and for their introduction into more sectors of society (Gandhi, 1976).

Such extensions of the accounting domain have had major implications for the development of both accounting thought and practice. As the theorists of management control (Anthony, 1965) now recognize, accounting can no longer be regarded as a mere collection of techniques for the assessment of individual economic magnitudes. Whilst procedures for the derivation of various categories of cost and economic surplus are still important, the growth of the modern business enterprise has resulted in their incorporation into more all embracing forms of organizational practice which can enable the co-ordinated and centralized control of the functional (Litterer, 1961 and 1963), divisionalized (Johnson, 1978) and now, the matrix and project oriented organization (Ansari, 1979; Chapman, 1973; Sayles & Chandler, 1971). Similarly the increasing demands for financial information made by the capital markets, agencies of the state and organizations within the accounting profession itself have resulted in more extensive and rigorous approaches to financial reporting and disclosure (Benston, 1976; Hawkins, 1963). Accounting problems have seemingly got ever more detailed, precise and interdependent, resulting not only in the need to articulate new practice but also to formally explicate what previously had been implicit in practice.

As a result of such developments accounting has gained its current organizational and social significance. No longer seen as a mere assembly of calculative routines, it now functions as a cohesive and influential mechanism for economic and social management. But why should this be the case? Why should accounting have grown in complexity and significance? What have been the underlying pressures for its growth and development? Just what roles has it come to serve in organizations and societies? And why? All too unfortunately such questions very easily take one into uncharted terrain. For although there has been an enormous investment of effort in improving the accounting craft and even in charting its technical development, very few attempts have been made to probe into the rationales for the existence and development of accounting itself. Be that as it may, the present paper will attempt to make a preliminary excursion into the field of the unknown. Whilst recognizing that with so few prior studies to appeal to our conclusions can be tentative at best, we nevertheless believe that it is important at least to start questioning what has not been questioned and thereby possibly to make problematic what may have been taken for granted.

Our argument starts with a discussion of two important tendencies underlying the development of accounting as we now know it: the increasing institutionalization of the accounting craft and the growing abstraction or objectification of accounting knowledge. On this basis we consider how these and other pressures might have stimulated a search for explicitly stated rationales for accounting – for expressions of the roles which it serves in organizations and societies. After discussing at least some of the more commonly articulated roles which accounting is claimed to perform, we attempt to analyse the adequacy of such functional imperatives, using both observations and the research studies that are available to demonstrate how purposes are implicated in action rather than being essential to the craft itself. To reinforce these arguments more particular consideration is given to the variety of roles which are created for accounting both within organizations and the societies of which they are a part. The paper concludes with a discussion of the implications of our arguments for the future study of accounting.

INSTITUTIONALIZATION, ABSTRACTION AND THE SEARCH FOR RATIONALES

It is possible to identify many tendencies underlying the development of the accounting craft. One could point to particular aspects of the emerging bodies of knowledge and practice or to the changing patterns of influence on them. Alternatively one could highlight developments in the organizational and social significance which accounting has had or changes in the organization of accounting itself. For the purpose of the present argument two particular tendencies are identified: the increasing institutionalization of the craft and the growing objectification and abstraction of accounting knowledge.[1] Both of these tendencies are important for gaining an understanding of the present state of accounting, the roles which it serves and those which are claimed for it. Moreover together they have resulted in the creation of new forums both for accounting deliberation and debate and for the introduction of accounting change, forms of occupational specialization within organizations which have provided bases on which accounting practitioners have searched for as well as responded to organizational needs and meanings, and the continued extension of the domains of both accounting practice and thought.

The institutionalization of accounting has occurred at both the organizational and societal levels. Within both business and governmental organizations, bookkeeping came to take on a new significance and influence as accounting became a more all embracing form of organizational practice (Garner, 1954; Pollard, 1965). Implicated in budgeting and standard costing, organizational segmentation and control, and planning and resource allocation, the accountant came to be an increasingly respected member of the management cadre. Accounting departments were created, specialist staff recruited, emergent accounting systems formalized, standardized and codified, and links with other forms of management practice established. Moreover, accounting itself came to be a more fragmented endeavour with the growing separation of the preparation of the financial accounts from the presentation of internal financial information and the management of corporate liquidity and financial structure.

Such organizational developments were themselves intertwined with the professionalization of the accounting craft. Almost from their birth, the professional institutes provided an interface between the growing agencies of the state and business enterprises. In continental Europe accountants were involved with the administration of the early commercial codes (ten Have, 1976) and in England and Wales the profession derived a large part of its initial rationale from those extensions to the accounting domain which had been created by successive companies and bankruptcy acts and legislation which provided for the regulation of sectors such as railways, building societies and municipal utilities (Brown, 1905; Chatfield, 1977; Edey & Panitpakdi, 1956; Littleton, 1933). And although the U.S. context was not so regulated in the earliest days of the profession, the latter nevertheless came to flourish on the basis of subsequent governmental interventions (Chatfield, 1977). Indeed with the establishment of professional accounting institutes, many of the subsequent institutional innovations in the accounting area in the U.S.A. and the U.K. were to arise at the interface between them and the expanding regulatory agencies of the state. So, initially at least, the Securities and Exchange Commission in the U.S.A. made rather limited use of its regulatory powers in the accounting area, allowing the profession to invest in that chain of institutional mechanisms for the explication, standardization and codification of financial accounting practice which would progress through the Accounting Principles Board to the Financial Accounting Standards Board. Not dissimilar developments occurred later in the U.K. with the Accounting Standards Steering Committee being created in response to governmental pressure and the desire of the professional institutes to preserve their powers of self-regulation. Elsewhere, however, the institutionalization of accounting was a more direct result of the activities of the state. In pre-war Germany, for example, legal and institutional mechanisms for the standardization of enterprise accounting were introduced in the context of the mobilization of the national

[1] The distinction between institutionalization, and objectification and abstraction parallels similar distinctions made by Popper, Kuhn and Foucault. Popper (1972), for instance, characterises objective knowledge ("that massive fabric of statements which exists in journals and books stored in libraries, discussions, computer memories, etc.") as a world – "world 3" – which is largely autonomous of the world of the senses – "world 2" – and the physical world – "world 1". See also Hacking (1975). Similarly Kuhn (1970) distinguishes between paradigms 1 and 2, the former relating to the logical, conceptual and discursive aspects of a science and the latter to the social and institutional conditions under which the science exists. Foucault (1977) likewise operates with a distinction between knowledge and power, with the latter referring to the complex of social relations – the "regime" – in which knowledge is embedded.

economy for war (Singer, 1943) and in France these innovations were adapted after the war to provide the information which was required for microeconomic planning by agencies of the state.

Important though such a pattern of institutionalized development may be in its own right, we are particularly interested in a number of the implications which it has had for the functioning of accounting and for understanding the roles which it has come to serve. First, the emergence of accounting as is recognized and influential occupational specialization in organizations gave some measure of autonomy to accounting practice. With the creation of accounting departments and the recruitment of cosmopolitan (Gouldner, 1957) specialists who were receptive to accounting developments elsewhere, the development of accounting systems could become intertwined with the management and growth of the accounting function in an organization. Accounting could take its place in the organizational "garbage can" (Cohen *et al.*, 1972), with its development stemming, in part at least from the fact that it existed. Rather than merely having to respond to preconceived organizational needs, accounting practitioners could search for organizational opportunities for the expansion of accounting practice. Roles could now be created for accounting, with accountants pointing to the potential of their systems and seeking to establish connections between accounting and other forms of organizational practice, particularly that of production management. Second, the emergence of professional institutes and specialized bodies for the standardization and codification of accounting practice provided new forums in which accounting deliberations and debates could take place and from which changes in accounting practice could emanate. Developments in financial accounting were no longer necessarily an outcome of the direct interplay between business enterprises and the institutions of the capital market or even the state. Pressures for change could stem from the relationships between the professional institutes, the bodies concerned with the regulation of accounting practice, the dominant partnerships of the accounting profession and the interested agencies of the state, and then be imposed, comfortably or otherwise, on business or other organizations. So yet again the creation of roles for accounting practice became a much more complex endeavour, with the pressures for change being quite capable of stemming from very different institutional arenas than those in which the new practices were to function. Thirdly the changing institutional structure within which accounting operated created new possibilities for the autonomous development of accounting knowledge.[2] Within organizations, accounting procedures came to be codified in charts and manuals. With their interests in training, examining and regulating, the professional institutes provided a further stimulus for an interest in accounting discourse that could be separated from the practice of the craft. And the growing interest of the state in enterprise accounting also resulted in the formalization of the craft as disclosure requirements started to be laid down and concerns with accounting standardization emerge. As Chatfield (1977, p. 121) notes:

> In coming to grips with problems of capital, income and asset created by the industrial corporation and absentee ownership, the auditor was forced to reason beyond existing rules of thumb and finally to elaborate his ideas of proper treatment into accounting principles. His scrutiny of financial statements ultimately rationalized bookkeeping itself, not only through the use of internal control procedures but more directly by refining transaction analysis, account classifications, and the rules of financial statement disclosure. English social conditions had created a need for audit services and had produced accountants more highly skilled than any before them. By subjecting customary methods to analysis, these auditors gave accounting theory some of its earliest practical applications. And in attempting to standardize British practice, Parliament through the companies acts codified parts of this theory.

In such ways accounting became an identifiable form of organizational and social practice. It could

[2] The relationship between the institutional setting of accounting and the development of accounting knowledge is very complex, particularly when one considers that institutions are no less discursive in nature than knowledge itself. A profession, for example, can be conceived as a mass of regulations, categories, procedures, norms and laws, etc. The differentiation and relationship between the two levels of analysis therefore needs to be handled with care. As both Popper (1972) and Foucault (1977) point out in their different ways, it is all too easy to seek to explain "abstractions", "paradigm 1" or "knowledge" by reference to "institutions", "paradigm 2" or "power". Rather than arguing that institutionalization gives rise to abstraction, or vice versa, we prefer to observe the conjuncture of the two. So, for example, formalized accounting knowledge can be seen as a condition for the possibility of the professionalization of accounting, and that professionalization in turn changes the conditions underlying the elaboration and development of accounting knowledge.

be described and codified, debated and challenged, and ultimately changed. The discourse of accounting could be influenced by pressures very different from those which impinged on its practical application. Other bodies of thought which had no necessary *a priori* relationship to the accounting craft could influence the development of accounting thought, often in institutions which were far removed from the practices of accounting. So, for example, accounting thought could come to be intertwined with that of economics (Baxter, 1978) and production engineering (Wells, 1978), and with the concerns of the scientific management movement (Epstein, 1973). And such discursive developments could provide a basis for changing the practice of accounting itself, either by direct application or through the influences which they had on the requirements and pronouncements of the state, the professional institutes and the bodies concerned with the standardization of the craft and independent commentators and analysts.

Together the institutionalization and abstraction of accounting also provided bases on which people might seek to formally explicate roles which accounting served. As in other areas of human endeavour (Hacking, 1975; Popper, 1972), the existence of an abstract and objective body of thought stimulates a search for its nature and rationale.[3] Just what is accounting and what functions does it serve were questions that started to be considered. And with the growing significance of the craft and the increasing complexity of the institutional processes through which changes emerged, such questions might have had a particular relevance for many of those concerned with its practice, regulation and development.

Given that the sources of accounting change were increasingly distant from the arenas in which the new practices were to function, there was no reason to expect why those rationales which had been used in the initial justification and development of any change should provide effective rationales for its public implementation. For in a social context, public actions need to have either a political means for their enforcement (Moonitz, 1974) or a wider social significance and legitimacy (Posner, 1974). In the latter case, they need to be seen as being orientated towards some desirable or acceptable social end or ends. Action needs, in other words, to have an explicit and public rationale (Watts & Zimmerman, 1979) – a formal expression of the aims and intentions that might be regarded as being embodied within it.

Certainly the state came to act on accounting in the name of both accountability and the furtherance of organizational and social efficiency (Searle, 1971). Professional institutes and those agencies concerned with accounting regulation adopted a similar stance, although they also emphasised the role which accounting could serve in improving the flow of information useful for the investment decisions of shareholders. And those practicing accounting within organizations came to point to its relevancy in improving organizational efficiency and the maintenance of organizational control.

Such roles were not necessarily mere interpretations of accounting practice. Roles could emerge at a distance from practice, often shaped by very different institutional contexts and bodies of thought, and thereafter serve as bases for changing practice. Providing the imperatives for accounting, their relationship to the practice of accounting need be only indirect.

THE IMPERATIVES OF ACCOUNTING

We are all familiar with those stated roles of accounting which grace the introductions to accounting texts, professional pronouncements and the statements of those concerned with the regulation and development of the craft. Latterday equivalents of the preambles of old which appealed more directly to Heavenly virtue and authority (Yamey, 1974), they attempt to provide a more secular basis for the accounting mission. In such contexts, accounting is seen to have an essence, a core of functional claims and pretentions.[4] It is, or so we are led to believe, essentially concerned with the provision of

[3] Equally the explication of roles for accounting can serve as an inducement for the elaboration of accounting knowledge and practice in particular directions.

[4] The search for a rationale in progress is illustrated by Littleton (1953, p. 18): "There *must* be some basic concept which makes accounting different from all other methods of quantitative analysis, there *must* be some central idea which expresses better than others the objectives, effects, results, ends, aims that are characteristic of accounting – a 'centre of gravity' so to speak" (emphasis added).

"relevant information for decision making", with the achievement of a "rational allocation of resources" and with the maintenance of institutional "accountability" and "stewardship". Such functional attributes are seen as being fundamental to the accounting endeavour. Justifying the existence of the craft, they provide rationales for continued accounting action.

Another rather different set of imperatives for accounting has originated from those scholars who have seen accounting systems as mirrors of the societies or organizations in which they are implicated. At the societal level, this has involved seeing accounting as essentially reflective of the organization of social relationships. Feudal societies are seen to require feudal accounting systems; capitalist societies, capitalist modes of accounting (Rose, 1977); and the era of the post-industrial society necessitates a new framework for the accounting craft (Gandhi, 1976). The translation of such thinking to the organizational level has been more recent, influenced by the emergence of contingency schools of thought in the study of organizational behaviour (Bruns & Waterhouse, 1975; Hopwood, 1974; Sathe, 1975; Waterhouse & Tiessen, 1978; Watson, 1975). However some would now see accounting systems as being essential products of such characteristics as the complexity, noxity or uncertainty of the organizational environment (Galbraith, 1973; Khandwalla, 1972), the technology of the enterprise (Daft & MacIntosh, 1978) or the strategy of corporate management (Chandler, 1962). Although the evidence in support of such broad normative theories of accounting is either non-existent or equivocal at best (see Hopwood, 1978), this has not prevented their growing popularity and influence. The fact that they are largely silent about the mechanisms that might create such an essential relationship between accounting and its presumed organizational and social determinants has not been seen as problematic by those who wish to point to either the necessity for change or the elegance of design which underlies accounting in action. Nor has the fact that so many of the underlying organizational theories depend for their validity on the presumption that such contingent designs further the achievement of higher order but defined, consistent and agreed organizational goals – goals which are in part made objective by the very accounting systems which they are supposed to explain (Pfeffer, 1978).

However rather than further delineating either the particular or the more general normative claims for accounting, we choose to focus on a number of their characteristics.

The stated roles of accounting have served to provide a normative structure for accounting thought. Addressing themselves to the accounting mission, they have provided a statement of what accounting is and ought to be about. And, on this basis, they have facilitated the appraisal of accounting practice. Accounting has been challenged and changed in the name of the roles which it is seen as serving. People have sought to extend accounting in order to promote "corporate accountability" and to further "rational decision making". Others have pointed to the challenges which social change necessarily creates for accounting practice (Gilling, 1976). Recognizing, however, the equivocal relationship between the roles and practices of accounting, the former have been used as vehicles for identifying the disparity of the latter and, on this basis, for correcting what have been seen to be errors in practice.

Indeed many of the functional claims that have been made for accounting have emerged at a distance from the practice of accounting. Emanating from professional institutes, bodies concerned with the regulation of the accounting craft, agencies of the state and not least in importance, the academy itself, they very often reflect the pressures on those bodies and their need for a public legitimacy and rationale for action. Formulated in the context of particular institutional needs and actions, the functional claims attempt to provide rather particular interpretations of the accounting mission. In the academy in particular the public roles that have been articulated have often reflected the influence of other bodies of thought and practice with which accounting as an autonomous body of knowledge has become intertwined. The influences of conventional economic discourse and administrative theory have been particularly important in this respect.

In fact it should be borne in mind that there is little in the development of accounting as practised that would lead one to describe its essential rationale in terms of the furtherance of economic efficiency or rationality. Not only are the concepts which it is claimed to further extremely difficult to define (Winston & Hall, 1959) but also it has been the practice of accounting which has itself provided some of the operational understandings of the pre-given economic ends which it is supposed to serve.[5] What relationships there are between accounting thought and economic discourse have stemmed from those accounting, management and economic theorists who have sought to analyse and guide the accounting task rather than from any pre-given essential attributes of either of the two bodies of knowledge and practice.

Finally it is worth noting that although the publically stated roles of accounting have been used to identify errors in practice, that very divergence of practice has rarely problematized the roles which are stated for it. Emanating from very different social contexts, the roles have remained absolute. Acting like guardians of the secular accounting mission, they have seemingly defied questioning and rarely been brought into confrontation with accounting as it is.

Hence we can tentatively conclude that the roles which have been attributed to accounting may tell us a great deal about how people have come to see accounting, the influences on accounting discourse and the bases from which people have sought publically to influence accounting. The roles of accounting have been used to change the practice of accounting and no doubt they have been influenced by practice. However that is not to say that they are descriptive of practice. As Argyris and Schon (1974) have pointed out in another context, espoused theories are very different from theories in use. At best the roles of accounting and the practice of accounting would appear to have a rather equivocal relationship.

THE COMPLEXITIES OF ACCOUNTING PRACTICE

More recently, however, we have witnessed what might be the beginning of a reappraisal of the pregiven imperatives of the accounting mission. Pressures stemming from both academic inquiry and the problems of practical action have encouraged some observers to recognize and analyse the complexities of accounting in action and, on this basis, to start questioning what has not been questioned and make problematic what so far has been taken for granted. For different reasons and on different bases these tendencies have been evident in both the financial and management accounting areas.

The sustained and influential body of research on the impact of accounting data on the capital markets (Dyckman, Downes & Magee, 1975) has provided one basis on which the actual functioning of accounting has come to be reconsidered. The findings that investors do not necessarily take accounting data at their face value and that much of the information content of corporate annual reports and accounts is reflected in share prices prior to their public announcement (Ball & Brown, 1968) have highlighted the existence of a highly competitive market in information on corporate performance, of which accounting reports are only a part. Investors appraise, question and corroborate accounting information. Rather than being mere passive recipients, they inquire into its significance for the decisions they are taking, bringing to bear their own standards of relevancy. Now other research is starting to recognize the multiplicity of interests in accounting information within even the investor community, let alone elsewhere. Based on conceptions drawn from the study of the economics of information search and use, it is pointing to the difficulty, if not the impossibility (Demski, 1973), of operationalizing general conceptions of decision relevancy and incorporating them into the selection of a body of information prior to its use in an actual decision situation. Like the empirical research on actual investor behaviours, it too suggests that the relevancy of information is determined within the context in which it is used rather than by the foresight of those who determine the form which it should take.

In which case what influences the nature of the accounting information which is provided, if not used? Unfortunately very little is known about this at the level of the individual enterprise. Whilst consideration is being given to the ways in which information disclosure might be implicated in the formation and operation of agency relationships, the empirical adequacy of such views remains to be tested. However one set of observations which is starting to provide us with at least a partial appreciation of the forces at work at the level of the regulatory institution rather than the individual enterprise has stemmed from analyses of

[5] The latter was particularly the case in the context of the efficiency and scientific management movements at the turn of the present century. See Haber, 1964; Hayes, 1959; and Searle, 1971.

accounting policy formulation. Both Moonitz (1974) and Horngren (1973) have provided insider views which have emphasised the political dimensions of the process. The technical components of accounting regulation and specification were seen as being embodied within a complex pattern of institutional and other influences and the search for technical solutions as being complemented by a search for institutional and political support. Arising from these studies, there is now a growing awareness of the need to understand the bases on which interests in accounting are determined, articulated and deliberated (Watts & Zimmerman, 1978, 1979). For instance, consideration is now being given to how such interests might stem from the ways in which an accounting of the corporate economy of the past can influence the economy of the future (Zeff, 1978). And with the capital markets no longer being seen as the only or indeed the most significant users of accounting data, more emphasis is also being given to the roles played by agencies of the state.

Financial accounting and reporting are coming to be seen as outgrowths of institutional processes of enormous and still uncharted complexity (Burchell *et al.*, forthcoming). More importantly for the present argument, the roles which they serve are starting to be recognized as being shaped by the pressures which give rise to accounting innovation and change rather than any essence of the accounting mission.

A similar problematization of the accounting craft is slowly starting to emerge from organizational and behavioural inquiries into the ways in which management accounting systems function. Some have questioned the extent to which accounting information is actually used in organizations (Mintzberg, 1973, 1975). Others have pointed to their symbolic rather than technical uses (Gambling, 1977; Meyer & Rowan, 1978). And yet others have emphasised the ways in which uses are created for accounting systems within the context of particular organizational environments (Cammann, 1976; Hopwood, 1973; Otley, 1978; Rahman & McCosh, 1976). Rather than the consequences of accounting systems being determined by their mere existence, they are now being seen as stemming from those organizational processes which give them a particular meaning and significance (Pettigrew, 1973, 1977). Already consideration has been given to the roles played by management styles and philosophies (Argyris, 1977; Hedberg & Mumford, 1975; Hopwood, 1973), organizational normative environments (Otley, 1978), power and influence structures (Argyris, 1971; Pettigrew, 1973, 1977), organizational mechanisms for the diffusion of information (Shortell & Brown, 1976), organizational mechanisms for the diffusion of information (Shortell & Brown, 1976) and external pressures and constraints (Meyer & Rowan, 1978; Olofsson & Svalander, 1975). Other researchers have given more attention to how accounting systems both arise from and function within the context of those micropolitical processes which constitute the organization as we know it (Pfeffer, 1978). Wildavsky (1965, 1978), for instance, has provided us with particularly vivid insights into how political processes influence how sophisticated budgeting systems function in practice. Equally detailed descriptions of the ways in which organizational resource allocations are a product of the intertwining of budgeting and planning systems and political processes have been provided by Pfeffer and Salancik (1974) and Dalton (1959), and similar findings in the context of the capital budgeting process have been reported by Bower (1970).

Organizational research is also starting to question those automatic presumptions of a positive and causal relationship between accounting systems and effective organizational performance which implicitly or explicitly grace accounting texts and the pronouncements of practitioners and consultants. Albeit slowly, we are starting to move beyond those questioning pleas from the heart that were uttered by Ackoff (1967) over a decade ago. Whilst accounting systems are most certainly centrally implicated in the design and functioning of organizations as we know them, even enabling the existence of particular forms of organizational segmentation and management (Braverman, 1974; Johnson, 1978), some all too tentative studies (Child, 1973, 1974, 1975; Rosner, 1968; Turcotte, 1974) would at the very least suggest that the financially successful might well avoid many of the rigors of the more sophisticated accounting, information and control systems. Seemingly they revel and flourish within the context of informal planning and assessment practices (Child, 1974), multiple and overlapping flows of information (Baumler, 1971; Grinyer & Norburn, 1975) and continually renegotiated exchanges between organizational participants (Georgiou, 1973). Indeed it might be the "newly poor" (Olofsson & Svalander, 1975) or the externally threatened (Khandwalla, 1978; Meyer & Rowan, 1978) that invest heavily in additional mechanisms for internal visibility and control as they attempt both to allocate their ever more scarce resources or to negotiate a new legitimacy with external agents.

Although we still know all too little about how accounting systems function in practice, the studies that are available do enable us to question the descriptive accuracy of many of the functional imperatives that are claimed on behalf of both financial and management accounting systems. Whilst they may be introduced in the name of particular conceptions of social and organizational efficiency, rationality and relevance, in practice accounting systems function in a diversity of ways, intertwined with institutional political processes and the operation of other forms of organizational and calculative practice. Accounting, it would appear, is made to be purposive rather than being inherently purposeful. At the very least research suggests that in laying down the pretentions of the accounting craft we have uncritically adopted a rather particular set of views of human, organizational and social rationality and the relationships between accounting, decision making and organizational action. Whilst such presumptions might have legitimized the accounting mission, provided the means for acting on accounting and simplified the accounting system design and implementation process, their relationship to the realities of organizational and social life is questionable at best.

Unfortunately the tentativeness of our knowledge of accounting in action precludes any comprehensive and analytical discussion of the way in which accounting systems function in practice. In this essay we can do no more than be suggestive of the roles which they serve. We do this by first focusing on how accounting systems are implicated in organizational practice, choosing to pay particular attention to their involvement in organizational decision making processes. Thereafter we made some even more tentative observations on the social as distinct from organizational functioning of accounting.

ACCOUNTING SYSTEMS AND ORGANIZATIONAL PRACTICE

The relationship between accounting and organizational decision making has been an influential basis for the analysis, development and articulation of normative accounting roles and "solutions". So many writers have pointed to the roles which accounting systems can and should play in providing relevant information for decision making, improving the rationality of the decision making process and maintaining the organization in what is seen as a state of control. However one problem with such a perspective is that the relationship between accounting information and decision making rarely has been examined critically. The link has, in other words, been presumed rather than described. It has been assumed, for instance, that the specification, design and use of accounting systems precedes decision making, that the roles played by accounting systems in decision making can be invariate across a multitude of different decision situations and that accounting information is there to facilitate and ease rather than more actively to influence and shape the decision making process. However whilst such assumptions might point to the potential of the accounting mission, they have a much more complex relationship to the ways in which accounting functions in practice.

Recognizing that the present state of knowledge precludes either a comprehensive or an authoritative account of the ways in which accounting information is implicated in the processes of organizational decision making, we base our own analysis on the rather particular understandings of decision making in organizations formulated by Thompson and Tuden (1959). Whilst overly simple, their perspective nevertheless added to the traditional view by characterizing various states of uncertainty and, as a consequence, a range of possible approaches to decision making. By so doing it provides a basis for discussing at least some of the diverse ways in which interests in accounting can arise out of the processes of organizational decision making.

As can be seen in Fig. 1, Thompson and Tuden

		Uncertainty of objectives	
		Low	High
Uncertainty of cause and effect	Low	Decision by computation	Decision by compromise
	High	Decision by judgement	Decision by inspiration

Fig. 1. Decision making and the location of organizational uncertainty.

distinguished between uncertainty (or disagreement, for that has the same effects at the organizational level) over the objectives for organizational action and uncertainty over the patterns of causation which determine the consequences of action. When objectives are clear and undisputed, and the consequences of action are presumed to be known, Thompson and Tuden highlighted the potential for decision making by computation. In such circumstances it is possible to compute whether the consequence of the action or set of actions being considered will or will not satisfy the objectives that have been laid down and agreed beforehand. As cause and effect relationships become more uncertain however, the potential for computation diminishes. Thompson and Tuden then saw decisions being made in a judgemental manner, with organizational participants subjectively appraising the array of possible consequences in the light of the relatively certain objectives. Just as the introduction of uncertainty into the specification of the consequences of action resulted in a different approach to decision making, so did the acknowledgement of debate or uncertainty over the objectives themselves. With cause and effect relationships presumed to be known, Thompson and Tuden thought that disagreement or uncertainty over the objectives of action would result in a political rather than computational rationale for the decision making process. A range of interests in action are articulated in such circumstances and decision making, as a result, tends to be characterized by bargaining and compromise. When even patterns of causation are uncertain, Thompson and Tuden pointed out that decision making tends to be of an inspirational nature. With so little known beforehand rationales for action were seen as emerging in the course of the decision making process itself.

By being based on a richer characterization of the ways in which uncertainties and indeed conflicts are perceived and located in organizations the array of approaches to decision making articulated by Thompson and Tuden offers some possibility for trying to understand the different roles which accounting and other information systems serve in organizations. Moreover their framework, whilst simple, does relate to the views of those who have seen information processing mechanisms as means for uncertainty reduction (Galbraith, 1973) and information value as the degree to which uncertainty is reduced. However rather than presuming any such link between information and uncertainty, let us consider the roles which accounting systems might play in the different decision situations. How, in other words, does accounting relate to the computational, the judgemental, the political and the inspirational?

Using an all too unsatisfactory "machine" analogy, Fig. 2 outlines a set of organizational roles which might help us to appreciate some of the ways in which accounting systems function in practice (Earl & Hopwood, 1979; Hopwood, forthcoming). Given low uncertainty over both the consequences of action and the objectives for action, we approach the management scientist's definition of certainty, where algorithms, formulae and rules can be derived to solve problems by computation. Alternatively this situation might represent what Simon (1960) has called structured decision making, where the intelligence, design and choice phases are all programmable. In either case, accounting systems can serve as "answer machines", providing the simple investment appraisal methods, stock control systems and credit control routines which grace many management accounting texts.

With clear objectives but uncertain causation, the situation is more complex. One might expect that this is where organizational participants would need to explore problems, ask questions,

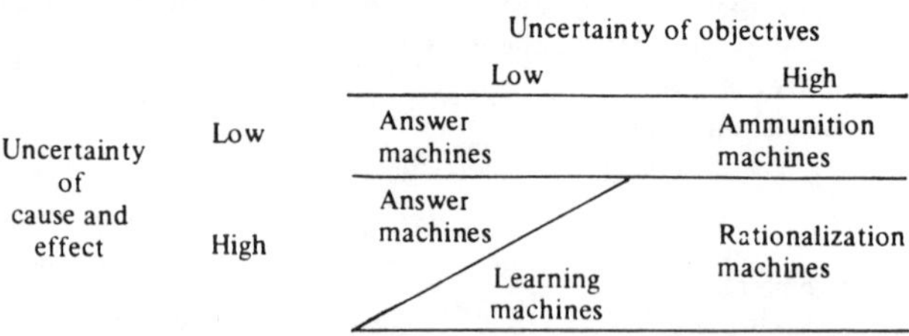

Fig. 2. Uncertainty, decision making and the roles of accounting practice.

explicate presumptions, analyse the analysable and finally resort to judgement. Rather than providing answers, accounting systems might be expected to provide assistance through what Gorry and Scott-Morton (1971) have called decision support systems and Churchman (1971) calls inquiry systems. In fact we do find such "learning machine" uses of the accounting function: access facilities, *ad hoc* analyses, what-if models and sensitivity analyses are available and used in organizations. However this is also the area of decision making where we have seen enormous extensions of more traditional approaches to computation practice. For the uncertainty, some would claim, has been seen as a threatening but not inevitable state of the world, needing to be masked, if not reduced, by an investment in the advancement of calculative systems. Accordingly the accountant has devised systems which can themselves absorb rather than convey the surrounding uncertainties. Together with the management scientist, optimizing models and modes of probabilistic and risk analysis have been developed and applied. Often trying to inculcate an aura of relative certainty, the "answer machine" extensions to the accounting craft often have presumed or imposed particular forms of economic and scientific rationality which have an equivocal relationship at best to those rationalities which are implicated in the processes of organizational decision making.

Given uncertainty or disagreement over objectives but relative certainty over causation, values, principles, perspectives and interests conflict. Standards for appraisal and criteria for guiding the organizational task are inherently problematic. Here political processes are important in the decision making process and modes of accounting can arise as "ammunition machines" by which and through which interested parties seek to promote their own particular positions. Striving to articulate the desirability of particular conceptions of the organizational mission (Batstone, 1978) and to selectively channel the distribution of information (Pettigrew, 1973), parties implicated in organized action can introduce new mechanisms for organizational control and the management of information flows.

Similarly we suspect that the uncertainties inherent in decision making by inspiration can create the need for accounting systems to serve as organizational "rationalization machines". Seeking to legitimize and justify actions that already have been decided upon, in such circumstances an accounting for the past can have a rather particular organizational significance and value.

Admittedly simplistic, our framework of accounting roles is nonetheless suggestive. By pointing to the different ways in which the accounting craft might be used to create particular conceptions of organizational clarity, it enables us to articulate a variety of roles which accounting systems might serve. However rather than discussing all of these, we will assume that at least the "answer machine" and "learning machine" roles are adequately covered in the existing literature. Our subsequent discussion therefore focusses on those extensions of computational practice which seemingly have extended the scope of "answer machine" approaches, the emergence and use of organizational "ammunition machines" and the roles which accounting might play in the rationalization of organizational action.

The extension of computational practice

The reasons behind the extension of computational practice into the realms of the judgemental remain largely uncharted. However we can point to at least two underlying factors. The first stems from the increasing formalization and objectification of management knowledge and the second from the growing extent to which accounting practices have become implicated in the development of new and more complex forms of organizational segmentation and management.

Organizational management has become the focus of a great deal of abstract investigation in the last few decades. Drawing on the perspectives and methods of economics, mathematics and statistics, in particular, formal representations have been made of management problems. Searching for algorithms, formulae and standardized rules, the investigations of an array of practitioners, consultants and scholars increasingly have enabled the reconstitution of significant portions of organizational decision making into programmed, highly specified forms (Galbraith, 1967; Simon, 1960). To varying extents, computational practices have been developed which can complement, if not replace, the exercise of human judgement.

Accounting has been implicated in the design and implementation of many of these changes in management practice. The increasing formalization of investment appraisals and planning processes has increased the sphere and extent of financial calculation. On occasions the financial risks and uncertainties which were important foci for managerial judgement are now being quantified, with the decisions taking more of a computational form. Developments in accounting practice have enabled the operationalization of particular conceptions of organizational efficiency and performance, allowing the objectives for action to be stated in seemingly less ambiguous terms. Advances in the practice of budgeting and planning have provided means for the co-ordination of organizational activities by computational means. Production and marketing operations, for instance, can be integrated in rather particular ways, inventory policies evaluated and amended in the light of envisaged organizational circumstances, and the consequences of planned actions for particular organizational resources, such as cash, calculated and evaluated. Similarly the introduction of production and inventory control procedures has resulted in demands for far more detailed financial and other information as the domain of computational practice has been extended.

The extension of computational practice has also been implicated in the development of other approaches to organizational management. The emergence of particular forms of organizational segmentation, for instance, has been enabled by extensions of the accounting craft. Certainly the creation of the divisionalized (Chandler, 1962; Johnson, 1978) and the project orientated (Sayles & Chandler, 1971) organization has been facilitated by the ability to create accounting representations of the newly emergent organizational maps, to measure the performance of organizational sub-units in ways which could be seen as relating to the objectives articulated by central management and to cope in informative and reporting terms with the complex array of organizational interdependencies created by such strategies of segmentation. The use of organization designs to isolate the technical core of the organization from environmental fluctuations (Thompson, 1967) also has enabled and often required the development of computational practices to aid both the control of the technical and the management of organizational buffers such as inventory. Similarly the emergence of accounting procedures for the measurement and assessment of performance has been intertwined with the development of practices for the evaluation and reward of organizational participants, with the emphasis which accounting has allowed to be put on operational concepts of efficiency and productivity being particularly important in this respect. In ways such as these the organizational rationales for accounting have stemmed increasingly from what it can achieve in conjunction with other approaches to the management task. Rather than having an independent and essential role to play, accounting systems have become ever more implicated with the functioning of more all-embracing forms of organizational practice.

Whilst a discussion of the wider organizational, let alone social, conditions which have facilitated the extension of computational practice is beyond the scope of the present discussion,[6] some of the dynamics which are inherent in the development of such practice at least can be noted. The growing extent of the computational domain, for instance, has resulted in the recruitment of specialists who can search for, as well as respond to, organizational roles. More importantly, however, computational developments can themselves provide the conditions for subsequent changes in both accounting and organizational practice which need be related only tenuously to the rationales in the name of which the initial changes were introduced. By creating a new pattern of organizational visibility, for instance, computational practices can often significantly change organizational participants' perceptions of the problematic and the possible. As a result, new systems of computation might emerge to complement the perceived inadequacies of the old (Jones & Lakin, 1978, pp. 89–96). Of possibly greater significance, however, the new patterns of visibility can change the conditions underlying the existence and functioning of other management practices. Measures of efficiency, for instance, can create possibilities for new targets for managerial intervention and new bases for organizational rewards. Similarly, means for the accounting representation of organizational segments can provide the conditions for the reorganization of the enterprise and the changing locus of power and

[6] Clearly the technical possibility for an accounting is not a sufficient condition for its organizational implementation and use. For discussions of some of the organizational and social considerations involved in the process of accounting change see the literature on the efficiency movement (Haber, 1964; Hayes, 1959; and Searle, 1971) and our analysis of the emergence of value added accounting in the U.K. (Burchell *et al.*, forthcoming).

influence. In ways such as these a rather complex dynamic can be introduced into the development of computational practice. New practices can themselves create possibilities for the development of yet further practices, the emergence and functioning of which may be governed by entirely different forces than those which guided the original changes.

Organizational "ammunition machines"

Rather than creating a basis for dialogue and interchange in situations where objectives are uncertain or in dispute, accounting systems are often used to articulate and promote particular interested positions and values. For the organization is almost invariably characterized by conflicts over both basic orientations and the organizational means which are likely to achieve particular ends. Rather than being cohesive mechanisms for rational action, organizations are constituted as coalitions of interests (Cyert & March, 1963). They are arenas in which people and groups participate with a diversity of interests with political processes being an endemic feature of organizational life. The mobilization and control of the organization, in the name of any interest, are problematic endeavours.

Mechanisms for organizational control are now starting to be seen as arising out of the political and conflictive nature of organizational life. As Pfeffer (1978) has stated:

> Structure, it would appear, is not just the outcome of a managerial process in which (organizational) designs are selected to ensure higher profit. Structure, rather, is itself the outcome of a process in which conflicting interests are mediated so that decisions emerge as to what criteria the organization will seek to satisfy. Organizational structures can be viewed as the outcome of a contest for control and influence occurring within the organization. Organizational structural arrangements are as likely to be the outcomes of political processes as are organizational resource allocation decisions.

The design of information and accounting systems are also implicated in the management of these political processes.

For out of the mass of organizational actions and their consequences, accounting systems can influence those which become relatively more visible (Becker & Neuheuser, 1975), particularly to senior management groups. And the visibility so established is very often an asymmetric one. The powerful are helped to observe the less powerful, but not vice versa, as a rather particular mode of surveillance is established. The centralized co-ordination of activities can thereby be established. Equally, however, demands, requirements, pressures and influences can be more readily passed down the organization, particularly in the spheres of the financial and the economic because of the disaggregative arithmetical properties of the accounting art (Hopwood, 1973). Budgeting, planning and reporting practices can together provide a framework within which a measured and observed delegation of authority can take place. A pattern of expectations can be articulated and even motivations influenced, as the visibility which is created provides a basis for organizational rewards and sanctions. Moreover by influencing the accepted language of negotiation and debate, accounting systems can help to shape what is regarded as problematic, what can be deemed a credible solution and, perhaps most important of all, the criteria which are used in their selection. For rather than being solely orientated towards the provision of information for decision making, accounting systems can influence the criteria by which other information is sifted, marshalled and evaluated.

However the consequences which accounting systems have cannot be considered to be simple reflections of the interests which might have given rise to their creation. New systems certainly can arise out of particular interests and concerns. They can be designed to make particular phenomena visible, to inculcate a particular mission or form of organizational consciousness and to help establish a particular chain of command. Indeed accountants themselves use a language which is suggestive of such ends. Nevertheless the rationales underlying their operation and functioning can differ from those which entered into their design and implementation. For once in operation, accounting systems are organizational phenomena. Indeed having their own *modus operandi* they themselves can impose constraints on organizational functioning, often contributing in the process to the effective definition of interests rather than simply expressing those which are pregiven. So although they might be able to be influenced by particular participants, accounting systems can rarely, if ever, be the exclusive domain of a single interest. Rather they become mechanisms around which interests are negotiated, counter claims articulated and political processes explicated. They may influence the language, categories, form and even timing of debate, but they can rarely exclusively influence its outcomes.

Accounting and the rationalization of action

The imperatives of the accounting mission have focused exclusively on roles for accounting which precede decision making. Even accountings for the past have been given a future rationale. However in organizations, decisions, once made, need to be justified, legitimized and rationalized. Often arising out of complex organizational processes of which few, if any, organizational participants have a comprehensive understanding (Weick, 1979) or out of those inspirational situations where both aims and causal relationships are in a state of flux (Thompson & Tuden, 1959), there is often a need for a retrospective understanding of the emergence of action, for an expression of a more synoptic organizational rationale or at least one which is seemingly consistent with formal expressions of organizational aims. And this particularly might be the case where there are dominant external interests in the decision making process (Meyer & Rowan, 1978).

Accounting systems can be and often are implicated in such organizational processes. As Bower (1970) and others have discovered, the widespread use of capital budgeting procedures has resulted in the availability of justification devices for proposals for organizational action which have gained early commitment and support as well as the simple provision of information for and prior to decision making for those proposals which remain problematic to the end. Similarly budgets and plans can be built around what is to be. Arguing more generally Meyer and Rowan (1978) note that:

> Much of the irrationality of life in modern organizations arises because the organization itself must maintain a rational corporate persona: We find planners and economists who will waste their time legitimizing plans we have already made, accounts to justify our prices, and human relations professionals to deflect blame from our conflicts. Life in modern organizations is a constant interplay between the activities that we need to carry on and the organizational accounts we need to give.

Indeed our own inquiries and those of others suggest that quite complex accounting developments can arise out of the need to justify and legitimize. For instance Pringle (1978) has described how the pioneering work on cost-benefit analysis by British officials in mid-nineteenth century India was orientated towards justifying rather than deciding what was to be done.

> Then, as now, the main *raison d'être* of cost benefit analysis, as practised, has been aimed at justifying projects rather than as a tool for investment planning . . . The main impetus seems to have come from the need of British civil servants in India to make a case for state investment. Given a relatively interventionist economic role recommended to the state, the development of a methodology for project evaluation was essential. It was necessary to show and to take into account the gains from state investment which did not accrue to the investing authority. Thus cost-benefit analysis served, in the case of nineteenth century India, to convince a sceptical government of the benefits, both to investors and to the society, of infra-structural projects.

In such circumstances an accounting rose to mediate between divergent interests in an organized endeavour, to legitimize and justify particular stances and, above all, to create a symbolic structure within which discourse could take place and through which action could be achieved.

Our discussion of the organizational functioning of accounting has been partial. Utilizing a particular frame of reference and a limited number of rather simple organizational metaphors, we have sought to illustrate some of the ways in which accounting is implicated in organizational action, but ignored others which might be equally vital. We have also focused on the organizational roles which accounting serves in a piecemeal fashion, discussing them sequentially rather than in combination, yet it is conceivable and indeed probable that within an organizational coalition support for accounting developments and change emerges from a variety of rationales (Banbury & Nahapiet, 1979) and that once implemented, the same accounting system can be used to serve even a different variety of ends as it is used by different actors in different ways (Hopwood, 1973). Moreover our discussion also has been restricted by the sheer lack of studies of accounting as it operates in organizations: there is so much that we do not know.

Hopefully, however, we have succeeded in demonstrating the divergence between the functional claims that are made on behalf of the accounting craft and the roles which it serves in practice. Whilst accounting can be and is acted upon in the name of its essential imperatives, it functions within that complex of political processes which constitute the organization. We have at least pointed to how the pressures to account can arise out of organizational functioning, how accounting can strive to shape conceptions of organizational reality and, in turn, how accountings and accounting systems can reflect as well as shape the pressures of action. Rather than being essential to the accounting mission, the roles which accounting serves in organizations are created, shaped and changed by the pressures of organizational life. They are implicated in action, rather than being prior to it.

ACCOUNTING AND SOCIAL PRACTICE

Accounting cannot be conceived as purely an organizational phenomenon however. Whilst arising out of organizational and institutional pressures, it is also a prevalent feature of the societies in which we live. Few accounting systems are unique to particular organizations for very long. Indeed many of the more important accounting innovations have occurred within numerous organizations at more or less the same time (Burchell *et al.*, forthcoming). Seemingly they satisfy more general searches for the extension of calculative practice which are embodied within the societies of which organizations are a part. Certainly the development of accounting itself has paralleled the emergence of numerous other specialized mechanisms for information processing and social and economic calculation, including *stat(e)*istics, the compilation of information for social and economic administration, and instruments for social and economic categorization in medicine, psychiatry, education, law and business and economic life (Baritz, 1960; Cullen, 1975; Kamin, 1974; Kendrick, 1970; Sutherland, 1977). Moreover accounting change increasingly emanates from the interplay between a series of institutions which claim a broader social significance. Often operating at a distance from the arenas in which their innovations function, those regulatory bodies, professional institutes, formal representatives of social interests and agencies of the state which increasingly shape the accounting domain are open to a very different array of social, political and economic pressures than those which directly impact on the business corporation.

Accounting, it would appear, can be intertwined with social as well as organizational practice. Unfortunately, however, very little is known about either the social nature of accounting thought and practice or the interplay between the social and the organizational. Some scholars have made occasional comments which have pointed to the social origins and significance of the accounting craft, although these have either not remained uncontested for very long or else have not been subjected to further inquiry. Yet other insights have been provided in more general historical studies of social and economic development (Kula, 1976), but those of direct relevance to accounting rarely have been explicated at length. So being all too conscious of such uncertainties, we do not intend to venture too far into the field of the unknown. Our comments on the social in accounting are brief, focusing first on the suggestions of those who have tried to appreciate the social significance of the accounting craft and thereafter on some of the implications for the development of accounting of those bodies which have claimed to have a broader social rationale.

The social significance of accounting

A multitude of different social significances have been attached to accounting. For Marx, accounting served as an ideological phenomenon. Perpetrating a form of false consciousness, it provided a means for mystifying rather than revealing the true nature of the social relationships which constitute productive endeavour.[7] Others, whilst adopting a less dogmatic stance, have nonetheless pointed to the mythical, symbolic and ritualistic roles of accounting (Coppock, 1977; Douglas, 1977; Gambling, 1977; Meyer, 1979; Wildavsky, 1976). In such a context accounting has been seen as implicated in the operationalization of dominant economic and social distinctions,

[7] Marx saw accounting as a perfectly adequate tool for rational decision-making on the part of capitalists. This is the aspect of his thinking taken up by Most (1963) and Bailey (1978), Most even lamenting that Marx did not jetison his ideological baggage and concentrate on management accounting. However, it is important to note that Marx claimed to reveal the *social* rationality of accounting which, as is pointed out in the text, consists of its mystification of the true nature of social relationships. In *Capital*, Vol. III, Part I, p. 45, Marx states:

"The way in which surplus value is transformed into the form of profit by way of the rate of profit is, however, a further development of the inversion of subject and object that takes place already in the process of production. In the latter, we have seen, the subjective productive forces of labour appear as productive forces of capital. On the one hand, the value, or the past labour which dominates living labour, is incarnated in the capitalist. On the other hand, the labourer appears as bare material labour-power, as a commodity. Even in the simple relations of production this inverted relationship necessarily produces certain correspondingly inverted conceptions . . ."

the creation of symbolic boundaries between competing social agents and the provision of a basis on which rationales and missions can be constructed and furthered. Conveying a pattern of economic and social meanings, it has been seen to be at least partially fulfilling demands for the construction of a symbolic order within which social agents can interact.

The contribution which accounting has made to the emergence and maintenance of the particular order inherent in economic rationality was emphasised by Weber (1969) to whom (Vol. 1, p. 86):

> From a purely technical point of view, money is the most "perfect" means of economic calculation. That is, it is formally the most rational means of orienting economic activity.

In fact Weber went so far as to see rationality in terms of the calculative means which might bring it about, defining the "formal rationality of economic action" as "the extent of quantitative calculation or accounting which is technically possible and which is actually applied" (1969, Vol. 1, p. 85). Whilst distinguishing between such a formal rationality and the "substantive rationality" which is implicit in action, Weber thought that the former provided an adequate means to achieve the latter. In the words of a recent commentator (Hirst, 1976, pp. 98-99):

> Only formal rationality can adjust means to ends in terms of efficiency since it provides a quantitative measure of efficiency; a *qualitative* measure of the *efficiency* of use of resources is logically impossible. *All* economic action therefore requires formal rationality and is modelled on formal rationality; resources cannot be "rationally oriented" to economic ends without quantitative calculation. *The definition of economic action defines it in terms of formal rationality.* Formal and substantive rationality are not alternative and equally "rational" calculations; end-rational action in the economic sphere requires formal calculation (emphasis in original).

The implications of that economic rationality which might be embodied within the perspectives and practices of accounting are more uncertain however. Whilst for Weber it was most likely an achievement for the good,[8] for Schumpeter (1950) it might contain the germs of the decline of the business civilization as we know it. That rational, calculating frame of mind which had served capitalism well when its rise was opposed by the "irrational" privileges of an aristocratic order could, he thought, undermine it as its critical intellectuality continued to develop, revealing "the pretensions of property to be as empty as those of the nobility" (Heilbroner, 1977). In his own words (1950, pp. 123-124):

> Once hammered in, the rational habit spreads under the pedagogic influence of favourable experiences to ... other spheres and there also opens eyes for that amazing thing, the Fact ... capitalist practice turns the unit of money into a tool of rational cost-profit calculations, of which the towering monument is double entry book-keeping ... primarily a product of the evolution of economic rationality, the cost-profit calculus in turn reacts upon that rationality; by crystallizing and defining numerically, it powerfully propels the logic of enterprise. And thus defined and quantified for the economic sector, this type of logic or attitude or method then starts upon its conqueror's career subjugating – rationa. :ing – man's tools and philosophies, his medical practice, his picture of the cosmos, his outlook on life, everything in fact including his concepts of beauty and justice and his spiritual ambitions.

Other commentators on the social roles and significance of accounting have adopted a less macroscopic stance, often emphasising the enabling functions of the accounting craft. Although some have stressed the roles which it plays in allowing the devolution and decentralization of economic decision making, others have pointed to the rather different internal pressures to account when decision making is centralized, either in the hands of the monolithic enterprise (Chandler, 1962) or the state (Bettleheim, 1976). And consideration has been given to the ways in which accounting has enabled the operationalization and furtherance of particular concepts of efficiency through the introduction of management methods which have reconstituted the enterprise, separating the conception and control

[8] It may be noted that Weber did allow for the possibility of formal calculative rationality actually subverting substantive rationality by reducing the world to an arid, soulless domain of mechanical calculation. In *The Protestant Ethic and the Spirit of Capitalism* (1958, p. 182) he commented:

"In the field of its highest development, in the United States, the pursuit of wealth, stripped of its religious and ethical meaning, tends to become associated with purely mundane passions, which often actually give it the character of sport. No-one knows who will live in this cage in the future, or whether at the end of this tremendous development entirely new prophets will arise, or there will be a great rebirth of old ideas and ideals, or, if neither, mechanized petrification, embellished with a sort of convulsive self-importance. For at the last stage of this cultural development, it might well be truly said: 'Specialists without spirit, sensualists without heart; this nullity imagines that it has attained a level of civilization never before achieved.' "

of the task from its practical execution (Braverman, 1974).

In this arena of inquiry the thoughts of a few undoubtedly have constructed an agenda of enormous complexity and potential significance, the validity of a lot of which remains to be tested. Looking beyond the immediate implications of the accounting craft, they have searched for a more general social significance, often, as non accountants, seeing accounting as an agent for the furtherance of particular concepts of rational action. Accounting has been seen as both reflecting and enabling the construction of society as we now know it, with both institutional forms and modes of social action intertwined with its emergence and development.

Accounting and the institutions for the regulation of the accounting craft

Very different aspects of the social functioning of accounting have been highlighted by our growing awareness of the processes inherent in accounting regulation. At one time seen in terms of technical elucidation and standardization, attention has now been devoted to the institutional and political components of the regulatory endeavour. For operating as they do at the nexus between the institutions of a professionalized craft, centralized bodies for the representation of social interests, the dominant partnerships of the accounting profession and the interested agencies of the state, those organizations which have a claim to regulate and standardize accounting are open to very different pressures from those which impinge on the organizations in which accounting is practiced. With the locus and form of regulation being subject to debate and change, the technical components of standardization have become intertwined with the desire to gain institutional legitimacy and support. Attention has had to be given to the origins of a diverse array of interests in the development of accounting and, as this has happened, the roles embodied in accounting change have been seen as being ever more implicated in the political pressures which have given rise to its emergence.

In the United Kingdom, for instance, we have witnessed how the institutional mechanisms for accounting regulation arose at the interface between a critical media, concerned agencies of the state and a profession concerned with preserving its powers of self-regulation and control (Zeff, 1972). And although often formally advocated in the name of the user's interests, the articulation of accounting standards has continued to reflect the dynamics of the institutional context of which they are an outgrowth.

The case of inflation accounting is a particularly interesting example of such forces at work. Here the fact of an inflationary economy was certainly a stimulus for change (Mumford, 1979). But that fact alone is not enough to provide an understanding of the emergence of the issue, the processes of the debate or its provisional outcomes. For arising out of the questioning of the state of accounting regulation and the emergent relationships between the accounting profession, the agencies of the state and industrial and commercial interests, the development of methods for the adjustment of financial accounting in an inflationary context has been influenced by a varied and changing number of issues and interests which either stimulated action or were called upon to legitimize particular stances and proposals. In this constellation, the changing interests of the state have been particularly important. At first inflation accounting was of interest to those administrative agencies which were concerned with the taxation of corporate income and the formulation of policies for macro-economic management. In those contexts, it was seen as being able to play rather particular roles, which could be favourably or unfavourably evaluated. Thereafter, however, other agencies of the state started to devote more explicit attention to the roles which inflation accounting might play in the implementation and furtherance of micro-economic policies for industrial recovery and growth. During its turbulent career other interested parties also have devoted attention to the roles which inflation accounting might or might not play in coping with both an economic crisis and a concurrent threat of a changing social power structure. Embodied within such a context, the inflation accounting debate has reflected pressures at both the social and the organizational levels. Some of the issues with which it has become implicated had no *a priori* relationship to the accounting craft and others have stemmed from the pressures of accounting regulation rather than its organizational practice. In such ways the potential roles which have at times given momentum to the debate have changed in both scope and level of institutional significance. Indeed only together rather than singly can they offer some basis for gaining an appreciation of the dynamics of the debate and those technical changes in accounting which are (or are not) likely to emerge.

Other accounting changes have had not dissimilar patterns of development. In some European countries, for instance, the centralization of accounting policy making has both enhanced and been enabled by the growing interest of the organized labour movement in information disclosure. And elsewhere we have noted the pressures which have created roles for accounting and accounting changes in the context of the conduct of war and the management of the national economy (Hopwood *et al.*, 1979).

In a regulatory environment, the conditions for accounting change are complex indeed. Whilst both technical and conceptual developments are required, to be influential they have to root themselves in a dynamic constellation of issues which constitutes the accounting context. In that constellation, both practice and the roles and functions which it serves and is seen as serving are subject to change as new issues emerge, new linkages to accounting established and new needs for the standardization of accounting practice arise. With so many of these pressures emerging from institutions which at least claim a broader social significance, the roles which can be associated with an accounting change can be different from those which subsequently might be implicated with its actual operation and use.

CONCLUSION AND IMPLICATIONS FOR THE PURSUIT OF ACCOUNTING RESEARCH

Our discussion of the organizational and social roles of accounting has tried to identify an area of enormous and largely uncharted complexity. Whilst the development of accounting has resulted in the attribution of formal roles for accounting which can be and are used to evaluate and change the accounting craft, our analyses have attempted to show how the actual practice of accounting can be implicated with the furtherance of many and very different sets of human and social ends. At the organizational level, we have emphasised how roles can be created for accounting within the context of the development of other forms of management practice, how accounting systems, as modes of organizational control, can arise out of the interplay of political processes both within the organization and at its interface with dominant external agents, and how accountings can emerge out of decisions rather than necessarily having to precede them. At the societal level, our discussion has been more tentative. However we have at least considered some of the views of those who have attributed quite a substantive social significance to the functioning of accounting. In a far more provisional manner, consideration also has been given to the roles which accounting change can play in a regulatory context.

In these ways we have chosen to give particular emphasis to the distinction between the imperatives which are articulated on behalf of accounting and those roles which it is made to serve in the context of organizational and social functioning. Whilst the former are inherently purposeful, often being used to give rise to accounting change, we have emphasised how organizational and social actors making accounting purposive. Seeing thereby the roles which accounting serves as being intertwined in the contexts in which it operates, we also have pointed to the diversity of functions which can be associated with even a single accounting. The pressures which give rise to its existence can themselves be both numerous and conflicting, and different from those which are used for its formal justification. Once implemented, an accounting becomes an organizational and social phenomenon, there to be used for a variety of ends by a range of actors in an organization.

Unfortunately our thoughts have had to remain tentative and suggestive for as yet all too little is known about accounting in action. The number of empirical studies of the organizational operation of accounting systems is few indeed, and even less is known about either the operation of regulatory bodies in the accounting area or the broader social context of accounting development and change. Until recently scholars interested in accounting have been seemingly content to accept the ends which have been claimed on its behalf, focusing their efforts on the further refinement of the craft. We do not necessarily criticize such an orientation, but we would claim that a case also can be made for the study *of* accounting as a social and organizational phenomenon to complement the more prevalent analyses which operate *within* the accounting context.

Not that such studies would be without problems. As we are already becoming aware, a questioning of what has not been questioned can be challenging to existing interests. Like other modes of inquiry, it too has the potential to change our conceptions of the accounting craft.

However, assuming that there is some willingness to investigate accounting as it functions, what types of inquiries might be required? There is, we think, a real need for more historical studies of the development of accounting. Just how has accounting come to function as we now know it? What social issues and agents have been involved with its emergence and development? How has it become intertwined with other aspects of social life? And what consequences might it be seen as having had? For until recently, we should remember, there have been relatively few social analyses of accounting change and the emergence of the new. Rather than inquiring into the mechanisms of change, scholars apparently have been more interested in studying the sequence and correlates of change. More emphasis has been placed on chronological accounts of technical developments *per se* than on the processes which gave rise to their existence and significance. And similar needs exist at the organizational level. In fact it is quite staggering to reflect on how few studies there are of the organizational functioning of accounting, particularly in light of the fact that most of what do exist have adopted a relatively short time horizon, focusing on the uses which are made and not made of accounting systems rather than the conditions which gave rise to their existence. Just how, we wonder, has accounting become implicated in the functioning of the modern large scale, hierarchical organization? How have particular systems arisen out of organizational processes and actions? What actions have been involved with their design, implementation and operation? And what have been the mechanisms for innovation, change and diffusion?

Such inquiries call for theoretical as well as methodological innovation. Scholars of the behavioural in accounting, for instance, would have to be prepared to move beyond the social psychological perspectives which have dominated their inquiries to date. In searching for the organizational and social significance rather than the human use of their craft they would have to be willing to confront those uncertainties which still characterize our knowledge of organizational behaviour and social action. Consideration would need to be given to the roles which information and accounting play in the political processes which characterize organizational and social life, to those forces which have constituted the organization as we now know it and to the ways in which the social and the organization in accounting intertwine with each other. Appeals would have to be made to very different frames of reference and bodies of knowledge. And above all it would have to be recognized that for the foreseeable future at least the different perspectives which are conceivable and available would produce very different insights, problems and leads.

Initially such developments cannot help but produce enormous uncertainties for accounting inquiry. And for that reason alone, some may not want to venture along the route. We nevertheless believe that such changes in orientation are required if scholarly inquiry is to explicate theories of accounting which can help us to appreciate the social and organizational significances which it has had and is capable of having.

BIBLIOGRAPHY

Ackoff, R. L., Management Misinformation Systems, *Management Science* (October, 1967), pp. B147–156.

Ansari, S. L., Towards an Open Systems Approach to Budgeting, *Accounting, Organizations and Society* (1979), pp. 149–161;

Anthony, R. N., *Planning and Control Systems: A Framework for Analysis* (Harvard Business School, 1965).

Argyris, C., Management Information Systems: The Challenge to Rationality and Emotionality, *Management Science* (1971), pp. B275–292.

Argyris, C., Single Loop and Double Loop Models in Research on Decision Making, *Administrative Science Quarterly* (September, 1976), pp. 363–375.

Argyris, C., Organizational Learning and Management Information Systems, *Accounting, Organizations and Society* (1977), pp. 113–123.

Argyris, C. & Schon, D. A., *Organizational Learning: A Theory of Action Perspective* (Addison-Wesley, 1974).

Bailey, D. T., Marx on Accounting, *The Accountant* (January 5th, 1978).

Ball, R. & Brown, P., An Empirical Evaluation of Accounting Income Numbers, *Journal of Accounting Research* (Autumn, 1968), pp. 159–178.

Banbury, J. & Nahapiet, J. E., Towards a Framework for the Study of the Antecedents and Consequences of Information Systems in Organizations, *Accounting, Organizations and Society* (1979), pp. 163–177.

Bariff, M. L. & Galbraith, J., Intraorganizational Power Considerations for Designing Information Systems, *Accounting, Organizations and Society* (1978), pp. 15–28.

Baritz, L., *The Servants of Power* (Wesleyn University Press, 1960).

Batstone, E., Management and Industrial Democracy, in *Industrial Democracy: International Views* (Industrial Relations Research Unit, Warwick University, 1978).

Baumler, J. V., Defined Criteria of Performance in Organizational Control, *Administrative Science Quarterly* (September, 1971), pp. 340–350.

Baxter,, W. T., Introduction, in W. T. Baxter (ed.) *Selected Papers on Accounting* (Arno Press, 1978).

Becker, S. W. & Neuheuser, D., *The Efficient Organization* (North-Holland, 1975).

Benston, G. J., *Corporate Financial Disclosure in the UK and the USA* (Saxon House, 1976).

Bettleheim, C., *Economic Calculation and Forms of Property* (Routledge & Kegan Paul, 1976).

Bowe, C. (ed.), *Industrial Efficiency and the Role of Government* (London, H.M.S.O., 1977).

Bower, J., *Managing the Resource Allocation Process* (Graduate School of Business Administration, Harvard University, 1970).

Braverman, H., *Labour and Monopoly Capital* (Monthly Review Press, 1974).

Brown, R. (ed.), *History of Accounting and Accountants* (Jack, 1905).

Bruns, W. J. & Waterhouse, J. H., Budgetary Control and Organization Structure, *Journal of Accounting Research* (Autumn, 1975), pp. 177–203.

Burchell, S., Clubb, C. & Hopwood, A. G., Accounting in Its Social Context: Towards a History of Value Added in the UK (forthcoming).

Cammann, C., Effects of the Use of Control Systems, *Accounting, Organizations and Society* (1976), pp. 301–313.

Chandler, A., *Strategy and Structure* (MIT Press, 1962).

Chandler, A. & Daems, H., Administrative Co-ordination, Allocation and Monitoring: A Comparative Analysis of the Emergence of Accounting and Organization in the USA and Europe, *Accounting, Organizations and Society* (1979), pp. 3–20.

Chapman, R. L., *Project Management in NASA: The System and the Men* (NASA, 1973).

Chatfield, M., *The History of Accounting Thought* (Krieger, 1977).

Child, J., Strategies of Control and Organization Behaviour, *Administrative Science Quarterly* (1973), pp. 1–17.

Child, J., Management and Organizational Factors Associated with Company Performance – Part I, *Journal of Management Studies* (1974), pp. 175–189.

Child, J., Management and Organizational Factors Associated with Company Performance – Part II, *Journal of Management Studies* (1975), pp. 12–27.

Churchman, C. W., *The Design of Inquiring Systems* (Basic Books, 1971).

Cohen, M. D., March, J. G. & Olsen, J. P., A Garbage Can Model of Organizational Choice, *Administrative Science Quarterly* (March, 1972), pp. 1–25.

Coppock, R., Life Among the Environmentalists, *Accounting, Organizations and Society* (1977), pp. 125–130.

Cullen, M. J., *The Statistical Movement in Early Victorian Britain* (Harvester, 1975).

Cyert, R. M. & March, J. G., *A Behavioural Theory of the Firm* (Prentice-Hall, 1963).

Daft, R. L. & MacIntosh, N. B., A New Approach to Design and Use of Management Information, *California Management Review* (Fall, 1978), pp. 82–92.

Dalton, M., *Men Who Manage* (Wiley, 1959).

Demski, J. S., The General Impossibility of Normative Accounting Standards, *The Accounting Review* (October, 1973), pp. 718–723).

Douglas, M., Accounting and Anthropology. Unpublished opening address to the Social Science Research Council Conference on Accounting Research, Oxford, 1977.

Dyckman, T., Downes, D. & Magee, R. P., *Efficient Capital Markets and Accounting: A Critical Analysis* (Prentice-Hall, 1975).

Earl, M. J. & Hopwood, A. G., From Management Information to Information Management. A paper presented to the IFIP TC8-WG8.2 Working Conference on the Information Systems Environment, Bonn, 1979.

Edey, H. C. & Panitpakdi, P., British Company Accounting and the Law, in A. C. Littleton and B. S. Yamey, *Studies in the History of Accounting* (Irwin, 1956).

Epstein, M. J., *The Effect of Scientific Management on the Development of the Standard Cost System.* Doctoral Dissertation, University of Oregon, 1973.

Foucault, M., *Discipline and Punish* (Allen Lane, 1977).
Galbraith, J., *Designing Complex Organizations* (Addison-Wesley, 1973).
Galbraith, J. K., *The New Industrial State* (Houghton Mifflin, 1967).
Gambling, T., Magic, Accounting and Morale, *Accounting, Organizations and Society* (1977), pp. 141-153.
Gandhi, N. W., The Emergence of the Postindustrial Society and the Future of the Accounting Function, *The International Journal of Accounting Education and Research* (Spring, 1976), pp. 33-50.
Garner, S. P., *Evolution of Cost Accounting to 1925* (University of Alabama Press, 1954).
Georgiou, P., The Goal Paradigm and Notes Towards a Counter Paradigm, *Administrative Science Quarterly* (1973), pp. 291-310.
Gilling, D. M., Accounting and Social Change, *The International Journal of Accounting Education and Research* (Spring, 1976), pp. 59-72.
Gorry, G. A. & Scott-Morton, M. S., A Framework for Management Information Systems, *Sloan Management Review* (Fall, 1971).
Gouldner, A. W., Cosmopolitans and Locals: Toward an Analysis of Latent Social Roles, *Administrative Science Quarterly* (1957), pp. 281-306.
Grinyer, P. & Norburn, D., Planning for Existing Markets: Perceptions of Executive and Financial Performance, *Journal of the Royal Statistical Society* (Series A, 1975), pp. 70-97.
Haber, S., *Efficiency and Uplift* (University of Chicago Press, 1964).
Hacking, I., *Why Does Language Matter to Philosophy?* (Cambridge University Press, 1975).
Hawkins, D. F., The Development of Modern Financial Reporting Practices Among American Manufacturing Corporations, *Business History Review* (Autumn, 1963), pp. 135-168.
Hays, S., *Conservation and the Gospel of Efficiency* (Harvard University Press, 1959).
Hedberg, B. & Mumford, E., The Design of Computer Systems: Man's Vision of Man as an Integral Part of the System Design Process, in E. Mumford and H. Sackman (eds.), *Human Choice and Computers* (North-Holland, 1975).
Heilbroner, R. L., *Business Civilization in Decline* (Penguin Books, 1977).
Heydebrand, W., Organizational Contradictions in Public Bureaucracies: Toward a Marxian Theory of Organizations, in J. K. Benson (ed.), *Organizational Analysis: Critique and Innovation* (Sage Publications, 1977).
Hirst, P. Q., *Social Evolution and Sociological Categories* (George Allen and Unwin, 1976).
Hopwood, A. G., *An Accounting System and Managerial Behaviour* (Saxon House and Lexington, 1973).
Hopwood, A. G., *Accounting and Human Behaviour* (Haymarket Publishing, 1974).
Hopwood, A. G., Towards an Organizational Perspective for the Study of Accounting and Information Systems, *Accounting, Organizations and Society* (1978), pp. 3-14.
Hopwood, A. G., Information Systems and Organizational Reality, Occasional Paper No. 5, Thames Valley Regional Management Centre, forthcoming.
Hopwood, A. G., Burchell, S., Clubb, C., The Development of Accounting in its International Context: Past Concerns and Emergent Issues. A paper presented at the Third Charles Waldo Haskins Seminar on Accounting History, Atlanta, April 20, 1979.
Horngren, C. T., The Marketing of Accounting Standards, *The Journal of Accountancy* (October, 1973).
Johnson, H. T., Management Accounting in an Early Multinational Organization: General Motors in the 1920's, *Business History Review* (1978), pp. 490-517.
Jones, R. & Lakin, C., *The Carpetmakers* (McGraw-Hill, 1978).
Kamin, L. J., *The Science and Politics of IQ* (Penguin, 1974).
Kendrick, J. W., The Historical Development of National Income Accounts, *History of Political Economy* (1970), Vol. 2, No. 3.
Khandwalla, P. N., The Effect of Different Types of Competition on the Use of Management Controls, *Journal of Accounting Research* (Autumn, 1972), pp. 275-285.
Khandwalla, P., Crisis Responses of Competing Versus Noncompeting Organizations, in C. F. Smart and W. T. Stanbury (eds.), *Studies in Crisis Management* (Institute for Research on Public Policy, Toronto, 1978), pp. 151-178.
Kuhn, T., *The Structure of Scientific Revolutions* (2nd Edition, enlarged; University of Chicago Press, 1970).
Kula, W., *An Economic Theory of the Feudal System* (New Left Books, 1976).
Litterer, J. A., Systematic Management: The Search for Order and Integration, *Business History Review* (1961), pp. 461-476.
Litterer, J. A., Systematic Management: Design for Organizational Recoupling in American Manufacturing Firms, *Business History Review* (1963), pp. 369-391.
Littleton, A. C., *Accounting Evolution to 1900* (American Institute Publishing Co., 1933).
Littleton, A. C., *Structure of Accounting Theory* (American Accounting Association, 1953).

Meyer, J. & Rowan, B., The Structure of Educational Organizations, in M. W. Meyer *et al.* (eds.), *Environments and Organizations* (Jossey-Bass, 1978).

Meyer, J., Environmental and Internal Origins of Symbolic Structure in Organizations. Paper presented at the Seminar on Organizations as Ideological Systems, Stockholm, 1979.

Mintzberg, H., *The Nature of Managerial Work* (Harper and Row, 1973).

Mitzberg, H., *Impediments to the Use of Management Information* (NAA, 1975).

Moonitz, M., *Obtaining Agreement on Standards in the Accounting Profession* (American Accounting Association, 1974).

Most, K. S., Marx and Management Accounting, *The Accountant* (August 17, 1963).

Mumford, M., The End of a Familiar Inflation Accounting Cycle, *Accounting and Business Research* (Spring, 1979), pp. 98–104.

Otley, D. T., Budget Use and Managerial Performance, *Journal of Accounting Research* (Spring, 1978), pp. 122–149.

Olofsson, C. & Svalander, P. A., The Medical Services Change Over to a Poor Environment – "New Poor" Behaviour. Unpublished working paper, University of Linköping, 1975.

Pettigrew, A. M., *The Politics of Organizational Decision Making* (Tavistock, 1973).

Pettigrew, A. M., The Creation of Organizational Cultures. Working Paper, European Institute for Advanced Studies in Management, Brussels, 1977.

Pfeffer, J., The Micropolitics of Organizations, in M. W. Meyer, *Environment and Organizations* (Jossey-Bass, 1978).

Pfeffer, J. & Salancik, G. R., Organizational Decision Making as a Political Process, *Administrative Science Quarterly* (June, 1974), pp. 135–151.

Pollard, S., *The Genesis of Modern Management* (Edward Arnold, 1965).

Popper, K. P., *Objective Knowledge: An Evolutionary Approach* (Oxford University Press, 1972).

Posner, R. A., Theories of Economic Regulation, *The Bell Journal of Economics and Management Science* (Autumn, 1974), pp. 335–359.

Pringle, G., The Early Development of Cost-Benefit Analysis, *Journal of Agricultural Economics* (January, 1978), pp. 63–71.

Rahman, M. & McCosh, A. M., The Influence of Organizational and Personal Factors on the Use of Accounting Information: An Empirical Study, *Accounting, Organizations and Society* (1976), pp. 339–355.

Rose, N., Fetishism and Ideology: A Review of Theoretical Problems, *Ideology and Consciousness* (Autumn, 1977).

Rosner, M. M., Administrative Controls and Innovation, *Behavioural Science* (1968), pp. 36–43.

Sathe, V., Contemporary Theory of Organization Structure, in J. L. Livingstone (ed.), *Managerial Accounting: The Behavioural Foundations* (Grid Publishing, 1975).

Sayles, L., & Chandler, M. K., *Managing Large Systems* (Harper and Row, 1971).

Schumpeter, J. A., *Capitalism, Socialism and Democracy* (3rd ed.; Harper and Row, 1950).

Searle, G. R., *The Quest for National Efficiency* (Blackwell, 1971).

Shortell, S. M. & Brown, M. (eds.), *Organizational Research in Hospitals* (Blue Cross, 1976).

Simon, H. A., *The New Science of Management Decision* (Harper and Row, 1960).

Singer, H. W., *Standardized Accounting in Germany* (National Institute for Economic and Social Research Occasional Paper V; Cambridge University Press, 1943).

Studenski, P., *The Income of Nations* (New York: 1959).

Sutherland, G., The Magic of Measurement, *Transactions of the Royal Historical Society*, 5th Series, Vol. 27 (1977).

ten Have, O., *The History of Accountancy* (Bay Books, 1976).

Thompson, J. D., *Organizations in Action* (McGraw-Hill, 1967).

Thompson, J. D. & Tuden, A., Strategies, Structures and Processes of Organizational Decision, in J. D. Thompson *et al.* (eds.), *Comparative Studies in Administration* (University of Pittsburgh Press, 1959).

Turcotte, W. E., Control Systems, Performance and Satisfaction in Two State Agencies, *Administrative Science Quarterly* (1974), pp. 60–73.

Waterhouse, J. H. & Teissen, P., A Contingency Framework for Management Accounting Systems Research, *Accounting, Organizations and Society* (1978), pp. 65–76.

Watson, D. J. H., Contingency Formulations of Organizational Structure: Implications for Managerial Accounting, in J. L. Livingstone, *Managerial Accounting: The Behavioural Foundations* (Grid, 1975).

Watts, R. & Zimmerman, J. L., Towards a Positive Theory of the Determination of Accounting Standards, *The Accounting Review* (January, 1978, pp. 112–134.

Watts, R. & Zimmerman, J. L., The Demand for and Supply of Accounting Theories: The Market for Excuses, *The Accounting Review* (April, 1979), pp. 273–305.

Weber, M., *The Protestant Ethic and the Spirit of Capitalism* (Charles Scribner & Sons, 1958).

Weber, M., *Economy and Society* (3 Vols) (Bedminster Press, 1969).

Weick, K., *The Social Psychology of Organizing* (2nd ed., Addison-Wesley, 1979).

Wells, M. C., *Accounting for Common Costs* (International Centre for Accounting Education and Research, 1978).
Wildavsky, A., *The Politics of the Budgetary Process* (Little, Brown, 1965).
Wildavsky, A., Economy and Environment/Rationality and Ritual: A Review Essay, *Accounting, Organizations and Society* (1976), pp. 117-129.
Wildavsky, A., Policy Analysis is What Information Systems are Not, *Accounting, Organizations and Society* (1978), pp. 77-88.
Winston, C. & Hall, M., The Ambiguous Notion of Efficiency, *The Economic Journal* (1959).
Yamey, B. S., Pious Inscriptions: Confused Accounts; Classification of Accounts: Three Historical Notes, in H. Edey and B. S. Yamey (eds.), *Debits, Credits, Finance and Profits* (Sweet and Maxwell, 1974).
Zeff, S. A., *Forging Accounting Principles in Five Countries: A History and an Analysis of Trends* (Stipes Publishing Company, 1972).
Zeff, S. A., The Rise of Economic Consequences, *The Journal of Accountancy* (December, 1978), pp. 56-63.

On trying to account for accounting
Commentary on
Research on monitoring the accounting standard setting process

Anthony G Hopwood
Institute of Chartered Accountants Professor of Accounting and Financial Reporting, London Graduate School of Business Studies

In the last few decades accounting issues have come to be debated more frequently and more forcefully in the public arena. What had previously been regarded as an aspect of ordinary commercial practice increasingly has come to be seen in wider public terms. Although it is recognized that complex technical issues remain to be resolved, increasingly these issues too are being seen in broader social and political as well as purely technical terms.

Such developments have resulted in a new series of institutions being established to provide forums for debates on the social-technical nature of both present accounting practice and the suggestions which are made for its reform and change. In the UK we now have the Accounting Standards Committee; in the USA there is the Financial Accounting Standard Board and many other western industrialized nations now have a variety of bodies for the regulation of the accounting craft. Of course, such bodies are not completely new. In many countries of continental Europe there have long been institutional arrangements for influencing and changing accounting practice in the name of the social, as has been repeatedly illustrated in the papers presented at this conference. Moreover, in the USA the broader nature of the potential influences on accounting was recognized in the period after the Great Crash. The establishment of the Securities and Exchange Commission, and its endowment with a responsibility for the regulation of accounting practice, represented a major recognition by the state and the political establishment of the need for a wider set of influences on accounting practices and institutions.

Despite the presence of such views, it is only in comparatively recent times that a more strategic view of accounting has come to be explicitly promulgated. Accounting, seemingly, is no longer a mere grouping of prevailing techniques and practices, or even technical alternatives to received knowledge. As a result of discussions initiated in the media, the institutions of political life and even in the business community itself, the accounting representation of organizational performance is seen as having consequences for the recognition of particular organizational problems, for the focusing of social and economic debate and, at times, for the allocation of economic resources. With such a different view of accounting, an explicit sphere of accounting policy making is now recognized. Accounting, from such a perspective, is no longer just a technical phenomenon. The technical intersects with the economic, the social and the political in such a way that a new and very different area of policy formulation is isolated (Zeff, 1978).

Such developments, whether appropriate or not, undoubtedly have contributed to the recognition of the role which knowledge and research can play in the accounting policy-making process. Again, I would not like to be interpreted as saying that this is a completely new development. It is not. There are numerous examples of more abstract notions of knowledge and research being called upon in the determination of accounting changes. However, I do think that this is becoming a more prevalent phenomenon. As accounting comes to be debated, and changed, in institutional arenas distanced from the domains in which it is practised, more abstract notions of both accounting and the conceptions of the social, economic and political roles which it has, does and might serve are coming to play a more significant role. 381

Beaver's paper should be seen in this context. Quite explicitly he offers just such an abstract characterization of the role of accounting in economic life. Accepting the institutional embodiments for the discussion and determination of accounting change, he also accepts, and indeed tries to further, a view of the accounting policy-making domain. In so doing, he recognizes that research and other abstract notions of the accounting craft have a vital role to play. Indeed his paper is of particular interest because he explicitly seeks to further that role; he strives to identify those spheres of the accounting policy-making endeavour to which accounting research can contribute.

Before proceeding further it is of interest to summarize some aspects of Beaver's characterization of the accounting policy-making sphere.

1 Accounting activities, according to Beaver, are centrally implicated in the guidance of the industrial and commercial investment process.
2 Given this, he sees the relevant constituencies in the accounting policy process as being the investors themselves, and financial intermediaries, information intermediaries, management and auditors.
3 Although recognizing that accounting policy processes reside in the social domain because of the consequences they might have for the distribution of wealth among members of society, he nevertheless provides a rather traditional characterization of the policy making process—one that is seen in terms of a rational specification of objectives, anticipated consequences and an analysis of outcomes.
4 Finally, research, according to Beaver, is something that will enhance the rationality of this process. It will help with the formulation and specification of the objectives, the understanding of anticipated consequences and the feedback of information on what has, or has not, been achieved.

Although all aspects of such a characterization conform to the dominant prevailing view of the accounting policy-making domain, I nevertheless think that all are subject to question and debate. By any standard Beaver's suggested view of the roles of accounting is a partial one. By emphasizing the involvement of accounting in corporate investment decision making, Beaver ignores the other interests which the state has had in accounting for many reasons over many years (Hopwood, Burchell and Clubb, 1979). He also ignores the ways in which attempts to delineate corporate performance are implicated in wider debates in society, for instance between those who control the distribution of capital and those who seek to negotiate in the interests of labour (Tinker, Merino and Neimark, 1982). Not too surprisingly, Beaver also provides both a very partial view of the constituents interested in the accounting domain and a conventionally rational description of the accounting policy-making process and the roles which research can play in this. In Beaver's eyes, the policy process is seen in
382 predominantly technical, managerial terms. Through whatever means, and Beaver himself has doubts on this, the technical can remain isolated from the social and the political. Research and information accordingly can illuminate the process rather than more actively shape it.

Perhaps it is not surprising that such views prevail at such an early stage in the public recognition of the public nature of accounting policy. However research orientated towards illuminating and enlightening discussions of public policy is not a new phenomenon, particularly in the USA where there is now a history of over three decades' involvement in policy orientated and evaluation research.

Now is not the appropriate occasion on which to delineate the problems that such an extended history presents us with, nor the lessons that can be learnt. However, as the 'evaluation research' community is now at pains to recognize, the interface between research and the public discussion of practice is not an easy one to infiltrate or manage.

Objectives are rarely precisely delineated or non-conflicting. The policy-making process is itself subject to conflicting rationalities. More technical rationalities, of the type described by Beaver, have some role to play. However, as much recent research has at least illustrated in an accounting context, alternative and conflicting rationalities are also at work (Watts and Zimmerman 1979). Finally, the delineation of actual consequences also is a difficult endeavour, particularly when many of the desired aims of policy changes might be implicit rather than explicit and when in the social domain eventual outcomes invariably combine both the anticipated and the unanticipated, with the latter at times being more significant than the former. A few of the problems raised by such a different perspective can be illustrated by the situation that confronts those seeking to evaluate the inflation accounting debate in the UK.

I would locate the debate's origins in the attempts of the accounting profession to secure its role in the regulation of accounting practice. Concerned

that the state might intervene, an institution for the regulation of accounting was established within the professional structure—the Accounting Standards Steering Committee. The initiative so gained by the profession on the policy nexus operating between the profession and the state was an uncertain one however, at least in the 1970s. Both sides recognized that further developments were required to solidify the achievement and the growing awareness of the inflationary 'problem'. Higham and Tomlinson, (1982), provided one context in which this could be done. Only history will inform us on which side the primary initiative was taken; however, we already know that many of the complicating factors were introduced by the machinery of the state. Inflation accounting was not seen in either unitary or stable terms by the different agencies of the state. Some saw it as a sign of the progressive development of accounting practice. Others more negatively related it to the macro-economic concerns of the state, both in terms of the problems of economic indexation and the difficulties of tax collection. Only subsequently did yet
others see it more positively in terms of the role that it might be able to play in highlighting the problems of under-investment in the context of a micro-economic industrial strategy.

The inflation accounting debate also involved the intertwining of such macro-institutional and national issues with the concerns of industrial and commercial management on whom the solution eventually would impact. Faced with the problems of enhanced profitability in an era of growing trade union power and of financing in a time of economic and, in particular, price constraint, the images presented by financial disclosure began to be seen in more strategic terms. In addition, as Bill Hyde notes in his commentary on Whittington's paper, the perceived interests of the business community were not identical. So a different forum for conflicting discussions was superimposed on that prevailing at a more macro level.

Faced with such a scenario, what role can research in general and evaluation research in particular play?

Research and knowledge dissemination processes all too clearly can play an active, albeit indirect, role, as Whittington demonstrates so well. Indeed with the discussion of accounting concepts so abstracted from the conventional contexts of accounting practice, it might be easier for research to play such a role. However the precise roles played will be influenced by a number of more specific aspects of the accounting policy making process

1 Many of the significant objectives lying behind accounting policy deliberations do not enter into the public arena. Little explicit mention is given to concerns with the institutional regulation of accounting, the divergent interests of the state in accounting, and the roles which accounting plays in the creation of persuasive images of corporate performance.

2 The multiple levels of the accounting policy process also are rarely discussed. Even though it is known that the institutional nexus between the state and the accounting profession, between the latter and its members, and between these and corporate management, are all important, few, if any, of these enter into the public rationales for accounting change.
3 Many of the conventional rationales for accounting change do not play a significant role in the process, at least in its early stages. Indeed, given this, there paradoxically might even be a greater need for research to illuminate such seemingly more obvious rationales as the advantages for capital market and corporate management decision making as the time for implementation gets near. A recent publication by the ASC illustrates that such research also has a role to play when implementation is contested (Carsberg, 1982).

384 When the accounting policy-making process is seen in such terms, the roles which research can play are both initially less obvious and subsequently more diverse. In the latter respect, I would like briefly to mention two such roles.

First, research can become involved in the creation of an institutional legitimacy for those bodies explicitly concerned with the regulation of the accounting craft. In many countries we have seen such institutions newly emerge at an interface between the accounting profession and the state. So distanced from the spheres in which accounting is practised, that interface is not an easy one to manage. Perhaps, therefore, it is not surprising that we have seen the FASB adopt a great deal of the public vocabulary of American federal institutions. Its concern with the establishment of 'due process' might be a part of this. More specifically, such institutions have difficulty in establishing a rationale for action. They can appeal to neither the traditions of the profession nor the perogatives of the state. Faced with such a dilemma, perhaps it is not surprising that many are seeking to establish a more scientific, knowledge based rationale, be this called a 'conceptual framework' or whatever.

A second role for evaluation research in particular stems more directly from the detailed decision processes surrounding particular policy initiatives. Faced with such an uneasy institutional legtimacy for action, agreement often can only be reached for constrained periods of time. Conflicting interests may be made to support a particular policy initiative if it is seen as, in part at least, a temporary one and if agreement is made to evaluate the consequences of its implementation. A degree of openness thereby is introduced into the decision making process. Seen in such terms, the *post-hoc* evaluation research endeavour is part of the *ex-ante* decision process!

Such a rationale might well have entered in the decision process on FAS No. 33. Again this should not be too surprising. Similar rationales provided a basis for the very earliest evaluation research endeavours in the USA when a provisional congressional agreement was made to launch the post World War II veterans' programmes.

No doubt others could provide further rationales for the growing politicization of research and knowledge processes in the accounting policy-making forum (Watts and Zimmerman, 1979). Unlike some, I do not see this in negative terms. Not only do I accept the inevitability of such political processes but also I positively value the role that they serve within the context of our democratic tradition. With due provision being made for the greater openness of the underlying processes, I would even go so far as supporting the role of the political rather than the purely technical. However, now is not an appropriate moment to take that particular argument further.

In the context of the present discussion I would like to conclude by making two points. First, I do welcome the type of evaluative research that Beaver outlines. The fact that it is to be so professionally conducted must
ensure that we stand to learn a great deal about the consequences of
accounting change. For that reason alone, the FASB is to be congratulated on initiating such an ambitious evaluation exercise. Second, however, my own discussion has tried to illustrate how little we know of accounting policy making processes and, in particular, the role which research and abstract knowledge serves in these. Although the type of evaluation exercises outlined by Beaver most likely will provide us with some further insights, I think that there also is an important role to be played by more direct research initiatives.

References

Carsberg, Bryan, *The Usefulness of Current Cost Accounting,* The Accounting Standards Committee, (1982).

Higham, D., and J. Tomlinson, 'Why do governments worry about inflation?', *National Westminster Bank Quarterly Review,* (May 1982).

Hopwood, A. G., S. Burchell, and C. Clubb, 'The development of accounting in the international context: past concerns and emergent issues' in A. Roberts (ed.) *An Historical and Contemporary Review of the Development of International Accounting*, Georgia State University, (1979).

Tinker, A. M., B. D. Merino, and M. D. Neimark, 'The normative origins of positive theories: ideology and accounting thought', *Accounting, Organizations and Society*, (1982).

Watts, R., and J. L. Zimmerman, 'The demand for and supply of accounting theories: the market for excuses', *The Accounting Review*, (April 1979).

Zeff, S. A., 'The rise of economic consequences', *The Journal of Accountancy* (December 1978).

THE DEVELOPMENT OF ACCOUNTING IN ITS INTERNATIONAL CONTEXT: PAST CONCERNS AND EMERGENT ISSUES 387

ANTHONY G. HOPWOOD,
STUART BURCHELL AND
COLIN CLUBB

As both accounting scholars and practitioners have explored beyond the constraints of their own national contexts, unitary views of the nature and purposes of accounting have come to be set aside. Comparative as well as historical analyses have shown accounting to be a heterogeneous phenomenon, varying in form, content, organization and function across both time and space. As a consequence, accounting is not seen to include a multitude of different practices, the nature of which has changed quite radically over time.

For the scholar such a view of accounting has provided yet further support for gaining a more detailed comparative appreciation of the accounting craft. Just how is one manifestation of accounting different from another? How do they function in both technical and institutional terms? And what are the practical consequences of the differences so observed? Just how, in other words, do the resultant accounts differ and what are the implications of such a differentiated view for understanding the development and functioning of accounting in practice?

Such questions, and many others like them, have provided the basis for a growing number of comparative and internationally orientated research inquiries (see Houghton, 1979; Kubin and Mueller, 1973), the findings of which are playing a valuable role in further extending the boundaries of accounting inquiry. By documenting the extent of accounting diversity, they have helped to problematise many prevailing conceptions of accounting practice. As a consequence, particular manifestations of the accounting craft increasingly are being seen in terms of the contexts in which they have emerged and now function rather than in terms of any absolute standard of accounting truth.

In such ways comparative analyses are helping to pose a rather different set of more general questions for scholars interested in the development and significance of the accounting craft. Having provided even a partial documentation of the extent of accounting diversity, increasing consideration now is being given to understanding the institutional, social, economic and political conditions which might have given rise to different accountings. And interestingly enough, other more pressing contemporary issues also are resulting in similar questionings of the broader pressures which have resulted and indeed might now be resulting in accounting change. Increasing concerns with accounting standardization (Merino, 1978; Moonitz, 1974; Watts and Zimmermann, 1978), the emergence of new interests in the accounting domain (Carlsson et al., 1978; Cooper and Essex, 1977; Gold, Levie and Moore, 1979) and the growing complexities of organizational life (Ansari, 1977; Waterhouse and Tiessen, 1978) are all resulting in an interest in accounting in terms other than its technical adequacy and functioning. Whether or not adopting an explicit comparative perspective, an increasing number of scholars are now actively recognizing the need to orchestrate social, economic, political and historical modes of inquiry in

---

The authors would like to acknowledge the comments of Simon Archer of the University of Lancaster, John Hughes of the London Graduate School of Business Studies and Janine Nahapiet of the Oxford Centre for Management Studies. The financial support of the Anglo-German Foundation for the Study of Industrial Society is also gratefully acknowledged.

the search for a better understanding of the accounting condition. Rather than being content to explore <u>within</u> any particular accounting context, they are striving to gain an understanding <u>of</u> how particular accountings have come to be as they now are and the processes by which they, in turn, will change.

A RANGE OF INQUIRIES

In the comparative accounting area, for a time some scholars sought to relate accounting to its social setting by trying to classify the array of internationally diverse accounting practices in terms of the institutional contexts in which they emerged and now function (cf. Mueller, 1967). Seeking to create a more readily comprehensible order, they sought to distribute accounting into a number of mutually exclusive categories. At that stage in the development of our knowledge certain major dimensions of differentiation appeared to exist and for a time the resultant simplicity was found to be useful, even if tentative. It did seem helpful, for instance, to contrast those countries where the development of accounting could be seen as being steered by professional associations and business enterprises with those where accounting was a more explicit instrument of the state, taking the form of either codified and standardized practice or an active instrument
390 of national economic and social management. However in the social arena such static forms of categorical knowledge are rarely satisfactory for long. For one thing, the very acceptance of such major dimensions of differentiation focuses inquiry onto the exceptions and the border line cases. More importantly however, practice itself is emergent, not having to follow the bounds of intellectual categorizations. So at the very time when such simplifying conceptions were being articulated, the shifting structures of many economies started to put greater emphasis on the role of accounting in the public as well as the private domain and in many countries the state itself started to challenge more actively the basis of professional autonomy and power in the accounting area. So before too long, a new diversity was in the process of being created, demanding afresh a means for its comprehension and understanding.

Perhaps aware of such difficulties, other scholars have placed more direct emphasis on understanding the conditions giving rise to particular manifestations of accounting and the processes inherent in accounting change. Although often operating outside of any explicit comparative context, they nevertheless have started to probe into the processes through which particular accountings have developed and gained their significance, and the social and institutional conditions which have been associated with their emergence and functioning. As a result of such discrete inquiries we are now starting to gain some useful insights into the roles which accounting played in enabling the creation and development of the modern business enterprise (Chandler, 1962; Chandler and Daems, 1979; Johnson, 1975 and 1978; Litterer, 1961 and 1963; Hughes, 1979), the ways in which accounting practices furthered the dissemination of the broader social concerns which were reflected in the early 20th century "efficiency movement" (Litterer, 1961; Wells, 1978) and into the institutional processes of accounting standard setting and regulation (Benst^n, 1976; Horngren, 1973; Moonitz, 1974; Watts and Zimmermann, 1979; Zeff, 1972).

All of these studies, and others like them, are helping to provide a basis for a wider consideration of the accounting craft. By seeing its roles and effects as being contingent upon the institutional nexus within which any particular manifestation of accounting temporarily resides, such scholars are trying to articulate theories of accounting which provide some understanding of the extent of accounting diversity and the processes of accounting development and change.

Our own investigations seek to further such inquiries by providing some understandings of the social nature of the accounting craft. The substantive problem of our current research concerns the simultaneous emergence of interest in and forms of practice of what has come to be called "social accounting," "social reporting" and "social auditing" in a number of major industrial nations. We very quickly discovered, however, that it was difficult to understand such phenomena without having a quite detailed appreciation of the social conditions underlying their emergence and current functioning. Not only did the common labels used in the area disguise major differences in contemporary national concerns, orientations and practices, and therefore the very different social meanings which were being given to the technical practices, but also the phenomena themselves, although so often seen as new, perhaps not too surprisingly had antecedents which could have influenced current conceptions of what was possible and desirable. Our desire to understand the emergence and functioning of a variety of "social accountings" therefore gave rise to a wider interest in understanding accounting as a social rather than technical practice--a form of practice which gains its significance from the networks of social relationships in which it is embedded. Social and historical perspectives were quite explicitly introduced into a comparative study of the novel and the new in order to illuminate the processes of emergence and change.

To date more detailed consideration has been given to the growing interest in value added accounting in the United Kingdom (considered in some European countries as a constituent part of a corporate social report); to the emergence of social accounting practice and theory in the USA; and to the relationship between changes in work organization (particularly the development of so-called semi-autonomous working groups) and the emergence of forms of socio-economic calculation in Sweden. At this stage in our inquiries only partial consideration has been given to how social, political and legislative changes have influenced accounting for and to labour; to the emergence, particularly in the United Kingdom, of forms of "counter-accountings" as other social interests, including the organized labour movement, have attempted to provide their own accountings of corporate actions; to the ways in which the development of accounting has been related to the progressive extension of the interventionist roles of the state; and to the political economy of inflation accounting.

Whilst these studies remain emergent, often serving to extend rather than reduce the agenda of the unknown and the problematic, nevertheless already they have provided rich insights into the complexity of the accounting context. However for the present discussion of some aspects of the international development of accounting in the 20th century we can do no more than point to a few tentative issues which have emerged during the course of these investigations.

We start by considering those institutional arenas for the development of accounting discourse and practice which entered into the present century--the organization, be it in the private or the public domain; the interface between the business organization and the capital markets; the interventionist platforms of the state; and the institutions of professional accounting practice. Thereafter we discuss how each of these arenas has continued to serve as a platform for the development of accounting in the present century, often becoming, in the process, increasingly interdependent in effect. Some of these developments have had a life and autonomy of their own. The employment of accounting specialists in organizations, for example, provided a basis for the further extension of organizational accounting practice (à la Parkinson?); the institutionalisation of capital market disclosure and the use of accounting information for tax purposes themselves resulted in further identifiable changes in accounting practice; and the professionalization of the accounting craft provided the basis for further developments as a result of the needs for professional regulation, control and even education. However other developments in accounting practice and discourse have emanated from the involvement of some or all of these institutional arenas in the articulation and attempted resolution of more general issues and concerns. To illustrate such processes, some brief consideration is given to the ways in which accounting practice has become implicated in the management of national economic policy, in conditions of both growth and decline, the conduct of war and the emergence of pressures for greater organizational accountability and the extension of democracy and participation into new areas of social life. Finally, to illustrate the interplay between such issues, the institutional arenas and of accounting change, some consideration will be given to the emergence and development of some specific forms of accounting practice.

The discussion is implicitly rather than explicitly international in orientation. Our discussion points to a number of tendencies in the development of accounting in industrialised nations. Hopefully, however, it will illustrate how a comparative analysis of the ways in which accounting has become implicated in wider issues and concerns has at least the potential to provide a better understanding of the functioning of accounting as a form of social calculative practice.

THE 20th CENTURY INHERITANCE

The changing institutional structure of social and economic life in the 18th and 19th centuries provided the basis for the more rapid development of the accounting craft. The emergence of the factory and later of the public company (or its equivalents), the crystallization of the modern state and the institutionalization of areas of professional life, education and the mechanisms for corporate financing resulted in an enormous increase in the demand for formal flows of information and associated techniques for information collection, processing and reporting. Such information was needed to manage and regulate the emergent institutions, to provide for their internal coherence and integration, to shape the distribution of valued resources and to establish those patterns of visibility on which particular forms of dominance and power could be based. This development of accounting had a role to play in satisfying most of these demands, but by no means a unique one. The same period witnessed the emergence or further development of numerous other specialised mechanisms for information processing, including that of stat(e)istics itself (Wilcox, 1934), of the compilation of information for social and economic administration and of instruments for social and economic categorization in the law, in medicine and in business and economic life.

As a result of these developments, 20th century industrialised nations inherited a great deal of accounting as we now know it, including most of those institutional arenas which now influence the development of accounting practice and discourse.

Accounting and Organizational Management

In both the business organization and in the machinery of the state many of the bases for present day accounting had been laid by quite early in the present century. Costing practices, for instance, had been developed which could cope with new forms of technology and organizational practice, often in the latter case playing both an enabling as well as a responsive role. The role of internal accounting in the establishment of particular patterns of order and motivated action had been established, particularly in the context of the development of the efficiency movement and of forms of scientific management (Wells, 1978). Indeed such developments came to constitute an important element of the substance of formal rationality in organizations (Weber, 1978). In addition, through the creation of partial but strategic patterns of internal visibility and of mechanisms for co-ordination and control (Litterer, 1963), accounting had started to demonstrate that it had a role to play in forging a more centralised control of diverse operations, a potentially important achievement in an era of growing organizational size and complexity. In ways such as these what had started as a rather specific organizational craft based on the routine of internal financial administration began to establish a basis for itself as a more significant, influential and pervasive form of organizational practice; a basis which when once achieved could perhaps provide for its continued development and expansion as a more autonomous (that is, less explicitly and precisely dependent on either other practices within the organization or its continual justification) form of practice.

Accounting and the Establishment of External Accountability

Whilst interpretations of the historical development of the disclosure of accounting information to the capital markets remain contested, in some countries at least, the fact of disclosure does not. Whether resulting from the calculated acts of an interested corporate management or the intervention of the state, accounting practice had become associated with the ambiguous ideals of corporate disclosure and accountability.

Moreover the history of the struggles for the release of corporate information (Hughes, 1979), accounting and otherwise, reveals that the concept of accountability was, and remains, one that was far broader in scope than the practice of accounting itself. Even early demands for the provision of accounting information had been articulated alongside possibilities for changing the patterns of corporate governance, for the more informal dissemination of information to privileged agents of financial interests, for audits, independent or otherwise, and for changes in the regulatory role of the state. Then, as now, accounting represented a rather particular tactic in a wider and more all embracing strategic debate.

Accounting and the Developing Interventionist Role of the State

From the perspective of today it is tempting to presume that only recently has the state taken an interest in accounting practice. An examination of the historical record provides many bases for questioning such a

presumption however. From the very earliest days the administrative concerns of the state had implicated it, often centrally so, in the development of accounting practice, with the administration of taxation being particularly important in this respect. Indeed there is reason to believe that the role which corporate accounting information served as a basis for the taxation of business enterprises already had started to influence the norms of accepted practice and principles for the recognition of revenues and expenses by the turn of the century, in some countries at least. In other contexts the state already had started to adopt a more explicit and direct interest in the practice of bookkeeping and commercial accounting, providing, in many cases, a direct stimulus for technical developments. Whilst many of the factors behind such interventionist concerns have still to be documented and analysed, even at this stage in the development of our understanding we can point to the problems stemming from the conduct of war (with accounting being implicated in the administration of naval shipyards, for example, and the control of a constrained war-time economy) and the management of economic crisis (with early French requirements for financial disclosure being implicated in the response to a period of severe economic decline (ten Have, 1976)). Certainly the presumed modern origins of the establishment of the state as an arena for the development of accounting discourse and practice need to be reconsidered as the many
394 and varied roles played by forms of economic calculation in the nexus between the state and the institutions of the community come to be recognised and studied.

The Professionalisation of the Accounting Craft

More recent developments have demonstrated the significance which the 19th and early 20th century institutions of a professionalised accounting have had as arenas for the conduct of accounting deliberation and debate. Juxtaposed between the practice of the craft and other agents and agencies striving for its regulation and control, paradoxically their establishment might have represented an early stimulus for the development of a body of accounting discourse (and possibly "theory") which could be abstracted from the intriquacies of its practical commercial setting. Today such a role is attributed, however imprecisely, almost exclusively to academicians. However the emergent needs of a profession to train, to regulate and to codify might themselves have provided a basis for a powerful interest in a more abstract body of accounting thought. Certainly more contemporary developments have demonstrated the way in which these emergent institutional structures have survived to serve such roles.

The accounting inheritance received by the present century was a substantial one. Although there remains a desperate need for further detailed historical inquiry, it would nevertheless appear that many of the institutional arenas in which subsequent international accounting discourse and practice were to take place had been established by the turn of the century, even if the issues which triggered their establishment and development might be different from those which were to foster their continuation and subsequent influence. To some of those subsequent issues we now turn.

SOME ISSUES FOR CHANGE AND DEVELOPMENT

The establishment of such institutional arenas itself provided a basis for the continued development of the accounting craft. Within organizations accounting had started to become a specialised endeavour.

Although we know all too little of the early ways in which the practice of accounting was organized and structured in business organizations, and of how these did and still do vary from country to country, the rapid expansion of a media for practical debate and illumination itself points to the emergent possibilities for forms of practical interchange and diffusion which increasingly had modes of existence and functioning of their own (Jenks, 1960). Practice could therefore develop some autonomy, searching for, as well as responding to, organizational needs and meanings. And the growing professionalization of the craft only furthered such tendencies as embryonic professional and educational institutions started to concern themselves with the training of apprentice members. Similarly the acceptance of the interests of the capital markets and of the state in the accounting domain provided a further basis for developments. Dissatisfactions could then be articulated and correcting actions taken. And the state, in particular, had a basis on which it could start to elaborate its interests in the roles which economic calculations, including forms of accounting practice, could play in its own economic management and interventionist policies.

We would venture to suggest that in ways such as these accounting started to develop a life of its own. Given its embodiment in such powerful institutional arenas, the continued significance and expansion of ac- 395
counting could stem from the fact that it existed rather than from any precise roles which it eigher might or should serve. Indeed such roles were now actively to be created, with many, including some writers of academic texts, thereafter striving to attribute and inculcate underlying rationalities and meanings to these (Burchell et al., 1980; Watts and Zimmerman, 1979).

However other accounting developments of the present century were to be more dependent on an active inter-change between accounting and other forms of organizational and social practice. Problems were to arise which, although perhaps not necessitating, at least could provide a basis for the elaboration and expansion of the accounting craft. Consideration is given in the present paper to three such issues or problems from amongst the many that could be cited: the conduct of war, the management of national economic policy in conditions of both growth and decline, and the emergence of pressures for greater organizational accountability and the extension of democracy and participation into new areas of social life. In each case we will attempt briefly to illustrate how the issues activated accounting developments in all or many of the institutional arenas.

The Conduct of War

The contribution which the conduct of war has made to management practice has yet to be analysed. Many indicators point to its immensity however. For instance in the UK and the USA, at least, personnel administration was initially to flourish, even if thereafter to temporarily decline, during the 1st World War as a consequence of the extremely tight labour market conditions, explicit government interventions requiring the establishment of personnel departments and the carrying out of manpower planning in plants manufacturing munitions, war supplies and ships, and the "discovery" shortly before the war of personnel turnover (Eilbert, 1959). Indeed the U. S. army even went so far as commissioning an assessment of economic consequences of the latter--an early form of human resource accounting! Many of the practices which now constitute personnel management, such as recruitment procedures and attitude testing, also owe their early development to the military organizations of such times (Baritz, 1960). In the 2nd World War the bases of operational research were established and the conduct of the "Cold War" stimulated the development in NASA and other aero-space organizations of many of today's more complex forms of organization, including matrix and project structures and their attendant information and control systems (Chandler and Sayles, 1971).

The administration of war has had a no less influential effect on accounting practice, both directly and indirectly. The constaints which the conduct of war introduces into an economy increase the salience of many forms of economic information. At the level of the state there is a need to plan, to allocate, to restrict and to divert. Such needs provided a basis for a renewed interest in the development of standardized flows of enterprise level accounting information in a militarised Germany in the 1930's (Singer, 1943), for instance, and were also to stimulate the development of forms of both national accounting and performance budgeting in the UK and the USA during the 2nd World War. Similar pressures had been evident in earlier confrontations. Then the state in many countries had not only shown an interest in the financial administration of its own military operations (Crick, 1950; Walkland and Hicks, 1960)
396 but had also gained an interest in the efficiency of organizations manufacturing war supplies on its behalf, often directly demonstrating the possibilities by installing financial control procedures in governmental operations and urging, or in some cases requiring, similar innovations in other organizations. The practice so established often then went on to provide a precedent for subsequent industrial and commercial practice.

Indeed military preparation has continued to be a source of innovation in the cost and management accounting area. With an increased scale of expenditure, and continued pressures for political and civilian control, questions of both management and accountability have been raised. The latter have given rise to more thorough mechanisms for both financial and operational audit and often, as in the USA for example, a renewed interest in uniform accounting practice (Shakleton, 1977). However the management problems have been no less significant. Indeed one could argue that many of the most significant developments in management accounting and control practice have emanated from the defence, and particularly the aero-space, sectors. The role of the RAND corporation in the development of PPBS and cost-effectiveness analysis must be noted in this respect, as well as the development of project orientated planning, information and control procedures in NASA.

No doubt further inquiry could isolate other linkages between the conduct of war and the development of accounting practice both in business organizations and the agencies of the state, and at the interfaces between them. As yet, for instance, we know all too little about the stimulus which periods of high wartime profitability, and taxation, might have given to financial accounting practice or to the ways in which debates over the morality of such receipts might have furthered debates over the accountability of the enterprise. Nor are we familiar with the processes through which accounting innovations originating in the context of war and military preparation have been diffused into other institutional arenas and problem areas. Such questions only serve to point to the potential for further enquiry into what has been a surprisingly neglected, although seemingly influential, area of practice.

The Management of National Economic Policy

The present century has given a particular prominence to economic matters in national deliberations and debates. Be it in the context of the formulation of policies orientated towards economic recovery or the continuation of growth, "the economy" as such has been constituted as a special object for intervention and management by agencies of the state. Such policies have naturally resulted in greater significance being given to modes of economic calculation. Measurements of GNP, for instance, have become more important as they have come to be seen as objectives of political policy rather than as instruments for economic management and control. And in trying to articulate and further such economic policies, the state has provided a basis for significant elaborations of mechanisms for economic calculation either directly by requiring the provision of information to itself or others or indirectly by formulating policies, the implementation of which requires extensions of calculative practice.

The impacts which economic crises have had on accounting are familiar to us all. The crises in Germany in the 1920's, for instance, provided the stimulus for at least the consideration of inflation accounting. And whilst the wisdom of the establishment of the SEC in the USA in the 1930's has been, and is still being, questioned, its basis in the Great Crash and its subsequent influence are not. Elsewhere too the corporate collapses and failures which have signalled the arrival of economic downturns have repeatedly resulted in examinations of the adequacy of accounting practice and renewed endeavours by both professional bodies and the state to regulate and order the practice of the accounting craft and its "conceptual" and legal underpinnings.

Perhaps no less influential has been the impact which such crises have had on the practice of management accounting. For the phenomenon of being "newly poor," as some researchers in Sweden (Olafsson and Svalander, 1975) have called it, has proved to be an influential stimulus to the introduction of elaborated systems of financial administration and control in business and, as more recently demonstrated in many countries, public organizations alike. In both cases, however, the effects which such elaborations have had on financial effectiveness remain equivocal as yet since neither research nor practice has managed to untangle the complexities of the desirable trade-offs between constraint and flexibility in such situations of crisis.

The state itself may have been a more active agent for the development of accounting practice in the context of policies for economic recovery and growth, particularly in the post World War II era. Numerous European governments, for instance, invested heavily, although with unknown success, in mechanisms for propagating the desirability of management accounting practices as instruments for the achievement of industrial efficiency and competitiveness. Similarly, with the aim of stimulating industrial investment, many direct modifications were made in national accounting practices for depreciation and reserves, including in some instances early, if not prolonged, experiments in inflation adjusted accounting, and more indirect changes, and problems one might add, have stemmed from the increasing use of the corporate taxation system as an active instrument of national econonic policy. The increasing use of microeconomic policies orientated towards intervention in the setting of wages and prices, for instance, also has resulted in further elaborations of calculative and accounting practice in business organizations, agencies of the state and at the interface between them. In the United Kingdom, for instance, claims have been made that the activities of the Price Commission have served as an important stimulus for the development of costing practice and the repeated use of national incomes policies has not only highlighted the significance of accounting for labour costs directly but also has resulted in a renewed interest in accounting for both the achievement and distribution of productivity.

Such examples serve to illustrate how accounting practice has operated and developed within the context of a problem arena of enormous complexity and significance, the connections of which to accounting were created rather than given. Also in demonstrating how accounting, as a form of calculative practice, has operated at the nexus between the institutions of business, the state and professional life, they point to the need for richer understandings of the conditions under which accounting has functioned and changed, and continues to do so.

Organizational Accountability and Demands for the Extension of Economic Democracy

398 Many of the struggles for financial accounting change have been conducted under the name of accountability. On this basis early representatives of financial interests claimed to have the right to receive accounting reports and the state often intervened under a similar banner. Accountability, however, is an emergent rather than determined concept, subject to continued reinterpretation. Therefore claims for greater accountability, and accounting disclosure, have continued to be made. Indeed many legislative interventions in the accounting area still reflect the contentiousness of such ends.

However financial interests have not been the only ones either to press such claims or, thereby, to have an influence, direct or otherwise, on accounting practice. In the last century the state increasingly started to act in the name of the "community" or the "public at large," requiring changes in management practice and behaviour, in employment policies in particular. Even such early changes are claimed to have resulted in an awareness of the interface between the economic and the social. As Stacey notes in English Accountancy: 1800-1954 (pp. 16-17):

> Humanitarian feelings and the pursuit of industrial efficiency rarely have a common denominator but in the case of the Factory Acts it would be difficult not to acknowledge their interdependence. Much of the legislation of the nineteenth century generally was to bestow greater freedom on sections of the population hitherto lacking social and economic status. Employees were less and less capable of exploitation. In an oblique way legislation of this type hastened the everwidening use of accountancy. The reasons for this belief are not far to seek. The costs of production rose as soon as a brake was put on the indiscriminate employment of children and adults. The profit margins of power-driven factory production in its salad days could doubtless absorb the inroads made into them as a result of the increased wages bill, but at the same time entrepreneurs had to exercise stricter control over outgoings to effect all possible savings in the process of manufacturing. This economy

drive could not be put into practice without some rudimentary information culled from the accounts. The larger the undertaking, the greater were the opportunities for saving and the importance of keeping accurate records of costs grew *pro tanto*.

Wider claims for organizational accountability certainly have been a characteristic of more recent debates and have now started to influence accounting practice in both the private and public sectors. Pressures for greater governmental accountability, for instance, are resulting in quite substantial innovations in state audit practices in many nations. And pressures for the greater accountability of the business enterprise have started to result in the greater disclosure of social and environmental as well as economic information and a growing number of experiments with forms of social accounting, reporting and auditing. Initially starting in the USA, by now experiments have been made in France (where the publication of the Bilan Social is now required by law), Germany (where companies are starting to standardize practice), Japan, the Netherlands, Sweden, Switzerland and, from without rather than from within the organization itself, the UK. As yet such practice remains at too early a stage to justify an appraisal. The ideals have still to be crystallized, the stimuli for action are widely variant and methodologies remain diverse, emanating as they do, from a mixture of the needs to legitimise, to respond and to inform. Nonetheless the widespeead diffusion of interest in and experimentation with the concept itself points to the changes that might be taking place in our concepts of the social location of the business enterprise and the roles which accounting practice might serve.

Perhaps in many countries the nature of accounting as a social artifact is in the process of being illustrated in an even more pronounced way as a result of the increasing articulation of the interests of the labour movement. Of course accounting practice has always had to grapple with the complexities of accounting *for* labour. Technological and organizational changes which affected the status of labour gave rise to new methodologies for its accounting characterization and analysis, even in the last century. More recently, however, not only have such changes continued, but accountants have also been forced to give more explicit attention to accounting *to* labour and, in a few places, at least, to responding to accounts produced *by* the labour movement itself.

Not too long ago human resource accounting could still be seen as a rather bizarre phenomenon, the creation of a group of missionary academicians rather than something which could claim to have direct relevance to current practices. In fact that still might be the view of the majority of the specific and highly specialised practices which have come to be advanced under the HRA label. But not, we would venture to suggest, of the broad problem areas which human resource accounting sought to address. For the advancing pace of social legislation which has sought to improve conditions of work and security of employment, and the developing interests of both the state and enterprises themselves in the training (Oatey, 1970) and mobility of labour as a resource, have served to problematise many current practices for accounting for labour. Not only is the status of labour as a "variable cost" now highly uncertain, if not actually superceded in many cases, but we also have witnessed a renewed interest in the technical aspects of accounting for such matters as training and the consequences of absenteeism and turnover, in the means for isolating the contribution of labour to productivity improvements, and in related concepts such as human capital. Practice as well as theory is certainly developing in such areas in most industrialized nations and in a recent poll of management accountants in the United Kingdom, such concerns were seen as the most important ones at the present time.

The changing social position of labour has also resulted in an interest in the means of disclosing information to employees and trade unions. In this area practice has often proceeded the law, as management has sought independently to inculcate the advantages of the profit motive. Increasingly, however, accounting for labour is being seen in terms broader than the mere communication of aims and intent. Under the banner of the rights of labour to participate in corporate management, legislation has strived to provide a basis on which representatives of labour could receive that information which is necessary for the conduct of collective bargaining and often, for the participation of labour in corporate policy formulation and decision making. Indeed in some countries requirements, if not practices, are now starting to move beyond those that can be readily characterised under the disclosure label. In Sweden, for instance, trade unions now have certain rights to access corporate information.

Indeed the recent Swedish changes already are stimulating interest in
400 whether it is possible to formulate a view of accounting from the perspective of labour. Research has been commissioned by the Swedish Accounting Standards Board to such ends. In Germany the trade unions themselves have issued a counter social report, challenging the facts and interpretations given in a management initiated version, and consideration also is being given to the possibilities for generalising such experiences. And in the United Kingdom continued economic decline has resulted in a whole series of "counter-accountings" of corporate actions and performance. Often stemming from the threats of redundancy, these, and the other aforementioned experiments, point to the ways in which issues of organizational accountability might be giving rise to questions related to the means by which accountings might be made by interests in the organization being considered alongside the more traditional concerns with accountings for and to such interests.

ISSUES, ARENAS AND THE CONDITIONS FOR ACCOUNTING CHANGE

The intricate ways in which changes in accounting practice emanate from the interrelationships between the institutional arenas in which practice flourishes and the issues which create the pressures for and the possibilities of change are little understood. Research has hardly started to unravel either the complexities which surely exist at the descriptive level or the conceptual structures and schemas which might help us at least to appreciate the processes involved, if not actively master them for our own ends. Yet, we would venture to suggest, the need to understand is a real one for so many of the crises and debates which currently afflict the accounting craft are so richly embedded in the nexus of issues and institutional interrelationships that simple procedural and technical understandings in isolation are nc longer sufficient either to illuminate or to guide.

Take, for example, the case of inflation accounting in the United Kingdom. The fact of an inflationary economy (itself "known" through accounting means and significant because of the policies of the state) certainly was a stimulus for change. But that fact alone is not sufficient for providing an understanding of either the processes of the debate or its outcomes. Such an understanding would require an appreciation of the arenas in which the debate was conducted and the varied and changing issues which either stimulated action or were called upon to legitimise particular stances and proposals. The debate would need to be seen in the context of those problems which gave rise to a questioning of the state of accounting regulation and the establishment of a standard setting machinery controlled by the professional bodies, of the emergent relationships between the agencies of the state and a procession seeking to preserve its own autonomy, and of the shifting internal interests within the state itself. In the latter respect, consideration would have to be given to the changing issues with which inflation accounting was related, to those of accounting regulation, of taxation, of the role of indexation in macro-economic management and its possibly competing functions in the implementation of micro-economic policies for industrial recovery and growth. And as if that was not enough, attention also would have to be directed towards understanding the many different and often conflicting pressures which both national economic circumstances and the concurrent threat of a changing social power structure placed on the management of enterprises in different industrial and commercial sectors, the roles which calculative practice was seen as capable of serving to alleviate these, and the varied influence which the sectors had in the institutions which determined accounting policies.

Needless to say such an analysis has yet to be done! Even we still talk of the potential of a study of the political economy of inflation accounting. Not only would it require enormous effort, and a multitude of perspectives and skills, but it also surely would lead to a questioning of many preconceived notions of the roles which accounting practice serves and the ways in which it functions and changes, a hazardous endeavour at the best of times.

Our own preliminary analyses of the development of value added accounting in the UK certainly point to such possibilities (Berchell, Clubb and Hopwood, 1980). Selected because of the interest in the topic throughout Europe and the strength of the claims made for it as a "new" form of social practice in the accounting area, the analysis of the conditions of its emergence has pointed to the intricate ways in which it arose out of a varied constellation of issues, institutional arenas and bodies of knowledge. Although finally coming into prominence, in the UK at least, within the context of accounting standard setting and the consideration of ways for furthering corporate disclosure, the practice of value added accounting had also functioned within the context of the management of the conflicting pressures for efficiency and participation in enterprises and the effects which economic management policies of the state had had on enterprise level management practices. An investigation of the latter even enabled us to question the claims made for the novelty of the practice since abundant examples of its use were discovered in the immediate post World War II era.

When seen in such terms the emergence of a particular form of accounting "innovation" can appear to have as much to do with the application of prevailing bodes of knowledge in industrial relations, organizational psychology and economics as well as of accounting itself. Indeed so intertwined can be the emergence of practice in such contexts that conventional notions of cause and effect can be used to little avail in the analysis of such phenomena. Accounting change needs to be socially located in much more complex ways.

Similar insights are emerging from our studies of the development of forms of socio-economic calculation in Sweden. Early steps were made within the context of a management response to the labour market problems of the 1970's. Calculative innovation was intertwined with experimentation with new forms of work organization, part of a new alliance or configuration of the activities of personnel administration, financial management and production engineering, which strived to engender greater flexibility and resilience in existing modes of organization and management. But practice which was so created could be, and was, used in the context of other issues. With growing pressures for greater corporate accountability and for participation and co-determination, the same forms of socio-economic calculation, or developments thereof, were to serve new roles. In this way attempts were, and still are, being made to forge new internal and external reporting practices and, in one instance at least, to provide a calculative basis for the possibility of modified financial relationships between the enterprise and the state.

The conditions for accounting change are complex indeed. Whilst both technical and conceptual developments are required, to be influential they have to root themselves in that dynamic constellation of institutions and issues which constitutes the accounting context. In that constellation, both practice and the roles and functions which it serves are subject to change as new issues emerge, new linkages to accounting established and new needs for economic and other forms of calculation arise. On the surface, such changes often have the appearance of the novel and the new. In most cases, however, that represents the mere tip of that little known iceberg which constitutes accounting practice in its social setting. And where the claims for novelty can be made with some justification, the discontinuity that exists is invariably one that is set at the complex of interfaces between accounting and other forms of social practice.

CONCLUSION

The growing recognition of the diverse nature of accounting practice across both time and space is providing a new agenda for those interested in understanding the development and functioning of the accounting craft. Rather than focusing exclusively on its technical adequacy and the determination of procedural rationales, scholars are now starting to ask questions about how particular accounts have come to be as they now are, how they have functioned and now function in social and institutional terms, and the consequences which they might have for both social and economic action.

What, for instance, are the conditions which stimulate accounting innovation? Just how are pressures for change articulated, and by whom? How, for example, has accounting come to be implicated in issues of broad social and economic significance? And what have been the consequences of such calculative innovations? In particular, what enabling roles might accounting have played? How, for instance, has it contributed to the emergence and functioning of the institutions of business and national life? Indeed how has it contributed to the very constitution of such discussive categories as "the state," "the organization," "the economy," and the criteria such as "efficiency" which are used in their assessment?

Unfortunately, for the time being, such questions only serve to illustrate the paucity of our existing appreciations of the accounting domain. Whilst we have a growing wealth of descriptive materials, we still have relatively few insights into the ways in which we might appreciate their significance. Prevalent conceptions *within* accounting which so often adopt an essentially unproblematic view of the craft are of little help in trying to understand the conditions under which accounting practice exists and changes. To do this we need appreciations *of* accounting which can problematise what has been taken for granted, locating, thereby, accounting within a nexus of social relationships and institutions, and illuminating, in the process, forces which provide bases for development and change.

The adoption of an international perspective is clearly not the only or necessarily the best way of achieving such an end. However it does have some potential. Just as the comparative analysis of religions provides a basis for isolating and studying the religious rather than the theological (see Hacking (1975) for a similar argument in relation to the history of science), so the study of the various manifestations of accounting practice might provide a powerful way for both scholars and practitioners to move beyond the intellectual constraints which are so often imposed by a focus on the mere practice of the craft itself. In such studies cultural, historical and social perspectives would all have vital roles to play.

Whether such studies will ever provide a basis for predicting, let alone steering, the future course of accounting development remains an open question however. At present their potential seems to reside within the hermeneutic rather than the technical tradition. Certainly the task of helping to illuminate and understand "what is" rather than either forecasting or creating "what might be" remains at least our primary concern.

If, however, we were nevertheless to cast our eyes towards the future, we can see no reason why many of the issues and concerns which have created the accounting present should not continue to forge the accounting future. Certainly questions concerning the regulation of the craft are as germane as they ever have been. The role of the state, and increasingly or supranational bodies such as the EEC, OECD and UN, continues to advance, implicating, in the process, both financial and management accounting practice. And we are witnessing the growing impact of the advancing claims for organizational accountability and, increasingly, the articulation of the right to receive information with which to influence, if not manage. The displacement of the centrality and potency of issues such as these indeed would require a radical discontinuity in both conceptions and practice.

Perhaps, however, at least some accounting research ought to consider the possibility of just such a radical discontinuity. Is it possible, we wonder, for more critical attention to be devoted to the entire accounting mission? More directly, could the accounting domain be radically different than it is now?

Certainly to date we appear to have uncritically accepted a seemingly never ending elaboration of accounting practice. Often in the name of admirable, although sometimes quite ambiguous ends, it has progressively invaded an ever expanding array of institutional arenas and social issues. Whether appealing to conceptions of efficiency, accountability, democracy or even, more recently, the quality of working life, accounting has become ever more deeply implicated in organizational practice. Moreover the organizational and social consequences of this constant extension of the accounting domain have tended to be assumed to be good. Rarely questioning the canons of conventional wisdom, we have tended to accept the prevalent explanations of both the advance of practice and its consequences.

And yet existing historical studies, of the "efficiency movement" for instance (Haber, 1964; Hays, 1959; Searle, 1971; Wells, 1978), suggest that accounting norms, in particular the one of "efficiency," do not provide an adequate basis for understanding the processes by which such an enormous investment has been made in calculative technology in organizations; nor do they provide anything like a sufficient basis on which to appraise the wider organizational and social consequences of that investment. More generally, we have remarkably few insights into whether today's accounting has or has not furthered those objectives in the name of which they were introduced (Hopwood, 1979).

Perhaps reflecting on how much of today's accounting mission is accepted uncritically, some research might at least move towards adopting a more critical stance. Just what processes, we wonder, have been involved in accounting's seemingly endless march forward? And what have been its consequences for organizational and social life? Ambitious and challenging though such questions may be, research orientated towards illuminating them might have at least some potential to make accounting become yet again what it is not, but in a very different sense than which this has occurred in the past.

BIBLIOGRAPHY

Ansari, S. L., "An Integrated Approach to Control System Design," Accounting, Organizations and Society, Vol. 2, No. 2 (1977).

Baritz, L., The Servants of Power (Wesleyan University Press, 1960).

Benston, G. J., Corporate Financial Disclosure in the UK and the USA (Saxon House, 1976).

Burchell, S., Clubb, C., Hopwood, A. G., Hughes, J., and Nahapiet, J., "The Roles of Accounting in Organizations and Society," Accounting, Organizations and Society (1980).

Carlsson, J., Ehn, P., Erlander, B., Perby, M-L., and Sandberg, A., "Planning and Control from the perspective of labour: a short presentation of the DEMOS project," Accounting Organizations and Society, (1978).

Chandler, A., Strategy and Structure (MIT Press, 1962).

Chandler, A., and Daems, H., "Administrative Co-ordination, Allocation and Monitoring: A Comparative Analysis of the Emergence of Accounting and Organization in the USA and Europe," Accounting, Organizations and Society (1979).

Chandler, M. K., and Sayles, L., Managing Large Systems (Harper & Row, 1971).

Cooper, D. and Essex, S., "Accounting Information and Employee Decision Making," Accounting, Organizations and Society, (1977).

Crick Report, The Report of the Committee on the Form of Government Accounts (H.M.S.O., Cmnd. 7969, 1950).

Eilbert, H., "The Development of Personnel Management in the United States," Business History Review (Autumn, 1959).

Gold, M., Levie, H. and Moore, R., The Shop Stewards' Guide to the Use of Company Information (Spokesman Books, 1979).

Haber, S., Efficiency and Uplift (University of Chicago Press, 1964).

Hacking, I., The Emergence of Probability (Cambridge University Press, 1975).

Hays, S., Conservatism and the Gospel of Efficiency (1959).

Hopwood, A. G., "Criteria of Corporate Effectiveness," in M. Brodie and R. Bennett, Managerial Effectiveness (Thames Valley Regional Management Centre, 1979).

Horngeen, C. T., "The Marketing of Accounting Standards," The Journal of Accountancy (October, 1973).

Houghton, K. A., European Accounting: An Annotated Bibliography (Institute of European Finance, University College of North Wales, 1979).

Hughes, J., The Rise of Directorial Capitalism and the Railway Industry: 1835-1865, Working Paper No. 79/2, Oxford Centre for Management Studies, 1979.

Jenks, L. H., "Early Phases of the Management Movement," Administrative Science Quarterly (December, 1960).

Johnson, H. T., "Management Accountancy in an Early Integrated Industrial: El du Pont de Nemours Powder Company 1903-1912," Business History Review (Vol. 49, 1975).

Johnson, H. T., "Management Accounting in an Early Multinational Organization: General Motors in the 1920's," Business History Review (1978).

Kubin, K. W., and Mueller, G. G., A Bibliography of International Accounting (3rd ed.; Graduate School of Business Administration, University of Washington, 1973).

406 Litterer, J. A., "Systematic Management: The Search for Order and Integration," Business History Review (1961).

Litterer, J. A., "Systematic Management: Design for Organizational Recoupling in American Manufacturing Firms," Business History Review (1963).

Merino, B., and Coe, T. L., "Uniformity in Accounting: A Historical Pesppective," Journal of Accountancy (August, 1978).

Moonitz, M., Obtaining Agreement on Standards in the Accounting Profession (American Accounting Association, 1974).

Mueller, G. G., International Accounting (Macmillan, 1967).

Oatey, M., "The Economics of Training With Respect to the Firm," British Journal of Industrial Relations (1970).

Olafsson, C., and Svalander, P. A., The Medical Services Change Over to a Poor Environment--"New Poor" Behaviour. Unpublished working paper, University of Linköping, 1975.

Searle, G. R., The Quest for Efficiency (Blackwell, 1971).

Shakleton, K., "Government Involvement in Developing Accounting Standards: (1) The Framework; (2) The Responses," Management Accounting (January and February, 1977).

Singer, H. W., Standardized Accounting in Germany (National Institute of Economic and Social Research, 1943).

Stacey, N. A. H., English Accountancy: A Study in Social and Economic History (Gee & Co., 1954).

Ten Have, O., The History of Accountancy (Bay Books, 1976).

Walkland, S. A., and Hicks, I., "Cost Accounting in British Government," *Public Administration* (Spring 1960).

Waterhouse, H. J., and Tiessen, P., "A Contingency Framework for Management Accounting Systems Research," *Accounting, Organizations and Society* (1978).

Watts, R., and Zimmermann, J. L., "The Demand for and Supply of Accounting Theories: The Market for Excuses," *The Accounting Review* (April, 1979).

Weber, M., *Economy and Society* (University of California Press, 1978).

Wells, M. C., *Accounting for Common Costs* (International Centre for Accounting Education and Research, University of Illinois, 1978).

Wilcox, W. F., "Statistics: History," *Encyclopedia of the Social Sciences* (Macmillan, 1934).

Zeff, S. A., *Forging Accounting Principles in Five Countries: A History and an Analysis of Trends* (Stipes Publishing Company, 1972).

Accounting, Organizations and Society, Vol. 10, No. 4, pp. 381–413, 1985
Printed in Great Britain

0361–3682/85 $3.00+.00
Pergamon Press Ltd

ACCOUNTING IN ITS SOCIAL CONTEXT: TOWARDS A HISTORY OF VALUE ADDED IN THE UNITED KINGDOM

STUART BURCHELL
Borough of Greenwich

COLIN CLUBB
Department of Management Science, Imperial College, London

and

ANTHONY G. HOPWOOD
London Business School

Abstract

Although the relationship between accounting and society has been posited frequently, it has been subjected to little systematic analysis. This paper reviews some existing theories of the social nature of accounting practice and, by so doing, identifies a number of significant conceptual problems. Using the case of the rise of interest in value added accounting in the United Kingdom in the 1970s, the paper conducts a social analysis of this particular event and then seeks to draw out the theoretical issues and problems which emerge from this exercise. Finally, the implications of these for the social analysis of accounting are discussed.

Accounting is coming to be seen as a social rather than a purely technical phenomenon. The social contexts of the accounting craft are starting to be both recognised and made more problematic. Albeit slowly, the ways in which accounting both emerges from and itself gives rise to the wider contexts in which it operates are starting to be appreciated. Accounting, in turn, also has come to be more actively and explicitly recognised as an instrument for social management and change. Attempts have been made to reform accounting in the name of its social potential. Proposals have been made for accounting to embrace the realm of the social as well as the economic, to objectify, quantify and thereby give a particular insight into the social functioning of organizations. To this end, attempts have been made to orchestrate social accountings, social reports, social audits, socio-economic statements, social cost–benefit analyses and accountings of the human resource.

However, despite such apparent manifestations of an intertwining of accounting with the social, relatively little is known of the social functioning of the accounting craft (Hopwood, 1985). Accounting seemingly remains embedded in the realm of the technical. Although it is now recognised that the social can influence the

* We wish to acknowledge the helpful comments of George Benston, Wai Fong Chua, David Cooper, Jeremy Dent, Dick Hoffman, John Hughes, Janine Nahapiet and Ted O'Leary. The financial support of the Anglo-German Foundation for the Study of Industrial Society is gratefully appreciated. One of the authors wishes to acknowledge the facilitative and supportive environment provided by the College of Business Administration, Pennsylvania State University, which greatly eased the final writing up of this study.

technical practice of accounting and that that, in turn, can mobilise and change the world of the social, the processes by which these intersections take place have been subject to hardly any investigation. Accounting has not been explored in the name of its social functioning or potential. The social has been brought into contact with accounting but the intermingling of the two has not been explored. As a result, little is known of how the technical practices of accounting are tethered to the social, of how wider social forces can impinge upon and change accounting, and of how accounting itself functions in the realm of the social, influencing as well as merely reacting to it. For to date the relationship of accounting to the social has tended to be stated and presumed rather than described and analysed.[1]

410 Recognising the very significant gap in present understandings, the present discussion merely aims to illustrate and discuss one specific instance of the intertwining of accounting and the social, namely the rise of interest in value added accounting in the United Kingdom during the 1970s. The contours of this event are outlined and an analysis conducted of the wider arenas in which such a form of accounting came to function. Drawing on this analysis, an attempt thereafter is made to explicate some of the implications for an understanding of the emergence of value added accounting in particular and the social functioning of accounting more generally. Initially, however, we discuss some existing understandings of accounting's relationship to the social. Our aim in so doing is to provide a basis for appreciating both the possibilities for and the difficulties of conducting a social investigation of the accounting craft.

ACCOUNTING AND SOCIAL CHANGE

No doubt reflecting the more general concerns of the social responsibility movement (Ackerman & Bauer, 1976; Vogel, 1978), a literature emerged during the 1970s which concerned itself more or less directly with the impact of social change on accounting (e.g. Bedford, 1970; Estes, 1973; Gambling, 1974; Gordon, 1978; Livingstone & Gunn, 1974; Vangermeersch, 1972). However, although a social challenge to accounting thereby was recognised, most of this literature accepted both the fact of social change and its relevance to accounting, seeking primarily to change and reform accounting in the name of its social context. Despite a proliferation in pleas, suggestions and possibilities for different accountings, very few attempts were made to explicate and develop any general description and characterisation of the processes involved in the interaction of accounting with its social context. Technical reform took precedence over social understanding once a necessity for change had been stated.

Gilling (1976) was one exception to this tendency. Although he too notes the fact of and argues the necessity for accounting change under the impact of environmental (social and technical) change, Gilling also attempted to provide some understanding of the underlying social and institutional forces at work. His animating concern was the lag that he perceived to have arisen in the adaptation process. Gilling argued that accounting change was lagging behind environmental change as a consequence of the incapacity of the accounting professions to decide, or rather agree, on the appropriate modifications to be made in accounting practice. This immobilisation of the agency of accounting change stemmed in turn from the absence of any one dominant point of view on accounting, or of what Gilling termed accounting "ideology"[2]. Thus the process of adjustment of accounting practice to changes in its environment was blocked not because accounting theory was in some sense inadequate but because of the clash of interests as they were

[1] One noteworthy exception to this tendency has been the work of Tinker. See Tinker (1980), Tinker *et al.* (1982), Tinker (1984) and Neimark & Tinker (forthcoming). Although there are a number of significant differences between the work of Tinker and ourselves, we nevertheless recognise the pioneering attempts he and his colleagues have made to investigate the social origins and functioning of accounting practice. Also see Cooper (1981).

represented by the different accounting ideologies. Each of these alone "could provide order and direction to accounting endeavour" (p. 70) but each also "provides little possibility of reconciliation or comprise with other views". According to Gilling the net effect of this impasse was that both the autonomy and the expertise of the accounting professions were under challenge — there existed a crisis:

> As a result of its failure to react to new environmental circumstances the accounting profession is facing something of a crisis; a crisis in part of public confidence and in part of identity (Gilling, 1976, p. 64).

Thus within Gilling's framework, accounting appears as something marked off from its environment. With the passage of time, the latter requires the former to change. Accounting thereby is seen to be something that is and certainly should be a reflective phenomenon. As the environment develops or evolves it requires accounting to fulfil different needs. The process of accounting change passes through the accounting professions and depends on their perceptions to determine precisely what adjustment is necessary. These perceptions are, in turn, structured by particular world views or ideologies which amongst other things are characterised by a number of assumptions concerning the basic properties, purposes and functions of accounting.[3]

Such a contingent perspective of accounting change is common to most discussions of the topic (see, for example, Bedford, 1970; Chambers, 1966; Flint, 1971). It is, however, open to enormous variation in its details, with considerable differences in the specification of the environmental changes to which accounting must respond.[4] Gilling's own specification was not very precise. He argued that the principal environment change in the last forty years has been "the recognition of the public character of accounting information" (Gilling, 1976, p. 65). This, he continued, had arisen out of public concern over the activities of the business corporation, as evidenced at the time of his writing by the debate over corporate social responsibility. The consequent search by the accounting profession for ways to improve the accuracy and utility of published financial statements resulted in, amongst other things, the creation of institutions for accounting standardization and regulation, themselves a significant new part of the accounting environment.[5] Others have identified the growing power of labour (Barratt

---

[2] Gilling (1976, p. 69) defined ideology in the following terms:

> All professions have a defining ideology, which in a general sense establishes a pattern of thought and a way of looking at the world for the profession. This pattern of thought defines the activity of the profession, its problems, and appropriate ways of approaching those problems. The behaviour of a profession towards its environment is a matter of perception of that environment. Once an image of that environment has been established, then behaviour will be determined by that image and the frame of reference that it creates. As long as image and perception are appropriate to the real world, behaviour will be appropriate to the real world. If perception does not correspond to the real world, behaviour will be inappropriate and irrelevant.

[3] Gilling (1976, p. 69) elaborated his views on the different and conflicting ideologies of accounting in the following way:

> Within accounting there is a latent ideological clash, frequently on issues of topical and lasting concern, between those who support the utilitarian view of accounting with its consequent piecemeal, case-by-case approach to the development of principles and practices, and those who seek to provide a sound, consistent theoretical base, to which all principles and practices can be related. Within those who are theory-orientated there exists further considerable differences of opinion between the current cash equivalents, the value to the owner, and the replacement cost schools of thought. To further cloud the issues there is the clash between those who see accounting as technology and those who see it as policy making.

[4] Even when there is some agreement over the specification of the environmental change, the significance attached to it may vary. There is, for example, no sense of threat or crisis in Churchill's (1973) comments on the search for corporate social responsibility and the concomitant emergence of a plethora of different social indicators and measurement techniques. There is rather a sense of an opportunity for the expansion of the accounting domain.

[5] Other commentators and theorists would fully agree with Gilling in identifying the emergence of such institutions of accounting regulation as being crucial for the subsequent development of accounting practice. However, different analyses

Brown, 1978; Carlsson *et al.*, 1978; Gold *et al.*, 1979; Hird, 1975), the increasing recognition of consumer rights (Medawar, 1978; Vogel, 1978), the acknowledgment of significant enternalities associated with the conduct of business (Estes, 1976; Frankel, 1978; Ramanathan, 1976) and changing political conceptions of corporate accountability as being amongst the important environmental changes which have influenced or should influence accounting theory and practice. Moreover for Gandhi (1976, 1978), environmental developments were characterised in terms of the emergence of the non-market economy. For him, the significance of this development was that it has increasingly made accounting an inadequate means of rational action given its unidimensional monetary
412 character. Gandhi exhorted accountants to "come to a collective realization that there is more to performance evaluation than financial indicators" (Gandhi, 1978).

The notion of the environment implicit in such contingent theories of accounting change is therefore a diffuse and only partially articulated one. Given the significance attached to accounting being or desirably being a reflective phenomenon, this introduces a large element of indeterminacy into such understandings of accounting change. Whilst , imperatives for change are recognised[6], the means for their explication and influence remain imprecise and relatively unexamined.

A different perspective on accounting change is provided by Wells (1976). In a sense Wells turns the contingency model on its head. He argues that the present crisis in accounting is less a question of a lack of adaption, on the part of accounting, to a changing environment, but more a product of virtually autonomous developments within accounting theory. Basing his analysis on the work of Kuhn (1970), Wells argues that a distinct, identifiable accounting disciplinary matrix emerged for the first time in the 1940s. This disciplinary matrix provided the framework for the work of normal science which subsequently, under the impact of criticism "by scholars, businessmen and in the courts", brought to light a number of anomalies within the body of accounting theory and it is these anomalies which engendered a crisis. During the 1960s and 1970s, so the argument goes, a series of *ad hoc* attempts were made to deal with the anomalies and criticisms. In part, at least, this resulted in a more general concern for the theoretical basis of accounting which, amongst other things, led to the 1960s being described as the "golden age in the history of *a priori* research in accounting" (Nelson, 1973, p. 4). However, far from resolving difficulties, these works of high theory instead served to "highlight the defects of the disciplinary matrix and loosen the grip of tradition". As a result there emerged a number of different schools of thought which tended to have different axiomatic starting points and were thus difficult to compare.[7] Each of these schools is in principle a candidate for a new disciplinary matrix, however, and Wells looks forward to the next stage in the development of accounting thought in which, according to Kuhn's schema, there "will be 'an increasing shift in allegiances' in favour of one of the alternatives" (Wells, 1976, p. 480).

would put the functioning of these bodies in an altogether different light. For Watts & Zimmerman (1978, 1979), for instance, accounting regulation appears as a wasteful and ill-fated maladaption. (Also see Watts, 1977.) The search for an agreed set of accounting principles on which to base regulation is doomed to failure because the different accounting ideologies discussed by Gilling mask a mass of necessarily different interests which are rooted in the different positions individuals occupy in the business environment. Further, the accounting standards actually reduce social welfare because of the existence of significant political transactions costs wich mean that bureaucrats cannot in general be assumed to act in the public interest. Also see Benston (1969, 1976, 1983). For a different view of the emergence and functioning of these bodies and their interest in and utilization of knowledge, see Hopwood (1984).

[6] For a critique of the notion of accounting imperatives see Burchell *et al.* (1980).

[7] One important aspect of the differences between the different approaches is that members of competing schools have different views of the phenomena which were the subject of their discipline. In particular, there were represented in the different schools of accounting theory, different conceptions of the business enterprise.

Wells' arguments are suggestive of the constitutive capacities of accounting. Rather than simply reflecting the context in which it operates, accounting has a power to influence its own context. Difficulties and disputes within accounting can engender accounting developments and a perception of crisis both internal and external to the specifically accounting domain. Accounting thereby is seen to give rise to developments which shape the context in which it operates. The environment of accounting can become, in part, at least, contingent upon the accountings of it.

In fact both Gilling (1976) and Wells (1976) move towards recognising the duality of accounting change. For although it is the constitutive capacities of accounting that tend to be stressed by Wells as compared to the reflective capacities which are highlighted in Gilling, both these writers offer some initial insights into a dialectic of accounting (in the case of Wells, accounting *theory*) and its environment. The environment, having previously partly been created by accounting, calls for changes in accounting:

> He [Kuhn] argues that the change takes place only after a serious malfunction has occurred in the sense that 'existing institutions (or practices) have ceased adequately to meet the problems posed by an environment that they have in part created' (Wells, 1976, p. 472).

> The interdependency of accounting and its environment results in change being brought about by a process of mutual adaption. Environmental demands lead to changes in accounting practice and changes in accounting practice lead to changes in environmental demands and expectations (Gilling, 1976, p. 61).

It would appear that however the tale is told, the environment–accounting contingency model cannot avoid tackling the seemingly indeterminate dualistic character of the process of accounting change that it proposes.[8]

Our study of value added accounting attempts to cast a little more light on the character of just such an accounting–society interdependence. In our case, however, it would perhaps be better to speak of an accounting–society interpenetration. In the discussion of value added accounting which follows we have not employed the categories of "accounting" and "society" as if they denoted two distinct, mutually exclusive domains. Rather attention has been focused on the specific practices and institutions in which the category "value added" appeared and functioned and on the contexts and the manner in which it has been mentioned and discussed. It will be seen that the social, or the environment, as it were, passes through accounting. Conversely, accounting ramifies, extends and shapes the social. 413

THE VALUE ADDED EVENT

The particular object of interest in this paper is "the sudden upsurge of interest in value added" (Cameron, 1977b) that occurred in the United Kingdom during the late 1970s.[9] The general contours of this event appear to be fairly uncontroversial and they therefore compromise the basic facts of the matter. These facts are that the concept "value added" appeared as an indicator of the value created by the activities of an enterprise in a number of different sites (private companies, newspapers, government bodies, trade unions, employer associations, professional accountancy bodies, etc.), functioning in a number of different practices (financial reporting, payment systems, profit sharing schemes, economic analyses, information disclosure to employees and trade unions, etc.), where before it had been largely absent or, at the most, an object of very limited sectional interest.

---

[8] A further discussion of the reflective and constitutive aspects of accounting change is given in Hopwood (1985). Also see Roberts & Scapens (1985).

[9] The discussion in this paper focuses on value added accounting in the U.K. However, at the same time attention also was being given to it in other European countries. See McLeay (1983). For developments in German see Dierkes (1979), Reichmann & Lange (1981), Schreuder (1979) and Ullmann (1979). For the Netherlands see Dijksma & Vander Wal (1984). In France interest was expressed in the idea of surplus accounting (see Maitre, 1978; Rey, 1978, pp. 132–134).

The widespread discussion of value added within the ranks of professional accountants commenced with its appearance in *The Corporate Report*, a discussion paper prepared by a working party drawn from the accountancy bodies, which was published by the Accounting Standards Steering Committee (now the Accounting Standards Committee) in August 1975. At least for accountants, this was the official debut of value added.

The Corporate Report recommended, amongst other things, a "statement of value added, showing how the benefits of the efforts of an enterprise are shared between employees, providers of capital, the state and reinvestment" (ASSC, 1975, p. 48). Subsequently a first draft of a consultative document entitled "Aims and scope of company reports", prepared by the Department of Trade, was issued on 9 June, 1976 for comment. This paper, which reads very much as a commentary on *The Corporate Report*, states:

> . . . our preliminary view is that the subjects identified in *The Corporate Report* which should be given highest priority for further consideration as candidates for new statutory disclosure requirements are:
> (a) Added Value;
> (b) Employee Report;
> (c) Future Prospects;
> (d) Corporate Objectives (*The Accountant*, 1 July, 1976, p. 13).

When the Government's Green Paper on *The Future of Company Reports* finally appeared in July 1977, one of the legislative proposals contained in it was for a statement of value added (Department of Trade, 1977b, pp. 7–8).

This policy debate in the realm of accounting regulation was paralleled by the phenomena of a number of companies using value added statements in their company reports and for reporting to employees. Fourteen companies (out of 300) in the Institute of Chartered Accountants in England and Wales' *Survey of Published Accounts* included value added statements in their annual reports for the year 1975–6 (ICAEW, 1978). This figure grew to 67 for 1977–78, 84 for 1978–79 and 90 for 1979–80 before declining to 88 in 1980–81, 77 for 1981–82 and 64 for 1982–83 (ICAEW, 1980; Skerratt & Tonkin, 1982; Tonkin & Skerratt, 1983). Other surveys indicate that more than one-fifth of the largest U.K. companies produced value added statements in the late 1970s (Gray & Maunders, 1980).

The exact incidence of the use of added value in employee reports is unclear, although several commentators mentioned its popularity in this context (e.g. Fanning, 1978). It also is of interest to note its use by several winners of the *Accountancy Age* competition for the best employee report, its advocacy for the purposes of explaining company performance to employees by the Engineering Employers' Federation (EEF, 1977) and its mention by the Trades Union Congress as a possible performance indicator in the context of a discussion of information disclosure to employees (TUC, 1974).

The Engineering Employers' Federation's advocacy of value added was a development of its position as presented in an earlier document, *Business Performance and Industrial Relations: Added Value as an Instrument of Management Discipline*, published by the Federation in 1972. As the title suggests, added value appears in this document as part of a discussion concerned with its use "as a practical tool of management" rather than simply as a form of presentation of financial information in company and employee reports. The particular area of decision making in which it was envisaged this "practical tool" could be brought into play was the one concerned with the utilisation of and payment for labour:

> The Federation therefore aims to encourage the use of added value as a discipline, so that all managers, with or without experience of accounting practices will appreciate the financial environment within which decisions affecting manpower are taken (EFF, 1972).

In the later 1977 EEF pamphlet the discussion of the applications of value added is taken further. Examination of its uses has shifted from simply describing how it may serve as a guide to management when formulating wages policy to describing how it may be linked more directly to earnings when serving as the basis of a value added incentive payment scheme (VAIPS). Moreover it should be noted that VAIPS's themselves became the focus of considerable interest. It has been estimated that 200–300 companies were operating, or about to operate, added value schemes in 1978 (Woodmansay, 1978).

In addition to the above uses of value added as a vehicle for information disclosure and as a basis for determining rewards at the level of the enterprise, the category also has appeared on several occasions in the context of policy discussions concerned with the performance of British industry (Jones, 1976, 1978; New, 1978). In addition it has been canvassed as the means of reforming company wide profit sharing schemes (Cameron, 1977a) and appears in stockbroker reports (Vickers da Costa, 1979) as a means of faciliating financial performance analysis.

The value added event, as we term it, already has stimulated some research and analytical reflection. In particular, four of the leading U.K. accountancy bodies — the Institute of Chartered Accountants in England and Wales, The Institute of Chartered Accountants of Scotland, the Institute of Cost and Management Accountants and the Association of Certified Accountants, commissioned and issued research reports on the subject of value added (respectively, Renshall *et al.*, 1979; Morley, 1978; Cox, 1979; Gray & Maunders, 1980). Our concerns however are somewhat different from those which motivated and characterise these reports. In each they very largely take for granted "the sudden upsurge of interest in value added". Value added is discussed in terms of its possible uses and the principles of measurement and forms of presentation that may be employed. As such, this discussion may be considered to be as much part or continuation of the value added event as it is a reflection on it. Insofar as an attempt is made to explain why this event took place, its occurrence is attributed to the phenomenon of social change:

> Accountants have reported on profit for many centuries. Why do we now need to report on Value Added as well? One answer is that the Value Added Statement reflects a social change: shareholders have become less powerful and central Government and organized labour have become more powerful (Morley, 1978, p. 3).

Indeed in the case of value added this is not an uncommon theme (see Pakenham-Walsh, 1964; Wilsher, 1974; Robertson, 1974) and it is precisely our interest in the relation between accounting change and social change that motivates this study of value added.

VALUE ADDED AND THE SOCIAL

On the face of it, the basic facts of the value added event appear clear enough. However, on closer inspection the picture becomes more complex and somewhat enigmatic. To begin with just what is value added? Rutherford (1977) responds to this question by advancing a definition drawn from Ruggles & Ruggles (1965, p. 50):

> The value added by a firm; i.e. the value created by the activities of the firm and its employees, can be measured by the difference between the market value of the goods that have been turned out by the firm and the cost of those goods and materials purchased from other producers. This measure will exclude the contribution made by other producers to the total value of this firm's production, so that it is essentially equal to the market value created by this firm. The value added measure assesses the net contribution made by each firm to the total value of production; by adding up all these contributions, therefore it is possible to arrive at a total for the whole economy.

However, as Rutherford goes on to point out, this definition does not provide a detailed prescription for the *calculation* of valued added. Indeed, he has pointed out elsewhere (Rutherford, 1978), as have other writers (Vickers da Costa, 1979; Morley, 1978), that calculative practice is very diverse. The treatment of depreciation varies (McLeay, 1983). A great deal of discretion exists as to the treatment of taxation, and so on. Futhermore, this calculative diversity is compounded by the fact that value added statements are presented in a number of different formats (tables, graphs, pie charts, pictures, etc.) which in turn bear a variety of different names ("value added", "wealth created", "where the money goes", etc) (see Fanning, 1978). There are clearly very many different value addeds.

Another curious feature emerges on inspecting the purported advantages of using value added. We already have indicated that the uses of value added are multiple — payment systems, company reporting, information disclosure to employees and trade unions, economic analysis, etc. What, however, is only rarely discussed is that the descriptions or specifications of the functioning of value added in any given organizational practice are commonly characterised by a form of duality. Value added is seen as a system of both determination and representation.

416 In the case of, for example, an incentive payment system (see Bentley Associates, 1975; Smith, 1978) value added is specified as a clearly defined financial category, the magnitude of which determines, according to certain well defined calculative procedures, a component of labour income. However, in addition to such a description of a particular system of *determination* there is usually associated a description of a system of *representation*, albeit that the latter is usually thoroughly intertwined with the former. The system of representation is itself composed of two strands. On the one hand, value added, it is argued, represents wealth; to be precise it represents the wealth created in the accounting entity concerned. Furthermore, so the argument goes, this representational property provides a basis for the improved calculation of certain important indices of enterprise performance, namely efficiency and productivity (e.g. Ball, 1968). On the other hand, it also is claimed that value added has the property of revealing (or representing) something about the social character of production, something which is occluded by traditional profit and loss accounting. Value added reveals that the wealth created in production is the consequence of the combined efforts of a number of agents who together form a cooperating team: "Value Added measures the wealth creation which has been built up by the cooperative efforts of shareholders, lenders, workers and the Government" (Morley, 1978, p. 3). It follows, therefore, that value added "puts profit into proper perspective vis-a-vis the whole enterprise as a collective effort by capital, management and employees" (ASSC, 1975, p. 49). Together these representational properties of value added are presumed to make it a means for both the more rational control of production and the achievement of a more harmonious and cooperative productive endeavour.

Now these expressive properties of value added, properties which provide it with both a technical and a social rationality, create a dilemma. For in order for value added to be able to represent the company as a cooperating team, the company must first have been constituted as such. On further investigation, however, it transpires that value added is seen as being able to serve as one means to this end. Value added therefore does not simply represent the company as a cooperating team, it also is seen as playing a positive role in the creation of this cooperative harmony. This is a point that was made very clearly some time before value added became such a widespread object of interest:

> The growth we are interested in is a growth of the national product, growth of the national product is achieved by making changes which lead to increased production by business undertakings. This will not be realised until production is seen by managers to be the central purpose of business and until the accounting profession re-orients its practices to this view. The profit and loss orientations of accounts, and notably of published accounts, is inimical to the improvement of industrial relations without which the growth in production desired will be attenuated.
>
> Although the antagonism between capital and labour has declined in recent years, the basic division of interest between maximising profits and providing maximum rewards for labour will continue to afflict industrial relations, unless we cease to see profits as the objective (Pakenham-Walsh, 1964, p. 268).

In such a context accounting is seen as a means of vision. A change in accounting implies a change in what is seen and hence a change in action. Social harmony might therefore not so much be revealed by value added as constituted by it. We are on the horns of the very dilemma which, as we already have indicated, is central to the society–accounting contingency model. On the one hand, it is asserted that value added may be accounted for by reference to wider changes and shifts in society (see Morley, 1978; Robertson, 1974; Wilsher, 1974). On the other hand, it now appears that this same social change might not be independent of the existence of value added. Value added is thus called upon to provide at least some of its own preconditions.

Whatever may be the logical problems that arise from the circularity that characterises attempts to explain accounting innovations in terms of their purported roles (also see Burchell *et al.*, 1980), it also is important to note that there does not exist any unanimous agreement over what the roles of value added are in the first place. The roles we have described above by no means exhaust the significance of this particular accounting innovation. In respect of its social rationality — value added as an expression of production as team production — it has been pointed out by Stolliday & Attwood (1978) that there is no obvious logical reason why the use of value added should not serve as a spur to workers in their attempts to totally eliminate the claims of others in its distribution. In this case value added still functions to reveal a "truth" about production, albeit a rather different one from production as teamwork. From yet another standpoint, the use of value added is viewed as a way of "misleading the workers" in an attempt to gloss "over the problem of profits" (see Hird, 1980; *Labour Research*, 1978). In this case value added serves as a device for *mis*representing reality. It presents a picture of a unity of interests in the financial performance of a given business organization, whereas in fact there exists a basic conflict of interests. Value added, it seems, is a distinctly equivocal social indicator.

There is yet another problem concerning the roles of value added and the statuses attributed to them. We have already pointed to calculative diversity as an important feature of the event we are seeking to unravel. Virtually all those writers who comment on it see this calculative diversity as subversive of those very properties that are often deemed to characterise value added:

> ... published statements of value added have, to date, been characterised by ambiguous terminology and by the treatment of items in ways inconsistent with the model of value added, and inconsistent within and between individual statements. The impression received by lay users of SVAs must be one of confusion — together possibly, with a conviction that value added, like profit can be made to mean whatever the accountant wishes it to mean (Rutherford, 1978, p. 52).

> The advantages offered by the Value Added Statement are, however, currently jeopardised by great diversity of practice (Morley, 1978, p. 141).

> Most of those [value-added statements] available seem to be designed to show, often by a "sales-cake" diagram, how much of the value-added goes to the employees themselves, how much the Government absorbs and how little the shareholder receives (Vickers da Costa, 1979).

Rather than shedding light, reducing conflict, etc. value added statements appear to be equally conducive to confusion, doubt and suspicion. This state of affairs problematises not only the social rationality of value added but also its technical rationality. Clearly there may be as many productivities and efficiences as there are added values. Thus value added is always more or less inadequate to its roles and the value added event cannot therefore be viewed simply as either the dawning of economic enlightenment or the expression of a particular social transformation.

The general upshot of this discussion is that the roles of value added do not of themselves provide a very satisfactory explanation of "the sudden upsurge of interest in value added". To summarise the argument so far: we encounter logical problems if we attempt to explain the widespread use of value added in terms of its roles; in any case, the precise specification of these roles is controversial; and, finally, the value addeds we actually encounter do not function flawlessly to achieve their appointed end. It is therefore suggested that these roles would be better considered as part of the phenomena to be explained and with this idea in mind it is possible to specify in rather greater detail our object of investigation and certain problems in respect of it which we wish to solve.

To the basic facts of the value added event we

now have to add that it was not a sudden and massive outbreak of a single, unambiguous concept of value added that occurred during the 1970s. There occurred instead the widespread discussion and use of a range of very particular, differentiated value addeds. These value addeds vary in definition and form of presentation and they came into the world in association with a number of properties. However historically contingent this association may be, the value addeds that we are interested in do not exist independently of these, their properties — namely the various roles that are imputed to value added and in the name of which it is frequently advanced. Although there is no unanimity in respect of these roles (or rationales), two have tended to predominate in the discussion and debate surrounding value added. It is frequently argued that value added is a superior means of the measurement, and hence pursuit, of wealth, productivity and efficiency. In addition it is also argued that it is the measure of income appropriate to production seen as a process involving the action of a team of cooperators. Finally, the circularity which is involved when seeking to explain the appearance of value added in terms of its roles coupled with the lack of general agreement over the specification of these roles enables value added to serve as the focus of a widely differentiated field of political interest. The very ambiguity of value added might, in other words, be implicated in its emergence and functioning. Depending on the point at which the circle of reasoning is entered, value added may be seen as a determining factor in the process of social change, a harbinger of social change or a consequence of social change. As Morley (1978, pp. 5–6) has expressed it:

> In saying that the Value Added Statement reflects social change one does not necessarily approve of the phenomenon. Indeed, one can distinguish three very different views on this:
>
> (i) One might report Value Added in order to hurry the change along and to give impetus to the movement of power from capital owners towards labour and central Government.
>
> (ii) One might report Value Added in order to alert the business community to this change, hoping that it may thereby be reversed.
>
> (iii) One might report Value Added in the hope that it would help one's 'new' masters to make sensible decisions.
>
> These three attitudes may perhaps explain why Value Added enthusiasts are to be found at both ends of the political spectrum. One encounters both left and right wingers who support this new Statement though their expectations from it differ greatly.

It is precisely this high differentiated social space within which the value added event took place that is our object of investigation. In what follows we have attempted to discover some of its preconditions — the factors that made possible the value added event. This work of description and analysis has been carried out by delineating three arenas, or complexes of issues, institutions, bodies of knowledge, practices and actions, within each of which there may be traced a descent — a succession of phases in the trajectory of a social movement. These movements intersected in the 1970s with value added serving as an important element in the triple conjucture. No doubt arenas other than the ones that we have outlined could be constructed. However the aim of this paper is *not* to provide an exhaustive description of the genesis and development of value added. Such a study would in any case take us back to before the Industrial Revolution and is therefore a task beyond the scope of the present paper (see, for example, Crum, 1982). The aim here is more modest: it is merely to shed a little descriptive and analytical light on the processes of accounting change.

THREE ARENAS

Each of the three arenas discussed below marks out a particular field of operations, namely the explication of standards for corporate financial reporting, the management of the national economy and the functioning of the system of industrial relations. Within each arena there has been charted the shifting patterns of relations between the various agencies functioning in these fields, e.g. the government, trade unions, the accounting profession, and the changes in their modes of operation and objects of concern, e.g. productivity, strikes, accounting standards. In each case some emphasis is placed on the interest in economic calculation and reporting in general and in value added in particular.

At this stage in the argument the movement in each arena, along with its associated "problems" and "solutions", has been handled as if it had a trajectory which was largely independent of those in the other arenas. This is no doubt an oversimplification. Clearly, macro-economic management concerns with payment systems were not without their implications for industrial relations. Conversely, the interest in industrial relations reform was not unrelated to certain postulated negative consequences of the existing structure of industrial relations for national economic performance. Similarly developments in accounting standardisation were related to both macro-economic issues, not least in the context of the inflation prevailing in the period, and the management of industrial relations in a time of a perceived growth in the power of the trade union movement. However the approach which we adopt at this stage does in our opinion have the merits not only of enabling the field of social relations in each of the arenas to be analysed more readily, allowing, in the process, both their autonomies and their interdependencies to be recognised, but also of facilitating an investigation of how issues such as economic performance and calculation were brought into relation with those of the status of employees and trade unions rather than presuming any *a priori* necessity for this to happen.[10]

The debate surrounding economic performance and industrial relations spilled over into a *pre-existing* debate in the area of corporate reporting which was concerned with determining the appropriate categories, principles and forms of presentation and distribution of corporate reports. While our treatment of accounting as a separate domain or arena has been motivated by a prior commitment not to handle accounting solely in a reductive or reflective manner, the discussion below goes some way towards indicating in a more positive fashion not only the components of this domain but also its articulations with other fields of action.

Accounting standards

As we already have observed, value added is characterised by considerable calculative diversity.[11] In a survey of published value added statements it was concluded that "It is difficult to capture systematically the degree of diversity present in the construction of statements of Value Added" (Rutherford, 1980). Moreover, such a heterogeneity of practice was seen as problematic for the roles, rationales and purposes that value added was seen and mobilised to serve. Rather than promoting efficient, harmonious, productive activity, the motley collection of value addeds was seen as subverting the very roles allocated to them precisely as a consequence of their variegated character. Amongst other things, the calculative diversity opened management to the charge of manipulation and bias. In the case of employee newsletters, for example, it was asserted that "most of those available seem to be designed to show . . . how much of the value added goes to the employees themselves, how much the Government absorbs and how little the shareholder receives" (*The Accountant*, 1978, p. 373).

One consequence of the perception that the practice of value added was not adequate to the roles commonly attributed to it was a call for its standardisation (Fanning, 1979; Vickers da

[10] We would argue that there is after all no obvious way in which notions of efficiency should be related to those of democracy. The nature of such a relationship has been subject to very little analysis and investigation, with the two notions inhabiting two distinct orders of discourse, namely those of economic and political theory. The same point applies to the relationship between the various practices concerned with the measurement and pursuit of efficiency and those concerned with the representation of interests.

[11] We would not wish to claim that value added is unusual in this respect. Most other key accounting indicators are subject to a similar ambiguity of definition and diversity of practice. In fact this characteristic of so seemingly an objective phenomenon could provide an interesting perspective for both technical and social analyses of the accounting craft.

Costa, 1979). The relevant agency in this respect was the Accounting Standards Committee. As a result of these and other[12] pressures, four of the accountancy bodies represented on the Accounting Standards Committee commissioned research studies of value added. The reports issued by both the Institute of Chartered Accountants in England and Wales (Renshall *et al.*, 1979) and the Institute of Chartered Accountants in Scotland (Morley, 1978) conclude in favour of value added reporting but add the caveat that "Standardisation of practice is a necessary precondition to any formal requirement" (Renshall *et al.*, 1979, p. 38), so as "to bring comparability to Value Added Statements and so safeguard the confidence of readers in the Statement" (Morley, 1978, p. 141). The study prepared for the Institute of Cost and Management Accountants was notably less enthusiastic and presented value added as just one more addition to the kitbag of management tools which may be usefully employed in connection with employee payment systems and public relations (Cox, 1979). The issue of standardisation was not raised in the report. The Association of Certified Accountants' study investigated the information needs of potential users of value added statements and reviewed existing corporate practice in the area before discussing measurement and disclosure policy (Gray & Maunders, 1980). Two approaches to the measurement of value added were identified, and although it was stated that "conceptually it would seem desirable that a consistent approach be adopted one way or the other" (p. 28), it also was argued that value added reporting should be "placed outside the restrictions established by convention" in order to facilitate its "imaginative development" according to the decision requirements of its potential users (p. 37).

There are two points of note concerning these four research studies. First, although all the reports commented on the sudden growth of interest in value added, an interest which provided the pretext for their discussions, none of them investigated the factors underlying this phenomenon. They all provided some sort of inventory of the various alleged advantages of using value added but none of them asked why these should have been perceived so suddenly or so late in the day. This point is important because if it can be shown that the emergence of value added was deeply implicated in certain wider socio-economic processes peculiar to a particular historical conjuncture, processes which moreover might have imbued value added with a particular historically contingent significance, then under different conditions debating the potential uses and advantages of value added might well be quite irrelevant. The second point relates to the fact that accounting policy in relation to the formulation of financial accounting standards has been fairly narrowly constrained to issues of measurement and forms of presentation. Until recently (Zeff, 1978), these problems have been deliberated very largely without reference to the likely implications of introducing particular standards. Indeed, in relation to the American experience, it has been argued that the dominant means of discourse in this domain — those furnished by accounting theory — have served to obscure the political character of the standard setting process and thereby have rendered ineffectual certain procedural reforms and research initiatives aimed at resolving the problem of obtaining agreement on accounting standards (Moonitz, 1974; Watts & Zimmerman, 1979; Zeff, 1978). In this sense it is ironic that the difficulties encountered by the Accounting Standards Committee in its standard setting programme — difficulties which could well have extended to any attempt to standardize value added should that ever have appeared on the agenda — provided an important impetus to the publication of *The Corporate Report* in which value added first entered the ranks of the accountancy profession.

The present arrangements for setting account-

[12] By initiating these research studies at least three of the four accountancy bodies also were responding to the Labour Government's threat of legislation requiring the reporting of value added. Given that the concept was a new part of the official accounting discourse, they were quite strategically investing in enhancing their understanding of the category.

ing standards in the U.K. were established at the end of the 1960s in the aftermath of the considerable controversy and debate surrounding a series of company collapses and take-over battles (Zeff, 1972). The standards setting programme very quickly ran into trouble however, not least in relation to its stated aim of narrowing the areas of difference and variety in accounting practice (ICAEW, 1969). This was most dramatically exemplified in the case of the inflation accounting debate (Whittington, 1983), but the same difficulties also applied to a number of other areas of accounting standardisation.

Although initiated to maintain professional control over accounting standardisation, the inflation accounting proposals of the then Accounting Standards Steering Committee quickly engendered such a breadth and intensity of debate that the Conservative Government of the time established a committee of inquiry in the area — the Sandiland's Committee (1975) (for an initial analysis of the context see Hopwood *et al.*, 1980; Hopwood, 1984). That in itself was perceived by the profession as a threat to the traditional division of responsibility between the professional bodies and the government concerning the determination of the content and form of presentation of and the measurement principles employed in corporate reports. The sense of professional crisis was further intensified by the fact that the committee was anticipated to report in a not uncritical manner during a new Labour administration whose opposition Green Paper, *The Community and the Company* (1974), had also threatened the existing framework of professional self-regulation with its proposals for the setting up of a powerful Companies Commission for regulating companies and financial institutions.

In anticipation of the report of the Sandilands Committee, the Accounting Standards Steering Committee established a committee to re-examine "the scope and aims of published financial reports in the light of modern needs and conditions" (ASSC, 1975) — something which had until then been ignored by the standard setters.[13] The committee's findings were published as *The Corporate Report*. In appraising current reporting practices, *The Corporate Report* evinces some concern for what it considers to be an over-emphasis on profit and goes on to argue that:

> The simplest and most immediate way of putting profit into proper perspective vis-a-vis the whole enterprise as a collective effort by capital, management and employees is by the presentation of a statement of value added (that is, sales income less materials and services purchased). Value added is the wealth the reporting entity has been able to create by its own and its employees efforts. This statement would show how value added has been used to pay those contributing to its creation. It usefully elaborates on the profit and loss account and in time may come to be regarded as a preferable way of describing performance (ASSC, 1975, p. 49).

In this way value added entered the discourse of accounting policy making.[14]

Value added was seen as a performance criterion that put employees on a par with other interests in the enterprise. Moreover this claim for an equality of status was reinforced by the stakeholder model adopted in *The Corporate Report*. Where before there only existed the shareholder (Sharp, 1971), there now stood a number of stakeholders, each of which is deemed to have "a reasonable right to information concerning the reporting entity" (ASSC, 1975, p. 17). The employee group constituted one such stakeholder. The report makes the point that "it is likely that employees will more suitably obtain the information they need by means of special purpose reports at plant or site level" (p. 22). However, it goes on to argue that

---

[13] In-depth research had been mentioned as one aspect of the standard setting programme, but no concrete steps had been taken in this area until the establishment of *The Corporate Report* Working Party. For an insider's comments on the establishment and functioning of this group see Stamp (1985).

[14] One reviewer suggested that further effort be put into tracing the origins of the interest in value added by *The Corporate Report* Working Party. Our investigations revealed that one of the authors of the present paper might have been influential in this respect! If this is so, it further reinforces our concluding observations on the non-monolithic and unanticipated nature of accounting change.

corporate reports could be used as a check on the reliability of these special purpose documents and could be useful to employees in evaluating managerial efficiency, estimating the future prospects of the entity and of individual establishments within a group.

The merits of value added as an alternative or complementary performance indicator had not been advanced in a vacuum, however. Two very important contextual considerations that should be borne in mind in connection with conditions in the United Kingdom during the second half of the 1970s were the debates, legislation and practical initiatives concerned with incomes policy and information disclosure to employees and trades unions. Although value added was new to the accounting policy making arena, it was functioning as a practice in both of these other two contexts.

Macro-economic management

Income policies have been linked to the use of the value added category by a number of writers (Beddoe, 1978; Cameron, 1978; IDS, 1977; Low, 1977). In every case the connection has been made via a discussion of value added incentive payment schemes (VAIPSs). VAIPSs are group bonus schemes which are usually operated on a plant basis, thus covering both blue- and white-collar employees. The bonus pool available for distribution to the employees is related to the value added of the plant. This pool may, for example, be determined by a certain agreed percentage of any increase in the value added per pound of payroll costs, over some agreed base figure for this ratio. These schemes came very much to the fore during the period of the 1974–79 Labour Government. With the inception of Stage III of that Government's pay policy in August 1977 there was imposed a 10% limit on wage settlements with the provision for agreements above this level where self-financing productivity deals had been implemented. VAIPSs, which had been introduced into the U.K. during the 1950s, were already functioning in a number of firms and were strongly advocated by a number of management consultants, are almost by definition self-financing and thus were well placed under Stage III to become more widely adopted.

One of the most important conditions of this particular conjuncture of value added and national incomes policy was that constituted by the practices of government management of the national economy. The "national economy" as an object of government intervention and "macro-economic policy" as a domain wherein this intervention is deliberated, planned and conducted were only constituted in the U.K., in the sense that we understand them today, during and immediately after the Second World War (Tomlinson, 1981). For a long time this field of action remained very much as it was initially structured by the conditions under which it emerged. This was particularly the case for the problem of productivity. "Before the war productivity was largely confined to academic discussion", Leyland (1953, p. 381) observed. "Today," he went on to add, "it is common currency". Such an interest is not hard to understand. Under conditions of full employment, improving productivity had been the only source of economic growth. It also faciliated the maintenance of an external balance without reducing domestic consumption or investment — both painful exercises with hazardous side effects for the government of the day. Moreover productivity also provided an indicator for gauging the competitive position of the manufacturing sector — a factor given continuing attention in the U.K. in the post-war era.[15] In short, productivity growth appeared to be a key to

[15] In the second half of the 1970s value added was itself increasingly used in political and media discussions of national economic performance and policy (Jones, 1976, 1978; New, 1978). Indeed productivity tended to be seen as something that was, if not synonymous with value added, at least very closely related to it. From this perspective discussions focused on the need for income policies, increased investment, particularly in "high value added sectors", and policies on the proportion of value added devoted to industrial research and development. In these ways value added appeared to simultaneously function as a way of describing the economy, elucidating policy problems and, in the context of VAIPSs, facilitating the solution of the problems so identified.

economic success.

While productivity and, more generally, economic efficiency have been continuing concerns of government, as evidenced by agencies such as the National Economic Development Office and earlier, the Anglo-American Productivity Council, neither these bodies nor the means of intervention associated with monetary and fiscal policy afforded governments a very effective purchase on these key economic variables. However, a rather more direct form of intervention has been provided from time to time by government incomes policies. These have been introduced, usually reluctantly and *in extremis*, in order to attempt to resolve one of the central presumed dilemmas of modern demand management, namely how is it possible to reconcile the objectives of price stability and full employment using only the instruments of fiscal and monetary policy. What is interesting here is that productivity growth has re-occurred as an important criterion for judging wage increase throughout the various phases of the post-war history of incomes policies.

Productivity was so emphasised during the incomes policies of 1961 and 1962. The theme re-emerged during the life of the National Board of Prices and Incomes (NBPI) established by the Labour Government in 1965 and wound up on 31 March, 1971. The NBPI was assigned the task of examining "particular cases in order to advise whether or not the behaviour of prices, salaries or other money incomes was in the national interest . . ." (see Fels, 1972, Chapter 3). "The national interest" was first specified in the White Paper, *Prices and Incomes Policy*, of April 1965 and was subsequently elaborated and modified in a series of White Papers until 1970. Initially it required that there should be an incomes "norm", i.e. a maximum percentage by which the wages and salaries of individuals should increase. A figure of 3–3½% per annum was derived from the expected annual rate of growth of productivity per head. In addition certain exceptional circumstances in which increases above the norm were considered justifiable were also defined. Amongst these there was one which allowed for above-norm increases in pay where employees had made a direct contribution towards an increase in productivity. For certain periods during the life of the NBPI there was imposed a zero norm and the exceptional criteria became the only permissable grounds for obtaining an increase in pay. It was under this regime that productivity agreements became very popular. The NBPI's third report on productivity agreements showed that 25% of all workers had been involved in productivity agreements, mainly in 1968 and 1969 (NBPI, 1968).

Subsequent investigation of these productivity deals led certain commentators to conclude that many of them were bogus, i.e. "the productivity increase was mostly that which would have happened in any case; so that what many so-called 'productivity bargains' really did was to use this to justify an exceptional wage increase" (Turner, 1970, p. 203). This experience plus the *ad hoc*, piecemeal character of many productivity deals which tended to be self-perpetuating thereafter (Elliott, 1978) and, perhaps more importantly, the lack of any mechanism relating the increases in hourly rates paid to the increase in productivity actually achieved were the cause of some concern on the part of both Government and the Confederation of British Industry in the discussions over the arrangements to be brought into effect with the expiry of Stage II of the 1974–79 Labour Government's incomes policy. At that time the Government was keen to build a productivity element into the provisions for Stage III. In this context VAIPSs could be presented as model schemes. They were comprehensive in character and maintained a continuous link between performance and reward. VAIPSs therefore involved the use of a measurement technology that offered a solution to many of the problems that had created difficulties for the NBPI in its attempts to audit the productivity deals of the late sixties. However, it is important to note that the force of the claims made on behalf of VAIPSs did not rest on these features alone.

In discussions of VAIPSs it is rare to find their merits presented solely in terms of their scope, self-financing character or measurement technology. In a number of different ways, the point was nearly always made that the effective functioning of these schemes presupposes a number of changes in the intra-organisational relations of the enterprise concerned. Further, it was often made clear that these changes were considered to be of positive value in their own right. The relevant organisational changes were usually discussed in terms of "information disclosure" and "participation". As one leading management consultant in this area put it:

> the contribution of Added Value requires:
> (a) an open management style that will "open the books" and welcome the increased questioning that will ensure
> (b) a preference for a more participative and less autocratic way of getting results (Binder, Hamlyn, Fry & Co., 1978, p. 18).

The underlying reasoning appears to be that given that the relevant unit of performance for determining bonus is a company or plant rather than a single machine, improved performance and hence bonus presupposes cooperation across functions and different activities and occupational groups within functions. This cooperation, so the argument goes, can only be achieved by means of the widespread disclosure of detailed company information which then provides the basis for discussion and agreement on the appropriate action for attempting to improve performance. Thus, in the case of the Bentley plan — a particular British varient of the VAIPS — the scheme "is initiated through a fully representative employee management council. A structure which will establish employee involvement and participation in a wider range of problems and enable profits, productivity and earnings to be rationally discussed and improved" (Bentley Associates, 1975, p. 12). In one group of companies in which a VAIPS was introduced the scheme in each company in the group was administered by a company consultative council. These bodies included representatives from senior and junior management and from all shop floor departments. Each council was given the details of its company's performance for the preceding month. Council members then reported back on the figures to colleagues in their own sectors (Cameron, 1977b; also see Woodmansay, 1978, p. 13). It is interesting to note that although the trade union response to VAIPSs was somewhat guarded it was suggested that if unions did enter such schemes they would require, amongst other things, complete access to all the relevant data (Beddoe, 1978).

The positive value of all these changes was generally seen in terms of the improvement in industrial relations that they were said to effect. It was argued that flexible working arrangements would become more likely and employees would become positively motivated to cut costs and improve efficiency. As a result there would be some amelioration in the repeated confrontation between workers and managers over working practices (Marchington, 1977; Cameron, 1977b). Now it was for very similar reasons that the NBPI was earlier so interested in productivity deals. It has been argued that the "NBPI's recommendations on pay policy often required changes in the machinery of wage determination; in addition, the incomes policy was often used as a Trojan horse to bring about reforms in collective bargaining institutions" (Fels, 1972, p. 150). The productivity deal was one of the principle means whereby the NBPI sought to supplant the hold of traditional factors in income determination and give practical effect to its own criteria.

However, in the 1970s there occurred a significant change in the character of the discussion surrounding the intra-organizational changes associated with the reform of payment systems. The productivity deals of the NBPI period were discussed wholly in terms of the rhetoric of management control:

> . . . genuine productivity agreements, for example, would have very useful side effects, such as improving management by increasing cost-consciousness, by providing new information about performance and information about performance and new methods of assessing it, and by directing attention to the possibility of changing methods of work. Management negotiations were brought into closer touch with unions, and more managers became aware of the implications for industrial relations of technical and financial decisions. The experience

> of applying the agreements with their provisions on overtime, flexibility, manning and so on often brought a revolution in managerial control over working hours and practices. There were changes in organisation, personnel and the provision of training, and senior and other managers were better informed and organised than before the agreements (Fels, 1972, p. 133).

While the discussion of VAIPSs during the second half of the 1970s still contained this thread concerned with management control and the efficiency of enterprise operations, it was also conducted according to the rhetoric of employee participation and industrial democracy. Indeed it became possible to completely invert the normal order of presentation and use the issue of industrial democracy as a springboard for advancing the claims of VAIPSs (e.g. Marchington, 1977). The significance acquired by and emphasis placed on the participative characteristics of VAIPSs at this time was rooted in a number of parallel developments occurring within the area of industrial relations.

Industrial relations and information disclosure

During the 1960s there commenced a significant shift in the conditions of trade union activity in the U.K. The pre-existing voluntary system of "free collective bargaining" was displaced by a progressively elaborated object of government intervention — an object increasingly overlaid by a network of legal relations and inset with a variety of new institutions concerned with the investigation, regulation and normalisation of industrial relations (see Crouch, 1979). This shift was preceded by two events of some interest. In 1961 there commenced the production of a record of unofficial strikes and in 1965 the Labour Government appointed a Royal Commission on Trade Unions and Employers' Associations — the Donovan Commission (Donovan, 1968). Thus there occurred the production of a key statistic, to be read a little later as a sign of a "central defect in British industrial relations" (Crouch, 1979, p. 264). In addition to its work of diagnosis, the Donovan Report contained a clearly articulated conceptual framework which would serve as a means of generating programmes of intervention designed to rectify this "defect".

A singular feature of the interventions into industrial relations that occurred during the period of the 1974–79 Labour Government was the degree to which the discussions and debates surrounding them were organised around the theme of industrial democracy (Elliott, 1978). Despite its apparent centrality, "industrial democracy" is an extremely difficult concept to pin down. According to one commentator "the term 'industrial democracy' is incapable of definition" (Kahn-Freund, 1977) and Elliott (1978, p. 6) has noted that:

> Despite its central semi-political theme of increasing the role and status of workers in an industrial society, industrial democracy means different things to different people. To some on the far left it is perceived as a path to full workers' control, while for many employers and Conservative politicians, who dislike its political connotations, it should be called simply "employee participation" and only involve a partnership between employer and employee in making the company and the present social and economic system work more efficiently and productively, without any changes in power relationships.

As for value added itself, it is perhaps precisely *because* of its equivocal character that industrial democracy was able to serve as a key point of articulation between a number of distinct conceptions of enterprise and industrial relations reform. The ambiguity might be required if the concept is to orchestrate the considerable number of positions that can be argued concerning the specification of individual and group interests and their political representations (Pitkin, 1967).[16]

An inquiry into industrial democracy chaired by Lord Bullock (Department of Trade, 1977a) and the enactment of the Employment Protection Act of 1975 were important elements in the programme of industrial relations reform of the

[16] "Industrial democracy" may be thought of as functioning in two different ways. Firstly it is the name attached to particular palpable regimes of industrial democracy. For example, in the name of industrial democracy, the Trades Union Congress

1974–79 Labour Government. However its democratic content may be judged, this programme implied a change in the information economies of private companies. Amongst other things it entailed the creation of new agents and bodies for the receipt and relay of information, new rights of access for certain existing bodies and the setting up of certain national agencies to oversee and supervise the implementation and functioning of the new provisions. The Employment Protection Act of 1975 gave statutory form to the Advisory, Conciliation and Arbitration Service (ACAS)[17] which was "charged with the general duty of promoting the improvement of industrial relations". To this end it was empowered to issue Codes of Practice containing practical guidance for promoting the improve-
426 ment of industrial relations. A Code of Practice on the disclosure of information to trade unions was issued by ACAS and came into effect on 22 August 1977. The disclosure provisions placed a general duty on an employer to disclose information to representatives of independent recognised trade unions, "(a) without which the trade union representatives would be to a material extent impeded in carrying on with him . . . collective bargaining, and (b) which it would be in accordance with good industrial relations practice that he would disclose to them for the purposes of collective bargaining". Although the Bullock Report did not result in any legislation, parallel developments in the areas of occupational pension schemes (Lucas, 1979) and health and safety took some steps towards taking workers into the sphere of management decision-making. The Health and Safety at Work Act was enacted in 1975. It provided for the appointment of employee safety representatives with functions of representation and consultation, workplace inspection and investigation and rights of access to certain documents and information. As one writer put it: "For the first time in law, the Regulations have given trade unions decision-making rights in their workplaces" (Stuttard, 1979).

It was in this context, in which the relative status of management personnel vis-a-vis trade unionists had come under considerable pressure, both in respect of information access and decision-making, that there developed a considerable amount of interest in employee reporting. Popular versions of companies' annual reports to shareholders were prepared in an attempt to make them understandable to employees (Hussey, 1978, 1979; Holmes, 1977). Around these corporate initiatives there had in turn grown up a parallel literature of prescription and advice emanating from such bodies as the Institute of Personnel Management, the ICAEW and the CBI. In addition to the use of employee reports, information also was disseminated to employees by means of personal presentations by company chairmen to mass meetings, slide and video presentations and small group briefing sessions. It was within this area of corporate communication with employees that value added frequently appeared and was discussed as a preferred form of presentation (Hopkins, 1975; EEF, 1977; Smith, 1978; Hilton, 1978). The Trades Union Congress, in its statement of policy on industrial democracy, had itself suggested that companies should provide information on value added to their employees (TUC, 1974, p. 33).

One final strand of interest in the industrial democracy debate is that of profit sharing. As a result of undertakings made to the Liberal Party during the formation of the "Lib-Lab" alliance, profit sharing was encouraged by provisions

advanced a comprehensive set of proposals for developing trade union activity at the level of the economy, industry, company and the plant (TUC, 1974). A rather different set of proposals are to be found in the evidence of the Confederation of British Industry to the Bullock Committee. There is thus a wide range of institutional and procedural arrangements that can lay claim to being democratic. In its second mode of functioning industrial democracy serves as a criterion for critically evaluating given institutions and procedures for their democratic content — the extent to which the arrangements in question may be considered to represent the interests of all the persons concerned. Thus Gospel appraises the provisions of the Employment Protection Act 1975 (Gospel, 1976) and the signatories of the minority report take their stand in relation to the majority report of the Bullock Committee (Department of Trade, 1977a, p. 175, para. 23).

[17] ACAS was first established on an administrative basis in 1974.

introduced in the Finance Act 1978 (Elliott, 1978). This particular innovation is one that was continued under the Conservative administration which came to power in 1979. The Confederation of British Industry viewed financial participation schemes as a means of obtaining a "sense of purpose, at least at company level" and "as a useful contribution to an employee participation programme" (CBI, 1978). Of particular interest here are the changes introduced by ICI into its own profit sharing scheme. This scheme had been running since 1953 and covered nearly 100,000 monthly and weekly paid staff who received an annual profit related share allocation. In 1976 an ICI working party report proposed that the right of the ICI board to unilaterally fix the annual bonus should be replaced by a formula based on an added value concept (Cameron, 1977a). This scheme differed from a VAIPS in that it operated at the company level as opposed to the plant level and it was not viewed as a major productivity incentive. The stated objectives were "(1) to help encourage the cooperation and involvement of all employees in improving the business performance of the company; (2) to provide tangible evidence of the unity of interests of employees and stockholders in the continued existence of ICI as a strong and financially viable company; (3) to help focus the interest of the employees towards being part of a more effective company, by being involved as stockholders" (Wellens, 1977).

It is perhaps no surprise therefore that VAIPSs having been introduced into the U.K. during the 1950s and effectively incubated during the 1960s then came into their own in the 1970s. While the topics of information disclosure to employees and economic performance were by no means new (see for example BIM, 1957; Searle, 1971), the discussion of them took place within and was driven forward by the rhetoric of industrial democracy which tended to place in the foreground the issue of the relative status of economic agents. It is precisely under these conditions, formed by the intersection of a number of different developments in the fields of setting accounting standards, the management of the national economy and the regulation and reform of industrial relations, that profit and its associated connotations could appear as a problem — an "awkward term" — and value added could establish its claim as an alternative performance indicator.

THE ACCOUNTING CONSTELLATION

Our concern is to discover the pre-conditions of the social space within which the value added event took place. As we indicated earlier, this particular social space is, amongst other things, characterised by the fact that the discussions concerning efficiency and productivity that took place within it during the second half of the 1970s were extensively intertwined with those concerning employee participation. The language of economic performance was strongly inflected with that of industrial representation and democracy. In the literature of the period concerned with such enterprise administrative practices as accounting and payments systems, problems were diagnosed and solutions proposed according to the terms of a discourse which was organized around the notions of efficiency and democracy. However these two ideas function as a pair of values the commensurability of which is far from clear. Just how is "efficiency" to be brought into relation with "democracy"? One solution to this problem seemingly was offered by value added. Value added was repeatedly presented as a means of achieving a felicitous combination of participation, if not democracy, and efficiency. Within the network of statements generated by the efficiency–democracy discourse, value added functioned as one strategic node or point of inter-relation.

Notions of efficiency and participation did not exist as a pair of pre-given, disembodied categories however. Nor did the debates and discussions concerning them simply consist of a series of words and statements, lacking any historical or contextual specification save that of the dates between which they occurred. In our discussion of the three arenas we have attempted to outline a three branched genealogy (Foucault, 1977) of the specific social space within which value added appeared and developed. As a consequence of tracing this genealogy, the space which the value added event occupied is seen to be comprised of a very particular field of relations which existed between certain institutions, economic and administrative processes, bodies of knowledge, systems of norms and measurement, and classification techniques. We have called such a field an accounting constellation. It was in the network of intersecting practices, processes and institutions which constituted this constellation that value added was caught and it was this network that governed how it might function as a calculative, administrative and discursive practice. In this latter sense the constellation also operates as a regime — one which governs the production, distribution and use of value added statements. Business organizations themselves appear within this regime as dense concentrations of social relations — a chain or archipelago of individual information economies set into a web of more dispersed, loosely knit relations.

We have described the development of activities along three strands of this web and how these three strands or arenas together made it possible for a number of mutually reinforcing interventions to be relayed into the information economies of individual enterprises during the 1970s in the United Kingdom. These interventions associated with incomes policies and the management of the national economy, company and labour law and the reform of industrial relations, accounting regulation and the standardisation of financial reporting, simultaneously affected a number of different aspects of the business enterprise. For example, productivity deals in general and VAIPSs in particular resulted in a significant elaboration of a firm's administrative apparatus. Moreover this elaboration was aimed at increasing its pervasiveness in order to secure greater unity in the combined action of the component parts of the enterprise. It also has been argued that productivity deals were seen to offer workers the scope for greater involvement and participation in decision making giving rise to the application of wage-work rules (McKersie & Hunter, 1973, pp. 21–23), an implication that was particularly apparent in many of the discourses that were associated with VAIPSs. Overall, therefore, these diverse strategies and interventions together had the possibility to intensify the regime of economic information within an enterprise and to move towards some reconstitution of the patterns of social relations. One interesting index of such an overall change was the widespread concern shown for the general level of financial and commercial literacy. Indeed the disclosure of corporate information to employees was often discussed as if it were part and parcel of an exercise in business education. A shift in the pattern of distribution and consumption of corporate information implied, or at least in this particular case was becoming increasingly associated with, a change in the distribution of the cultural resources commonly associated with the receipt and use of this information.

In many respects the appearance of value added statements in company annual reports was merely the tip of the iceberg in relation to the more general shift which had taken place in and around the enterprise in the processing of information. Although further investigation undoubtedly would provide interesting insights, we have not sought to uncover the precise mechanisms whereby value added was written into *The Corporate Report*, for instance. Instead we have attempted to indicate how it was necessary to speak about value added, to adopt a certain style of discourse, if what was basically a very marginal calculative elaboration of existing accounting practice was to generate such widespread interest and debate. Ours, therefore, is a history of possibilities, an account of how and why value added came to be a significant even if technically marginal accounting elaboration. From our perspective the necessity of talking about value added in a particular way arose as a result of the conditions that made the value added event possible — conditions we wish to encapsulate within our notion of an accounting constellation.

It is this idea of an accounting constellation, along with the processes of its formation, modification and dissolution which now appears as our prime object of interest. As yet, however, it remains a vague and ill-specified idea. The series of inter-connected observations which follow seek to clarify certain of its more general features.

The specificity of the constellation

It is important to note first of all that the accounting constellation discussed here has been constructed in response to a particular problem concerning the value added event. There is no presupposition whatsoever that it encompasses the field of relations governing the production, distribution and use of all accounting statements. An examination of, for example, the conditions of possibility of the debates surrounding accounting for depreciation, deferred taxation or inflation accounting[18] would no doubt reveal an accounting constellation that only partly coincided with that associated with value added. Indeed, this might also be true if one examined an aspect of the value added event other than the one addressed here, e.g. the appearance of value added in a particular firm.

To so argue for the specificity of a particular accounting constellation does not reduce the significance of our general method of analysis. It is merely to recognise the diverse and changing factors that can intermingle with the processes of accounting change (also see Hopwood, forthcoming). However, although advising caution on the transference of any specific accounting constellation to the domains of other accounting innovations and changes, we nevertheless would seek to argue for the general mode of analysis adopted in the present study, not least in respect of its genealogical emphasis, its mobilising theoretical and practical concerns, and the very real theoretical cautions which resulted in the use of this approach rather than any other.

The pursuit of interests and unintended consequences

The accounting constellation as we have described it was very much an *unintended* phenomenon. The field of action that we have outlined in relation to value added was not designed by anyone, and no blueprint for its construction can be found. It was produced as the consequence of the intersection of a great many events, some famous, and, as a consequence, well documented, and others unnoticed and possibly lost to history forever. Most of these events were produced by people with clear views of what they were doing — negotiating a wages settlement; conforming to an Act of Parliament; fighting inflation; seeking information; informing workers of the facts of economic reality — and no thought at all for an accounting constellation. Although there were identifiable causes to that which eventually emerged, they were ones which operated without any reference to certain of their effects.

Admittedly such a view differs from other notions of the interested nature of accounting practice. While, as we have stated, we do not seek to deny the purposive nature of accounting action, we are concerned to emphasise the potential multitude of different actors acting on accounting in purposive ways in an array of different arenas, each having specific, often non-overlapping and sometimes conflicting interests in the accounting practice they are utilising and only partial knowledge of both its consequences

[18] For some brief but related comments on the emergence and functioning of the inflation accounting debate see Burchell *et al.* (1980) and Hopwood (1984). Inflation accounting occupies some of the same accounting constellation as the value added event, albeit that different aspects are emphasised. Indeed in the accounting standards arena discussions of the two were intertwined at particular junctures in the politics surrounding the processes of accounting regulation. Inflation accounting also was implicated in debates on macro-economic management, although in somewhat different policy arenas than those which explicitly related to value added. (The emphasis was on questions of indexation, albeit a problem that had arisen in the context of incomes policies, and the performance of the manufacturing sector.) Moreover in the context of a wider politics surrounding the techniques for surplus declaration, the inflation accounting debate became intertwined with industrial relations issues. In addition to such partial overlaps, however, other significant arenas also became involved with the development and functioning of inflation accounting, including questions of taxation policy, debates on the relative performance of different sectors of the U.K. economy, a questioning of the high levels of profitability of financial institutions and discussions and developments within the academic community.

and the resistance that its use will engender (Hindess, 1982). Although at any particular moment of time there may be some mobilisation of consequences that relates to the interests in the name of which accounting is advanced, in our analysis there is no assumption as to either any functional orchestration of these diverse initiatives or their precise effectivity in realising the objectives which were stated for them. Accounting may, in other words, be purposive but whether it is purposeful is a matter for detailed and careful investigation across the diverse arenas in which specific accountings can become intertwined.

A non-monolithic constellation

One consequence of being the unintended
430 product of a large number of different purposive actions is that the accounting constellation is non-monolithic in character. Although an accounting constellation may well govern the form of reasoning concerning certain of the decisions confronting enterprise management, such as, for example, the choice of the form of accounting and payment system to be adopted, there still remains considerable scope for conflict and disagreement. It is possible to imagine a situation in which workers and management of a firm are both agreed on the desirability of introducing VAIPS and yet for both sides to violently disagree on virtually all the procedural and organizational details which would effectively constitute the new payment system. In an analogous way, a particular mode of reasoning and institutional milieu can be said to organise the conflictual debates that have occurred in the area of accounting standard setting (Zeff, 1978). In the case of value added, we have indicated how a field of action was laid down by the intersection of developments in three distinct arenas — developments which in each case proceeded without reference to certain of the possibilities and consequences of their interaction in mind. One aspect of this meshing of these developments, in fact one of the very ways in which they were articulated with one another, was that certain systems such as VAIPSs and certain categories such as value added functioned as the vehicle for a number of different interests and purposes. They were overdetermined phenomena, equivocality and ambiguity being central to their functioning. Seen in such terms an accounting constellation is less a system or an entity which is usually understood in relation to some unambiguous governing principle, role or function, than a garbage can (Cohen *et al.*, 1972).

Accounting's embeddedness in the organisational and the social

Our model of accounting change is still in many ways a contingency model. We have not suggested or discovered any general theory of accounting change. Everything all depends on the circumstances under which change occurs. There are, however, important differences with the accounting–environment contingency model of change discussed earlier. For a start, we have not attempted to separate out two domains called accounting and the environment and then conduct the analysis in terms of this prior distinction. Instead we have attempted to outline a network of social relations throughout which there may be found in the process of their emergence and functioning a certain class of statements — value added statements, company reports, employee reports, financial statements, statements concerning financial statements, etc. Within this network accounting can be found providing the conditions of existence of certain social relations, such as helping to define the rights, duties and field of action of certain agents and playing a role in the specification of both organizational boundaries and intra-organizational segments. Accounting, so seen, is intimately implicated in the construction and facilitation of the contexts in which it operates. It cannot be extracted from its environment like an individual organism from its habitat. Of course it is possible to discuss categories such as profit and indeed value added in a general abstract manner without any reference to the law, organizational rules and functioning, and the rights and duties of agents. However the added values we are interested in, the added values featuring in the value added event, did not exist thus. To attempt to investigate them in such an abstract fashion would be to investigate a different problem. We have been concerned to capture and analyse the way value added exists and functions as an integral part of and inscribed within certain social relations.[19]

The accounting constellation and networks of social relations and organizational practices

We have frequently described the set of social relations pertinent to the emergence and functioning of value added as a network. Our use of this term is very similar to the way in which it is deployed in organizational theory (Aldrich, 1979). There the idea of a network of organizations has opened up research perspectives which tend to cut across the organization – environment dichotomy. Interest focusses less on the intra-organizational problems of adaptation to a changing environment than of the properties of a network of inter-organizational relations.

In our analysis the formation of a network of social relations has been described as a means of accounting for the outbreak of value added which during the 1970s characterised financial statements emerging from a wide range of sources. Although we have not analysed the properties of this network in any detail, it is important to note that in certain respects we conceive the accounting constellation rather differently from the way networks are specified in organizational theory. The main components of our network are not individual organizations, but rather particular systems or processes — payment systems, financial reporting systems, information systems. We have indicated how these systems are caught up and elaborated in networks of relations existing between various agents, agencies and the systems themselves. Moreover these networks were uncovered by studying developments in three arenas, each of which could be characterised in terms of specific fields of action, and targets and agents of intervention, along with their means of surveillance and intervention and associated bodies of knowledge. The developments within each arena were then seen as involving the formation of relations between particular agents, agencies and administrative practices as a consequence of the various interventions taking place. Finally, the accounting constellation was itself specified as a network by noting the often unintended interdependencies between the processes and the practices in the separate arenas.

In this way we provided an account of the emergence and functioning of value added across a diverse social space with developments in particular fields of action both changing the preconditions for developments elsewhere and enabling or constraining specific innovations to take place. Thus the arena of accounting standard setting was shown not to be independent of developments taking place in the arenas of macro-economic management and the conduct of industrial relations. Although each of these arenas had its own trajectory of change, the notion of a network enabled us to locate the possibilities for their interpenetration and mutually dependent functioning.

We attempted to use such a perspective in order to avoid giving a privileged ontological status to the notion of an organization as a discrete bounded entity with a well defined interior and exterior. Clearly such notions do exist and certain agents act in their name and are engaged in their fabrication and maintenance. What is important to note, however, is that the

[19] In a very different context (that of the emergence of prisons), Patton (1979) similarly noted that "... the abstract machine, however, can only function by means of concrete social machines which give it content". He elaborated this idea in the following way: "... each concrete social machine is composed of both discursive and non-discursive elements. While the abstract machine only functions through its concrete forms, it is nevertheless that which renders possible the emergence of those concrete social machines. It plays the role of immanent cause, which 'selects' a particular machine according to its own design". In the case of value added the actual historical emergence of the abstract discursive category is so intimately bound up with its social functioning that it is difficult to disentangle the two. In other areas of accounting, however, it might be possible to more readily conduct an analysis of the interrelationship between the discursive and non-discursive components. Inflation accounting comes to mind in this respect.

conditions of possibility for the actions of organization builders are *not* contained in that which they are attempting to build. An organization can hardly be presupposed as a means for its own (auto-) generation. Aware of such problems, by focussing on certain administrative systems and their position within each of the arenas we have studied, we hope to have indicated how the very substance of organizations is constructed by processes which cut across any single distinction that might be made between organizational members and non-members. In a similar way Litterer (1961; 1963) has indicated how the organizational phenomenon of "Big Business" (Chandler, 1962) was made possible by the emplacement of cost accounting, production and inventory control systems as joint effects of the systematic management movement.[20]

In a similar manner the developments in each of our arenas also amount to the elaboration and development of certain dimensions of those complex entities we call the economy, society and the environment (see Donzelot, 1979). The interventions within the different arenas, which are conducted according to a variety of different principles, single out and privilege certain agents and their means of action. In the process of being used to intervene in the organization, practices for the management of the social and the economic are elaborated and changed. "The organization" thereby designates a particular site of intersection of practices conducted in the name of the social and the economic, amongst other things. It represents a common nodal point in a number of different networks, each having different objects and means of intervention. And it also represents a site where people in attempting to draw boundaries seek to coordinate the actions of those enclosed within them, striving to fashion out of the diverse processes and interventions at work a machine for pursuing certain goals and performing certain functions. Seen in such terms the organization and society and the economy are not independent realms. Rather than residing without, the social and the economic pass through the organization in the course of their own formation, as we have seen in the case of the value added event.

The mode of investigation

Finally, it is worth making some comments concerning the mode of investigation that we employed. The choice of arenas around which the investigation has been organized was a product of the particular origins and history of a more general inquiry of which this paper is one (unintended) outcome. It was not determined at the beginning on the basis of any general theoretical principles or model. However the decision to attempt to divide the accounting context into a number of arenas — whatever they might have been — and to consider the process of development within each as *sui generis*, marching to its own drummer, was motivated by a prior theoretical concern to attempt to avoid the problems entailed in adopting an enterprise–environment and/or an accounting–environment model of change.

Having identified three arenas, our mode of investigation was in many ways very similar to those conducted by the authorities — Depart-

[20] Unlike Chandler (1962, 1977) who merely provides a rationale for certain organizational forms by reference to general economic developments (railways, markets, etc.), Litterer (and others) describe some of the processes and mechanisms at work in the construction of the large bureaucratic firm. The systematic and scientific management movements and the welfare movement were very specific, describable forms of intervention in the enterprise involving very specific agents (engineers, welfare secretaries, foremen) which coalesced around a number of measurement techniques and administrative procedures (cost accounting, inventory and production control systems, measurement of efficiency and personnel turnover) and emerged and functioned under very specific social, political and economic conditions. These different movements were not unified in their goals and encountered resistance to their attempts to implement their programmes, clashing with one another and with certain of the agents they attempted to (re-) construct (the foreman, the labourer, etc.). As Jenks (1960, p. 421) has said: "The contemporary institutionalization of business management development through the convergence of an indeterminate number of distinct movements of thought and action." He went on to add: "Perhaps it would be well to think of several origins for the management movement, each of limited scope but some possible overlap . . ." (p. 427). Such a form of analysis is very consistent with our own.

ment of Trade Inspectors — when investigating irregularities in the affairs of a company. The irregularity that we set out to investigate was the outbreak of added value during the second half of the 1970s. How was this phenomenon or event possible? What did it signify? Now Department of Trade Inspectors in their investigations presuppose and attempt to reconstruct the accounting regime — system of book-keeping, accounting and internal control — existing in the particular company under investigation. Such a regime must have served as the condition of possibility for the irregularities which precipitated the investigation. We have been concerned with a considerably more widespread and heterogeneous set of phenomena than those normally addressed by Department of Trade Inspectors. However we have argued that certain features of the value added event were only possible given the existence of a set of conditions — the accounting constellation — which together also comprise a regime of sorts. It is however a regime which no one designed, and is never audited.

The enquiries of the authorities are also of interest because they must of necessity study accounting systems in terms other than the roles or functions, e.g. stewardship, that are commonly attributed to them. It is not enough merely to register the fact of irregularities, errors, and anomalies in the operation of an accounting system. In order to refine and elaborate accounting systems so as to prevent such irregularities occurring again in the future it is necessary to discover the positive determinants of errors and anomalies. How is it that something that is assumed to function as a means of accountability, served instead as a mechanism for financial irregularity? In the case of the value added event we have pointed to the multiplicity of roles attributed to value added statements and commented on the seeming inadequacy of any given statement as to its purported role(s). Our genealogical study of the event attempts to show how certain roles came to be attributed to a number of processes within which value added could be found functioning. We have attempted throughout to avoid making any assumptions concerning the essential or proper functions of accounting practice.

ON EMERGENCE AND DECLINE

Having discussed the nature, significance and specificity of the constellation which provided the conditions for the value added event, it is now of interest to note that the attention given to value added subsequently waned during the early 1980s. With the election of a new Conservative Government in 1979 the three arenas of the value added constellation were suddenly ruptured and transformed. Different policies were introduced for the management of the national economy. Industrial relations came quite quickly to be seen and conducted in fundamentally different terms. And albeit with a lag, the specification of accounting standards was no longer seen to be subject to so real a possibility of government intervention. In these ways the specific significances which had been attached to value added were no longer salient. With its context so radically changed, the functioning of value added in social relations started to approximate to its technical marginality. Value added started to become a phenomenon of the past.

Although the state of the British economy was still such that economic performance remained a fundamental governmental policy concern, the new administration attempted to deal with this in very different ways. Emphasis was placed on the roles that could be served by monetary policies, financial stringency and the enhancement of competitive pressures. The level of wage settlements was still seen as problematic, but incomes policies did not enter into the explicit political repertoire. Market pressures in an increasingly high unemployment economy were seen to offer more effective means for income control. Productivity and efficiency also remained important objects of government attention. Here too, however, very different interventionist strategies were used. A reemergence of the managerial prerogative was seen as being capable of enhancing the efficiency of British industry. Gone were the days when conceptions of cooperation and participation were interwoven into the vocabulary and practice of economic management. Stress was placed on the positive roles that could be played by a reemphasis of competitive pressures, increased training, the shedding of "surplus" labour and increased investment, particularly in areas of high technology and capital intensity. Related changes were taking place in the industrial relations arena. Discussions of industrial democracy, participation and the enhancement of worker rights ceased. Indeed efforts were made to repeal or not to enforce legislative rights conveyed by the previous administration. The relevance of a relationship between democracy and efficiency was no longer seen. The vocabulary of change focussed on competition, free markets and the ending of restrictive practices and monopoly powers. Certain economic rather than more widespread social and political rights came to be emphasised. More significance was attached to decisive and entrepreneurial action rather than cooperation and persuasion. Leadership rather than participation was the order of the day.

The accounting profession was slow to recognise the relevance of the changes taking place. The fear of government intervention had been a very deeply felt and widely articulated one. Eventually, however, it came to realise that it was no longer subject to the same intensity of threat. Although still very much concerned with very visible remnants of an era past in the form of inflation accounting, the profession in general and the Accounting Standards Committee in particular started to adjust itself to the new political situation. Representatives of wider industrial and financial constituencies were brought on to the Accounting Standards Committee now that its legitimacy as a protector of the profession from an interventionist State was no longer apparent. New investments were made in the potential legitimising roles of knowledge (see Hopwood, 1984). And the agenda of future areas of standard setting was radically curtailed. Amongst other things, value added was removed from the agenda for future deliberation and action.

The time for value added was no longer. The specific constellation which had resulted in its emergence, significance and development had been ruptured. The arenas out of which value added had emerged had been subject to significant discontinuities. The social context of value added had mutated. Devoid of its specific social conditions of possibility, value added was little more than a mere technical accounting possibility — perhaps something to be mentioned in the footnotes of accounting texts. The factors that had endowed it with a wider significance and momentum for development had disappeared.

Such a waning of interest in value added was not a new phenomenon however. Value added also had had a period of temporary significance in the United Kingdom in the late 1940s and early 1950s. Then, as in the mid 1970s, there also was conjoined a considerable interest in employee communication and information disclosure and a concern for the performance of the British economy. It was in this context that value added also appeared in company reporting practices in a way which also completely anticipated the practices of the late 1970s (Burchell *et al.*, 1981). Between those two periods there was little if any discussion of value added however.

The immediate backcloth to this earlier, proto-value added event was the Second World War. War-time mobilization resulted in trade unionists being heavily involved at all levels in the administration of social and economic policy (Pelling, 1971). Many of these war-time arrangements continued after the war when the problems of post-war reconstruction and the sudden ending of American "lend-lease" assistance led to a continued concentration on production and productivity. The winter fuel crisis of 1947 brought things to a head. In response to the Government's call for cooperation, the General Council of the Trades Union Congress urged the reconstitution of the joint production committees in the factories, most of which had faded away after the war. In addition, the issue of wage restraint came very much to the fore. One aspect of this period, as evidenced by the work of the Anglo-American Productivity Council and the contents of *Target*, a Central Office of Information publication, was the extent to which attempts were made to propagate the value of more systematic management practices. What is particularly interesting is that this discussion of enterprise practices was shot through with the imagery of cooperative endeavour. Cooperation and participation were presented as the means of underpinning improved economic performance and were to be secured by the disclosure of information. In the words of a *Target* editorial statement (*Target*, 1948):

> There is undoubtedly widespread misapprehension among working men and women upon the subject of wages and profits. The points made by the Chancellor of the Exchequer . . . at the recent Trades Union Congress need further elaboration and emphasis. The subject must be dealt with fully and frankly if workers generally are to be satisfied on the issues involved . . . the worker, who suspects that the shareholders are reaping large rewards while he, the man who produces the goods, is denied his dues, should be given the facts. More often than not a full and frank explanation will remove such misconceptions . . . if we are going to stand on our own feet by the time American aid comes to an end — by 1952 at the latest — we must concentrate on productivity . . . if workers can be made to feel that they really are partners in this all-out effort to put this country of ours on its feet again, they are surely entitled to the full facts?

Target functioned as a means of communication between companies on the problems of raising productivity. During the first eight months of its existence it focussed on works information schemes before being designated the official means of communication between the Anglo-American Productivity Council and British industry in February, 1949. Before this happened readers of the publication were greeted by such headlines as "Telling workers the facts"; "Scottish firm tells the workers 'what and why'"; "More firms who say where the money goes"; "The facts about factory economics"; and even "Workers had all the facts — up went efficiency".

Many of the employee communication schemes of companies featured in *Target* were organised around forms of distribution accounting, very reminiscent of the value added statements used nowadays in employee newspapers. Information was presented in order to reveal "how each pound of revenue . . . is paid out to the various costs of manufacture or remain as profits". It was at this juncture that value added made its entry in a booklet entitled *Added Value* produced by Metal Box Company Ltd (written by Sir Robert Barlow, the company's chairman). "In spite of paper difficulties", a copy of *Added Value* was sent to every man and woman on the weekly staff and to hourly-paid workers in certain long service grades. Its publication was timed to coincide with the issue of the company's 1948 annual report which was sent to every member of each factory's work committee. Writing in the booklet, Sir Robert commented that:

> There is . . . a great deal of misconception about profits, or, as they might properly be called, earnings. There is even a danger that they may be regarded as evil in themselves — hence that those who earn them are engaged in anti-social activities.
>
> Writing from the standpoint of productive industry, we say that this is the opposite of truth: that a profit which arises from the efficient working of a worthwhile enterprise is legitimate, desirable and necessary. For the alternative to a profit is a loss, and who, may it be asked, will be the better for that? Not the shareholders, not the employees, not the management, nor the State, for all of these benefit from a profit and would suffer from a loss. Least of all, perhaps, the customer; for no enterprise, operating at a loss, can supply him with what he will need in a market competitive in quality and price.
>
> The object of this booklet is to demonstrate this from facts; to go further and to show that from the operations of an industrial concern there arises an added value which is shared by all. For when a man performs a useful piece of work he creates wealth in its real sense. Once a body of men are actuated to perform their part of a common task in a better than normal way, and when from their efforts there flows a continually expanding activity, wealth is created to a considerably increased degree. Profit ceases to be, if indeed it ever has been, the dominating motive, and pride in work and an ensuing sense of responsibility takes its place (Metal Box Company Ltd, 1948).

In the name of such ideas, Metal Box introduced a whole array of strategies and practices to communicate the facts of business life to the workers

[21] For a discussion of other related schemes at this time see Burchell *et al.* (1981).

in order "to explain the significance of . . . various points, their impact on the company, what the organization as a whole and the men and women who make it work, can do to help."[21]

The existence of such a proto-value added enables us to reinforce the point concerning the way the functioning and very existance of accounting categories is conditioned by a complex set of circumstances. It also enables us to emphasise the highly specific and contingent nature of those circumstances. For in the early 1950s, as in the early 1980s, interest in value added was to wane. Again with a different political context and, in this case, the emergence of relative economic prosperity rather than the use of very different policies for the continued management of adversity, the value added constellation was ruptured and subjected to significant discontinuities. The very decline of interest in value added thereby serves to reinforce the theoretical perspective developed in this paper.

CONCLUSION

We have sought to indicate how the value added event arose out of a complex interplay of institutions, issues and processes. The study of this particular accounting change has enabled us not only to move towards grounding accounting in the specific social contexts in which it operates but also to raise and discuss what we see to be some important theoretical issues which have to be faced when seeking to understand the social functioning of the accounting craft.

Zeff (1978), albeit in a different way from ourselves, is another who has pointed to the need for such richer and more contextual appreciations of accounting in action. Focussing solely on the setting of accounting standards he points to the myriad political factors which have intruded in the setting (and subsequent criticism) of standards, factors the impact of which is not registered in the accounting model which has traditionally provided the dominant frame of reference for discussing accounting practices and the reasons for adopting them. Zeff argues that the economic and social consequences of accounting practices "may no longer be ignored as a substantive issue in the setting of accounting standards" (Zeff, 1978) and *inter alia* points to the importance of developing our theoretical resources in order to be able to adequately confront this issue.

Recently there has been developed a theoretical approach to accounting based on the agency model of the firm (Jensen & Meckling, 1976) which may be seen as a direct response to the problem articulated by Zeff. This approach has been employed in the analysis of the standard setting process (Watts & Zimmerman, 1978), the status and form of accounting theory (Watts & Zimmerman, 1979) and the form of particular accounting procedures (Zimmerman, 1979). By way of concluding, it is worthwhile to indicate briefly in what ways the approach we have adopted differs from that of the agency theorists and the associated implications for accounting research.

In general terms the differences between the two approaches can be clearly stated. In the case of the agency theorists, financial statements are viewed as economic goods for which there exists a certain demand and the production of which entails certain costs. The function of financial statements is that of a means of determining the magnitude of certain wealth transfers such as dividends, tax credits, loan payments, management renumeration and agency costs. Accounting procedures differ in their impact on these wealth transfers, and it is argued that individuals and groups are therefore not indifferent as to the particular procedures used. These individuals and groups calculate the effect on their wealth of using any given procedure and take up positions accordingly — whether it be in an unregulated market for financial statements or in relation to some regulatory agency. We do not doubt that individual agents do attempt to estimate the financial effects of proposed changes in accounting practice as part of their process of decision-making in relation to the choice of accounting procedures. We, however, are more interested in the processes whereby a particular configuration of interest groups, or rather groups with an interest in accounting, comes into existence. The agency theorists only distinguish between such configurations to the extent that they distinguish between regulated and unregulated economies. Clearly state intervention into the economy has been of enormous importance for the development of accounting (see Hopwood *et al.*, 1980). This, however, does not mean that it is impossible to construct a more nuanced picture than that which the dichotomy between a regulated and unregulated state allows and, at the same time, study in greater detail the processes of change. Amongst other things we would include amongst these processes those whereby accounting, or particular categories and statements, came to feature within the field of interest of certain agents and the *means* whereby the position of these agents with respect to these novel objects is deliberated and calculated: how was it that value added surfaced within the field of industrial relations and how was it evaluated once it had appeared there?

Thus our focus rests on the processes of change whereas the agency theorists attempt to establish correlations between certain classes of action, such as positions adopted on proposed accounting standards, and estimates of the interests of those adopting the positions. The agency theorists present their model as a self-interest theory whereas we are concerned to discover how self-interests, or particular policy positions, are in fact established — including the role which specific economic calculations and accountings rather than the generality of an economic calculus play in this process. The agency theorists privilege a particular mode of calculating (self-) interests derived from economic theory and a particular role for financial statements. Their analysis presupposes the existence of a meta-accounting which somehow guides rational economic action and their studies seek to explore specific explications and elaborations of such an accounting. Our analysis aims to make no such presumption of a primaeval account. Rather than being viewed by us as revelatory of particular administrative and policy making practices, the role and mode of calculation are instead viewed as functioning discursive components *within* these practices.

We have in this paper adopted a historical, genealogical approach as a device to avoid the assumption that accounting has some essential role or function. Our working principle in this has been that "the cause of the origin of a thing and its eventual unity, its actual employment and place in a system of purposes, are worlds apart" (Nietzsche, 1969, p. 77 as quoted in Minson, 1980). It has been suggested elsewhere that the organization of our concepts and the philosophical difficulties that arise from them, have to do with their historical origins. When there occurs a transformation of ideas, whatever made the transformation possible leaves its mark on subsequent reasoning. It is as if concepts have memories (Hacking, 1981). Indeed the study by Wells of the origins of accounting for overhead costs is written in just such a vein (Wells, 1978). In a similar way we have attempted to indicate how the processes underlying the value added event determined the character of discourse bearing the category value added.

BIBLIOGRAPHY

Aims and Scope of Company Reports, *The Accountant* (1 July, 1976) pp. 12–14.

Accounting Standards Steering Committee, *The Corporate Report* (ASSC, 1975).

Ackerman, R. & Bauer, R., *Corporate Social Responsiveness: The Modern Dilemma* (Englewood Cliffs, NJ: Prentice-Hall, 1976).

Aldrich, H. E., *Organizations and their Environments* (Englewood Cliffs, NJ: Prentice-Hall, 1979).

Ball, R. J., The Use of Value Added in Measuring Managerial Efficiency, *Business Ratios* (Summer 1968) pp. 5-11.

Barratt Brown, M., *Information at Work* (Arrow Books, 1978).

Beddoe, R., *Value Added and Payment Systems*, Technical note no. 42 (Oxford: The Trade Union Research Unit, Ruskin College, 1978).

Bedford, N. M., *The Future of Accounting in a Changing Society* (Champaign, IL: Stipes, 1970).

Benston, G. J., An Analysis of the Role of Accounting Standards for Enhancing Corporate Governance and Social Responsibility, in Bromwich, M., and Hopwood, A. G. (eds) *Accounting Standard Setting: An International Perspective* (Pitman, 1983).

Benston, G. J., *Corporate Financial Disclosure in the UK and the USA* (Saxon House, 1976).

Benston, G. J., The Value of the SEC's Accounting Disclosure Requirements, *The Accounting Review* (July 1969) pp. 515–532.

Bentley Associates, *A Dynamic Pay Policy for Growth* (Brighton: Bentley Associates, 1975).

Binder, Hamlyn and Fry & Co., *Added Value as a Concept* (Binder, Hamlyn and Fry, 1978).

British Institute of Management, *The Disclosure of Financial Information to Employees* (BIM, 1957).

Burchell, S., Clubb, C. & Hopwood, A., 'A Message From Mars' — and other Reminiscences From the Past, *Accountancy* (October 1981) pp. 96, 98, 100.

Burchell, S., Clubb, C., Hopwood, A. G., Hughes, J. & Nahapiet, J., The Roles of Accounting in Organizations and Society, *Accounting, Organizations and Society* (1980) pp. 5–27.

Cameron, S., Added Value Plan for Distributing ICI's Wealth, *Financial Times* (7 January, 1977a).

Cameron, S., Adding Value to Britain, *Financial Times* (31 May, 1977b).

Cameron, S., Breeding a New Type of Productivity Deal, *Financial Times* (3 April, 1978).

Carlsson, J., Ehn, P., Erlander, B., Perby, M-L. & Sandberg, Å., Planning and Control from the Perspective of Labour: A Short Presentation of the DEMOS Project, *Accounting, Organizations and Society* (1978) pp. 249–260.

Chambers, R. J., *Accounting, Evaluation and Economic Behaviour* (Englewood Cliffs, NJ: Prentice-Hall, 1966).

Chandler, A. D., *Strategy and Structure* (Cambridge, MA: M.I.T. Press, 1962).

Chandler, A. D., *The Visible Hand: The Managerial Revolution in American Business* (Harvard University Press, 1977).

Churchill, N. C., The Accountant's Role in Social Responsibility, in Stone, W. E., *The Accountant in a Changing Business Environment* (University of Florida Press, 1973) pp. 14–27.

Cohen, M. D., March, J. G., Olsen, J. P., A Garbage Can Model of Organizational Choice, *Administrative Science Quarterly* (March 1972) pp. 1–25.

Confederation of British Industry, *Financial Participation in Companies: An Introductory Booklet* (CBI, 1978).

Cooper, D., A Social and Organizational View of Management Accounting, in Bromwich, M. and Hopwood, A. G. (eds) *Essays in British Accounting Research* (Pitman, 1981).

Cox, B., *Value Added: An Appreciation for the Accountant Concerned with Industry* (Heinemann in association with the Institute of Cost and Management Accountants, 1979).

Crouch, C., *The Politics of Industrial Relations* (Fontana, 1979).

Crum, R. P., Added-Value Taxation: The Roots Run Deep into Colonial and Early America, *The Accounting Historians Journal* (Fall 1982) pp. 25–42.

Department of Trade, *Committee of Inquiry on Industrial Democracy* (Chairman: Lord Bullock) Cmnd 6706 (1977a).

Department of Trade, *The Future of Company Reports* (London: H.M.S.O., 1977b).

Dierkes, M., Corporate Social Reporting in Germany: Conceptual Developments and Practical Experience, *Accounting, Organizations and Society* (1979) pp. 87–100.

Dijksma, J. & Van der Wal, R., Value Added in Dutch Corporate Annual Reports 1980–1982. Working paper of the Faculteit der Economische Wetenschappen, Erasmus University, Rotterdam (1984).

Donovan, Lord, *Royal Commission on Trade Unions,* (Cmnd 3623, London: H.M.S.O., 1968).

Donzelot, J., *The Policing of Families* (Pantheon, 1979).

Elliot, J., The Liberals Make Their Point, *Financial Times* (3 February, 1978).

Engineering Employers Federation, *Business Performance and Industrial Relations* (Kogan Page, 1972).

Engineering Employers Federation, *Practical Applications of Added Value* (Archway Press, 1977).

Estes, R., *Accounting and Society* (Melville Publishing Company, 1973).

Estes, R. W., *Corporate Social Accounting* (New York: John Wiley, 1976).

Fanning, D., Banishing Confusion from the Added Value Equation, *Financial Times* (13 December, 1978) p. 11.

Fels, A., *The British Prices and Incomes Board* (Cambridge University Press, 1972).

Flint, D., The Role of the Auditor in Modern Society: An Exploratory Essay, *Accounting and Business Research* (Autumn 1971) pp. 287–293.

Foucault, M., Nietzsche, Genealogy, History, in Foucault M., (ed. by D. F. Bouchard), *Language, Counter-Memory, Practice* (Oxford: Basil Blackwell, 1977).

Frankel, M., *The Social Audit Pollution Handbook* (Macmillan, 1978).

Gambling, T., *Societal Accounting* (Macmillan, 1974).

Gandhi, N. M., The Emergence of the Postindustrial Society and the Future of the Accounting Function, *International Journal of Accounting* (Spring 1976) pp. 33–49.

Gandhi, N. M., Accounting in a Non Market Economy: A Futuristic Look, in Gordon, L. A. (ed.), *Accounting and Corporate Responsibility* (University of Kansas, 1978).

Gilling, D. M., Accounting and Social Change, *International Journal of Accounting* (Spring 1976) pp. 59–71.

Gold, M., Levie, H. & Moore, R., *The Shop Stewards' Guide to the Use of Company Information* (Spokesman Books, 1979).

Gordon, L. A. (ed) *Accounting and Corporate Social Responsibility* (University of Kansas, 1978).

Gospel, H., Disclosure of Information to Trade Unions, *Industrial Law Journal* (1976).

Gray, S. I. & Maunders, K. T., *Value Added Reporting: Uses and Measurement* (Association of Certified Accountants, 1980).

Hacking, I., How Should we do the History of Statistics, *Ideology and Consciousness* (Spring 1981) pp. 15–26.

Hilton, A., *Employee Reports: How to Communicate Financial Information to Employees* (Woodhead-Faulkner, 1978).

Hindess, B., Power, Interests and the Outcomes of Struggles, *Sociology* (November 1982) pp. 498–511.

Hird, C., Beware of Added Value, *New Statesman* (4 August, 1980).

Hird, C., *Your Employers' Profits* (Pluto Press, 1975).

Holmes, G., How UK Companies Report Their Employees, *Accountancy* (November 1977) pp. 64–68.

Hopkins, L., Value Added, *Accountancy Age* (7 November, 1975).

Hopwood, A. G., Accounting Research and Accounting Practice: The Ambiguous Relationship Between the Two. Paper presentation to the conference on New Challenges for Management Research, Leuven, Belgium (1984).

Hopwood, A. G., The Tale of a Committee that Never Reported: Disagreements on Intertwining Accounting with the Social, *Accounting, Organizations and Society* (1985) pp. 361–377.

Hopwood, A. G., The Archeology of Accounting Systems, *Accounting, Organizations and Society* (forthcoming).

Hopwood, A. G., Burchell, S. & Clubb, C., The Development of Accounting in its International Context: Past Concerns and Emergent Issues, In A. Roberts, ed., *A Historical and Contempory Review of the Development of International Accounting* (Georgia State University, 1980).

Hussey, R., *Employees and the Employment Report — A Research Paper* (Touche Ross & Co., 1978).

Hussey, R., *Who Reads Employee Reports?* (Touche Ross & Co., 1979).

Incomes Data Report, New Thoughts on Profit Sharing at ICI, *Report 251* (February 1977) p. 21.

Institute of Chartered Accountants in England and Wales, Statement of Intent on Accounting Standards in the 1970s, *The Accountant* (18 December, 1969) pp. 842–843.

Institute of Chartered Accountants in England and Wales (ICAEW), *Survey of Published Accounts 1977* (ICAEW, 1978).

Institute of Chartered Accountants in England and Wales (ICAEW), *Survey of Published Accounts 1979* (ICAEW, 1980).

Jenks, L. H., Early Phases of the Management Movement, *Administrative Science Quarterly* (1960) pp. 421–447.

Jensen, M. C. & Meckling, W. H., Theory of the Firm: Managerial Behaviour, Agency Costs and Ownership Structure, *Journal of Financial Economics* (1976), pp. 305–360.

Jones, F. C., *The Economic Ingredients of Industrial Success* (James Clayton Lecture, The Institution of Mechanical Engineers, 1976).

Jones, F. T., Our Manufacturing Industry — The Missing £100,000 million, *National Westminster Bank Quarterly Review* (May 1978) pp. 8–17.

Kahn-Freud, O., Industrial Democracy, *Industrial Law Journal* (1977) pp. 75–76.

Kuhn, T., *The Structure of Scientific Revolutions* 2nd Ed. (University of Chicago Press, 1970).

Labour Party, *The Community and the Company* (1974).

Value Added, *Labour Research* (February, 1978).

Leyland, N. H., Productivity, in Warswick and Ady, *The British Economy 1945–1950* (Oxford: The

Clarendon Press, 1952).

Litterer, J., Systematic Management: Design for Organizational Recoupling in American Manufacturing Firms, *Business History Review* (1963) pp. 369–391.

Litterer, J., Systematic Management: The Search for Order and Integration, *Business History Review* (1961) pp. 461–476.

Livingstone, J. L. & Gunn, S. C., *Accounting For Social Goals: Budgeting and Analysis of Non Market Projects* (Harper & Row, 1974).

Low, E., Forget Piecework and Develop a Fair Way to Reward Employees, *Accountants Weekly* (6 May, 1977) pp. 16–17.

Lucas, R. J., *Pension Planning Within a Major Company: A Case Study of the Negotiation of the British Leyland Pension Plan for Manual Workers* (Oxford: Pergamon Press, 1979).

Maitre, P., The Measurement of the Creation and Distribution of Wealth in a Firm by the Method of Surplus Accounts, *Accounting, Organizations and Society* (1978) pp. 227–236.

Marchington, M. P., Worker Participation and Plant-wide Incentive Systems, *Personnel Review* (Summer 1977) pp. 35–38.

McKersie, R. B. & Hunter, L. C., *Pay Productivity and Collective Bargaining* (Macmillan, 1973).

McLeay, S., Value Added: A Comparative Study, *Accounting, Organizations and Society* (1983) pp. 31–56.

Medawar, C., *The Social Audit Consumer Handbook* (Macmillan, 1978).

Metal Box Company Limited, *Added Value* (London: Metal Box Company Ltd., 1948).

440 Minson, J., Stragegies for Socialists? Foucault's Conception of Power, *Economy and Society* (1980).

Moonitz, M., *Obtaining Agreement on Standards in the Accounting Profession*, Studies in Accounting Research No. 8 (American Accounting Association, 1974).

Morley, M. F., *The Value Added Statement* (Gee & Co. for the Institute of Chartered Accountants of Scotland, 1978).

National Board for Prices and Incomes, *General Report, August 1967 – July 1968*, (Cmnd 3715 London: H.M.S.O., 1968).

Neimark, M. D. & Tinker, A. M., The Social Construction of Management Control Systems, *Accounting, Organizations and Society* (forthcoming).

Nelson, C. L., *A Priori* Research in Accounting, in Dopuch, N. and Revsine, L. (eds) *Accounting Research 1960 – 1970: A Critical Evaluation* (Center for International Education and Research in Accounting, 1973).

New, C., Factors in Productivity that Should Not be Overlooked, *The Times* (1 February, 1978).

Nietzche, F., *On the Genealogy of Morals*, Kaufmann, W. (trans.) (Vintage Books, 1969).

Pakenham-Walsh, A. A., Spanners in the Growth Engine, *The Cost Accountant* (July 1964) pp. 260–268.

Patton, P., Of Power and Prisons, in Morris, M. & Patton, P. (eds.) *Michel Foucault: Power, Truth, Strategy* (Sydney: Feral Publications, 1979).

Pelling, A., *A History of British Trade Unionism* (Harmondsworth: Penguin Books, 1971).

Pitkin, H. F., *The Concept of Representation* (University of California Press, 1967).

Ramanathan, K. V., Theory of Corporate Social Accounting, *The Accounting Review* (July 1976) pp. 516–528.

Reichmann, T. & Lange, C., The Value Added Statement as Part of Corporate Social Reporting, *Management International Review* (1981).

Renshall, M., Allan, R. & Nicholson, K., *Added Value in External Financial Reporting* (Institute of Chartered Accountants in England and Wales, 1979).

Rey, F., *Introduction a la Comptabilite Sociale: Domaines, Techniques et Applications* (Paris: Enterprise Moderne d'Edition, 1978).

Roberts, J. & Scapens, R., Accounting Systems and Systems of Accountability – Understanding Accounting Practices in Their Organizational Contexts, *Accounting, Organizations and Society* (1985) pp. 443–456.

Robertson, J., Can we have a Non-Profit Society, *The Sunday Times* (19 May, 1974).

Ruggles, R. & Ruggles, N. D., *National Income Accounts and Income Analysis*, 2nd Ed.(New York: McGraw Hill, 1965).

Rutherford, B. A., Value Added as a Focus of Attention for Financial Reporting: Some Conceptual Problems, *Accounting and Business Research* (Summer 1977) pp. 215–220.

Rutherford, B. A., Examining Some Value Added Statements, *Accountancy* (July 1978) pp. 48–52.

Rutherford, B. A., Published Statements of Value Added: A Survey of Three Year's Experience, *Accounting and Business Review* (Winter, 1980), pp. 15–28.

Sandilands Committee, *Inflation Accounting: Report of the Inflation Accounting Committee,* (Cmnd 6225 London: H.M.S.O., 1975).

Schreuder, H., Corporate Social Reporting in the Federal Republic of Germany: an Overview, *Accounting, Organizations and Society* (1979) pp. 109–122.

Searle, G. R., *The Quest for National Efficiency* (Oxford: Basil Blackwell, 1971).

Sharp, K., Accounting Standards After 12 months, *Accountancy* (May 1971) pp. 239–245.

Skerratt, L. C. L. & Tonkin, D. J., *Financial Reporting 1982–83: A Survey of U.K. Published Accounts* (Institute of Chartered Accountants in England and Wales, 1982).

Smith, G., *Wealth Creation — the Added Value Concept* (Institute of Practitioners in Work Study, Organizations and Methods, 1978).

Stamp, E., The Politics of Professional Accounting Research: Some Personal Reflections, *Accounting, Organizations and Society* (1985).

Stolliday, I. & Attwood, M., Financial Inducement and Productivity Bargaining, *Industrial and Commercial Training* (1978).

Stuttard, G., Industrial Democracy by the Back Door, *Financial Times* (21 March, 1979).

Target, The Facts About Factory Economics (November 1948).

Tinker, A. M., The Naturalization of Accounting: Social Ideology and the Genesis of Agency Theory. Working paper, New York University (1984).

Tinker, A. M., Towards a Political Economy of Accounting: An Empirical Illustration of the Cambridge Controversies, *Accounting, Organizations and Society* (1980) pp. 147–160.

Tinker, A. M., Merino, B. D. & Neimark, M. D., The Normative Origins of Positive Theories: Ideology and Accounting Thought, *Accounting, Organizations and Society* (1982) pp. 167–200.

Tomlinson, J., *Problems of British Economic Policy, 1870–1945* (Metheun, 1981).

Tonkin, D. J. & Skerratt, L. C. L., *Financial Reporting 1983–84: A Survey of U.K. Published Accounts* (Institute of Chartered Accountants in England and Wales, 1983).

Trades Union Congress, *Industrial Democracy* (TUC, 1974).

Turner, H. A., Collective Bargaining and the Eclipse of Incomes Policies: Retrospect, Prospect and Possibilities, *British Journal of Industrial Relations* (July 1970).

Ullman, A. A., Corporate Social Reporting: Political Interests and Conflicts in Germany, *Accounting, Organizations and Society* (1979) pp. 123–133.

Vangermeersch, R. G. J., *Accounting: Social Responsible and Socially Relevant* (Harper and Row, 1972).

Vickers da Costa, *Testing for Success* (London: Mimeo, 1979).

Vogel, D., *Lobbying the Corporation: Citizen Challenges to Business Authority* (Basic Books, 1978).

Watts, R. L., Corporate Financial Statements: A Product of the Market and Political Processes, *Australian Journal of Management* (April 1977) pp. 53–75.

Watts, R. L., & Zimmerman, J. L., The Demand for the Supply of Accounting Theories: The Market for Excuses, *The Accounting Review* (April 1979) pp. 273–305.

Watts, R. L. & Zimmerman, J. L., Towards a Positive Theory of the Determination of Accounting Standards, *The Accounting Review* (January 1978) pp. 112–134.

Wellens, J., An ICI Experiment in Company-wide Communication, *Industrial and Commercial Training* (July 1977) pp. 271–278.

Wells, M. C., *Accounting for Common Costs* (International Centre for Accounting Education and Research, University of Illinois, 1978).

Wells, M. C., A Revolution in Accounting Thought, *The Accounting Review* (July 1976) pp. 471–482.

Whittington, G., *Inflation Accounting: An Introduction to the Debate* (Cambridge University Press, 1983).

Wilsher, P., How do you cut your Profit and Save Prosperity, *Sunday Times* (30 June, 1974).

Woodmansay, M., *Added Value: An Introduction to Productivity Schemes* (British Institute of Management, 1978).

Zeff, S. A., *Forging Accounting Principles in Five Countries* (Stipes, 1972).

Zeff, S. A., The Rise of Economic Consequences, *Journal of Accountancy* (December 1978).

Zimmerman, J. L., The Cost and Benefits of Cost Allocations, *The Accounting Review* (1979) pp. 504–521.

Accounting, Organizations and Society, Vol. 12, No. 3, pp. 207–234, 1987
Printed in Great Britain

0361-3682/87 $3.00+.00
Pergamon Journals Ltd.

THE ARCHAEOLOGY OF ACCOUNTING SYSTEMS*

ANTHONY G. HOPWOOD
London School of Economics and Political Science

Abstract

Accounting systems change over time. However relatively little is known of the preconditions for such change, the process of change or its organisational consequences. Existing perspectives on accounting change are reviewed and evaluated in this article. Thereafter three examples of accounting change are discussed. Based on these cases, a number of theoretical issues relating to the understanding of the process of accounting change are examined. Emphasis is placed on the diversity of factors implicated in accounting change, the constitutive as well as reflective roles of accounting and the ways in which accounting change can shift the preconditions for subsequent organisational changes.

Accounting is not a static phenomenon. Over time, it repeatedly has changed. New techniques have been incorporated into the accounting craft. It has been called upon to serve an ever greater variety of different and changing purposes. Different accounts have been provided of organisational activities, processes and outcomes. Different emphases have been incorporated into accounting practices. Over time, accounting has been implicated in the creation of very different patterns of organisational segmentation. New patterns of organisational autonomy and interdependency have been highlighted, if not more actively created by accounting means. Different managerial functions have come to be emphasized by the changing accounting representation of them.

When seen in such terms, accounting continually has had a tendency to become what it was not. A fluid and emergent craft, its techniques and their attendant perspectives have been implicated in a number of very different ways in organisational and social transformations. Unfortunately, however, very little is known of the processes of accounting change. As of now we have only a limited understanding of the conditions which provide the possibility for particular conceptions of the accounting craft, the forces that put accounting into motion, the processes accompanying accounting elaboration and diffusion, and the varied human, organisational and social consequences that can stem from changing accounting regimes.

Although a great deal of attention has been devoted to the history of accounting (American Accounting Association, 1970; Baladouni, 1977; Parker, 1977, 1981), most of the studies that are available have adopted a rather technical perspective delineating the residues of the accounting past rather than more actively probing into the underlying processes and forces at work. Antiquarianism has reigned supreme. Much of the significance for accounting of the wider economic and social setting of the organisation has

* The financial support of the Anglo-German Foundation for the Study of Industrial Society and the Foundation for Management Education is greatly acknowledged. The paper has benefited enormously from discussions with Stuart Burchell, Colin Clubb, John Hughes and Janine Nahapiet. The more specific comments of Shahid Ansari, Simon Archer, Mark Covaleski, Mark Dirsmith, Graeme Harrison, Pat Keating, Brendan McSweeney, Peter Miller, Ted O'Leary, Charles Perrow and Ross Stewart have greatly assisted in the revision process. Finally, I wish to acknowledge the facilitative environment provided by my Summer colleagues at Pennsylvania State University which helped the preparation of the final draft of the article.

been ignored. The roles which organisational accounts might have played in the emergence of organisations as we now know them, the external and internal boundaries which they are conceived of having, and the relationships which they have to other bodies and interests have been subjected to very little investigation. Relatively little consideration has been given to the ways in which accounting has become implicated in, and, in turn, shaped by, the emergence of processes of organisational governance and management. For until recently (Armstrong, 1985, 1987; Hoskin & Macve, 1986; Loft, 1986a; Merino & Neimark, 1982; Miller & O'Leary, 1987), most historical analyses of the accounting phenomenon, if not adopting a quite atheoretical stance, have been content to see ac-
444 counting change as a process of technical elaboration and, almost invariably, improvement.

Rather than being perceived as an outcome of processes that could make accounting what it was not, accounting has more frequently been seen as becoming what it should be. A teleological trajectory of development has provided a basis for understanding changes in the accounting craft. Discursive conceptions of technical or economic rationality and purpose have been called upon to make sense of the emergence of practical developments in the accounting arena.[1] Instead of being interrogated in the name of the factors that either impinge upon accounting or are changed as a result of it, a relatively unproblematic progressive and functionalist interest has been imposed all too readily on the residues of the accounting past.

A not dissimilar perspective also has tended to pervade many of the attempts that have been made to gain a more explicit organisational understanding of the accounting phenomenon. Relatively little has been done to advance our understanding of the pressures that impinge on accounting in practice; we have few insights into how the very practice of accounting might itself create a dynamic for accounting change and reform; and little is known of the precarious and often uncertain relationships which the practice of accounting has with the potential in the name of which it is advanced.[2] Despite the fact that accounting has and still does become what it is not, despite the fact that accounting can be quite centrally implicated in wider processes of organisational functioning, and despite the fact that accounting gets mobilised in the name of ends that do not enter into its own justification (Burchell *et al.*, 1980), many organisational enquiries into accounting have tended to see and study it in ways that are disconnected from the contexts in which it operates. It is still perceived

[1] For a somewhat more detailed discussion of the relationship between accounting (and related) discourses and accounting practice see Hopwood (1984b). Also see Miller & O'Leary (1986, 1987). A fuller consideration of the practical consequences of accounting discourse also would probe into the discursive cohesion given to disparate accounting practices by textbooks and manuals, the diffusion roles served by these sources, and the significance for the development of an accounting rhetoric of the extension of accounting discourse into the arena of the organizational and, particularly, the managerial uses of accounting techniques. Accounting discourses also have played an influential role in interpreting the heterogeneous nature of practice, isolating from amongst the diversity examples of both "good" and "bad". By so appealing to conceptions of practice that are not in any sense implicit in the craft itself, the accounting discourse articulates a normalising logic that concerns itself with the achievement of what is seen to be accounting and organizational improvement. For a further discussion of these points see Hopwood (1986a).

[2] Although many enquiries have sought to identify the dysfunctional aspects of accounting functioning, these usually have been seen as phenomena to be confronted and changed in the name of an accounting potential rather than manifestations of the organizational tensions and conflicts created by the increasing encroachment of the accounting craft on other aspects of organizational life. As such, analyses of dysfunctions have tended to tell us much about the conceptions of the ideal from which practice is deemed to have deviated as they do about the functioning of accounting systems in practice. Indeed such a primary concern with the accounting potential rather than its actuality also is reflected in the increasingly sophisiticated attempts that have been made to utilize behavioural understandings to fine-tune the sociotechnical practice of accounting. Rather than seeking to confront the technical practice of accounting, and the aims that are attributed to it, with insights gained from an appreciation of its organizational emergence, functioning and consequences, many behavioural and organizational studies have tended to be used to mobilize the technical interest.

as a relatively static technical phenomenon that enables rather than more actively shapes organisational functioning as we now know it.

The need for an alternative view of accounting in action is now a very real one, however. On the other hand, there are a number of quite significant pressures on accounting to change. Questions are being raised about the relationship which accounting might have to different organisational forms and processes (den Hertog, 1978; Hedberg & Jönsson, 1978; Hopwood, 1977, 1979). Increasingly accounting is being interrogated in the name of a more strategic conception of organisational management (Goold, 1986; Simmonds, 1983). Accounts are being demanded of different organisations, not least those residing outside the domain of the "private" (Hopwood, 1984a). Different information technologies are creating the potential for continued shifts in the locus and organisational significance of the accounting craft. And, not least in significance, increasingly accounting is being examined in terms of the consequences which it actually has rather than those to which it continues to aspire (Hopwood, 1986; Kaplan, 1985). So albeit slowly, the factors implicated in accounting change, its organisational advancement and the actual consequences of the accounting craft are startingto enter the research agenda. On the other hand, the research perspectives from which accounting is examined also are starting to change. Rather than necessarily seeking to advance only the technical rationality of the craft, there are signs of both more appreciative and more critical stances emerging within the research community. Not unrelated to this, very different questions are starting to be asked of accounting. Rather than accepting its technical rationality, such research is beginning to probe into the wider organisational and social origins of accounting as we now know it. Questions are being asked of the variety of organisational pressures and rationales underlying the accounting craft. Consideration is being given to the ways in which conflicting interests are intertwined with the development of forms of economic calculation, such as accounting. And with accounting no longer seen as a disinterested endeavour, but as one that creates a very particular visibility and pattern of organisational significance, more explicit attention is being given to its consequences for both organisational and social action.

When seen in such terms, the agenda for research is a large one. The technical and static emphases of the past stand in stark contrast to the emerging interest in a wider view of accounting dynamics. Recognising, however, that such an agenda is beyond the scope of any single analysis and review, the present discussion has a number of more particular objectives. Initially some existing perspectives, both explicit and implicit, on accounting change are examined. The aim is to consider their adequacy for understanding both the forces that put accounting into motion and the ways in which the accounting craft becomes intertwined with organisational and social action. Thereafter, an appeal is made to a number of illustrative cases, both historical and contemporary, in order to illuminate at least some of the pressures and processes involved in accounting change. Rather than striving to present comprehensive analyses of accounting becoming what it was not, the objective of the case discussions is the more tentative one of trying to tease out some bases for an alternative questioning of the accounting craft. Based on these case analyses, a number of important issues relevant for an understanding of accounting change are identified and discussed. The aim of the analysis as a whole is to move towards a more questioning, a more organisationally grounded and a more dynamic understanding of the accounting craft.

SOME PERSPECTIVES ON ACCOUNTING CHANGE

Accounting and organisational improvement

As has been made clear already, the majority of conventional discussions of accounting change see it in terms of organisational reform and improvement. Accounting is changed in order to get better. Albeit slowly, the craft is seen as having progressed. Analysis, enquiry and experiential learning together are seen as having resulted in the increasing realisation of an accounting potential. In becoming what it was not, accounting has been seen to be in the process of becoming what it should be.

Such characterisations of accounting change invariably appeal to the role which accounting is seen as playing in the enhancement of organisational performance. Organisational economy, efficiency and effectiveness are seen not only as being capable of being improved by accounting means but also as having an existence independent of the accounting or other calculative representations of them. Moreover, the positive roles which accounting plays in organisational functioning also tend to be defined prior to and

independently of the specific organisational practices by which they are effected. Accounting is seen as being implicated in processes of direction, planning, decision making, co-ordination, control and the management of motivation, amongst other things. In all of these areas specific practices of accounting can be, and indeed are, compared with abstract conceptualisations of what they essentially should be about.

In such ways conceptual bodies of knowledge play a powerful role in informing our understandings of the accounting craft. Accounting, even in the conventional view, is not a mere technique. Knowledge does not stand outside of accounting. Our appreciations of the technical nature of accounting are infused by a rhetoric of economic and managerial rationality and functioning. Appeals are made to a "conceptual network" (Foucault, 1972) of ideas, categories and theories that are seen to illuminate and give guidance to the pragmatic accounting task. Actual accounting practices thereby can be seen as manifestations of the realisation or frustration of these abstract imperatives. They can be seen as being more or less adequate in ways that are not solely dependent on their specific functioning in specific organisations. And because of this, attempts can be made to improve accounting in the name of what it should be rather than what it is.

As a discipline, accounting has invested a great deal in the articulation of abstract bodies of knowledge concerned with what it should be.[3] Ideas exist as to good, indeed, "best", costing practice, good planning, good modes of management reporting and good approaches to the appraisal of new investment possibilities. Attempts have been made to tease out the abstract characteristics of good co-ordination and direction, and their implications for the reform of accounting practice. Both economic and cognitive conceptions of decision making and its rationality have been related to the accounting concrete. Regimes of thought thereby have been developed which have an existence and dynamic of change which are not dependent on the practice of the accounting craft. By drawing on bodies of knowledge from such more autonomous discourses as economics, political theory, public administration and psychology or emergent notions of strategic management, as well as by abstracting from the practice and functioning of the craft itself, accounting can be evaluated in terms of what it is not. Specific practices can be appraised on the basis of their conformity to more general notions of management and the manageable. An abstract external body of knowledge can be imposed on them in order both to assess their adequacy and to reform them so that they can become what they really should be. Accounting is seen as being able to be mobilised and changed in the name of an abstract image of its real potential.[4]

[3] Such understandings are not only future orientated. Very particular appreciations of the past also have informed our view of what accounting is and might become. As has been discussed already, quite specific trajectories of emergence have been imposed on accounting developments, at times creating a basis for a powerful continuity between what accounting was and what it should become. For more general discussions of the mobilization of understandings of the past see Hobsbawm & Ranger (1983), Lowenthal (1985) and Wright (1985).

[4] In the area of financial accounting, the debates over inflation accounting would provide an interesting arena in which to study such processes at work.

Undoubtedly much accounting change has resulted from such conceptions of an accounting potential. However, as a basis for understanding either the process or the consequences of such change, conventional views are severely limited. For rather than providing a history of the emergence of accounting as it now is, they provide the basis for the compilation of a history of inadequacy, ignorance and obsolescence when accounting was not what it should be, peppered with only occasional moments of enlightenment when accounting moved nearer to realising its potential. Presuming that the functions of accounting exist independently of its practice, that its practice is orientated towards particular goals that themselves are autonomous of the accountings that are made of them and that the problem of practice is to reform organisational procedures so that their intrinsic goals are achieved, accounting change is described and evaluated by reference to a body of knowledge that is assumed to be external to accounting itself. So, whilst the realisation of the accounting potential may be problematic, the potential itself is only rarely, if ever, seen in either problematic or emergent terms. It is endowed with a privileged epistemological status such that although accounting is seen as being laboriously constructed, its essence is not. Rather than enquiring into their own patterns of emergence, the means by which they have gained a current significance and the circumstances under which they come to be intertwined with the specifics of technical change, accounting has taken for granted the discourses that are credited with mobilising change.

Such a view of accounting development also ignores the duality of the interactions between accounting and ideas of its potential. In both historical and organisational terms the apparatus of organising has played a profound role in influencing our conceptions of the organisation. Ideas about organisational goals, functions and functioning have emerged amidst the development of specific means of organisational action and calculation. Equally, organisational participants have not been defined externally to the practices in which they are engaged. The concepts of management and the manager were actively constructed in a particular way at a particular socio-historical juncture and are inseparable from the practical means of administration and calculation which were, and still are, implicated in their emergence and functioning. There was no *a priori* manager to whom one can appeal as having interests and needs which can mobilise the development of management practices. Equally, there was no primeval concept of accounting which shaped the development of accounting as we now know it. Accounting has emerged in a more positive way than the mere realisation of an essence. Indeed, in part, the present imperatives of accounting which can and do guide its development have emerged from the practice of the craft. And, in similar terms, accounting practice needs to be seen as playing a more active role in creating rather than merely enabling organised endeavour. Accounting change is as much a history of organisational construction as organisation realisation and enablement.[5]

That is not to deny that external discourses of an accounting potential can and do mobilise accounting change. They provide an incentive for action and an understanding of specific organisational targets for intervention can be constructed on their bases (Nahapiet, 1984). They can also provide criteria for both gauging the presumed need for change and reading its effects. But such appreciations of the roles served by discourses which can direct and facilitate change still do not help us to understand the mechanisms of change, the forces mobilising the deployment of different accountings and different accounting rhetorics, the precise practices involved, the resistances which they engender and the actual organisational consequences which they gave rise to. For it would be inap-

[5] Such a point is emphasized by Litterer (1963) in his discussion of the emergence of systematic management in American manufacturing firms. He states that "in fact, it is systems such as those we have been discussing and many others like them which constitute the great bulk of managerial activities" (p. 388, also see p. 391).

propriate to assume that there is any invariant relationship between a rhetoric and discourse of accounting and a programme of intervention in the organisation conducted in the name of it. The variety of forms that such a relationship can take should be a problem for investigation rather than presumption.

Accounting and the construction of an organisational order

Increasingly accounting practice has itself become the focus of research interest. Realising the ambiguous relationship between the abstract discourse of an accounting potential and the specifics of accounting as it functions in organisations, research has come to be more concerned with analysing and understanding accounting in action (Hopwood, 1978, 1983; Kaplan, 1983; Scapens, 1983, 1984). In the vast majority of such investigations, however, the phenomenon of accounting change has not been emphasized explicitly. Primary consideration has been given to the present diversity of the accounting craft and the use made of the resultant accountings at any particular point in time.

Although studies have started to investigate the organisational tensions engendered by the use of accounting systems, comparatively little consideration has been given to how these might provide bases for a re-appraisal and change of the accounting craft. Some histories of accounting resistance and dysfunctions have been written, but, with relatively few exceptions (Argyris, 1977; Berry *et al.*, 1985), little or no consideration has been given to the counter histories of accounting elaboration and change as attempts are made to ensure the continued integrity, legitimacy, effectiveness and power of the craft. So, although accounting is starting to be examined in its organisational context, the underlying perspective remains a relatively static one. The analyses that have been made of accounting diversity are not dissimilar. Although the differences in the contemporaneous practice of the craft have provided an incentive for the analysis of some of the factors that impinge on the forms that accounting takes, the resultant contingent analyses have many of the characteristics of an exercise in comparative studies (Otley, 1980). Accounting is seen as it was and as it is rather than in the process of becoming. Moreover the organisational calculus implicit in accounting adaptation is still one that is posited on the functional roles that accounting plays in the enhancement of a neutral and highly generalised concept of organisational performance. Little role is acknowledged for management discretion and choice (Child, 1972; Thompson, forthcoming), let alone the active exercise of politics and power (Cooper, 1981; Pettigrew, 1972). Accounting change also is seen as a reflective rather than a constructive organisational endeavour. With accounting conceived of as enabling rather than more actively shaping organisational affairs, other organisational factors are seen as impinging on it, but accounting seemingly is seen as having no similarly active role to play. Different accountings are seen as reflecting different circumstances rather than themselves being implicated in a more positive process by which accounting becomes what it was not. The analysis of accounting diversity thereby has resulted only in a presumption of change rather than more specific analyses of the processes involved which make no prior assumptions as to either the underlying logics at work or the organisational roles and consequences of the accounting craft.

Still, such organisational appreciations have been useful. Despite the many problems to which they are subject (Dent, 1986; Otley, 1980), accounting at least is being shown as a craft that is embedded in the functioning of the organisation, co-existing and interdependent with such other aspects of the organisation as its strategy, structure, approaches to the segmentation of work and other organisational technologies and practices. Not existing as an isolated craft, accounting is shown as being an organisational practice that is constructed and used amidst the configuration of a specific culture, be it organisational or national (Horovitz, 1980), a specific organisational environment and a specific set of approaches to the management of the organisational task. Accounting has at least been grounded in the organisational contexts in which it operates. And by being seen as a phenomenon that is so interdependent with its context and subject thereby to the vicissitudes of other organisational practices and concerns, the possibility is at least opened up that accounting is not necessarily adequate to the ends in the name of which it is advanced (Argyris, 1977; Kaplan, 1983). So although the perspectives remain preliminary and partial, abstract conceptions of the potential of the craft are nevertheless being faced by a growing understanding of its practices.

Accounting and the construction of a social order

Preliminary though they are, organisational insights into accounting all still see accounting as a practice that has a rationale that can be understood purely in terms of the needs and requirements of the specific organisations in which it functions. Accounting is seen as having its origins within the problems created by the need to co-ordinate and manage a complex process of transformation within the context of a particular regime of organisational constraints and objectives. More recent inquiries are starting to question such an organisationally isolated view however. Increasingly accounting is coming to be seen as having some of its origins in the social conflicts which are enacted in the organisational arena (Cooper, 1980, 1981; Hopper *et al.*, 1986; Tinker, 1980; Tinker *et al.*, 1982). Rather than seeing organisational accounts as a technical reflection of the pregiven economic imperatives facing organisational administration, they are now being seen to be more actively constructed in order to create a particular economic visibility within the organisation and a powerful means for positively enabling the governance and control of the organisation along economic lines (Clawson, 1980). Accounting, when seen in such terms, is not a passive instrument of technical administration, a neutral means for merely revealing the pregiven aspects of organisational functioning. Instead its origins are seen to reside in the exercising of social power both within and without the organisation. It is seen as being implicated in the forging, indeed the active creation, of a particular regime of economic calculation within the organisation in order to make real and powerful quite particular conceptions of economic and social ends.

From such a perspective, organisational options, decisions and actions are seen as being positively shaped by the ways in which they intersect with accounting practices. Accounting is seen as having played a very positive role in the creation of a manageable organisational domain. A regime of economic visibility and calculation has positively enabled the creation and operation of an organisation which facilitates the exercising of particular social conceptions of power. Economic motives have been made real and influential by their incorporation into legitimate and accepted economic facts. The labour process in the organisation has been exposed, ordered and physically and socially distributed. The resultant organisational facts, calculations, schedules and plans have positively enabled the construction of a management regime abstracted and distanced from the operation of the work process itself.

So, although functioning within the organisation, accounting is best seen from such a perspective as an artifact residing in the domain of the social rather than the narrowly organisational. It has been implicated in the radical transformation of the organisation in the name of the social. Indeed, accounting is considered as one of the important means by which the organisation is incorporated into the social domain.

Accounting change is clearly a specific focus of attention from such a viewpoint. Not only has the development of accounting practice been addressed quite explicitly but also a particular trajectory of development sometimes has been imposed upon it. Indeed, in some senses, accounting, when seen from such a perspective, still has an essence, a mission which mobilises its development. Accounting, from such a stance, is still a revelatory endeavour, making real, by the active construction of the organisation as we know it, interests which are independent of both the accounting and the organisational representation of them. And, like the more conventional presumptions of accounting in motion, it can still be seen as an endeavour that is adequate to the ends in the name of which it is advanced. Accounting is seen to be both purposive and purposeful.

Towards a view of accounting in motion

Albeit slowly, our understanding of accounting change nevertheless is advancing. Attempts are being made to confront the conventional view of accounting improvement with insights from analyses of the organisational and social functioning of the craft. Accounting is in the process of being seen as an organisational practice in motion, the changes and consequences of which are dependent on its intertwining with other approaches to the creation of a manageable organisational regime. A very real start has
450 been made on locating the construction and functioning of accounting in the domains of the organisational and the social rather than purely the technical.

As has been discussed above, existing approaches are still preliminary however. Relatively few attempts have been made to confront the specifics of accounting in action. Reference still tends to be made to the mobilising potential of general tendencies for organisational, environmental or social change (Burchell *et al.*, 1985). Little has been done to uncover and describe the precise mechanisms of accounting change. The domains of the organisational and the social also have tended to remain independent ones. Few attempts have been made to delineate the both overlapping and interdependent spheres of the two, to appreciate how accounting might enable the concerns of the social to pass through and thereby transform the organisation and, in turn, to create organisational practices which can be influential in the construction of the world of the social as we know it. Be it from an organisational or social perspective, the roles of accounting are still defined externally to the practice of the craft. Organisational agents are still seen as existing in isolation of the practices in which they are engaged. Possibly because of the distancing of inquiry from practice, only the reflective rather than the constitutive tendencies of accounting (Burchell *et al.*, 1985; Hopwood, 1985b) have been emphasised in the accounts that we now have of accounting change.

In the context of such an agenda for development, the subsequent discussion has only a modest aim. Using some instances of accounting change, an attempt is made to tease out some of the processes at work at the organisational level. By drawing on some specific illustrations of accounting in action, the aim is to illuminate some of the factors that are implicated in the processes by which organisational accountings become what they are not. No attempt is made to construct an alternative theory of accounting change however. The aim is the much more modest one of delineating a few of the issues and problems that any such theory or theories would need to address. The intention is merely one of expanding the conceptual arena rather than of seeking its resolution.

ON PUTTING ACCOUNTING WHERE ACCOUNTING WAS NOT

It rarely is possible to witness the birth pains of a newly emergent accounting. Normally we have to content ourselves with observing the process of accounting elaboration, as one organisational account is extended and refined as it becomes transformed into another. However, in the case of Josiah Wedgwood, the eighteenth century English potter, is is possible to do this indirectly by means of the extensive correspondence and records that have been preserved (McKendrick, 1960, 1961a, b, 1964, 1973).[6]

Wedgwood was a successful entrepreneur in the early days of the British industrial revolution.

[6] I do not wish to imply in any way whatsoever that the "protean manifestations" of cost accounting "sprang full-grown" from Wedgwood's initiatives (Jenks, 1960, p. 423), nor that there were no precedents. That clearly was not the case. Although earlier costing systems have been poorly documented and analysed (see, however, Jones, 1985), a costing craft was emergent. In addition, and of particular significance, I think, a relevant more general economic discourse was available to serve as an

A man of scientific and analytical temperament, as well as acute commercial acumen, he created one of the first British industrial (as distinct from craft) manufacturies of pottery, pioneering not only in production methods (McKendrick, 1961a) but also in product design, the application of scientific research (Schofield, 1956) and the commercial exploitation of his products (McKendrick, 1960, 1961b). Wedgwood quickly established himself as the supplier of pottery to the wealthy. His business quickly became a very profitable and rapidly expanding one.

Initially Wedgwood made little use of accounting, particularly for what would now be seen as management purposes. Accounting information did not inform his product and pricing decisions or the selection of his methods of work. As McKendrick (1973, p. 48) has observed:

> So handsome were the profit margins which he could normally expect, and so high the prices which he could regularly charge, that the incentives towards anything more than routine costing were usually rather slight.

Indeed Wedgwood himself admitted that "he could do little more than guess at costs" and "further conceded that his attempts at total costing were out by a factor of two" (McKendrick, 1973, p. 49).

That situation was to change however. In 1772 the expansion came to an abrupt end. The pottery industry was caught in a major economic recession. "Panic spread through most of the cities of northern Europe", according to Ashton (1959, p. 128). Prices, profits, wages and employment all fell sharply, and bankruptcies soared in the pottery industry as elsewhere. Wedgwood, like others, was well aware of the impending difficulty:

> The evidence of accumulating stock and falling sales mounted miserably through the autumn, as the slackening demand, so evident in London, spread farther afield. In November he reported very poor sales in Edinburgh. "Mr. Ferrier . . . has sold nothing at all since the month of June" . . . And as sales slackened, production at Eturia had to be cut back to a dangerous level. Reluctant as Wedgwood was to recognise the drop in demand, he finally *had* to recognise it. He stopped overtime only when "we have not work for them the common hours". At this stage Wedgwood refused to believe that the situation was "in such a desperate way and that we should set our best hands adrift to the establishment of our antagonists" . . . Wedgwood was determined to hang on to the men he had taken such pains to train but already many of his men were out of work — "our Gilders have not a piece to do and are all at play". With the coming of Winter things grew steadily worse. On 19 September Wedgwood wrote that "any opening" should "be pursued with all our might". On Boxing Day any trivial aspect of fashion was being frantically exploited . . . Two days later he announced with relief that he was laying off the men for Christmas, but three weeks later the situation was even worse. "We begin, after 3 weeks rest, to work again on Monday. If you can make us any orders pray send them, for I really do not know what to set them to work upon, however they must begin for they attacked me in a body yesterday morning and insisted on being either employ'd or discharg'd" (McKendrick, 1973, p. 63).

In times of such crisis business methods often are re-examined. With such an aim in mind, Wedgwood started to turn his attention to the level of his production expenses. And it was in this context that his cost accounts were born.

Wedgwood had the idea that he might better survive the recession if he could lower his prices in order to stimulate demand. Such a view was conditioned, however, by the need to ensure that the price still exceeded the cost. And there the problem arose. For although a concept of cost entered into the discourse of commerce and trade, and could thereby mobilise action, there was no well established apparatus for operationalising the discursive category. Cost remained an idea, not a fact.

It was the facts of costing that Wedgwood set

---

incentive for the production of a new visibility (Tribe, 1978). Costs could be talked about, if not observed. So despite the fact that, to use Jenks' (1960) characterization of the process of change in a somewhat later era, "problems of organization . . . were solved *ad hoc* empirically for each establishment", resulting in the development of "little clusters of socially sustained norms and concepts, whose communication beyond the individual firm was rare, accidental, or the result of individual transfer of employment" (p. 424), we nevertheless should recognize the important discursive and practical conditions of possibility underlying such innovative steps.

out to discover. As he noted to Bentley, his business partner:

> It will deserve our serious discussion whether we shd not lower the prices of Pebble and Gilt Vases very considerably, for this purpose I am forming a price book of Workmanship &c which is to include every expence of Vase making as near as possible from the Crude materials, to your Counter in London, upon each sort of Vases, of this we will send you a specimen & you will then be able to judge better what we can do in this respect, what will be most prudent is the next question for our Consideration (McKendrick, 1973, p. 49).

The task was not an easy one. No established procedures were available for observing the inner workings of the organisation through the accounting eye. The organisation could not be
452 readily penetrated. The facts of costing had to be laboriously created rather than merely revealed.

> I have been puzzling my brains all the last week (Wedgwood wrote to Bentley on 23 August 1772) to find out proper data, and methods of calculating the expence of manufacturing, Sale, loss &c to be laid upon each article of our Manufacture & a very tedious business it has been, but what is worse I find what I have done is wrong — somewhere, very essentially so, but do not know where or how to amend it though I shall not give up being sensible of the importance of the enquiry, and what I now send you is only to shew you what steps I have taken & the grounds I have gone upon, & to desire you will sit down some morning & consider the subject & try to put me in a better way, for it will be of the greatest use for us to establish some such scale as I have now been attempting to examine all our new articles by, that we may not fix the prices so high as to prevent sale, nor so low as to leave no profit upon them (McKendrick, 1973, p. 49).

Such endeavours resulted in the construction of an increasingly detailed account. Still, however, Wedgwood was not satisfied with his efforts.

> Some of my difficultys I have laid before you, but what perplexeth me most is, that although I am very positive what I have allowed for the expences of making & selling our goods is quite enough yet it appears from comparing this expence of Manufacture for a year, with the amot of goods made, to be little more than half the real expence attending the making & selling so many goods (McKendrick, 1973, p. 53).

Shortly thereafter, however, he was to obtain some insight into some of the reasons for his uneasiness. Comparing his financial accounts with his emergent costings, he found that the two did not agree.

> This Acc^{t} is very exact as to the *whole* but we cannot make it agree with its parts viz the separate pieces — It agrees with the small Vases very well but those we sell at 2 or 3 G-s do not appear to cost us 1/10 of that money. We are now taking a stock & shall then try another method (McKendrick, 1973, p. 61).

Being of a curious disposition, Wedgwood soon discovered why the various parts of his accounting experiments did not mesh together. His inquiries revealed "a history of embezzlement, blackmail, chicanery, and what Wedgwood called 'extravagance and dissipation'" (McKendrick, 1973, p. 61). His head clerk, Ben, whom he had "long been uneasy on this account being fully perswaded (*sic*) that matters were not right with . . . His Case acc^{ts} being always several months behind, & yet to jump exactly right when he did Ballance them" (McKendrick, 1973, p. 61), had had his hand in the till. On further investigation, Wedgwood found that "the plan of our House in Newport St.", where the clerks resided, "is rather unfavourable to Virtue & good order in young men", "that the housekeeper was frolicking with the cashier", "that the head clerk was ill with 'the foul Disease' and had 'long been in a course of extravagance and dissipation far beyond anything he has from us (in a lawfull way) wd. be able to support'" (McKendrick, 1973, p.61).

Only after such revelations as to the sources of accounting inconsistency did Wedgwood feel confident in his newly fledged facts. As he went on to report:

> Our House may be looked upon as unfixed, & afloat, the first Clerk and Cashier being remov'd, it seems the properest time to introduce any new regulations we may think proper, or to change the whole plan if we can adopt a better . . . now we know that all goods *sold for money* & not *brought to account* must appear as *increase of* stock in *stateing the* acc^{ts} & we have such strong reasons for suspecting our Head Clerks fidelity such an amazing increase of stock is an alarming circumstance & I shall not be easy 'till the stock is taken to clear my doubts in this respect (McKendrick, 1973, p. 61, emphasis in original).

Immediate steps were taken to correct the matter. A new clerk was installed and, in order "to put the necessary business of collecting into a way of *perpetual motion*" (McKendrick, 1973, p. 62, emphasis in original), a routine of weekly accounts implemented.

The birth of Wedgwood's accounts had been difficult and laborious. There had been no easy relationship between the idea of costing and a specific programme of intervention in the organisation conducted in the name of that idea. Costs had had to be constructed rather than merely revealed. An organisational economy grounded in a domain of accounting facts had to be forged painstakingly rather than merely exposed.

Once constructed, however, Wedgwood had a powerful instrument for observing the organisation in economic terms. His strategic conception of the role which records could play in the management of crisis had resulted in a means by which he could penetrate the inner workings of the organisation. A new visibility had been created. The organisation had been colonised by economic facts (Patton, 1979). A calculative means had been found for conceiving the functioning of the organisation in different terms. An accounting eye had provided Wedgwood with a new means for intervening in the organisation.

And intervene he did. As we have seen, the administration and control of the financial records was reformed. More substantially, during the depression, prices were actively changed in the name of the new knowledge of costs and profits[7] (McKendrick, 1964, 1973). A basis for a more systematic consideration of marketing policies was created (McKendrick, 1960, 1961, 1973). The newly emergent facts of the economic provided a basis for re-appraising the organisation of the manufacturing processes, the advantages of large volume production, and the calculation of piece rates, wages and bonus's (McKendrick, 1960, 1961a, 1973). The inner workings of the organisation had been made amenable to a new form of economic analysis.

Wedgwood's discovery of the advantages of large scale production illustrates this well. Faced with his newly emergent costing facts, Wedgwood noted that:

> If you turn to the columns of calculation & see how large a share, Modeling and Moulds, & the three next columns bear in the expense of Manufacturing out goods, & consider that these expenses move like clockwork, & are much the same whether the quantity of goods be large or small, you will see the vast consequence in most manufacturers of *making the greatest quantity possible at a given time* (Wedgwood's italics). Rent goes on whether we do much or little in the time. Wages to the Boys and Odd Men, Warehouse Men & Book-keeper who are a kind of Satalites to the Makers (Throwers, Turners &c.) is nearly the same whether we make 20 doz of Vases or 10 doz per week & will therefore be a double expence upon the later number. The same may be said in regard to most of the incidental expences . . . .
>
> We now have upwards of 100 Good forms of Vases, for all of which we have the moulds, handles & ornaments & we cd. make them almost as currently as useful ware, & at half the expence we have hitherto done, provided I durst set the Men to make abo[t] 6 to 13 doz of a sort; perhaps (as the first expence of all these apparatus's is over, & our Men in full practice, and many have some fears of losing a good branch of business) at much less than half.
>
> The first expence will be all sunk if we do not proceed in the business this apparatus is adapted for.
>
> The Great People have had these Vases in their Palaces long enough for them to be seen & admired by the Middling Classes of People, which Class we know are vastly, I had almost said, infinitely superior in number to the Great, & though a great *price* was, I believe, at first necessary to make the Vases esteemed *Ornament for Palaces*, that reason no longer exists. Their character is established, & the Middling People wd. probably by [sic] quantitys of them at a reduced price (McKendrick, 1973, p. 55).

[7] Outside periods of depression, Wedgwood was well aware that in an imperfect market, with explicit strategies for product differentiation, there was no necessary relationship between cost and price. As McKendrick (1964, p. 29) points out: "The phrase 'The prices Mr Bentley will regulate as he thinks proper' occurs so frequently in letters on pricing that one soon recognizes it as a familiar refrain". As Wedgwood himself put it, "When I fix a price upon any new article, please to remember that I have more regard to the *Expence of workmanship* than the *apparent and comparative value* with other things so you'll correct it by the latter which is often most essential" (emphasis in original). In McKendrick's (1964, p. 29) words, Wedgwood judged "the cost of production, the difficulty of making, and the number he could easily make, and then Bentley would decide at which market to aim them, at what price to charge them and in what quantities to make them".

As McKendrick (1973, p. 54) notes, Wedgwood's costing "had other more permanent repercussions on his business management". In often unanticipated ways, the organisation was changed in the name of the knowledge of it. For "by his own persistence, by an unfailing attention to detail, by founding, if not creating, the traditions of a foreman class and equipping it with rules and regulations, he transformed a collection of what in 1765 he called, 'dilatory, drunken, idle, worthless workmen' into what ten years later he allowed to be 'a very good sett of hands'" (McKendrick, 1961a, p. 46). What is more, Wedgwood's observations could now be conducted indirectly. No longer did he have to rely solely on walking around the pottery constantly on the lookout for "unhandiness", scold-
454 ing those individuals who did not follow his instructions (McKendrick, 1961a, pp. 43–44). Such personal observation and supervision could start to be complemented by the exercising of control at a distance, both in time and space.[8] Wedgwood now had available to him the basis of a more anonymous and continuous means of surveillance.

Although born amidst crisis and doubt, the consequences of Wedgwood's accounting system started to be quite profound. Initiated to reveal what had been presumed to be there already, once established, it provided a basis for significantly changing, if not eventually transforming, the functioning of the enterprise. The newly established accounting system enabled a different set of dynamics to be set into motion. The fine details of the production process could now be related to the aims and performance of the organisation as a whole.[9] Policies created at the top of the organisation could be related to specific aspects of organisational functioning. The organisation could be observed and managed in terms different from those in which it functioned. Attempts could be made to co-ordinate and plan divergent parts of the organisation in the name of the economic. An organisational economy could start to be emergent. As Patton (1979) has said in a very different context:

> The emergence of [a practice] cannot be explained by the functions it subsequently comes to fulfil; new roles may be forced upon it, foreign to those it was introduced to bear.

ACCOUNTING, ORGANISING AND THE ORGANISATION[10]

Turning to an organisation which already has a long history of accounting, the aim is to consider in a little more detail some of the processes through which organisational accounts change as they become intertwined with the organisation itself. By examining another case of accounting change, an illustration is provided of

[8] In his detailed study of the history of Boulton and Watts' Soho engineering factory, opened in 1796, Roll (1930, p. 250) also notes how the introduction of time sheets for workmen started to serve a number of different roles. In addition to providing a basis for ascertaining the workers' wages and entering into the determination of prices by calculating the labour costs of the engines being made, Roll commented on the ways in which the new detailed visibility of wage costs influenced the organization of work and the relationships between effort and remuneration. The data provided a starting point for making changes in the methods of production, suggesting possibilities for speeding up work and introducing further machinery. The new records also served to establish a standard or a norm for efficiency in the enterprise, enabling wages to become more related to detailed task performance. Here, as with Wedgwood, the newly established visibility of the economic itself created a dynamic for changing the organization of which it was presumed to be a reflection.

[9] Loft (1986b, pp. 93–94) usefully notes the interdependence between production methods and record keeping, with each facilitating the construction of the other. As she comments: "Sophisticated cost accounting systems go hand in hand with the standardization of products and production methods. The 'facts' which cost accounting systems demand can only be created with enormous difficulty where work is carried on in a disordered, anarchic way. The opposite also applies, for the operation of a complex and detailed system of organization may be virtually impossible without records. Roll (1930, p. 252) points this out, noting that many aspects of the re-organized Soho Works (of Boulton and Watt) were such as to make any check except that through written records impossible".

[10] I acknowledge the help of John Hughes (now of the Open University) in assisting with the research on which this case study is based. The analysis also has benefited from discussions with Sten Jönsson.

some of the ways in which the processes, practices and perspectives that characterise organisational life impinge on accounting. Continuing the theme introduced in the analysis of Wedgwood, consideration also is given to the ways in which accounting, in turn, impinges on the process of organising.

M was established in the early days of the present century. In the business of industrial component manufacturing, it quickly established itself as an international enterprise with manufacturing and marketing establishments in a wide variety of countries throughout the Western world. *M* grew rapidly, not least during the 1950s. Those were years of prosperity and expansion with good profits and a high return on assets employed. But this situation changed after 1960. Although product demand eased slightly, change was most evident on the supply side of the industry. In particular, the entry of Japanese manufacturers into the world market ushered in a decade of fierce competition. During the 1960s the total value of Japanese output rose by over 350% but their exports increased by almost 1,700%. Suddenly *M* was exposed to intense competition and this was greatest at the volume end of the market where, on certain individual products, the Japanese selling price was below M's calculated unit cost.

A growing awareness of the dangers of Japanese competition and a dissatisfaction with the measured performance of the company caused a major re-appraisal of the company's competitive position to be undertaken. During the early 1970s a number of working parties were established to undertake a thorough investigation of the problems facing the company.

The first problem to be identified was, perhaps paradoxically, that of giving too good a service to customers. *M* had prided itself on providing for any application "the right (component), at the right price — regardless of cost". Special design departments, part of the marketing function, liaised with customers to produce components for each and every application with little company-wide engineering and design collaboration because of the semi-autonomous nature of the organisation's constituent plants. The result was a proliferation of marginally different components produced in different plants in a number of different countries. Moreover, the decentralised strategy of organising also resulted in the same or similar products being produced in each country where there was a market for them, with a consequent duplication of tooling, set-up and other manufacturing costs for each operation and a high value of work-in-progress because of the large decentralised stocks. The problems were further exacerbated by the sheer proliferation of manufacturing plants, there often being many in the same country. During the highly profitable 1950s these problems had been of relatively little concern. Faced with a very different competitive situation, however, *M* decided to reduce considerably the number of product variants. 455

The perception of an external market threat thereby resulted in a detailed examination of internal manufacturing operations. At that time the batch production methods used by *M* gave a large measure of independence to the separate functions of the manufacturing process. This resulted in a great deal of operational flexibility. Rush orders could be injected easily into the system and the ramifications of machine breakdowns minimised. Such an approach was not suited to more concentrated and, consequently, higher volume production, however. The lack of inter-operation handling equipment resulted in long throughput times and high inventories. Moreover batch production of this type put a heavy burden on local production control systems, stores personnel, operators, inspectors and factory supervisors. So very active consideration was given to alternative production methods.

M decided to move, as far as possible, to production organised by means of multi-machine lines. Under this arrangement a number of similar machines are connected individually with an extensive inter-operational conveyor system. The latter provided not only transportation but also a buffer storage, enabling machine groups to work at different paces and the effects of a breakdown to be relatively contained. The capital costs of this type of plant were high, but production speeds were increased, throughput time was reduced and, as a consequence, inventory requirements were reduced also. However those advantages were gained not only at the expense of higher capital investment but also at the loss of considerable operational flexibility. The production systems would have to become more autonomous of the market, the very turbulence of which had been the initial stimulus for change.

Originally each of *M*'s plants had produced a full range of products to meet the demands of the local market. However, if production costs were to be reduced, as the international market was perceived to necessitate, it was decided that multi-product lines would have to be introduced. In turn, this meant that production runs 456 needed to be longer if the economies of scale were to materialise. One way of doing this was to reduce the number of variants produced, but in the fiercely competitive market of the late 1960s and early 1970s this in itself was not sufficient. It was decided therefore that the manufacturing of each type of product should be concentrated in one location to maximise production volume and reduce costs.

A new production strategy gradually emerged from these examinations and discussions, and it was formally agreed in 1971. The method of implementing and achieving these aims was laborious however. The initial allocation of production represented a significant balancing problem and discussions went on for a number of years. "Weeding out" non-essential variants was also a large task as each final product variety was tested for commercial, financial and technical viability. In 1973 all variants were classified on the basis of sales value, thus identifying those which had such low sales that they were probably unprofitable. Each candidate for elimination was then examined individually. In parallel with the commercial examination, once again a technical assessment was carried out. The design, quality and materials of each were examined critically. Manufacturing and marketing considerations also entered into this assessment. Together these processes enabled *M* to reduce its product range from 50,000 final variants in 1972 to 20,000 in 1978. Over the same period the average annual volume per final variant rose by 300%. An additional category of product, namely "special" products, was also introduced, enabling products to be produced to customer specifications, but at extra cost. Overall, *M*'s managements considered that the product range concentration had reduced market coverage by only 1% but that this had eliminated what had been the unprofitable sectors of the operation.

Production methods, product policies and production locations were thereby all radically changed in the name of cost. All of these strategic considerations had been infused not only by the language of cost, however, but also by the specific accounting calculations in use at *M*. The reduction of a ***measured*** notion of cost had been a primary aim. In the deliberations and policy intitiatives cost had operated not only as an influential abstract category entering into the language of strategy but also as a seemingly precise outcome of a specific set of accounting procedures.

In such ways the technical practices of accounting became intertwined with the managerial functioning of *M*. Organisational policies came to be interdependent with the accounting representation of them. For a complex set of accounting rules defined what was and was not to be regarded as costly. Definitions of "productive" and "unproductive" cost categories influenced the changes made to specific production locations and eventually, the production of specific products. Rules by which overhead costs were to be allocated to production operations, and by what means, had a significant impact on reported cost levels. Debates over the capacity assumptions on which overhead costs were to be allocated were similarly influential in the highly detailed cost assessments, as were the technical procedures for determining how frequently standard costs were to be updated to take account of inflation and exchange rate fluctuations. Also of great importance were the procedures for accounting for operational change in *M*. For although the problems of the company had orginated from the perception of a changing environment, *M*'s accounting system operated under assumptions of steady state production. The calculation and reporting of set-up and order costs and operation start costs were such that although the financial ramifications of stable production were made clearly visible, the equally significant implications of production changes were much less visible and the costs of operational flexibility and inflexibility did not enter into the accounting calculations at all. In all of these ways not only did the rhetoric of accounting come to play a significant mediating role in the policy deliberations but also the very particular physical, spatial and temporal assumptions and biases incorporated into *M*'s formal accounting systems came to influence the relative preferences assigned to the various production strategies. The accounting system started to be not only reflective of *M* but also constitutive of its options and policies (Burchell *et al.*, 1985).

However the network of changes at work in *M* was such that accounting itself came to be subject to pressures to change. Not only had it played a significant role in mediating the relationship between managerial perceptions of a strategic need for change and the operational responses decided upon but also *M*'s formal information systems, including those of an accounting nature, were also to be significantly changed by the different production policies that had followed the recognition of a market crisis. Under the old system of multiple local production the relationship between marketing and manufacturing had been dealt with at a local (national) level. Many of the relevant liaisons and linkages had been done informally. Although there were formal systematic flows of information, these were primarily local in nature. That was no longer adequate however. With geographically concentrated production, the marketing and manufacturing functions had been uncoupled. A new way had to be found to aggregate total forecast and actual demand for every product variant in order to plan the utilisation of capacity in each plant. What had previously been informal had now to become formal. The new production strategy had given rise to the need for a new mode of organising and radically different formal flows of information.

To deal with these problems, two new organisational structures were established. A central co-ordinating committee was set up to judge market demand and decide upon appropriate production levels in line with available capacity, inventories and strategic and operating policies. The interface between marketing and manufacturing thereby became subject to much more centralised control and new functional staff groups were set up in the head office to support this new influence structure. Also, with these rather crucial decisions requiring accurate and up-to-date information, a new management information system was established with its operating team based in a central geographical location. Utilising the forecast parameters established by the co-ordinating group, the new central information office decided upon capacity booking, factory loading, assembly scheduling and distribution instructions. To facilitate this process, feedback of actual levels of manufacturing, sales and stocks was required to be made monthly by all local establishments via *M*'s new computer-based data transmission systems. The increasingly centralised interdependent decision making and control processes were investing in a great deal of formal information (Galbraith, 1973). *M* was in the process of becoming a more information intensive and information dependent organisation.

As a result of these changes, consideration also had to be given to the formal organisational structure of *M*. Previously the company had been structured around the national manufacturing and marketing units. As relatively self-contained entitities, they had constituted useful business responsibility units. Performance was measured on an annual basis in traditional balance sheet and income statement terms. Longer term planning of the enterprise as a whole had been attempted but had proved a difficult and unsatisfactory endeavour. Now, however, *M* was a more integrated and centralised organisation. The relationships between local marketing and manufacturing had been severed. Local sales were no longer dependent on local production. Performance in total was more dependent on central decision making. With this in mind, the whole organisation started to be structured along product lines.

In the midst of such organisational changes it was recognised that the previous rudimentary controls were no longer adequate. Consideration had to be given to a more frequent, more disaggregated reporting system. Budgeting became a more iterative and time consuming process. Even when arrived at, the budget was updated by a regular series of quarterly plans. The centre now needed to be much more closely informed of local developments and revisions in local expectations. Local performance, in turn, was assessed monthly with the previous summary financial information now being replaced by an extremely detailed reporting of financial, marketing, operating and even personnel re-
458 sults. And, in such a newly centralised enterprise, even local performance was now conditioned by centrally mediated and much contested accounting policies for transfer prices and the allocation of costs.[11]

As is shown in Fig. 1, the accounting system and its resultant problems now started to be a complex residue of marketing, production and organisational strategies. Just as accounting had mediated some of the early crucial policy decisions, now accounting was itself subject to the implications of some of its own effects.

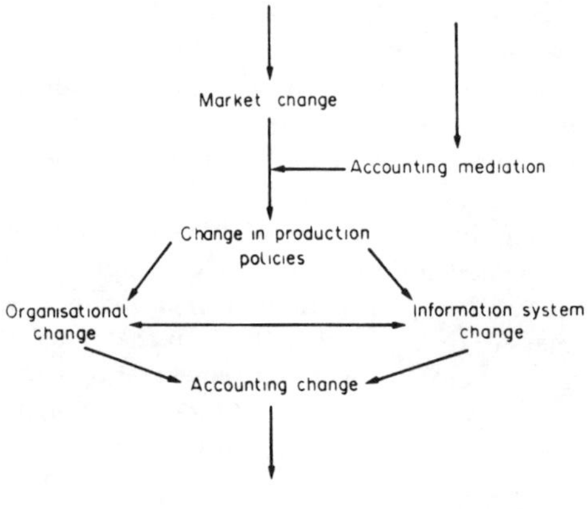

Fig. 1. Accounting implicated in organisational action.

Accounting was firmly embedded in the organisation rather than being any clearly separable part of it. The organisation was not independent of the accountings of it. Although at a point in time the practices of accounting could be identified, their functioning was intertwined with that of the organisation in both reflective and constitutive ways. Other important aspects of organisational functioning had impinged on accounting, providing pressures for it to change. In this sense accounting was a residue of past strategic choices, past decisions on models of organising and past commitments to policies for making visible, and thereby potentially governable (Miller & O'Leary, 1987), particular aspects of organisational action. All of these activities of the past had played a role in undermining the accountings of the past and creating the possibility for the accountings of today. Accounting, however, had not only been a passive phenomenon. It was not only a reflection of other aspects of organisational life but also had played a more positive constructive role in organisational functioning. Accounting had provided an operational and influential language of economic motive, its calculations had infused and influenced important policy decisions, and the visibilities it created played an important role in making real particular segmentations of the organisational arena. Accounting not only reflected the organisation as it had been but it also played a not insignificant role in positively making the organisation as it now is.

ACCOUNTING AND THE RESIDUES OF THE ORGANISATIONAL PAST

The constitutive roles of accounting provide a major focus for analysing *Q*, also a major manufacturing enterprise. Like *M*, it also had to face

[11] With increasing emphasis being placed on the control function of local performance reports, "fairness" rather than decision relevance was an important criterion for evaluating such accounting practices and changes in them. I am grateful to Sten Jönsson for bringing this point to my attention.

extreme market turbulence and change. Increasing competition, changing consumer expectations and a squeezing of profit margins also engendered in *Q* a sense of organisational crisis.

As an organisation, *Q* is even more information intensive than *M*. It has invested heavily in formal information and control systems, paying particular attention to those of a financial and accounting nature. The tentacles of these systems penetrate deep into the manufacturing, marketing, distribution and administrative functions of the enterprise. Detailed aspects of the organisation are made economically visible on a very regular basis. Standards, budgets and plans play a central role in the co-ordination and integration of a very large, functionally specialised and geographically dispersed organisation. Indeed it is through the formal flows of economic information that many important aspects of *Q* come to be known, managed and assessed. No pockets of local autonomy are consciously allowed to exist. Not only are all the parts of the vast, dispersed and varied enterprise drawn together by the information systems which provide the basis for the operational governance of *Q* but also the rhythms of the accounting year thereby become very influential components of the organisational construction and management of time.[12] The accounting eye is indeed a significant and omnipresent one.

The information economy of *Q* had been elaborated and refined during periods of growth and relative prosperity. Although difficulties had been encountered with this vast and expensive machinery of abstract information and administration, conditions of stable growth had rarely placed these at a premium. The abstract categories of cost and profit had been deemed to provide an adequate portrayal of the functioning of the organisation. The management of the general rather than the particular had not been seen as problematic. The resulting periodisation of governance had not created any insurmountable difficulties in the context of relative stability. The systems, for there were a vast number of only partially integrated ones, had been fine tuned and developed in relation to specific problems and presumed needs. In this way the information regime of *Q* had marched ever forward, gaining, in the process, an increasing measure of autonomy and further creating the basis for a detached, specialised and abstract arena of management that seemingly had less and less direct contact with the operational specifics of the enterprise.

The market crisis was to make such an information regime increasingly problematic however. With mounting uncertainty, the need for information that was not collected became ever greater. The senior management of *Q* started to realise that what it had been regarding as a detached and independent source of illumination — information — was in fact a direct reflection and an integral component of its system of administration and governance. What had been controlled — costs, profits, variances and volume — had given rise to an information residue. What had not been controlled, but what was now seen to be in need of control, was unreflected in the organisation's battery of information systems. The previously unmanaged — quality, detailed aspects of the functioning of the production process, employee and managerial commitment and motivation, throughput times and operational inventory holdings, technological progress, the detail of customer responsiveness — resided in the domain of the unknown. The visibilities of the present were partial, reflecting only the locus of past problems, past controls and past patterns of authority. However significant it might be, in *Q* the new had enormous difficulty filtering through the old. The dimensions of concern were just so different.

The organisation of the present was thereby tethered to the concerns of the past. The information systems of *Q* had become not only so detailed, so seemingly precise and so apparently comprehensive but also so fundamentally intertwined with the present organisation of *Q* that for a long time they had served to deny the legitimate existence of alternatives. Not only had their very technical quality come to be seen

[12] For a further discussion of the role of accounting in the construction of conceptions of time see Hopwood (1986b).

as so high and so all embracing that gaps had not been perceived but also the present information and control flows had become co-determinous with the enterprise itself. In an important way the accounting system of *Q* had become isomorphic with the organisation. Both had changed such that each was now both dependent on and reflective of the other. What had once been direct and specifically identifiable bureaucratic controls had, over time, become much more unobtrusive ones (Perrow, 1986), a central part of *Q* itself. Now they were implicated in the establishment of the very premises of decision making, "the control of the cognitive premises underlying action" (Perrow, 1986, p. 129), determining at a very basic level the structure of meaning and significance in the organisation.[13]
460 Change is extremely difficult in such a context. It is only with great difficulty that people can start to conceive of doing anything differently. The new has few means to penetrate the consciousness established by the old.

Eventually, however, circumstances were such in *Q* that the radically changed environment was recognised. It slowly started to be reflected in even the traditional indicators. And although delayed, investigations prompted by this provided a basis on which some members of the organisation started to realise the significance of the changes underway.

In the context of such a perception of crisis important aspects of the organisation of *Q* that had been positively shaped by its regime of information systems started to be regarded as problematic. The batteries of standards, budgets and plans were seen as creating a relatively inflexible and inward looking enterprise. The phrase "paralysis by analysis" started to enter the organisational vocabulary. It was perceived that emphasis had been placed on the management of the normal rather than the irregular. The management of the abstract had created an organisation that found it difficult, if not positively traumatic, to respond to the particular. The systems of information also were recognised as having played a very crucial role in the creation of conceptions of time in *Q*. No only was the continual stream of organisational action periodised in a very particular way but also the regime of routine planning and reporting had resulted in a celebration of the present and the short-term. By extensive processes of budgeting and planning, the future had been brought into the present, seemingly becoming more certain, less contingent, less debatable and, possibly, less readily subject to influence in the process. After an era of emphasising the immediate in many aspects of its management, *Q* now found it extremely difficult to instill a more proactive conception of an influencable and manageable longer term future.

As in *M*, important features of organisational life had become intertwined with the functioning of an accounting system. Accounting had developed such that is was embedded in the organisational fabric, both reflecting and creating the contexts in which it operated. In *Q*, however, this process had gone much further. While such tendencies clearly were at work in *M*, in *Q* they had become fully realised. Although autonomous developments could and did take place in the design and functioning of *Q*'s accounting systems (and which by feeding into the functioning of the organisation, could subsequently lose their autonomy), accounting in *Q* had become a phenomenon that could not be regarded as being in any sense separable from the enterprise as a whole.

Past investments in a finely tuned economic visibility had radically increased the salience of the economies that could be gained from functional specialisation, geographical dispersion and a regime of administrative co-ordination. The accounting eye had become a very strategic one. The organisation had been mobilised in the name of what was known of it. Economic objectives and strategies for meeting them had been

[13] As Perrow (1986) points out, with unobtrusive control, what he terms the "control of premises," organizational participants "*voluntarily* restrict the range of stimuli that will be attended to ('Those sorts of things are irrelevant', or 'What has that got to do with the matter?') and the range of alternatives that would be considered ('It would never occur to me to do that')". (Perrow, 1986, p. 129; emphasis in original). Such attitudes were indeed prevalent in *Q*.

given a very precise meaning. Investments had been made in the context of a very particular economic knowledge. As a result, *Q* was now composed of different machines and different people with different skills located in different places, and subject to a different management regime. What is more, *Q* now needed its accounting systems in order to function as it did. They satisfied needs that they had played a role in creating (Ignatieff, 1984). The present structuring of the organisation presumed the existence of accounting. No longer just discrete technical procedures, the accounting systems were infused into the organisation itself.

The creation of accounting residues that, in turn, played a role in creating the organisation in which the accountings functioned had been an important part of *Q*'s development. A visibility had become a reality. But that visibility had not always been so centrally implicated in the functioning of *Q*. It had been born amidst a different reality, serving different purposes than those now required of it. The accounting residues had been laid down in an organisation different from that which *Q* now is.

Important features of the emergent economic visibility had been created in the context of attempts to control the labour process (Clawson, 1980). A conflictful and organised work force had provided one significant base for the rise of a regime of economic calculation and administration in *Q*. The control of economically orientated effort had been a mobilising problem. Investments had been made in the specification of work expectations, in the linking of effort to reward and in the measurement and control of actual performance. A regime of detailed economic calculation had been created in order to render visible in a quite particular manner the functioning of the operational core of the organisation. The social control of work had provided an important incentive for *Q*'s investment in an enhanced visibility of the economic.[14] Now, however, that socially constructed visibility had created an enterprise organisationally dependent on the resultant knowledge. The organisation had been reformed in the name of the knowledge of it. A managerial regime based on facts and analysis had arisen (although in a different corporate context, see Geneen, 1984). More precise articulations of objectives had been made, and these had been diffused throughout the organisation by means of the accounting calculus. New segmentations of work had been initiated in the organisation and new bases for administrative expertise forged. What had been initiated in the organisation in the name of the social came to function in the name of both the organisational and the social.

ON THE CONSIDERATION OF ACCOUNTING IN MOTION 461

Together the cases illustrate not only that accounting can be conceived as being in motion but also that such a perspective provides a rich insight into the organisational practice of accounting and its consequences for action. What conventionally have been seen to be the statics of the accounting craft have been seen to be in the process of changing, becoming thereby, what they were not. And such a portrayal has enabled an analysis of some of the ways in which accounting, by intersecting with other organisational processes and practices, influences the patterns of organisational visibility, significance, structure and action.

In the case of Wedgwood the emergence of a new accounting was observed. The categories and inter-relationships of an economic discourse and rhetoric (McCloskey, 1985) provided an incentive for the creation of a practical means for observing the organisation in economic terms, so making seemingly real what previously had been abstract. Although initiated as a tool for deciding upon prices and product volumes, a means thereby was created for interven-

[14] Several independent and very detailed historical studies support this conclusion. Moreover these have been conducted from a number of different theoretical perspectives. However, in the name of preserving the anonymity of *Q*, no references are given.

ing in and transforming the organisation in the name of the new economic knowledge of it. As we left our consideration of Wedgwood a basis was starting to be established upon which the accounting craft would become a more powerful means for organisational intervention and governance, able to play a more active role in the shaping of the trajectory of organisational development. Initiated to reveal what was presumed to be, the accounting eye was starting to be suggestive of organisational reform.

Such a proactive role for accounting was seen in operation in the early days of the formulation of *M*'s response to a market crisis. The otherwise abstract languages of economic motive and managerial analysis had been made into a more precise calculus for the assessment of organisational
462 change by the accountings that had been laid down in *M* in times past. In this way, the quite specific properties of the accounting system played an active role in mediating the organisational response to the perceived need to change. The mobilising potential inherent in the early costings of Wedgwood was now seen in action, helping to shape in quite particular ways the marketing, production, and thereafter, the organisational, information and even accounting strategies in *M*. For accounting, by becoming more embedded in the organisation, not only shaped other important aspects of organisational life, but it, in turn, also was influenced by them, overtime thereby playing some role in creating the possibilities and conditions for its own transformation.

In *Q* the organisational embeddedness of accounting was such that it played a significant and extremely influential role in the functioning of the organisation. Although created over a long period of time and originally appealed to for reasons different from its present functioning, the accounting and other related information and control systems now created the dominant means of visibility in *Q*. The organisation was seen and managed through an accounting eye. The selective patterns of accounting visibility had provided a means for mobilising and changing the organisation such that it not only was dependent upon but also almost synonymous with the particular flows of information which had become intertwined with its development and current mode of functioning.

For all three organisations accounting had played some role in their transformation. The processes through which their accountings had become what they were not were starting to become, or already were, embedded in the very fabric of their functioning. Particular regimes of accounting facts had been created. An operational significance was given to economic and managerial categories and rhetoric. A seemingly precise and specific calculus had entered into organisational deliberations and debate. Accounting, in being propagated and changed, had become implicated in wider processes of organisational perception, governance and strategic mobilisation.

The consequences of such a trajectory of development were significant for all the organisations, providing, in the case of *M*, an important mediating influence at a time of a key strategic change, and, in *Q*, creating a form of organisational dependency that was to constrain and thereby, for a time, to influence the organisation's responsiveness to environmental turbulence.

Such consequences are amongst those that have provided the basis for a more widespread development of "worrying about management accounting" (Hopwood, 1985a). As was discussed earlier, there is now an increasing tendency for accounting systems to be assessed in terms of their actual as well as their intended organisational consequences. The full range of impacts that they can have on organisations is now starting to be discussed. If only because of this it is important to try to tease out and analyse in a little more detail some of the issues inherent in the cases, albeit that they have to be expressed in a tentative and partial manner at this stage in the development of our knowledge of the organisational nature of the accounting practice. For when seen in such terms, the cases are suggestive of a number of considerations which have a wider significance for the ways in which we can conceive of accounting in action and the processes of accounting elaboration and change.

Perhaps most importantly, the changes we have analysed have not reflected any simple, linear pattern of accounting development. Although abstract rhetorics of change have played a role in disturbing a prevailing status quo, no unitary mobilising force, be it an economic rationality, a social intent or a political will, has been found to be silently embedded within the shifting course of accounting's subsequent path of modification. Indeed in Wedgwood there was no easy and obvious relationship between an abstract economic category and a programme of intervention in the organisation conducted in the name of it. A diversity of quite specific issues, rationales and constraints impinged on the course of accounting change in *M*, together providing a means by which accounting could both shape the perception of problems and their solutions, and itself be adjusted by the shifting patterns of other organisational phenomena. In *Q* accounting had become so firmly embedded in both the structure and the consciousness of the organisation that it, for a time, defined what was perceived to be of economic significance. So in none of the companies were the accounts marching forward towards a conception of what they should become. No unproblematic pattern of accounting progress has been charted. The changes were specific ones, orientated to the resolution of quite particular problems and issues. Although there were most certainly doubts and uncertainties accompanying the path of accounting change, equally there was no evidence that some pre-existing accounting order was merely masked by the ignorance of the particular organisational participants we have considered. Complex, nuanced and subtle though they sometimes may have been, the processes of organisational functioning have not been shown to have hidden any abstract *a priori* path of accounting improvement.

The emergence of a particular account has been shown to be neither an unproblematic reflection of a more abstract intent nor a sudden discovery or transformation. Rather the cases have illustrated the more positive ways in which specific local origins moderated the path of accounting development and the multiple and even conflicting conditions of possibility that gave rise to particular manifestations of the accounting craft. They have pointed to the manner in which particular configurations of issues, problems and other organisational structures and practices both provided a context for and shaped the development of specific accounting changes. Some of the ways in which the particular meanings and significances attached to accounting information influenced the pattern of its transformation have been illuminated, as have the manner in which accidents, errors and deviations left their marks on the accounts that emerged. So although appeals were made to a body of accounting knowledge and technical practice, and to mobilising accounting and wider rationales, taken together the cases point to the need to see the resultant accounting changes as a combined result of both these and a multiplicity of other often minor changes in disparate parts of the organisational arena, each of which was itself engaged in for a diversity of local, tactical and conjectural reasons.

Although the process of accounting change thereby has been shown to be complex, the cases hopefully have demonstrated that such a local and contingent pattern of change is an intelligible one. An appreciation of accounting change has been shown as being able to be grounded in the circumstances in which it occurs. However, as the above discussion has tried to make clear, intelligibility is not to be confused with necessity. In none of the cases was any imperative driving a particular outcome. Nor could any be constructed on the basis of the organisational circumstances which resulted in accounting change. Rather than either assuming what accounting must be or deriving any retrospective view of the necessity of what happened, the cases demonstrate the need for an appreciation of change to be based on a more detailed awareness of the means through which accounting comes to be embedded within an organisation and the processes which provide a basis for accounting solutions to be related to other organisational problems and phenomena. They also point to the need to understand the more pro-active ways in which accounting can shift the con-

figuration of organisational practices and processes, thereby itself providing a context for modification and change. Of equal importance, they are suggestive of the need to appreciate both the contingent and interactive nature of the circumstances surrounding those processes in any particular setting. Seen in such terms, the intelligibility which we seek to advance is shown to be dependent on the means by which we can question, interpret and interrogate the organisational functioning of the accounting craft and, thereby, on those conceptual concerns and modes of investigation and analysis which provide a basis for the appreciation of both the accounting particular and the accounting general rather than an appeal to any overarching rationale that is deemed to be implicit in either
464 accounting practices or the circumstances that force them to change. Whilst it is recognised that organisational life involves a continuous dialogue between the possible and the actual, and that thereby conceptions of an accounting potential can play a role in mobilising accounting change, this is not to attach an obviousness, a priority or an imperative to the rhetorical claims that are associated with the accounting craft or to provide them with any privileged role in enabling accounting to become what it was not. What effects such claims have need to be seen as arising from their interaction with the other circumstances that characterise organisational life rather than an all embracing, powerfully penetrating and unproblematic logic.[15]

Reflecting the need to articulate a wider appreciation of accounting in action and the processes by which it changes, the analysis of the cases has been conducted in terms of a number of analytical themes. Emphasis has been placed on the particular visibilities created by accounting systems and the means by which they, in turn, shifted perceptions of organisational functioning, mediated the recognition of problems and the options available for their resolution, and infused the patterns of language, meaning and significance within the organisation. From such a stance, attention was directed to the constitutive as well as the reflective roles of accounting. For although it was recognised that a diverse array of other factors could and did impinge upon the accounting craft, at times causing it to shift its focus of attention and locus of organisational embodiment, equally the analyses were undertaken with an awareness of the more enabling properties of accounting itself. By moulding the patterns of organisational visibility, by extending the range of influence patterns within the organisation, by creating different patterns of interaction and interdependence and by enabling new forms of organisational segmentation to exist, accounting was seen as being able to play a positive role in both shifting the preconditions for organisational change and influencing its outcomes, even including the possibilities for its own transformation. Through such mutual processes of interaction, accounting was conceived as a phenomenon embedded within the organisation rather than as something that had a meaningful independent existence. The forms that it took and the influences that it had were not seen as being able to be appreciated outside of the context of the other organisational practices, functions and processes with which it became intertwined. Together they reflected a particular specificity of alignments and although it was sometimes possible to distinguish one organisational phenomenon influencing another, the analysis was conducted in terms of the possibility for, but not the necessity of, such influences since the mobilising factors were often so numerous, diverse, ambiguous

[15] Keat & Urry (1982, pp. 245–246) make a similar point in their more general consideration of social phenomena:

> . . . the profound interdependence of social entities . . . is important . . . (because) the conditions under which the causal powers of important social entities are realized consist in fact of other social entities and of the at least partial realization of their powers. This fundamental interdependence of such entities thus means that the causal powers of some entities constitute the conditions necessary for the realization of the powers of other entities. And this, of course, means that the empirical events which then come to be generated are the product of highly complex interdependent processes . . . Moreover, these processes are not merely to be listed so that they can be "added up" — rather they are to be *synthesized* so that their combination qualitatively modifies each constitutive entity (emphasis in original).

and uncertain, and had such an equivocal *a priori* relationship to the craft of accounting, that change, be it accounting or otherwise, was seen as being something that was created rather than determined. Moreover, as organisational practices and processes over time changed together, it appeared more useful to understand the configurations of which they all formed a part since the presence of any one practice came to presuppose the existence of the others. Perhaps hardly surprisingly, such analytical themes were also sensitive to the nuances and uncertainties which moderated the trajectories of accounting change and to the ways in which the interdependent nature of the resultant organisational processes gave rise to the unintended, the unanticipated and the problematic.

The constitutive roles of accounting are worthy of particular attention, not least because they have been little appreciated or discussed.

For as we have seen, at times accounting can play a significant role in the creation of the possibilities for other organisational phenomena to become what they are not. Through its interwining with the discursive notions of accountability and responsibility, accounting can play a role in the reconstitution of organisational agents, enabling different configurations of organisational arrangements to exist. By its routinisation of information flows and the ways in which it imposes a spatialisation on time, it can change conceptions of the past, the present and the future, contributing different saliences to each which can, in turn, moderate temporal preferences and emphases, and thereby, organisational actions. Creating quite particular objectifications of the otherwise vague and abstract, and particular conceptions of economic facts, accounting also can create not only a context in which the conditions exist for other organisational practices to change but also a means by which a particular organisational visibility can compete for or be imposed upon managerial attention and, if such strategies succeed, perhaps even eventually exclude the visibility and significance of other ways of characterising the organisational terrain, as in *Q*. If such developments occur, the transformational potential of accounting is only enhanced, as the facts created by the craft give rise to an influential language and set of categories for conceiving and changing the organisation in economic terms. As Foucault (1972, p. 167) has noted:

> a succession of events may . . . become an object of discourse, be recorded, described, explained, elaborated into concepts, and provide the opportunity for a theoretical choice.

So although not frequently analysed, the importance of accounting's constitutive roles should not be under-emphasised. They represent one of the significant ways in which accounting becomes embedded in the organisation of which it is a part.

Indeed accounting can become so integral a part of a configuration of organisational practices that it can create some of the possibilities that provide the basis for changing the conditions that themselves mobilise accounting change, as we saw in both *M* and *Q*. In *M* it mediated the selection of not unproblematic marketing and production strategies that provided the context in which the subsequent organisational changes created new information and accounting problems. And in *Q*, a particular regime of economic visibility laid down in the context of one set of organisational problems played its role in creating an economic awareness that transformed the organisation and created a basis for its own dependence on a much elaborated regime of accounting facts. Such illustrations point to not only the transformational potential of accounting but also some of the ways in which accounting can become a part of the factors that impinge upon it.

Central to such a view of accounting is the possibility of there being an equivocal relationship between the aims in the name of which the craft is advanced and its actual organisational consequences (also see Burchell *et al.*, 1985; Hopwood, 1983, 1986b). Not least because the generality of the accounting rhetoric can have difficulty interfacing with the detail, the complexity, the diversity and the specificity of organisational action, some of the anticipated consequences of a particular accounting intervention may not be realised (see Hopwood, 1986a).

Moreover, a whole domain of the unanticipated can realise itself as accounting intersects with other organisational practices and processes, as it actively creates a new sphere of organisational visibility, objectivity and potential significance, and as, in the process of so doing, it engenders resistances to the strategies and interventions which it seeks to further.[16] As all the case analyses have illustrated, the consequences of accounting interventions in the organisation can disturb, disrupt and displace the organisational arena that was presumed in their formulation, thereby having the power to transform rather than merely modify the processes of organisational change.

From such a perspective accounting also can be conceived of as creating residues of organisational consequences that can change the preconditions for subsequent organisational change. It is as if organisational transformations deposit sediments which not only interact with the organisational past but also modify the possibilities for the organisational present, and its future. In this sense "the present really does contain the past which preceded it", although as Gross (1981–82, p. 76) went on to add, "this may be unperceived". A temporal interdependency is so built into organisational life and the task of analysis, as reflected in the cases, in part becomes one of delving through the residues of organisational affairs to illuminate the patterns of pre-conditions that moderate the accounting craft.

It was with such metaphors in mind that the task of analysis was seen to be an archaeological one of carefully and cautiously sorting through the sediments of organisational history, however recent, to reconstruct the ways in which the present emerged from the past.[17] However, as Foucault (1972, 1977) has come to use the terms, the mode of analysis mobilised in the present discussion has features of both a genealogy and an archaeology. An "archaeology tries to outline particular configurations" (Foucault, 1972, p. 157) in order to reveal "relations between discursive formations and non-discursive domains (institutional, political events, economic practices and processes)" (p. 162). As in the present analysis, an archaeology strives to isolate the conditions of possibility of social and organisational practices and bodies of knowledge aiming to reconstruct "a heterogeneous system of relations and effects whose contingent interlocking" (Gordon, 1980, p. 243) constitute the basis on which practice is formed, functions and has its effects. Moreover, it is the active construction of an archaeology that creates a sensitivity to the power creating potential of bodies of knowledge and organisational and social practices that come to create a conception of reality within which they function. Genealogy, on the other hand, concerns itself with ruptures and transitions whereby words, categories, practices and institutions adopt new meanings and significances as they become intertwined with new purposes and new wills, an equally important theme of the present discussion. With its emphasis on change, it is the genealogical perspective that serves to alert us to the dangers of assuming any underlying coherence, tendency or

[16] The observations of Hirschman (1977, p. 131) are interesting in this respect:

> On the one hand, there is no doubt that human actions and social decisions tend to have consequences that were entirely unintended at the outset. But, on the other hand, these actions and decisions are often taken because they are earnestly and fully expected to have certain effects that then wholly fail to materialize. The latter phenomenon, while being the structural obverse of the former, is also likely to be one of its causes; the illusory expectations that are associated with certain social decisions at the time of adoption may keep their *real* future effects from view. Moreover, once these desired effects fail to happen and refuse to come into the world, the fact that they were originally counted on is likely to be not only forgotten but actively repressed (emphasis in original).

[17] In fact the imagery of archaeology emerged from the initial field work in *M* and provided a basis for analysing and structuring the observations made there. At that time I was unfamiliar with Foucault's theorizing and used the metaphor in a more primitive sense. Subsequently the mobilization and structuring of the arguments in this and related articles (see, e.g. Burchell *et al.*, 1985) have been informed by an awareness of the powerful analytics proposed by Foucault (1967, 1972, 1973, 1977, 1979). However, even though it may result in a little confusion for some, the archaeological metaphor is preserved in the title out of both a sense of loyalty to the original formulation and a sense of ease with the imagery in the present context.

logic, such as progress, mobilising patterns of historical and organisational transformation towards some ultimate fulfilment or conclusion. As Foucault (1977, p. 146) made clear, genealogy "does not pretend to go back in time to restore an unbroken continuity that operates beyond the dispersion of forgotten things".

Although the present investigations have been both more focused and constrained than the inquiries undertaken by Foucault, they nevertheless have provided an appreciation of some of the ways in which accounting can both be transformed by and serve as a vehicle for the transformation of the wider organisation. Both a fluidity and a specificity have been introduced into our understanding of accounting in action. The significances attached to accounting have been shown in the process of their reformulation. The craft has been seen as becoming embedded in different organisational configurations and serving very different organisational functions in the process of its change. The mobilising vehicles for these changes have been seen as residing in a very diverse number of organisational processes and practices and, not least, in accounting itself.

However, at this stage in our understanding it is still important to exercise some element of interpretative caution, not least in respect of the mobilising factors that can put accounting into motion. For although the cases have provided a rich insight into at least some of the internal processes of accounting elaboration and change, together they provide less of an understanding of the means through which the external might be able to recast the internal. Tempting though it may be to suggest an analysis in terms of the mobilising potential of a perception of crisis, not least an economic crisis, some care needs to be exercised before too strong a theory is articulated on this basis. Undoubtedly crisis and economic restraint can and do generate action, not least in the accounting area (Khandwalla, 1973; Olofsson & Svalander, 1975). However, the analysis of the cases suggests that the relationship is far from being a straightforward one. In Wedgwood economic recession did provide a stimulus for change, although the relationship between an economic rhetoric of change and its implementation was not unproblematic, requiring, as it did, an intersection with operational bodies of knowledge and specific organisational practices. In *M* accounting mediated the response to a major market change, although it was only itself changed after marketing, production and organisational changes had created a new organisational configuration and a new set of accounting problems. And in *Q*, so unobtrusive and embedded within the structure and consciousness of the organisation had accounting become that initially it served to constrain change by masking the exact nature of the turbulent environment. So together the cases certainly provide no basis for any general theory of crisis driven accounting change. Indeed the mode of analysis that has been articulated should moderate our desire to state any such general view. Instead it should encourage a more precise and careful investigation of the ways in which either the perception or the actuality of external events can disturb the organisational configurations of which accounting forms a part (see Czarniawska & Hedberg, 1985). Seen in terms of the possibility to so shift the organisational terrain and the visibilities that form a part of it, a role exists for the mobilising potential, but certainly not necessity, of a whole series of intrusions into the organisation. Alongside a more nuanced view of the role of crisis (also see Brunson, 1985), we need to appreciate the ways in which new bodies of knowledge, new specialists associated with their practice, government regulatory attempts, changing theoretical and practical conceptions of organisational governance and order, and even the development of a different accounting rhetoric can provide a basis for action and change.

All too clearly there is a need for a great deal more research and a very considerable elaboration of the theoretical and analytical premises on which it might take place. Hopefully, however, the present investigation at least has served to illustrate the possibility for an analysis of accounting change that is not dependent on abstract conceptions of potential and does not impose any unifying orchestration of action. It also aims to have indicated the ways in which historical (however recent that means) analyses can give insight into accounting dynamics and, by recognising that the roles that accounting serves cannot be considered in isolation of the practices of the craft, the need for appreciations of the specific practices that constitute the craft and the organisational processes which endow them with a significance and meaning.

BIBLIOGRAPHY

American Accounting Association, Report of the Committee on Accounting History, *Acccounting Review* Suppl. to Vol. 45 (1970).

Argyris, C., Organizational Learning and Management Information Systems, *Accounting, Organizations and Society* (1977) pp. 113–124.

Armstrong, P., Changing Management Control Strategies: The Role of Competition Between Accounting and other Organizational Professions, *Accounting, Organizations and Society* (1985) pp. 124–148.

Armstrong, P., The Rise of Acccounting Controls in British Capitalist Enterprises, *Accounting, Organizations and Society* (in press).

Ashton, T. S., *Economic Fluctuations in England, 1700–1800* (Oxford University Press, 1959).

Baladouni, V., The Study of Accounting History, *International Journal of Accounting* (Spring 1977), pp. 53–67.

Berry, A. J., Capps, T., Cooper, D., Ferguson, P., Hopper, T. & Lowe, E. A., Management Control in an Area of the N.C.B.: Rationales of Accounting Practice in a Public Enterprise, *Accounting, Organizations and Society* (1985) pp. 3–28.

Brunsson, N., *The Irrational Organization: Irrationality as a Basis for Organizational Action and Change* (John Wiley, 1985).

Burchell, S., Clubb, C., Hopwood, A. G., Hughes, J. & Nahapiet, J., The Roles of Accounting in Organizations and Society, *Accounting, Organizations and Society* (1980) pp. 5–27.

Burchell, S., Clubb, C. & Hopwood, A. G., Accounting in Its Social Context: Towards a History of Value Added in the United Kingdom, *Accounting, Organizations and Society* (1985) pp. 381–413.

Child, J., Organization Structure, Environment and Performance: The Role of Strategic Choice, *Sociology* (January 1972) pp. 1–22.

Clawson, D., *Bureaucracy and the Labour Process* (Monthly Review Press, 1980).

Cooper, D., Discussion of Towards a Political Economy of Accounting, *Accounting, Organizations and Society* (1980) pp. 161–166.

Cooper, D., A Social and Organizational View of Management Accounting, in Bromwich, M. and Hopwood, A. G. (eds), *Essays in British Accounting Research* (Pitman, 1981).

Czarniawska, B. & Hedberg, B., Control Cycles Responses to Decline, *Scandinavian Journal of Management Studies* (August 1985) pp. 19–39.

den Hertog, J. F., The Role of Information and Control Systems in the Process of Organizational Renewal — Roadblock or Road Bridge?, *Accounting, Organizations and Society* (1978) pp. 29–46.

Dent, J., Organizational Research in Accounting: Perspectives, Issues and a Commentary, in Bromwich, M. and Hopwood, A. G. (eds), *Research and Current Issues in Management Accounting* (Pitman, 1986).

Di Maggio, P. J. & Powell, W. W., The Iron Cage Revisited: Institutional Isomorphism and Collective Rationality in Organizational Fields, *American Sociological Review* (April 1983) pp. 147–160.

Foucault, M., *Madness and Civilization* (Tavistock, 1967).

Foucault, M., *The Archaeology of Knowledge* (Tavistock 1972).

Foucault, M., *The Birth of the Clinic* (Tavistock, 1973).

Foucault, M., *Language, Counter-Memory, Practice* (Basil Blackwell, 1977).

Foucault, M., *Discipline and Punish: The Birth of the Prison* (Tavistock, 1979).

Foucault, M., *History of Sexuality* Vol. 1. (Allen Lane, 1979).

Galbraith, J., *Designing Complex Organizations* (Addison-Wesley, 1973).

Geneen, H. S., The Case for Management by the Numbers, *Fort une* (October 1984) pp. 78–81.

Goold, M., Accounting and Strategy, in Bromwich, M. and Hopwood, A. G. (eds) *Research and Current Issues in Management Acccounting*, (Pitman, 1986).

Gordon, C., Afterword, in Foucault, M., *Power/Knowledge* (Harvester, 1980).

Gross, D., Space, Time, and Modern Culture, *Telos* (1981–82), pp. 59–78.

Hedberg, B. & Jönsson, S., Designing Semi-Confusing Information Systems for Organizations in Changing Environments, *Accounting, Organizations and Society* (1978), pp. 47–64.

Hirschman, A., *The Passions and the Interests: Political Arguments for Capitalism before its Triumph* (Princeton University Press, 1977).

Hobsbawm, E. & Ranger, T. (eds) *The Invention of Tradition* (Cambridge University Press, 1983).

Hopper, T., Cooper, D., Lowe, T., Capps, T. & Mouritsen, J., Management Control and Worker Resistance in the National Coal Board, in Knights, D. and Willmott, H. (eds) *Managing the Labour Process* (London: Gower, 1986).

Hopwood, A. G., Information Systems in Matrix Organizations, in Knight, K. (ed.) *Matrix Management* (Saxon House, 1977).

Hopwood, A. G., Towards an Organizational Perspective for the Study of Accounting and Information Systems, *Accounting, Organizations and Society* (1978), pp. 3–14.

Hopwood, A. G., Economic Costs and Benefits of New Forms of Work Organization, in *New Forms of Work Organizations*, Vol. 2, (International Labour Office, 1979).

Hopwood, A. G., On Trying to Study Accounting in the Contexts in which it Operates. *Accounting, Organizations and Society* (1983) pp. 287–305.

Hopwood, A. G., Accounting and the Pursuit of Efficiency, in Hopwood, A. G. and Tomkins, C. (eds) *Issues in Public Sector Acccounting* (Philip Allan, 1984a).

Hopwood, A. G., Accounting Research and Accounting Practice: The Ambiguous Relationship Between the Two. A paper presented at the Conference on New Challenges to Management Research (Leuven, 1984b).

Hopwood, A. G., The Development of "Worrying" About Management Accounting, in Clark, K. B., Hayes, R. H. and Lorenz, C. (eds) *The Uneasy Alliance: Managing the Productivity — Technology Dilemma* (Harvard Business School Press, 1985a).

Hopwood, A. G., The Tale of a Committee that Never Reported: Disagreements on Intertwining Accounting With the Social, *Accounting, Organizations and Society* (1985b), pp. 361–377.

Hopwood, A. G., Accounting and Organizational Action. A paper presented at the Annual Meeting of the American Accounting Association, New York, August 1986a.

Hopwood, A. G., Management Accounting and Organizational Action: An Introduction, in Bromwich M. and Hopwood A. G. (eds.), *Research and Current Issues in Management Accounting* (Pitman, 1986b).

Horovitz, J., *Top Management Control in Europe* (Macmillan, 1980).

Hoskin, K. W. & Macve, R. H., Accounting and the Examination: A Genealogy of Disciplinary Power, *Accounting, Organizations and Society* (1986) pp. 105–136.

Ignatieff, M., Michel Foucault, *University Publishing* (Summer 1984) pp. 1–2.

Jenks, L. H., Early Phases of the Management Movement, *Administrative Science Quarterly* (1960) pp. 421–447.

Jones, H., *Accounting, Costing and Cost Estimation* (University of Wales Press, 1985).

Kaplan, R. S., Measuring Manufacturing Performance: A New Challenge for Managerial Accounting Research, *The Accounting Review* (1983) pp. 686–705.

Kaplan, R.S., Accounting Lag: The Obsolescence of Cost Accounting Systems, in Clark, K. B., Hayes, R. H., and Lorenz, C. (eds) *The Uneasy Alliance: Managing the Productivity — Technology Dilemma* (Harvard Business School Press, 1985).

Keat, R. & Urry, J., *Social Theory as Science* 2nd edn (Routledge & Kegan Paul, 1982).

Khandwalla, P. N., Effect of Competition on the Structure of Top Management Control, *Academy of Management Journal* (1973) pp. 285–295.

Litterer, J. A., Systematic Management: Design for Organizational Recoupling in American Manufacturing Firms, *Business History Review* (1963) pp. 369–391.

Loft, A., Towards a Critical Understanding of Accounting: The Case of Cost Accounting in the U.K., 1914–1925, *Accounting, Organizations and Society* (1986a) pp. 137–169.

Loft, A., Understanding Accounting in its Social and Historical Context: The Case of Cost Accounting in Britain, 1914–1975. Unpublished Ph.D. Thesis, University of London, 1986b.

Lowenthal, D., *The Past is a Foreign Country* (Cambridge University Press, 1985).

McCloskey, D. N., *The Rhetoric of Economics* (University of Wisconsin Press, 1985).

McKendrick, N., Josiah Wedgwood: An Eighteenth Century Entrepreneur in Salemanship and Marketing Techniques, *Economic History Review*, 2nd. Series (1960) pp. 408–433.

McKendrick, N., Josiah Wedgwood and Factory Discipline, *The Historical Journal* (1961a) pp. 30–55.

McKendrick, N., Josiah Wedgwood: 18th Century Salesman, *Proceedings of the Wedgwood Society*

(1961b) pp. 161–189.

McKendrick, N., Josiah Wedgwood and Thomas Bentley: An Inventor — Entrepreneur Partnership in the Industrial Revolution, *Transactions of the Royal Historical Society*, 5th Series (1964), pp. 1–33.

McKendrick, N., Josiah Wedgwood and Cost Accounting in the Industrial Revolution *Journal of Economic History* (1973) pp. 45–67.

Merino, B. D. & Neimark, D. M., Disclosure, Regulation and Public Policy: A Socio-Historical Re-appraisal, *Journal of Accounting and Public Policy* (1982), pp. 33–57.

Miller, P. & O'Leary, T., Hierarchies and Ideals. Unpublished Working Paper, Department of Accounting, University of Illinois at Urbana-Champaign, 1986.

Miller, P. & O'Leary, T., Accounting and the Construction of the Governable Person, *Accounting, Organizations and Society* (1987) pp. 235–265.

Nahapiet, J., The Rhetoric and Reality of an Accounting Change: A Study of Resource Allocation. Paper presented to the First International Conference on Organizational Symbolism and Corporate Culture, University of Lund, Sweden, 1984.

Olofsson, C. & Svalander, P. A., The Medical Services Change over to a Poor Environment. Unpublished Working Paper, University of Linköping, 1975.

Otley, D. T., The Contingency Theory of Management Accounting: Achievement and Prognosis, *Accounting, Organizations and Society* (1980) pp. 413–428.

Parker, R. H., Research Needs in Accounting History, *Accounting Historians Journal* (Fall 1977), pp. 1–28.

Parker, R. H., The Study of Accounting History, in Bromwich, M. and Hopwood, A. G. (eds) *Essays in British*
470 *Accounting Research* (Pitman, 1981).

Patton, P., Of Power and Prisons, in Morris, M. and Patton, P., (eds) *Michel Foucault: Power, Truth, Strategy* (Sydney: Ferel Publications, 1979).

Perrow, C., Complex Organizations: A Critical Essay 3rd edn (Random House, 1986).

Pettigrew, A., Information as a Power Resource, *Sociology* (1972) pp. 187–204.

Roll, E., *An Early Experiment in Industrial Organization: Being a History of the Firm of Boulton and Watt, 1775–1805* (Longmans, 1930).

Scapens, R. W., Closing the Gap Between Theory and Practice, *Management Accounting* (January 1983), pp. 34–36.

Scapens, R. W., Management Accounting: A Survey, in Scapens, R. W., Otley, D. T. and Lister, R. J. (eds) *Management Accounting, Organizational Theory and Capital Budgeting* (Macmillan, 1984).

Schofield, R. E., Josiah Wedgwood and a Proposed Eighteenth-Century Research Organization, *Isis* (1956) pp. 16–19.

Simmonds, K., Strategic Management Accounting, in Fanning, D. (ed) *Handbook of Management Accounting* (Gower, 1983).

Thompson, G., Inflation Accounting in a Theory of Calculation, *Accounting, Organizations and Society* (forthcoming).

Tinker, A. M., Towards a Political Economy of Accounting: An Empirical Illustration of the Cambridge Controversies, *Accounting, Organizations and Society* (1980) pp. 147–160.

Tinker, A. M., Merino, B. D. & Neimark, M. D., The Normative Origins of Positive Theories: Ideology and Accounting Thought, *Accounting, Organizations and Society* (1982) pp. 167–200.

Tribe, K., *Land, Labour and Economic Discourse* (Routledge & Kegan Paul, 1978).

Wright, P., *On Living in an Old Country: The National Past in Contemporary Britain* (Verso, 1985).

Reflections on the Research Endeavour

Accounting research in the United Kingdom*

Anthony G. Hopwood
London Business School

Michael Bromwich
University of Reading

1. INTRODUCTION

Accounting research has developed rapidly in the United Kingdom since 1970. As a result, there is now a lively and quite active research community. Intellectually as well as physically located between the research communities of the United States, with which it shares a common language, and Continental Europe, with which it is slowly forging more substantive academic links, British accounting research has come to reflect both concerns which have developed inside its own boundaries and the interests of its intellectual partners. Although still developing, the resultant research activities are varied and often cumulative. In several areas of investigation there are now quite distinctive British schools of thought; in many other areas there is a British presence and frequently a British contribution.

The diversity and extent of the interests of the British accounting research community are now such that it is difficult to summarize succinctly its achievements and current preoccupations. A short review can only emphasize some of the more important and interesting of the developments. Bearing this inevitable restriction in mind, this review will focus on the institutional context which has given rise to the current research interests, those areas of inquiry which have been traditionally emphasized in the UK and some of the significant directions for research which have emerged in the last decade.

2. THE INSTITUTIONAL CONTEXT

The serious academic study of accounting is of fairly recent origin in the UK. Nevertheless some early beginnings deserve recognition. In 1902 the first Faculty of Commerce in England was created at the University of Birmingham with Lawrence Dicksee, an accounting practitioner with scholarly interests (see Kitchen and Parker, 1980, 51-63), being appointed to the first chair in accounting established in any British university. The chair was a part-time one, however, and Dicksee's occupancy of the post was to be short-lived, too. In 1906 he resigned to move to the London School of Economics and Political Science where the teaching of accounting had commenced in 1904-1905. At the School Dicksee was appointed to a

*We wish to acknowledge the contributions of the many colleagues whose efforts have had to remain anonymous within the confines of this general review.

part-time professorship of accounting in 1914 and to the Sir Ernest Cassel Chair in Accounting and Business Methods, also on a part-time basis, in 1919. In 1926 he was succeeded in the latter post by F.R.M. de Paula, another active practitioner scholar who previously had held a readership in accounting at the School since 1924 (Kitchen and Parker, 1980).

Part-time chairs of accounting also were created at the Universities of Edinburgh and Glasgow in 1919 and 1925, respectively, reflecting, no doubt, the traditional Scottish interest in the university education of its professional cadre. In 1930, however, the London chair lapsed; the Birmingham chair also remained vacant for many years around this time. Indeed no professor of accounting worked again in London until William Baxter's appointment to a full-time chair in 1947 – the only full professorship in the subject in the UK until one at Bristol was established in 1955 (Dev, 1980; Solomons and Berridge, 1974).[1]

474 However, the intervening period was not without developments which influenced the future conduct of accounting research in the UK. Indeed what was for many years the dominant British tradition of scholarly inquiry into accounting, as distinct from the teaching of its current practice (Edey, 1974), started to be developed at the London School of Economics during the late 1930s. Accounting at that time became an object of interest to a group of British economists. With the appointment of Ronald Edwards, a professionally qualified accountant and economist, to the small team of economists at the School who worked in the area of business administration (Dev, 1980) a basis was established for the more systematic study of both the nature of costing (Coase, 1938; Edwards 1937a, 1937b) and the theory of income measurement (Edwards, 1938). Economic theory and modes of analysis were brought to bear on the investigation of accounting problems. Substantive issues in accounting thereby came to be recognized as significant to a wider research community, and a way had been found to conduct research into accounting that was independent of the need to propigate the current mode of its practice. Moreover, the foundation had been laid for the important role which the London School of Economics was to play in the development of a British academic accounting commnunity in the post-war era when Baxter, Solomons, Edey and others were to continue to develop the theoretical project launched by their economist colleagues.

Such intellectual developments were not initially matched by more manifest signs of the growing maturity of accounting research, however. Other early attempts 'to raise the standard of British academic accounting', to quote Zeff (1981), 'had not been marked by conspicuous success'. The Accounting Research Association, founded by Edwards, amongst others, failed to survive the war. The program of research developed by the Incorporated Accountants Research Committee and the promising research journal, *Accounting Research*, established by those associated with that committee, did not survive the integration of the Society of Incorporated Accountants and the Institute of Chartered Accountants in England and Wales in 1957. Indeed in 1961 the Parker report on the education and training policies of the combined institute actively discouraged any efforts to bring universities and the accounting profession together.

The situation was to change, however. During the 1960s not only was there a rapid expansion of university education in general but also a growing student demand for university accounting courses. One by one universities, including the new universities founded at that time, established accounting departments. Often these were associated with departments of economics, following the precedent established by the influential London School of Economics whose younger staff and graduates were to occupy many of the newly created chairs. However, over time, the parallel growth in university courses in business and management studies provided an opportunity for accounting teaching and research to be placed in a very different context. The two major business schools at London and Manchester were established in 1965 following the recommendations of the Franks' Report. The subsequent rapid development of both undergraduate and postgraduate studies in management provided increasing opportunities for accounting to be studied and researched alongside management functions and disciplines other than the 475
purely economic. Over time this pattern of development, together with the growing absolute size of the university accounting sector, provided the basis on which the previous hegemony of the London School of Economics was broken, such that the latter institution is now merely one of many.

By the end of 1974 there were 28 professors of accounting, plus two vacant chairs. All of these professors were members of professional accounting bodies (Parker, 1975). That growth continued, and in 1983 there are over 40 such professors, including several who were not members of any of the professional bodies.

Although the newly expanded group of British accounting academics were much occupied with heavy teaching loads and the administrative problems associated with establishing rapidly growing departments, an interest in research nevertheless developed. Indeed a number of new research journals were established to cater for the increasing demand for scholarly forms of publication. In 1970 *Accounting and Business Research* was launched by the Institute of Chartered Accountants in England and Wales, and in 1974 the still young *Journal of Business Finance* was renamed the *Journal of Business Finance and Accounting*. The more specialist research journal, *Accounting, Organizations and Society*, was founded in the UK in 1976 and has since developed a significant international reputation. In fact by 1976 the interest in accounting research was such that the national Social Science Research Council launched an Accounting Research Initiative to build upon and further direct the research basis already established. Based on the recommendations of the 1975 Tricker report on *Research in Accounting – Strategy for Further Work*, the initiative has sought to provide both general and specific stimuli to accounting research, with funds being made available for particular areas of research, the establishment of research networks and the discussion of research in progress.[2] In subsequent years most of the main professional accounting institutes have created or developed their own capabilities in the accounting research area, with the English Institute establishing its own Director of Research in 1981 – a position held part-time by a senior accounting academic.

The net result of these developments is that there is now a sounder institutional basis for accounting research in the UK. The research community, although still not large, has gained academic recognition and now has its own professional literature and access to both national and professional sources of research funding. A viable basis appears to have been established for a more active and rigorous research tradition.

3. THE BRITISH ACCOUNTING RESEARCH TRADITION

Although there were relatively few British accounting academics until the 1970s, the research inquiries undertaken in earlier periods nevertheless have had a pronounced impact on subsequent research emphases and approaches. Together they provided a basis for more recent concerns with advancing economic understandings of accounting issues, for a pragmatic and theoretically eclectic approach to
476 accounting research and for a concern with the historical appreciation of accounting practice.

3.1 *Income theory and measurement*

The British concern with the theoretical bases for the definition of income and the alternative approaches to its measurement stems from the work of both accountants and economists. Edwards, one of the early group of applied economists working on accounting problems at the London School of Economics in the 1930s, played a role in introducing the problem to the accounting research community (Edwards, 1938; see Baxter, 1978). Thereafter influential early work in the area was undertaken by both the accounting academics who subsequently worked at the School (Baxter, 1959, 1967, 1971 and 1975; Edey, 1974; Solomons, 1961), economists from the School and elsewhere (e.g., Hicks, 1946; Kaldor, 1955) and later by numerous other British academic accountants and economists. An overall insight into these contributions can be found in the collection of readings edited by Parker and Harcourt (1969), the introduction to which provides an influential synthesis of much of the early work. Other useful reviews of the contributions and the debates which these have engendered are to be found in Lee (1974) and Whittington (1981, 1983a, 1983b).

Hicks (1946, 173-174) provided an early and subsequently influential statement of the problem of defining income. He offered three different definitions of *ex ante* income:

1. 'Income No. 1 is .... the maximum amount which can be spent during a period if there is to be an expectation of maintaining intact the capital value of prospective receipts (in money terms).'
2. 'Income No. 2 .... (is) the maximum amount the individual can spend this week, and still expect to be able to spend the same amount in each ensuing week.'
3. 'Income No. 3 must be defined as the maximum amount of money which the individual can spend this week, and still expect to be able to spend the same amount in *real terms* in each ensuing week.'

With these definitions Hicks encapsulated many of the problems which have served as foci for subsequent British research in the area. At a very basic level, he highlighted the ambiguous nature of the income concept and the variety of approaches available for its definition, let alone measurement. His discussion not only emphasized the dependency of the definition of income on an underlying concept of capital maintenance but also provided a basis for the increasing recognition of the intractable problems involved in offering any general definition of income which might provide a basis for the practical assessment of the economic performance of a business enterprise. As Hicks (1946, 176) himself concluded: 'We shall be well advised to eschew *income* .... (it is a) bad tool, which break(s) in our hands.'[3]

Aware also of the additional difficulties of characterizing income in conditions of uncertainty, both Kaldor (1955) and Solomons (1961) reached pessimistic conclusions about the practical usefulness of the income concept, in Kaldor's case 477
as a basis for taxation and for Solomons as a measure of economic performance. Indeed Solomons went so far as to conclude that 'so far as accounting is concerned, the next twenty-five years, may subsequently be seen to have been the twilight of income measurement'. That pessimism has continued to be part of the British accounting research tradition. Arguing from a more theoretically rigorous stance, both Bromwich (1977b) and Peasnell (1977) came to the conclusion that 'there is no reason to suppose that accountants have a comparative advantage in measuring income' and that they therefore should 'concentrate on reporting those items of information about the entity of which they have special knowledge and which enter into the process of income measurement, rather than carrying out the final evaluation' (Whittington, 1981).

Hardly surprisingly given such conclusions, British work in the area of income measurement thereafter focused on ways of facilitating the practical assessment of the economic performance of an enterprise. In addition, because of the increasing awareness that no single income measurement can serve all purposes, emphasis shifted to attempts to relate income measures to the specific purposes for which they might be used (see Edwards, 1938, for an early discussion of this theme). Together, these emphases paved the way for a more 'user oriented' approach to income measurement.

Although a variety of approaches have been utilized, a great deal of emphasis has been placed on those derived from the use of asset valuations based on 'value to the owner' (Baxter, 1967; Stamp, 1971) or 'deprival value', the latter being Baxter's (1971) term for the same concept. Essentially an eclectic approach to the valuation problem, value to the owner can involve the use of net realisable value (NRV), replacement cost (RC) or discounted value in present use (PV) as a basis for asset valuations (Parker and Harcourt, 1969). With the aim of establishing the loss which a firm would suffer if deprived of an asset (for the debate on the problem of aggregation, see Edey, 1974; Ma, 1976; Peasnell, 1978), replacement cost is considered as placing a ceiling on the value to the owner in those cases in which it would be worthwhile replacing the asset. If the asset would not be replaced, it would be valued at the present value of the expected net cash receipts where it is being held for use (PV > NRV) or at net realisable value where it is being held for resale (NRV > PV). However, with replacement cost thus providing the basis for the general valuation rule, the value to the owner approach has often been used to justify using replacement cost as a general basis for asset valuation (Parker and Harcourt, 1969; Gee and Peasnell, 1976; also see the more complex approach outlined by Stamp, 1971).

The value to the owner approach has not been uncontroversial (Chambers, 1966), and it is certainly not without both theoretical and practical problems (see Bromwich, 1977b; Whittington, 1983b). However, its British advocates have tended to justify its use on pragmatic grounds. Baxter (1975), for instance, claimed that it was 'grounded in common sense', and its use would avoid the anomalies that would result from the application of a single valuation method in all circumstances.
478 Perhaps for these reasons, value to the owner was adopted by the Sandilands Committee, the government initiated inquiry into inflation accounting that reported in 1975.

Overall, therefore, the British tradition in the area of income theory and measurement can be characterized as one that has tried to emphasize the need for a pragmatically useful approach. Although grounded in an economic mode of analysis, a pessimistic view was taken of the possibility of general theoretical solutions to the problem. Accepting, however, prevailing notions of the economic nature of enterprise performance assessment, emphasis was placed on the need to supply information which is seen to be useful to the users of accounting reports. Increasingly the need for theoretical coherence and closure within an accounting context alone was seen to be of less significance.

3.2 *Cost theory*

Another area where economic analysis had a major impact on British accounting research was in the area of cost theory and, in particular, on discussions of the determination of appropriate costs for decision making. Again a strong contribution came from the applied economists working at the London School of Economics. In a series of articles published in the 1930s, Edwards (1937a, 1937b, 1937c), Coase (1938) and Baxter (1938) outlined an approach to both the appraisal of prevailing modes of costing which relied on the collection and allocation of historic costs and their replacement by more economically oriented costing principles. Emphasizing the significance in a decision-making context of marginal, future oriented and opportunity costs, these authors and later colleagues at the School (see Buchanan and Thirlby, 1973) together provided the outline of a general approach to cost determination that has had a major impact on subsequent accounting research and university education in accounting in the UK (Arnold and Scapens, 1981; Scapens, in press).

Summarizing the contribution of the 'London tradition of costing' (Buchanan, 1969), Arnold and Scapens (1981, 150-151) commented as follows:

> Collectively, they made three main contributions. The first was to recognise the fundamental importance of defining cost in terms of the choice to be made; . . . The second contribution was to adopt a 'common sense' approach to costing for decisions, based on providing relevant information for decision models. . . . Their third contribution was to apply the cost concepts they developed to real world business problems.

Again the research approach was pragmatic in nature rather than being theoretically refined and self-contained. As Gould (1974, 1977) subsequently pointed out, opportunity costs cannot be calculated until sufficient information is already available to make a decision. The aim of the costing research project was not theoretical elegance and closure, however, but rather the articulation of an approach that might provide a useful guide to the better derivation of costs in the world of practice. So once again British pragmatism ruled supreme.

Subsequent research extended opportunity costing ideas into the areas of mathematical programing (Samuels, 1965), transfer pricing (Gould, 1964) and the analy- 479
sis of planning variances (Bromwich, 1969).

3.3 *Accounting and organizational structure*

The concern with the improvement of costing practice came about as a result of attempts to use administrative and calculative means to increase the rationality and efficiency of decision making in large bureaucratic organizations where decisions were not subject to the direct influence of the market. Another quite influential area of accounting research had a similar origin, namely, that concerned with the role of accounting in the measurement and control of the performance of divisionalized organizations. Here the aim of research was to improve the internal measurement of performance at the divisional (profit or investment center) level so that actions aimed at improving an index of divisional performance would benefit the organization as a whole.

The problem arose when Solomons (1965) pointed out that the generally accepted measurement of divisional performance on the basis of return on capital employed did not necessarily encourage managers to take optimal investment decisions. Prevailing accounting practices seemingly did not further the economic rationality of decision making. In order to avoid some of these problems Solomons (1965) preferred the use of residual income ('the excess of net earnings over the cost of capital'), with divisions being charged with the opportunity cost of the capital resources used in their operations. However, Amey (1969b, 5) argued that 'the introduction of interest in evaluating past performance is . . . unnecessary or positively misleading, depending on the divisional objective'. He believed that once investment decisions are taken they represent sunk costs which are irrelevant for the appraisal of operating performances (Amey, 1969a). The resulting debate attracted the attention of numerous British academics (Amey, 1975; Bromwich, 1973; Flower, 1971; Scapens, 1979; Tomkins, 1975).

Although the primary concerns were seemingly technical, the research conducted in this area had a wider significance: it provided the first context in which

British accounting research had addressed issues of management control (to refer to the more all-embracing American term for the appreciation of management accounting in its organizational context) rather than just technical accounting practice. Although the discussions made no specific appeal to organizational research, consideration nevertheless started to be given to the interface between organizational structures and appropriate accounting practices. Some attention was given to the problems involved in the joint design of patterns of organizational responsibility and accounting measures of performance. Questions relating to the impact of accounting measurements on the time scale of management attention came under discussion. And managerial motivations *vis-à-vis* indices of organizational performance were no longer seen as being completely unproblematic. Although the analysis of these and related issues in organizational control remained more implicit than explicit, a basis nevertheless had been established for the
480 intermingling of organizational and accounting issues.

3.4 *The historical appreciation of the accounting craft*

One final strand of the British accounting research tradition is worthy of separate mention, namely, the attempts that have been made to forge an historic appreciation of the accounting craft. Over the years, numerous British accounting academics (and other interested colleagues) have demonstrated an interest in documenting and describing the emergence of accounting practice (Baxter, 1945; Parker, 1969; Solomons, 1952; Stacey, 1954; Yamey, 1978; also see the collection of studies which appeared in Littleton and Yamey, 1956). As outlined in Parker's (1981) review of British research in this area, particular consideration has been given to the history of double-entry bookkeeping, the earlier stages of the development of corporate financial reporting and the emergence and early functioning of the institutions of a professionalized accounting craft.

The reasons for such a historical interest are difficult to decipher. Some of the founding fathers of British accounting research had a personal interest in historical inquiry (Baxter, 1945; Solomons, 1952) which they successfully transferred to their colleagues and students (de St. Croix, 1956; Yamey, 1978, amongst many others). An historical interest also might have furthered their desire to present accounting as a significant area of intellectual inquiry, much as Hatfield (1924) had formulated his own 'historical defence of bookkeeping' in the USA at an earlier stage of the development of an academic accounting. Moreover, the traditional British interest in the antiquarian also might have had a role to play, not least because many of the historical studies undertaken focused on the early history of the craft in isolation from any explicit attempt to understand its current functioning and processes of change.

Whatever the reasons for its emergence, the resultant historical backcloth to accounting research has offered a number of advantages. Through it accounting has come to be more generally recognized as a contingent phenomenon, dependent on the contexts in which it emerged. However, the historical emphasis was not without its problems. The vast majority of studies were atheoretical in nature, implicitly adopting very particular views of historical development and change. Few explicit attempts were made to unmask the specific relationships that accounting might have to the wider organizational and social fabric. Accounting, in other words, was rarely seen as a problematic endeavor, implicated in organizational and social struggles to define and allocate the surpluses generated in the corporate domain. Rather, emphasis was placed on describing the progressive development and achievements of the technical accounting art. Be that as it may, the early British concern with accounting history nevertheless usefully extended the arena of research inquiry. The fact of, if not the rationale for, accounting change was at least placed on the table for subsequent deliberation and debate.

3.5 *The creation of a research community*

Stemming, as they did, from a small research community, the early emphases of British accounting research nevertheless succeeded in creating a foundation for subsequent inquiries. A legitimate basis was established for research and scholarly deliberation which had some autonomy from the articulation and propagation of current accounting practice. An academic accounting community was emergent. Moreover, the concerns of accounting research had been related to those of other substantive social sciences, notably economics. A wider basis thereby had been established for accounting inquiry. The approach was a pragmatic one, however. Theories, both accounting and otherwise, were related to what were seen to be significant problems and dilemmas facing accounting practice. Rather than striving to create a comprehensive theory of the accounting endeavor, the aim was to develop and articulate reasoned but useful approaches to accounting debate and reform. Nevertheless accounting could start to be investigated from without as well as in terms of its own internal rationale and logic.

4. 1970-1980: A DECADE OF DEVELOPMENT AND CHANGE

During the 1970s the academic accounting community in the UK was to grow rapidly. A large number of new departments were established, and many new recruits joined the ranks of the academic community. Although traditions continued to be influential in both teaching[4] and research, the new growth not only ensured their continued development but also provided the conditions for them to evolve.

The new recruits to the academic accounting community brought with them new interests, skills and backgrounds. A more diverse research community was being created. University accounting departments also started to have different institutional settings. Rather than necessarily residing in or alongside departments of economics (and law), the relationship to other management functions increasingly was recognized, and quite explicitly so in the growing number of business schools and departments. A basis thereby was created for very different intellectual and practice interests to be brought to bear on accounting inquiry. Moreover important aspects of the context of accounting in practice also were changing in ways that were to have quite important implications for the interests of the research community. The state of accounting practice became an issue for wider public concern and debate. Accounting quite explicitly came to be seen as something in need of development and change. In the form of the Accounting Standards Committee an institutional platform for the discussion and reform of accounting was established (Leach and Stamp, 1981). This, in turn, was to provide an influential basis for a more abstract discussion of the state of the accounting art and proposals for its reform. During the 1970s a need for accounting knowledge thereby came to be recognized even in professional circles – a major change by British standards.

Change was no less significant, even if less explicit, in the area of management accounting. As the debates on accounting for divisionalized enterprises had fore-
482 warned, there was increasing practical and academic interest on the articulation and integration of the techniques of internal accounting in the more comprehensive contexts of overall financial or management control. We now turn to these developments.

4.1 *Income measurement theory and some subsequent research developments*

The sudden announcement by the (then) Accounting Standards Steering Committee in 1974 of their proposal that all companies should publish a statement of accounts adjusted for the effects of inflation provided the basis for the first major public discussion of the state of accounting practice and knowledge in the UK. Was it appropriate for inflation to be accounted for in terms of a current purchasing power adjustment, as proposed by the professional standard-setting body, or could stronger arguments be made for a replacement-cost approach that would introduce a more significant discontinuity into accounting practice? Could the two approaches even be combined? The intensity of the debate was such that the government established a committee of inquiry into the subject, the Sandilands Committee, which reported in 1975. That and the debates which followed, and still continue, provided a continued platform for both the practical and theoretical discussion of the nature and measurement of income.

Hardly surprisingly this significant policy debate on accounting provided a major stimulus for research. Past traditions were reexamined, refined and developed and criticized. Some new approaches emerged, as we will discuss. All told, a massive literature of mainly theoretical debate resulted, much of which is expertly and succinctly surveyed by Whittington (1981, 1983a, 1983b). Continued research attention was given to the alternative valuation bases available (Kennedy, 1978), both the further refinement of the concept of value to the owner (Baxter, 1975) and the bases for its applicability (Bromwich, 1977a, 1977b), and the role which accounting might or might not play in the delineation of a useful basis for gauging the distribution profits of an enterprise (Eggington, 1980; Sale and Scapens, 1978).

The one relatively new topic that did attract a considerable amount of research as a result of the public discussion of inflation accounting was the gearing adjustment. Although research on this had been conducted in Germany in the 1920s and 1930s, it would appear that the concept was 'reinvented, apparently independently' (Whittington, 1981, 19) by a number of British researchers (Gibbs, 1975, 1976; Godley and Wood, 1974; Kennedy, 1978). Aiming to recognize some of the impact of general price-level changes within the context of a replacement-cost accounting system, interest in the gearing adjustment resulted from the public discussion of first, the accounting implications of the corporate liquidity crisis of 1974 (Merrett and Sykes, 1974) and, subsequently, the system of replacement cost accounting proposed by the Sandilands Committee. As a result of these discussions, research attention was given to the need for and the means of dealing with the recognition of gains on borrowing and losses on monetary assets within a current-cost accounting system.

Within an amazingly short period of time, a form of gearing adjustment was 483
incorporated into both the Hyde Guidelines (ASC, 1977), which attempted to reconcile conflicting views on inflation accounting, and the subsequently proposed and adopted accounting standard, ED 24 and SSAP 16, although it is fair to say that none of these practical proposals did justice to the full range of issues raised in the theoretical discussions of the topic (for a review of which see Whittington, 1983a).

Although relatively new to the theoretical discussion of the measurement of income in Britain, the arguments for the inclusion of a gearing adjustment nevertheless reflected a number of the characteristics of the previous British research work in this area. As Whittington (1981, 19) points out: 'it ... shares the less desirable attribute of being somewhat imperfectly related to specific information needs of users of financial reports. It is another example of a "general purpose" technique which has been developed to deal with a specific problem.'

Increasingly aware of the very real difficulties with both new and more traditional approaches to income theory, many British accounting researchers had begun to place more emphasis on the possibilities of providing what was thought to be useful information on components of income rather than attempting to provide any comprehensive assessment of the concept as a whole. The ideal of *the* income therefore has been a receding one. In its place many researchers seemingly have been content with the possibility of disaggregating income measures into useful components so as to help the user make his or her own assessment of the income relevant in a particular context. Recognizing both the diversity of users and decision contexts, the need to provide a coherent theoretical *a priori* integration of the elements of income began to be seen by many as being less crucial.

However, the anarchic tendencies of such an approach also have been recognized, implicitly if not explicitly. Accordingly, research has tended to place much greater emphasis on a new mobilizing rationale – the information needs of the users of accounting information. Indeed in a very short period of time the concept of the 'user' has come to play a much more significant role in both academic and practical discussions of accounting. Accounting discourse is now peppered with the terminology of 'users', 'usefulness', 'user information needs' and 'user decisions'. The derivation and articulation of user needs for information has come to be seen by many as a way of overcoming the theoretical difficulties encountered in attempts to apply more traditional approaches to accounting reform. Rather than seeking to impose a new accounting from without, the user approach seemingly offers the possibility of providing a more grounded, empirical and pragmatic approach to accounting evaluation and reform that avoids the difficulties inherent in high accounting theorizing.

Accounting research in Britain is still at the stage of embracing and developing this new orientation. However, some theoretical contributions to the new approach have been made (Carsberg, Hope and Scapens, 1974; Peasnell, 1974a, 1974b), and attempts also have been made to point to the empirical research needs inherent in such an approach to accounting evaluation and reform. As Carsberg
484 (Carsberg and Hope, 1977, 267) has pointed out:

> ... the main reason for undertaking empirical studies of the ways in which accounting reports are used at the present time is in the need to obtain insight into the objectives which the decision-takers are seeking. We cannot judge what information would be useful until we understand these objectives.

Although empirical research has not been a strong point of the British accounting research tradition (Peasnell, 1981), some attempts nevertheless have been made to identify the users of accounting information, to study their information processing behavior (see especially the studies undertaken by Lee and Tweedie, 1977) and to investigate some of the decision effects of accounting information. Much of this research is ably reviewed by Peasnell (1981). More recently this newly emergent approach to research has been used by the Institute of Chartered Accountants in England and Wales in order to evaluate the utility of the inflation accounting standard (Carsberg, in press). Although undertaken in a very short period of time, an attempt nevertheless was made to explore the use made of inflation accounting information by significant groups of users, including institutional investors, share analysts, the media, government agencies and corporate management. In a separate ICAEW sponsored study Archer and Steel (1983) also surveyed the views of senior corporate financial executives.

The range of reactions to such policy oriented empirical studies of accounting users and use (at present of necessity confined to the more popular accounting media) points to the preliminary nature of research in this area. The methodologies are still emergent. More significant are the difficulties in interpreting the results, regardless of the quite legitimate questions of sample size, selection and generalizability. Just how can the findings of such detailed investigations be brought to bear on policy deliberation? As yet little consideration has been given to these important issues by the research community.

Therefore at the present stage of British research in the area of income measurement, traditional theoretical approaches are subject to question, newer empirical approaches are at a very early stage of development and no consideration has been given to the relationship between the two. This, combined with the growing tendency to see accounting policy-making in political terms – a factor that will be discussed below, may provide a basis for the views of those researchers who increasingly see the need to cast questions of accounting regulation and reform in more legalistic terms (see Leach and Stamp, 1981). Although such an approach does not deny the relevance and utility of more conventional research strategies, it does add to the research agenda an important new element, namely, the need to consider and debate both the technical and wider socioeconomic aspects of the alternative institutional settings in which accounting policy-making can and should take place (Bromwich and Hopwood, 1983a).

4.2 *Cash flow accounting*

The theoretical and practical problems associated with the income concept also 485
resulted in another important strand of research, namely, that concerned with cash-flow reporting. In this area the British research contribution has been a significant one. Associated with his early critique of the income concept, Solomons (1961) suggested the possible relevance of cash-flow or funds-flow reporting. Edey (1963) reinforced the arguments in favor of this approach. However, most of the exploration, development and refinement of cash-flow reporting was undertaken by Lawson and Lee in a significant series of papers which are succinctly summarized and reviewed by Ashton (1976) and Lee (1981). Basing their arguments on the greater decision relevance of an approach that is not posited on the arbitrary inter-temporal allocations that are a feature of conventional income approaches, Lawson and Lee have sought to advance both the theoretical basis for their approach and develop a sound framework for practical measurement and presentation. In addition, they have both invested in the provision of empirical materials which are suggestive of both its utility and practicality. The net result of these sustained endeavors is that cash-flow reporting is now recognized as a suggestive alternative to present approaches to corporate reporting. Its raw materials are those items which lie at the heart of enterprise financial decision-making. In addition to avoiding many of the problems of conventional accounting, it is forward looking, easy to understand and graphically portrays many of the key financial problems faced by enterprise management. Still, however, it has not been accepted by the practicing profession!

4.3 *Accounting standards and the standard-setting process*

The 1970s in the United Kingdom was the era of accounting standard setting. As has already been shown in the arena of inflation accounting, such professional concerns provided an influential backcloth for a great deal of the research conducted in the area of financial accounting. Researchers attempted to provide critical analyses of some of the areas of accounting where individual standards were being formulated and discussed. Recognizing that all too little was known of the current state of the accounting art, let alone the proposals for its reform and standardization, surveys have been conducted of the state of accounting practice. And increasingly aware of the partial nature of many proposals for accounting reform, researchers also have started to inquire into both the factors that result in accounting as it is and the institutional processes through which proposals for its change emerge.

In such ways the standardization of accounting has now come to be seen as a not unproblematic endeavor. Albeit slowly, the research community is starting to adopt a more independent and questioning but far from coherent and well-articulated stance *vis-à-vis* the standardization project. The present diversity of accounting practice has been sympathetically explored. The conceptual validity of alternative bases for accounting reform has been recognized. Consideration slowly is being given to the relationship which the reality of standard setting has to the
486 aims and objectives that were, and still are, articulated on its behalf. Even the central premises of the standardization mission have themselves been analyzed and questioned.

Given the constraints of a general survey, it is difficult to do justice to the large amount of research that has been conducted in individual areas of financial accounting. During the 1970s a mass of such articles and monographs were published by British accounting researchers, many in the more professional sections of the accounting literature. Suffice it to say that the pragmatic debates in professional circles stimulated some significant research analyses, with important work being done in areas like foreign exchange accounting (see the survey papers by Patz, 1977, and Nobes, 1980) and segmental reporting (Emmanuel and Gray, 1977, 1978; Hatherly, 1979). Also in the context of the work of the Accounting Standards Committee, research has been conducted into such new areas of accounting as the value added statement (see, for example, Rutherford, 1977) and employment reporting (Maunders, 1982), and more recently increased attention is being given to the problem encountered as a result of attempts to extend the scope of accounting standardization to the public sector (Jones, 1982; Jones and Pendelbury, 1982; Lapsley, 1981). In such ways accounting research increasingly has come to confront important and often contentious aspects of the operation and reform of accounting in practice.

One reason for the difficulty of surveying the diverse research contributions in the area of financial accounting is that accounting research, like accounting practice, lacks a coherent framework. Individual topics and problems have been investigated in isolation from other aspects of the accounting craft. There has been neither an orchestrating theory of accounting nor a unifying rationale for its practice.

Aware of this situation and stimulated by US concerns with the development of a conceptual framework to guide policy making in accounting, the British profession enlisted the aid of a researcher (Macve, 1981; also see Macve, 1983) to investigate the possibilities for articulating a more comprehensive perspective for organizing and formulating the diverse elements of the accounting art. To many, however, the results were not encouraging. Certainly the view of most British researchers remains that attempts to seek to base the authority for accounting standards on an agreed conceptual framework are bound to fail. Not only do they invariably ignore vital elements of the political process of standard setting, but they cannot confront the inherent conceptual difficulties involved in trying to meaningfully standardize important components of a practical economic calculus. As Bromwich (1981, 54) has said, '. . . . the problems facing accounting standard-setters are far greater than is, perhaps, apparent to those who consider their endeavours from a practical and pragmatic stance'.

Although much lip service increasingly is paid to the political nature of accounting standard setting, at present this remains an area where the verbal interests and inclinations of the research community have not resulted in very much sustained inquiry. There are now some signs of a more systematic interest, however (Hope, 1979). Attempts are being made to carefully analyze the processes involved in 487
particular instances of accounting change with a view to understanding the forces that seem to be at work (Hope and Briggs, 1982; Hope and Gray, 1982). However, more detailed consideration has been given to some of the general theoretical problems inherent in accounting standard setting which might provide a basis for coming to a better understanding of the political resolutions observed in practice. Drawing on economic theory, serious attempts have been made to explicate the social-choice assumptions implicit in standardization proposals and the limited circumstances under which standard accounts can be deemed to unproblematically increase general economic and social welfare (Bromwich, 1977b; 1980). Indeed the British work in this area anticipated recent American findings that ideal accounting standards cannot, in general, exist in a world of market failure where there is an inability to market all commodities (Bromwich, 1981).

4.4 *Management accounting and the rise of an organizational interest*

Although conducted by different researchers in different contexts drawing on very different theoretical frameworks, some of the developments in British management accounting have mirrored those taking place in the financial accounting area.

Management accounting research also has witnessed a growing disillusionment with the traditional theoretical framework (Scapens, in press). Concerns have been expressed about their internal coherence (Gould, 1974, 1977), their emphasis on questions of cost accounting rather than more widespread notions of financial control in complex organizations and the seemingly equivocal relationship which they have to practice (Scapens, 1983, in press). Research in the area of management accounting also went through a period of fragmentation as it sought to address an increasingly diverse array of both practical and theoretical problems and possibilities (Bhaskar, 1981; Hart, 1981; Scapens, in press), often with very few researchers working in any single area. Issues related to budgeting, standard costing and variance analysis and financial planning and investment appraisal (see the research review by Lister, in press) were considered alongside the more traditional concerns with costing. Slowly the problems involved in the design of financial control systems appeared on the research agenda (Lowe and Machin, 1983; Lowe and McInnes, 1971; Otley, 1983). More and more frequently, research insights are drawn from quantitative methods (Bhaskar, 1981), systems analysis (Otley, 1983), behavioral science and organization theory (Cooper, 1981; Otley, in press), in addition to the traditional concern with economic theory. Finally, management accounting research also has started to confront the problems of trying to appreciate and understand the complexities, difficulties and seemingly different rationales of practice (Scapens, 1983, in press). As in the financial accounting area, there are now very real signs of interest in the factors that have resulted in today's management accounts, the processes through which they change and their organizational and social consequences (see Hopwood, 1983).

Of course there also are differences between the two areas. In total, management
488 accounting has not attracted anywhere near as much research attention in the UK as has financial accounting. There are also fewer areas of management accounting research where there are sustained, cumulative traditions of inquiry. On the other hand, attempts to confront theory in the name of practice in all probability started earlier in the management accounting area. Certainly at the present time the research which they gave rise to tends to be recognized as a more legitimate component of research into and the knowledge basis of management accounting than related studies in the area of financial accounting.

The more traditional areas of management accounting research already have been ably surveyed by Arnold and Scapens (1981), Bhaskar (1981) and particularly by Scapens (in press; see also the review by Hart, 1981). Such reviews suggest that in recent years emphasis tends to have been placed on the refinement of existing perspectives and procedures. More sophisticated quantitative approaches have been used; more explicit efforts have been made to allow for the effects of uncertainty; attempts have been made to incorporate an awareness of the costs of information into the analytical frameworks being proposed. Although there were some early significant British contributions to this literature, e.g., Samuels (1965), the surveys of Scapens (in press), Bhaskar (1981) and Hart (1981) all demonstrate that British research has tended to operate within the paradigms established in the USA.

Regardless of origin, however, the net result of past research contributions increasingly is being seen as a body of knowledge that is distanced from both the practice of management accounting and the problems that it faces (Scapens, 1983, in press; see also the contributions in Arnold, Cooper and Scapens, 1983). Surveys repeatedly demonstrate that the sophisticated procedures provided by research are not used in practice (see the review in Scapens, 1983; for more recent UK research see Coates *et al.*, 1980, and Scapens *et al.*, in press). Researchers in other management disciplines point to the need for different research strategies to address the problems of today (Simmonds, 1983). Even some of the research developments themselves are now pointing to the bases for an organizational interest in simple management accounting procedures in conditions of uncertainty where the cost of information is recognized explicitly (Scapens, in press) – far from unfamiliar circumstances. Increasingly, therefore, both the extension of past economic research perspectives and the growing interest in the organizational bases for and functioning of management accounting systems is pointing towards the formulation of a new interest in the area – an interest which seeks to appreciate, understand and possibly guide the emergence, functioning and consequences of management accounting in the contexts in which it operates (Hopwood, 1983).

British research has played a significant role in the delineation of an organizational interest in management accounting. Although initially influenced by American research on the behavioral aspects of accounting (Hopwood, 1972, 1973; McRae, 1972), the United Kingdom quickly provided a receptive, nurturing and independent environment for the study of management accounting in the organizational contexts in which it operates (Cooper, 1975; Dew and Gee, 1973; Lowe and Shaw, 1968). The American 'behavioral' interest was soon supplanted by a British interest in the 'organizational' and, increasingly, the 'social'. Concerns with individual and group responses to accounting information were superceded by an interest in the organizational construction and functioning of accounting systems.

Some useful surveys of the British research contribution in this area are already available (Cooper, 1981; Otley, 1977, in press), as are other relevant commentaries (Colville, 1981; Hopwood, 1978, 1983; Lowe and Machin, 1983; Scapens, in press). Given this, here we only seek to identify some of the more important features of this body of research.

1. The understanding of how accounting information is used in organizational settings has been an important mobilizing concern of British research. Initially consideration was given to moderating roles played by budgetary pressures (Lowe and Shaw, 1968), management styles and different approaches to performance appraisal (Hopwood, 1972; Otley, 1978), and management structures and other important aspects of the internal organizational environment (Dew and Gee, 1973). More recently, attempts have been made to locate the use made of accounting information more centrally in the context of on-going processes of organizing (Colville, 1981; Tomkins *et al.*, 1980). More detailed consideration is now being given to such areas as the functioning of accounting systems in times of economic restraint (Tomkins *et al.*, 1980) and the role which accounting plays in the operation and control of complex organizational structures (Berry *et al.*, 1983).
2. British research has attempted to understand not only how accounting systems are embodied in organizations but also how their design and functioning is conditioned by other important aspects of the organizational environment, including the nature of the task, the technologies in use and the uncertainties prevalent in both the external and internal environments of the organization. Along with such interests, consideration has been given to the relevance of contingency theories of organization for understanding the observed diversity of accounting systems and their modes of use (Cooper, 1977; Hopwood, 1978;

Lowe and Tinker, 1976; Otley, 1978). The use of such a contingent perspective has not been seen as unproblematic, however (Cooper, 1981; Otley, 1980). Growing recognition also has been given to the need to understand both the detailed processes by which accounting systems emerge and change and the ways in which managerial interests in the design and use of management accounting systems are exercised.

3. More explicit attention increasingly has been given to the control functions of accounting (Otley and Berry, 1980). Control, however, is recognized as having a variety of useful meanings. Although consideration is still being given to refining the more technical implications of the managerial guidance notions of control (Lowe and Machin, 1983), increasing attention is being paid by British researchers to the wider connotations of control procedures and strategies (Cooper, 1981, 1983; Hopwood, in press).

490 The ways in which management accounting systems are implicated in the exercise of organizational and social power are now being investigated quite explicitly. Attention has been directed towards the ways in which accountings can emerge from the politics of organizational life (Burchell *et al.*, 1980). The ritualistic and symbolic uses of accounting information have been explored (Batstone, 1979; Cooper, 1981; Gambling, 1977). The interested nature of accounting practices is being recognized (Willmot, 1983). 'Power' has entered the accounting research vocabulary. Albeit slowly, research efforts are now being directed towards understanding how accounting systems have been constructed in the context of the design and functioning of modes of organizing that have a significant role to play in the establishment of both organizational and social patterns of power, influence and domination.

In these ways even management accounting is coming to be understood as both an organizational and social phenomenon (Hopwood, 1983). Although functioning in organizational settings, its origins are being seen to reside both within and outside the organization. Seemingly the social can pass through the organizational in the construction of management accounts (Burchell *et al.*, in press), although little is known of the processes by which this takes place.

4. Theoretical considerations have loomed large in organizational research on management accounting, as in so many other areas of British accounting research. Although empirical studies have been undertaken, the investigation of the empirical domain has been relegated to a less significant role than elsewhere, for instance, in the USA and Scandinavia.

The relative neglect of the empirical has both advantages and disadvantages. On the positive side, it has facilitated the use of new theoretical perspectives from other of the human and social sciences. It is true to say that British research in the area has been characterized by a theoretical openness and an awareness of new developments in other relevant disciplines. The concentration on theoretical concerns also has furthered the exploration of the wider organizational and social nature of accounting practice. Accounting has not been explored on its own terms. Conceptions of its organizational roles and consequences have been

> critically assessed and even reformulated (Burchell *et al.*, 1980). Theories 'of' rather than 'in' accounting have emerged that have sought to distance themselves from prevalent internal conceptions of the accounting craft. So much of the richness and vitality of research in the area has stemmed from the emphasis given to conceptual and theoretical questions. Those gains have been achieved at a large cost, however. Despite the investment that has been made in advancing an organizational understanding of accounting, relatively little is empirically known of accounting in action. Many of the theories have few precise empirical referents. Studies of accounting change and use are sparce; little is known of the detailed ways in which accounting intersects with other aspects of organizational life. At present we have few bases for appraising the consequences of accounting in action.
>
> However there are some encouraging signs of change (Berry *et al.*, 1983; Tomkins *et al.*, 1980). Empirical work appears to be winning a higher priority. Its significance at this stage of theoretical development is being recognized (Otley, in press; Scapens, in press). Moreover the previous theoretical emphases seemingly are having a significant effect on the nature of the empirical task that is being delineated. A more problematic view of the empirical domain appears to be emergent (Tomkins and Groves, 1983; Willmot, 1983). Conventional positivistic notions of the empirical are being set aside by some members of the research community. The need to recognize the interplay between the theoretical and the empirical seems increasingly clear. The indications are that future empirical work will emphasize the qualitative, the interpretative and the theory-generating aspects of the research craft.

In total, organizational research on management accounting has played a not unimportant role in highlighting the gap that exists between traditional research perspectives and the practice of the craft (Scapens, 1983). By emphasizing the need to understand accounting as it is, such research has helped to make problematic more conventionally normative traditions of inquiry. Interestingly, however, as has already been discussed, an interest in the organizational practice of accounting also emerged from within the traditional perspectives themselves. As research placed greater emphasis on the study of the design of management accounting systems in conditions of uncertainty and as the costs of information were recognized explicitly, a basis came to be established for appreciating rather than necessarily reforming the accounting craft. Subsequent research developments in the areas of the economics of information and organization, and their application to accounting, have encouraged further work from such a perspective (Scapens, in press). The result is that now accounting also is being explored in the context of its organizational linkages and functioning from an economic as well as social viewpoint. That complementarity is to be welcomed, although great care needs to be exercised in presuming that the assumptions underpinning the seemingly different but nevertheless overlapping inquiries are similar, as Cooper (1983) makes clear.

4.5 *Accounting and the pursuit of social interests*

A number of factors have contributed to an increasing recognition of the interested nature of accounting practice among some members of the British accounting research community. The debates surrounding the development of new financial accounting standards have provided a context in which to at least observe from a distance the interest which different parties seemingly have in accounting and the public vestiges of the subsequent negotiation process. Research on the political process of standard setting is now seeking to clarify those relationships. Other researchers also have established an interest in the processes. Organizational and social inquiries also are giving rise to an understanding of how interests in economic calculations and forms of regulation and control shape the development of the accounting craft. Research in these areas is slowly becoming more significant. In
492 addition, during the 1970s accounting in practice itself sought specifically to address its relationship to wider social interests. A questioning of the bases for regulating accounting practice, a more powerful labor movement, a wider interest in questions of accountability and democracy together provided a platform on which questions such as the disclosure of information to employees and trade unions, the relationship which accounting has and might have to the enhancement of accountability and the extension of accounting to include a consideration of the social as well as the economic were considered explicitly (see, for example, ASSC, 1975).

Political, social and economic circumstances have since changed! There is currently relatively little professional interest in such matters. However, the earlier discussions did stimulate a number of research studies, and there are signs that the questions which they gave rise to have left a residue of interest in the British accounting research community in both the social nature of accounting practice and the interests which underlie it.

The early research on the disclosure of information to employees and trade unions was of two forms. The more academic variety emphasized the need to create an analytical framework for the consideration of policy options in the area. Attention was given to the construction of a rational decision-oriented approach which might facilitate the identification of the newly emergent 'user needs' for information in the context of decision areas such as wage bargaining (Climo, 1976, Cooper and Essex, 1977; Foley and Maunders, 1977). In sharp contrast, others adopted a more immediately pragmatic approach, directly attempting to assist trade union members and others in using company financial information. With the rallying cry of 'open the books', Barratt Brown (1968) provided an early example of the alternative approach. As subsequent work illustrated, the aim was to help active trade unionists to ask for relevant accounting information, to demystify its seemingly neutral technical nature (Irvine, Miles and Evans, 1979) and to use it to assist in the furtherance of their own ends (Gold, Levie and Moore, 1979; Hird, 1975).

It was this latter, action-oriented research which was to provide a basis for a minority but sustained tradition of inquiry in the area. Firmly established outside the academic walls, a pattern of 'counter accountings' emerged to challenge the bases and implications of conventional accountings from the perspective of the labor movement. Often concerned with an immediate need to provide information in the context of wage claims (Trade Union Research Unit, 1978), redundancies and proposed factory closures (e.g., Barratt Brown, 1978; North Tyneside Community Development Project, 1978; Wainwright and Elliot, 1982), this blend of unofficial research sought to undermine rather than understand or even reform conventional accountings. It was oriented towards making explicit the partiality of the official accounts, identifying their interested nature and demonstrating the wider economic as well as social ramifications of corporate decision-making based on traditional accounting calculations.

It was in these contexts that a British interest in social auditing and accounting emerged. Indeed in 1968 Barratt Brown had proposed that workers' control groups 493
'would act as social audit groups for their particular factory'. Although subsequently other agencies were established with a remit in the social audit and accounting area (e.g., the Public Interest Research Group and Counter Information Services), they, too, saw their role as challenging rather than merely supplementing the conventional financial accounts. Indeed, the fact that social accounting in the UK emerged from, and remained identified with, the labor and, to some extent, the consumer movements goes some way to explaining why there was a relative absence of either practical management or academic research interest in the UK compared with the USA and many continental European countries. With a few exceptions, social accounting in Britain came to be seen as an area where action was more important than words.

Faced with such a situation, accounting researchers had a number of options. First, they could stay clear of the area! Most did just that. Second, they could join the ranks of the converted. A few did this (Bryer *et al.*, 1982). Third, they could seek to further the understanding of the social nature and consequences of accounting practice. A task more compatible with traditional conceptions of academic inquiry, research has advanced along this route, as has been discussed already. Finally, research could be directed towards examining and understanding the organizational and social processes involved in actual disclosure situations. Gradually, some research is beginning to adopt this latter strategy (Levie and Moore, 1977; Jackson-Cox *et al.*, in press), in the process providing some useful insights into the factors which influence organizational information disclosure policies, the processes which influence information use and the impact that legal intervention in the area has had. Although much more research remains to be done, the specificity and richness of the available findings provide a useful palliative to more general social theorizing in the area.

4.6 *Other areas of interest*

The diversity of British accounting research is such that it is difficult for one survey to embrace all areas and issues. Fortunately, a number of other surveys provide insights into some of the more important areas not included in the above discussion. Both recent research in auditing and the need for further inquiries are reviewed in Bromwich, Hopwood and Shaw (1983). The increasingly important area of public sector accounting is surveyed by Perrin (1981), Tomkins (1981) and Hopwood and Tomkins (in press). Gray (1982) provides a review of British research in the area of international accounting, and Parker (1981) discusses both past and present historical research. Finally, the British use of computers in accounting education is discussed by Bhaskar (1982).

5. CONCLUSION

The 1970s witnessed a major expansion in the British academic accounting re-
494 search community. During that decade the subject became established in most institutions of higher education. The cadre of academic accountants increased correspondingly. Relevant research journals were founded, and after a short period networks of researchers began to be established. By the end of the decade what had previously been a very small group of researchers had developed into a sizeable community of academics interested in systematic inquiry into the accounting craft.

The research contribution provided by the expansion is more difficult to articulate. There undoubtedly has been a significant increase in the volume of research. However, without any unifying theoretical framework, contributions almost inevitably have been diverse. On the one hand, past traditions and concerns still have had an impact. On the other, the rapid expansion of the institutional basis of research has brought to bear a very different array of subjects and problems. Accounting has been made to confront the perspectives of other management subjects. Increasingly, the perspectives of economics have been complemented by those of the human and social sciences. Even in the more traditional areas of inquiry, the standardizing concerns of the profession increasingly have served to encourage reflective as well as technical inquiries. Accounting quite explicitly has been seen to be subject to a wide array of institutional, social and political as well as economic influences. The net result of all of these pressures is very similar to what Whitley (1983) has called a 'fragmented adhocracy' in the context of his analysis of the development of management studies more generally defined.

Be that as it may, there are very real and encouraging signs that accounting research in the UK is in the process of identifying a viable and interesting agenda for the future. There are no grounds for complacency, however. Not all accounting academics have research interests. Many areas of inquiry are still dominated by American perspectives, with British work playing a relatively minor role. And the relationship between research and practice remains a tense and uncertain one. So the future will not be without its own difficulties and problems. Even so, it is fair to say that past endeavors have provided a sounder basis for accounting inquiry. We can only hope that some more of that potential comes to be realized in the years ahead.

NOTES

1. It should be pointed out that accounting was not alone in respect to the paucity of attention given to it by UK universities prior to the 1960s. British universities were also slow to concede that business and management studies were suitable components of a university education, despite repeated pleas for the recognition of their national importance since the end of the nineteenth century (Searle, 1971; Wiener, 1981). However, even one member of the profession has admitted that the record of accountancy was even more dismal than that for business administration in general (Stacey, 1954). Such a situation was borne out by Solomons' and Berridge's survey of the size of full-time academic staff in professional departments in twelve British universities in 1972 (Solomons and Berridge, 1974). Compared with engineering (124; 1005) and law (35; 163), accounting only had 13 professors and 66 other academic staff. Accounting, in particular, and business and management studies, in general, tended to be regarded as subjects more suitable for study in lower-level educational institutions, particularly in the locally controlled higher educational sector. In this respect pioneering roles were played by such institutions as the Manchester Municipal Technical College and its successor, The Institute of Science and Technology, and the Birmingham Technical College, which subsequently became the Birmingham College of Advanced Technology and, thereafter, the University of Aston. In many respects British accounting academics are still dealing with the attitudes reflected in and furthered by such institutional segmentation.
2. Further information on the SSRC initiative is given in Bromwich and Hopwood (1981) and Hopwood and Bromwich (in press). Among the studies resulting from the initiative are Bromwich and Hopwood (1981; 1983a), Hopwood, Bromwich and Shaw (1983), Arnold, Cooper and Scapens (1983), Lister, Otley and Scapens (in press), Lowe and Machin (1983), Whittington (1983b) and Whittington and Tweedie (in press).
3. In view of the subsequent discussion of the emphasis which accounting research placed on the derivation of a practically useful measurement of income it is interesting to note Hicks' (1946, 179-180) advice to economists:
'It seems to follow that anyone who seeks to make a statistical calculation of social income is confronted with a dilemma. The income he can calculate is not the true income he seeks; the income he seeks cannot be calculated. From this dilemma there is only one way out; it is of course the way that has to be taken in practice. He must take his objective magnitude, the social income *ex post*, and proceed to adjust it, in some way that seems plausible or reasonable, for those changes in capital values which look as if they have had the character of windfalls. This sort of estimation is normal statistical procedure, and on its own ground it is wholly justified. But it can only result in a statistical estimate; by its very nature, it is not the measurement of an economic quantity'.
4. Traditionally the teaching of accounting in British universities has been much influenced by the body of accounting research. Rather than emphasizing the propagation of current accounting technique, attention was placed on the articulation of a more theoretical structure for the accounting craft. In this context the research undertaken in the areas of income and cost theory played an important role in accounting education in British universities. It also should be pointed out that in many British universities (but less frequently in the business schools), finance is taught alongside accounting.

REFERENCES

Accounting Standards Steering Committee (1975), *The Corporate Report*. A discussion paper published for comment by the ASSC. London, ASSC.

Accounting Standards Committee (1977), *Inflation Accounting – An Interim Recommendation by the Accounting Standards Committee*. London.

Amey, L.R. (1965a), *The Efficiency of Business Enterprises*. London, George Allen and Unwin.

Amey, L.R. (1965b), Divisional performance measurement and interest on capital, *Journal of Busines Finance* (Spring).

Amey, L.R. (1975), Tomkins on 'residual income', *Journal of Business Finance and Accounting* (Spring).

Archer, S., and A. Steele, (1983), *Management Accounting Research and Practice*. London, Institute of Cost and Management Accountants.

Arnold, J., and R. Scapens (1981), The British contribution to opportunity cost theory, in: M. Bromwich and A.G. Hopwood, eds., *Essays in British Accounting Research*. London, Pitman, 155-173.

Arnold, J., D. Cooper and R. Scapens (1983), *Management Accounting Research and Practice*. London, Institute of Cost and Management Accountants.

Ashton, R. (1976), Cash flow accounting: A review and critique, *Journal of Business Finance and Accounting* (Winter).

Barratt Brown, M. (1968), *Opening the Books*. Nottingham, Institute for Workers' Control.

Barratt Brown, M. (1978), USC: The social audit, in: K. Coates, ed., *The Right to Useful Work: Planning by the People*. Nottingham, Spokesman Books.

Batstone, E. (1979), Systems of domination, accommodation, and industrial democracy, in: T.R. Burns, L.E. Karlsson and V. Rus, eds., *Work and Power*. London, Sage, 249-272.

496 Baxter, W.T. (1938), A note on the allocation of costs between departments, *The Accountant* (5 November).

Baxter, W.T. (1945), *House of Hancock*. Boston, Harvard University Press.

Baxter, W.T. (1959), Inflation and the accounts of steel companies, *Accountancy* (May and June), 250-257, 308-314.

Baxter, W.T. (1967), Accounting values: Sale price versus replacement cost, *Journal of Accounting Research* (Autumn), 208-214.

Baxter, W.T. (1971), *Depreciation*. London, Sweet & Maxwell.

Baxter, W.T. (1975), *Accounting Values and Inflation*. London, McGraw-Hill.

Baxter, W.T. (1978), *Collected Papers on Accounting*. New York, Arno Press.

Berry, T., T. Capps, D. Cooper, P. Ferguson, T. Hopper and T. Lowe (1983), Management control in an area of the national coal board. Unpublished paper.

Bhaskar, K.N. (1981), Quantitative aspects of management accounting, in: M. Bromwich and A.G. Hopwood, eds., *Essays in British Accounting Research*. London, Pitman.

Bhaskar, K.N. (1982), Use of computers in accountancy courses, *Accounting and Business Research* (Winter).

Bromwich, M. (1969), Standard costing for planning and control, *The Accountant* (19 April, 26 April, 3 May).

Bromwich, M. (1973), Measurement of divisional performance: A comment and extension, *Accounting and Business Research* (Spring).

Bromwich, M. (1977a), The use of present value valuation models in published accounting reports, *The Accounting Review* (July), 587-596.

Bromwich, M. (1977b), The general validity of certain 'current' value asset valuation bases, *Accounting and Business Research* (Autumn), 242-249.

Bromwich, M. (1980), The possibility of partial accounting standards, *The Accounting Review* (April).

Bromwich, M. (1981), The setting of accounting standards: The contribution of research, in: M. Bromwich and A.G. Hopwood, eds., *Essays in British Accounting Research*. London, Pitman.

Bromwich, M., and A.G. Hopwood, eds. (1981), *Essays in British Accounting Research*. London, Pitman.

Bromwich, M., and A.G. Hopwood, eds. (1983a), *Accounting Standards Setting: An International Perspective*. London, Pitman.

Bromwich, M., and A.G. Hopwood (1983b), Some issues in accounting standard setting: An introductory essay, in: M. Bromwich and A.G. Hopwood, eds., *Accounting Standards Setting: An International Perspective*. Pitman v-xxiv.

Bromwich, M., A.G. Hopwood and J. Shaw (1983), *Auditing Research: Issues and Opportunities*. London, Pitman.

Bryer, R.A., T.J. Brignall and A.R. Maunders (1982), *Accounting for British Steel*. Aldershot, Gower.

Buchanan, J.M. (1969), *Cost and Choice: An Inquiry in Economic Theory*. Chicago, University of Chicago Press.

Buchanan, J.M., and G.F. Thirlby (1973), *LSE Essays on Cost*. London, Weidenfeld and Nicolson.

Burchell, S., C. Clubb, A. Hopwood, J. Highes and J. Nahapiet (1980), The roles of accounting in organizations and society, *Accounting, Organizations and Society*, 5-27.

Burchell, S., A.G. Hopwood, C. Clubb (in press), Accounting in its social context: Towards a history of value added in the UK, *Accounting, Organizations and Society*.

Carsberg, B.V. (in press), *Studies of Inflation Accounting* (title to be finalized). London, Institute of Chartered Acountants in England and Wales.

Carsberg, B.V., A. Hope and R.W. Scapens (1974), The objectives of published accounting reports, *Accounting and Business Research* (Summer).

Carsberg, B.V., and T. Hope (1977), *Current Issues in Accounting*. Oxford, Philip Allen.

Chambers, R.J. (1966), *Accounting, Evaluation and Economic Behavior*. Englewood Cliffs, N.J., Prentice-Hall.

Climo, T. (1976), Disclosure of information to employees' representatives: A wage bargaining model. Unpublished paper, University of Kent.

Coase, R.H. (1938), Business organization and the accountant, *The Accountant* (1 October 17 December).

Coates, J.B., J.E. Smith and R.J. Stacey (1980), Results of a preliminary survey into the structures of divisionalised companies, divisionalised performance appraisal and the asociated role of management accounting. Paper presented at the Management Accounting Research Conference, Manchester Business School.

Colville, I. (1981), Reconstructing 'behavioural accounting', *Accounting, Organizations and Society*, 119-132.

Cooper, D. (1975), Rationality and investment appraisal, *Accounting and Business Research* (Summer).

Cooper, D. (1977), Organizational aspects of budgetary control, in: J.E. Lewis and G. Dickinson, eds., *Handbook of Financial Management*. London, Kluwer-Harrap.

Cooper, D. (1981), A social and organizational view of management accounting, in: M. Bromwich and A.G. Hopwood, eds., *Essays in British Accounting Research*. London, Pitman, 178-205.

Cooper, D. (1983), Tidiness, muddle and things: Commonalities and divergencies in two approaches to management accounting research, *Accounting, Organizations and Society*, 269-286.

Cooper, D., and S. Essex (1977), Accounting information and employee decision making, *Accounting, Organizations and Society*, 201-217.

de St. Croix, G.E.M. (1956), Greek and Roman accounting, in: A.C. Littleton and B.S. Yamey, eds., *Studies in the History of Accounting*. Homewood, Illinois, Irwin.

Dev, S. (1980), *Accounting and the LSE Tradition*. London, London School of Economics and Political Science.

Dew, R.B., and K.P. Gee (1973), *Management Control and Information*. London, Macmillan.

Edey, H.C. (1963), Accounting principles and business reality, *Accountancy* (November), 998-1002; (December), 1083-1088.

Edey, H.C. (1974), The department of accounting, *LSE* (June), 1-2.

Edey, H.C. (1974), Deprival value and financial accounting, in: H.C. Edey and B.S. Yamey, eds., *Debits, Credits, Finance and Profits*. London, Sweet & Maxwell, 75-83.

Edwards, R.S. (1937a), The rationale of cost accounting. Lecture given at the London School of Economics, represented in: D. Solomons, ed., *Studies in Costing*. London, Sweet and Maxwell, 1952.

Edwards, R.S. (1937b), Cost accounting and joint production. *The Practising Accountant and Secretary* (7 May).

Edwards, R.S. (1937c), The approach to budgetary control, *The Practising Accountant and Secretary* (23 July and 6 August).

Edwards, R.S. (1938), The nature and measurement of income, *The Accountant* (July-September).

Eggington, D.A., (1980), Distributable profit and the pursuit of prudence, *Accounting and Business Research*, (Winter), 1-14.

Emmanuel, C.R., and S.J. Gray (1977), Segmented disclosures and the segment identification problem, *Accounting and Business Research* (Winter), 37-50.

Emmanuel, C.R., and S.J. Gray (1978), Segmental disclosure by multibusiness multinational companies: A proposal, *Accounting and Business Research* (Summer).

Flower, J.F., (1971), Measurement of divisional performance, *Accounting and Business Research* (Summer).

Foley, B.J., and K.T. Maunders (1977), *Accounting Information, Disclosure and Collective Bargaining*. London, Macmillan.

Gambling, T. (1977), Magic, accounting and morale, *Accounting, Organizations and Society*.

Gee, K., and K.V. Peasnell (1967), A pragmatic defence of replacement cost, *Accounting and Business Research* (Autumn), 242-249.

Gibbs, M. (1975), Why Sandilands is not the full answer, *The Times* (18 September).

Gibbs, M. (1976), A better answer to the problem of inflation accounting, *The Times* (23 February).

Godley, W., and A. Wood (1974), Stock appreciation and the crisis of British industry. Working paper, Department of Applied Economics, Cambridge.

Gold, M., H. Levie and R. Moore (1979), *The Shop Stewards' Guide to the Use of Company Information*. Nottingham, Spokesman Books.

498 Gould, J.R. (1964), Internal pricing in firms where there are costs of using an outside market, *Journal of Business* (January).

Gould, J.R. (1974), Opportunity cost: The London tradition, in: H.C. Edey and B.S. Yamey, eds., *Debits, Credits, Finance and Profits*. London, Sweet and Maxwell.

Gould, J.R. (1977), The economist's cost concept and business problems, in: W.T. Baxter and S. Davidson, eds., *Studies in Accounting*. London, Institute of Chartered Accountants in England and Wales.

Gray, S. (1982), International accounting: A review of research in the UK. Paper presented to the European Accounting Association.

Hart, H. (1981), A review of some major recent developments in the management accounting field, *Accounting and Business Research* (Spring).

Hatfield, H.N. (1924), An historical defense of bookkeeping, *Journal of Accountancy* (April), 241-253.

Hatherly, D. (1979), Segmentation and the audit process, *Accounting and Business Research* (Spring).

Hicks, J.R. (1946), *Value and Capital*. Oxford, Clarendon Press.

Hird, C. (1975), *Your Employer's Profits*. London, Pluto Press.

Hope, A. (1979), Accounting policy: Theory or pragmatism or both, *Submissions on the Accounting Standard Committee's Document: Setting Accounting Standards*, vol. 2. London, Accounting Standards Committee.

Hope, A., and J. Briggs (1982), Accounting policy making – Some lessons from the deferred taxation debate, *Accounting and Business Research* (Spring).

Hope, A., and R. Gray (1982), Power and policy making: The development of an R + D standard, *Journal of Business Finance and Accounting* (Winter).

Hopwood, A.G. (1972), *An Accounting System and Managerial Behavior*. Farnborough, Saxon House.

Hopwood, A.G. (1973), *Accounting and Human Behavior*. London, Accountancy Age Books.

Hopwood, A.G. (1978), Towards an organizational perspective for the study of accounting and information systems, *Accounting, Organizations and Society*, 3-13.

Hopwood, A.G. (1983), On trying to study accounting in the contexts in which it operates, *Accounting, Organizations and Society*.

Hopwood, A.G. (in press), Accounting and the pursuit of efficiency, in: A.G. Hopwood and C. Tomkins, eds., *Current Issues in Public Sector Accounting*. Oxford, Philip Allen.

Hopwood, A.G., and M. Bromwich (in press), Emerging patterns of management accounting research, in: R. Lister, D.T. Otley and R.W. Scapens, eds., *Management Accounting, Organizational Theory and Capital Budgeting*. London, Macmillan.

Hopwood, A.G., M. Bromwich and J. Shaw, eds. (1983), *Auditing Research: Issues and Opportunities*. London, Pitman.

Hopwood, A.G., and C. Tomkins (in press), *Current Issues in Public Sector Accounting*. Oxford, Philip Allen.

Irvine, J., I. Miles and J. Evans (1979), *Demystifying Social Statistics*. London, Pluto Press.

Jackson-Cox, J., J.E.M. Thinkell, and J. McQueeney (in press), The disclosure of company information to trade unions, *Accounting, Organizations and Society*.

Jones, R.H. (1982), Financial reporting in non-business organizations, *Accounting and Business Research* (Autumn).

Jones, R.H., and M. Pendlebury (1982), Uniformity v. flexibility in the published accounts of local authorities: The UK problem and some European solutions, *Accounting and Business Research* (Spring).

Kaldor, N. (1955), *An Expenditure Tax*. London, Allen & Unwin.

Kennedy, C. (1978), Inflation accounting: Retrospect and prospect, *Cambridge Economic Policy Review*.

Kitchen, J., and R.H. Parker (1980), *Accounting Thought and Education: Six English Pioneers*. London, Institute of Chartered Accountants in England and Wales.

Lapsley, I. (1981), A case for depreciation accounting in UK health authorities, *Accounting and Business Research* (Winter).

Leach, R., and E. Stamp (1981), *British Accounting Standards: The First 10 Years*. Cambridge, Faulkner - Woodhead.

Lee, T.A. (1974), *Income and Value Measurement: Theory and Practice*. London, Nelson.

Lee, T.A. (1981), Cash flow accounting and corporate financial reporting, in: M. Bromwich and A.G. Hopwood, eds., *Essays in British Accounting Research*. London, Pitman, 63-78.

Lee, T.A., and D.P. Tweedie (1977), *The Private Shareholder and the Corporate Report*. London, The Institute of Chartered Accountants.

Levie, H., and R. Moore (1977), *Interim Reports of the Research Project on the Acquisition and Use of Company Information by Trade Unions*. Oxford, Trade Union Research Unit.

Lister, R. (in press), Capital budgeting: A survey, *SSRC Reviews of Management Accounting Research*. London, Macmillan.

Lister, R., D.T. Otley and R.W. Scapens (in press), *SSRC Reviews of Management Accounting Research*. London, Macmillan.

Littleton, A.C., and B.S. Yamey (1956), *Studies in the History of Accounting*. Homewood, Illinois, Irwin.

Lowe, E.A., and Machin, J., eds. (1983), *New Perspectives in Management Control*. London, Macmillan.

Lowe, E.A., and J.M. McInnes (1971), Control of socio-economic organizations: A rationale for the design of management control systems (Part 1), *Journal of Management Studies*, 213-27.

Lowe, E.A., and R.W. Shaw (1968), An analysis of managerial biasing: Evidence from a company's budgeting process, *Journal of Management Studies* (October).

Lowe, E.A., and A.M. Tinker (1976), The architecture of requisite variety, Parts 1 and 2, *Kybernetes*.

Ma, R. (1976), Value to the owner revisited, *Abacus* (December), 159-165.

Macve, R.H. (1981), *A Conceptual Framework for Financial Accounting and Reporting: The Possibilities for an Agreed Structure*. London, Institute of Chartered Accountants in England and Wales.

Macve, R.H. (1983), The FASB's conceptual framework - Vision, tool or threat? Paper presented to the Arthur Young Professor's Roundtable.

Maunders, K. (1982), *The Employment Report*. London, Institute of Chartered Accountants in England and Wales.

McRae, T.W. (1972), The behavioural critique of accounting, *Accounting and Business Research* (Spring).

Merrett, A.J., and A. Sykes (1974), Article in *The Financial Times* (30 September).

Nobes, C.W. (1980), A review of the translation debate, *Accounting and Business* (Autumn).

North Tyneside Community Development Project (1978), *North Shields: Living With Industrial Change*. Newcastle, NTCDP.

Otley, D.T. (1977), Behavioural aspects of budgeting, *Accountants Digest* 49. London, Institute of Chartered Accountants in England and Wales.

Otley, D.T. (1978), Budget use and managerial performance, *Journal of Accounting Research* (Spring).

Otley, D.T. (1980), The contingency theory of management accounting: Achievement and prognosis, *Accounting, Organizations and Society*, 413-428.

Otley, D.T. (1983), Concepts of control: The contribution of cybernetics and systems theory to management control, in: E.A. Lowe and J. Machin, eds., *New Perspectives in Management Control*. London, Macmillan, 59-87.

Otley, D.T. (in press), Management accounting and organization theory: A review of their interrelationship, *SSRC Review of Management Accounting Research*. London, Macmillan.

Otley, D.T., and A.J. Berry (1980), Control, organization and accounting, *Accounting, Organizations and Society*, 231-244.

Parker, R.H. (1969), *Management Accounting: An Historical Perspective*. London, Macmillan.

Parker, R.H. (1975), Room at the top for more academic accountants, *The Times Higher Education Supplement* (17th January).

Parker, R.H. (1981), The study of accounting history, in: M. Bromwich and A.G. Hopwood, eds., *Essays in British Accounting Research*. London, Pitman.

Parker, R.H., and G.C. Harcourt (1969), *Readings in the Concept and Measurement of Income*. Cambridge, Cambridge University Press.

500 Patz, D.H. (1977), The state of the art in translation theory, *Journal of Business Finance and Accounting*.

Peasnell, K.V. (1974a), *The Usefulness of Accounting Information to Investors*. International Centre for Research in Accounting, University of Lancaster.

Peasnell, K.V. (1974b), The objectives of published accounting reports: A comment, *Accounting and Business Research* (Winter).

Peasnell, K.V. (1977), A note on the discounted present value concept, *The Accounting Review* (January), 186-189.

Peasnell, K.V. (1978), Interaction effects in CCA accounting, *Accounting and Business Research* (Spring), 82-91.

Peasnell, K.V. (1981), Empirical research in accounting, in: M. Bromwich and A.G. Hopwood, eds., *Essays in British Accounting Research*. London, Pitman, 104-129.

Perrin, J.R. (1981), Accounting research in the public sector, in: M. Bromwich and A.G. Hopwood, eds., *Essays in British Accounting Research*. London, Pitman, 297-322.

Rutherford, B.A. (1977), Value added as a focus of attention for financial reporting: Some conceptual problems, *Accounting and Business Research* (Summer).

Sale, T., and R.W. Scapens (1978), Current cost accounting as a surrogate for dividend paying ability, *Accounting and Business Research* (Summer).

Samuels, J.M. (1965), Opportunity costing: An application of mathematical programming, *Journal of Accounting Research* (Autumn).

Scapens, R.W. (1979), Profit measurement in divisionalised companies, *Journal of Business Finance and Accounting* (Autumn).

Scapens, R.W. (1983), Closing the gap between theory and practice, *Management Accounting* (January), 34-36.

Scapens, R.W. (in press), Management accounting – A survey paper, *SSRC Reviews of Management Accounting Research*. London, Macmillan.

Scapens, R.W., J.T. Sale, and P.A. Tikkas (in press), *Financial Control of Divisional Capital Investment*. London, Institute of Cost and Management Accountants.

Searle, G.R. (1971), *The Quest for National Efficiency*. Oxford, Blackwell.

Simmonds, K. (1983), Strategic management accounting, in: D. Fanning, ed., *Handbook of Management Accounting*. London Gower Press.

Solomons, D. (1952), The historical development 'of costing', in: D. Solomons, ed., *Studies in Costing*. London, Sweet and Maxwell.

Solomons, D. (1961), Economic and accounting concepts of income, *The Accounting Review*, 374-83.

Solomons, D. (1965), *Divisional Performance: Measurement and Control*. New York, Irwin.

Solomons, D., and T. Berridge (1974), *Prospectus for a Profession: The Report of the Long Range Enquiry into Education and Training for the Accounting Profession*. London, Advisory Board of Accountancy Education.

Stacey, N.A.H. (1954), *English Accountancy: A Study in Social and Economic History, 1800-1954.* London, Gee.

Stamp, E. (1971), Income and value determination and changing price levels: An essay towards a theory, *The Accountants Magazine* (June), 277-292.

Tomkins, C.R. (1975), Another look at residual income, *Journal of Business Finance and Accounting* (Spring).

Tomkins, C. (1981), Financial control in local authorities: Potential research, in: M. Bromwich and A.G. Hopwood, eds., *Essays in British Accounting Research.* London, Pitman, 323-336.

Tomkins, C., D. Rosenberg and I. Colville (1980), The social process of research: Some reflections on developing a multi-disciplinary accounting project, *Accounting, Organizations and Society*, 247-262.

Tomkins, C., and R. Groves (1983), The everyday accountant and researching his reality, *Accounting, Organizations and Society*, 361-374.

Trade Union Research Unit (1978), *Why Ford UK Can't Afford to Pay.* Oxford, TURU.

Tricker, R.I. (1975), *Research in Accountancy – A Strategy for Further Work.* London, Social Science Research Council.

Wainwright, H., and D. Elliot (1982), *The Lucas Plan: A New Trade Unionism in the Making?* London, Allison and Busby.

Weiner, M.J. (1981), *English Culture and the Decline of the Industrial Spirit, 1950-1980.* Cambridge, Cambridge University Press.

Whitley, R. (1983), The development of management studies as a fragmented adhocracy. Unpublished working paper, Manchester Business School.

Whittington, G. (1981), The British contribution to income theory, in: M. Bromwich and A.G. Hopwood, eds., *Essays in British Accounting Research.* London, Pitman.

Whittington, G. (1983a), The role of research in setting accounting standards: The case of inflation accounting, *Accounting Standards Setting: An International Perspective.* London, Pitman.

Whittington, G. (1983b), *Inflation Accounting: An Introduction to the Debate.* Cambridge, Cambridge University Press.

Whittington, G., and D. Tweedie (in press), *The Debate on Inflation Accounting.* Cambridge, Cambridge University Press.

Willmot, H. (1983), Paradigms for accounting research: Critical reflections on Tomkins and Groves 'The everyday accountant and researching his reality', *Accounting, Organizations and Society* 407-415.

Yamey, B.S. (1978), *Essays on the History of Accounting.* New York, Arno Press.

Zeff, S.A. (1981), Preface, in: M. Bromwich and A.G. Hopwood, eds., *Essays in British Accounting Research.* London, Pitman, vi-ix.

Introduction

Issues facing auditing research in the UK

Michael Bromwich, *Professor of Accounting, University of Reading*
and
Anthony G. Hopwood, *Institute of Chartered Accountants', Professor of Accounting and Financial Reporting, London Graduate School of Business Studies.*

Auditing has come recently to play an important role in the processes through which attempts are made to make institutional management accountable to a wider range of constituencies than has been usual in the past. Growing out of the early efforts to establish reliable information flows between management and the providers of investment finance, the audit function is called upon to serve an ever expanding number of social roles. Although it developed rapidly during the emergence of the modern form of corporate structure, auditing still remains under pressure to adapt to new institutional forms, information processing technologies and changing social pressures. It is not and cannot be a static social endeavour. Indeed, today efforts are being made to extend the roles which auditing plays in the public sector and, in both the public and private sectors, to increase the number of social groups on behalf of whom audits are conducted.

Until now, auditing has developed in a pragmatic manner. There have been few attempts at systematic research and inquiry. As new demands have been made, auditors have attempted to balance the competing pressures for change, sometimes initiating new audit practices and procedures in the process. More recently however, some attempts have been made to provide a more systematic basis for both understanding the audit function and directing its future development. No doubt aware of the still growing pressures for auditing to change, the contribution which systematic research might be able to make has come to be recognised, initially in the US but subsequently, albeit slowly, elsewhere.

The papers in this volume seek to make a contribution to this process. Growing out of a symposium which brought together senior practitioners and academics, the papers provide an overview of auditing research issues currently being addressed in the UK as well as some topics for further inquiry.

Before discussing the issues considered in the papers, we first briefly consider the nature of the accounting and auditing research community from which these issues emerge, review some of the factors which have determined the relationship between research and practice in accounting in the UK and consider the current pressures on auditing which might encourage a more active interest in the roles which research can play.

The accounting research community

Over the last fifteen years accounting research has come to be seen as a legitimate and useful activity in both British universities and organizations concerned with the practice of accounting. Within the academic community, the efforts devoted to accounting research have increased considerably. Indeed it is quite widely recognised that these endeavours, although not yet strong and mature, now provide a sound basis for further growth and development. At the same time, the technical and research activities of the larger public accounting firms and the similar functions in major industrial companies have experienced equal, if not greater, growth. An applied research function is now a recognised part of all major public accounting firms and many of the accounting departments of major companies. These functions were established as a result of the pressures on accounting to respond to the accounting crises of the late 1960s, to standardise accounting practice, to reflect the consequences of inflation in their reports to management and the public, and to implement government policies in areas such as price and wage control.

The vast majority of these academic and practitioner attempts to gain a greater understanding of accounting have developed in parallel, but separately. There has been little evidence of either complementarity or synergy. More recently however, plans have been made for co-operation between the different accounting research communities and there have been some attempts to encourage an exchange of views and needs, of which the conference on which the following papers are based is an example. For instance a number of the accounting firms have organized meetings with members of the academic community and there also has been a growth in the support, both financial and otherwise, given to the accounting departments of universities. So far, however, this type of co-operation has not gone as far as it has in the US. In addition to the activities of separate firms, the appropriate committees of the professional bodies recently have acquired a number of academic members and together they and the professional members have sought to encourage relevant research. Finally, the Social Science Research Council's Accounting Research Initiative also has attempted to encourage rigorous academic research addressed to society's current accounting concerns.

Although all such efforts are important and need to be encouraged, it is still difficult to avoid the view that much needs to be done to unite the various efforts of the profession and the academic community to understand the nature of accounting problems and to search for their solutions. Until recently, at least, the two communities have remained separate for the most part, with few exchanges of views or needs and relatively little opportunity for the concerns of one to influence the efforts of the other.

The relationship between research and practice

More recently, however, there have been some indications that the accountancy profession is becoming more interested in the potential of research. Although there are many reasons for this emergence of interest, not least in importance have been the pressures on accounting to explicate the nature of its practice. Because of both governmental and other social pressures to improve, regulate and standardise accounting, the profession has had to give increasing attention to the statement and justification as well as the mere practice of accounting. In the process, the practice of accounting has had to become intertwined with the statement of a more formal body of knowledge about itself. It is now no longer sufficient that accounting is merely done or even seen to be done. The practice, and increasingly the desirable practice, of accounting must now be explicitly stated and subject to wider consideration and debate. Accounting principles, standards and even the conceptual frameworks which might be deemed to underlie them have to be stated in terms abstracted from the specific contexts in which they operate. Similarly auditing principles and standards are now being debated and formulated, and more explicit consideration is having to be given to the rationales for auditing and its practices, particularly when there are pressures for or interests in the extension of those practices, such as into the public and governmental domain.

As distanced though such pressures might initially appear to be from the realms of research, they nevertheless have brought accounting practice into contact with more abstract notions of the knowledge basis on which it does or might operate. Such steps at least offer the possibility for a more active interchange between practice and research.

If nothing else, the inflation accounting debate in the UK has forcefully illustrated that such possibilities can become real. In that debate there were very real pressures to set out the nature and functions of the accounting craft. Indeed in the process of this debate accounting practice was confronted with notions about what it might or even should be about. Although it would be difficult to claim that research played a direct role in these deliberations, there is no doubt that the products of systematic and sustained inquiry did influence the language in which that debate took place, the options that were formulated and the choices, although of a political nature, that were exercised. This experience does indicate the substantial impact that research which has matured, which has been exposed to the profession (and others) for a substantial period of time and which can be expressed in a way which can be understood by those willing to make the effort can have on the profession's deliberations.

An increasing amount of evidence points to the possibility that attempts to solve the problems confronting the accountancy profession will require that research of possible relevance be at least considered. However this evidence also suggests that for the present, at least, such research, having been considered, is often - indeed usually might be thought to be the more appropriate word - rejected by the profession. Such an observation should neither cause great surprise nor should it be regarded as evidence that academic research in accounting is of little enduring value.

For one thing, accounting research in the UK is still a very new activity and one which is carried out in brief periods stolen from heavy teaching and administrative duties. Many researchers have no rigorous training in research methods and are having to learn as they go. This has often meant that much of what purports to be research amounts to little more than review articles, rehearsing, and perhaps polishing, well-known arguments in a language often borrowed from other disciplines. In addition a fair amount of the research literature of accounting comprises exchanges about value judgements which are usually stronger in their criticisms of other views than in the rigour of the arguments supporting their authors' preferred views. Whatever their role may be in the academic community, research attempts of this type are unlikely to dissuade practitioners from their own views which reflect their own perceived experiences obtained at considerable personal cost.

Those research endeavours which do make a rigorous contribution to the greater understanding of accounting problems are likely to be expressed in languages difficult for practitioners to understand. In order to make any contribution to the understanding of a complex world, research often has to use abstract models expressed in rather difficult symbolic language, and models and theories from other disciplines which are often at the edge of knowledge in the parent disciplines. Examples of this type of research are those which seek to apply information economics, the latest results in the theory of finance and current social theories to the accounting area. Much of this research is often incomprehensible to practioners. Moreover it often is addressed not to specific problems of current practical interest but rather appears to be more concerned with questioning practitioners' hard-earned views of the world by continually questioning the fundamental assumptions used in practical accounting.

Perhaps the inability to communicate new theories is not a long term problem. In the world of the social, at least, the success and maturity of new theories has often been judged on the ability of their proponents eventually to express them in language comprehensible to the relevant professional groups. However, the tendency of research to question, if not shake, the foundations of current accounting beliefs might be a more serious barrier for attempts to 'ground' research efforts more solidly in the practical domain. Successful research is often likely to make today's practitioners uncomfortable. Moreover this general problem, which is faced by all researchers, is intensified for those working in the accounting area because of the short period of time over which the subject has been intensively researched. The outcome of research when it is focussed on a given problem for the first time often tends to be negative, introducing new problems which have not been considered previously without indicating any obvious positive way forward. Such findings are hardly likely to commend themselves to, or be acted on by, practitioners who still have to address the problems that cross their desks using whatever current tools are thought useful. Casting doubt on those tools is unlikely to earn much applause.

It should be remembered that research articles, and even text books, tend to be consulted by the professional community only with a specific problem in mind. Often the literature considered will be written from a different viewpoint and, therefore, thought not to be relevant to the problem under consideration. Indeed there may be few articles in existence related to any specific problem and again the cry of non-relevance can justifiably arise. It is frequently forgotten that the lag between an academic taking up a problem and publication may be three to five years. Thus if academics did seek to address today's specific problems, their eventual findings, even if satisfactory to the practising community, are likely to be thought to lack relevance to the specific problems which are then plaguing the profession.

This problem is intensified by the natural tendency of the practising side of the profession to seek to solve their problems by considering the alternative procedures which are available and selecting that which best suits their view as to what accounting is about and which is likely to achieve a professional consensus. Solutions also have to satisfy those being advised and the societal responsibilities of the profession as understood at the time. The work of the FASB and the ASC often seems to exemplify this approach. Academic research which reminds those proceeding this way that their accounting choices should be related to the fundamental objectives of accounting, without suggesting how this might be done and without considering how the resultant choices might achieve acceptance in the relevant parts of the community, is unlikely to be welcome.

The accounting and auditing research symposium

One of the objectives of the symposium on which the papers in this volume are based was to help to bridge the gaps between accounting practitioners and academic researchers by allowing them to meet in a relatively small group to discuss subjects of common interest and to explore areas for fruitful co-operation. The intention was for practitioners and researchers to discuss the state of the art as they both saw it in a variety of areas and to identify future research needs.

This symposium, which is believed to be the first of this type in the UK, builds on a series of conferences sponsored by the Social Science Research Council as part of its accounting research initiative. Other elements of this initiative included actively seeking researchers to address accounting problems which the SSRC considered to be in urgent need of attention (e.g. inflation accounting and accounting for employees), sponsoring a management accounting research group and another group concerned with the political and social aspects of accounting, and finally financing a two-year professorial fellowship to study inflation accounting.

The series of conferences financed by the SSRC on a pump-priming basis culminated in a conference in late 1979 which reviewed the state of British accounting research, the proceedings of which have now been published under the title Essays in British Accounting Research. (Pitmans, 1981). Deloitte Haskins & Sells took over the major financing of these conferences in 1980, although the SSRC continues to act as a co-sponsor. Their aim was to provide a forum for the discussion of accounting research and to facilitate dialogue between senior members of the professional and academic communities. Deloitte Haskins & Sells also have undertaken to finance these conferences on a pump-priming basis in the hope that long term finance for them may become available from a wider sector of the profession. The seminars are thus to be seen as a contribution to the development of the profession in general.

Auditing: the subject of the first accounting and auditing research symposium

The selection of auditing as the first topic for the symposium was apt in a number of ways. First because it illustrates in an extreme way the above arguments concerning the gap between researchers and practitioners. It has been estimated that some 45,000 to 50,000 people are engaged in the public auditing profession and that the total annual economic cost of external audit in the UK is well in excess of £500 million. Most accounting graduates from universities and polytechnics obtain their training in this sector of the profession. However, few of these institutions teach auditing in any serious way. In this respect it is interesting to note that Chambers in his paper in this volume says that one of the recognised tests of a profession is whether it has accumulated a body of knowledge which is taught and researched in universities. The usual reasons given for this lack of attention to auditing are that it is a technical subject and its teaching would be of a descriptive character which is more successfully carried out during the student's professional training. Given this view it is not surprising that little academic research on auditing is proceeding in the UK and that the same is true of most other countries. Even in the US, auditing research has, with the notable exception of Mautz and one or two others, tended to address mainly statistical issues and it has often been handled in a very mathematical way. Only recently have American academics begun to look at more fundamental aspects of the auditing process.

One useful role of this symposium was, therefore, to allow a number of auditing practitioners in both the private and public sectors to describe the state of their art and their views as to the needs for accounting research. One role of research in auditing would be to subject these views to empirical test. In this respect the seminar's proceedings suggest that auditing is a rich field for research and one in which research findings cannot easily be regarded as irrelevant to the profession.

It is our view, supported by many of the papers in this volume, that many of the results of such research will cause some discomfort to the profession. One of our reasons for taking this view formed yet another argument for the selection of auditing as the first topic for the accounting and auditing symposium. In many ways the fundamental objectives and philosophy of auditing have remained implicit and probably unquestioned as part of the ethos and motivation of the professional firms. Research will attempt to make these explicit and therefore expose them to critical questioning.

Another reason for our view that auditing was an especially suitable subject for consideration at the symposium is the existence of a number of premonitions of varying strengths of a crisis ahead for the auditing fraternity which serious research may help forestall.

The crisis in auditing

There is beginning to be a questioning of what services external auditors actually do perform for their clients. The basic reasons for having an audit, ignoring any legal duty, are fairly well understood. The management of all organisations is likely to have greater information than the other elements of society to which they are held to be accountable (until recently the social partners especially in mind were the shareholders and creditors of companies). In the absence of an independent check, they could, therefore, utilise this superior knowledge to confuse these other parties. Unless the eventual outcome of management's performance can be clearly and definitely revealed, some independent check is required to ensure that management has not sought to maximise their own benefits at the expense of other parties in the organisation. This would be the case even if management bound themselves to certain conduct (as is often required under debt agreements) where the other parties to the agreement do not have special access to inside information.

The historical development of auditing indicates this need for auditing was recognised, for this service was in some demand by the capital markets prior to an audit becoming statutorily necessary, though these demands were met imperfectly. Kitchen's paper indicates that shareholder auditors came to be regarded as unsatisfactory because of their lack of technical skill even though one might have thought that such auditors, if their preferences and beliefs were representative of those of other shareholders, would be better able to evaluate management's conduct from the shareholders' point of view than accountants with different backgrounds and possibly different preferences.

Indeed, Skerratt in his paper analysing the academic literature addressing auditing indicates that a number of studies have suggested that the audit certificate per se has little value to the users of accounts. (Unfortunately the literature referred to does not indicate how it might be possible to test this assertion when all firms have to produce such certificates.) However, he does point out that audit qualifications may affect share prices. A more commonplace test of the worth of audits, at least to the business community with their existing viewpoint, is that there are few complaints concerning the fundamental need for audits or their costs in resource terms (other than the general grumbles caused by the inflationary environment).

It is well accepted that one major function of an external audit is to give credibility to the firm's accounts. The auditor's unqualified opinion implies that management has met its responsibility towards its security holders and has made a full and frank disclosure of the financial results of its actions and decisions and has satisfied the requirements imposed by the law and other relevant agencies.

It can be argued that this definition of the function of audits does not get us very far in analysing the contribution auditors offer to society. First, how is this credibility bestowed? It would not seem to flow from public knowledge of the detailed procedures of the audit firms. These are not generally available even to the business community. Nor is it clear that the procedures of all audit firms are the same, though as Skerratt indicates there is some evidence that this is, in general, the case. The type of credibility given also seems to have an absolute quality about it; there is no suggestion that one audit firm produces more or less credibility than another.

Auditors also have superior information relative to others in the business community and,apart from seemingly glaring errors, there are no clear definitive results of the auditors' operations which will be clearly revealed to the community with the passage of time. Given this and that the operating procedures of auditors are not generally available for inspection we need to ask from where is the authority to certify accounts derived? This is especially so as some recent
510 theoretical analysis would suggest that audit firms would not necessarily maximise their own welfare by carrying out their tasks in the most efficient way. The outputs of different audit firms cannot be distinguished easily by the business community nor can this community easily monitor the differential inputs of the various firms. This suggests that those audit firms which believe that they have superior services to offer may have no incentive to offer these services. All firms will be regarded as close substitutes and will be rewarded in the same way.If superior services cannot be observed by the business community in some way, this would suggest that all audit firms would tend to offer approximately the same services. This might suggest a positive role for some type of advertising but this advertising is not obviously that which is currently allowed.

One obvious qualification to this theory is that enterprise management may be in a better position to evaluate the services of the firm's auditors. However, this argument needs to be carefully examined by rigorous research for management may well take actions, including changing auditors, for reasons that may not be in the best interests of the shareholders and the business community. This possibility is argued in the literature as one reason for having independent auditors. Another qualification to the theory is that audit firms might attempt to provide non-auditing services, where success is, perhaps, more visible, in the hope that any such success will improve the relative perceived prestige of their auditing services.

Thus one possible challenge to the auditing professions, which has already been partly made in the US by the Metcalfe Committee, is to show both from where their authority for certifying accounts is derived and that they are carrying out the necessary duties to fulfil their functions as perceived by society.

There is a rich ground for research here as the likely answer to these types of challenges is to emphasise the importance of the auditing profession's independence and professionalism. The former of these defences is also under challenge. Professor Stamp and others have suggested that the present independence rules for the profession are not sufficiently stringent. However, the degree of dependency between auditors and their clients is difficult to appraise in any quantitative way. Indeed it is difficult to evaluate the problems of any given relationship between auditors and their clients without considering the reigning social environment. As the paper by the former Comptroller and Auditor General indicates, the resources for his service flow from the government, but few would question his independence and some would use his office as an example of the type of independence to which the auditing profession might aspire. The penalty attached to attempting to minimise any possible controversial relationship between auditors and their clients is a likely reduction in the auditor's intimate knowledge of the business which is being audited (see Tomkins' plea in this volume for the public sector auditor to be deeply involved in the organisations being audited).

In the end, it is difficult to avoid the conclusion that the auditor's authority must stem from society's belief that the profession is able on a self-regulating basis to carry out its responsibility. (For more on this, see Flint's article in this collection). It may be easier for society to reach a judgement on the profession as a whole by, for example, considering its codes of practice and ethical codes and how breaches of these are handled, rather than attempting to ascertain, without adequate knowledge, the success or failure of specific members of the profession in specific settings. For in the latter case, with the existing state of accounting knowledge, society would often be attempting to evaluate the value judgements of individual auditors. Independence therefore does seem a subject for fruitful research and of some present interest to the profession.

However, the professionalism of the auditing profession is also subject to several challenges, each of which is susceptible to research efforts. A number of parties within society are suggesting that the auditors' charge to monitor the accountability of firms for shareholders and creditors needs to be extended to other members of society such as the workforce and consumers. Others feel that the activities of auditors are not geared to the true interests of even their conventional interest groups. The argument is that investors and creditors really require information which may help them assess the future and yet the UK audit profession seems somewhat unwilling, for good reasons, to give an opinion on forecasts or on the other reports which make up the overall financial reports of a company and which may be more relevant than the accounts proper to investors and creditors. Many doubt whether the existing skills of auditors give them any comparative advantages in these new tasks which are being suggested, other than their ability to command society's acceptance of their certification. Whether this acceptance will carry over to these new tasks is an open question.

Similarly there have been some calls for what have been called in the public sector "management" audits or "value-for-money" audits. The implicit view underlying these demands is that accountability monitoring for society cannot be discharged without an attempted evaluation of managerial efficiency. The advocates of this view have never really explained how this might be done. It would seem that the consultancy arms of the professional accounting firms are probably as qualified as other challengers for this job. Whether the firms can undertake this task without damaging their independence and professionalism is, however, by no means clear. It is difficult to see how such a task can be undertaken without both a very close involvement with enterprise management and the employment of a substantial number of specialists who are unlikely to be accountants and, therefore, to be subject to the profession's ethical code.

A number of additional forces can also be felt, as yet only tentatively, which may limit the future exercise of the auditor's professionalism. There seems to be a trend towards greater legislation on accounting matters in the UK, and the EEC seems likely increasingly to regulate both accounting and auditing. Moreover, past experience suggests that many of the matters being legislated for in North America will in due
512 course be given consideration in Britain. Of course such legislation is not an unmixed problem to the profession for it may well produce more work, but it may also act to restrict opportunities for the exercise of professional judgement. These arguments would seem to apply equally to the output of the ASC and FASB and of the bodies which lay down audit standards. Finally, any move towards the American idea of audit committees with members including prestigious non-accountants may also affect opportunities for the unquestioned exercise of professional judgement.

None of these factors may necessarily be bad things but they may dilute the professional status of the profession. Certainly these are matters which are likely to be illuminated by research. There are a number of other challenges to the auditing profession which are mentioned in the papers in this volume. Both Chambers and van Zutphen highlight the dangers and promises provided for the auditor by existing and future developments in information processing technology. This is equally true of advances in statistical sampling theory and in computer software Yet further challenges are on the horizon. It has been argued that the market for audit services in the US has now reached maturity. It is not clear that this is yet the case, at least for the larger firms, in the UK. There is, however, no doubt that British auditing firms would be wise to consider their future growth strategy. It is difficult to see that many strategies exist which do not, for the reason suggested earlier, endanger their independence and professionalism.

American experience also suggests that audit firms may, if they stick to their traditional last, find it more difficult to attract high quality students who might find that MBA degrees and careers in finance will better meet their aspirations.

It is to some of the above issues that the papers in this volume address themselves.

The contents of this volume

Jack Shaw in his preface to this collection of papers attempts to set out briefly what auditing is presently understood to be, and why it is important. He introduces a major concern of the symposium - the lack of research into auditing. He claims that a major function of research is to provide a better understanding of auditing and to place auditing in a wider context. Another important question he raises is the need to research whether the practice of auditing meets the expectations society holds concerning an instrument to aid in rendering organisations accountable to the various concerned social parties.

Professor Kitchen attempts to place the current practice of auditing in its historical context. He argues that historical study is indispensable if, in the absence of an agreed conceptual framework, we wish to understand how accounting as we know it today has developed. Such developments are likely to be found to be rooted in responses to changing technology, and the economic and social environments which surrounded their birth and growth. He reminds us that auditing as we know it today is a relatively young subject. Although many of today's accepted principles emerged early, these were often lost from sight as the profession responded to what was thought to be permissible accounting in a given age.

Bob Tricker reinforces Kitchen's argument when he, again using historical analysis, suggests that auditing practices over time have reflected society's changing demands for organisational accountability. He hypothesises that changes in these demands are highly correlated with corporate crisis. On this basis he reviews briefly the various theories concerning the nature of managerial power and authority within society and suggests that changes in society's views on this are likely to cause demands for audits with wider terms of reference.

Skerratt's charge was to review the academic literature on auditing. He indicates that some understanding of auditing can be obtained by adopting an agency perspective, where auditing is seen as one way of moderating the relationship between the shareholder principal and the management agent. Thereafter he goes on to consider those few papers which have sought to ascertain whether auditing is regarded as useful and carried out effectively. A major part of his review covers those studies which have attempted to answer the questions of what should be audited and how much auditing is enough. He tentatively suggests that more information should be given in the audit report.

David Flint considers in some detail the role of the audit, paying special attention to the social and ethical issues involved. He is especially interested in the social function of auditing, and shares with other contributors to this volume a concern as to whether the attestation function alone can satisfy society. The auditor's role involves considerable value judgements and the judgements rendered by auditors will be acceptable to society only if they correctly reflect the accountability concerns of society. Flint also assesses a number of important issues of current relevance to the audit profession, including independence and the profession's vulnerability to litigation. He concludes with a list of aspects of auditing which are likely to provide fruitful fields for research.

Looking at internal rather than external auditing, Andrew Chambers starts his paper by considering whether internal auditing meets the usual criteria for a profession. A similar analysis could have interesting consequences for the external auditing profession. A major part of his paper is addressed to the need for research to consider whether the internal auditor has more in common in his objectives with the external auditor than with enterprise management. Finally, he argues the need to research the behavioural aspects of the internal auditing function, and raises many problems which may well need to be considered by the external auditing profession in the future.

After these wide ranging papers the next group of papers focusses on aspects of auditing which are of great practical concern today. All are contributed by senior members of the auditing profession.

Graham Stacey provides a succinct discussion of the auditing needs of the larger professional firms. Taking for granted the general need for a research competence, he considers the roles which research can play in establishing and maintaining existing auditing standards, in helping the professional firm to adapt to external changes which affect its clients and in keeping up with and developing new audit techniques. His discussion of the resources which the larger professional firms are able to devote to these tasks provides some interesting insights for the outsider and his views on the role which academics might play could stimulate debate for some time to come.

The specific area of research on auditing techniques is addressed by David Smith. Confirming the more general point which we made above, he demonstrates how research on statistical sampling has forced the profession to confront more problems than they had imagined to exist. However his experiences have remained positive ones and his paper goes on to address areas where further research is required.

Luc van Zutphen reviews likely developments in the area of electronic data processing and EDP auditing. It is clear that EDP auditing has a close relationship with both internal auditing and with operational data processing. He charts the flood of new developments in data processing. He suggests that the only way to cope with this in EDP auditing is to encourage auditors to specialise in specific auditing tasks. He has in mind differentiating, for example, between EDP auditors and program and software auditors. The need to obtain a supply of such people makes for a difficult timing problem and the need to maintain the close relationship between EDP auditors and external auditors are two other major problems considered.

The final three papers in this collection consider the very exciting area of public sector auditing. Many of society's increased demands for more accountability are focused on this area. It is also an area where many believe that considerable additional auditing skills are needed. Indeed it may be here that many of the developments suggested in these proceedings are likely to come to fruition.

The former Comptroller and Auditor General's paper first sketches the developments in public audit in a number of countries and indicates the functions of his department, distinguishing between financial and regularity audit and what has been called 'value for money' audit. He indicates the difficulty that evaluation of policy decisions causes in attempting the latter function and the possibility for conflict to be engendered by attempts at this type of audit. The paper by Sir Norman Price sets out the very difficult problems in the transnational auditing of EEC payments and receipts. One of the major difficulties faced by the European Court of Auditors, of which he is a member, is that of the very different traditions rooted in the law of auditing in countries within the EEC. This is a problem which already plagues those private auditing firms which have sought to expand their services to non-domestic environments. The differing social and economic environments of different countries mean that many of the problems suggested in this collection of papers to be of growing importance are already being encountered in full force by such international auditing firms. This makes research into these problems a matter of immediate urgency.

These two public sector papers throw some light on the vexed problem of independence. The independence of the auditor in the public sector seems beyond challenge, though suggestions that the C and AG might be subject to some direction concerning the areas that he audits might be thought by some to endanger his independence. Whether there are any lessons here for private sector accounting firms concerned to safeguard their independence is another open question.

The final paper in this collection is that of Tomkins who is concerned to give a perhaps less establishment view of the process and dynamics of public sector auditing. He does this by comparing and contrasting private and public sector auditing and by reviewing the state of the public sector audit in a number of countries. He gives the reasons for his view that, contrary to what many believe, there is very little effectiveness auditing in the public sector. The paper argues strongly for the adoption of a new paradigm for auditing and implicitly for accounting. The suggestion is that the auditor should not have preconceived aims and hypotheses, but rather should first attempt to gather data and understand the phenomenon being audited before reaching judgements about organisational effectiveness. Some might wonder whether this approach may not intensify concerns about auditor independence.

Conclusions

This book makes it clear that the auditing profession may face some very severe challenges. The continued success of the profession depends in part on its response to these challenges. Research has a role in clarifying the nature of these challenges and in exploring the possible responses. To do this successfully, this research has to explore fundamental questions about why and where the auditor's authority and power in society reside and how this location changes over time. To understand what is expected of auditors by society requires detailed studies of society's changing accountability. The requirements society places on a professional body before it is allowed to exercise certification power also represents a fruitful area for research. The importance of independence in allowing the exercise of this power is a matter for investigation, for there are reasons to think that without the constraint that professionalism is held to impose on auditors, they might well maximise their well-being at the expense of others in society. These are some areas which the papers in this volume suggest might be susceptible to research. If nothing else these papers indicate that auditing is a dynamic subject and research in this area will have immediate practical relevance.

Some issues in accounting standard setting: an introductory essay

Michael Bromwich
University of Reading
and
Anthony Hopwood
London Graduate School of Business Studies

Questions of accounting policy can no longer be considered in national isolation. The international nature of the industrial and commercial communities has placed increasing pressures on accounting policy makers to see their task in a wider context. International patterns of investment, financing and ownership now all create an interest in the comparability of the vital sources of corporate economic intelligence which accounting reports provide. Moreover the creation and often growing power of transnational government agencies have reinforced the tendencies emanating from the business community itself.

Aware of these pressures, the conference on which the present volume is based sought to address the international aspects of accounting standard setting in two ways. First, papers were presented on the experiences of a number of countries representative of different ways of tackling the problem of regulating external financial reports. This allowed some useful comparative assessments to be made, a process which was aided by the deliberate attempts of the authors to provide comparative critiques of the systems they were addressing. Second, the international perspective was enhanced by a set of papers which considered major existing attempts to harmonize accounting standards across countries. In addition, the attempt to provide a comparative evaluation of the different systems for regulating accounting reports was strengthened by selecting discussants who had experience of different regulatory environments to that of the author on whom they were commenting. It was thought that the papers by Sprouse and Burggraaff introduced so many of the key themes of the conference that the discussion of their contributions was best dealt with as part of this introductory scene-setting paper.

A British conference addressed to the international aspects of accounting standard setting is especially apt at the present time. Not only has the Accounting Standards Committee (the British standard setting body) recently been reorganized after celebrating its tenth anniversary, but also the 1980 and 1981 Companies Acts have increased continental European influences on British accounting and seem likely to restrict further the future freedom of standard setting in the UK. It is probably fair to say that British accounting policy makers have not yet come to grips with this major European influence which, at least on the surface, seems to strengthen the importance of the law in accounting, to give legal support to the more conservative aspects of accounting, and to codify the information given and the valuations used in accounting reports.

The continental European influence, outwardly at least, seems to be in direct contradiction to the efforts of the Financial Accounting Standards Board in the United States of America to develop a conceptual framework orientated towards helping investors and creditors to make better decisions—another potential if not actual influence on UK policy. The aim of the FASB is to choose accounting standards which help the estimation of the amounts, timing and uncertainty associated with the future cash flows to be generated by enterprises. Given that these American efforts have now been prosecuted for some eight years and have absorbed some 40 per cent of FASB's resources over this period, the time would now seem ripe to appraise these endeavours. The paper by Robert Sprouse, Vice-Chairman of the
518 FASB, helps in this evaluation, even though, interestingly, he mainly concentrates on the features of the Board which he believes should ensure its survival relative to that of previous American standard setting bodies. These features bear a considerable similarity to those which produce the 'independence' we associate with courts of law. Some of these same influences can be seen in recent developments in the ASC's procedures. Additional emphasis has been placed on 'due process', with wide discussions prior to the compilation of an Exposure Draft, a widespread distribution of such drafts and the use of public hearings to allow all who wish their 'day in court'.

In contrast, the papers from France and Germany do not show such a great concern for a legalistic due process, perhaps because of the greater impact which the law already has in these countries by its provision of a fairly detailed structure on which accounting policy makers can build.

Some might feel that British standard setters sit uneasily between the American efforts to produce more decision-orientated accounts and continental European legal influences. However, this dilemma is felt by other European accounting policy makers, as is illustrated by their debates on 'substance over form'. There, to put it simply, the 'substance' of an accounting issue represents the conceptual frameworks utilized by the policy makers, while the 'form' represents the restraining influences of both the law and conservative custom. As von Wysocki illustrates, the non-acceptability of the proposed treatment of accounting for leasing to accounting policy makers in Germany was based on such substance over form arguments, demonstrating once again the very real problem of resolving the conflicting pressures to help accounting users make 'better' decisions while at the same time complying with legal requirements and societal influences.

The problem over leasing accounting in Germany was encountered even though the proposal was consistent with the recommendations of the International Accounting Standards Committee, which is attempting to harmonize accounting standards internationally, and whose recommendations many countries have said they will attempt either to follow or to integrate into their own accounting standards. The existence of this body is another reason why a conference to consider accounting standards internationally is timely. Now that the number of international standards is well into double figures, the endeavours of the IASC also are ripe for re-evaluation. Many of these international standards are ostensibly able to encompass controversial matters, but only at the cost of phrasing standards so that all the existing treatments favoured by different countries remain mainly undisturbed. Mr J. Burggraaff, Chairman of the IASC at the time of the conference, discusses these and other problems in his paper. The paper by Coleman and Petite indicates that the EEC faces similar problems in dealing with accounting treatments in its Directives.

The EEC and the IASC are not the only two bodies seeking to harmonize accounting practices internationally. Both the United Nations and the Organization for Economic Cooperation and Development have attempted to lay down codes or guidelines for accounting. Both organizations are mainly concerned with the accounting reports of multinational organizations, and these endeavours seem addressed to producing standards which should give host countries some general all-purpose information which will aid them in obtaining the maximum benefit from providing bases for multinational enterprises. It is fair to say that both attempts are subject to major political arguments, the UNO being more prey to these problems than the OECD. The delegations from many countries see in these guidelines some hope of obtaining information which will allow some control of the 'exploitation' they believe they are subjected to by multinational companies.

Such deliberations indicate that there is some strength in the arguments of those who believe that accounting standards may be set for political purposes and also of those who oppose this on the ground that it will deny accounting one major attribute—its independence from any given group's desired view. For there is reason to believe that such political influences work in national as well as international forums, including those in the USA and the UK. Oil reserve accounting provides, so it is said, an American example and the government's intervention in the search for an inflation accounting standard seems to provide a British example.

The above are some of the reasons why it was felt that a conference addressed to comparing and contrasting accounting standards in a number of countries was timely. A final reason was that a survey of standard setting practice in a number of countries may help both the ASC in its new form and other national accounting bodies to better achieve their objectives.

Some important themes

A number of important themes run throughout the discussions in this volume. A number of these can be summarized in the following manner:

1 Although research efforts have so far been unable to clearly chart how accounting information either is used by society's members or how it benefits society, accounting policy makers, the preparers of accounting reports and governments still remain convinced that accounting can have a major impact on society and should be regulated in some way.

2 Self-regulation by the profession and regulation by the government are not presently alternatives. All the countries reviewed in this volume are subject to what might be called 'mixed regulation' in the same sense as we refer to a mixed economy. Different countries are located at different places on a spectrum of more or less state control.

3 A similar situation prevails in respect of the role of statute law relative to that of professional guidance concerning standards.

4 There is reason to believe that accounting standards and regulations
520 often reflect the concerns of society with a substantial lag. In other words, today's accounting reflects yesterday's concerns. Moreover, those concerns which ultimately impact on accounting are rarely stated in an explicit way, with the result that often the accounting policy making process can only respond to them in a rather nebulous manner.

5 The social concerns which are deemed to have relevance for accounting differ substantially between societies. As a result, the international accounting context is not a homogeneous domain.

6 It is doubtful whether those accounting policy makers who operate on the international scene can hope to have any explicit objectives other than to produce some agreed output as a first step in the process of setting international standards. This need to obtain consensus is, of course, present in all standard setting exercises, though societies that rely more on statute law might possibly have less need to generate consensus *de nova* for each standard because the law provides a substantial foundation which all are willing to respect.

7 The need to obtain consensus within and between standard setting bodies, the accounting profession and, more generally, society at large, is one reason why accounting standards are regarded as political. Another reason for this is the view that accounting standards may redistribute income and wealth between different social interests. For example, better informed potential investors may make decisions that augment their wealth relative to existing security holders and management. Accounting standards also may make it more difficult for management to pursue their own objectives protected by their 'inside' knowledge. Not least in significance is the role which accounting might play in moderating the conflicting interests of labour and capital.

Almost all the authors in this volume are addressing what might be called general-purpose standards and accounting reports. Given this, it is difficult to see how accounting standards can really satisfy those with differing preferences unless they are so bland that they offend no one (or, at least, no entity in society sufficiently powerful to resist any issued standard or, perhaps, to put the future of the standard setting body in the balance). In fact the limited evidence available suggests that, at least, the British and American standard setting bodies do make value judgements favouring one section of the community over others.

Few of the papers in this book really address these political problem points other than tangentially. This may be because most of the authors have practical experience of standard setting and are loath to deal with the more overt conflict which might follow attempts to make these political matters more explicit. It may equally reflect the lack of academic research in this area—at least until very recently. There is no doubt that research in this area which fulfils the usual criteria for social science research is difficult to mount. Having of necessity to reflect on issues of a political nature, much of the literature which has tried to address these points can appear to be rather polemical in nature.

In addition to the above points, a number of other themes are discussed in the papers, but frequently in a more implicit manner. Given the significance which these have both for understanding accounting standard setting processes and increasing the acceptability of their outcomes, some further more detailed consideration is justified.

Why accounting standards?

Few of the authors in this volume have any doubts concerning the need for the regulation of external accounting reports. Equally, most seem to support the system of regulation practised in their own countries, regarding this as at least no worse than the alternatives prevailing elsewhere. Only Benston questions whether accounting standards should be enforceable. Rather than so fundamentally questioning the status quo, the other authors concern themselves with whether the contents of accounting reports should be laid down by law (including those provisions of commercial and tax legislation which deem acceptable for their purposes only accounting reports that follow the rules specified by such laws), as is commonly held to be the situation in France and Germany (see Collins and Pham, and von Wysocki), or whether it is sufficient to allow some non-governmental body, usually associated with the accounting profession, to promulgate accounting standards which flesh out the fairly minimal reporting requirements which would be imposed by the law in such a setting, as was the case in Britain, at least until recently (see R. Leach and E. Stamp, *Accounting Standards: The First Ten Years*, Woodhouse-Faulkner, 1981).

The debate between these two latter options dominates the present volume, even though the arguments generally remain implicit.

In some ways it is surprising that the debate over the alternative modes of regulating accounting arises at all because most authors accept, again implicitly, that the regulation of accounting reports is an exercise in making social choice decisions. (see, however, Benston and Solomons.) Given this, one might have assumed that such social choices would have been dealt with in the usual way in each society.

That accounting choices involve social choices is easily shown. Different accounting rules will aid different parties in society. Unregulated accounts would aid those with greater knowledge in achieving their own objectives. In such an economy, management would tend to use its greater knowledge about enterprises to report in a way which is favourable to their own objectives even though these may well be at variance with interests of others in the economy. It is easy to construct examples of such activities. In the accounting environments of Britain and America, for example, there is a fair amount of evidence that management choose accounting methods which smooth income figures because investors are presumed to prefer such smooth trends rather than abrupt changes. Another example is provided by the relatively low level of voluntary disclosure of accounting statements adjusted for inflation. There are, of course, a number of reasons for the lack of such reports, including a belief that users would not only be confused by such statements but also would gain little benefit from them, a feeling that the cost of provision might thereby exceed the benefits available, and a wish not to reduce reported profits and returns on investment. However such arguments themselves illustrate that management is making judgements about the preferences of other members of society.

In contrast to those who argue for or against different modes of dealing with the social choice problem, Benston argues that the problem should not arise in well-organized markets. In such markets, those managers who sought to maximize profits and who did not disclose information for which people would be willing to pay its marginal costs, would find that investors would invest in other fuller disclosure, profit maximizing firms. Funds would not be available to non-disclosing firms at the going market rates and they also would be liable to take-over bids. In such markets the managers of profit-maximizing firms would, over the longer run, do better than those managers who followed non-profit maximizing behaviour and who did not provide disclosure for which there is effective demand.

However, even in such perfect markets the need for political judgements may well remain because the results so generated may involve what are seen to be undesirable transfers of wealth. It could be argued that the correction or avoidance of these could justify regulatory action. This may be a legitimate argument for intervention by the legislature, but it would not seem to support regulation by the profession who cannot, in general, claim any real mandate for making such judgements on the transference of wealth.

In less perfect markets, there seem to be strong arguments for the more general regulation of financial accounting reports (see Bromwich, 'The Setting of Accounting Standards: The Contribution of Research' in *Essays in British Accounting Research*, op. cit.). It is argued that these stem from major imperfections in the market for accounting information. The concern in most developed countries to avoid 'insider trading' has led to attempts to ensure that all users of accounting information, including those outside the enterprise, have equal access to identical public information at very low cost. With such a system, there is no market mechanism for expressing effective demands for additional accounting information. Moreover, even if such a mechanism did exist, it would not be used because restrictions on inside trading imply that any information made available to an outside user who is willing to pay the cost of the information must, or should at least, be made available to all at no cost. No one, therefore, will be willing to pay for any additional information. Similarly, it is argued that the market will not bid up the shares of enterprises which voluntarily give additional information relative to similar non-disclosing firms because no market actor can use this information for private profits.

The supply side of the accounting information market is also held to be imperfect. These problems result from the presence of what are called 'external' effects which flow from the activities of market transactors but which affect people other than those making transactions in the market place. Such effects may cause good or harm, but they will not enter into the calculus of the people directly undertaking the transactions. The effect on the market of rules to avoid 'insider' trading also provide an example of this.

It is also argued that accounting information once generated for one person or, indeed, for enterprise management can be provided to others at little or no additional cost. In a well-organized market such information would be provided to all willing to bear this cost. Enterprises in the practical world will be reluctant to do this unless forced to by, say, the government or profession for at such prices they will not cover the average cost of providing the information.

All of the above points suggest that some type of regulation of accounting information is required because without it management would be able to provide the information which would further their own interests without concerning themselves with the desires of its ultimate users. Be that as it may, the opponents of this view still believe that the market can be relied upon to provide the required accounting information. Yet others would accept the above characterization of the market for accounting information but would argue that even an imperfect market will do better for the welfare of the users of accounts than would any regulatory regime. If nothing else, the conflicting perspectives suggest that there is a clear need for further research in this area.

However, in the meantime, whatever view one takes of the market versus regulation issue, it is clear that any such regulation will involve social choices which can favour one sector of society over another. Moreover, in a democracy such important social choices usually are made by the legislature, or delegated by it. When seen in this way, the arguments for regulation do not obviously seem to support self-regulation by the accounting profession, other than where the choices are of a 'purely' technical nature. And even this latter argument may not seem convincing, first because of the other highly technical issues which legislatures already deal with, and secondly, because few accounting issues are purely of an isolated technical nature. A better argument for leaving accounting matters to the profession might rest on the seeming indifference of politicians to many accounting issues.

The legitimacy of accounting standard setters

Past and existing arrangements for self-regulation by the profession do not seem to include obvious mechanisms for making social choice decisions. Most of the bodies that do exist are mainly comprised of accountants who, however hard they try, cannot reflect either the views of society as a whole or of every sector in society.

Of course in some countries in continental Europe the accounting profession has no such general mandate. Those who seek to develop accounting standards in these countries generally attempt to change the law via the legislature. Such reliance on the legislature to regulate accounting overcomes the problems of seeking to show from whence comes the mandate of accounting standard setters. Value judgements concerning accounting are made in the same way as the other value judgements made by the society's political system. The problem of enforcement also is solved under such a system of regulation. In laying down accounting regulations the legislature also provides whatever penalties they feel necessary for non-compliance with these regulations. There are, however, clear potential difficulties with such systems. Accounting issues may be decided on the basis of the political views of the political faction in power at any time. More importantly, it can be argued that given the vast number of issues facing politicians, accounting matters may not be regarded as an urgent use of limited resources. Thus the legislature may be seen as generally rubber-stamping the ideas of interested civil servants and those who have influence on civil servants and politicians. That this is a better method of standard setting for society than self-regulation is questioned by many. There is little reason to doubt (see Wysocki) both that this process of standard setting is even lengthier and less flexible than other methods and that because of constraints on legislative time only those items judged of considerable importance will be pursued.

Even the establishment of the view that a given issue is important enough to be considered by the legislature also takes time. Moreover, given the difficulties of issuing accounting regulations under this system, attempts to change extant regulations are likely to be discouraged and the process of obtaining change likely to be long. Basing his remarks on Germany, Professor von Wysocki suggests that the results obtained from such a system are very similar to those achieved by other systems and, at least, no worse than the results of these other systems. However, evidence of dissatisfaction with the German system is given by the existence of a large number of other bodies in Germany concerned to alter existing accounting regulations and to introduce regulations new to the law.

In the UK, Australia, New Zealand and with the earlier American standard setting process, standard setters have no authority to set accounting standards for society. Where their authority resides is not clear, but many would say it must flow from the influence in society of the accounting profession and in the importance attached to accounting reports which are seen as too technical for the usual political processes.

One major weakness of self-regulation is said to be that the standard setting bodies have to achieve consensus for each standard among those who have the power to ignore it if they so wish, such as large professional firms of auditors and large enterprises. This may explain the concern of the ASC to increase its enforcement powers which currently involve only resort to the disciplinary procedures of the various accounting bodies. Without the ability to enforce standards, those issued may have to be tempered to achieve the acceptance of those influential bodies who can challenge the authority and the existence of the standard setting body by not complying with its edicts. Users and some others affected by accounting reports do not seem to have this power and, indeed, in general, tend to be unrepresented on accounting standard setting bodies, including the ASC.

Another suggested weakness of self-regulation is that to obtain consensus the standard setting bodies have to demonstrate that each of the issues with which they are dealing is of crucial importance both to the community and to those parties who, by their behaviour, can influence the acceptability of exposure drafts and of issued standards. Past experience of standard setting in America, Australia and the United Kingdom indicates that in order to obtain acceptability for their conclusions standard setting bodies direct their efforts towards damping down whatever brush fires are regarded as of importance in accounting at any specific time, thereby expecting to show that their activities are of relevance to society. However, in practice, the process of issuing exposure drafts and standards can be a very lengthy one (see Whittington for a description of the time taken to achieve an 'inflation' accounting standard)—a fact that may destroy the claimed advantages of concentrating on the immediate rather than the substantive.

So often, controversial issues have altered by the time the standards which have attempted to deal with them have come to fruition.

Another possible weakness of the need to obtain consensus is that it may encourage overflexibility by the standard setters. Either a standard that has been issued may be changed if there are strong feelings among those affected by it or a similar flexibility may prevail during the process of promulgating a standard. In either case, critics of the standard setting bodies see such flexibility as a weakness because they see it as a sign of the willingness to respond to particular powerful interests. To reinforce their claims they point to the process of developing standards for depreciation and research and development expenditures in the UK and oil and gas accounting in the USA. However those who support the standard setting bodies see this very same 'malleability' as evidence of a willingness to respond to 'good' arguments and the 'logic of experience'. Research certainly could serve an important role in such debates by casting some further
526 light on both the forces at play and their ultimate consequences for corporate reporting.

In the USA, the FASB has a delegated authority from the legislature. However, some might think that this authority is a weak one because it is subcontracted to the FASB by the Securities and Exchange Commission. Certainly both the legislature and the SEC have been unwilling to abstain from threats and sometimes actions to overrride FASB pronouncements. When seen in such terms, the FASB, with its concern for 'due process' and its attempt to see a generally agreed conceptual framework, might be seen as trying to defend itself from such challenges by strengthening its authority to lay down accounting standards, although Sprouse gives an alternative rationale for these and other concerns.

Canadian standard setters presently seem to have the most explicit mandate for accounting reform because accounting standards there promulgated in the authorized way become part of the statute law. Be that as it may, few attempts have been made in Canada to ensure that the bodies involved in standard setting reflect the multi-faceted views of society.

The myth of a 'self-regulating' profession

One issue made explicit by the discussions in this volume is that accounting regulations imposed by law cannot be treated as separate from accounting standards generated by the profession. When considering the degree of regulation placed on accounting reports in any country, the activities of the law makers, the judiciary and the standard setters have all to be considered together. The idea that setting standards is the preserve of a 'self-regulating' profession seems not to stand up to examination. In all the countries surveyed in this volume, standard setting builds on the law and generally deals only with areas which have not yet been addressed by the legislature.

That standard setting mechanisms reflect the social, political and economic environments of the country in which they are being set is clear from all the articles in this book. On the surface, at least, American standard setters seem to have considerable freedom. In fact, the American Securities and Exchange Commission's requirements on quoted companies, not to mention both federal and state legislation and the possibility, and sometimes the actuality, of SEC intervention, restricts the Financial Accounting Standards Board's freedom. Similar constraints arise from the large number of governmental bodies which may be lobbied to overturn a standard when it falls within their domain, and yet further restrictions arise from the ever-present possibility of the intervention of Congress itself.

It is not so much the actual intervention in standard setting by more powerful bodies than the FASB which restricts its freedom, but rather the knowledge that those discontented with, or jealous of its activities, can turn to these bodies to restrict FASB activities. For example, it is difficult to see what incentives can be given to other bodies with interests in accounting standards to accept a conceptual framework when such an acceptance amounts to a reduction of their power in society as a result of the consequent narrowing of their right to comment.

Until the passing of the 1980 and 1981 Companies Acts, standard setters in the United Kingdom have been less constrained than their American colleagues. The legislation relating to accounting has not been too detailed, the courts have tended to rely on the profession for evidence of 'good practice' and other bodies, such as government departments, seem to have generally been fairly uninterested in accounting matters (with only inflation accounting providing a counter example of the latter). As a result, the threats of intervention by government have only been of a fairly general nature—a fact that has probably strengthened the argument of those who wish to have standard setting take place outside government by allowing them to suggest that the only alternative to self-regulation is complete government takeover. The Accounting Standards Committee, therefore, has been able to devote its attention to getting its voluntary standards accepted by the preparers of accounting reports and the practising sector of the profession. However, the reverse of this lack of restriction has meant that the ASC has no really obvious mandate for its activities from the government. Support from government has been only of a very general nature. The recent greater interest of ASC in consultation and 'due process' may be seen as a search for an alternative basis for its mandate.

Different environmental contexts also may explain why the British Accounting Standards Committee has not followed the FASB in its search for a conceptual framework. *The Corporate Report* (published by the Accounting Standards Committee in 1975) suggests that the roles seen for accounting reports in Britain are far wider than those the FASB have in mind. This is likely to make the generation of a generally agreed conceptual framework even more difficult in Britain than in America, even though most British commentators actively interested in accounting standards have argued the continuing need for such a framework. Any such framework would have to make explicit and public choices aiding the welfare of different members of society, including those who do not even use the accounting reports, at least directly. However, attempts to derive a generally agreed conceptual framework in situations where such social choices are to be made may merely make explicit conflict which might otherwise remain implicit. It should be remembered that it is often possible for people with different views to agree on a given issue (on accounting standards in our case) even though they see it as achieving very different objectives and thereby could not agree on any joint overriding objective for action.

In any case, recent legislation, especially the 1980 and 1981 Companies Acts, has moved the environment in which British standard setters have to operate away from that of the USA and towards that of continental
528 Europe. For example, parts of the 1980 Act make only realized profits distributable but they leave the definition of realized profits to generally accepted accounting principles. In these circumstances it would seem reasonable to assume that the courts may well take the view that accounting standards provide good evidence of what are generally accepted accounting principles. This Act taken on its own would thus seem to strengthen the hand of the ASC. However, it is generally accepted that to be realized profits must be passed through the profit and loss account. This has tended to strengthen the case for the use of historic cost accounting, with its emphasis on objectivity and prudence, relative to mixed systems, including those which necessitate the revaluation of some assets. This concern with objectivity and prudence has been reinforced by the 1981 Companies Act which enacted the EEC Fourth Directive into British law. Some see this Act as introducing considerable continental European influences into British accounting. The major European characteristics imported by the Act include a much more complete codification of accounts, with fairly complete rules for the valuations to be used in any permissible revaluation of an asset or assets, more concern with accounts as giving objective evidence of enterprise results in order that creditors and investors can see whether their shares in the enterprise have been protected, and less concern with accounts as aids to decision making by the users of accounts. Moreover, the form of accounts laid down in the Act is fairly detailed and seems to increase somewhat the disclosure requirements of UK companies. It also lays down valuation rules for all categories of assets which make explicit the primacy of historical cost valuation rules.

Together these Acts may restrict the activities of British standard setters. This constraint is doubled if, as some suggest, the Department of Trade has taken on the role of guardian of the Fourth Directive and therefore stresses prudency and objectivity in accounts. Some evidence for this view is provided by the Department's resistance to some parts of the contemplated

ASC Foreign Exchange Exposure Draft. Views of this type must militate against accounts being orientated towards improved decision making and the impact of the Fourth and other Directives must make it less easy for British standard setters to move down the American path of primarily seeking to aid investors in decision making.

It has been argued that the role of British accounting standard setters will be seen to be unclear when sufficient time has passed for the provisions of the 1981 Act to be fully appreciated. Detailed disclosure requirements imposed by standard setters could be resisted in the courts on the ground that standard setters have no right to promulgate additional disclosure requirements over and above what are now fairly detailed legal disclosure requirements. A case could be made that if the legislature had wished to foster the objectives given in the *Statement of Intent on Accounting Standards in the 1970s*, that is to reduce the differences and variety of accounting principles, to encourage the disclosure of accounting bases and to obtain the disclosure of, or departures from, definitive accounting standards (*Accounting*, January 1970), one could suppose that they would have done so. Certainly the argument that the profession must seek these objectives on a self-regulating basis in order to fill the gap left because the government and the courts preferred to leave technical accounting matters to the experts is weakened. The Act also lays down quite comprehensive valuation rules and it is not entirely clear by what right the ASC can seek to augment these valuation rules.

However, the Act does not define a true and fair view, the achievement of which is stated in the Act to be a dominant statutory requirement. There is a role for the profession here in dealing with situations where resort is required to the true and fair override. As part of the process of ensuring a true and fair view accounting standards also may be required where the 'substance' of an accounting item is not conveyed by adhering strictly to accounting 'form'.

Taken to extremes, the above difficulties facing those who seek to set accounting standards in the current legal environment would suggest that, apart from situations where the government explicitly expected legislation to be augmented by accounting standards (mergers and acquisitions provide an example of this), standard setters should be concerned mainly with information additional to the statutory accounts. Current cost and flows of funds statements might provide examples of the latter. Certainly continental experience suggests that additional statements may also help to meet the demands for information by those sectors of society not generally seen as aided by published accounts. However, the European experience also suggests that such supplementary statements which have proved themselves over a long period may be taken into legislation.

European experience also suggests there still is need for consultative bodies which seek opinion on possible changes to the accounting law (see the papers by Collins and Pham and by von Wysocki). The Accounting

Standards Committee would seem to be one eminent candidate for this role. Continental European countries also find the need to have a variety of bodies to suggest and recommend new and altered accounting methods. Again, the ASC could expect to play an authoritative part in this process.

Specific international aspects

A number of papers in this volume are addressed to the variety of relatively recent bodies seeking to co-ordinate accounting standards internationally. These bodies address different geographical areas and different issues. The most ambitious of these is, of course, the International Accounting Standards Committee which seeks to harmonize accounting standards over all its constituent member countries and to expand the number of its members
530 (see Burggraaff). Coleman and Petite write about the problems of attempting to harmonize accounting treatments within the EEC. The OECD and UNO attempts at international standard setting have rather different aims. Zünd's paper dealing with these two organizations implies that here the major aim is to require multinational companies to disclose information which host countries think would be helpful in controlling them. Such activities have to be on an international level for multinationals seem able to overcome national accounting requirements by, for example, adopting a system of transfer pricing that reduces the information given and an organizational structure of buying and selling that achieves the same purposes.

The problems encountered in national standard setting indicate that any attempt at international standard setting is likely to be plagued by the problem of reconciling accounting systems which are addressed to very different objectives and are at different stages of development. Moreover, these accounting systems also may be based on very different intellectual foundations, of which the difference between legal based systems and user orientated approaches provide a vivid example. The problems of international standard setting are often further intensified because the standards so produced only have the authority that each of the countries involved wish to give them. Faced with such difficulties, it is difficult to see how these bodies can proceed other than by seeking consensus over very long periods of time. Certainly the activities of the EEC and the International Accounting Standards Committee have been so consensus orientated and, at least until recently, their outputs have had little effect on national standards.

As Busse von Colbe suggests, whether the OECD and UNO can do better than other international standard setting bodies is doubtful. Their aims are perhaps less ambitious but their proceedings seem more vulnerable to disputes caused by the very different cultural and political views of the countries which participate in these endeavours.

The role of research

A number of suggestions for research in the area of accounting standards already have been made in this introduction. Others are given in the other papers collected in this volume, particularly in the one by Beaver. In the following remarks we seek both to summarize these and to suggest some additional areas where research might have a role to play.

A number of authors suggest that a major role for accounting research is to assess existing and potential standards for their conceptual and logical consistency. Although such studies have not been favoured by academics, at least in the United Kingdom or the USA, there does seem to be some considerable potential for studies which seek to evaluate the consistency of standards both within themselves and with other standards. Evaluations of the conceptual bases of standards are likely to present more difficult problems however, because few standards make their conceptual foundations explicit and few standard setting bodies make overt the conceptual 531
frameworks they are using. Such problems would be particularly acute where accounting regulations depend heavily on the law since legislatures so rarely make explicit all the rationales for their action. However, research of this nature might be encouraged in the USA if the FASB succeeds in compiling its Conceptual Framework.

It also has been suggested that academics should concern themselves with ascertaining the empirical influences and effects of accounting standards. Outside of the USA there have been few attempts to undertake such studies (see Beaver for a description of a very comprehensive study of the FASB's standard on changing price levels), although this is potentially an area of great promise for research, if only because the rationales given for so many standards are stated in terms of the consequences which they are presumed to have. For example, the various standards that have been proposed for lease accounting are all based on a view that disclosing the economic value of leases would help the users of accounts in their decision making. The constraints placed on merger accounting by many standard setting bodies similarly presume that without them merger accounting may be used to reduce the information given to users. Of course, attempting to trace the ramifications of any particular accounting standard is not an easy endeavour, as the conflicting findings of a number of American studies of the economic consequences of standards illustrate (see particularly the evidence presented in the oil and gas accounting debate). Be that as it may, such studies are of significance because they might provide a basis for monitoring the performance of standard setting bodies and therefore could serve as their own management accounting systems.

Other suggestions for research focus on the need to make more operational some of the fundamental concepts which enter into accounting policy discussions. One obvious candidate for this is the concept of 'substance over form'. Although many suggested solutions to accounting problems appeal to this notion (accounting for leases is said to offer an example), so little is really known about either the meaning or the consequences of the phrase. Indeed even the rules for determining the substance of any accounting matter are quite unknown. With present knowledge (or level of critical assessment), the concept continues to be used in a fairly free way, often with no degree of consistency across different issues, and sometimes with the very ambiguity of the phrase being used to mask differences of opinion or treatment. Potentially, however, some think that the consideration of 'substance over form' may be an indirect way of introducing conceptual frameworks into standards setting debates since any notion of substance must be derived, it is argued, from some view of the objectives served by accounts. Regardless of the ultimate usefulness of such a view relative to that of a more direct attempt to explicate the conceptual underpinnings of the accounting craft, research could play a most useful role in examining the nature of concepts such as this which enter into the everyday justification of accounting change.

The above suggestions for research all seek to facilitate existing modes for regulating accounting standards. Accepting the nature of the accounting 'problem', they aim to improve the analysis and evaluation of accounting alternatives. Other proposals for research adopt a rather different perspective however, seeking to further our understanding of the organizational processes from which accounting standards emerge, the prevailing and alternative institutional arenas for the specification of such standards, the nature and implications of the economic, social and political influences on the standard setting bodies, and indeed, the origins of the interest in standardizing what might seemingly be regarded as an aspect of ordinary commercial practice.

Some of the rationales for the latter type of research have already been suggested by our own discussions of the cultural nature of the accounting craft, the often conflicting interests of the state and the accountancy profession in its regulation and control, the social legitimacy of the regulatory agents and the variety of other influences, both actual and potential, on financial accounting as we now know it. Although all of these issues are central to debates on accounting policy at both the national and the international levels, remarkably few insights are available into them. Indeed it is fair to say that some of the most crucial aspects of the accounting craft still remain in the realm of the mysterious, with little information and even fewer theories being available to those who wish to see them in more secular terms.

Such research is beginning to emerge however, albeit slowly, both in Europe and the USA. Often controversial and invariably tentative, it nevertheless is starting to demonstrate the potential for a range of alternative ways of viewing the accountancy standard setting endeavour, some, at least, of which are not cast in conventional accountancy terms. Questioning what was previously taken for granted and seeking to understand rather than initially to improve, such research might eventually offer bases for more fundamental appraisals of the issues which concern the authors of the papers in this book.

Even on the basis of present knowledge, one clear view that emerges from the present volume is that accounting standard setting is a far more complex and difficult endeavour than its critics suggest. Therefore, from whatever perspective research into it is pursued, it is unlikely that progress will be either quick or straightforward—an assessment which can also be made about the efforts taking place in the world of practice.

The contents of this volume

In his opening scene-setting paper on 'The political dimensions of accounting standards setting in Europe', Burggraaff emphasizes the need to see accounting in international terms. By noting the differences between

the nature and functions of accounting in socialist and capitalist countries and, in the latter, between those countries where accounting rules emanate from the state, compared with those which are more of a reflection of commercial practice, he demonstrates how accounting is implicated in wider social and political realities. Turning to examine in more detail some of the political aspects of accounting, Burggraaff focuses on and introduces the issue of the influence of interest groups on the processes of change and some of the ways in which attempts have been made to contain them. In the latter category he discusses the attempts that have been made to involve interest groups in the standard setting process, efforts orientated towards establishing the underlying concepts of accounting and the roles which multiple-base reports might play. Although aware of the political dimensions of the accounting craft, Burggraaff certainly distances himself from the desirability of them. To him, accounting still needs to be distanced from the pressures which characterize political life if it is to play an economic and social role.

In the first of two papers which attempt to relate accounting standards to the prevailing concepts of corporate governance and corporate social responsibility, Benston also tries to provide a discussion of accounting standards that distance them from a wider political context. He, however, adopts a very different perspective to that used by Burggraaff. While admitting that attempts have been made to use accounting standards to improve the level of corporate reporting so that managers would have an enhanced concern for their shareholders and/or society at large, he argues that this is not a beneficial role for accounting to serve. He bases this conclusion on the fact that the required measurements for useful standards cannot generally be made, a limitation which he sees as being a decisive one with respect to social responsibility concerns. He recognizes that accounting standards might be useful, in the area of corporate governance, primarily for preventing potentially fraudulent dealings and similar misuses of shareholder's assets by corporate managers. But even here, the costs of accounting standards are likely to exceed their benefits, according to Benston.

In contrast Tricker, in the second paper exploring the relationship between corporate governance, adopts a more institutional perspective. He discusses how conceptions of accountability and corporate governance have evolved and, in so doing, emphasizes that processes of accounting standard setting cannot be isolated from wider social and even philosophical issues. With particular relevance to the present discussion, Tricker discusses the widely divergent philosophical differences between the Anglo-American and the continental European views of the nature of the corporation in society and the way in which it should be managed and regulated. For these reasons, if for no others, he sees major difficulties arising from any attempts to harmonize such differing perspectives.

534 After these more general discussions of the contexts of accounting standard setting, the subsequent group of papers focus on the experiences in a number of different representative countries.

Sprouse starts by discussing briefly the three major episodes in the history of accounting standard setting in the USA, concentrating on a consideration of the present role of the Financial Accounting Standards Board. In his discussion of the latter, he emphasizes the attempts that have been made to ensure its independence from any special interest groups, a broad basis for participation in its decision processes and the authoritative nature of its pronouncements. He gives particular emphasis to the role which research has played and is now playing in the achievement of these aims, not least in the context of the conceptual framework studies. It is Sprouse's opinion that such research efforts can play a key role in ensuring that the FASB can achieve 'something more pervasive and long-lasting than specific responses to the hot issues of the day'.

The very different context of accounting standard setting in Germany is described by von Wysocki. In a paper that does much to illuminate the processes at work in that country, he emphasizes the dominating role that is played by the commercial and tax laws. However, although he sees such legal processes as being slow and relatively inflexible, he thinks that the resultant financial statements cannot be regarded as being worse than those resulting from very different standard setting processes. Von Wysocki's paper also provides an interesting and contrasting view of the role which research can play in the process. Accepting the legitimacy of the present political and institutional bases for accounting change, he provides a more cautious assessment of the potential which more scientific approaches might offer.

Another continental European view of accounting standard setting is provided by Collins and Pham. In their overview of the situation in France, they illustrate the long, although often contradictory, tradition of state influences on the specification of accounting procedures and the rather minimal role played by either the pressures or the institutions of the capital markets. To emphasize further the differences from Anglo-American conceptions, they conclude by noting how accounting in France is now developing along the lines of a more socially orientated information system, involved more directly in questions of national social and economic policy than its equivalent in the UK and the USA.

Stamp in his paper briefly introduces another method of seeking accounting principles based on his study for the Canadian Institute of Chartered Accountants (*Corporate Reporting: Its Future Evolution*, CICA, 1980), and another role for research to play in the standard setting process. His emphasis is on achieving a consensus on the criteria with which accounting standards need to comply to satisfy a wide range of constituencies. This attempt is seen as one which utilizes the proven methods of the judiciary to arrive at a conceptual framework, rather than trying to adapt scientific method to this task, as Stamp considers the FASB are seeking to

do in their search for a conceptual framework. The additional role he suggests for research is to use questionnaires to see what agreement exists among different groups as to the relative weightings of a number of criteria applicable to accounting standards. That he finds statistically significant agreement between the rankings accorded to his criteria by the members of ASC and participants at this conference suggests the promise of this approach.

From the perspective of the European Economic Community, Coleman and Petite discuss both the rationale for transnational influence and the nature of the harmonization task. Zünd thereafter discusses the more truly international influences, or rather attempted influences, of the OECD and the United Nations. Speaking from the perspective of a participant in these discussions, he provides some insight into the complexities of the political forces at work. However, like many of the other authors in this volume, he is aware of the ways in which present accounting practices remain embedded in very different national institutions and culture. If only because of such problems he remains sceptical of what can be achieved at such an international level.

Although many of the previous papers have discussed the roles which research has, can and might play in accounting standard setting, Whittington and Beaver focus more particularly on this interface.

By examining in some detail the development of the inflation accounting debate in the UK, Whittington demonstrates, perhaps to the surprise of many practitioners, that accounting scholarship and research has had a not insignificant influence on the shape of practical affairs: but he makes a point of stressing that the influence has rarely been a direct or obvious one. Referring to the famous quotation of Keynes, his paper shows how 'practical men, who believe themselves to be quite exempt from any intellectual influences' have on many occasions been influenced by 'some academic scribbler of a few years back'. However, Whittington, like Keynes before him, recognizes that those influences are often unknown and invariably separated by a long period of gestation in which the ideas slowly and often anonymously permeate the fabric of institutional life. Although aware of such an indirect influence, Whittington believes that accounting research does have a number of distinct and important roles to play, varying from the provision of 'excuses', through the clarification of assumptions and efforts to secure logical consistency, to more empirical investigations of both accounting as it is and the consequences which it has.

The latter role of accounting research is the primary concern of Beaver. Adopting a rational rather than political characterization of the accounting standard setting process, he discusses how research can help to develop the objectives which are attributed to the accounting craft, to illuminate the consequences which might stem from attempts to change it, and to provide some feedback to the accounting policy-making process by analyzing the
536 actual consequences of accounting changes. The latter role is discussed in greater detail in the context of the FASB's current attempts to evaluate the implementation of FAS No. 33. However, although favouring the increased rationality which research seemingly might contribute to the accounting standard setting process, Beaver is nevertheless aware of those institutional and political factors which constrain the acceptance of research results. Like so many of the other authors represented in this volume, he concludes by emphasizing both the political forces which determine the shape of practical affairs and our limited understanding of their operation and effects.

Solomons was given the Herculean task of synthesizing the many contributions. He manages to do this with authority and style, emphasizing the differing traditions of both accounting practice and inquiry and the underlying concerns with standardization and harmonization. Although admitting the social and political forces which do and must enter into these latter debates, Solomons distances himself from those who want to recognize an explicit primary political component of the accounting craft. Preferring to emphasize what an accepted conceptual framework might achieve, he concludes by discussing the important roles which research can play in the accounting setting area. In his opinion, such research really does have the potential to provide a useful and productive interface between the domains of practice and the academic world—an issue which provided the primary motive for the conference on which these papers are based.

European accounting research: An introduction

Anthony G. Hopwood and **Hein Schreuder**
Editors

1. INTRODUCTION

Accounting research in Europe is characterized by a great deal of diversity. There are very different theoretical traditions of inquiry and different emphases on the legal, professional and managerial aspects of the subject. A diverse array of approaches to the methodology of accounting research are evident, and very different appeals have been made to such other disciplines as economics, jurisprudence, history and the human sciences in order to illuminate and advance the accounting craft. Indeed, almost regardless of which dimensions of inquiry and scholarship are emphasized, European accounting research displays a diversity of strategies, approaches and substantive concerns.

Until now no attempt has been made to chart even the diversity of European accounting research in any systematic way, let alone understand the reasons for the differences or their consequences for both accounting thought and practice. The former task provides the focus for the present volume, however. The papers included build upon a smaller and more preliminary set presented at the accounting research workshop which formed part of the conference organized by the European Institute for Advanced Studies in Management in 1982 to celebrate its tenth anniversary. Although they do not provide a comprehensive review of all accounting research in all European countries, taken together they nevertheless provide some indication of the different research strategies in use in Europe, the relative emphases and concerns of accounting research in a large number of European countries and some of the achievements and understandings that are now available.

Initially, however, it is useful to consider some aspects of the European research community and some of the factors which are, gradually, encouraging a greater awareness of European traditions and modes of inquiry.

2. DIVERSE TRADITIONS

Until recently, accounting research in Europe had developed within quite tightly defined national boundaries. As has already been noted, the substantive research concerns and strategies were often very different. Education and research training and funding tended to be purely national concerns. The research and professional journals which existed were primarily nationally oriented and, if only for reasons of language, had quite narrowly circumscribed national readerships. With a few notable exceptions,[1] there was little or no systematic cross fertilization. Few attempts even had been made to create any awareness of the diversity of research traditions and approaches, and, at a quite basic level, few accounting researchers even knew their peers in other European countries.

Of course language played an important role in reinforcing, if not creating, this pattern of segmentation. It is difficult to believe, however, that language played the leading role. Other disciplines in management as well as in the social and natural sciences have succeeded in achieving a much greater degree of international awareness and even an active interchange of ideas. Both the origins of and the reinforcing conditions for the peculiarly national orientation of accounting research, therefore, must be sought elsewhere.

A key factor undoubtedly has been the national orientation of accounting itself, for although there are recognizable similarities in the technical language and practice of accounting among European countries, very significant differences also abound in both technical and contextual terms. Indeed the difficulties which have faced the accounting harmonization endeavors of the European Community themselves point to the substantive nature of the differences among national practices with respect not only to particular valuation and measurement rules but also in the extent of corporate disclosure, the constituencies which the accounting craft is seen to serve, the structure and roles of the accounting profession and the institutional arrangements of accounting practice and policy making (see Burggraaff, 1983; von Wysocki, 1983; Coleman and Petite, 1983; and especially Busse von Colbe, 1983). Moreover, even apparent technical similarities can mask the fact that European accounting practices have developed in very different nexi between the enterprise, the capital markets, the state, the accounting profession and others claiming an interest in the development of accounting systems. Faced with such differences, academic accountants have dealt with quite disparate educational tasks and problem agendas. National concerns were, as a result, generally much more significant than either international or comparative ones. Accounting academics accordingly tended to look inwards to their own national practices and contexts rather than outwards to accounting in the world at large.

3. An emerging international perspective

That situation has started to change in recent years. The growing internationalization of the business community has resulted in a greater need to appreciate the diversity of accounting in practice. Equally, the growing significance of transnational bodies such as the European Community has encouraged an interest in and even some progress towards a degree of harmonization of that practice.

In educational and research terms these developments have furthered an interest in international and comparative accounting practice. Both textbooks and research studies now seek to document, describe and understand the differences which characterize European and other forms of accounting (Ashton, 1981; Beeney, 1975, 1976; Beeney and Chastney, 1978; Choi and Mueller, 1978; Ernst and Whinney, 1980; Lafferty and Cairns, 1980; Macharzina, 1981; Nobes and Parker, 1981; Stillwell, 1976). Albeit slowly, European accounting teaching is now beginning to reflect a growing international awareness, and research has begun to consider both comparative issues and the specifically international in accounting.

Valuable though such developments have been in helping to further an awareness of the different national contexts of accounting practice, they have done relatively little to create an awareness of the variety of national research traditions or to stimulate the establishment of a more European accounting research community. The achievement of the latter has depended on a very different set of institutional developments occurring within the research community itself.

4. A EUROPEAN INVISIBLE COLLEGE

New developments in knowledge depend a great deal on the existence of informal networks of active researchers through which ideas can flow and be subject to discussion, criticism and review. Such 'invisible colleges' (Crane, 1972) in the research community play a vital role in serving as an essential complement to the more official channels of dialogue and communication. They provide a basis for researchers to informally discuss their tentative ideas and impressions, to elaborate upon the more official accounts of research findings that are published in scholarly journals and to test out with appreciative and knowledgeable colleagues their ideas for the development and reform of both theoretical and empirical findings. Not only do the invisible colleges of the research community speed up the transference of ideas, but they also provide an institutional structure which, whilst facilitative, can also accommodate the debates and disagreements which are a feature of the research process. Equally, they are able to convey both the richness and the contingent nature of ideas which are so vital in all discussions of the novel and the new.

Until very recently the invisible colleges of European accounting research, like their more formal counterparts, were almost exclusively nationally oriented. Unlike many in professional, industrial and commercial accounting,[2] very few accounting researchers had any contacts which bridged national boundaries (and most of those that did exist were oriented towards the USA rather than internally within Europe). Whilst often effective in their own domestic contexts, the informal as well as the formal organization of the research community nevertheless served to reinforce the already predominantly national orientation of European accounting research.

The possibility for that situation to change emerged with the establishment of the European Institute for Advanced Studies in Management in Brussels in 1971 (Naert, 1982). Initially emphasizing its role as a facilitator of European doctoral research in management, the Institute quite quickly assumed a number of other significant roles. It became a meeting place for European management teachers, researchers and research students. It began to organize research meetings and workshops which quickly attracted many of the more active researchers from a wide variety of European countries. And later it served as the catalyst for the establishment of a series of Pan-European professional associations for teachers and researchers in a number of different management disciplines and subject areas. In this way the European Institute for Advanced Studies in Management became the institutional nodal point for a growing network of teachers and researchers in many management subjects in most European countries. It thereby provided the basis for the development of a whole series of transnational invisible colleges. As a result, people began to know and respect one another, national research traditions were exposed and discussed, and, albeit more slowly, ideas began to be transferred from one country to another.

Accounting was recognized at an early stage by the European Institute. In 1971 Edmond Marquès of the Centre d'Enseignement Supérieur des Affaires in France and subsequently Anthony Hopwood, then of the Manchester Business School in the UK, were invited to become visiting members of the faculty of the Institute with the aim of developing a series of European accounting research workshops. Starting with a major one on human resource accounting organized by Marquès[3]
540 and subsequently incorporating workshops on comparative accounting practice in Europe, the social and political nature of accounting and information and control systems, the accounting workshops of the Institute quickly became successful, well-attended events. Through them, a growing group of European researchers started not only to know one another but also to understand and appreciate each other's research interests and the traditions from which they emerged. At long last the transnational invisible college which is now an increasingly important feature of the European accounting research community was in the process of being formed. A basis had been established for the movement of research ideas across European national boundaries.

Rather than reciting the detailed history of the accounting activities of the European Institute, it is sufficient to note a number of more substantive issues relating to their development:

1. Many of the Institute's initiatives in the accounting area have focused, perhaps initially unconsciously so, on areas and topics where there are either no or very small national research groups. Indeed, in the early days of the initiative, it proved extremely difficult to mount workshops in areas where there were already adequate national networks. Initially, at least, the roles that wider meetings could serve in these latter areas apparently were not evident. More recently, however, with the growing awareness of the Institute's accounting activities, the growth of an informal network of researchers and a greater interest in sharing more widely research ideas and findings, that situation has changed, not least in relation to research related to those areas of accounting where the harmonization activities of the European Community are now having an impact.

   Earlier, however, by providing at a European level almost the only forums for discussion, debate and the presentation of research proposals and findings, the Institute played a not insignificant role in stimulating research into areas such as comparative accounting, human resource accounting, social accounting and the organizational and social aspects of accounting systems. Indeed in some of these areas, and particularly the latter, there is evidence that the resultant interminglings of research perspectives have resulted in a distinctive European approach to the subject.

2. Together the series of workshops organized under the auspices of the European Institute have resulted in a large number of papers describing – for most European countries, including some in Eastern Europe – accounting practices, their historical development and the current pressures for them to change. Similar papers have outlined many of the different traditions of research, the divergent theoretical perspectives and the implications which some of these have had for accounting practice. In fact, a new literature has been created largely for the purpose of helping others to understand and appreciate particular national contexts.

   In the main, such papers have not been published in more official channels, although there are a number of exceptions to this rule. Together, however, they have played a most useful role in the creation of a more European accounting research community. Although often short and written in an all-too-unfamiliar foreign language, in many cases they nevertheless have provided the only means available for trying to understand the contexts and concerns of others. If for no other reason than this, many of these papers have been widely cited in the writings of others, entering thereby the official literature through more indirect means.
3. The workshops have also served a very different role by providing a less hierarchical context for the discussion of research, both intended and completed. Compared with almost all equivalent national forums, the workshops offer the senior and the junior, the student and the supervisor, an environment emphasizing the originality of ideas and the commitment to research rather than academic status and position. The very ambiguity created by the mixing of different academic systems and labels of differentiation was used positively to further lateral and knowledge-based interchanges. That in itself is a significant innovation in a European context, and one that already has most likely had a significant, even if largely invisible, impact.

Appreciable though these accomplishments may be, perhaps one of the main achievements of the network of contacts created by the accounting workshops of the European Institute has been the establishment of the European Accounting Association. Emerging directly from discussions which took place at one of the Institute workshops, the Association has rapidly become a well-established organization in its own right. Its annual congresses now occupy an important place on the European accounting calendar. Its newsletter provides a means for the exchange of information throughout Europe. Already, in fact, the European Accounting Association is the largest of the European professional associations (Naert, 1982), with members from virtually all European countries, and further afield. It has now held its annual congresses in Paris (1978), Cologne, Amsterdam, Barcelona, Aarhus, Glasgow and St. Gallen (1984). Indeed the very geographical rotation of its meetings reflects the Association's deliberate aim to involve accounting researchers from all over Europe and to transcend the local boundaries which have characterized European accounting research in the past.

One small measure of the transnational contacts which have resulted from the joint activities of the European Accounting Association and the European Institute is the coming together of the authors of the present volume. Without these organizations few, if any, of the contributing researchers would even have heard of, let alone have known, one another. Being, thereby, a product of the invisible college created by these organizations, it is our hope that the surveys of accounting research throughout Europe which are contained in this volume will serve to further encourage the development of a European accounting research community.

5. THE CONTENTS OF THIS VOLUME

The contents of this book are organized into two different sections. In the first section, overviews of accounting research are presented on a country-by-country
542 basis. In the second section, three papers offer observations on the relationships between accounting research and practice. Some introductory comments on both sections are in order.

5.1. *The national surveys*

Unfortunately, it has not been possible to provide a discussion of all European accounting research. Most notably absent is Eastern Europe. Equally, a number of Western European countries have not been covered, including Belgium, Greece and Portugal. A number of reasons account for the partial coverage, including the size restrictions placed on the book, the different degree of participation in the evolving European accounting research network by the various communities of accounting scholars and the unfamiliarity of the editors with some of the national communities. Thus the omission of certain countries from this volume in no way reflects upon the potential importance of their accounting research. Indeed it is hoped that subsequent volumes will fill the gaps that we have had to leave.

For many of the countries included in this book, the present papers represent the first published attempts to provide an overview of their national accounting research in the English language. Given this, we thought that it was important for the authors not only to describe the substance of the research undertaken but also to discuss it as far as possible in its own historical, social and institutional context. Why are certain research themes emphasized in one country and completely ignored in another? What explains the diversity and the eclecticism of research in a number of countries, while in others a common frame of reference does seem to exist? To what extent is present accounting research a continuation of historical developments or, alternatively, a reaction to them? And what roles are played by practice, by the accounting profession, by the organizational setting of accounting researchers or by other institutional factors in shaping the development of research? We felt that many readers would inevitably face such questions in reflecting upon the nature of European accounting research. Hence, we thought it would be useful to simultaneously present as much of the relevant background information as possible.

Of course, this approach implied that a trade-off had to be made between the substantive discussion of research and the presentation of background information. We generally have left the resolution of this trade-off to the authors, supplying them only with the following suggestion as to the elements of the overview:

1. Historical background.
2. Present institutional context, particularly the research context.
3. Accounting research in the last decade: Main classifications and trends.
4. Personal assessment of the author.
5. References: Literature, journals, organizations, etc.

In editing the papers we have further attempted to ensure that comparative information on these points would be provided for all countries. However, the actual structure adopted for the paper as well as the emphases placed on certain elements at the expense of others were entirely at the authors' discretion. The choices made are themselves quite informative in that they reveal which factors are considered most important for describing and explaining the accounting research situation in a particular country. The amount of attention devoted, for instance, to historical developments is indicative of the current significance of the research tradition in that country. In some countries (such as Italy) current research seems strongly influenced by such traditions, while in other countries their influence seems either waning (The Netherlands) or virtually absent (France). In a sense, then, the selection of topics *not* to be discussed in a national overview may be just as informative as the choice of elements to be covered.

In yet another respect, the mode of presentation of a national overview reveals some important characteristics of the research itself. We refer to the concepts, the terminology and the style used. Consider, for instance, the difficulties of translating the Italian *economia aziendale* or the Dutch *bedrijfseconomie* into English. Both terms denote the overall discipline in which accounting is embedded. An English translation could be 'business administration'. However, an Italian would protest that this translation robs the term of many of its connotations which are regarded as essential in the Italian tradition to which it refers. As Galassi explains in his contribution, it is therefore necessary to literally translate the term into 'concern economics', even though the latter is somewhat awkward English usage. For the Dutch *bedrijfseconomie*, the best translation is 'business economics' since this reflects the Dutch tradition of regarding business studies primarily as a subdiscipline of economics. As Klaassen and Schreuder note in their overview, though, this translation should not misguide the reader into thinking that the Dutch *bedrijfseconomie* resembles the Anglo-American 'industrial economics'. In actual content it is much closer to business administration, yet this term would be regarded as too managerial by many Dutch academics.

These examples suggest how the terms and concepts used in the overviews correspond to different worlds of thought. The translation problems are only the surface manifestations of deeper conceptual differences. The conceptualization of research problems in business studies and accounting appears to differ across countries. Since the conceptual (and terminological) systems are, therefore, to some extent incommensurable, the main problem of authors – and editors – of national overviews is *to correctly convey the local world of thought* to a foreign audience. This cannot be achieved by forcing all contributions into the same stylistic mold which is, for instance, required by the prominent Anglo-American research journals. This would strip them of all *couleur locale* and hence be counterproductive. In editing these papers we therefore have tried to strike a balance between preserving the character of the original world of thought and at the same time affording accessibility and readability to an international audience. However, the latter cannot be achieved to the extent possible within one accounting community. As a consequence, the reader will have to expend more than normal effort to ascertain the true meaning and message of some of the contributions. The benefits are, however, proportionately larger too: the glimpse of 'another world' and the corresponding awareness of the relative and local significance of one's own notions.

5.2. *Research and practice*

The second section offers three papers on the relationships of theory and practice. Schreuder's paper is methodological. It investigates the roles of values in accounting theorizing. This issue is especially significant in the European context where so many different cultural values exert their influence on accounting research and practice. The second paper, by Dent *et al.*, examines the relationship of management accounting research to practice from the perspective of academia. It explores the roles played by accounting theories and research by means of the challenging notion of 'myth cycles', a concept which is used to reflect the degree of consensus in the world view which underlies such theories and research. The paper by Muis adopts the practitioner's perspective and deals primarily with financial accounting. It describes the different worlds of accounting research and practice but argues that ultimately the two are mutually dependent. The paradox of this relationship is, however, that neither can contribute much to the other if it is not accorded a substantial degree of autonomy. As an illustration of the difficulties of European rule-making, Muis describes the development of the EEC Fourth Directive. His vivid account of this process is bound to amuse all those familiar with the intricacies of the European environment.

6. SOME EUROPEAN EMPHASES

It is difficult to offer an overall view of European accounting research. Diverse approaches and perspectives are utilized in different countries. Very different schools of thought have emerged from the different institutional bases for research prevailing in the different countries. Nevertheless, despite such obvious signs of diversity, a few points of commonality do emerge, at least when the European contributions are contrasted with those prevailing elsewhere. We now turn to a brief consideration of these.

One characteristic of the European accounting research community is that it is relatively 'long in experience and short in [empirical] research training' (*cf.* Peasnell, 1981, 121). As is evident from many of the contributions to this book researchers are generally well aware of the historical development of their discipline and tend to assess its current status from this perspective. What is more, in this historical perspective accounting is frequently seen as part of a wider discipline, usually a branch of economics dealing specifically with (business) organizations. Consequently, research is also evaluated from this broader point of view. The central focus is on its *incremental* contribution to our understanding of (business) organizations as this has developed over time and across disciplines. Hence, one can often detect some annoyance with research studies which display an insensitivity towards these historical and comparative dimensions. In the last decade this has perhaps been most evident in the inflation accounting debate. Those commentators familiar with the European research traditions in this area could not help but note the frequent reinvention of the wheel in the international inflation accounting literature.

New modes or strands of research are similarly assessed from this broader perspective. Traditionally, there has been a concern to preserve the coherence of the overall (economic) discipline of business studies. Hence, there has often been some reluctance in immediately adopting any new views or techniques becoming available. Perhaps this also helps to explain why empirical research has developed more slowly in Europe in the last decade than in the United States (although it has now become quite widespread across countries and research sites).

However, this is at best only a partial explanation. At least as important are some other differences in central research orientations, most of which are not restricted to accounting or business studies but reflect more general cultural differences (see Hofstede, 1980; Kassem, 1976). One such difference is that European social research is rather markedly theory-oriented as opposed to technique-oriented. In other words, problem understanding dominates problem solution and the 'know-why' takes precedence over the 'know-how' (Kassem, 1976). There is an uneasiness about research programs which mainly consist of the collection of empirical 'facts' without adequate theoretical underpinnings. There is a profound awareness of the contingent nature of factual knowledge, both because of the impossibility of theory-free observation and because of the influence of our different cultural values upon our implicit or explicit theories. Indeed, one of the major advantages of living and working in the European environment may be the continuous exposure to the different values and presuppositions which the various cultures generate. The resulting awareness of the highly contingent nature of our knowledge claims leads to a natural skepticism concerning any 'one best way' to solve problems. Thus, to more pragmatically inclined observers, European debates may seem to unnecessarily problematize accounting problems instead of working toward their solutions. It is only against the background of our highly diverse social, political and institutional environments that this attitude becomes understandable.

The very conceptualization of organizations to account for is similarly affected by this background. As organization theorists have noted (see Hofstede and Kassem, 1976), European theories tend to emphasize the organization-in-society. The focus is thus not only on the internal functioning of organizations, but also on their relationships with the social environment. A diverse array of social interests are recognized. Any monolithic conception of the organization is therefore inadequate. As a consequence, the answer to the question 'what to account for?' becomes dependent upon the conceptualization of this 'interested' nature of accounting. In addition, the question 'to whom should accounts be directed?' naturally arises, as well as the question 'by whom?'. Again, the contingent nature of the answers to these questions is highly apparent in the socio-political laboratory we call Europe.

Finally, we wish to note the methodological and epistemological debates which
546 seem to be more prevalent in Europe than elsewhere. In view of the discussion above, this should come as no surprise. Partly they are a consequence of our research traditions and our historical-comparative perspective. Partly, also, they are the result of the continuous doubt cast on the validity of social knowledge claims when assessed from a different socio-political or cultural point of view. The appropriate methods for gathering social knowledge and proper justifications of its validity then become an inevitable preoccupation.

Of course, this synopsis can only represent a somewhat crude generalization – or even an oversimplification – of some of the commonalities we observe in the various European research traditions. Not one of those traditions will have been appropriately characterized by this description. Nevertheless, we think that collectively the European traditions exhibit the features indicated above. What is more, we venture that these features will become more pronounced as the inter-European contacts grow in number and intensity through the institutional mechanisms created in the last decade. And we believe that this is exactly how European accounting research may make its profoundest international contribution: by developing the awareness of our diversity into an understanding of it. If this book provides a small step in that direction, it will have been a valuable undertaking.

7. ACKNOWLEDGEMENTS

We would like to conclude this introduction by acknowledging the help and support provided by a number of individuals and organizations.

The role of the European Institute for Advanced Studies in Management has been a particularly important one. Not only did it organize the conference out of which the present volume emerged, but it has also continued to demonstrate a concern for extending the dialogue between accounting researchers in Europe. In this respect we would particularly like to mention the efforts of all the Directors of the Institute, Richard van Horne, Bob Graves, Per Jonas Eliaeson, Alain Bensoussan and particularly the present Director, Philippe Naert. We also would like to thank Gerry Dirickx for her continued help, advice and support.

It is difficult to imagine the present volume ever emerging from conception to reality without the editorial support of Joyce Muis-Lowery. She has devoted days of effort to working on the style and language of the various drafts submitted by the authors. Both we, as editors, and the authors are extremely grateful for the caring attention she has given to the preparation of the volume.

We also would like to thank Ernst and Whinney for their support, both financial and otherwise, for the preparation and publication of this volume. In this respect the contributions of Jules Muis and Eddy Bartholomew are particularly appreciated. Also, we have been fortunate to have the services of an accommodating publisher in the person of Frans Grijzenhout of the Vrije Universiteit Boekhandel/ Uitgeverij.

It also is appropriate to thank the authors who have contributed to this volume. Many did not realize just how much work would be involved. All have given unsparingly of their time and effort. We hope that the collective product does justice to the individual efforts that they have made towards its compilation. 547

Last, but by no means least, we would like to thank our secretaries, Mary Scott-Fleming and Ria de Swart-van Doornewaard, as well as the secretarial staff of the University of Washington, where Hein Schreuder was a Visiting Scholar in 1982-1983. All have helped considerably in dealing efficiently with the seemingly endless correspondence generated by the editorial process. So great was this that after a while the storage point for the correspondence became known as the 'European book project *pile*'.

NOTES

1. For instance, German theories of accounting had a significant influence on accounting thought and education in the Scandinavian countries earlier in this century. Domestic influences are more dominant now, however.
2. The increasing internationalization of industry and commerce and the growth of international professional accounting practice provided a strong basis for the development of a growing community of internationally oriented practising accountants. For some time the existence of the UEC had also facilitated transnational accounting dialogue in Europe, and there had been a history of periodic bilateral meetings between senior members of European professional institutes. The consultative procedures established as part of the EEC also played a significant role in the development of a European network of practitioners, particularly through the Groupe d'Etudes des Experts Comptables de la CEE.
3. Some of the papers presented at this workshop were published in the special issue on Human Resource Accounting, *Accounting , Organizations and Society* (vol. 1, no. 2/3).

REFERENCES

Ashton, R.K. (1981), *The Use and Extent of Replacement Value Accounting in the Netherlands.* London, Institute of Chartered Accountants in England and Wales.

Beeney, J.H. (1975), *European Financial Reporting: 1. West Germany.* London, Institute of Chartered Accountants in England and Wales.

Beeney, J.H. (1976), *European Financial Reporting: 2. France.* London, Institute of Chartered Accountants in England and Wales.

Beeney, J.H., and J.G. Chastney (1978), *European Financial Reporting: 4. The Netherlands.* London, Institute of Chartered Accountants in England and Wales.

Burggraaff, J.A. (1983), The political dimensions of accounting standards setting in Europe, in: M. Bromwich and A.G. Hopwood, eds., *Accounting Standards Setting: An International Perspective.* London, Pitman, 1-12.

Busse von Colbe, W. (1983), A discussion of international issues in accounting standard setting, in: M. Bromwich and A.G. Hopwood, eds., *Accounting Standards Setting: An International Perspective.* London, Pitman, 121-126.

Choi, F.D.S., and G.G. Mueller (1978), *An Introduction to Multi-National Accounting.* Hemel Hempstead, Prentice-Hall.

Coleman, R.J., and M. Petite (1983), Accounting and auditing research and the European Community, in: M. Bromwich and A.G. Hopwood, eds., *Accounting Standards Setting: An International Perspective.* London, Pitman, 98-105.

Crane, D. (1972), *Invisible Colleges.* London, University of Chicago Press.

Ernst and Whinney (1980), *Consolidated Accounts in Europe.* London, Financial Times Business Information Ltd.

Hofstede, G.H. (1980), *Culture's Consequences: International Differences in Work-Related Values.* Beverly Hills, Sage Publications.

Hofstede, G.H., and M.S. Kassem (1976), *European Contributions to Organization Theory.* Assen, Van Gorcum.

Kassem, M.S. (1976), Introduction: European versus American organization theories, in: G.H. Hofstede and M.S. Kassem, eds., *European Contributions to Organization Theory.* Assen, Van Gorcum.

Lafferty, M., and D. Cairns (1980), *1980 Financial Times Survey of 100 Major European Companies' Reports and Accounts.* London, Financial Times Business Publishing Ltd.

Macharzina, K. (1981), Grenzen einer internationalen Vereinheitlichung der Rechnungslegung, in: E. Ruhli and J.P. Thommen, eds., *Unternehmensführung aus finanz-und bankwirtschaftlicher Sicht.* Stuttgart, Poeschel, 365-385.

Naert, P.A. (1982), Ten years' European Institute for Advanced Studies in Management: Evaluation and perspectives, Institute Report 82-4. Brussels, European Institute for Advanced Studies in Management.

Nobes, C.W., and R.H. Parker (1981), *Comparative International Accounting.* Oxford, Philip Allan.

Peasnell, K.V. (1981), Empirical research in financial accounting, in: M. Bromwich and A.G. Hopwood, eds., *Essays in British Accounting Research.* London, Pitman.

Stillwell, M.L. (1976), *European Financial Reporting: 3. Italy.* London, Institute of Chartered Accountants in England and Wales.

von Wysocki, K. (1983), Research into the processes of accounting standard setting in the Federal Republic of Germany, in: M. Bromwich and A.G. Hopwood, eds., *Accounting Standards Setting: An International Perspective.* London, Pitman, 57-67

THE DELOITTE, HASKINS & SELLS ACCOUNTING LECTURES
AT
THE UNIVERSITY COLLEGE OF WALES, ABERYSTWYTH

ACCOUNTING RESEARCH AND ACCOUNTING PRACTICE: THE AMBIGUOUS RELATIONSHIP BETWEEN THE TWO

by
Professor Anthony G Hopwood
London School of Economics and Political Science

The lecture was delivered at Aberystwyth on 27 October 1983 and has been subsequently revised for publication

Although the relationship between research and practice should be of central concern to the accounting academic community, it has only rarely been specifically addressed[1]. Of course there have been pleas for more research to be conducted on the seemingly problematic areas of accounting practice (Alexander and Carsberg, 1981; Carty, 1982; Coleman and Petite, 1983; Flint and Shaw, 1981). Indeed such a theme now seems to dominate most occasions when practitioners address academic audiences [however see Stacey (1982) for one exception]. Equally, academics have tended to articulate a view that practice can and should be guided by the findings of systematic research to a greater extent than is currently the case (Kaplan, 1981; Kinney, 1981; Tricker, 1978), often recognising, in the process, that the achievement of this would require quite major changes in research (Abdel-Khalik, 1981; Kaplan, 1983; Santocki, 1980; Tomkins and Groves, 1983) and educational (Sterling, 1974) practices. Nevertheless, despite a history of such pleas and presumptions, and even the identification of an assumed "schism" between the worlds of the scholarly and the practical, the relationship which accounting research does and might have to accounting practice has tended to be presumed rather than specifically analysed. The desirability, indeed often the necessity, of an intermingling of the two has been stated but the processes and mechanisms through which that either is or might be achieved have not been subjected to any detailed inquiry. Research into the relationship between the academy and accounting practice has tended to be ignored.

There are a few encouraging signs that this is starting to change, however. The quite explicit use of some of the language, categories and concepts of academic accounting in the context of the eminently practical debates on inflation accounting has encouraged some exploration of a very particular intermingling of the scholarly and the practical (Tweedie and Whittington, 1984; Whittington, 1983a; 1983b). In the same context, research also has been called upon to observe (and even evaluate) accounting in practice and there are some signs that this is providing, both directly and indirectly, a basis for a more explicit recognition and analysis of the complexity of the relationships which research can and does have to practical action (Beaver, 1983; Beaver et al, 1982; Carsberg and Page, 1984; Hopwood, 1983; in a wider context also see Dyckman and Zeff, 1984; and Stamp, 1985). Accounting research itself also is slowly starting to be seen in ways which more actively facilitate reflection upon its relationship to the world of practical affairs. Rather than being seen as a relatively unproblematic revelation of the real and the true, the more proactive possibility that theories might not only reflect but also produce and reproduce the contexts in which accounting operates is coming to be recognised (Crawford, 1984; Burchell et al, 1985). Attention has been drawn to the significance of some of the internal dynamics and changes in the world of accounting scholarship for our perception, appreciation and understanding of both accounting functioning and the possibilities for change in the accounting domain (Christenson, 1983; Wells, 1976). Equally, but more controversially, increasing consideration is being given to the nature of some of the practical interests and social and institutional structures and processes that underlie the development of theories both in and of accounting (Cooper, 1981; Hopwood, forthcoming; Tinker et al, 1982).

Such tendencies to see the relationship between research and practice in very different ways have been reinforced by a number of factors. On the side of practice, a stimulus has been given by the opportunities to witness and reflect upon the processes and language of accounting change which the increasingly institutionalised and public nature of accounting undoubtedly has provided. Although a lot remains firmly hidden within the accounting policy-making closet, particularly in the UK, more and more of the body of accounting, as it is, is starting to be seen. The resultant processes of consultation and deliberation, drafting and reviewing have served to stimulate the imagination of at least some of those concerned with understanding accounting in action. The ways in which quite specific accounting practices are related to, and, in turn, reflected in, more general notions of the rationales, roles and potential of the accounting craft are coming to be observed and meditated upon. Increasingly accounting change is coming to be seen in terms of a process that can quite positively value and utilise certain types of ideas and knowledge. By identifying the rise of a wider economic rhetoric of the consequences of accounting, Zeff (1978), for instance, has started to explore the changing nature of the discourses in which specific accounting reforms come to be embedded. Watts and Zimmerman (1979), in turn, have pointed quite specifically to the roles which abstract accounting theorizing plays in both the pursuit and justification of practical accounting change[2].

On the side of research, different and even competing forces have been at play.
552 On the one hand, secular pressures have resulted in an expanded intellectual discourse that is expressed in terms of "applied", "action" and "useful" research. At least part of the academy is now more interested in mingling with the affairs of practice. On the other hand, accounting also has witnessed the development of a more reflective research stance grounded in the substantive disciplines of the human sciences. Rather than trying to improve the rationality of accounting on its own terms, this strand of inquiry is more interested in understanding, appreciating and even problematising the practice of accounting as it has come to be. With many such researchers not being prepared to take for granted the accounting domain that has been established, varieties of theorizing of, rather than within, accounting are now emerging.

As a result of such developments, at least some of the axes on which the realms of the practical and the scholarly might be related are coming to be investigated. Albeit slowly, there nevertheless are signs that bases are emerging on which our understandings of the intermingling of research and practice can start to advance. Rather than presuming a separation of the two, a distancing, in other words, of the practical from the abstract such that one has consciously to strive to meet the other, we are coming towards gaining insights into both the abstract bases of practical developments and the pragmatic influences on abstract theories. A view of a much greater potential for an interrelationship between research and practice is slowly arising out of a series of quite disparate and still very tentative research contributions and observations.

Already these insights into the interdependent realms of the abstract and the practical are starting to offer a challenging view of some of the knowledge processes involved in accounting change, not least to those whose calls for a greater relationship between the two arise from a comfortable impression of the enormous gap that must be overcome. Indeed it is perhaps to just such celebrations of the gap that the present comments are addressed. Although no systematic overview of the relationship between accounting research and practice is offered, since that is beyond the possibilities of present research in the area, an attempt nevertheless is made to outline some of the situations which have served to provoke my own thoughts on the topic and some of the general implications which I see as arising from these.

AN EMERGING UNDERSTANDING

My own thoughts on the relationship between accounting research and practice have been developing and changing for some time. On the one hand, I have held quite traditional notions of the appreciative and even reformist roles which scholarly inquiry can serve in the sphere of practical action. And I still do see a role for research to tease into the premises, both conceptual and pragmatic, underlying accounting practice. On the other hand, for both practical and theoretical reasons, I have become even more impressed by the abstract nature of much practical accounting, by the repeated instances, both minor and substantive, on which practice has been changed, if not in the name of theory, at least in the name of quite abstract notions of its roles, potential and functioning, and, not least in significance, by the numerous signs of a growing practical interest in accounting research. The net result of these influences has been an increasing interest in what might be at stake in an intermingling of research and practice in the accounting domain, a growing realisation of the quite ambiguous and little understood relationship between the two, and a slowly evolving desire to confront the practical and the scholarly interests in accounting.

On several occasions in the past I almost have put pen to paper on the matter, not, as it would happen, for more scholarly outlets but rather for the popular accounting media. Caution repeatedly got the better of me; that is something which I now regret.

The first such occasion almost resulted in a short article on "The Politicization of Accounting Research". My aim was to analyse some of the reasons that led me to predict a quite substantial increase in interest by the British accountancy profession in accounting research. Given that I was envisaging such an article before the Institute of Chartered Accountants in England and Wales had appointed (or even thought of appointing) a Director of Accounting Research and before the Accounting Standards Committee had explicitly considered the roles which research could play, such a paper would have been a quite explicit predictive test of my own understanding of the institutional dynamics of the standard setting project, what I saw to be the uneasy legitimacy established for that exercise and a consequent growing pragmatic interest in the legitimising roles that research could play. In retrospect it is easy to be wise. At the time, I can only presume that caution and discretion won the day.

Regret also surrounds my decision not to go ahead with another popular article that was to have been written under the title "Are you the person on the Clapham Omnibus?" After being privy to a series of meetings which one major organisation held to evaluate and reform its management accounting systems, I became fascinated by the highly abstract notions of managerial process which underlay accounting change. Participants in the exercise repeatedly dissociated themselves personally from the imperatives which they saw pushing for change. However, change was still contemplated and eventually agreed, not in the name of any specific practical use or user but rather in the name of a 'person' whom I came to see as residing in the (empty) middle of the committee table --- the 'person' I later described as the Person on the Clapham Omnibus[3].

Rather than explicitly acknowledging the operative interests in a centralisation of influence, an information flow that would further increase the salience of economic factors and a central concern for increasing the structured component of the management task, participants repeatedly referred to the decision needs of a 'person' whom they admitted had very different information desires than themselves. The article I had in mind was to have elaborated the practical interest in seemingly impractical abstract conceptions and to have used this as a means for pointing to the ways in which a rhetoric of facilitating rational decision making can mask a variety of other interests in accounting change.

I am not sure if I have learnt the lessons of my past cautiousness. On this occasion, however, I will at least pretend that I have, using this as an excuse for trying to articulate a few preliminary thoughts on some of the relationships between accounting research and practice. One further caveat also is in order. That relates to the grounding of my ideas in the cultures of the UK and the USA, the former, in particular, having what I see as a very particular and long standing attitude towards knowledge and the new[4].

554 That being said, the argument can proceed. Some paradoxes underlying conventional notions of the relationship between research and practice are first considered. Thereafter, building on one of these relating to the growing practical interest in research, some of the institutional characteristics associated with a practical concern with the scholarly are discussed. Finally, some specific examples are described which illustrate some of the relationships outlined.

SOME CONFLICTING PERSPECTIVES ON RESEARCH AND THE PRACTICAL

I have come to question quite a number of what I think are commonly held views concerning the relationship between accounting practice and research. Some of these are of sufficient centrality to the debates on how research is and might be intertwined with the conduct of practical affairs that it is worthwhile to try to give an initial formulation of my views. I do this by contrasting a somewhat stereotyped outline of what I see to be present dominant perspectives on some important aspects of the relationship, both actual and potential, with a contrasting view that emerges from an analysis of my own observations of the relationship in practice.

Different Worlds vs. a Shared Viewpoint

It is frequently presumed that accounting researchers and practitioners hold very different views of the accounting domain. But is this really the case? Do not the vast majority of accounting academics and practitioners share a view of accounting as a set of devices which provide a neutral indicator of organisational performance and a technical means for facilitating the achievement of a relatively unproblematic view of rational decision making? Neither accounting academics nor practitioners generally look to the measurement of profit, for instance, as providing an indicator of the relative power of different social interests within the enterprise (Tinker, 1980). Few in either practice or the academy have views of costs and costliness, organisational efficiency and the efficient allocation of resources which see these and related concepts as having specific historical trajectories for their emergence which point to them having social, political and organisational bases (Callahan, 1962; Haber, 1964; Hays, 1959) as well as the more traditionally accepted economic and technical ones (Hopwood, 1984). With very few exceptions, both groups of accountants also accept conceptions of accounting performance measurements that quite frequently have an ambiguous relationship to the role which they play in even conventional economic theories as indicators of differential market power. Be they be in the world of the scholarly or that of practice, the majority of accountants appear to hold on to a well socialised notion of accounting as a neutral technical device, the design and functioning of which is distanced from the social and political bases of organisational life. Accounting is seen as something which seeks to realise a particular pre-given and unproblematic notion of organisational rationality. It is seen as being in the business of revealing rather than constructing a view of the economic and administrative functioning of the organisation (Loft, 1986). Although seen as an enabling technology, the consequences which accounting has are thought to reside almost solely in the realms of the economic and the managerial rather than those of the social and the political.

Of course there are many differences between accounting researchers and practitioners. In many senses they can legitimately be regarded as two different 555
groups, albeit that neither is homogeneous in orientation. However, I am still impressed by the many similarities in the conceptions of the accounting mission and craft that the vast majority of the members of the two groups share. I, at least, am tempted to argue that it is these similarities, rather than the differences in their intellectual orientation to the advancement of the craft and the means by which this is done, that have had and still do have a not insignificant impact on the development of accounting knowledge, be that ingrained in the conduct of practice or articulated in more abstract terms.

Abstract Accounting vs. Practical Abstractions

Another commonly held view is that accounting researchers operate in a world of abstractions whilst practitioners have to operate in the world of the specific and the concrete. Once again I would like to challenge such a sharp contrast. Although the two groups may now make quite different appeals to the general and the abstract, a great deal of accounting abstraction pragmatically emerged from the conduct of accounting practice.

The continued advance of accounting practice has resulted in a whole series of concerns with the ability to talk accounting as well as merely to do it. The professionalisation of the craft was particularly influential in this respect. To further the education of new entrants into the professional cadre, accounting practice came to be enshrined in abstract texts and manuals (Crawford, 1984). Examinations had to be conducted to test the aspiring entrants' ability to think and write accounting (see Hoskin and Macve, 1986). Professional concerns with the adequacy, uniformity and legitimacy of practice gave further impetus to the generalised abstraction of accounting from the specific and often highly contingent contexts in which it was practiced. As of yet, the history of the development of an accounting discourse remains to be written. But I think that it is possible to delineate some of the significant benchmarks along the route. In addition to the mobilising concerns already noted, it would be illuminating to analyse the history of a professionalised accounting's deliberations with the agencies of the State, increasingly the media, and those other bodies claiming an interest in the accounting domain. How did the rationales for accounting practice come to be articulated and changed in the midst of concerns with the legal requirement for audit, the uses made of economic calculation in both the regulatory and revenue raising activities of the State, the granting of a legal monopoly to a specific group of economic calculators and, more recently, the adequacy of the financial reporting of the corporate sector? Quite specific consideration also needs to be given to those cases where abstract notions of the accounting possible seemingly had (or almost had) an influential impact on the nature of accounting in practice. How, for instance, did conceptions of depreciation and, more recently, inflation accounting come to be brought to bear on accounting practice? What issues, interests and discursive developments furthered their advance? Just how did an abstract discursive domain of accounting seeingly mingle into, as well as arise out of, the practice of the craft? And how are these interrelationships developing in an era when specialised institutions such as the Accounting Standards Committee and the Financial Accounting Standards Board have been established in the name of practice for the discursive development of quite abstract notions of accounting?

Fig.1 - The Relationship between Accounting Discourse and Accounting Pracice

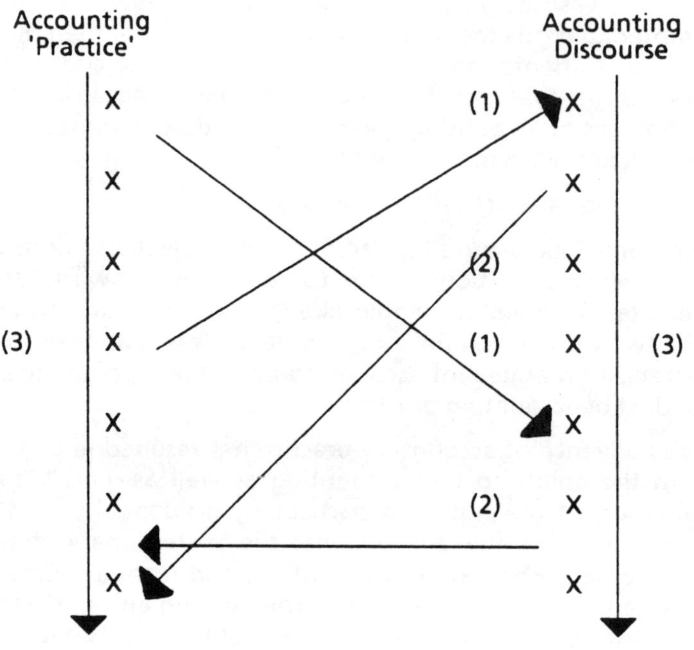

Although much remains to be known of the process of accounting abstraction, it nevertheless is useful to conceive of an interrelationship between the realms of the practical and the discursive as shown in Fig.1. Such a pictorial representation of what is undoubtedly a very complex process is quite obviously not without major limitations (see also Burchell et al, 1980, footnote 2, p.8), not least because the practice of accounting cannot be dissociated so readily from a discursive representation of it. However the figure nevertheless usefully alludes to: (1) the process of abstraction from the sphere of accounting practice, (2) the ability of practice to be reformulated and even reformed in the name of abstract discursive representations of it; and (3) the partial autonomies of the discursive and practical domains. In both the worlds of the scholarly and the practical a wide array of issues, problems, discourses and theories which have no a priori relationship to accounting can be and repeatedly are (as I illustrate in this work and elsewhere) brought to bear on the discursive representation of accounting (Burchell et al, 1985). Indeed it is because the two dimensions of the practical and the discursive can exist independently of one another that accounting discourse can be changed in the name of what accounting currently is not. And, on occasions, such seemingly alien abstractions also can be brought to bear on the practice of accounting, resulting, thereby, in accounting in practice also becoming what it was not (Hopwood, 1983b; 1987).

For the purpose of the present argument it is important to acknowledge the long-standing contribution which a practical accounting and its practitioners have made to the development of an abstract accounting discourse. In historical terms, I would want to argue that the contribution of accounting researchers is a much more recent and modest one. Of course to so point out the prior claims of the practitioners is not to say that the guardians of practice relish all the fruits of their own accomplishments! Quite obviously that is a different matter, not least at a time when practitioners have continued to create institutions which consume, further propagate and themselves give rise to partially autonomous accounting abstractions which have an ambiguous relationship to the practical conduct of their craft. As elsewhere, accounting practitioners are now starting to realise that the consequences of actions can be very different from those which entered into their original justifications (for a specific discussion of this see Burchell et al, 1985).

Accounting Change: Progressive or Otherwise?

The majority of both accounting practitioners and researchers share a conception of the generally progressive nature of accounting change. Rather than being seen as being buffeted around by the pressures of circumstances and the dominant interests of the day, the practice of accounting is regarded as having improved, and improved for the benefit of all rather than for any particular interests which its changing nature might be orientated toward furthering.

Such a conception of accounting change itself incorporates a poorly articulated view of accounting knowledge as well as its practice. To some, accounting has been able to learn the lessons of its own practice. It has been possible to reflect upon and abstract from the contingencies of particular circumstances in order to incorporate the lessons of history into the present functioning of accounting. Although rarely so expressed, an active interchange between the abstract and the practical is recognised and valued, albeit one that is little understood and seen by some as more legitimately taking place in the office than in the academy. Others attach even greater significance to the role which knowledge has played, and still remains to play, in accounting change. Although also recognising the ebbs and flows of circumstance which impact on accounting at any particular point in time, accounting nevertheless is seen as being in the process of becoming what it should be. An abstract notion of the accounting possible plays a pervasive role in evaluations of accounting in practice. Detached from many of the contingencies and pressures of the organisational and social functioning of the craft, such conceptions of accounting are based on a presumed understanding of the essential, even if at times frustrated, technical roles which accounting plays in economic life. However partial and imperfect such an understanding may be, from such a stance abstract ideas of accounting are recognised as being able to play an active and legitimate role in the process of accounting change. Their detachment from the specifics of organisational and social actions is not seen as constraining their practical role. Even those with a practical interest can so attribute to abstract notions of accounting a role in guiding the practice of the craft.

Both sides of the progressive intertwining of the practical and the abstract are usually grounded in a neutral technical view of accounting in action. Rather than facilitating particular interests (be they defined in individual, group or social terms), directly or indirectly, intentionally or otherwise, accounting is seen as playing a more general facilitative role. Abstracted from the particular organisational and social pressures which give rise to accounting innovations and change, such a view enables those in both the academy and practice who share it to ignore any consideration of the wider social origins and consequences of both accounting in action and the abstract notions of a general welfare enhancing economic rationality which are seen as being embedded within it. Accounting is indeed seen as having got better for the benefit of all.

The Practical Interest in Abstract Accounting

By now it should be clear that I think accounting abstractions not only can be, but are, implicated in practical processes of accounting change. Knowledge, as such, is not something that stands outside of accounting. It is incorporated not only in the institutionalised and professionalised practice of the craft but also into the multitude of processess through which accounting has been and still is being evaluated, changed and reformed in the name of notions of its potential that are not necessarily well articulated as part of the practical functioning of the craft and that often bear only a partial relationship to those pressures that change the craft.

Knowledge therefore is not something that needs to be imposed upon accounting. Be it of an experiential nature or, more importantly in the present context, subject, as research knowledge is, to external processes of validation and legitimation, there can be active practical interests in at least particular forms of accounting knowledge. Indeed, as I already have implied, for some time I have been conscious of a growing interest. Practical accounting seemingly is in the process of becoming a research consumer. Although still often masked by denunciations of the impractical nature of academic theories, of the need for accounting scholars to communicate better to their lay peers and, at times, of the almost inseparable gap between the two, there nevertheless are signs of a very real practical interest in even quite scholarly research, particularly in the context of the management of the accounting standard process[5].

Why should this be so? To understand some of the processes at work it is necessary to reflect on a number of aspects of the institutional nature of the accountancy profession (albeit in this discussion only those of the UK and USA), the pressures on it to change and, thereafter, on some of the roles which knowledge and particularly externally legitimated forms of knowledge can play[6].

THE ACCOUNTANCY PROFESSION IN ITS INSTITUTIONAL CONTEXT

A number of aspects of the institutional context of the accountancy profession are important for understanding the increasing interest in the role of abstract knowledge. In the following discussion particular emphasis is placed on four such factors:

(i) the axis of relationship between the institutions of a professionalised accounting and agencies of the State;

(ii) the organisations which have been created to manage the conflicts which arise on that axis;

(iii) the loose internal structure of the profession; and

(iv) the changing nature of the organisation of the professional firms which constitute the profession.

All too clearly there are other significant elements of the institutional network in which the accountancy profession is set which are important for appreciating the growth of an interest in accounting knowledge. The dynamics created by the fragmented nature of the British profession have been ignored even though they have a historical importance and even some contemporary significance (Willmott, 1986). The formation of interest and pressure groups around the standard setting process also has been ignored despite the fact that they provide valuable insights into the detailed processes of accounting regulation, the changing institutional forms and procedures of standard setting bodies and, in the context of the following discussion, some of the particular appeals that are made to knowledge (Watts and Zimmerman, 1979). Such a neglect should not be interpreted as implying the unimportance of the diverse constituents of the accountancy profession's institutional context, but merely that emphasis has been placed on delineating just a few of the significant elements and mobilising concerns.

The Accountancy Profession and the State

Conventional analyses of the relationship between the accountancy profession and agencies of the State emphasise the potential interventionist role of the State. Usually adopting a regulatory perspective, such analyses tend to conceive of the relationships in terms of a zero-sum game with phenomena being subject to either regulation by the State or the self-regulation of the profession. So conceived, the State has the potential to challenge and reduce the sphere of autonomy of the profession which is presumed to have resulted from the wider social recognition of its particular and valued knowledge, expertise and competence.

At any specific historical juncture such a perspective need not be too misleading. Ignoring those spheres where either ambiguity or discretion exist, it is possible to say what phenomena are subject to the control of which authority. Seen in such terms, there can be an axis of conflict between the profession and the State. Moreover, as is discussed later, many of the actors on the axis do conceive of the relationship in these terms, a not unimportant consideration when seeking to understand the processes and changes which such conflicts engender.

However, when seen in historical terms, such an understanding of the relationship between the profession and the State is far from adequate, suggesting, as it does, a moment of original professional independence followed by a subsequent history of State intervention and resistance to such intervention. For the accountancy profession, as for others (Felding and Portwood, 1980; Johnson, 1977), such a dream of original autonomy is far from the truth. Indeed the institutions of a professionalised accountancy were born amidst the administration of the bankruptcy and company laws of the State[7].

The professionalisation project so founded subsequently gained a legal
560 requirement for audit from the State and, at a later stage, a legal monopoly in its provision. Much of the subsequent activity of the profession has been engendered by the growing activities of the State, as is illustrated by the work undertaken in the areas of tax, business investigations and regulation, and more recently, the bringing to bear of economic calculations within the machinery of the State itself. So rather than professional status and autonomy being independent of the State, one requires a view of the State as being quite centrally implicated in the construction of today's conception of the accountancy profession and its powers, privileges and no doubt perquisites[8].

Just as the accountancy profession is not independent of the State in historical terms so, in turn, the State as we now know it is at least partially dependent on the profession. The consequences of the enabling roles served by a legitimate group of practitioners of economic calculation have yet to be investigated but I think that it is possible to point to their impact in important areas of tax administration, business regulation, the conduct of industrial relations and the internal administration of the State itself. Indeed in the latter area the accountancy profession is implicated in quite major attempts to change the nature of the British State away from being one that has had many of the attributes of a loosely coupled structure towards one that is more centrally, tightly and coherently managed in the name of economics and efficiency.

For the purpose of understanding the nature and functioning of the accountancy profession it therefore is important to emphasise the mutually constructive nature of its relationship with the State. The profession and its autonomy have emerged in the context of the formation and development of the State and, it, in turn, has played an integral role in the articulation of the State itself[9].

However, having such a view should not prevent us from recognising the very real conflicts that can arise on the axis between the profession and the State at any particular point in time, the significance of the images held of that axis by the members and officials of the professional bodies, and the strategies of resistance to some, at least, of what are seen to be the interventionist activities of the State.

A Loosely Coupled Profession

The accountancy profession has a loosely coupled structure (Weick, 1976). In the UK it is fragmented into a number of geographically and functionally specialised organisations and also tolerates some more direct competitive relationships between some of the constituent institutes. More importantly for the present argument, both in the UK and the USA the internal management structures of the professional organisations are poorly articulated. Significant power resides with the major audit firms rather than with the membership at large. Decision making can be influenced by the charisma and power of the elder statesmen (sic) of the profession, a small cadre of people who can be asked to play significant roles in times of crisis and stress. The basis for more managerial and bureaucratic control remains more rudimentarily developed and the professional institutes only exert rather loose surveillance and control over the main tasks of their membership, including that of auditing which provides the basis for their professional status. Despite more recent attempts to articulate standards of adequate audit work, the control of the core task of a professionalised accountancy remains highly decentralised. The specification, evaluation and reform of audit procedures still remains firmly in the control of the membership 561
of the relevant institutes in their capacity as participants in competitive professional partnerships. The upper echelons of the professional institutes have relatively few means for directly influencing the conduct of auditing and little or no legitimacy for doing so.

In recent years the audit profession has been subject to a great deal of change, however. In addition to responding collectively, or at least at a centralised level (the latter following from the loose coupling of the profession), to what have been seen as the interventionist policies of the State, the constituent professional firms themselves have been subject to increasing change. They have faced increased competitive pressures within the audit "business", a growing internationalisation of both their business and ownership and control structures, rapidly changing cost structures which have reflected the increased cost of training[10] and the increasing commitment that has been made to both the marketing of their services and their administrative coordination and control, a changing technological base and a more knowledge intensive task, and both the need and opportunity for a more strategic management of the composition and diversity of their product portfolio. The full ramifications of all these changes have yet to be realised. Already, however, there are very definite signs of an increasing centralisation of control within the larger audit firms in the profession as they adopt the bureaucratic management structures and control procedures characteristic of business firms operating in a competitive environment. Also, as is argued later, these changes are resulting in an enhanced awareness of both the task and the strategic relevance of forms of knowledge different from the more experiential varieties that have been utilised to date. Consideration even is being given to the use of more rigorous and extensive internal accounting controls!

The net result of these developments is an audit profession consisting of more centralised performance units which continue to operate in a loosely coupled professional context where the governing bodies have relatively few legitimate and effective bases for task control

The Development of Institutions on the State-Profession Axis

Despite the longer term symbiotic relationship between the State and the accountancy profession, at any particular moment in time the axis of relationship between the two can be subject to a great deal of tension and conflict. Questions can arise as to the appropriate locus of control over significant components of professional practice. The State can make, and certainly can be seen to make, interventionist acts vis-a-vis the conduct and regulation of the task activities of a professionalised accountancy. And because of this, strategies of professional resistance can be formulated and implemented, some of which can give rise to substantial organisational innovations in the professional accountancy institutional context.

Such pressures can be seen as accounting for the establishment of specialised bodies for the standardisation of the accounting rules used in enterprise reporting. In the USA, the Financial Accounting Standards Board was quite explicitly established to provide a mediating institution for the regulation of accounting which was located in neither the province of the profession nor of
562 the State. Arising out of the long standing tension between the SEC and the US accountancy profession (Zeff, 1972; Moran & Previts, 1984), the FASB was created to provide an institutional locus for the regulation of the accounting aspects of corporate reporting that could appeal to a legitimacy and authority wider than that of the institutions of a professionalised accountancy while still not being incorporated within the State itself. The related establishment of the then Accounting Standards Steering Committee had a not dissimilar origin, although without either the long standing history of State involvement and legislative responsibility in the area or the unfortunate experience of modified forms of professional control that were reflected in the US Accounting Principles Board (Zeff, 1972), the institutional developments in the UK could be based closer to the sources of professional authority, control and, one presumes, legitimacy.

Although there are such similarities between the institutional forms and foci of the standard setting bodies in the UK and the USA[11], this should not be seen as suggesting any obviousness about the particular institutional structures and their foci of attention which are developed in countries subject to some degree of conflict on the axis between the accounting profession and the State[12].

In the UK in particular, the focus of attention on the regulation of the accounting aspects of enterprise reporting was not implicit in the crisis of confidence in the state of professional accounting that emerged in the late 1960's. Although some of the accounting scandals did raise questions relating to the comparability and lack of standardisation of enterprise reporting practice and although these concerns were furthered both by the pressures of some influential industrialists and the prior US experiences, others of the so-called scandals could have been interpreted as raising questions about the adequacy of the audit function itself (also see Macve, 1983). If the latter interpretation had become the dominant one (through, for instance, a different perception and analysis on the part of the media), I suspect that the UK accountancy profession would have faced a much more serious crisis since it could have been asked to make substantial innovations in an area where its internal control structure and legitimacy for action was, and still is, weak. Indeed such an interpretation is reinforced by recent American developments where legal challenges have focused on the adequacy of audit procedures. As a result, innovations have been introduced, including the establishment of procedures for peer review and moves towards creating a basis for a heightened awareness of the formal content and legitimacy of the body of knowledge underlying auditing. In the UK, however, such a formulation of the problem did not occur and the profession was able to respond by innovating in an area where there were both domestic and external precedents for action (an important legitimising factor) and where it was less likely to face (at least immediate) internal challenges to its regulatory initiatives.

Still, however, bodies established on the axis between the State and the profession do face some very real difficulties in establishing a mandate for action that is accepted as legitimate by significant groups within their institutional network. Self regulation by the profession can still appeal to the legitimacy provided by professional expertise, perceived independence and status, although there is evidence of a longer term questioning of the bases of these sources of authority in many Western countries. Regulation by the State can appeal to the democratic mandate which is seen to underlie all governmental and quasi-governmental agencies, although once again there are signs of a growing ideological questioning of the authority of the State emanating from both the Right and the Left. However, intermediary bodies established between the profession and the State have no such present source of authority and legitimacy to which to appeal. Indeed when the commitment generated by the crises which resulted in their foundation starts to wane either by the passage of time or as a result of their own controversial activities, their legitimacy is even more problematic. It is in just such a context that research, as an externally validated and legitimated source of knowledge, is increasingly being appealed to as a source of authority. To the further examination of this I now turn.

THE RISE OF AN INTEREST IN KNOWLEDGE

The growth of interest in the role which knowledge can play in the accounting standard setting process has been more pronounced in the USA than in the UK. The FASB is more explicitly aiming to be independent of the institutes of the accountancy profession and so the latters' traditional sources of authority and legitimacy are not so readily available to it. Moreover, although the FASB has increasingly adopted many of the process characteristics of American federal government decision making, including its concern with a certain openness of the decision making process and allowing due process to be seen to be done, there are limits to the extent to which these accoutrements of the American State can provide a substantive basis for authority given the body's intermediary positioning on the axis between the profession and the State. So the question of the authority and legitimacy of the FASB has risen quite explicitly as an issue, fuelled no doubt by the more open process of challenging sources of authority that US legal and media practices stimulate. Also, compared with the UK, knowledge and appeals to research and science have a wider cultural potential to provide a legitimacy for action. A more widely educated business and professional elite, a legal system that attaches a greater authority to expert forms of reasoning, and a media and lobbying system that have histories of demanding a more open debate of the rationales, evidence and authority underlying action (what, in accounting, might be termed an account of accounting) have all provided an impetus for an interest in the role which externally validated knowledge can play in the construction of a legitimate basis for accounting authority. And I have few doubts that that impetus has been furthered by a quite genuine belief in the enabling and substantive rather than merely ritualistic roles of knowledge that is created by the American educational and social systems.

Interestingly, many related processes are at work in the larger individual firms of the US audit profession. Here, I suspect, the changing and increasingly centralised nature of the management structure of these firms is providing an enabling influence. As the market in audit services becomes increasingly competitive and subject to cost pressures, a more managerial interest is emerging in the role which more systematic knowledge might be able to play in both the control and restructuring of the audit work process and the development of differentiated forms of audit services. 'Brand X' auditing is now a very real phenomenon in which seemingly quite esoteric varieties of research knowledge already have had some influence on the development of
564 differentiated products in the audit market.

In addition to such competitive and business uses of knowledge, there is another major pressure towards the supplementing of traditional forms of experiential know-how in the US audit context. Externally validated forms of knowledge have been increasingly implicated in both the legal defence of the adequacy of audit practice and the anticipatory reform of that practice such that it is more likely to be more legally defensible. Still, however, despite such developments, many of the mysteries and indeterminancies of the audit black box remain and, I suspect, are likely to remain, given the roles that they play in the maintenance of the aura of a professional rather than a purely business craft. So research and knowledge are being appealed to by the larger auditing firms in much more general ways. Research into auditing is being funded on quite a significant scale (albeit sometimes with legal encouragement). Efforts are being made to make auditing into a legitimate focus for advanced study, teaching and research[13].

General, vague and ambiguous though such attempts may be, they still have the potential to create a different image, at least, and hopefully, a different basis of authority for a traditional craft which operates in a society which is showing some signs of demanding more modern bases for the authority and autonomy which that craft currently enjoys.

Technical and Strategic Knowledges

Returning to the increasing utilisation of research by accounting standard setting bodies, in order to further appreciate some of the factors behind this development it is useful to distinguish between three possible foci for such research:

(1) Research orientated towards providing an improved basis for the a priori analysis of accounting choices.

(2) Research orientated towards providing a basis for the ex post evaluation of an accounting choice.

(3) Research orientated towards providing a more general knowledge basis for accounting policy making.

Other things being equal, the more technical the research interest the more likely it is to focus on research of a type (1) and possibly a type (2) nature. A technical orientation also might result in type (3) research emerging from a cumulation of type (1) research initiatives rather than a more direct type (3) approach. In contrast, the more strategic and institutionally grounded is the research interest, the more likely it is to focus on research of a type (2) and certainly of a type (3) nature.

Type (1) research is seemingly attractive to those wishing to increase the technical rationality of specific accounting policy decisions. Interestingly, this is an area where the FASB, although devoting some resources to synthesising, understanding and appraising the present state of research and practical knowledge in some areas, has not invested a major share of its research resources. Certainly its efforts have not resulted in any major research innovations despite both the inadequate state of knowledge in many areas of enterprise reporting that have been and still are of direct interest to its operations and the potentially large research resources that are available. For although a search for an enhanced technical rationality might be able to delay the decision process and increase the authority and perceived objectivity of
specific accounting policy decisions once made, research of such a specificity has the potential to mingle poorly with the micro-politics of the individual decision making processes themselves, often removing rather than adding to the discretion that is available to the decision makers at the time the decisions are made. In addition, although an improved technical authority might be useful for increasing the legitimacy of decisions once made, even such appeals to type (1) research can become more problematic when the different interests and different states of knowledge operating on different decisions result in the need for seemingly incompatible technical rationalities (Watts and Zimmerman, 1979). Certainly such an incremental and highly specific research strategy is unlikely to result in a more coherent general type (3) research formulation that might be seen as being capable of endowing the whole accounting policy making process, rather than its separate component decisions, with a greater legitimacy and authority.

Seen in such terms, the fact that the major investment in research by the FASB has been devoted to types (2) and (3) research is interesting. Although type (2) evaluation research cannot and should not be dissociated from a genuine desire to learn from experience, it also has the potential to play other significant roles. It can provide a basis for relating to the development of an increasingly influential discourse of accounting policy making rather than technical accounting practice that places considerable emphasis on the economic, political and social consequences of accounting change (Zeff, 1978). Furthermore, type (2) evaluation research can relate more directly to the detailed decision processes surrounding particular accounting policy initiatives. Faced with both conflicting interests in accounting change and an uneasy institutional legitimacy for action, agreement often can only be reached for constrained periods of time (Hopwood, 1983a). In such circumstances the conflicting interests may be able to be persuaded to support a particular policy initiative if it can be seen as a temporary one and if an agreement is made to evaluate the consequences of its implementation. Anticipatory appeals to knowledge will be made; "given time, things will be worked out". A degree of openness thereby is introduced into the decision making process and the promise of an ex post type (2) evaluation research endeavour becomes a significant part of the decision process[14]. The FAS 33 and similar evaluation initiatives might well be seen in such terms.

The more general enabling role of type (3) research is more specifically orientated toward providing an institutional knowledge-based legitimacy for accounting policy making. Although such research might be able to infiltrate and guide the accounting policy making process in a context characterised by a technical rather than a political rationality, in the accounting world which is typified as much by the latter as the former rationality, such research does and must have an ambiguous relationship to the specifics of individual decisions. Rather than informing the particular, it is more concerned with communicating those generalities of accounting practice, both actual and desirable, that are seen to have a potential to create an aura of legitimacy for the specific decision making processes, enabling them to be grounded on appeals to either actual or potential knowledge and science as compared with either traditional notions of professional authority or the democratic mandate of the State. In this context, the wider external authority and validity of the knowledge claims are more
566 important than their specific technical enabling properties. The scope and comprehensiveness of the knowledge so generated are more important than the articulation of the means for its implementation. The aspirations of the research are as vital, if not more so, as the technical means for its integration with the specifics of current accounting practice. The fact that widely respected researchers, rather than just good or even excellent ones, are associated with the research process is significant, as are the appeals to the explicit imagery of rigorous and theoretical virtuosity. For there will be a quite explicit concern with the public nature of the research and the perceived potential that such forms of seemingly scientific advance have to relate to important accounting policy issues. Type (3) research invariably is not a private endeavour; openness and publicity are intimately associated with its foundation and progress.

The Conceptual Framework studies of the FASB have many of the characteristics of type (3) strategically orientated research. They are cast in general, even ambiguous, terms. The aspirations of the project are as yet more important than its specific technical enabling properties. Emphasis has been placed on scholarly respectability and the studies have been put into the public domain at an unusually early stage of their development. As McLuhan (McLuhan and Fiore, 1967) might have said, "the medium is (indeed) the message". Of course the Conceptual Framework research project has not exhibited all of the properties of the strategic nature of the type (3) research that have been described. That, however, might reflect the changing political context of the accountancy policy making process in the USA. The tension on the axis between the accounting profession and the State that resulted in the establishment of the FASB as an intermediary institution might no longer be so great. A change in political perspective has resulted in some diminution of the need to articulate a new authority for action. And a more cautious management of the issue agenda by the FASB itself also has diminished the potential for challenges to its authority; political learning has taken place. So, established to cope with circumstances past (although not necessarily ones that have disappeared completely and certainly not for ever), the FASB type (3) initiatives now operate at a somewhat lower level of strategic significance than might have been envisaged for them originally. That, however, does not detract from the basically institutional rather than technical nature of their aspirations - or potential.

Compared with the USA, relatively little use has been made of research, in the accounting policy making process in the UK, at least until relatively recently. Nevertheless there is now a respected Director of Accounting Research at the Institute of Chartered Accountants in England and Wales (who actively liaises with the Accounting Standards Committee), a prestigious Research Board at the same organisation, some elements of a programmatic, policy orientated approach to research and very definite signs of a growing awareness of the strategic potential of research in many of the other professional bodies that constitute the accounting profession in the UK. What is more, as in the USA, there are signs that more institutionally orientated type (2) and type (3) research is being furthered rather than the more technically enabling type (1) variety. So the American description is not inapplicable to the UK context, even though it reflects a much greater commitment to the powerful roles that knowledge can play.

The relative recency of a research based strategy for, or at least as a component
in, the management of the accounting policy making process in the UK is itself of 567
some interest for understanding the factors that influence the nature of the appeals that are or are not made to knowledge in the course of the practical development of accounting. A number of factors are of significance in this respect.

The accounting policy making body, the ASC, was itself established as being less independent of the accountancy profession. So legitimate appeals could still be made to traditional sources of authority, reducing, thereby, the urgency for the derivation of new ones. And in the UK, knowledge, as has already been said, is a less obvious source of authority and legitimacy for action. What is more, the debates on the one dominant issue on the accounting policy making agenda for most of the life of the ASC, namely inflation accounting, have been conducted in ways and over such a period of time that did not readily facilitate the extent to which the incorporation of more externally validated forms of generalised knowledge into them could endow any significant measure of authority and legitimacy. That is not to say that accounting research has not played an important role. It has. The almost alien language and categories of a research based interest in accounting have infused the rhetoric of pragmatic accounting deliberation. On occasions they have played quite significant roles by creating temporary resolutions of the debate via the introduction of new technical practices and subtleties. But such uses of research have been difficult to distinguish from the technical practice of accounting, utilised by particular interests at particular moments of time rather than endowing any more general authority to the policy discussions.

One reason for this is that accounting in general and inflation accounting in particular has been explicitly perceived and acted upon in the UK in terms that are much wider than are implicit in the conventional views that either accounting practitioners or researchers hold of their craft. At different stages in the inflation accounting debate the technical practice of accounting has been seen as an index of the professional propensity to innovate and "to look at the basics", as a variable in the regulation of tax policies, as a sign of creeping indexation in the context of macro-economic policy making and as an indicator of the revelation of the "true" state of the British manufacturing sector of relevance to the formulation of micro-economic industrial policies. The accountancy profession has not been able to maintain control of the discursive uses made of its craft and, what is more, the policy contexts in which inflation accounting has been debated have not been stable over time. Such factors have not served to increase the relevance of specifically commissioned research. Another factor operating in the same direction has been the fact that the public debates of inflation accounting in the UK have made quite explicit appeals to the role which accounting change can play in the politics of surplus declaration in the corporate sector. Such debates have taken place within the corporate sector itself between different industrial and commercial groups, and, in the early days at least, over the strategic significance of accounting in the management of industrial relations. More recently, the State has made appeals to the possibilities which different forms of economic calculation might play in its management of the nationalised sector (Wells, 1984). One result of such deliberations is that an ever present backcloth to the inflation accounting debate in the UK has been a potential for the practice of accounting adjustment to be seen in terms of both its political and economic consequences. Finally, a not insignificant component of the British inflation accounting debate has stemmed from the loose coupling of the accountancy profession itself. With challenges to the relevance of inflation accounting emanating from within the profession appealing to its technical complexity and theoretical pretentiousness, appeals could less usefully be made to the authority of an abstract research based knowledge.

Still, there are now some signs of a growing interest in the policy relevance of externally validated forms of accounting knowledge, albeit that they are far from fully institutionalised or stable. Although British accounting standards setting has not as yet experienced any really significant challenge to its legitimacy, tensions operating on its institutional axis with the State are ever present, not least in the mind of some of the officers and elder statesmen of the profession. Indeed there already are instances where appeals have been made to knowledge when threats to professional authority have been perceived as possible. Anticipating a critical government sponsored report on inflation accounting, the ASC invested in that peculiarly British vehicle of committee research which resulted in The Corporate Report (Stamp, 1985), an attempt to outline some of the possible implications for corporate reporting of a change in the social and political environment (Burchell et al, 1985). When, however, the anticipated threat to the profession's competence was perceived to be manageable through existing institutions, the report was treated with indifference. And although no Conceptual Framework study was initiated in the UK, at the time of a more intense questioning of the accounting standard setting project, the ASC invited an academic to investigate the potential for the UK of the American research in the area (Macve, 1981)[15].

Once again, however, the commissioning of the report was to prove more significant than its publication. However that same period of concern with the profession's mandate for accounting regulation did result in some external interests being incorporated into the governance structure of the ASC and a move towards acknowledging the potential role that knowledge can play by the appointment of a Director of Research. As it happened, these steps were taken before the profession had realised the implications of the changed political climate in the UK for the reduction of the pressures to which it had become so accustomed on its axis of relationship with the State. Still, however, questions of professional autonomy, power and accountability remain on the political agenda, all be they expressed in very different ways, and for the time being, at least, the profession cannot ignore the potential for its authority and bases of expertise to be discussed in the context of the wider consideration of the appropriate means of regulation of the capital markets.

The UK therefore now also has a basis for a professional interest in accounting research. Emergent from institutional pressures not dissimilar from those prevailing in the USA, the research interest already has focused on questions of a more strategic rather than purely technical relevance. It is, however, far too early to predict either the path of future development or the consequences of these initiatives in a cultural context where knowledge has traditionally had a more ambiguous role to play.

CONCLUSION

The primary aim of the above discussion has been to point to the complex and changing nature of the relationship between accounting practice and accounting research. Although there are many differences between members of the academic and practitioner communities, the view of a significant gap between them grossly oversimplifies the current state of affairs. Much of today's accounting practice has been infused and changed by abstract notions of the accounting possible and desirable, albeit ones that so far have tended to be developed in the office rather than in the academy. And more recently, there have been signs of a growing interest by practitioners in the roles that can be served by externally validated and legitimated forms of research. Faced with such tendencies, it is not useful to simply polarise the practical and the scholarly. The increasing knowledge intensity of accounting practices needs to be recognised much more explicitly.

The arguments that have been presented have emphasised the strategic rather than the technical roles of research knowledge. Rather than radically changing the accounting craft, there has been a tendency for externally legitimated forms of knowledge to be called upon to serve more institutional roles. Accounting research is becoming implicated in the construction of rationales for accounting action, in the discourses which emerge on the axis between the institutions of the accountancy profession and agencies of the State, and in the articulation of a conception of accounting practice that is more compatible with the requirements of a modern rational society. Over time, some of these changes might well infiltrate and change the actual practice of the accounting craft. For the time being, however, it is important to note the specific institutional origins of the emerging interest in accounting research, the externally rather than internally orientated roles which it is called upon to play, and the loose, indeed ambiguous relationship that such interests in research have to the detailed functioning of the accounting craft.

Such a particular interest in research itself reflects wider changes in the accounting profession. Although only loosely coupled to the technical practice of

accounting, increasingly the institutions of the profession nevertheless have been called upon to account for accounting and to regulate and control accounting. Crises in the corporate sector, changes in political perspectives and the growing involvement of economic calculation with the instrumental policies of the State have all created an awareness of both the significance and adequacy of the accounting craft. Accounting has been questioned, analysed and appraised as it never has before. Faced with such demands to account for itself, the profession increasingly has created centralised organisations, committees and task forces to anticipate, respond to and engage with the pressures that have been placed upon it. And it is these bodies that have started to articulate a demand for accounting research.Such newly emergent centralised components of the profession face several dilemmas. They have only weakly developed internal channels of influence and control. Despite the institutional changes which have occurred within the profession, it still remains a loosely coupled network of practitioners and firms, the members of which have considerable power of discretion. The new bodies therefore face very considerable problems in trying to engage in a detailed regulation and control of the accounting task. If anything, it is even in their own interest to deflect attention away from the core components of the task itself if their credibility and authority are not to be
570 questioned. In this respect it is interesting to reflect on how the newly emergent discourse of accounting regulation, what might indeed be called a discourse for accounting for accounting, almost exclusively focuses on accounting, and its involvement with enterprise reporting, rather than auditing, even though the latter still remains the core activity of a professionalised accountancy. Such difficulties also point to the equivocal legitimacy of such bodies, a legitimacy which is not only not taken for granted within the profession but also outside. So, aspiring to be perceived as authoritative and legitimate, such regulatory agencies have engaged in a number of adaptive strategies, including a growing interest in the role which externally validated forms of knowledge can play. Being both unable and unwilling to deal with the complexity and diversity of accounting and auditing as they are, they have shown increasing interest in formal, explicit and legitimate forms of knowledge. Rather than appealing to the historically complex and diverse ways in which the actual practices of accounting have been diffused to serve a multitude of often conflicting purposes, they have preferred to focus on simpler rationales for accounting change and reform which make an explicit appeal to modern conceptions of rational action.

By so engaging in the furtherance of a newly explicated rationale for accounting action, the agencies of a professionalised accounting have introduced new dynamics into accounting change. A new sphere of explicit accounting policy making has been created. New institutional interfaces have been created in the world of accounting action. New pressures have arisen for the practical to become intertwined with the abstract. And, as the increasing emphasis on the mythical "user" of accounting (a new person ready to board the Clapham Omnibus) demonstrates so well, new rationales are being articulated for the regulation, reform and furtherance of that action. All these represent interesting and indeed fascinating tendencies for the observer of the accounting craft. Not only are new dynamics being introduced but also those dynamics will almost invariably change accounting in ways that currently are unanticipated. For it is the fortune of most forgers of change to witness the creation of consequences which did not enter into their original justifications.

FOOTNOTES

[1] I am grateful for the helpful comments and suggestions provided by David Cooper, Hein Schreuder and the late Eddie Stamp. The ideas also have benefited from discussion at the Accounting Research Seminar of the University of Glasgow.

[2] In retrospect it is a pity that nearly all of the criticisms of the Watts and Zimmerman position have concentrated on their epistemological claims rather than the substance of their arguments (eg. Christenson, 1983; Schreuder, 1984; however see Lowe et al., 1983). This is not to imply that the resulting discussion has not been valuable. Exactly the opposite is the case. Nevertheless, it is surprising how little systematic attention has been given to their analysis of the interested nature of accounting knowledge utilisation. Although framed in quite particular epistemological terms and grounded in a narrow economistic logic, many of their ideas are nevertheless not incompatible with some of the views of even those who disparage them.

[3] 'The man (sic) on the Clapham Omnibus' is a British expression for the average person. He has had 1.3 wives and lives with his 2.2 children. Although non-existent, the world can be and is changed in his name, as also is illustrated by the
572 equally influential legal construct of the 'reasonable person' and the 'economic man' of economics.

[4] I can best summarise my own view of the traditional British interest in knowledge in terms of its perception as a consumption rather than an investment good. So frequently in the UK, knowledge tends to be seen as something which generates 'culture', a particular life style, rather than something which is a resource, a more proactive source of power. Although an analysis of the social utilisation of knowledge illustrates the very real practical relevance and significance of the latter alternative viewpoint, popular conceptions are still grounded in metaphors of consumption which are even propagated in the most ancient of universities. The net result is a cultured and educated elite who have a distrust of knowledge generation processes and a narrow conception of the role of the new. Also see Whitley (1986).

[5] The growing interest in research is by no means confined to the accounting standard setting domain however. In both the UK and the USA there have been practical interests in management accounting research. Although this also is an interesting area for investigation, this is not pursued in the present analysis.

[6] Although such an investigation goes well beyond the remit of the present analysis, the utilisation of knowledge could be seen as a central axis for examining the functioning of the accounting profession. Some even have analysed professions as occupational groupings which are subject to a high ratio of indeterminancy ir their knowledge and task structures (James and Peloille, 1970; also see Whitley, 1984). The application of such a perspective to the understanding of accounting requires further investigation however. Although the use of accounting knowledge in specific contexts is subject to some discretion, and thereby indeterminancy, much of the basic knowledge utilised in present professional accountancy is not of a very complex or advanced nature. Certainly the sheer size of the present profession in the UK and the USA, and in the UK, the relative recency of the transition from social to more educationally orientated criteria for recruitment suggest that the relevance of the

indeterminancy of the knowledge base may not have been as significant a factor behind the professional mobilisation of accountants as it was for other occupational groups which achieved professional status. If this is so, more detailed consideration might be given to the role which the monopolisation of competence rather than the lack of specification of its substance played in the creation of the specialised institutes of a professionalised accountancy (Larson,1977; for an example of such an investigation see Loft, 1986). Such a perspective seemingly is more compatible with the focus of the following argument on the role which knowledge plays in the moderation of the relationship between the accounting profession and the State since the latter is the primary source of the profession's monopolisation of the private sector audit function. Other possible explanatory factors should not be ignored however. At least for the UK, attention needs to be given to the changing exphasis placed by accountants on social versus meritocratic skills (Macdonald, 1984; 1985) and the implications for professional mobilisation and expansion of the traditional British preference for the generalist rather than the expert (see footnote 3). All these arguments point to the very real need for a much more substantial investigation of the functioning and control of knowledge in a professionalised accountancy.

[7] In the case of cost accountancy an important mobilising factor was the creation
of a new and legitimate cadre of economic calculators to enable the State's economic management and regulation of a wartime economy (Loft, 1986).

[8] Of course such a view of professional formation and functioning does not conform to the self-image propagated by the profession and held by the vast majority of its practitioners. In the present political context in the UK it is tempting to hypothesise that such a conflicting stance constitutes one basis for the attractiveness of the profession to the State: a group of loyal servants of the State who do not share a philosophy of Statism.

[9] I would not wish to imply that such processes are irreversible. Strategies for deregulating the capital market and increasing competition for professional services, both features of the present political context in the UK, could have the potential to considerably curtail professional autonomy.

[10] Interestingly, one response to the higher cost of professional training in the USA has been its partial externalisation onto the individual and the State by means of the establishment of specialised university Schools of Accountancy.

[11] There are also, of course, major differences between the two bodies. By emphasising the similarities at this stage in the argument I wish to stress the scenarios accompanying their foundation and their positioning on a particular institutional axis.

[12] Such a form of wording is intended to suggest a basis for distinguishing developments in the UK and the USA from those countries where the State is seen to have a legitimate and central role to play in the regulation of corporate financial accounting.

[13] For a discussion of the contrasting situation in the UK see Steele (1983) and Gwilliam (1984).

[14] Similar rationales provided a basis for the very earliest evaluation research endeavours in the US federal government when a provisional agreement was made to launch the post World War II Veteran's programmes.

[15] More recently a study similar in form to that of the US Conceptual Framework project has been commissioned, albeit with very modest resources.

REFERENCES

Abdel-Khalik, A.R., How Academic Research Should be Restructured for Impact, in J.W. Buckley, ed., *The Impact of Accounting Research on Policy and Practice* (Council of Arthur Young Professors, 1981).

Alexander, M.O., and Carsberg, B., Glory, Knock-Down Arguments, Impenetrability, in J.W. Buckley, ed., *The Impact of Accounting Research on Policy and Practice* (Council of Arthur Young Professors, 1981).

Beaver, W., Research on Monitoring the Accounting Standards Setting Process, in M. Bromwich and A.G. Hopwood, eds., *Accounting Standards Setting: An International Perspective* (Pitman, 1983).

Beaver, W., Griffin, P., and Landsman, W., The Incremental Information Content of Replacement Cost Earnings, *Journal of Accounting and Economics* (July, 1982), pp.15-39.

Burchell, S., Clubb, C., Hopwood, A.G., Hughes, J., and Nahapiet, J., The Role of Accounting in Organizations and Society, *Accounting, Organizations and Society* (1980), pp.5-27.

Burchell, S., Clubb, C., and Hopwood, A.G., Accounting in its Social Context:
Towards a History of Value Added in the United Kingdom, *Accounting,* 575
Organizations and Society (1985).

Callahan, R.E., *Education and the Cult of Efficiency* (University of Chicago Press, 1962).

Carsberg, B.V., and Page, M.J., eds., *Current Cost Accounting: The Benefits and the Costs* (Prentice Hall, 1984).

Carty, J., Accounting Standards: The Dismal Academic Contribution, *World Accounting Report* (April 2, 1982)

Christenson, C., The Methodology of Positive Accounting, *Accounting Review* (January, 1983), pp.1-22.

Coleman, R.J., and Petite, M., Accounting and Auditing Research and the European Community, in M. Bromwich and A.G. Hopwood, eds., *Accounting Standards Setting: An International Perspective* (Pitman, 1983).

Cooper, D., A Social and Organizational View of Management Accounting, in M. Bromwich and A.G. Hopwood, eds., *Essays in British Accounting Research* (Pitman, 1981).

Crawford, A., Cost Accounting, Work Control and the Development of Cost Accounting in Britain 1914-1925. Paper presented at the Congress of the European Accounting Association, St. Gallen, Switzerland, 1984.

Dyckman, T.R., and Zeff, S.A., Two Decades of the Journal of Accounting Research, *Journal of Accounting Research* (Spring, 1984), pp.225-297.

Felding, A.G., and Portwood, D., Professions and the State - Towards a Typology of Bureaucratic Professions, *Sociological Review* (1980), pp.23-53.

Flint, D., and Shaw, J., Accounting Research from the Perspective of Practice, in M. Bromwich and A.G. Hopwood, eds., *Essays in British Accounting Research* (Pitman, 1983).

Gwilliam, D.R., Current Developments in United Kingdom Auditing Research, in H.F. Stettler and N.A. Ford, eds., *Auditing Symposium VII: Proceedings of the 1984 Touche Ross/University of Kansas Symposium on Auditing Problems* (Univeristy of Kansas, 1984), pp.133-157.

Hays, S., *Conservation and the Gospel of Efficiency* (Harvard University Press, 1959).

Hopwood, A.G., On Trying to Account for Accounting, in M. Bromwich and A.G. Hopwood, eds., *Accounting Standards Setting: An International Perspective* (Pitman, 1983a).

Hopwood, A.G., On Trying to Study Accounting in the Contexts in Which it Operates, *Accounting, Organizations and Society* (1983b), pp.287-305.

Hopwood, A.G., Accounting and the Pursuit of Efficiency, in A.G. Hopwood and C. Tomkins, eds., *Issues in Public Sector Accounting* (Phillip Allen, 1984).

Hopwood, A.G., The Archaeology of Accounting Systems, *Accounting, Organizations and Society* (1987), pp.207-234.

Hopwood, A.G., Accounting and the Pursuit of Society Interests, in A. Lowe and A. Puxty, eds., *Critical Perspectives on Management Controls* (Macmillan, forthcoming).

Hoskin, K., and Macve, R., Accounting and the Examination: A Genealogy of Disciplinary Power, *Accounting, Organizations and Society* (1986), pp.105-136.

Jamous, H., and Peliolle, B., Professions or Self-Perpetuating Systems? Changes in the French University-Hospital System, in J.A. Jackson, ed., *Professions and Professionalisation* (Cambridge University Press, 1970).

Johnson, T.J., What is to be Known?, *Economy and Society* (1977), pp.194-233.

Kaplan, R.S., The Impact of Management Accounting Research on Policy and Practice, in J.W. Buckley, ed., *The Impact of Accounting Research on Policy and Practice* (Council of Arthur Young Professors, 1981).

Kaplan, R.S., Measuring Manufacturing Performance: A New Challenge for Management Accounting Research, *The Accounting Review* (1983), pp.686-705.

Kinney, W.R., The Impact of Auditing Research on Policy and Practice, in J.W. Buckley, ed., *The Impact of Accounting Research on Policy and Practice* (Council of Arthur Young Professors, 1981).

Larson, M.S., *The Rise of Professionalism* (University of California Press, 1977).

Loft, A., Towards a Critical Understanding of Accounting: The Case of Cost Accounting in the UK, 1914-1925, *Accounting, Organizations and Society* (1986), pp. 137-169.

Lowe, E.A., Puxty, A.G., and Laughlin, R.C., Simple Theories for Complex Processes: Accounting Policy and the Market for Myopia, *Journal of Accounting and Public Policy* (1983), pp.19-42.

Macdonald, K.M., Professional Formation: The Case of Scottish Accountants, *British Journal of Sociology* (June, 1984), pp.174-189.

Macdonald, K., Occupational Registration: Status, Control and Monopoly. Paper presented at the Conference on Interdisciplinary Perspectives on Accounting, University of Manchester, 1985.

Macve, R.H., *A Conceptual Framework for Financial Accounting and Reporting: The Possibilities for an Agreed Structure* (Institute of Chartered Accountants in England and Wales, 1981).

Macve, R.H., The FASB's Conceptual Framework - Vision, Tool or Threat? Paper presented at the Arthur Young Professors' Round Table, May, 1983.

McLuhan, M., and Fiore, Q., *The Medium is the Message: An Inventory of Effects* (Bantam Books, 1967).

Moran, M., and Previts, G., The SEC and the Profession, 1934-84: The Realities of Self-Regulation, *Journal of Accountancy* (July, 1984), pp.68-80.

Santocki, J., Accounting Research Attitudes, *Management Accounting* (UK) (April, 1980), pp.20-27.

Schreuder, H., Positively, Normative (Accounting) Theories, in A.G. Hopwood and H. Schreuder, eds., *European Contributions to Accounting Reseach: The Achievements of the Last Decade* (Free University of Amsterdam Press, 1984).

Stacey, G., Audit Research - the Needs and Resources of Professional Firms, in A.G. Hopwood, M. Bromwich and J. Shaw, eds., *Auditing Research: Issues and Opportunities* (Pitman, 1982).

Stamp, E., The Politics of Professional Accounting Research: Some Personal Reflections, *Accounting, Organizations and Society* (1985), pp.111-123.

Steele, A., The Market for Publicly Subsidised Research in Auditing: A UK Perspective: Unpublished working paper. Department of Accounting and Finance, University of Lancaster, (1983).

Sterling, R.R., Accounting Research, Education and Practice, *The International Accountant* (March, 1974), pp.3-8.

Tinker, A.M., Towards a Political Economy of Accounting: An Empirical Illustration of the Cambridge Controversies, *Accounting, Organizations and Society* (1980), pp.147-160.

Tinker, A.M., Merino, B.D., and Neimark, M.D., The Normative Origins of Positive Theories: Ideology and Accounting Thought, *Accounting, Organizations and Society* (1982), pp.167-200.

Tomkins, C., and Groves, R., The Everyday Accountant and Researching His Reality, *Accounting, Organizations and Society* (1983), pp.361-374.

Tricker, R.J., *Research in Accounting: Purpose, Process and Potential* (University of Glasgow, 1978).

Tweedie, D., and Whittington, G., *The Debate on Inflation Accounting* (Cambridge University Press, 1984).

Watts, R.L., and Zimmerman, J.L., The Demand for and Supply of Accounting Theories: The Market for Excuses, *The Accounting Review* (April, 1979), pp.273-305.

Weick, K., Educational Organizations as Loosely Coupled Systems, *Administrative Science Quarterly* (March, 1976), pp.1-19.

Wells, M.C., A Revolution in Accounting Thought, *The Accounting Review* (July, 1976), pp.471-482.

Wells, M.C., *Current Cost Accounting and the Nationalised Industries: An Analysis and a Proposal* (University of Glasgow, School of Financial Studies, 1984).

Whitley, R., *The Intellectual and Social Organization of the Sciences* (Oxford: The Clarendon Press, 1984).

Whitley, R., The Transformation of Business Finance into Financial Economics: The Roles of Academic Expansion and Changes in US Capital Markets, *Accounting, Organizations and Society* (1986), pp.171-192.

Whittington, G., The Role of Research in Setting Accounting Standards: The Case of Inflation Accounting, in M. Bromwich and A.G. Hopwood, eds., *Accounting Standards Setting: An International Perspective* (Pitman, 1983a).

Whittington, G., *Inflation Accounting: An Introduction to the Debate* (Cambridge University Press, 1983b).

Willmott, H., Organizing the Profession: A Theoretical and Historical Examination of the Development of the Major Accountancy Bodies in the UK, *Accounting, Organizations and Society* (1986), pp.555-580.

Zeff, S.A., *Forging Accounting Principles in Five Countries: A History and an Analysis of Trends* (Stipes Publishing Company, 1972).

Zeff, S.A., The Rise of Economic Consequences, *The Journal of Accountancy* (December, 1978). pp.56-63.

Selected Editorial Pontifications

Accounting, Organizations and Society, Vol. 1, No. 1, pp. 1-4. Pergamon Press, 1976. Printed in Great Britain.

EDITORIAL

THE PATH AHEAD

Accounting has played a vital role in the development of modern society. To this day it remains the most important formal means of collecting, analysing and communicating information on the financial activities and performance of all forms of organization. And the terminology and underlying calculus of "profits", "costs" and "assets" continue to exert a profound impact on human consciousness and action.

Unfortunately, however, although recognized as important, all too often accounting has been seen as a rather static and purely technical phenomenon. Nothing could be further from the truth. The purposes, processes and techniques of accounting, its human, organizational and social roles, and the way in which the resulting information is used have never been static. The economic distinctions drawn by accountants and the methods which they use are themselves creations of the human intellect and reflect social as well as economic evaluations. They have evolved, and continue to evolve, in relation to changes in the economic, social, technological and political environments of organizations.

ACCOUNTING IN TRANSITION

The recent inflationary era has provided one vivid illustration of the pressure for accounting methods to respond, and in some countries, including the United Kingdom, respond quite quickly, to an important change in the economic environment. But at the present time there are other equally significant economic, social and institutional changes which already are starting to have important implications for the development of accounting thought and practice.

Current social, environmental and political developments are focussing increasing attention on the wider accountability of organizations. A great deal of the consequent work on social accounting, social reporting and social auditing may be embryonic. Even the terminology is still imprecise and the present approaches reflect a diverse array of social and political values ranging all the way from the radical fringe to those held by the managerial elite. However, as Bowman & Haire, and Epstein, Flamholtz & McDonough discuss in their articles, these developments represent one way in which the accountant already is striving to respond to emerging social pressures for more comprehensive information on organizational activities and performance. Birnberg & Gandhi reflect related concerns. And, as Ullmann points out, the awareness of ecological problems is drawing attention to the necessity of developing accounting systems which can report on an organization's use of scarce resources. Energy and environmental accounting may well remain undeveloped arts, but increasingly they are being discussed at both the governmental and corporate level.

The debate on accountability is only one of the many issues which is focussing attention on the assumptions which accounting makes of social institutions, power structures and values. As our institutions and values change, these assumptions will become more evident. But in the process we can expect pressures for the processes and practices of accounting to change along with them.

Indeed this is already starting to happen. The disclosure of accounting information to employees and trade unions, for example, is now codified in the legislation of a growing number of industrial nations. Financial analysis already is starting to play a different role in collective bargaining in some countries. Also the increasing concentration of resources in the public sector is resulting in an awareness of the need for fundamental innovation and research in governmental accounting. But other changes are undoubtedly ahead of us. Already, for instance, in Europe interest is being expressed in the possibility of measuring the economic performance of business enterprises in terms of added value and reporting on the distribution of the added value amongst all the stakeholders in the enterprise. In this instance the technical aspects of changing from recognizing wages as a cost to seeing them as a distribution of surplus shade into insignificance beside the conceptual change in what might be implied for the relationships between the various parties involved in the enterprise.

Similarly, as has been so vividly documented in the writings of corporate and accounting historians, the design and use of accounting systems within the organization also respond to evolving circumstances. Market pressures, technological innovations, the increasing scale of activity and the consequent changes in management structures provided the impetus for developments in past eras. Indeed there is still a search for strategies which can improve the way in which accounting systems adapt to such changes. After engaging the energies of practitioners for so long, the problem is now starting to attract the interest of the research community. But even before accountants have responded to these pressures, new developments are apace. The full implications of advances in information technology and the growing internationalization of business have still to be digested. And the complexity of modern organizations provides an ever more important rationale for perspectives which can help to integrate the function and design of accounting systems with other approaches to information processing and the overall management task.

Social pressures are also resulting in a growing interest in the design of information systems for self management and control. Traditionally the accounting perspective may well have emphasized control and evaluation rather than problem solving and decision making. But both managerial and employee expectations are changing and there is a need to consider and study the traditional relationships that have existed between accounting and organizational power, authority and reward structures. Alternative approaches do exist but we know little about their practical effect and so far there has been little incentive to either experiment or innovate. Times may be changing however. With experiments on job restructuring, autonomous working groups and industrial democracy underway in almost every industrial nation, there is now an awareness of the need for designing accounting systems which facilitate rather than frustrate such initiatives.

All the above developments provide a renewed urgency for understanding the way in which all forms of accounting information are actually used. Just how do investors assimilate and process financial reports? What effects are new approaches to accounting such as social accounting and human resource accounting likely to have? And how are budgets and financial plans formulated and used? What roles do they play in organizational functioning? When, for instance, do financial analyses of investment projects exert a significant impact on the allocation of organizational resources? And when are they merely rationalizations of past decisions? One could go on and on. At present all too much of our knowledge is experiential and, on occasions, even mythical. But with new developments apace and an even more sophisticated accounting technology there is a need to move beyond the experiential to delve into the processes through which accounting does in fact gain its social and organizational significance.

THE NEEDS FOR RESEARCH

Accounting is a responsive subject and research into accounting, when seen in this context, is an essential means of ensuring its adaptiveness to developing needs. Indeed research which can facilitate accounting developments is doubly important. Not only can it assist the processes and techniques of accounting to respond more rapidly to emerging economic, social and organizational circumstances, but also the resultant changes in accounting can often help to further the underlying changes. Information is rarely neutral. New approaches to accounting are quite capable of influencing attitudes and behaviours through the feedback of information into the decision making process.

Is research into the social, organizational and behavioural aspects of accounting capable of responding to the challenges which lie ahead? Certainly the citation analysis reported by Hofstedt provides a rather disturbing view of the state of the art of behavioural research on accounting. Contrasting the behavioural literature in accounting with the security price literature, Hofstedt portrays a field which is still in an early stage of development with fragmented studies and few signs of a coherent research tradition.

The past difference is hardly surprising however. The magnitude of the intellectual jump between accounting and the social and behavioural sciences is great compared with that required for the integration of economic and quantitative perspectives which provided the basis for the substantive body of security price research in accounting. In the latter case many accounting academicians already had a firm grounding in the necessary disciplines and the intellectual leadership in the new area was firmly established in a few key university institutions. This was highly respectable research! The social and behavioural sciences, on the other hand, were less familiar to most accountants in terms of both the body of knowledge and the underlying values. And the integration of accounting and social perspectives was a very different endeavour than the integration of finance and accounting. Given the early choice of topics by accounting academicians, the resultant perspectives were often alien to the values of many social and behavioural scholars who preferred to forget the courtships which some of their predecessors had had with "the servants of power". As a result many of the early strivings into the unknown had to be undertaken without the intellectual support and assistance of colleagues in the relevant disciplines.

But there are encouraging signs of progress and I share Hofstedt's optimism for the future. A few areas of behavioural research on accounting are establishing a strong intellectual basis, and in the process, they are attracting the interest and involvement of scholars of the relevant social and behavioural sciences. Studies in the information processing area may well belong to this category. Albeit still controversial for many and strongly influenced by personal values, research on human resource accounting has moved forward, and in the process, is starting to stimulate the enquiries of other scholars who are now pursuing very different approaches to the underlying problem.

Even the substantial body of behavioural research on budgeting is now starting to display evident signs of progress. Early studies concentrated on the psychological and social psychological aspects. However by considering the organizational nature of the budgetary process later studies moved, albeit very slowly, towards providing a basis for organizational diagnosis, if not prescription. Perhaps more significantly, however, these later studies are now being replicated and extended in the U.S.A., Europe and elsewhere. We also have a series of studies of budgeting and resource allocation as a political process, although I fear that these are still very neglected by many accountants, and a few behavioural and organizational studies of the capital budgeting process. And more recently a number of independent studies have all moved towards the basis of what might be a contingent view of budgeting where the nature of the process and its effects depend on the organizational and environmental context in which the process operates.

There is growing interest in research on social accounting in Europe, the U.S.A., Japan and elsewhere. The increasing sophistication of accounting systems is itself providing an incentive for better understandings of the ways in which managers and employees actually use information. And there is a developing interest in studying the organization and activities of the accounting profession itself.

Progress could undoubtedly have been greater but the emerging directions of research may now allow, and hopefully encourage, more sustained research initiatives in the future.

There is now an urgent need for research which can provide a basis for seeing accounting as both a social and organizational phenomenon. More explicit consideration needs to be given to questions of power, influence and control. Even what might be the quite significant ritualistic role of many accounting systems needs to be recognized. And every opportunity should be taken to move beyond static forms of analysis to study the complexities of the evolving dynamic processes of accounting in action.

But before this can be done with any degree of confidence we need to move towards a more coherent research tradition where new developments can be seen as building on and extending prior foundations. I, at least, look forward to larger scale research projects which draw on a richer, wider and more rigorous array of research methodologies. But rigour and relevance should, and can, be seen as going together. So far the relationship between research and action has only been cautiously considered in this area. Increasingly, however, we need to see behavioural and social research as providing a basis for both diagnosis and prescription.

THE ROLE OF THE JOURNAL

Accounting, Organizations and Society exists not only to monitor these emerging developments but also to actively encourage new approaches and perspectives. Among many other topics, advances in social accounting for the use of scarce resources will be discussed alongside behavioural studies of how accounting information is actually used. Technical developments in areas such as human resource accounting will be reported. And the extension of financial reporting to employees, trade unions and other stakeholders will be both studied and debated. The more specific behavioural aspects of budgeting, capital investment appraisal and planning will be considered side by side with the development of organizational strategies for designing and using accounting systems. And inevitably in such an emergent area we can look forward with confidence to the development of new topics, approaches and areas for investigation and debate.

Articles will range from original theoretical and empirical contributions to reviews of the state-of-the-art in specific areas. The Biblioscene section will contain book reviews, short literature surveys, particularly of non-English language material, and specialized bibliographies. In addition, the Action Forum section of the journal aims to specifically emphasize the interplay between theory and practice. I hope to publish reports of new experiments and approaches, the process and politics of both research and implementation, and even unsolved practical problems. In this way the journal will seek to encourage a lively interchange between academicians and practitioners and hopefully accelerate an even more vital mutual dialogue.

The fact that researchers and practitioners now have a specialized forum for the publication of material on the behavioural, organizational and social aspects of accounting is itself indicative of an emerging maturity and significance. But more fundamental and exciting developments undoubtedly lie ahead. In stimulating these enquiries, reporting on the emerging perspectives, discoveries and the inevitable frustrations and disappointments, and helping to bring them all to the attention of a wider audience, *Accounting, Organizations and Society* has a challenging and valuable role to play.

Anthony G. Hopwood

Accounting, Organizations and Society, Vol. 1, No. 2-3, pp. 131-132. Pergamon Press, 1976. Printed in Great Britain

EDITORIAL

HUMAN RESOURCE ACCOUNTING

Human Resource Accounting has attracted an enormous amount of interest in a comparatively short period of time. Although many inquiries related to the behavioural and organizational aspects of accounting have developed in a rather hesitant manner, research, writings, enthusiasms and, to be honest, criticisms and disappointments have flourished in this one particular area. A diverse group of scholars, and increasingly practitioners, have been attracted to the topic and, as a result, there have been an equally diverse number of approaches, suggestions and criticisms. But in the midst of this almost frenzied array of activities and arguments at least some of the scholars have had the enthusiasm and commitment to create a substantive and cumulative body of knowledge.

Just why has interest in and research on Human Resource Accounting progressed at such a rate? Like in all other fields of human endeavour the role of individual personalities has been crucial. But however important individual energies may have been, I think that other more general factors have played a vital role. The original formulation of the organizational nature of the problem by Likert, and perhaps more importantly, its expression in accounting terms, captivated the imagination of a significant group of accounting academicians and practitioners. That this was done at a time when there was an increasing awareness of both the behavioural problems of accounting systems in particular and of more general changes in social values only contributed to the urgency of the debate.

Accountants, as well as interested observers from other social sciences, had for some time been all too well aware of the possible dysfunctional human consequences of many accounting systems in action. Conflicts and frustrations had been observed and nearly everyone who had been active in the field could point to undesirable decisions which had been taken in the light of accounting outcomes rather than more all embracing organizational needs. But the combined expression of these concerns with some initial thoughts on new ways in which enterprises might formally account for the human consequences of their activities played a vital role in attracting the interest of accounting scholars. For many this was a succinct and convincing articulation of a familiar although not unthreatening problem and, perhaps more significantly, a related and reasoned suggestion from a non accountant that one approach to a solution might take the form of an extension rather than a restriction of the focus of accounting systems. Indeed, in view of a number of previous comments on the general problem, the surprise, if not amazement, at the latter part of the argument might well have stimulated the energetic response. Perhaps equally significantly, at least at that early stage of the debate, the likely accounting developments were being discussed in terms that were not incompatible with existing practices. In retrospect the combination of ideas might be seen as powerful, even irresistable.

However, Human Resource Accounting has not been without its critics and at the present time at least the sceptics are most likely in a majority. Indeed as time passes some of the doubts are being more precisely reasoned and presented. Fundamental economic issues are being raised, although, to be fair, the relevance of many of the questions in this area extend far beyond this particular area into more traditional areas of accounting activity. Behavioural and organizational factors also are being considered but as a number of the articles in the present issue demonstrate, researchers in Human Resource Accounting are now moving towards investigating the impact which the new procedures are likely to have on attitudes and actions within the enterprise.

More fundamental ethical and even ideological

considerations lie immediately below the surface of many debates on the topic. With accounting being seen as a social process through which society, or more accurately, powerful groups in society, articulate their views of the significant, just what is implied by accounting for the human resource? Certainly Human Resource Accounting challenges very few, if any, prevailing ideologies or values. Should not, however, some have argued, we be more concerned with the development of resourceful humans than with the management of human resources? And increasingly, as the debate extends across ideological boundaries, some critics are beginning to point to the contrast between ideological systems which focus on the investment component of the human being and those that focus on the human component of investment.

Undoubtedly these questions, ranging all the way from issues relating to practical implementation to the cultural meaning of the calculations, will be debated in the forthcoming years. Because of this it is far too early a stage to provide a comprehensive assessment of either the conceptual or applied relevance of the ideas and practices. Too many practical, methodological, theoretical and even philosophical problems still have to be considered, let alone solved. Even the range of applicability of the underlying concepts and methods is still being considered as is demonstrated by the paper relating them to the context of current experiments orientated towards improving the quality of working life. There also have been far too few practical applications and even fewer comprehensive assessments of either the processes of designing and implementing or the personal and organizational consequences.

This issue of *Accounting, Organizations and Society* aims to present a collection of papers which reflect the range and variety of current approaches to Human Resource Accounting Differences, indeed striking comparisons, are immediately visible. But in a field of such potential significance and impact this is, I am convinced, a very healthy sign of vitality and progress.

In editing the issue I am grateful for the invaluable help and assistance of two co-editors, Eric Flamholtz and Edmond Marquès, and a large number of anonymous reviewers scattered across the continents.

Anthony G. Hopwood

Accounting, Organizations and Society, Vol. 1, No. 4, pp. 287–288. Pergamon Press, 1976. Printed in Great Britain.

EDITORIAL

Perhaps one of the most damaging weaknesses of the Western intellectual tradition has been the fragmentation of our perception and understanding of the world around us. Ever more specialised fields of intellectual endeavour have proliferated with amazing ease and speed, and although attempts have been made to pull them together through both interdisciplinary and problem oriented enquiries, many of these attempts have achieved only very partial success. As a result, at a time when the emerging complexities and interdependencies of the modern world place an ever greater premium on the need for a wider appreciation, our ability to provide this seems to be ever more distant.

These processes and problems are reflected in the study and practice of accounting as they are in other areas of human endeavour. Whilst our technical appreciations deepen, it would appear that we still lack those vital integrative understandings of the nature of accounting itself which are so necessary for guiding practice in today's demanding and uncertain environment. For despite the real progress that has undoubtedly been made, debates on the rationale of financial reporting become ever more intense and organizations in both the private and public sectors have even greater difficulty designing and implementing effective information policies.

In its early days the study of the behavioural and organizational aspects of accounting offered the potential of providing one wider, integrative appreciation of the organizational role of accounting. The pioneering writings of Carl Devine clearly reflected such a concern, as did the very very different enquiries undertaken by Chris Argyris and Herbert Simon and his colleagues. These scholars were striving in their own ways to see accounting processes as an integral part of organizational functioning.

Later scholars have carried this tradition forward. Wildavsky has studied in illuminating detail the political processes inherent in budgeting and planning. A rich description of the organizational processes surrounding investment decision making, including the final financial assessments, has been provided by Bower. Galbraith has formulated the outline of a way of seeing in information processing terms the relationships between accounting systems and other elements of organizational structure and process. And more recently, people like Donald Michael have shown the potential which a social psychological view of organizational and societal planning processes can offer.

However closely related these and many similar studies are to the consideration of accounting technologies and processes, in large part they have not been considered as part of the intellectual tradition underlying the study of the behavioural and organizational aspects of accounting. A great deal of the behavioural work on accounting focused on ever smaller problems at the very time that these wider perspectives continued to develop outside the accounting fraternity.

But the costs of this are real enough. We now have no systematic appreciation of the forces underlying the evolving role and practice of accounting that are so well documented in the works of corporate and economic historians. We recognise that environmental and organizational factors can shape how information is perceived and used, but we know very little about how such considerations have influenced the design of accounting systems. Indeed accountants have almost completely ignored the study of the processes that influence the design of their systems. Similarly we have very few insights into the organization of the accounting function itself. The early work of Herbert Simon and his colleagues is frequently cited but rarely pursued. And whilst researchers from other fields of interest have focused on the role that information plays in the political process within an organization, and how the political process affects the perceptions of and responses to information, such challenging and important issues have been ignored by most accounting scholars.

Rather than studying these wider questions, until recently the accounting academician has seemingly preferred to focus in a fragmented way on more detailed behavioural questions with little

consideration of their ongoing organizational and social context. In large part this reflects the pervasive impact that the very technology of accounting and its attendant power structures have had on intellectual vision and the recognition of fields for investigation and inquiry. Perhaps looking for immediate practical benefits, a great deal of the early behavioural work on accounting was orientated towards making the accounting technology more acceptable and influential. The technology itself, and so much of its immediate organizational context, was so often taken as given. But accounting techniques and structures are not given. They have evolved and continue to evolve, reflecting the pressures of their environment, emergent organizational missions and strategies, and those values which define the significant. By largely ignoring these wider issues
588 the behavioural and organizational study of accounting processes might well have limited its longer-term ability to contribute to the potential of accounting itself.

But enough of the past. There are now encouraging signs that research is slowly starting to broaden its vision and scope. Recent work on the behavioural aspects of budgeting have explicitly recognized the interplay of managerial and environmental factors. Investigations of the organizational circumstances that shape the design of accounting systems are now starting to map the complexities of the world of action. Yet again the organization of the accounting function is being studied. And particularly in the area of computerized information systems, consideration is being given to the nature of the design process itself.

The future content of *Accounting, Organizations and Society* undoubtedly will reflect these and other emerging concerns. And given that with this issue the journal's first year is complete, it is only appropriate to consider some of the hazards on the paths that we have already traversed and some of the sign posts to the paths that lie ahead.

Anthony G. Hopwood

Accounting, Organizations and Society, Vol. 2, No. 2, pp. 99–100. Pergamon Press, 1977. Printed in Great Britain.

EDITORIAL

> "The 'technical' question of forms of economic calculation and planning therefore opens up a field of investigations concerning the structure of the transitional economy and of the political, economic and ideological conditions of its transformation."
>
> B. Hindess, "Introduction" to C. Bettelheim, *Economic Calculation and Forms of Property* (Routledge & Kegan Paul, 1976).

Few fields of scholarly inquiry in accounting can have developed quite as rapidly as social accounting. From a few cautious inquiries undertaken a few years ago, studies of social accounting now have given rise to a vast array of articles, pamphlets, monographs, conference proceedings, edited collections, case studies and the social accounts themselves. And judging from the rate at which new material arrives on my desk, the expansion of the field is still taking place.

The interest in social accounting is also increasingly international in scope. On my shelves American Monographs sit side by side with volumes from France, Germany and the U.K. Publishers in France and Germany as well as the U.S. send me details of forthcoming books. The Commission des Opérations de Bourse in France, like the Securities and Exchange Commission in the U.S., has conducted its own inquiries. Professional accountancy bodies in the U.S. and the U.K. have issued reports which deal directly with the topic. Conference proceedings emanate from Belgium, France, Germany, the U.K. and the U.S. Pamphlets and reports also come from Canada, Japan and the Netherlands. And there are now a growing number of social accounts, audits and reports from France, Germany, the Netherlands, the U.K., the U.S. and more recently, Sweden.

The international diversity of the growing body of knowledge also illustrates the diverse agencies and factors that have stimulated and sustained interest in the area. In France, where it is quite likely that there will be a legal requirement for companies to prepare a social report by the end of this year, developments have been influenced by the endeavours of governmental commissions and agencies and the pioneering efforts of a few groups of employers. With few exceptions, individual companies were slow to innovate, although they now appear to be preparing to catch up, and with most of the discussion focusing on the assessment of the internal social environment of the enterprise, the accountancy profession has remained quiet. In the U.S., on the other hand, the first significant steps were taken by corporate managers themselves as they responded to the articulation of a new social consciousness by action groups, students and religious organizations. However, consultants and academicians quickly started to develop the necessary perspectives and measurement technologies and the accountancy profession has itself entered the debate in not an insignificant way. The German approach was not dissimilar although in this case the corporate activities were more clearly orientated towards responding to the development of governmental social policies and requirements and, from what I can gather, as yet there is little evidence of any sustained interest by the accountancy profession. In the U.K., on the other hand, corporate activity has been very spaced indeed, although rumour has it that a few things are now starting to take place behind closed doors. But the accountancy profession has at least started to discuss the broader problem of how accounting might respond to social and political change and some consultancy firms have identified what might be greener pastures in the future. The major initiatives in the U.K. to date, however, have emanated from such independent groups as the Public Interest Research Centre and Counter Information Services.

Not too surprisingly the developments in social accounting are following rather different paths in the different countries. In some countries greater emphasis seems to have been placed on the role that social accounting might play in encouraging social debate whilst in others it appears to have been seen primarily as a way of responding to social debate. Also different emphases are being placed on reporting on the internal social environment of the enterprise as against its wider social and environmental impacts. And in some countries social accounting is seen as a phenomenon that might rest side by side with the traditional financial accounts. Debates in other countries, in contrast, seem to be stressing the need for a greater degree of integration and in a few of the European countries the debates on social accounting are taking place alongside a more fundamental consideration of the social bases of the financial accounts.

Such differences serve to illustrate the fact that amidst all the hectic rush to "do", far too little consideration has been given to what social accounting stands for and its possible implications for broader issues in accountancy thought and practice. Perhaps the time is still too early for such an undertaking. Certainly at present it is difficult to disentangle the fashions and fads, which undoubtedly are present, from those innovations which might represent a less temporary part of accountancy's meandering path of social adaptation and development. But the potentiality as well as the need for a wider view might well be illustrated by those same international differences. For they clearly show how social accounting developments have responded to the differing social institutions, power structures and prevailing ideologies of the various countries.

Social accounting, in this way, merely illustrates the social nature of accountancy thought and practice. For the purpose, processes and techniques of accounting and its human, organizational and social roles have never been static. They have evolved, and continue to evolve in relation to changes in the social and political as well as economic and technological environments of organizations.

Fortunately research is slowly beginning to focus on questions relating to the social context of accounting development. The derivation of financial accounting standards is, for instance, now being studied as a process that is influenced by social and political circumstances as well as the search for economic "truth". Other research is starting to explore the role that accounting might play in influencing the social as well as economic consciousness of organizational participants. And accounting historians are starting to recognize the potential role that they might play in the development of organizational, social and intellectual history. But a lot more is needed before we even start to have a basis for deriving appreciations *of* accounting, that see accounting in context, rather than appreciations *in* accounting, where the context is taken as given. That, however, should be our goal.

Anthony G. Hopwood

Accounting, Organizations and Society, Vol. 2, No. 4, pp. 277–278. Pergamon Press, 1977. Printed in Great Britain.

EDITORIAL

The differences between accounting as promulgated in our textbooks and consulting manuals and accounting as practised, are indeed great. In the texts, effort is devoted to standardizing what is practised, searching in the process for the commonalities and points of agreement. But accounting in practice, in contrast, has responded and still does respond to the circumstances where it is applied.

Pressures from the external environment provide incentives for accounting change and innovation. Organizations search for financial information systems that complement the shifting demands of management structures and patterns of responsibilities. Differences in capital or labour intensiveness also influence the scope of managerial direction, what therefore is problematic, and hence managerial and other participant demands for information.

The evolving patterns of accounting thought a partially outlined in the writings of corporate and accounting historians. They provide insights into how the emerging competitive pressures in the early days of the industrial revolution provided the incentive for innovations in cost accounting. The origins of many of today's management accounting procedures are related to managerial attempts to maintain the integration and regularity of the increasingly large and diverse enterprises that started to emerge towards the end of the nineteenth century. And historical research also illustrates how changing patterns of social organization and control, and the related sets of values and ideologies, have influenced the development of accounting practices. For accounting has not only sought to map the economic implications of organizational decisions but also to present this information in ways that are meaningful in terms of the prevailing social as well as economic relationships and prevailing beliefs about accountability and distributive justice.

Accounting as currently practised, and its historical development, highlight the evolutionary and contingent nature of the subject in a way that is invariably absent from the manuals of received knowledge. Rather than being static and purely technocratic, accounting has had, and hopefully still has, the potential of being a responsive and adaptive calculative technology that can relate to and facilitate broader processes of enterprise and social development.

Such an evolutionary perspective raises many issues that are particularly salient at the present time. It encourages us to consider the institutional processes that can both facilitate and constrain the development of accounting. It might even point to the desirability of considering the impact that the professionalization of the accounting craft, and later governmental or regulatory standardization, had on the adaptability of the technology. The relationship of accounting to organizational power structures, and the attendent pressures to maintain the organizational status quo in terms of the preservation of existing organizational relationships, languages of discourse and ways of defining the scope of the problematic, also need further inquiry in this respect.

It might, however, be too easy to focus on the institutional and other forces that might be constraining the development of accounting at present, even though there might be growing incongruities between accounting practice and the patterns of economic and social development. For such incongruities themselves provide a basis for experiment and change.

And experiments there are. Such "spontaneous initiatives", as Charles Medawar termed them in a recent discussion, are increasingly evident throughout the accounting domain. Inflationary pressures have resulted in a questioning of traditional approaches to costing and budgeting, as well as income measurement. Not only have the more obvious components of accounting systems, both internal and external, been examined and changed, but also those equally essential aspects of the systems that provide the essential organizational linkages also have been re-examined. Reporting frequencies, levels of aggregation and modes of preparation and presentation have also responded to the changing nature of the economic environment.

The increasing uncertainties of the business

environment are also encouraging accountants and their managerial colleagues, to reconsider the role of accounting systems in planning and strategy formulation. What might have been acceptable in times of continued growth, is not necessarily relevant in today's environment. For the days of accounting "answer machines" are no longer with us: the need is for ways of facilitating managerial and organizational learning. As a consequence, some organizations, at least, are now starting to grapple with the problem of how they can consciously manage the information resource, rather than merely implement the bodies of received wisdom, and manage it in a way that is flexible and adaptive.

There is also evidence that accounting is starting to respond to wider social and political changes. Academicians are still exploring the basic rudi-
592 ments of new paradigms for accounting that might explicitly consider different patterns of social relationships and changing values, but an increasing number of organizations are actually having to start to experiment in this new and difficult domain. Questions relating to the possibilities of and approaches to disclosing financial information to employees and trade unions are being investigated. Designs for accounting systems in different organizational settings are being considered. The means for economically evaluating new methods of work organization, of facilitating the operation of autonomous working groups and of accounting for more broadly defined socio-economic ends are all starting to be explored. And, as the Social Report prepared for the Swedish Fortia Group (published in this issue) illustrates, a wide variety of experiments in accounting to social reporting are now underway.

So many of these experiments, or preliminary meanderings into the realm of the unknown, as we might prefer to call them, are tentative and inprecise. Mistakes and false leads are bound to be made. But nevertheless, like the other managerial attempts to relate accounting systems to changing organizational circumstances, they illustrate in a live and real way the developmental nature of accounting practice.

Unfortunately, research paradigms are presently unable to grapple with the issues raised by such a developmental perspective. Sadly, we lack even the outlines of a contingent view of the accounting domain and although issues such as social accounting and information disclosure are now being examined with increasing vigour, the essential social nature of all accounting remains hardly recognized and certainly under-researched.

The hope is that the moving nature of accounting practice, and the problems created by the application of static knowledge in changing circumstances, might themselves provide the incentive for enquiry and research. For it is precisely in those circumstances that there is a need for new knowledge, perspectives and technologies. And accounting research at least claims to be interested in providing these.

Anthony G. Hopwood

Accounting, Organizations and Society, Vol. 3, No. 2, pp. 93–95. Pergamon Press, 1978. Printed in Great Britain

EDITORIAL

ACCOUNTING RESEARCH AND THE WORLD OF ACTION

The relationship between research and practice should be of vital concern to all interested in the behavioural and social aspects of accounting. By their very nature it would appear that inquiries in these areas should be concerned with accounting in action; with how accounting systems do and do not function, with the factors that shape the form that they take and the influence which they have, with the circumstances which promote or constrain the effectiveness of the accounting function, and even with the bases for designing alternative forms of accounting.

Indeed some studies have tried to provide a basis for understanding, if not directly improving, the design, operation and use of accounting systems. And a few inquiries have claimed to have a more direct relationship to the improvement of practice either by focussing on rather precise pragmatic issues or by consciously striving to derive and articulate a more systematic basis for action.

However, despite the possibilities of inquiries such as these, the literature on the behavioural, organizational and social aspects of accounting tends to be noted for the absence rather than the presence of any systematic consideration of the relationship between research and practice. Such issues also all too rarely enter into research presentations and discussions. Even empirical, organizationally based research is sparce, and although such studies might be somewhat more prevalent than they used to be, rather amazingly they are far from being a firmly established part of the research tradition in the area. Furthermore there is little or no tradition of action research in accounting. We have few studies of accounting changes in organizations, of the factors that induced them, of the nature of the design and implementation processes and of their organizational impacts, and however much such studies might be considered as a substantive part of a design orientated discipline, such as accounting, we have hardly any examples of changes jointly designed and monitored by researchers and practitioners.

The absence of such studies is surprising to colleagues in other management and social science disciplines. Surely, they so frequently claim, studies of this type would and should constitute the essence of accounting research. Be that as it may, however, they are not.a prevalent mode of behavioural and organizational research. Interesting and important as it might be to ponder on the many and complex reasons for this, such considerations are beyond the possibilities of this short note.

However there are signs that the relationship between research and practice is being considered more actively and urgently in the organizational area of accounting, as in other areas of accounting and indeed in many other areas of management and social science inquiry. Not only is there an emerging interest on the part of researchers themselves, who increasingly want to see their knowledge and insights applied, influencing in the process, design orientations and system changes, and hopefully, no doubt, the availability of research funds in an increasingly constrained environment, but there are also indications of interest from organizational interest groups, both at the enterprise and societal levels. The need to respond to social and institutional pressures, and the desire to adapt to the increasing rate of both organizational and environmental change, themselves stimulate an interest in new knowledge, insights and procedures.

If such pressures continue we can anticipate a great deal more attention being given to the interface between research and practice. How might research be made more responsive to practical problems? What institutional forms can best stimulate an active interchange? What methodological and epistemological problems, and opportunities, might more action orientated modes of research create? And what new insights might be needed into the conduct and even politics of the research process itself? For although it is easy to point to the need for and virtues of a greater relationship between research and practice, many real and difficult problems will have to be confronted if we are to achieve this end.

For one thing, the immediate interest of practitioners is often in sharply focussed technical level research. How can they formulate an accounting standard in one particular area? How should they adjust capital budgeting procedures to allow for inflation? What, indeed, is the way in which inflation should enter into the regular costing and budgeting processes of the enterprise? And how might they overcome lower management resistance to the imposition of tighter financial controls? One could go on and on delineating such issues for they constitute the very substance of the professional nature of the accounting craft. However, as real and important as such problems might be for the conduct of accounting practice, it is an open question as to how they might provide the focus for accounting research, often lying, as they do, at the far developmental end of the spectrum of knowledge.

Certainly one wonders whether accounting research insights and skills are capable of adequately responding to the complexities of what constitutes a solution in an organizational setting. Depending, as it invariably does, on a complex interplay between the articulation of new insights and the grounding of these in the technical, managerial and even political circumstances of a particular organization or other arena of action, it is far from obvious what role new technical insights in isolation, be they research based or not, can and do play. At this stage it would appear that understanding the pragmatic processes of problem definition and solution in the accounting area is itself a significant challenge to the research community, for without this the researcher is in danger of serving as a rather detached, but hopefully high level, technician rather than as a person with an explicit understanding of the accounting process that goes substantially beyond what is currently implicit in practice.

The derivation of such descriptive appreciations of accounting in action and the process of accounting change might not be welcomed by many practitioners however. Whilst there might be demands for technical assistance there are few, if any, signs of interest in studies which question the organizational and social roles served by accounting information, the negotiated and political nature of technical accounting solutions and the way in which design options are constrained and shaped. For such studies *of* accounting, rather than *in* accounting, where accounting itself is regarded as a problematic organizational and social process influenced by, and in turn influencing many vital elements of the wider context in which it operates, are quite obviously capable of challenging the status quo by providing a basis on which to question what has not been questioned and what some would prefer not to be questioned. So whilst attempts to gain such insights might constitute an important aspect of more practically orientated research, it is far from obvious whether they will meet current practitioner demands.

Clearly the definition of research problems is a far more complex issue than is presumed in so many of the simplistic discussions of the relationship between research and practice. Not only can problems be more or less tightly defined, by researchers or practitioners, and more or less negotiable, but also the very definition of a problem incorporates, implicitly or otherwise, prior perspectives and interests which themselves may need to be articulated in the research process, however challenging or threatening this may be.

From what point of view is something problematic? Is it equally problematic from alternative perspectives? If not, why not and what might this say about the research context? And even if something is seen as problematic, just why should anyone be interested in research? What new knowledge are they interested in, what roles might it serve and, of equal importance, what role for the researchers is presumed? Indeed, one might also ask what role might the associated recognition of a present lack of knowledge also serve?

Questions such as these have been investigated seriously in some other areas of social science. Studies in the history of science, ideas and social and economic institutions not only show that they are issues of substance, requiring enormous scholarship and continued research, but also that they provide a vital context from which to consider the complexities of the relationship between research and practice and the role played by social interests, values and ideologies, institutional forms and power structures.

Unfortunately, such appreciations are sadly lacking in the accounting area. In the main, accounting historians, numerous as they might be, have tended to focus on documenting the flow of technical developments *per se* rather than on providing a basis for a social and ideological understanding of accounting. And other social scientists and historians have tended in the past to ignore the potentialities and richness of the accounting domain. However there are a few encouraging signs of change. A few social and economic historians and students of the history of ideas are starting to enquire into the ways in which different societies at different periods of time have tried to articulate their views of the significant in accounting systems; scholars of the labour process are beginning to question the nature and impacts of management practices, including accounting; and some political economists are slowly starting to probe more fundamentally into the meaning of forms of economic calculation. Even accounting researchers themselves are now investigating some of the processes inherent in the development of practical knowledge, however controversial this might be.

Research into the social nature of accounting knowledge is highlighting the importance of factors which rarely enter into the more superficial case for a closer relationship between research and practice. The institutional forms in which pressures for new knowledge arise, the locus of power and the relative access to information and expertise, and the relationship between knowledge and social interests, values and ideologies are essential aspects of the social as distinct from technical nature of the research process. Although, as yet, rarely discussed and researched, such factors none the less exert their influence on that interplay between research and practice which provides the basis for so much of the search for what is new and novel.

Some of the current social and political pressures for change are likely to increase the salience of issues such as these. Indeed, in Europe at least, many are now questioning the automatic presumption that accounting and accounting research are there to serve the interests of the managerial class and the professional power structure. Work orientated towards public policy and trade union and employee interests is slowly but surely progressing. And in the USA recent deliberations on the public role of accounting and the potentialities of accounting regulation also illustrate the selectivity with which research is both used and commissioned by the divergent interests in the debate. Examples such as these, and one could cite others, point to the emerging complexities of the relationship between research and practice in societies which are now explicitly recognised to be at the very least of a pluralistic nature.

Naturally many more issues could be, and need to be, considered for this is both an important and neglected area of concern. In this short discussion only a very superficial glimpse has been taken at some elements of the research process, the variety of the relationships which it does, can and might have to action, and some of the forces which influence and constrain the development of new insights and ideas. No consideration has been given to the equally significant methodological questions raised by applied and active research. However, limited though the discussion has been, hopefully it has illustrated that if there are to be more extensive discussions of the interface between accounting research and accounting practice, which seems highly likely, then there is an urgent need for accounting academicians, possibly with the help and advice of other social scientists, to gain a surer understanding of the complexities involved and the issues at stake.

Anthony G. Hopwood

Accounting, Organizations and Society, Vol. 4, No. 1/2, pp. 1–2.

EDITORIAL

Recently I have become ever more aware of a rather paradoxical situation concerning those substantive areas of accounting which *Accounting, Organizations and Society* seeks to cover. Whilst at no time before has there been such a seemingly receptive audience for social, organizational and behavioural understandings of accounting, substantive research in these areas remains in an uncertain state.

The interest in the social and human dimensions of accounting stems from many sources. At one level the explicit recognition by both professional and academic commentators of the negotiated nature of the accounting domain has encouraged a renewed series of debates. The legitimacy of those who seek to influence the accounting craft and the social and institutional processes through which accounting changes eventually emerge are now being considered. Rather than the social in accounting being confined to some seemingly esoteric new accountings, accounting itself is now starting to be seen as a social phenomenon, albeit one that is little understood. As this happens the traditional search for accounting truth is starting to be complemented by analyses of the factors which make accounting what it is rather than what it might be. More interest is being shown in historical understandings of accounting. Consideration is being given to the ways in which different social interests relate to accounting. And even those accounting theoreticians who have relied for their insights on understandings derived from neoclassical economics are slowly rejecting at least some of their unitary conceptions of the accounting craft as they start to analyse the ways in which accountings emanate from the interplay of a diverse array of actors with diverse and often changing interests.

An explicit recognition of the social and organizational bases of accounting thought and practice has also stemmed from the pressures for accounting to respond to changing social and political circumstances. Interests in wider forms of enterprise accountability and requirements to disclose information to new constituents, including, in Europe at least, employees and trade unions, have resulted in a new importance being given to questions of information presentation, interpretation and use and the mechanisms for accounting change. Moreover some members of the labour movement are now themselves questioning the prevailing conventional wisdom of enterprise level economic calculation. Pointing to its basis in particular economic interests, they are at least starting to suggest the possibility if not the actuality of forms of accounting which rest on very different socio-political presumptions.

Within individual enterprises questions relating to the organizational and behavioural aspects of accounting are no less meaningful. The explosion of information processing which occurred in the 1960s and early 1970s is now being considered in a slightly more detached way. Whilst many can still be impressed by the sophisticated technical advances that took place, others are equally aware of the mismatch between information provision and use. At least some commentators are beginning to ask more fundamental questions about the design of management information and control systems, including accounting systems, about the suitability of particular systems for particular organizational circumstances and about the relationship between the presumptions of economic rationality which are built into so many of today's systems and the norms and practices of managerial behaviour. With a lot of this questioning there is a willingness to acknowledge the significance of organizational and behavioural factors. Indeed for some of the commentators these are no longer regarded as appealing cosmetics which can be used to complement a given technical structure. With increasing frequency they are beginning to be recognized as key factors in system design, implementation and operation, and as this happens, there is emerging a more genuine interest in the state of knowledge in the area. Just what do we know about the behavioural and organizational aspects of the problem is a question that is being articulated with increasing frequency.

Past research endeavours have provided some understandings in these areas of current concern. Slowly the social nature of accounting practice is being not only recognized but also investigated and more consideration is being given to the institutional processes which give rise to accounting change. The pressures for accounting to respond to new social and political circumstances have also stimulated work on the possibility for new accountings and new forms of accounting disclosure. Although initially many thought that these were problems which could continue to be dealt with in technical isolation, increasing consideration is being given to both the broader social context in which such changes are embedded and the organizational and behavioural factors which contribute to their effectiveness. And the past decade or so of work on the behavioural aspects of accounting has indeed provided some insights into the factors which influence the use which is made of accounting information, the ways in which budgeting, capital budgeting and planning systems function in practice, the variety of organizational roles which these and other accounting systems serve and the ways in which wider organizational circumstances influence and constrain the possibilities for system design.

Nonetheless one cannot help to be impressed by the enormous gap between what is known and what we would like to know. Of course the area of investigation is a relatively new one and our expectations ought to be modest at this stage in its development. Moreover the areas of concern are ones of great complexity, requiring insights into the ways in which accounting systems arise from and intersect with other complex areas of organizational and social functioning. However despite such real difficulties, I still think that it is fair to say that research on the social, organizational and behavioural aspects of accounting has been characterized by an unwillingness to wander into many areas of seemingly great significance and a fragmentation of effort which is unusual in other areas of social enquiry.

Why should this be the case? For one thing, there has been a tendency for scholars working in the area to proceed from their attachment to the current accounting mission, often searching for understandings within accounting rather than appreciations of accounting. Wanting to overcome the resistance to accounting change or to improve the effectiveness with which current accounting information is used, psychological and social psychological rather than organizational and sociological aspects of problems have been emphasized. And such perspectives have been reinforced by both the institutional context in which research has been conducted and the reward structure of the academic world. For until recently psychological orientations to the study of business were much more firmly established in the business schools in which accounting research was pursued and very often enquiries grounded in these traditions could more readily produce a larger number of research reports that were regarded as methodologically acceptable by peers both within and without accounting. Other constraints on the social study of accounting have stemmed from the relative neglect of empirical inquiry and particularly of grounded observation. For what claims to be an eminently practical subject this is perhaps surprising. Be that as it may, much of the research in the area has proceeded from the application of the theoretical perspectives of other disciplines rather than more direct attempts to appreciate the complexity of accounting in action.

But such characteristics of the past should not constrain our awareness of the potential for future inquiry in the area. I think that there are now some signs of a wider diversity of perspectives being brought to bear on the social study of accounting. Earlier concerns with the psychological and social psychological determinants of the use of accounting information are being seen in a wider organizational context and even very recent attempts to improve the effectiveness of individual decision making are now seen to involve changes in factors which may have very different implications for the functioning of organizations than for the individuals within them. Moreover there is certainly a greater willingness to consider the social roles that accounting serves, the ways in which accounting institutions function and the variety of contributions which theoretical perspectives can make. As yet it would be wrong to point to a new vitality or mission for the area but one can nevertheless point to encouraging signs of change. As *Accounting, Organizations and Society* belatedly starts its fourth year of publication we can only hope that these will continue to flourish.

Anthony G. Hopwood

Accounting, Organizations and Society. Vol. 4, No. 3, pp. 145–147.

EDITORIAL

Recently I have become ever more aware of how little we know about the actual functioning of accounting systems in organizations. We certainly have had numerous pleas for either a behavioural or an organizational awareness of the accounting craft and a good number of scholarly reviews of the potential of past, present and emergent psychological and sociological insights. Moreover there is still a growing number of laboratory simulations of situations inspired by our prevailing understandings of the accounting mission. Yet as valuable as all these endeavours may have been in stimulating interest in the area, it has to be admitted that as yet we have precious few descriptions, let alone understandings of accounting systems as they operate in organizations.

Drawing on over two decades of scholarly effort, it is difficult to name more than a handful of organizationally based empirical investigations of the accounting craft. Moreover many of those which are available have been undertaken by organizational psychologists, sociologists, political scientists and industrial anthropologists rather than accounting scholars themselves, and perhaps because of this they are being incorporated only cautiously into the accounting corpus of knowledge. Where accounting academicians have tried to delve into understanding the complexities of accounting in action their studies have tended to focus on only a few aspects of the accounting craft. For a number of reasons, budgeting, and particularly the operation of participative processes in the budgetary context, has been singled out for special attention, with hardly any consideration being given to the functioning of other management control and reporting systems, to the use made of costing analyses, to those processes which constitute financial planning practices in organizations and to the role of financial appraisal in investment decision making.

Moreover there would appear to be few signs that the situation is changing. Whilst interest in the organizational and behavioural aspects of accounting is growing, a great deal of the scholarly writing in the area is still pointing to the potential of prevailing sociological and psychological insights rather than actually trying to realise that potential by empirical inquiry and analysis. And even where an empirical mode of investigation is adopted, there seems to be some tendency to rely from the very start on tools of indirect observation.

For some reason, the psychological laboratory remains peculiarly attractive to the accounting researcher in the USA. I do not want to belittle the role that laboratory research can play in accounting, let alone other areas of social investigation. Where we have a rather precise understanding of the variables operating in a particular context and of their main interrelationships, and when we seek to further our appreciation of the magnitude of the interrelationships and of secondary and interaction affects, laboratory methods may indeed have a role to play. But on the basis of our present appreciations of the ways in which accounting operates in an organizational setting, can we be so content with our understandings of the relevant concepts let alone variables that we can so readily proceed to a laboratory setting? Can we, for instance, presume that accounting information is used in such a rational, well structured decision context that simple, structured information processing exercises can provide us with insights into the ways in which accounting systems function in organizations rather than the ways in which human beings process information, be it accounting or not, in rather particular organizational contexts? On the basis of present understandings can we so readily dismiss or at least ignore the more symbolic roles which accounting plays in organizations, the more complex ways in which it might influence management consciousness and action, its relationship to the political processes which shape and constitute organizational life and to the articulation of mechanisms for achieving particular patterns of organizational (and indeed societal) control and influence? I think that at least a consideration of such issues should introduce some element of caution into our methodological choices. Apparently, however, such considerations are not as yet part of the research tradition in the accounting area.

Recently I had the opportunity of discussing

research interests and orientations with a number of young researchers interested in the organizational and behavioural aspects of accounting. There was no doubt in my mind that they could identify and structure problems of real significance and potential. But I was surprised by the extent to which that structuring, and indeed the subsequent methodological choices, had taken place without any attempt at least to expose themselves to the problem as it functions in actual organizations. Had they, I asked, tried to identify an organization in which they could observe their problem as it functioned in practice, if only for a few weeks before firming up the variable set and hypotheses on which their laboratory work would be based? Invariably, but fortunately not exclusively, the reply was made in the negative. All too apparently they had relied on those myths (which may or may not be useful) of the accounting craft which permeate our textbooks, on theoretical and empirical perspectives written up in organizational behaviour monographs and on their own intuitive views of what might (and on a few occasions, "what surely must") happen.

Similar problems are also detectable in a number of studies which have ventured into organizations in order to administer questionnaires. Such methodologies have many advantages. Recently, however, reviewers of several papers which have been submitted to the journal have commented on the obvious lack of prior investment in trying to understand the context of the research site or sites, the quite frequent tendency to see such research in terms of the replication of the administration of existing research instruments which were often developed to explore very different problems from the perspective of very different theoretical frameworks than those which are at least explicitly articulated in the introductory sections of the manuscripts submitted and the tendency for some researchers at least to rely on instruments which relate to organizational appreciations which have since been criticised, if not superceded, in their own parent disciplines. In some cases the reviewers have wondered why the researchers have not tried to exploit more fully the research opportunities which appear to be open to them. With access to organizations available and with managers and other employees being willing to devote at least some of their time to facilitating the research endeavour, why haven't the researchers tried to delve further into the organizational context in which the accounting systems they seek to study function?

All too clearly the lack of a tradition of organizationally grounded research in accounting suggests that a number of constraining circumstances must be at work. Some of these have been suggested, if not discussed, in previous editorials. Behavioural and organizational inquiry in accounting has been influenced more by the traditions and perspectives of pyschology than sociology, political science and anthropology. Emphasis has been placed on the rigor and sophistication of the research methodologies rather than on the formulation and analysis of research questions and perspectives. The reward structure of the academic community has encouraged low risk, short term research rather than more open ended and risky inquiry. Behavioural researchers themselves have also tended to want to explore issues which appear to be readily compatible with the existing conceptions of the accounting mission and its potential rather than question what has not been questioned, avoiding, thereby, any possibility of problematising in the process what has not been, and what may not want to be, problematic. And even where researchers have tried to delve into the complexities of accounting in action, access and the politics of organizational research have proved to be difficult. Organizations may be willing to accept technically orientated inquiries or more superficial organizational investigations, but it is far from obvious that they have encouraged or indeed are likely to encourage more questioning inquiries into the origins, nature and consequences of their management practices.

Nevertheless I think that the research community in accounting should at least become more conscious of what it has and has not explored and achieved, of the gaps in our understandings of the origins and operation of the accounting craft and of the ways in which methodological and epistemological preferences and choices are influenced and constrained by a wide range of social and institutional circumstances. Not that I would expect, a sudden rush of alternative investigations. For one thing, past constraints are hardly likely to erode so quickly. Their very success in the past points to their continuing role in the future. Moreover, I, at least, would like to preserve a healthy array of epistemological, theoretical and methodological alternatives. With so little known, it would be wrong to focus too much effort on one line of inquiry. And those researchers who do seek to reorientate their perspectives will most likely gain from the questioning, if not suspicion, that will inevitably greet their explorations and reports. I would, however, like to see at least some more research orientated towards describing and understanding accounting systems in action. For without it, I feel, the behavioural and organizational study of accounting will increasingly exist in a void, within a world grounded on the myths of the accounting mission rather than the achievements of accounting in practice.

The topics which I have discussed in this editorial are substantive and important ones. All too obviously they are not ones on which there is a consensus view. Different people concerned with the development of our understandings of the organizational and behavioural aspects of accounting have arrived at very different conclusions. However such differences themselves point to the need for further consideration and debate. If you, as a reader of *Accounting, Organizations and Society*, would like to make a contribution to such a debate I would be very happy to set aside a section of a future issue of the journal for an exchange of views on a topic of such significance.

Anthony G. Hopwood

Accounting, Organizations and Society, Vol. 10, No. 1, pp. 1–2, 1985
Printed in Great Britain

0361–3682/85 $3.00+0.00
Pergamon Press Ltd

EDITORIAL

With this issue, *Accounting, Organizations and Society* is ten years old. From the perspective of today, those years have rushed by. What was once a new journal, the first of the specialist research journals in the accounting area, has gained acceptance, respectability and a certain vitality and style of its own. A regular forum now has been created for the dissemination and discussion of research on the behavioural, organizational and social aspects of accounting.

I would like to think that quite a lot has been achieved in the last ten years. The behavioural analysis of accounting has been shown to be a legitimate and fruitful area of investigation. Organizational and social understandings of the emergence and functioning of the accounting craft have been developed. The need for and epistemological bases of different approaches to accounting research have been not only discussed but also demonstrated by exemplars of sound research. More substantive links have been forged with underlying social science disciplines. Accounting also has been shown to be a discipline in transition, with pressures for it to change emanating not only from the spheres of the economic but also from organizational, social and political pressures.

Although the agenda remains an open one, *Accounting, Organizations and Society* has played a positive role in furthering a questioning of the nature, functioning and consequences of the accounting craft. Attempts have been made to examine accounting in terms other than those on which it normally is advanced. Some of the wider factors implicated in the emergence and development of accounting as we now know it have been specified and analysed. Consideration has been given to the mediating roles played by human cognitive processes. The means by which accounting becomes embedded in organizational processes and action at least have been outlined. Accounting, in the process, has been shown to be a discipline implicated in the wider fabric of organizational and social life. Cognitive, organizational and social understandings have been brought to bear on furthering our appreciation of not only what accounting now is but also some of the directions for its future development.

When seen in such terms, the "path ahead" for the journal which was outlined in the first issue has not been ignored.

Such progress has not always been easy to achieve. Although a great deal of enthusiasm and goodwill accompanied the establishment of *Accounting, Organizations and Society*, the journal then had to live through the leaner years when its existence was a fact but when it still had to earn the acceptance and respect which provided it with a regular flow of high quality papers. Those more difficult days are now well behind us, however. A distinctive and widely utilized new forum has been created. The achievements of the past have provided us with a viable basis for dealing with the continuing research agenda which is the future.

Looking ahead, much remains to be achieved. Although a more adequate basis has been created for serious, cumulative research on the cognitive, organizational and social aspects of accounting, the vast majority of the emergent perspectives need further exploration and elaboration. In particular, there remains a very real need for the new approaches to confront more explicitly the intricacies and complexities of accounting as it now is. Although it has been useful, indeed essential, to observe, analyse and interrogate accounting from perspectives suggestive of its human, organizational and social functioning, the task of accounting for the specifics of its actual emergence, operation, development and consequences remains an open one. The new research traditions have yet to penetrate into the workings of the world of accounting in action.

Accounting, Organizations and Society hopefully will be able to continue to provide a sympathetic forum both for such further explorations of accounting as it is and for considered appreciations of the possibilities for continued accounting change. To further such aspirations, the journal itself will be changing in the forthcoming years:

Recognising the continuing development of research in the areas which it seeks to advance, as from 1986 *Accounting, Organizations and Society* will be published six times a year rather than the present four. As an interim move in this direction, the page budget for 1985 has also been significantly increased.

A renewed emphasis will be given to research on the cognitive aspects of accounting. Recognising that this is an area where considerable developments have taken place in the last decade, *Accounting, Organizations and Society* will seek to provide a forum where further research developments in this area can be disseminated, discussed and appraised. To this end, a number of editorial and other changes will be announced shortly.

Further emphasis will be placed on relating cognitive, organizational and social analyses of accounting to substantive developments occuring in associated social science disciplines. The successful series of conferences sponsored by the journal will be continued in order to highlight the very real potential of such research relationships. In the more immediate future, forthcoming issues will include the papers presented at the 1981 conference.

With such developments in hand, the future for *Accounting, Organizations and Society* promises to be as busy and exciting as its first ten years.

No review of the development of the journal could be complete without acknowledging the tremendous help and support of those who have devoted so much effort to ensuring that *Accounting, Organizations and Society* is as it now is. The contributions of all members of the Editorial Board, both past and present, have been enormous. Their unfailing support, encouragement, wisdom and sheer expenditure of time have provided the essential basis for the editorial process. The journal has also benefited from the help given by a very large number of editorial advisors from all over the world. Their contribution has also been a most important one, as has that of the publishing, editorial and production staff of Pergamon Press. Finally, I would like to acknowledge the very special contributions made by Jake Birnberg, David Cooper and Eric Flamholtz. Jake was a party to the very earliest discussions on whether a new journal should be established. Both then and subsequently, he has been a constant source of help, advice, encouragement and good humour. David, now, with Jake, an Associate Editor of the journal, has served as a sounding board for editorial policy discussions. In innumerable meetings we have discussed editorial options and problems. His advice has always been considered and welcomed. Eric played a different role. However, by suggesting the possibility of the first conference to be jointly sponsored by the journal he initiated a series of events which have had an important influence on the journal's development.

Anthony G. Hopwood

Accounting, Organizations and Society, Vol. 12, No. 1, pp. 65–69, 1987.
Printed in Great Britain

0361–3682/87 $3.00+.00
Pergamon Journals Ltd

ACCOUNTING AND GENDER: AN INTRODUCTION

For some, accounting and gender might not appear to be the most obvious axis on which to advance the wider understanding of the social functioning of accounting. Although there is a growing recognition of the shifting sexual composition of the practitioners of the accounting craft and the partialities of the past which thereby are illuminated (Wescott & Seiler, 1986), the issues which such developments raise still tend to be seen by many as being understandable in terms of prevailing conceptions of the institutional functioning of accounting and its perceived organizational and social roles. From such a stance, there is little or no reason to radically change our appreciations of what might be at stake in the advance of the particular forms of economic rationality and calculation with which accounting is associated or their organizational and social embodiment. Others, however, are aware not only of wider questions which such changes in the accounting labour market might expose but also of the possibilities for a more penetrating examination of what might be at stake in the accounting function when perceived from the perspective of gender and an explicitly feminist perspective on organizational and social functioning. Accounting, from such a view, is not a mere technical phenomenon, but one that has the potential for having a reciprocal relationship with the wider societies in which we live. It both can be infused by and can potentially, at least, partially shape organizational and social values, concerns and modes of operation, and their consequences. From such a perspective, it becomes more important to examine questions relating to the focus of accounting, the particular rationalities and decision calculi which it furthers, the conceptions of organizational and social functioning which can be implicit within it and the specific social and institutional contexts in which the practice of the craft is embodied. Gender, from such a stance, represents a new but a nevertheless significant axis on which to conduct an examination of accounting in action. While it can certainly help to illuminate changes in the sexual composition of accountants, as a basis for the wider interrogation of accounting, a concern with gender also reflects quite different changes in both the intellectual development of accounting itself and some of the bases on which wider analyses are conducted and understandings gained of influential bodies of knowledge and organizational and social practices. A concern with accounting and gender so conceived can reflect a genuine concern with expanding the account which we currently have of accounting.

AN EXPANDING ACCOUNT OF ACCOUNTING

Accounting is coming to be perceived and analysed in a number of very different ways. Whilst the technical practice of the craft continues to be advanced on its own terms by both practitioners and academic researchers, increasing attention also is being given to the exploration of the wider significances of the accounting craft. Rather than unproblematically accepting what technical rationalities might be deemed to be implicit within accounting, increasingly research is moving towards exploring the wider economic, organizational, social and even political rationalities with which the organizational practice of the craft can be seen as being associated.

From some of the newer perspectives the techniques of the accountant's art can be seen in terms of their significance for the co-ordination and integration of the diverse activities of that hierarchically organized activity that is the enterprise, for the more effective mobilisation of a contracting system within the organization and for the consequent monitoring of the performance of organizational members. Differently conceived from other perspectives, accounting is now starting to be seen in terms of the creation of a selective pattern of organizational visibility, the infusing of organizational language and systems of meaning with a quite specific economic significance, the advancement of a logic of economic action and the propagation of a system of organizational power and control. Yet other perspectives are emphasizing the roles which accounting serves in the active construction of a particular image of organizational reality, in establishing an economic legitimacy for organizational action and in integrating the operations of the enterprise into a wider set of values and interests prevailing in the environment.

Although many such perspectives clearly differ from those conventionally articulated within accounting's own discourses, they nevertheless represent attempts to explore in a serious manner the wider significance and consequences of the accounting craft. Rather than accepting conventional views of the relationships which accounting might have to highly generalised notions of organizational efficiency and control, accounting researchers, as social scientists rather than accounting technicians, have come to question, interrogate and appraise accounting in terms of its organizational, economic and social functioning. Whilst in the past external bodies of knowledge were applied to accounting in order to improve and advance its perceived rationality and technical modes of operation, now they are increasingly being used to analyse and examine accounting, to ask questions of its rationales, origins and both its organizational and social interdependencies. Of course accounting, as an influential organizational and social practice and an area of professional and thereby privileged expertise, is not alone in this respect. Indeed other significant spheres of professional endeavour, such as the law (Hirst, 1979; Kay & Mott, 1982; Rueschmeyer, 1972; White, 1973), medicine (Friedson, 1970a, b; Illich, 1975; Kennedy, 1983; Navarro, 1976, 1978; Wright & Treacher, 1982) and psychiatry (Foucault, 1967; Laing, 1967; Rothman, 1971, 1980; Strauss *et al.*, 1964), have a longer history of wider examination and questioning, and some other organizational practices (Baritz 1960; Watson, 1977) and forms of calculative technology (Sutherland, 1984) also have been subjected to more social and economic scrutiny. Sometimes such examinations have reflected a genuine desire to improve our understanding of influential bodies of knowledge and social practices. In such a context there have been explorations of the complexities of origins, analyses of the shifting patterns of social roles which have been both served and created, and attempts to understand the more contemporary ways in which wider social and economic forces both infuse particular practices and are often, in turn, shaped by them. It is now possible to identify such trends in accounting research. In other instances the urge to re-examine has emerged for more pragmatic reasons. A practical will to know has resulted from concerns about both the actual and the possible consequences of influential social practices, not least when they are perceived to be both unanticipated and dysfunctional (Boudon, 1982). Spurred on by the desire to improve, investigations have explored the ecology of cause and effects surrounding particular organizational and social interventions and the nature of the wider contexts which influence eventual outcomes. Once again, such inquiries are now evident in accounting, both in relation to the complexities of financial accounting policy formulation and implementation and the actualities of management accounting regimes. A concern with the actual consequences of social practices and bodies of knowledge also has stimulated more critical analyses which seek to expose the interested nature of social practices, to identify the interests behind them and to illuminate the partiality of their consequences. Such concerns are now visible in an accounting context and it is to such ends that an analysis of accounting from the perspective of gender is now being articulated.

GENDER AND THE ANALYSIS OF SOCIAL PRACTICES AND BODIES OF KNOWLEDGE

Although the analysis of accounting from the

perspective of gender is novel, there is now a significant, although still controversial, tradition of scholarship which seeks to explore the functioning of influential social practices and bodies of knowledge from a feminist perspective. Perhaps not surprisingly, many of the concerns have focused on the practices and institutionalized knowledges that are most intimately related to the feminine condition. So medicine (Oakley, 1980, 1984; Roberts, 1981b) and biology (Birke, 1986; Harding, 1986) have been interrogated from the perspective of gender, as have the portrayal of women in conventional psycho-analytic discourses (Felman, 1985; Gallop, 1982; Irigaray, 1985a,b; Kofman, 1985) and the aesthetic depiction of the female body (Jardine, 1985; Rubin-Suleiman, 1986; Turner, 1984). Building on such explorations, a more general feminist scholarship has now emerged addressing, albeit in a still controversial manner, issues such as the nature of scientific inquiry (Gornick, 1983; Harding, 1986; Keller, 1985), epistemology (Glennon, 1979; Harding & Hintikka, 1983; Keokane *et al.*, 1981), psychology (Henley, 1985), the decision calculus of morality (Gilligan, 1982; Noddings, 1984), and the specific problems of feminist research (Bell & Roberts, 1984; Graham, 1984; Roberts, 1981a). In this wider context a feminist literature on the organization (Balsamo, 1985; Ferguson, 1984; Kanter, 1977; Knights & Willmott, 1986; Wolff, 1977) and management (Goffee & Scase, 1985; Stead, 1985) is emergent. However, although there are occasional recognitions of the powerful potential of calculative technologies (Deacon, 1985), accounting as such has yet to be subjected to a feminist analysis and critique.

The bases from which such an alternative analysis of accounting could be conducted are numerous. Perhaps most obviously, the sexual composition of the occupations associated with accounting, and changes within them, could provide one axis from which to interrogate accounting as it is. For it is widely known that until recently the professional echelons of accounting were a male preserve (Wescott & Seiler, 1986), with women confined to the clerical and secretarial functions. Of course, such distinctions were not confined to accounting. Rather, they accompanied the more general emergence of the office as a locus for abstract management at a distance from the direct physicality of the transformation process (Delgado, 1979). Indeed one of the aims of the early professionalisation projects in accounting might be seen in terms of a solidification of the demarcation between the gentlemanly professional and the mere (and usually female) clerk, where previously the distinction had been vague and ambiguous, if existent at all. The history of the resultant discrimination has yet to be recorded, however, as have the variations in the subsequent changes by place and hierarchical level, and the diverse rationales which might lie behind them. More generally conceived, recent advances in feminist scholarship might be able to make some contribution to the illumination of issues such as the processes of objectification implicit in the accounting art, the conceptions of order and regulation that infuse accounting rhetoric and the partiality of the particular modes of decision rationality towards which accounting is seen as being orientated.

The contributions which follow aim to initiate such a critical endeavour. Each, however, offers a quite specific analysis rather than providing any general overview of either the practical or the research issues at stake from the perspective of gender. Neimark & Tinker provide an historical analysis of the ideological role which corporate reports play in both reflecting and advancing particular images of women. Burrell & Crompton were commissioned both to comment on the Neimark & Tinker contribution and to reflect more generally on the issues at stake and the wider agenda that an analysis of accounting and gender might construct. Taken together the discussions are designed to provide some initial views of an as yet invisible element of accounting's functioning.

Anthony G. Hopwood

BIBLIOGRAPHY

Balsamo, A., Beyond Female as Variable: Constructing a Feminist Perspective on Organizational Analysis. A paper presented at the Conference on Critical Perspectives in Organizational Analysis, Baruch College, CUNY, 1985.

Baritz, L., *The Servants of Power: A History of the Use of Social Science in American Industry* (Wesleyan University Press, 1960).

Bell, C. & Roberts, H., *Social Researching: Politics, Problems, Practices* (Routledge & Kegan Paul, 1984).

Birke, L., *Women, Feminism and Biology* (Wheatsheaf, 1986).

Boudon, R., *The Unintended Consequences of Social Action* (Macmillan, 1982).

Deacon, D., Political Arithmetic: The Nineteenth-Century Australian Census and the Construction of the Dependent Woman, *Signs* (Autumn 1985) pp. 27–47.

Delgado, A., *The Enormous File: A Social History of the Office* (Murray, 1979).

Felman, S., *Waiting and Madness* (Cornell University Press, 1985).

Ferguson, K. E., *The Feminist Case Against Bureaucracy* (Temple University Press, 1984).

Foucault, M., *Madness and Civilisation: A History of Insanity in the Age of Reason* (Tavistock, 1967).

French, J., 'It's Great to have Someone to Talk to': The Ethics and Politics of Interviewing Women, in Bell, C. and Roberts, H. (eds.) *Social Researching: Politics, Problems, Practice* (Routledge & Kegan Paul, 1984).

Friedson, E., *Profession of Medicine: A Study of the Sociology of Applied Knowledge* (Dodd, Mead, 1970a).

Friedson, E., *Professional Dominance: The Structure of Medical Care* (Aldine-Atherton, 1970b).

Gallop, J., *The Daughter's Seduction: Feminism and Psychoanalysis* (Cornell University Press, 1982).

Gilligan, C., *In a Different Voice: Psychological Theory and Women's Development* (Harvard University Press, 1982).

Glennon, L. M., *Women and Dualism: A Sociology of Knowledge* (Longman, 1979).

Goffee, R. & Scase, R., *Women in Charge: The Experiences of Female Entrepreneurs* (George Allen & Unwin, 1985).

Gornick, V., *Women in Science: Portraits from a World in Transition* (Simion & Schuster, 1983).

Graham, H., Surveying through Stories, in Bell, C. and Roberts, H. (eds) *Social Researching: Politics, Problems, Practices* (Routledge & Kegan Paul, 1984).

Harding, S., *The Science Question in Feminism* (Cornell University Press, 1986).

Harding, S. & Hintikka, M. B., *Discovering Reality: Feminist Perspectives on Epistomology, Metaphysics, Methodology and Philosophy of Science* (Reidel, 1983).

Henley, N. M., Psychology and Gender, *Signs* (Autumn 1985) pp. 101–119.

Hirst, P., *On Law and Ideology* (Macmillan, 1979).

Illich, I., *Medical Nemesis: The Expropriation of Health* (Calder & Boyars, 1975).

Irigaray, L., *Speculum of the Other Woman* (Cornell University Press, 1985a).

Irigaray, L., *This Sex Which is Not One* (Cornell University Press, 1985b).

Jardine, A. A., *Gynesis: Configurations of Woman and Modernity* (Cornell University Press, 1985).

Kanter, R. M., *Men and Women of the Corporation* (Basic Books, 1977).

Kay, G., & Mott, J., *Political Order and the Law of Labour* (Macmillan, 1982).

Keller, E. F., *Reflections on Gender and Science* (Yale University Press, 1985).

Kennedy, I., *The Unmasking of Medicine: A Searching Look at Health Care Today* (Paladin, 1983).

Keohane, N. O., Rosaldo, M. Z. & Gelpi, B. C. (eds), *Feminist Theory: A Critique of Ideology* (University of Chicago Press, 1981).

Kofman, S., *The Enigma of Woman — Woman in Freud's Writings* (Cornell University Press, 1985).

Knights, D. & Willmott, H., *Gender and the Labour Process* (Gower, 1986).

Laing, R. D., *The Politics of Experience* (Ballantine Books, 1967).

Navarro, V., *Medicine Under Capitalism* (Croom Helm, 1976).

Navarro, V., *Class Struggle, the State and Medicine* (Martin Robertson, 1978).

Noddings, N., *Caring: A Feminist Approach to Ethics and Moral Education* (University of California Press, 1984).

Oakley, A., *Women Confined: Towards a Sociology of Childbirth* (Martin Robertson, 1980).

Oakley, A., *The Captured Womb: A History of Medical Care of Pregnant Women* (Blackwell, 1984).

Roberts, H. (ed.), *Doing Feminist Research* (Routledge and Kegan Paul, 1981a).

Roberts, H., Women and their Doctors: Power and Powerlessness in the Research Process, in Roberts, H. (ed.), *Doing Feminist Research* (Routledge & Kegan Paul, 1981b).

Rothman, D. J., *The Discovery of the Asylum: Social Order and Disorder in the New Republic* (Little, Brown, 1971).

Rothman, D. J., *Conscience and Convenience: The Asylum and its Alternatives in Progressive America* (Little, Brown, 1980).

Rubin-Suleiman, S. (ed.), *The Female Body in Western Culture: Contemporary Perspectives* (Harvard University Press, 1986).

Rueschmeyer, D., *Lawyers and their Society: A Comparative Study of the Legal Profession in Germany and the United States* (Harvard University Press, 1973).

Stead, B. A., *Women in Management* (Prentice-Hall, 1985).

Strauss, A. L., Schatzman, L., Bucher, R., Ehrlich, D., & Sabshin, M., *Psychiatric Ideologies and Institutions* (Free Press, 1964).

Sutherland, G., *Ability, Merit and Measurement: Mental Testing and English Education* (Oxford University Press, 1984).

Turner, B. S., *The Body and Society* (Blackwell, 1984).

Watson, T. J., *The Personnel Managers: A Study in the Sociology of Work and Employment* (Routledge & Kegan Paul, 1977).

Wescott, S. H. & Seiler, R. E., *Women in the Accounting Profession* (Markus Wiener, 1986).

White, J. B., *The Legal Imagination* (University of Chicago Press, 1973).

Wolff, J., Women in Organizations, in Clegg, S. and Dunkerley, D. (eds.) *Critical Issues in Organizations* (Routledge & Kegan Paul, 1977).

Wright, P. & Treacher, A., *The Problem of Medical Knowledge: Examining the Social Construction of Medicine* (Edinburgh University Press, 1982).

Accounting Books Published by Garland

NEW BOOKS

- *Altman, Edward I., *The Prediction of Corporate Bankruptcy: A Discriminant Analysis.*
  New York, 1988.

- Ashton, Robert H., ed. *The Evolution of Accounting Behavior Research: An Overview.*
  New York, 1984.

- Ashton, Robert H., ed. *Some Early Contributions to the Study of Audit Judgement.*
  New York, 1984.

- *Bodenhorn, Diran. *Economic Accounting.*
  New York, 1988.

---

* Included in the Garland series Foundations of Accounting
† Included in the Academy of Accounting Historians, Classics Series, Gary John Previt, ed.

■ *Bougen, Philip D. *Accounting and Industrial Relations: Some Historical Evidence on Their Interaction.*
New York, 1988.

■ Brief, Richard P., ed. *Corporate Financial Reporting and Analysis in the Early 1900s.*
New York, 1986.

■ Brief, Richard P., ed. *Depreciation and Capital Maintenance.*
New York, 1984.

■ Brief, Richard P., ed. *Estimating the Economic Rate of Return from Accounting Data.*
New York, 1986.

■ Brief, Richard P., ed. *Four Classics on the Theory of Double-Entry Bookkeeping.*
New York, 1982.

■ Chambers, R. J., and G. W. Dean, eds. *Chambers on Accounting.*
New York, 1986.
Volume I: Accounting, Management and Finance.
Volume II: Accounting Practice and Education.
Volume III: Accounting Theory and Research.
Volume IV: Price Variation Accounting.
Volume V: Continuously Contemporary Accounting.

■ *Clark, John B. (with a new introduction by Donald Dewey). *Capital and Its Earnings.*
New York, 1988.

■ Clarke, F. L. *The Tangled Web of Price Variation Accounting: The Development of Ideas Underlying Professional Prescriptions in Six Countries.*
New York, 1982.

■ Coopers & Lybrand. *The Early History of Coopers & Lybrand.*
New York, 1984.

■ Craswell, Allen. *Audit Qualifications in Australia 1950 to 1979.*
New York, 1986.

■ Dean, G. W., and M. C. Wells, eds. *The Case for Continuously Contemporary Accounting.*
New York, 1984.

■ Dean, G. W. , and M. C. Wells, eds. *Forerunners of Realizable Values Accounting in Financial Reporting.*
New York, 1982.

■ Edey, Harold C. *Accounting Queries.*
New York, 1982.

■ Edwards, J. R., ed. *Legal Regulation of British Company Accounts 1836-1900.*
New York, 1986.

■ Edwards, J. R. ed. *Reporting Fixed Assets in Nineteenth-Century Company Accounts.*
New York, 1986.

■ Edwards, J. R., ed. *Studies of Company Records: 1830-1974.*
New York, 1984.

■ Fabricant, Solomon. *Studies in Social and Private Accounting.*
New York, 1982.

■ Gaffikin, Michael, and Michael Aitkin, eds. *The Development of Accounting Theory: Significant Contributors to Accounting Thought in the 20th Century.*
New York, 1982.

■ Hawawini, Gabriel A., ed. *Bond Duration and Immunization: Early Developments and Recent Contributions.*
New York, 1982.

■ Hawawini, Gabriel A., and Pierre A. Michel, eds. *European Equity Markets: Risk, Return, and Efficiency.*
New York, 1984.

■ Hawawini, Gabriel A., and Pierre Michel. *Mandatory Financial Information and Capital Market Equilibrium in Belgium.*
New York, 1986.

■ Hawkins, David F. *Corporate Financial Disclosure, 1900-1933: A Study of Management Inertia within a Rapidly Changing Environment.*
New York, 1986.

■ *Hopwood, Anthony G. *Accounting from the Outside: The Collected Papers of Anthony G. Hopwood.*
New York, 1988.

■ Johnson, H. Thomas. *A New Approach to Management Accounting History.*
New York, 1986.

■ Kinney, William R., ed. *Fifty Years of Statistical Auditing.*
New York, 1986.

■ Klemstine, Charles E., and Michael W. Maher. *Management Accounting Research: A Review and Annotated Bibliography.*
New York, 1984.

■ *Langenderfer, Harold Q., and Grover L. Porter, eds. *Rational Accounting Concepts: The Writings of Willard Graham.*
New York, 1988.

■ *Lee, T. A., ed. *The Evolution of Audit Thought and Practice.*
New York, 1988.

■ Lee, T. A., ed. *A Scottish Contribution to Accounting History.*
New York, 1986.

■ Lee, T. A. *Towards a Theory and Practice of Cash Flow Accounting.*
New York, 1986.

■ Lee, T. A., ed. *Transactions of the Chartered Accountants Students' Societies of Edinburgh and Glasgow: A Selection of Writings, 1886-1958.*
New York, 1984.

■ *Loft, Anne. *Understanding Accounting in Its Social and Historical Context: The Case of Cost Accounting in Britain, 1914-1925.*
New York, 1988.

▪ McKinnon, Jill L.. *The Historical Development and Operational Form of Corporate Reporting Regulation in Japan.*
New York, 1986.

▪ *McMickle, Peter L., and Paul H. Jensen, eds. *The Auditor's Guide of 1869: A Review and Computer Enhancement of Recently Discovered Old Microfilm of America's First Book on Auditing by H. J. Mettenheimer.*
New York, 1988.

▪ *McMickle, Peter L., and Paul H. Jensen, eds. *The Birth of American Accountancy: A Bibliographic Analysis of Works on Accounting Published in America through 1820.*
New York, 1988.

▪ *Mepham, M.-J. *Accounting in Eighteenth-Century Scotland.*
New York, 1988.

▪ *Mills, Patti A., trans. *The Legal Literature of Accounting: On Accounts by Diego del Castillo.*
New York, 1988.

▪ *Murphy, George J. *The Evolution of Canadian Corporate Reporting Practices: 1900-1970.*
New York, 1988.

▪ *Mumford, Michael J., ed. *Edward Stamp—Later Papers.*
New York, 1988.

▪ Nobes, Christopher, ed. *The Development of Double Entry: Selected Essays.*
New York, 1984.

- Nobes, Christopher. *Issues in International Accounting.*
  New York, 1986.

- Parker, Lee D. *Developing Control Concepts in the 20th Century.*
  New York, 1986.

- *Parker, Lee D., ed. *Financial Reporting to Employees: From Past to Present.*
  New York, 1988.

- *Parker, Lee D., and O. Finley Graves, eds. *Methodology and Method in History: A Bibliography.*
  New York, 1988.

- Parker, R. H. *Papers on Accounting History.*
  New York, 1984.

- Previts, Gary John, and Alfred R. Roberts, eds. *Federal Securities Law and Accounting 1933-1970: Selected Addresses.*
  New York, 1986.

- *Reid, Jean Margo, ed. *Law and Accounting: Nineteenth-Century American Legal Cases.*
  New York, 1988.

- *Sheldahl, Terry K., ed. *Accounting Literature in the United States before Mitchell and Jones (1796): Contributions by Four English Writers, through American Editions, and Two Pioneer Local Authors.*
  New York, 1988.

▪ Sheldahl, Terry K. *Beta Alpha Psi, from Alpha to Omega: Pursuing a Vision of Professional Education for Accountants, 1919-1945.*
New York, 1982.

▪ Sheldahl, Terry K. *Beta Alpha Psi, from Omega to Zeta Omega: The Making of a Comprehensive Accounting Fraternity, 1946-1984.*
New York, 1986.

▪ *Sheldahl, Terry K., ed. *Education for the Mercantile Countinghouse: Critical and Constructive Essays by Nine British Writers, 1716-1794.*
New York, 1988.

▪ Solomons, David. *Collected Papers on Accounting and Accounting Education (in two volumes).*
New York, 1984.

▪ Sprague, Charles F. *The General Principles of the Science of Accounts and the Accountancy of Investment.*
New York, 1984.

▪ Stamp, Edward. *Edward Stamp—Later Papers.* See Michael J. Mumford.

▪ Stamp, Edward. *Selected Papers on Accounting, Auditing, and Professional Problems.*
New York, 1984.

▪ *Staubus, George J. *Activity Costing for Decisions: Cost Accounting in the Decision Usefulness Framework.*
New York, 1988.

■ Storrar, Colin, ed. *The Accountant's Magazine—An Anthology.*
New York, 1986.

■ Tantral, Panadda. *Accounting Literature in Non-Accounting Journals: An Annotated Bibliography.*
New York, 1984.

■ *Vangermeersch, Richard G. *Alexander Hamilton Church: A Man of Ideas for All Seasons.*
New York, 1988.

■ Vangermeersch, Richard, ed. *The Contributions of Alexander Hamilton Church to Accounting and Management.*
New York, 1986.

■ Vangermeersch, Richard, ed. *Financial Accounting Milestones in the Annual Reports of the United States Steel Corporation—The First Seven Decades.*
New York, 1986.

■ *Walker, Stephen P. *The Society of Accountants in Edinburgh, 1854-1914: A Study of Recruitment to a New Profession.*
New York, 1988.

■ Whitmore, John. *Factory Accounts.*
New York, 1984.

■ *Whittred, Greg. *The Evolution of Consolidated Financial Reporting in Australia: An Evaluation of an Alternative Hypothesis.*
New York, 1988.

■ Yamey, Basil S. *Further Essays on the History of Accounting.*
New York, 1982.

■ Zeff, Stephen A., ed. *The Accounting Postulates and Principles Controversy of the 1960s.*
New York, 1982.

■ Zeff, Stephen A., ed. *Accounting Principles Through the Years: The Views of Professional and Academic Leaders 1938-1954.*
New York, 1982.

■ Zeff, Stephen A., and Maurice Moonitz, eds. *Sourcebook on Accounting Principles and Auditing Procedures: 1917-1953 (in two volumes).*
New York, 1984.

■ *Zeff, Stephen a., ed. *The U. S. Accounting Profession in the 1890s and Early 1900s.*
New York, 1988.

REPRINTED TITLES

■ *American Institute of Accountants. *Accountants Index, 1920* (in two volumes).
New York, 1921 (Garland reprint, 1988).

■ American Institute of Accountants. *Fiftieth Anniversary Celebration.*
Chicago, 1937 (Garland reprint, 1982).

■ American Institute of Accountants. *Library Catalogue.*
New York, 1919 (Garland reprint, 1982).

■ Arthur Andersen Company. *The First Fifty Years 1913-1963.*
Chicago, 1963 (Garland reprint, 1984).

■ Bevis, Herman W. *Corporate Financial Reporting in a Competitive Economy.*
New York, 1965 (Garland reprint, 1986).

■ Bonini,. Charles P., Robert K. Jaedicke, and Harvey M. Wagner, eds. *Management Controls: New Directions in Basic Research.*
New York, 1964 (Garland reprint, 1986).

■ **The Book-Keeper and the American Counting Room.*
New York, 1880-1884 (Garland reprint, 1988).

- Bray, F. Sewell. *Four Essays in Accounting Theory.* London, 1953. *Bound with* Institute of Chartered Accountants in England and Wales and the National Institute of Economic and Social Research. *Some Accounting Terms and Concepts.*
  Cambridge, 1951 (Garland reprint, 1982).

- Brown, R. Gene, and Kenneth S. Johnston. *Paciolo on Accounting.*
  New York, 1963 (Garland reprint, 1984).

- Carey, John L., and William O. Doherty, eds. *Ethical Standards of the Accounting Profession.*
  New York, 1966 (Garland reprint, 1986).

- Chambers, R. J. *Accounting in Disarray.*
  Melbourne, 1973 (Garland reprint, 1982).

- Cooper, Ernest. *Fifty-seven years in an Accountant's Office. See* Sir Russell Kettle.

- Couchman, Charles B. *The Balance-Sheet.*
  New York, 1924 (Garland reprint, 1982).

- Couper, Charles Tennant. *Report of the Trial ... Against the Directors and Manager of the City of Glasgow Bank.*
  Edinburgh, 1879 (Garland reprint, 1984).

- Cutforth, Arthur E. *Audits.*
  London, 1906 (Garland reprint, 1982).

- Cutforth, Arthur E. *Methods of Amalgamation.*
  London, 1926 (Garland reprint, 1982).

■ Deinzer, Harvey T. *Development of Accounting Thought.*
New York, 1965 (Garland reprint, 1984).

■ De Paula, F.R.M. *The Principles of Auditing.*
London, 1915 (Garland reprint, 1984).

■ Dickerson, R. W. *Accountants and the Law of Negligence.*
Toronto, 1966 (Garland reprint, 1982).

■ Dodson, James. *The Accountant, or, the Method of Bookkeeping Deduced from Clear Principles, and Illustrated by a Variety of Examples.*
London, 1750 (Garland reprint, 1984).

■ Dyer, S. *A Common Sense Method of Double Entry Bookkeeping, on First Principles, as Suggested by De Morgan. Part I, Theoretical.*
London, 1897 (Garland reprint, 1984).

■ *† Edwards, James Don. *History of Public Accounting in the United States.*
East Lansing, 1960 (Garland reprint, 1988).

■ *† Edwards, James Don, and Robert F. Salmonson. *Contributions of Four Accounting Pioneers: Kohler, Littleton, May, Paton.*
East Lancing, 1961 (Garland reprint, 1988).

■ *The Fifth International Congress on Accounting, 1938 [Kongress-Archiv 1938 des V. Internationalen Prüfungs- und Treuhand-Kongresses].*
Berlin, 1938 (Garland reprint, 1986).

▪ Finney, A. H. *Consolidated Statements.*
New York, 1922 (Garland reprint, 1982).

▪ Fisher, Irving. *The Rate of Interest.*
New York, 1907 (Garland reprint, 1982).

▪ Florence, P. Sargant. *Economics of Fatigue and Unrest and the Efficiency of Labour in English and American Industry.*
London, 1923 (Garland reprint, 1984).

▪ *Fourth International Congress on Accounting 1933.*
London, 1933 (Garland reprint, 1982).

▪ Foye, Arthur B. *Haskins & Sells: Our First Seventy-Five Years.*
New York, 1970 (Garland reprint, 1984).

▪ *† Garner, Paul S. *Evolution of Cost Accounting to 1925.*
University, Alabama, 1925 (Garland reprint, 1988).

▪ Garnsey, Sir Gilbert. *Holding Companies and Their Published Accounts.* London, 1923. *Bound with* Sir Gilbert Garnsey. *Limitations of a Balance Sheet.*
London, 1928 (Garland reprint, 1982).

▪ Garrett, A. A. *The History of the Society of Incorporated Accountants, 1885-1957.*
Oxford, 1961 (Garland reprint, 1984).

▪ Gilman, Stephen. *Accounting Concepts of Profit.*
New York, 1939 (Garland reprint, 1982).

▪ Gordon, William. *The Universal Accountant, and Complete Merchant* ... [Volume II].
Edinburgh, 1765 (Garland reprint, 1986).

▪ Green, Wilmer. *History and Survey of Accountancy.*
Brooklyn, 1930 (Garland reprint, 1986).

▪ Hamilton, Robert. *An Introduction to Merchandise, Parts IV and V (Italian Bookkeeping and Practical Bookkeeping).*
Edinburgh, 1788 (Garland reprint, 1982).

▪ Hatton, Edward. *The Merchant's Magazine; or, Tradesman's Treasury.* London, 1695 (Garland reprint, 1982).
Hills, George S. *The Law of Accounting and Financial Statements.*
Boston, 1957 (Garland reprint, 1982).

▪ *A History of Cooper Brothers & Co. 1854 to 1954.*
London, 1954 (Garland reprint, 1986).

▪ Hofstede, Geert. *The Game of Budget Control.*
Assen, 1967 (Garland reprint, 1984).

▪ Howitt, Sir Harold. *The History of the Institute of Chartered Accountants in England and Wales 1880-1965, and of Its Founder Accountancy Bodies 1870-1880.*
London, 1966 (Garland reprint, 1984).

▪ Institute of Chartered Accountants in England and Wales and The National Institute of Social and Economic Research. *Some Accounting Terms and Concepts.* *See* F. Sewell Bray.

▪ Institute of Chartered Accountants of Scotland. *History of the Chartered Accountants of Scotland from the Earliest Times to 1954.*
Edinburgh, 1954 (Garland reprint, 1984).

▪ *International Congress on Accounting 1929.*
New York, 1930 (Garland reprint, 1982).

▪ Jaedicke, Robert K., Yuji Ijiri, and Oswald Nielsen, eds. *Research in Accounting Measurement.*
American Accounting Association,
1966 (Garland reprint, 1986).

▪ Keats, Charles. *Magnificent Masquerade.*
New York, 1964 (Garland reprint, 1982).

▪ Kettle, Sir Russell. *Deloitte & Co. 1854-1956.* Oxford, 1958. *Bound with* Ernest Cooper. *Fifty-seven Years in an Accountant's Office.*
London, 1921 (Garland reprint, 1982).

▪ Kitchen, J., and R. H. Parker. *Accounting Thought and Education: Six English Pioneers.*
London, 1980 (Garland reprint, 1984).

▪ Lacey, Kenneth. *Profit Measurement and Price Changes.*
London, 1952 (Garland reprint, 1982).

▪ Lee, Chauncey. *The American Accomptant.*
Lansingburgh, 1797 (Garland reprint, 1982).

▪ Lee, T. A., and R. H. Parker. *The Evolution of Corporate Financial Reporting.*
Middlesex, 1979 (Garland reprint, 1984).

■ *† Littleton, A. C.. *Accounting Evolution to 1900.*
New York, 1933 (Garland reprint, 1988).

■ Malcolm, Alexander. *The Treatise of Book-Keeping, or, Merchants Accounts; In the Italian Method of Debtor and Creditor; Wherein the Fundamental Principles of That Curious and Approved Method Are Clearly and Fully Explained and Demonstrated ... To Which Are Added, Instructions for Gentlemen of Land Estates, and Their Stewards or Factors: With Directions Also for Retailers, and Other More Private Persons.*
London, 1731 (Garland reprint, 1986).

■ Meij, J. L., ed. *Depreciation and Replacement Policy.*
Chicago, 1961 (Garland reprint, 1986).

■ Newlove, George Hills. *Consolidated Balance Sheets.*
New York, 1926 (Garland reprint, 1982).

■ North, Roger. *The Gentleman Accomptant; or, An Essay to Unfold the Mystery of Accompts; By Way of Debtor and Creditor, Commonly Called Merchants Accompts, and Applying the Same to the Concerns of the Nobility and Gentry of England.*
London 1714 (Garland reprint, 1986).

■ **Proceedings of the Seventh International Congress of Accountants.* Amsterdam, 1957 (Garland reprint, 1988).

■ Pryce-Jones, Janet E., and R. H. Parker. *Accounting in Scotland: A Historical Bibliography.*
Edinburgh, 1976 (Garland reprint, 1984).

■ *Reynolds, W. B., and F. W. Thornton. *Duties of a Junior Accountant* [three editions].
New York, 1917, 1933, 1953
(Garland reprint, 1988).

■ Robinson, H. W. *A History of Accountants in Ireland.*
Dublin, 1964 (Garland edition, 1984).

■ Robson, T. B. *Consolidated and Other Group Accounts.*
London, 1950 (Garland reprint, 1982).

■ Rorem, C. Rufus. *Accounting Method.*
Chicago, 1928 (Garland reprint, 1982).

■ Saliers, Earl A., ed. *Accountants' Handbook.*
New York, 1923 (Garland reprint, 1986).

■ Samuel, Horace B. *Shareholder's Money.*
London, 1933 (Garland reprint, 1982).

■ *The Securitites and Exchange Commission in the Matter of McKesson & Robbins, Inc. Report on Investigation.*
Washington, D. C., 1940 (Garland reprint, 1982).

■ *The Securities and Exchange Commission in the Matter of McKesson & Robbins, Inc. Testimony of Expert Witnesses.*
Washington, D. C., 1939 (Garland reprint, 1982).

■ Shaplen, Roger. *Kreuger: Genius and Swindler.*
New York, 1960 (Garland reprint, 1986).

■ Singer, H. W. *Standardized Accountancy in Germany. (With a new appendix.)*
Cambridge, 1943 (Garland reprint, 1982).

■ *The Sixth International Congress on Accounting.*
London, 1952 (Garland reprint, 1984).

■ Stewart, Jas. C. (with a new introductory note by T. A. Lee). *Pioneers of a Profession: Chartered Accountants to 1879.*
Edinburgh, 1977 (Garland reprint, 1986).

■ Thompson, Wardbaugh. *The Accomptant's Oracle: or, a Key to Science, Being a Compleat Practical System of Book-keeping.*
York, 1777 (Garland reprint, 1984).

■ *Thornton, F. W. *Duties of the Senior Accountant.* New York, 1932. *Bound with.* John C. Martin. *Duties of Junior and Senior Accountants, Supplement of the CPA Handbook.*
New York, 1953 (Garland reprint, 1988).

■ Vatter, William J. *Managerial Accounting.*
New York, 1950 (Garland reprint, 1986).

■ Woolf, Arthur H. *A Short History of Accountants and Accountancy.*
London, 1912 (Garland reprint, 1986).

■ Yamey, B. S., H. C. Edey, and Hugh W. Thomson. *Accounting in England and Scotland: 1543-1800.*
London, 1963 (Garland reprint, 1982).